iLife '11 Made Simple

Glen Durdik

Apress®

iLife '11 Made Simple

ISBN 978-1-4302-3632-0

ISBN 978-1-4302-3633-7 (eBook)

Trademarked names, logos, and images may appear in this book. Rather than use a trademark symbol with every occurrence of a trademarked name, logo, or image we use the names, logos, and images only in an editorial fashion and to the benefit of the trademark owner, with no intention of infringement of the trademark.

The use in this publication of trade names, trademarks, service marks, and similar terms, even if they are not identified as such, is not to be taken as an expression of opinion as to whether or not they are subject to proprietary rights.

President and Publisher: Paul Manning
Lead Editor: Michelle Lowman
Development Editor: James Markham
Editorial Board: Steve Anglin, Mark Beckner, Ewan Buckingham, Gary Cornell, Jonathan Gennick, Jonathan Hassell, Michelle Lowman, Matthew Moodie, Jeff Olson, Jeffrey Pepper, Frank Pohlmann, Douglas Pundick, Ben Renow-Clarke, Dominic Shakeshaft, Matt Wade, Tom Welsh
Coordinating Editor: Kelly Moritz
Copy Editor: Tracy Brown
Compositor: MacPS, LLC
Indexer: BIM Indexing & Proofreading Services
Artist: SPi Global
Cover Designer: Anna Ishchenko

Distributed to the book trade worldwide by Springer Science+Business Media, LLC., 233 Spring Street, 6th Floor, New York, NY 10013. Phone 1-800-SPRINGER, fax (201) 348-4505, e-mail orders-ny@springer-sbm.com, or visit www.springeronline.com.

For information on translations, please e-mail rights@apress.com, or visit www.apress.com.

Apress and friends of ED books may be purchased in bulk for academic, corporate, or promotional use. eBook versions and licenses are also available for most titles. For more information, reference our Special Bulk Sales–eBook Licensing web page at www.apress.com/info/bulksales.

The information in this book is distributed on an "as is" basis, without warranty. Although every precaution has been taken in the preparation of this work, neither the authors nor Apress shall have any liability to any person or entity with respect to any loss or damage caused or alleged to be caused directly or indirectly by the information contained in this work.

I would like to dedicate this manual to my mother, who instilled in me both the value of hard work and the desire to pursue a path in life that I am passionate about.

Contents at a Glance

Contents

About the Author

Glen Durdik is an Apple Certified Macintosh Technician with a passion for all things Apple. He started his career in the Information Technology field by helping to get a University's first Macintosh classroom up and running while he was a student there. For the next two years, he helped hundreds of future graphic artists and teachers learn how to use the Macintosh, as well as the ins and outs of the programs they were using. He knew then that he wanted a career that would always give him the satisfaction of helping users in need. After graduation, he worked full-time at the University and helped expand the Macintosh presence on campus. He later moved on to work at an Apple–authorized training and service center. He was called upon to travel all over of Manhattan to resolve Mac issues and set up new hardware. However, the education environment again beckoned him. He is currently a desktop engineer, helping to support the largest New York school district outside of New York City. Once again, he is applying his years of teaching skills and technical knowledge to help teachers and students best use the technology they have available to them. Glen has been married to his beautiful wife, Elisa, since 2008. All of his spare time is currently dedicated to helping his wife take care of his first child, who was born in January 2011. Glen can be reached at gdurdik@mac.com.

About the Technical Reviewer

 **Thomas Olivieri** has been teaching computer graphics for over twenty five years on both the secondary and college level. He has been instrumental in developing curriculum in the areas of Fine and Applied Arts. Tom has also served as a Lab Consultant in his former Brentwood School District. Retired from public school instruction, he continues to maintain the District Website.

He has also been a multimedia independent producer for over thirty years. He currently produces college sports recruitment videos and player web pages. Tom resides in Smithtown, NY.

Acknowledgments

I would like to begin by thanking my wife for giving me the opportunity to write this book. Without her support, it would have been difficult to find the time and energy to do so. I would also like to thank all of the support staff who have worked hard on this project. Through our team effort, I feel we have put together a concise and easy-to-follow guide that will teach users what makes iLife so great – and in the process make them as passionate about the software as I am.

Part I

Quick Start Guide

To assist new users who have seen the light and purchased a Macintosh, this Quick Start Guide will help you jump right in and find information in this book—and learn the basics of how to get around your Mac and enjoy iLife right away. At the end of this section is a helpful little intro to keyboard shortcuts. As you become more familiar with the Macintosh platform and iLife….the highlighted shortcuts listed will make your time on the Mac much more efficient. Mac (and IOS devices!) and iLife…a perfect combination to perform all of your media tasks. After reading this Quick Start Guide…you are ready to begin your journey of learning in detail—how each great iLife application can make performing their designed tasks a breeze.

Getting Around Quickly

OK. You just got your brand new Mac, and you see that iLife is installed. And you ask yourself, "Do I need these applications?"

Well, I have to say, "YES!!!! Of course you do!!!!"

Apple has created mind-blowing applications to simplify all aspects of handling your digital assets. Most iLife programs serve many purposes. This could be simply storing your photos or combining many video clips into an amazing family video. Some iLife apps are geared towards creating just one type of output, such as a webpage or DVD. Whether it is a quick edit of a photo or easily sharing any of our iLife projects with the world, soon you will be saying, "How can I live without these apps?"

Let's start with a brief description of every iLife app and what it's used for. iTunes can be used to share your projects in most iLife apps, so I feel it is essential to cover this app, as well.

Table P1–1 highlights what I think are the key points in every iLife application. It also tells you in what chapter/s each application is detailed.

Table P1–1. *iLife's Apps—Plus iTunes*

Application	Description
 iPhoto	iPhoto is a great application for handling your digital photo or video library needs. It is truly a digital darkroom for the masses! It includes easy-to-use, yet powerful photo-editing tools. With just a few clicks, you can share your precious memories with a few friends or the whole world via the Internet. This is the first application I cover, and its amazingness is covered in Chapters 1–6.
 iDVD	iDVD's power lies in the fact that it makes it so easy to create a professional-looking DVD. With iDVD, iMovie, and GarageBand, you can spend only a few moments and create a great project. Or you can spend hours and hours taking your work to the next level. You have the power, so you decide: take things fast and easy to create a great looking project—or spend long hours creating the world's best DVDs. Get your creative juices ready and learn more about iDVD in Chapters 7–9.
 iWeb	You know what www.apple.com is, and you want to create your own amazing website. But what if have no idea how to create a webpage. Enter the iWeb app, which lets you create webpages in no time. Learn how to become your very own webmaster by browsing Chapters 10–12.
 iMovie	This is not your father's 8mm film projector. With iMovie, you are only limited by your imagination. Import video and a custom soundtrack, and suddenly your family memories are not what they used to be. You can now even create an awesome looking "Movie Trailer" from your media in just a few short steps. Learning how to become the next great director is covered in Chapters 13–15.
 GarageBand	Do you want to improve your guitar or piano skills or learn from accomplished artists? Is there an inner composer dying to come out? Look no further: GarageBand is designed for you. As with the other iLife apps, the more you explore, the more fun you'll have, and the better your skills and compositions will become. Learn how to "rock on" in Chapters 16–18.
 iTunes	Although not part of iLife '11, iTunes is automatically installed on your Mac, and it plays a role in several iLife applications. iTunes may seem simple: it provides a place to store your music, videos, and iOS apps. However, there is so, so much to learn about the inner-workings of iTunes that I included it in this manual. Learn how to master all that iTunes offers in Chapters 19–22.

Main Items of Interest

After you have launched an application, there are two main items to take note of. The first is the menu interface located at the top of every application's window (see

Figure P1–1). A few menu items like **File** and **Help** are found in every Macintosh application. Other choices are specific to that application.

Figure P1–1. *A sample of the menu interface on a Macintosh*

To access a menu choice, move your mouse over the menu you want to access, and then click and hold your mouse button over the title of that menu. Keep the mouse button pressed and move your mouse down to the option you want.

The second element is the workspace. Every application has its own workspace. In the chapters to follow, I will go over every element in each iLife application. In Figure P1–2, we see the workspace for GarageBand. Most items in the workspace require one click of the mouse button to access or trigger their functionality. Some applications have sliders. For example, iTunes has a slider for controlling the volume (see Figure P1–3). To change the setting in question, click and hold the mouse button over the small circle inside the slider.

Figure P1–2. *A sample GarageBand workspace*

Figure P1–3. *An example of a slider element*

There are also quite a few other items that are the same in every iLife application (and most other Macintosh apps). Table P1–2 covers a few additional items of interest to Macintosh users.

Table P1–2. *iLife Basics.*

Common item	Function of the item
	The Red, Orange, and Green Buttons: Every Macintosh window has these three round buttons (or dots) on the top-left corner. Each button has its own function, which I will discuss later in this table.
	The Red, Orange, and Green Buttons with Symbols: If you move your mouse over the three dots, you'll see that an "X" is placed in the red dot, a "-" is placed in the orange dot, and a "+" is placed in the green dot. This does not change their function, but it does give you another way of remembering what each button does.
	The Red Button (the dot on the far left): This is the **Close** button. If you want to close the window or document you are currently viewing, click this red dot. If you are working on a project, clicking this will raise a prompt that asks whether you want to save your work first.
	The Orange Button (the middle dot): This is the **Minimize** button. Clicking it will minimize your current window to the dock. Once the window is minimized, you can bring it back up by clicking the icon in the dock. An example of a minimized window is shown below. Notice that it has a small window of the project you are working on and a small icon of the application it is from. In this example, there is a small blue DVD icon—which is, of course, the icon for the iDVD app. 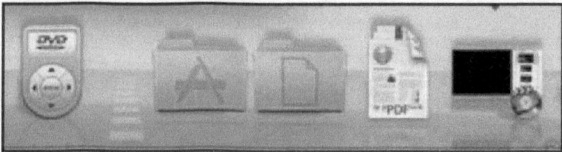 If you hold your mouse over the icon in the dock, it will display the name of the project, as shown in the following image. 
	The Green Button (the dot on the far right): This button toggles between the current size of the window you are working on and the full-size rendition of your window. For example, you might have reduced the size of your iPhoto window to do another task on your Mac. After you are done, you can click this button to restore the

Common item	Function of the item
	window to its full size.
	**The Window Resize Corner**: This corner is at the bottom right of every window. Click and hold the mouse button over the diagonal lines of this corner, and then drag to expand or decrease the size of the current window. As I just mentioned, clicking the green dot will return the window to its full size if you so desire.
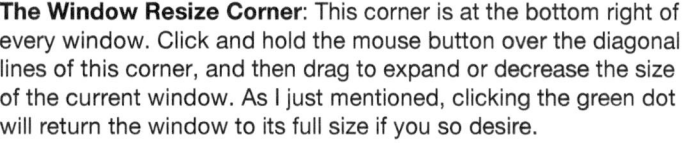	**The Current Application**: You will see a small blue dot below one of the application icons in the dock. This blue dot indicates the app currently in use. Please also notice that if you move your mouse over an icon in the Dock, that the application or folder name will appear. In this case "iDVD.
	**The Application Version**: Every application has a feature to tell you what version of the app you are running. This feature can be found in the **Application** menu. The example to the left shows the **iDVD** menu. In iPhoto, you would see the **iPhoto** menu. Menus are always found on the top of your screen. The **Application** menu is always one of the leftmost menus on your screen. To find out what version of the app you are running, go to the **Application** menu (the **iDVD** menu, in this example), and then click and hold your mouse button over the **Application** menu. While the mouse button is pressed, move your cursor down to the about application option (**About iDVD**, in this case). This will bring up a screen like the one shown below. 

Common item	Function of the item

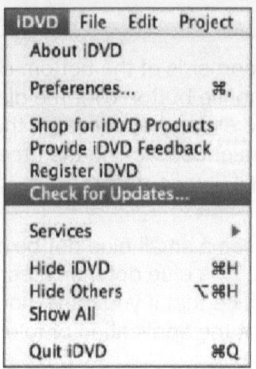

Check for Updates...: This is also found in the **Application** menu. Clicking this simply takes you online to Apple's website to check for updates. The process is shown below.

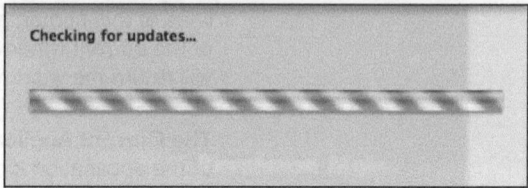

If the app is up-to-date, you will see a screen like the one below.

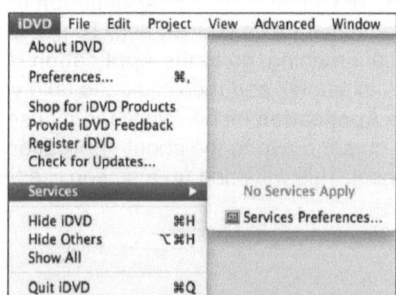

Services: If there are special features that an application can take advantage of, this is where you can access them. Notice in the example to the left that there are no services available for iDVD.

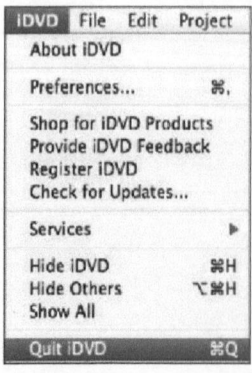

Quit: Clicking this option quits the application currently in use. If you have unsaved documents, you will be asked you if want to save your work first.

Common item	Function of the item

Page Setup…: If your application has printing features, this option will always be there. It is found in the **File** menu. You can see an example of this window in the image below.

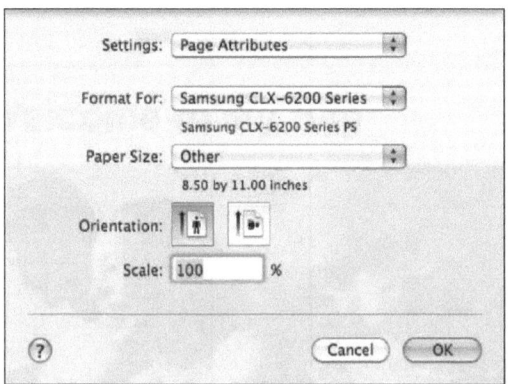

Print…: Like **Page Setup…**, this option appears in the **File** Menu if the application you are using has printing capabilities. The first screen that appears when you select this option is shown below. Please note the blue square with an arrow pointing down.

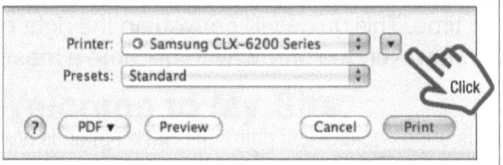

Clicking this blue square brings up the complete set of options for printing, as shown in the screenshot below.

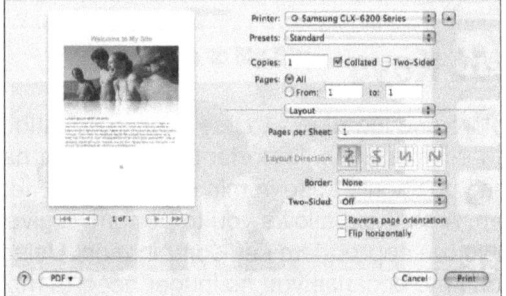

Common item	Function of the item
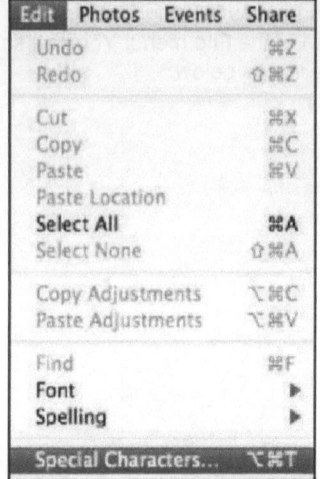	**Special Characters**: If you are looking for a special symbol or character, go to the **Edit** menu and select the **Special Characters...** option at the bottom of the menu. 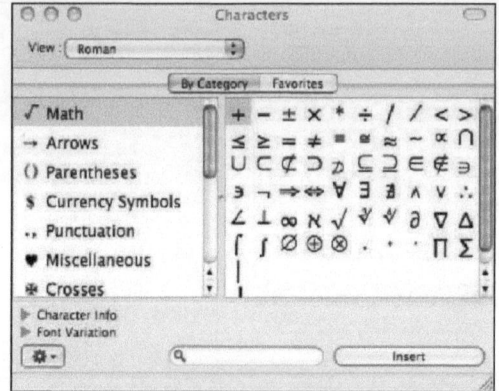

You will notice that many options are found in the same spot in every application. For example, you will always find the options to create a new project or open a saved one in the **File** menu. Similarly, the **Help** menu is always the last (i.e., rightmost) menu in every application. As you explore your new Mac and iLife, you will learn where everything is located in no time. This guide will get you on the right path to becoming an experienced iLife or Mac user. However, the only way to become a master is to EXPLORE and EXPERIMENT!!

> **NOTE:** This brings up one last point: the **Save** option is always found in the **File** menu. Be wise and save often!!! The Mac operating system is very stable, but application crashes do happen from time to time.

Shortcut Keys

As you explore and learn how to use each application, finding features become easier. However, there is one very important lesson about navigating through Macintosh applications you should keep in mind. Most menu items list a *shortcut* key combination next to them. A shortcut allows you to perform a given task—just by clicking and/or holding down the appropriate key combination. Using the keyboard to perform a task will save you time because you no longer need to move your mouse to perform that task. Each application contains many shortcuts. Table P1–3 contains shortcuts that are universal to virtually every Macintosh application. Once learned, these timesavers can be applied in almost any Mac app. In a similar vein, Tables P1–4 through P1–9 list the shortcuts you'll most likely use with various iLife applications.

> **NOTE:** Remember that the **Command** key is ⌘. There are **Command** keys located to the left and right of your **Spacebar** key.

Table P1–3. *The Shortcuts Found in Virtually Every Macintosh Application*

Task to Be Performed	Shortcut Keyboard Combination
New project or document	Command-N
Copy highlighted material	Command-C
Cut highlighted material	Command-X
Paste highlighted material	Command-V
Select all items in your workspace	Command-A
Save your project	Command-S
Undo last action	Command-Z
Redo last action	Shift-Command-Z
Minimize window	Command-M
Print your project	Command-P
Close your current open window	Command-W
Access the **Help** menu	Command-question mark (?)
Quit the application you are working in	Command-Q

Table P1–4. *The Most Commonly Used Shortcuts in iPhoto.*

Task to Be Performed	Shortcut Keyboard Combination
Import photos	Shift-Command-I
Export photos	Shift-Command-E
Create new folder	Option-Shift-Command-N
Create new (empty) album	Shift-Command-N
Create new album from a selection of photos	Command-N

Task to Be Performed	Shortcut Keyboard Combination
Create new Smart album	Option-Command-N
Go to next photo	Right Arrow
Go to previous photo	Left Arrow
Duplicate photo	Command-D
Open photo in edit view	Return
Enter or leave full-screen view	Option-Command-F
Show photo information	Command-I
Rotate photo	Command-R
Enter edit view	Command-E
Open crop tool	C
Open Effects pane	E
Open Adjust pane	A
Pause slideshow or resume playing	Spacebar
Move through a slideshow manually	Press the Right or Left Arrow keys

Table P1–5. *The Most Commonly Used Shortcuts in iDVD*

Task to Be Performed	Shortcut Keyboard Combination
Add submenu	Command-Shift-N
Add movie	Command-Shift-O
Add slideshow	Command-L
Add text	Command-K
Autofill drop zones	Command-Shift-F
Show project info	Command-I
Burn DVD	Command-R

Task to Be Performed	Shortcut Keyboard Combination
Save as disc image	Command-Shift-R
Show map	Command-Shift-M
Show Inspector	Command-I

Table P1–6. *The Most Commonly Used Shortcuts in iWeb.*

Task to Be Performed	Shortcut Keyboard Combination
Scroll to the top of the page	Home
Scroll to the end of the page	End
Show Fonts window	Command-T
Show Colors window	Shift-Command-C
Align text flush left	Shift-Command-left curly brace ({)
Align text flush right	Shift-Command-right curly brace (})
Center text	Shift-Command-vertical line (|)
Align text flush right and flush left (justify)	Shift-Command-Option-vertical line (|)
Edit hypertext without disabling hyperlinks	Arrow keys into text
Show/hide layout	Shift-Command-L
Show/hide Inspector	Option-Command-I
Rotate object	Command-drag handle
Mask/unmask object	Shift-Command-M
Exit mask mode	Return, Command-Return, Enter, double-click

Table P1–7. *The Most Commonly Used Shortcuts in iMovie.*

Task to Be Performed	Shortcut Keyboard Combination
Import from camera	Command-I
Play video beginning from the frame beneath the pointer	Spacebar

Task to Be Performed	Shortcut Keyboard Combination
Open Music and Sound Effects pane	Command-1
Open Photos pane	Command-2
Open Titles pane	Command-3
Open Transitions pane	Command-4
Open Map, Background, and Animatic browser	Command-5
Open crop, rotate, and Ken Burns effect editor	C
Open Clip Adjustments pane of Inspector	I
Open Video Adjustments pane of Inspector	V
Open Audio Adjustments panel of Inspector	A
Play the selected event or project full screen	Command-G
Exit full-screen mode	Escape (Esc) key
Play selection	Slash (/)
Play selected event or project from the beginning	Backslash (\)
Show fine-tuning controls	Command-Option
Export movie	Command-E

Table P1–8. *The Most Commonly Used Shortcuts in GarageBand*

Task to Be Performed	Shortcut Keyboard Combination
Start/stop recording	R
Split selected region at the playhead	Command-T
Join selected regions	Shift-Command-J
Start/stop playback	Spacebar
Show Track Info pane	Command-I
Show editor	Command-E

Task to Be Performed	Shortcut Keyboard Combination
Show Loop browser	Command-L
Show/hide Media browser	Command-R
Show onscreen keyboard	Command-K
Show Musical Typing window	Command-Shift-K
Create a new track	Command-Option-N
Create a new basic track	Command-Shift-N
Mute/unmute the selected track	M
Solo/unsolo the selected track	S
Lock/unlock the selected track	L
Turn snap to grid on/off	Command-G
Show/hide alignment guides	Command-Shift-G
Turn the metronome on/off	Command-U
Turn count in on/off	Command-Shift-U
Show track mixer	Command-Y
Show Track Info pane	Command-I
Show editor	Command-E
Show Loop browser	Command-L
Show/hide Media browser	Command-R
Show Chord mode in LCD	Command-F (with Software Instrument track selected)
Show Tuner mode in LCD	Command-F (with Real Instrument track selected)
Show Time mode in LCD	Command-Shift-F
Show Measures mode in LCD	Command-Option-F
Show Tempo mode in LCD	Command-Control-F

Table P1–9. *The Most Commonly Used Shortcuts in iTunes*

Task to Be Performed	Shortcut Keyboard Combination
Play the selected song immediately	Return
Stop or start playing the selected song	Spacebar
Create a new playlist	Command-N
Create a new playlist with the selected songs	Shift-Command-N
Create a new Smart playlist	Option-Command-N
Add a file to the Library	Command-O
Import a song, playlist, or library file	Shift-Command-O
Eject a CD	Command-E
Increase the volume	Command-Up Arrow
Decrease the volume	Command-Down Arrow
Show the currently playing song in the list	Command-L
Hide/show the song artwork	Command-G
View the Equalizer window	Option-Command-2
Make visual effects take up the entire screen (when visualizer is on)	Command-F
When a song is playing, play the next song in a list	Command-Right Arrow
When a song is playing, play the previous song in a list	Command-Left Arrow
Mute the sound (song keeps playing)	Option-Command-Down Arrow

Part II

Introduction

Welcome to iLife '11 and the book that tells you what you need to know to get the most out of it. In this part, I show you how the book is organized and where to go to find what you need, along with some great tips and tricks about iLife. With 18 chapters dedicated to iLife and four chapters on its necessary companion—iTunes...this introduction provides a more detailed layout of this book. It will allow you to quickly learn what sections you want to hit first! (but all the chapters are really informative—so don't skip them!)

Welcome to iLife '11!

This book contains 22 sleek chapters dedicated to learning the ways of the iLife apps. The bundled iLife apps are iPhoto, iDVD, iWeb, iMovie, and GarageBand. Additionally, having knowledge of the iTunes app (free and already installed on your Mac) is essential to getting the most out of iLife because it's used to share the work you create in the iLife apps. Therefore, I'm also including a section that covers the ins and outs of iTunes. This section on iTunes is formatted in the same way as the other app chapters, but it goes far beyond just the sharing features used by iLife.

To paint a more complete picture of the iLife experience, I am also including a pair of bonus pieces. The first covers the iPad versions of iMovie and GarageBand, and the other drills down on the upcoming rollout of the iCloud service from Apple.

Getting the Most out of *iLife '11 Made Simple*

This book covers each iLife application in a separate part. A typical part contains one chapter on an app's workspace and another on its menus. Depending on the application, additional chapters are included that discuss topics that are unique to that app. New users to the Mac platform will most likely want to read this book from cover to cover because it kicks off with the Quickstart Guide, which covers Macintosh OS basics. However, some users might be familiar with older versions of the applications covered, so they will only need to brush up on their skills or learn about new features. I feel that I have covered what makes each app so special and easy to use.

Navigating this Book

This book is divided into 10 parts. The rest of this chapter provides a breakdown of what is included in each section.

Part I: The Quickstart Guide

The Quickstart Guide covers several important topics of interest for people who are new to Macs and/or iLife. In this part, you will learn about all of the following:

- **Key elements of the Macintosh OS**: New Macintosh users will learn about the Macintosh OS interface, including essential facts about some of its basic features and common menu options.

- **Each iLife app**: You will learn about the general purpose of each iLife app. You will also learn which chapters contain more information about a given app.

- **Keyboard shortcuts**: You will learn everything you need to know to utilize keyboard shortcuts on a Mac. You'll begin by learning some basic shortcuts that work in virtually every app on the Mac. Next, you'll be shown the essential keyboard shortcuts for every iLife app.

Part II: Introduction

You are reading it.

Part III: Getting iLife into Your Life – Installing, Configuring, and Updating...

This part is also geared towards the new Mac user. It covers the initial installation from a DVD or the App Store, and then walks you through upgrading your software to the latest and greatest versions. The processes involved in this section are relevant for any other Macintosh software app, as well.

Part IV: iPhoto

iPhoto is the first iLife application I discuss. iPhoto is a great app for storing, editing, and sharing your photos and videos. This app contains many different features, so I broke the subject matter into six smaller "topic" chapters. For example, creating books and calendars is covered in one chapter, while the process of creating a slideshow is covered in another. For each of the applications in this book, I cover the main workspace environment and all of the app's menu options in separate chapters.

Part V: iDVD

iDVD was created to help streamline the process of creating DVDs based on your photos and videos. Actually, you can adopt a couple different approaches. First, you can choose to take your time and create a fully customized DVD. Alternatively, with just with a few mouse clicks, you can create a simple DVD. I cover the ways to create a DVD, the iDVD workspace, and the iDVD menu options in this part.

Part VI: iWeb

iWeb is designed for the individual who has little or no knowledge on how to create a website. This app contains many cool features to help a novice create a great looking website. It even makes the process of getting the website "live" on the Internet as simple as possible.

Part VII: iMovie

It's possible to have a lot digital videos, yet not know how to make them look good or how to share them easily with friends or family. iMovie can help. This is a video-editing program that is geared towards a novice user, constantly teaching this novice how to accomplish cool tasks and tricks. At the same time, this app also contains a lot of advanced features, so more experienced users will find the expected tools and features they're accustomed to using for video editing.

Part VIII: GarageBand

Are you musically inclined? GarageBand performs a few major music-related functions. For example, this program will help you do all of the following:

- Learn how to play the piano or guitar. (You can learn from an Apple instructor; or, for a fee, you can download a lesson from a professional music artist.)
- Create your own songs using either the digital software instruments included in GarageBand or an instrument that you attach to your Mac.
- Create iPhone ringtones.

Part VIX: iTunes

iTunes is the last the application covered in this book. This application is commonly used for downloading and storing music and video media. However, it is also used by many of the iLife apps to share your projects with the world, so I'm also covering it in this guide. iTunes began as a simple way to facilitate media storage – but it now encompasses a whole lot more. Even if you already use iTunes occasionally, I am sure you will learn a number of new and interesting things about the app in this book's chapters on it.

Part X: Bonus Pack

This part includes two appendices:

Appendix A: The iOS platform is gaining popularity by leaps and bounds. Apple feels that the iOS platform is the future, and it is constantly updating this operating system. It has also been porting its desktop software to this mobile platform. The mobile versions of iMovie and GarageBand are not as feature-packed as the desktop versions – but they can do a lot, and their potential in the future is wide open.

Appendix B: If you download a song or create a project, it is sent to a central location – the iCloud – and then sent to all of your devices. In other words, the iCloud provides access to what matters to you – anywhere. Plus, this feature functions as a great backup strategy, as well.

Getting Started

This part includes a section on how to install and upgrade iLife. And while this section is geared toward the novice Mac user, it is essential for all users to check for updates to their apps on a regular basis. This section covers two approaches for installing apps. It begins with the more commonly used approached, describing the steps required to install software from a program CD/DVD. It then tackles the method that Apple hopes will be the approach of the future—downloading and installing apps from the App Store. Finally, this part will cover checking for updates to your programs or OS. This is essential to keeping your Mac running without incident or gaining access to new features.

Getting iLife into Your Life: Installing, Configuring, and Updating...

Ready to unleash your creative side?

In this part, I will guide you through the installation process of iLife '11 and show you how to update your Apple software.

> **CAUTION:** Your Mac must have an Intel processor, at least 1 GB of RAM, at least 5 GB of disk space, a DVD drive, OS 10.6.3 or later, and a screen that can display at least 1280 by 768 pixels. Please make sure all these requirements are met before purchasing an iLife '11 upgrade.

Installing iLife onto Your Macintosh

There are three main ways of getting iLife '11 into your life:

- Installing it from a bundled DVD (it comes free with a new Mac purchase)

- Installing it from an upgrade DVD (purchased at the Apple Store or other retailer)

- Purchasing or installing it via the App Store (purchased as digital media only – no DVD)

> **NOTE:** You cannot purchase the iLife '11 Suite at the App Store, but iMovie, iPhoto, and GarageBand are sold individually. Unfortunately, you cannot purchase iWeb or iDVD from the App Store at present.

On the following pages, I will guide you through the installation process for each of these methods in detail.

If you've already installed the entire iLife Suite or just a few of the apps and want to learn how to upgrade the software, go to the "Updating iLife to the Latest Version" section.

Let's start by covering how to install the version of iLife '11 that comes bundled with every new Mac. Note that the first three steps differ only slightly from the installation process for an upgrade DVD, and starting at Step 4, the two processes are essentially the same.

Installing from a Bundled Disk

To install iLife '11 from a bundled disk, follow these steps:

1. Insert the **Applications Install Disc** into your CD drive.

2. Once the **Application Install Disc** icon appears on your desktop, double-click (two fast taps on the mouse button) the **DVD** icon. This icon is shown on the left in Figure P3–1.

3. Double-click the **Install Bundled Software** icon (see the right side of Figure P3–1).

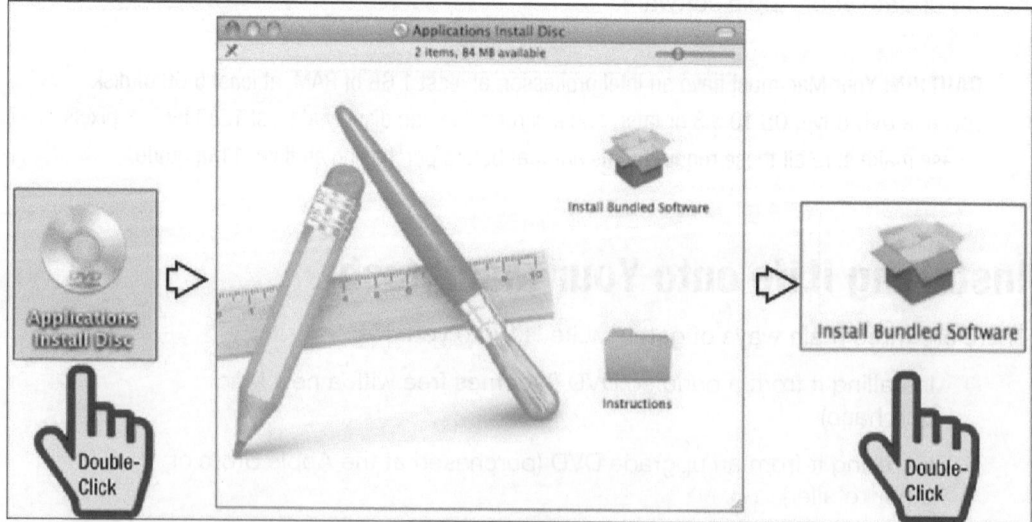

Figure P3–1. *The first three steps to install iLife from a bundled Application disk*

NOTE: The bundled software DVD that came with your Mac will only install on the Mac you just purchased. It will not work for a different Mac model. The error message below will appear if you try to install the software on a different model.

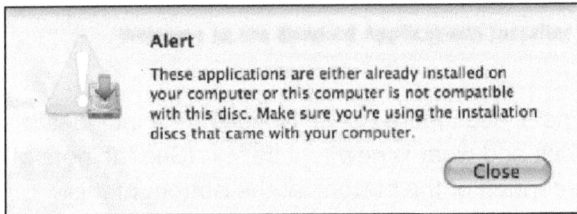

4. The **Welcome** screen then appears (see Figure P3–2). On the left of the window, please note of all the steps required before completion. These steps start with "Introduction" and end with "Summary."

Figure P3–2. *Installation – the **Introduction** window*

5. After reading the text, click (tap the mouse button once) **Continue**.

NOTE: After the installer is running, an **Installer** icon will appear in your Dock. The icon shown below is the same icon used for many Macintosh applications.

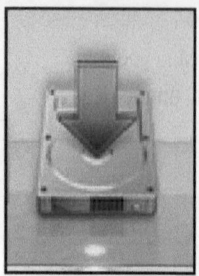

6. The **Read Me** window comes up next (see Figure P3–3). Notice that it includes a summary of what iLife encompasses and what is new to iLife '11. (See the note at the end of this step for a brief description of the buttons at the bottom of this screen.)

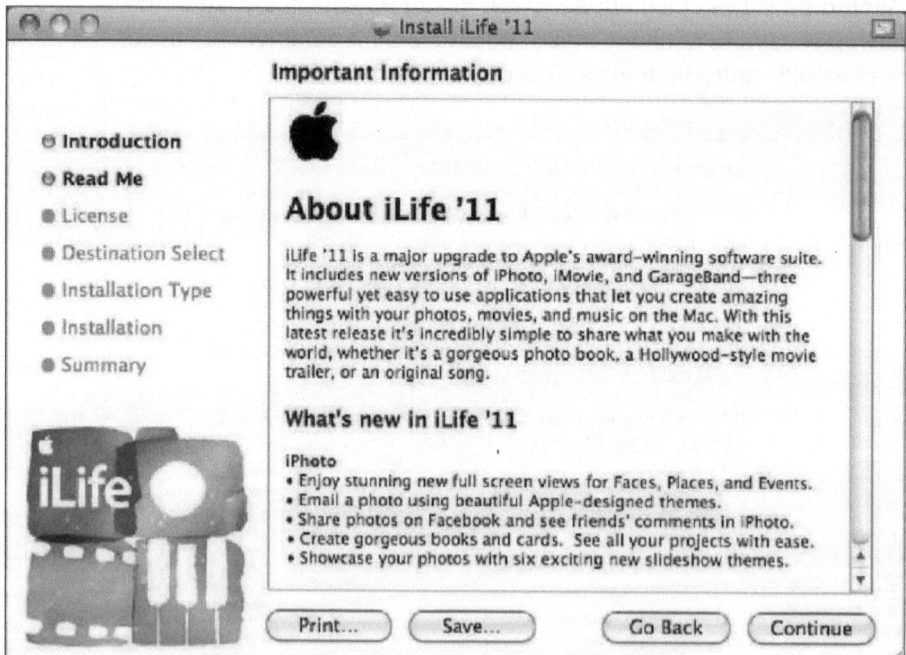

Figure P3–3. *The Read Me file for iLife '11*

NOTE: The following buttons appear at the bottom of the **Read Me** window:

Print: This allows you to print a hard copy of this file. This feature is available on some of the windows to follow in the installation process, as well.

Save…: This allows you to save this file to your hard drive. This feature is available on some of the installation windows to follow, as well.

Go Back: This appears here and on subsequent installation windows, as well. Clicking this icon takes you back to the previous window.

Continue: This button also appears on subsequent installation windows. After you have read through the text on the screen or modified the options available in the current window, clicking this icon takes you to the next window.

7.   Next, we come to the **License** window (see Figure P3–4). Please don't pirate software. If you agree to the terms outlined here, click **Continue**.

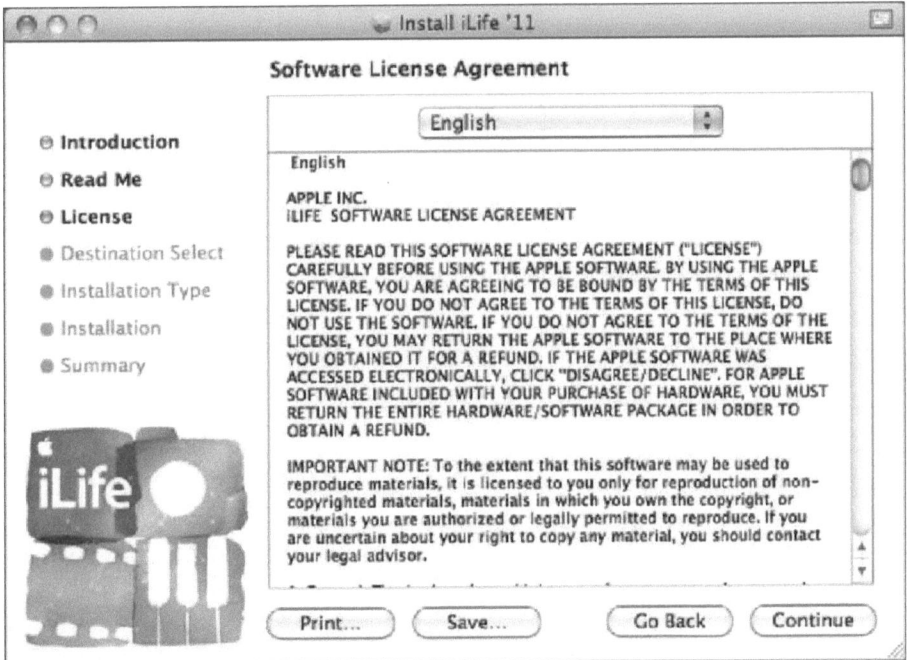

Figure P3–4. *The software license agreement (part 1)*

NOTE: If you click **English**, you can change the language of the agreement. For example, you can read the terms in French or German instead.

8. You are then asked to manually click **Agree** or **Disagree** (see Figure P3–5). If you click **Disagree**, then the installer quits and the installation process ends. You also have a chance to read the license again by clicking **Read License**. Click **Agree** to continue.

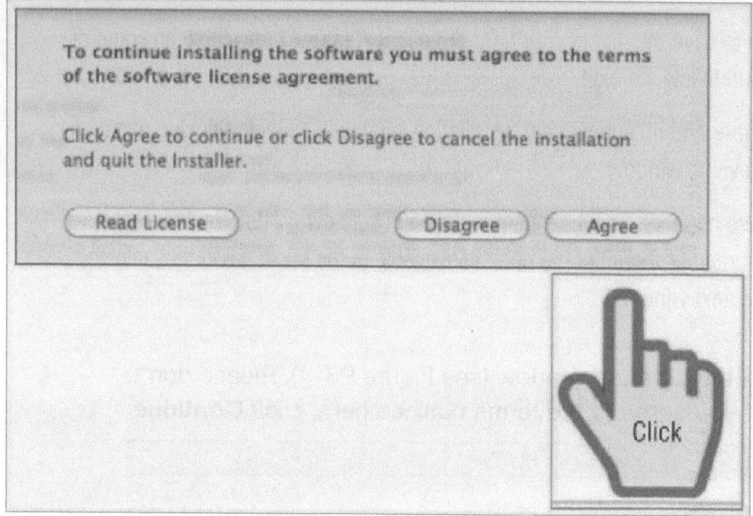

To continue installing the software you must agree to the terms of the software license agreement.

Click Agree to continue or click Disagree to cancel the installation and quit the Installer.

Read License   Disagree   Agree

Click

Figure P3–5. *The software license agreement (part 2)*

9. Now you need to configure the installation. The complete window is shown in Figure P3–6. Notice that this window states how much disk space the installation will take (4 GB, in this case). It also tells you where it is going to be installed ("Mac HD," in this case).

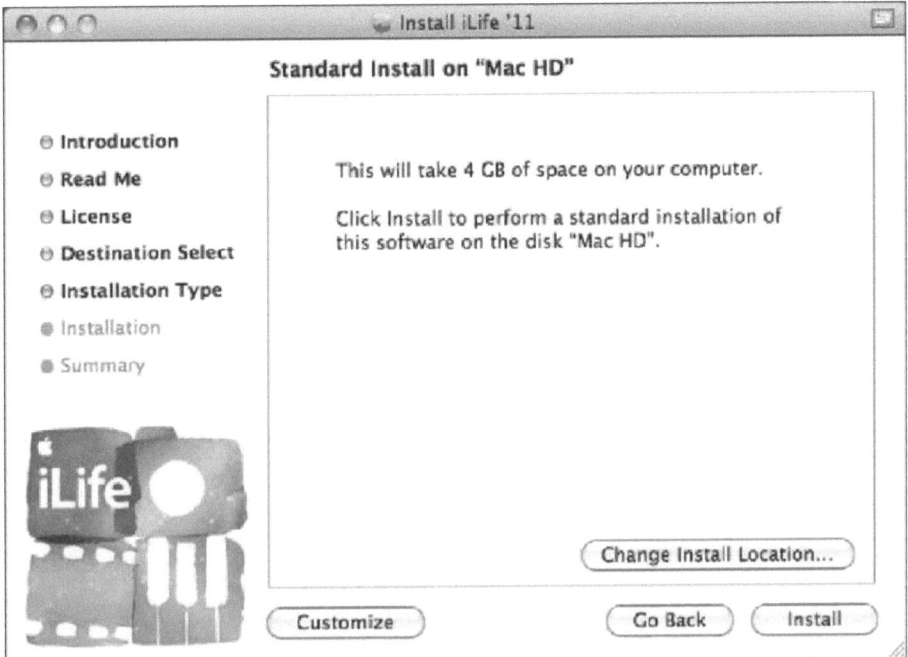

Figure P3–6. *The **Installation Type** window for iLife*

REVIEWING TWO KEY BUTTONS: CHANGE INSTALL LOCATION... AND CUSTOMIZE

> Change Install Location...

The **Change Install Location...** button allows you to change where you want to install iLife. Figure P3–7 shows the window that comes up if you click this button.

The green arrow in the **Mac HD** icon means that you can install iLife on this hard drive or hard drive partition. The yellow warning triangle in **Macintosh HD** icon means that you cannot install iLife there. In the example shown in Figure P3–7, I can't install iLife on "Macintosh HD" because iLife requires the Mac OS that is installed on the hard drive you want iLife to be on to be active and running.

If you click the **Customize** button [Customize], you can specify which applications you want or don't want to install. This window is shown in Figure P3–8. By default, all applications have a checkmark. If you want to install a given application, make sure that the small box next to the application name has a checkmark next to it. The size of every application is displayed here, as well. To get the most out of this book, it is recommended that you install all of the iLife applications.

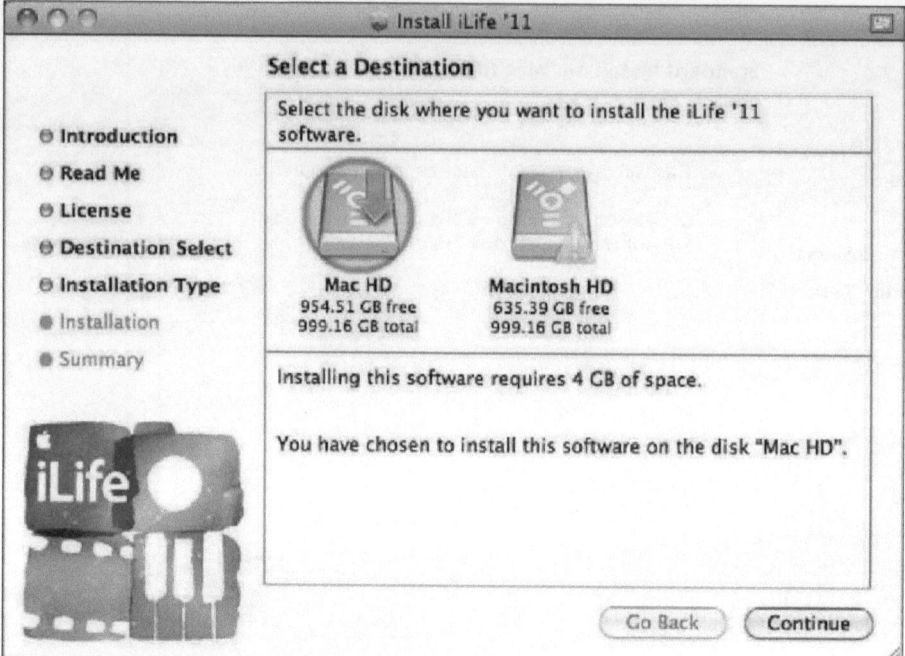

Figure P3–7. *The Select a Destination window*

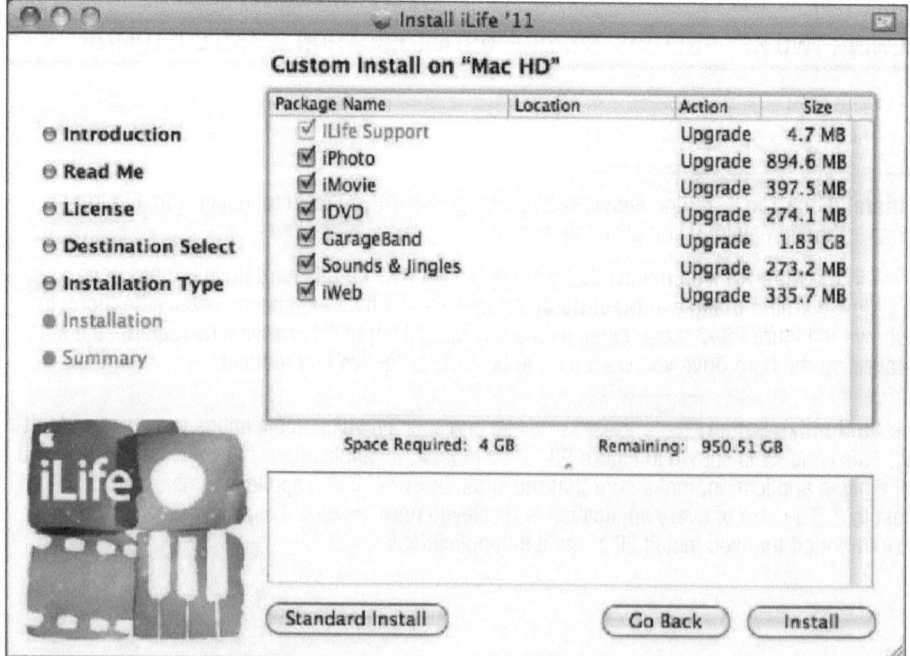

Figure P3–8. *The Custom Install window*

Figure P3–9 shows one other item of interest: the highlighted **Sounds and Jingles**. In the small box below the list of applications, you can see a description of the highlighted app.

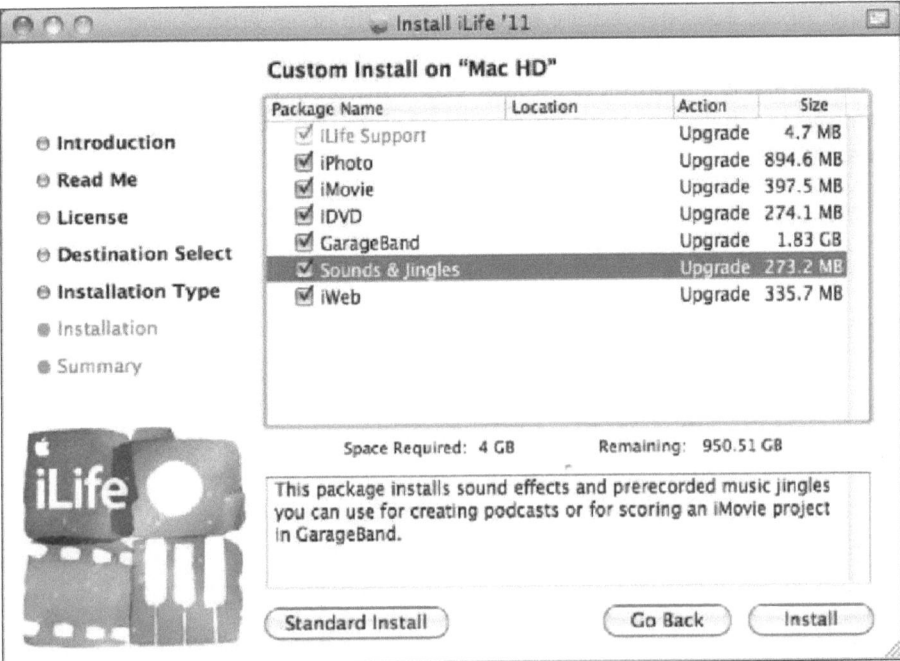

Figure P3–9. *An example of a selected item and its corresponding explanation in the box below*

If you want to go back to a "Standard Install," then click **Standard Install**.

10. Once you have determined what you want to install, click the **Install** button.

11. You must enter an Admin Username and Password to install most items on a Macintosh (see Figure P3–10).

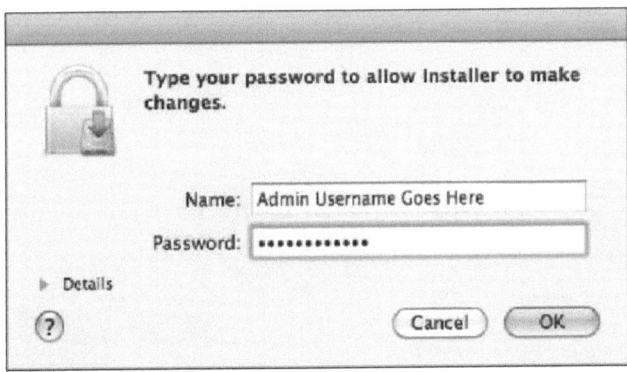

Figure P3–10. *A dialog box to enter an Admin Name and Password*

12. Click **OK** to start the actual installation process. Figures P3–11 through P3–15 show the last five screens of the installation process. You will notice that Apple does not require serial numbers to be entered during this process. Even though Apple does not keep track of its software via serial numbers, it is important to register your software if you want to be kept informed of the latest news about iLife or other important Apple updates.

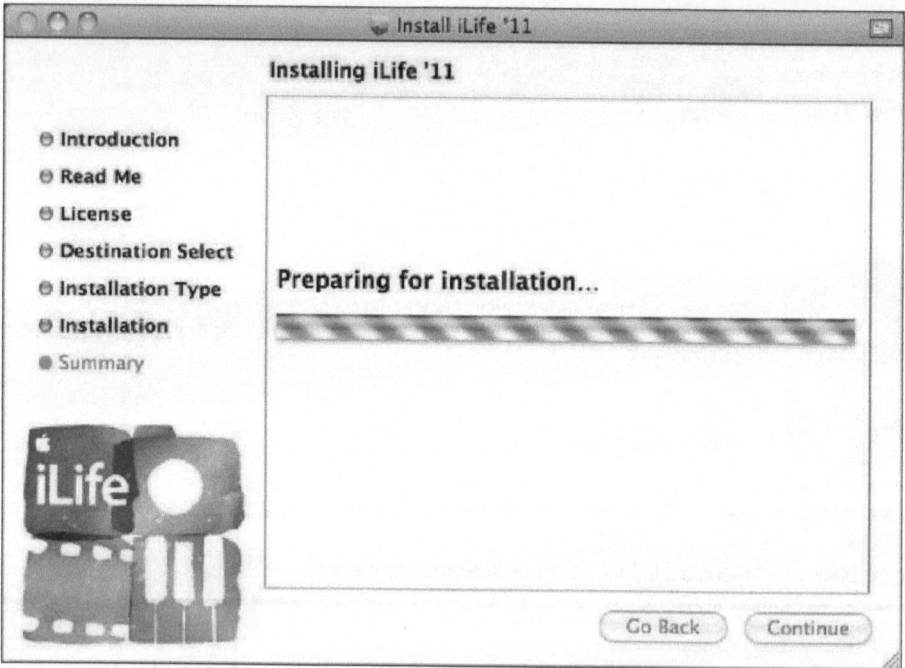

Figure P3–11. *The Preparing for installation window*

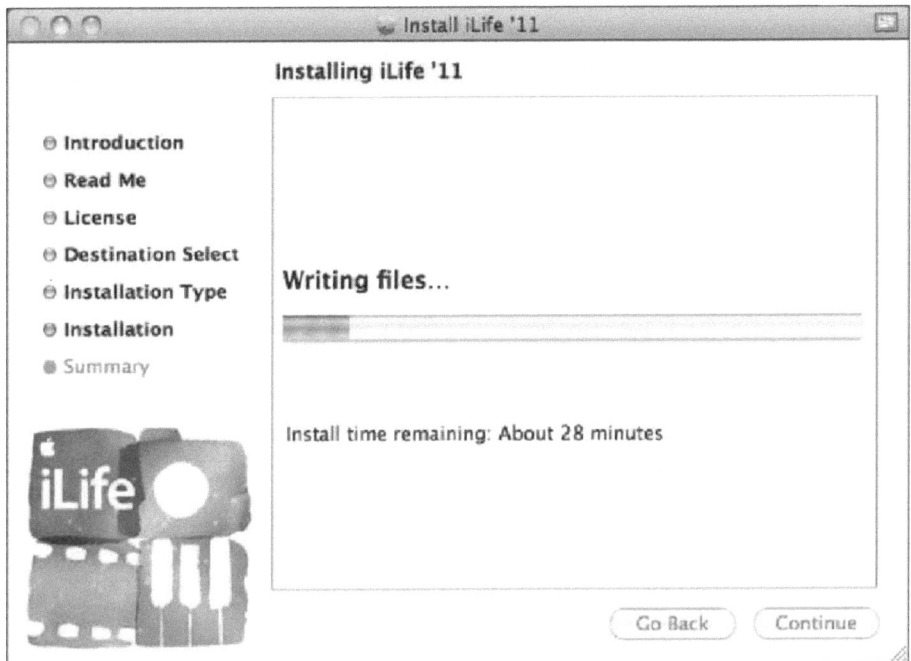

Figure P3–12. *The **Writing Files** window*

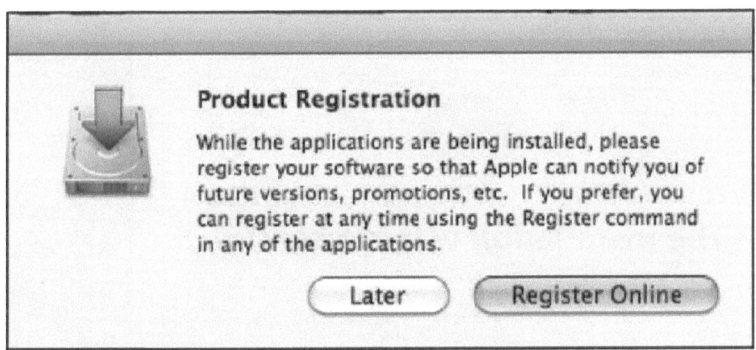

Figure P3–13. *The **Option to Register Online** window*

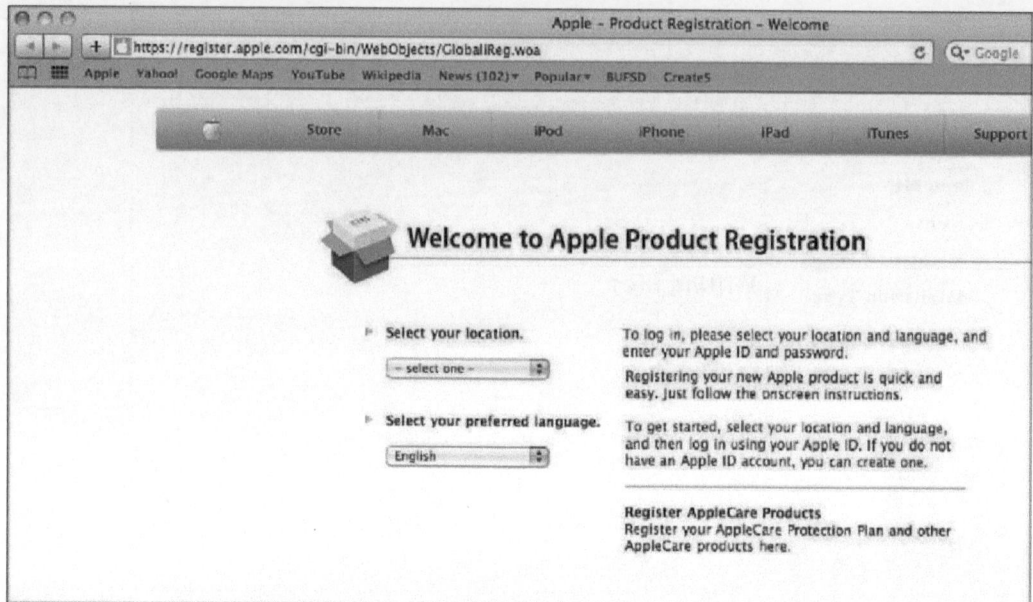

Figure P3–14. *Apple's* **Online Product Registration** *window*

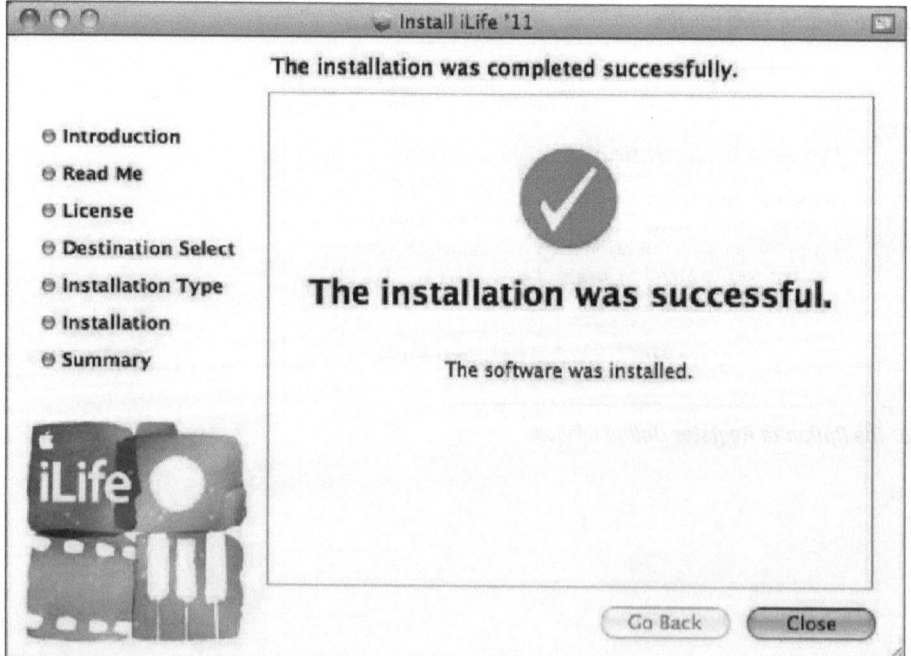

Figure P3–15. *The* **Installation was successful** *window*

13. Click the **Close** button to complete the process.

Installing from an Upgrade DVD

Installing iLife from an upgrade DVD is very similar to the process for installing from a bundled DVD, so I have abbreviated the steps here and referenced earlier figures when appropriate. To install iLife '11 from an upgrade DVD, follow these steps:

1. Insert the upgrade DVD into your DVD drive.

2. Double-click the **iLife '11 Install DVD** icon after it appears on your desktop (see Figure P3–16).

3. Double-click the **Install iLife** icon, which is also shown in Figure P3–16.

Figure P3–16. *The first three steps to installing iLife from an upgrade disk*

4. After you double-click the **Install iLife** icon, you are greeted with an **Introduction** (or **Welcome**) screen (see Figure P3–2).

5. The window that comes up next is the **Read Me** window. (Make sure you conform to the hardware/software requirements noted at the beginning of this chapter.)

6. Next, we come to the **License** window (see Figures P3–4 and P3–5). Configure the installation as desired (see Figure P3–6).

7. Once you have determined what you want to install, click the **Install** button.

8. You must enter an Admin Username and Password to install most items on a Macintosh; do so now (see Figure P3–10).

9. Click **OK** to start the actual install process (see Figures P3–11 through P3–15).

10. Click the **Close** button to complete the process.

Accessing Mac Software from the App Store

Purchasing Macintosh software can now be done in a much simpler way. If you are running Mac OS 10.6, you now have access to a new utility program called the **App Store**. The final version of this software will be included in Mac OS 10.7, which is scheduled to be released in July of 2011. Simply put: If you have an Apple ID, you can access this new digital-software warehouse and purchase the software you are looking for. As you will see, the installation process is also much simpler than installing software from a CDDVD. Apple is so confident of this new distribution method that, starting with Mac OS 10.7, all future major Macintosh OS upgrades will only be available through this store.

One of the major benefits of this new purchasing option is that you can install purchased apps on any of the Macs you own. This is really handy if you purchase a new Mac for a couple reasons. First, it gives you quick access to all the software you have purchased. Second, this approach enables you to install all of your licensed software with a just few mouse clicks. The only issue with the App Store from Apple is that certain applications are not yet—and may never be—available for purchase on it. The software installer CD/DVD will be around for awhile.

> **NOTE**: You cannot purchase software that is already installed on your Macintosh. For example, I purchased and installed the iLife Suite on my Mac quite some time ago. Therefore, I cannot repurchase any of the iLife apps for my Mac from the App Store.

Finding the New App Store on Your Mac

You can access the App Store in either of two ways. First, you can go to the **Apple** menu and choose the **App Store...** option (see Figure P3–17).

Figure P3–17. *Accessing the App Store via the **Apple** menu*

Second, you can go to your hard drive and locate the actual App Store application, which is found in your Applications folder. The **App Store** icon is shown in Figure P3–18.

Figure P3–18. *The **App Store** application icon if accessed via the hard drive*

Finding an App You Want

The App Store is a totally new digital marketplace for purchasing Mac software. In some respects, it looks and acts like the iTunes Store that many Mac and PC users are already familiar with. (The iTunes Store will be discussed in Chapter 19: "Navigating iTunes via its Sidebar and Different Workspace Views."

To demonstrate the various ways of finding an app, I will show you how to find the iPhoto app in the App Store. The first and easiest method for finding an app is to use the Search tool. But there are other ways as well, which I'll also list here:

- **Search:** The search tool is located at the far right of the App Store window – at very top of the screen. If you look at Figure P3–19, you can see "iPhoto" in the Search box and the results in the window below. Notice that the actual iPhoto app is listed at the far left of the screen, but several other apps that can be used with iPhoto also appear. The ability to access all the apps that might be useful with a given app is amazing because it might have taken hours of research on the Internet to find these other items.

Figure P3–19. *The Search tool*

- **Featured:** This section breaks down new releases into three sections: **New and Noteworthy**, **What's Hot**, and **Staff Favorites**. Since iPhoto was released quite some time ago, it was not found in the **Featured** section at the time of this guide's writing.

- **Top Charts:** This option breaks down the most popular apps that were recently purchased. It is broken down into three categories: **Top Paid**, **Top Free**, and **Top Grossing**. If you are looking for an app that has just been released, this is a great place to look. At the time of writing, iPhoto could be found in the **Top Paid** and **Top Grossing** sections.

- **Categories:** If you are searching for a type of program, but you don't know what specific programs are out there, then this is a good place to look for it. Software is broken down into 21 separate categories. From business apps to travel apps, this is a great place to look. You can find iPhoto in the **Photography** section, iMovie in the **Video** section, and GarageBand in the **Music** section. These sections also include other apps that can be used in conjunction with these iLife apps.

NOTE: **Purchased** and **Updates** are also options along the App Store's top toolbar. The **Purchased** section simply keeps track of all your purchases, while the **Updates** section alerts you if there any software upgrades to any of the software you have purchased previously from the store. **Updates** can even update several apps at once (assuming more than one app has an update available).

Installing iPhoto Via the App Store

Sticking with the iPhoto example, let's walk through the process of purchasing and installing an app:

1. Double-click the app you might want to purchase. In this case, click the iPhoto graphic shown below.

This brings up a screen with more details about the application; Figure P3–20 shows the info provided for iPhoto.

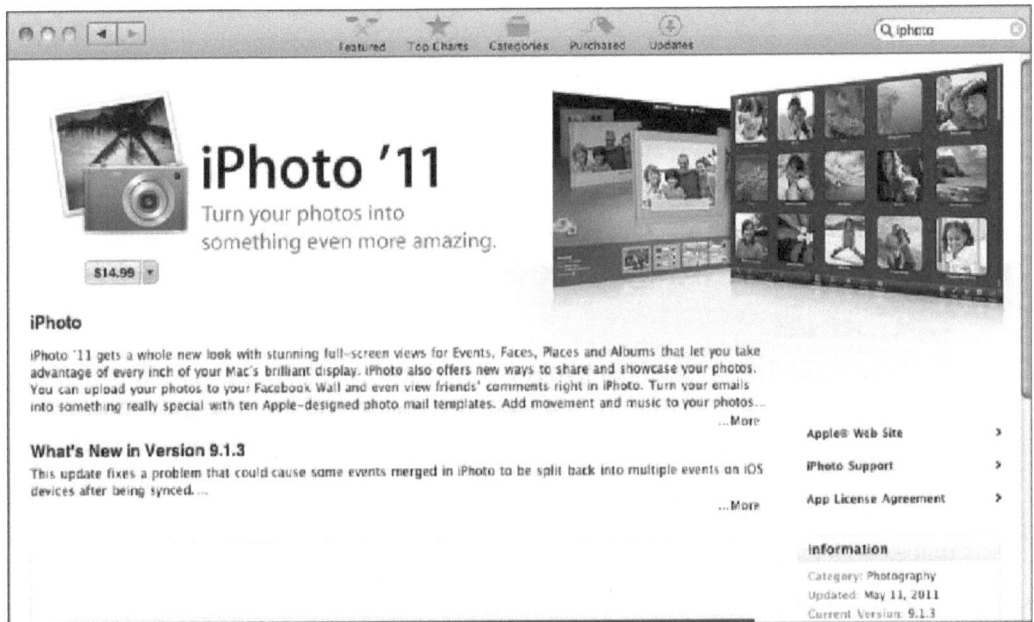

Figure P3–20. *A window that shows the full description of the app and provides the opportunity to purchase it*

2. If you decide to purchase the app, click the price of the app located below the app title. In Figure P3–20, the **Price** button looks like this: $14.99.

3. The **Price** button will then change to a **Buy App** button. Buy App. Click this button to continue the purchasing process.

4. You will then be asked to fill in your Apple ID, so that Apple can charge you for the purchase (see Figure P3–21).

Sign in to download from the App Store.

If you have an Apple ID, sign in with it here. If you have used the iTunes Store or MobileMe, for example, you have an Apple ID. If you don't have an Apple ID, click Create Apple ID.

Apple ID   Password   Forgot?

phoenix737@nyc.rr.com   •••••••••

(?)   (Create Apple ID)   (Cancel)   (Sign In)

Figure P3–21. *The login window, which is needed to provide the credentials to actually purchase the application*

5. Click the **Sign In** button to complete purchasing process.

6. If you entered the correct account info, the application will begin to install. The button you clicked to purchase the app will now become the **Installing** button.

    [Installing ▼]

7. The amount of time it takes to install an app depends on the size of the application you purchased. After the app is installed, the **Installing** button will become the **Installed** button. [Installed ▼]

8. The App Store automatically launches the app after the process is finished and places an icon for the app in the Dock.

Congratulations! iLife is now installed on your hard drive. You will notice that the **iPhoto**, **iMovie**, and **GarageBand** icons are now in your Dock, as shown in the figure below. These three apps are what I call the "three Amigos" of iLife '11 because these are the only applications added to the Dock automatically.

Although iWeb and iDVD apps are also installed, Apple decided not to put their icons in the Dock by default.

If you want to add iWeb and iDVD to the Dock, then you will have to go to the

Applications folder [Applications] on your hard drive and drag the icon for each to a location of your choosing on the Dock. The icons for these two applications are shown below.

Although iLife is installed now on your Mac, there are a few loose ends to take care of. First, when you initially launch iPhoto, there are a series of questions that need to be answered before you can fully access the application. Second, you need to make sure you have the latest versions of the iLife apps installed (hopefully all of them!). Learning how to check for updates is very important because it can help you avoid issues, as well as get access to new features in some cases. The next steps are to finish the iPhoto installation process and then update iLife with the latest changes.

Additional Questions Raised During the iPhoto Installation

The first question you have to answer is this: Do you want iPhoto to launch when a camera is attached? You are given three choices, as shown in Figure P3–22:

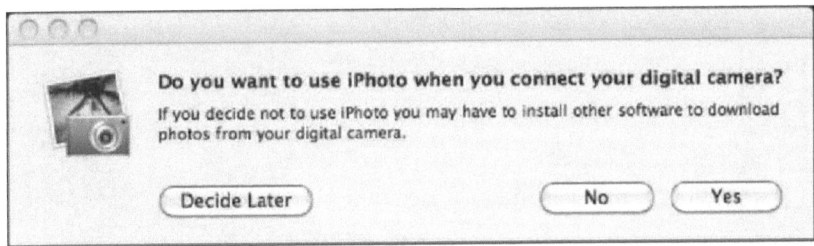

Figure P3–22. *Deciding whether you want iPhoto to automatically launch when connecting to a digital camera*

- **Decide Later**: This message will reappear the next time you launch iPhoto.

- **No**: iPhoto will not start up when a camera is detected.

- **Yes**: iPhoto will start up and automatically import your photos when a camera is detected.

The next option involves GPS (Global Positioning Satellite) data. iPhoto can take this info and add your photos to a map (see Figure P3–23).

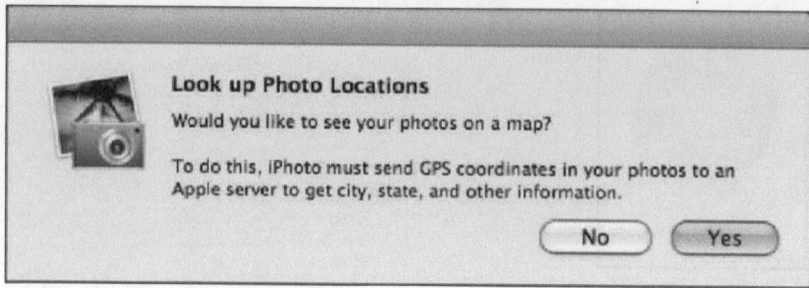

Figure P3–23. *Deciding whether you want to use GPS data*

After answering the preceding two questions , you'll see the screen shown in Figure P3–24. This screen basically lists your three choices for getting started. You can connect a camera or memory card, drag photos from a hard drive into iPhoto, or import photos using the **File** menu.

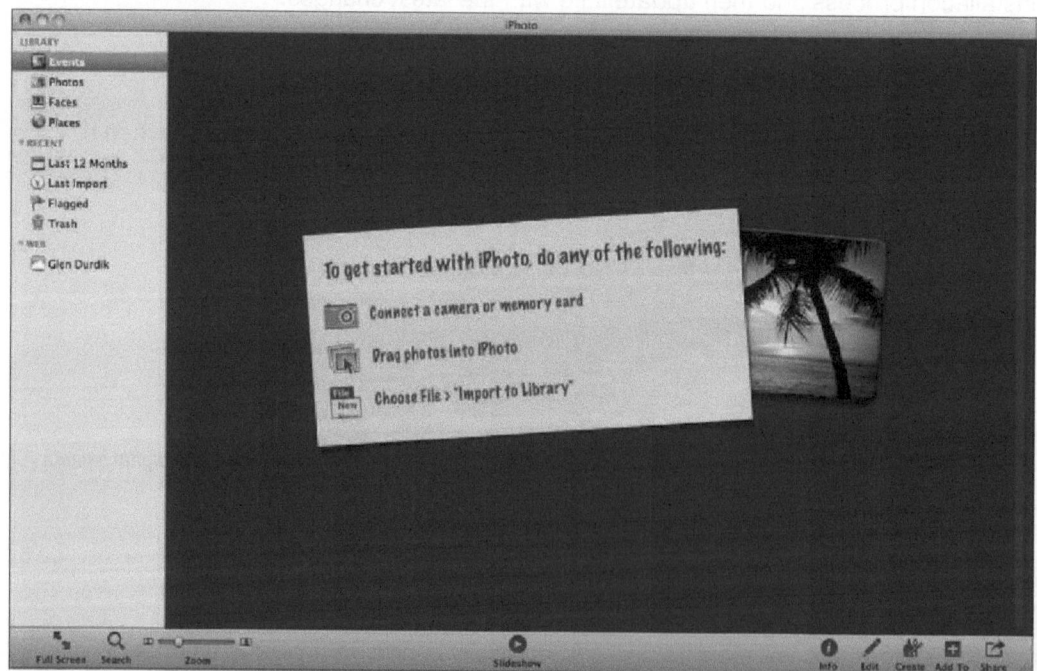

Figure P3–24. *The third screen that appears after you initially launch iPhoto*

Figure P3–25 appears when you first click the Faces feature in the sidebar's **Library** section. I will cover the Faces feature in detail in Chapter 5: "Faces and Places." This screen basically explains how to use this powerful feature of iPhoto. Once a person is tagged, iPhoto can find that individual in any existing or new photo.

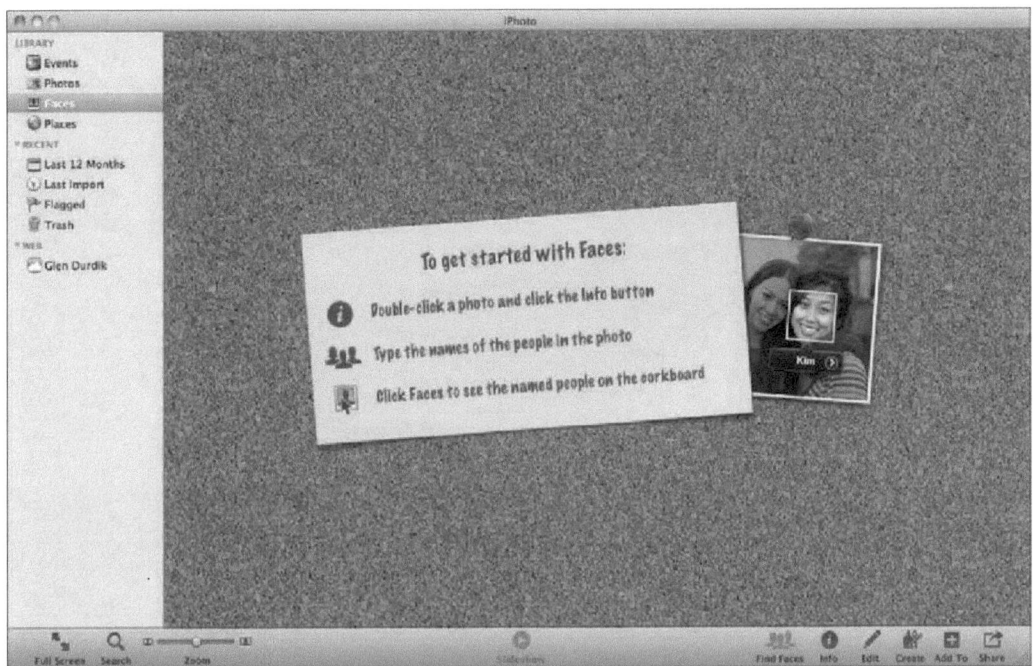

Figure P3–25. *The initial screen that appears when first choosing Faces in the **Library** section*

Figure P3–26 shows the initial screen you see after you click the Places feature in the sidebar's **Library** section. As with the Faces feature, the first time you click the Places feature brings up basic instructions on how to use this cool feature. The Places feature will be covered in detail in Chapter 5: "Faces and Places."

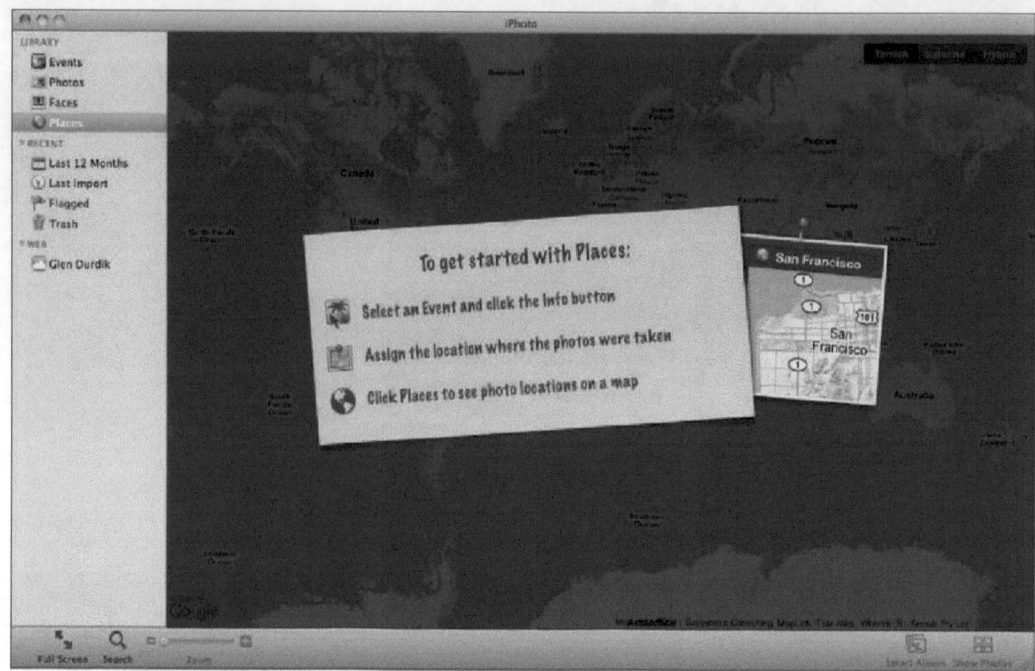

Figure P3–26. *The initial screen that appears when first choosing Places in the **Library** section*

Finally, you will see the **Welcome** screen (see Figure P3–27).

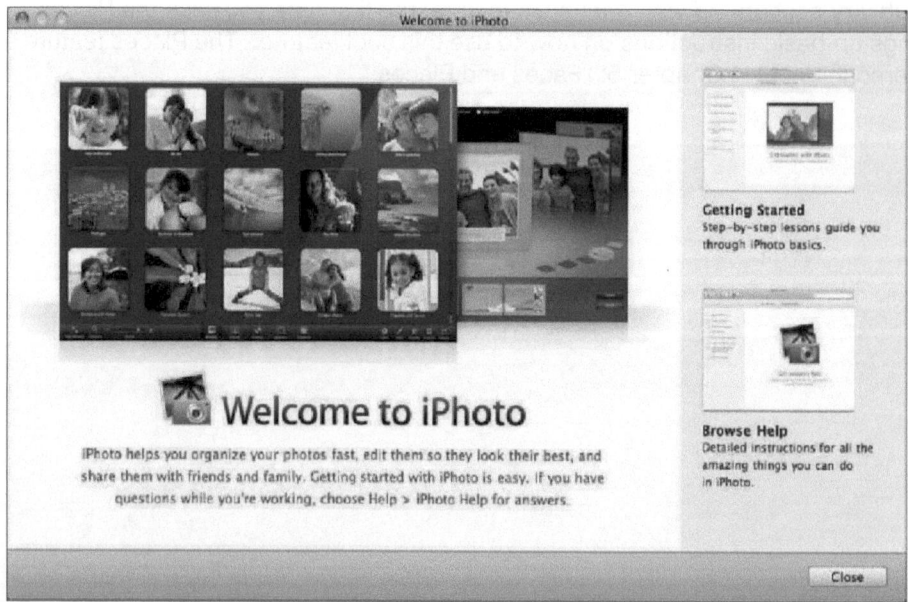

Figure P3–27. *The **Welcome to iPhoto** screen*

There are two items of interest in the **Welcome to iPhoto** window. Both assist you with using iPhoto. To access these items, go to the **Help** menu and choose **iPhoto Help**. You will see the following options:

- **Getting Started:** Shows you step-by-step how to perform several tasks in iPhoto.

- **Browse Help:** Shows you (by example) how to perform most tasks in iPhoto.

If you want to close this window, click the **Close** button.

Updating iLife to the Latest Version

Most of the time, there are updates available for a product when you purchase and install it. iLife is no different. Software fixes or new features might be added at any time, as well. It is important to check for updates periodically. In the next few pages, I will guide you through the update process for iLife. Similar steps are also taken to update your Macintosh operating system. Follow these steps to update the iLife Suite:

1. Go to the **Apple** menu (located at the top left of your display). Click and hold down the mouse button. This will bring up the menu shown in Figure P3–28.

Figure P3–28. *The Apple menu*

2. While still holding down your mouse button, move your pointer down to the **Software Update...** option.

3. Let go of the mouse button after the option is highlighted (see Figure P3–29). Your Mac will now contact Apple to see if there are any updates (see Figure P3–30).

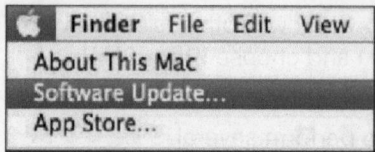

Figure P3–29. *Selecting the **Software Update...** option*

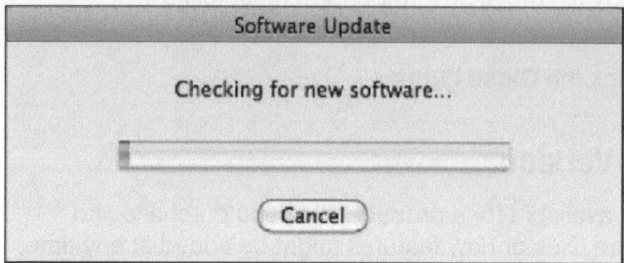

Figure P3–30. *The **Checking for new software...** window*

4. If there are updates for iLife (and/or your operating system), you should click **Show Details** on the bottom left of your screen (see Figure P3–31). Doing so brings you to the screen shown in Figure P3–32.

Figure P3–31. *Selecting the **Show Details** button*

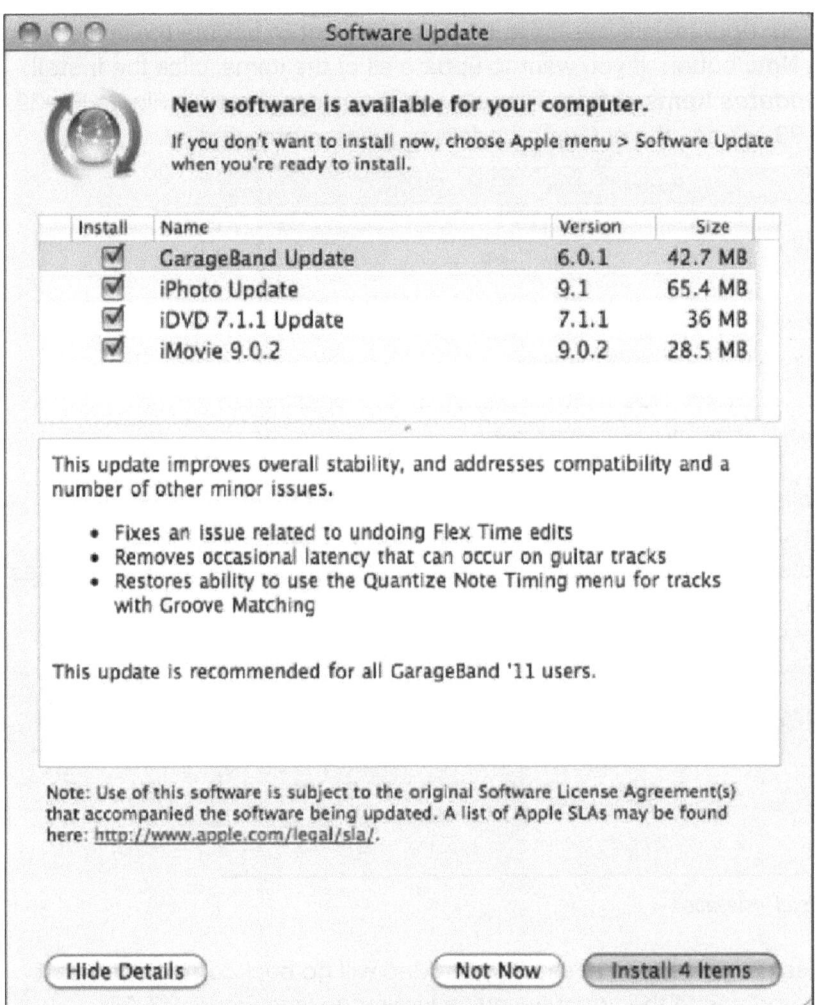

Figure P3–32. *The **New software is available for your computer** window*

NOTE: The small box next to the software title will have a blue checkmark in it if the app has an update available.

5. In this case, four updates are available. If you don't want to update the items, click the **Not Now** button. If you want to update all of the items, click the **Install** *number of updates* **Items** button. These two buttons are shown in Figure P3–32. In Figure P3–33, we see the software-update process in progress.

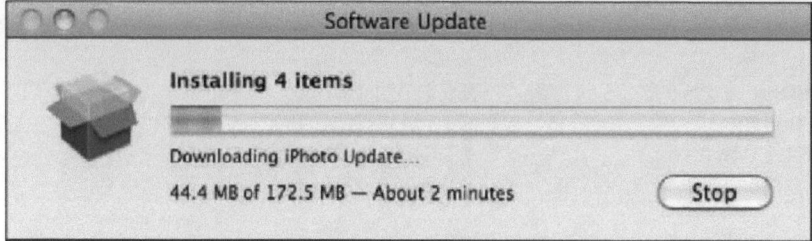

Figure P3–33. *The beginning of the software-update process*

6. After the Mac is done installing the updates, you will get the window shown in Figure P3–34. Just click **OK** and the process is done. If you are updating your operating system as well, you might be asked to restart your Mac for the changes to take place.

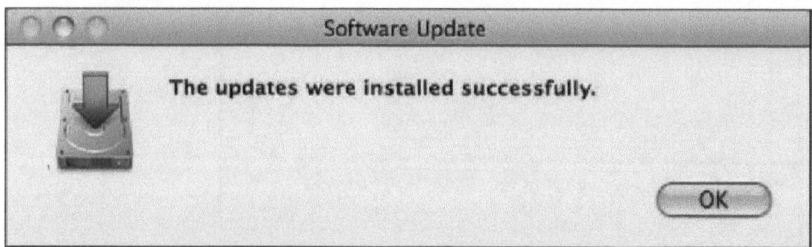

Figure P3–34. *A successful installation*

7. If your updates do *not* require a restart, your Mac will go back to Apple to see if there are any updates to the updates you've just made (see Figure P3–35).

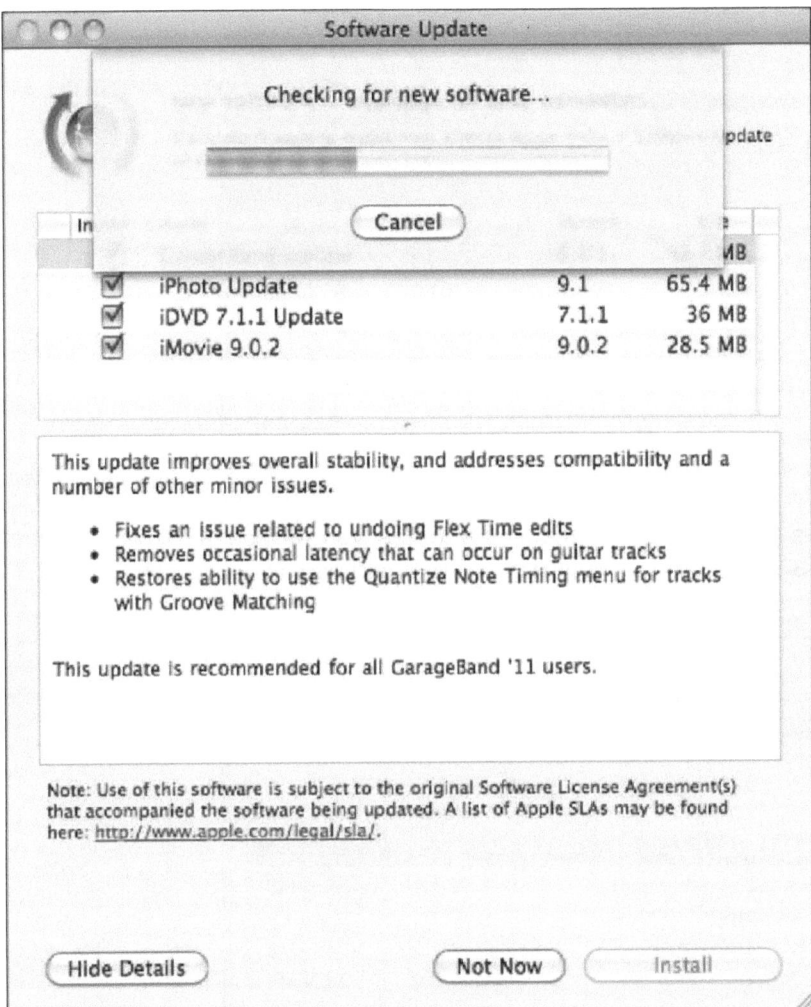

Figure P3–35. *The Rescan for new updates window*

8. If your Mac finds additional updates, it will display these in a blue box with a checkmark inside it next to the relevant applications (see Figure P3–36). Notice the green circles with a white checkmark. These items do not require updates.

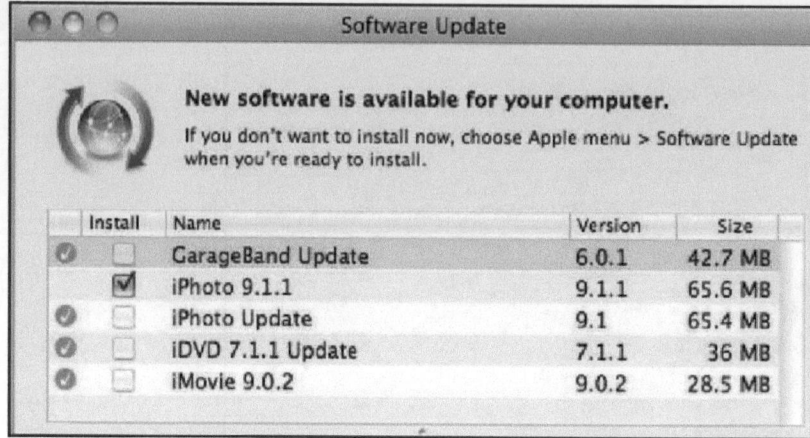

Figure P3–36. *A window showing several applications that do not need any additional updates and one that does*

9. After you have gone through the required updates, you will see the screen shown in Figure P3–37. Notice that it now states, "Your software is up to date."

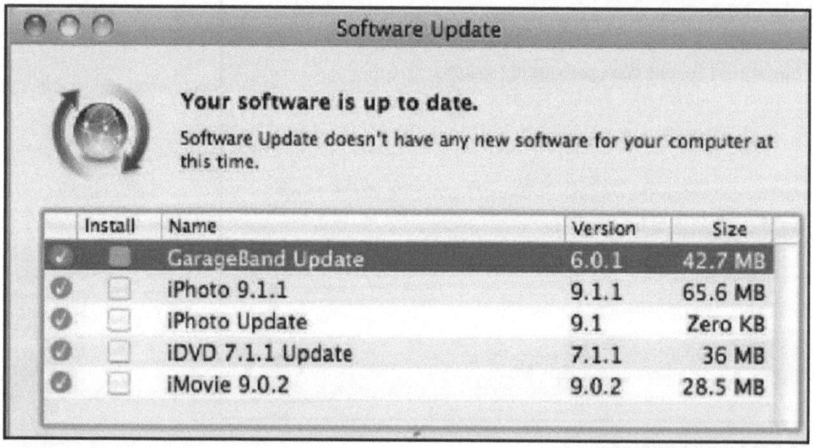

Figure P3–37. *The **Your software is up to date** window*

This might seem like a lot of steps, and the process can take a while to complete; however, I have never experienced any complications while performing these steps.

NOTE: Never update your operating system or software the moment an update comes out. Apple has made bad updates from time to time, and it is better to wait a few days to see if the update works as planned. I recommend searching the Web for Apple support sites and checking them whenever an update is released. It's much better to be safe than sorry.

Summary

OK, I admit that installing and upgrading software is not the most glamorous part of the book. However, many people just getting started with iLife are also brand new to the Macintosh environment. Covering how to install software via a DVD or the App Store is essential because the vast majority of Macintosh software is installed in the same fashion. Being aware of software updates is also critical in helping you to keep your Mac up and running. But – as I mentioned just before this summary – it is also critical that you wait a day or two to see if a new update causes more problems than it solves. Bad updates from any company are rare – but they do happen.

That said, turn on your Mac (if it isn't already on), turn the page, and start down the road to becoming a proficient iLife user. You are only limited by the vastness of your creativity.

Part **IV**

iPhoto

iPhoto is an application geared towards people who want to store, enhance, or share their precious memories with just a few clicks of the mouse. I've broken down iPhoto's environment, key edit features, and sharing capabilities into six chapters. iPhoto is a breeze to use... but there is a lot to learn to become comfortable with all the great aspects of the program.

Chapter 1

Getting Around Your Digital Darkroom

With how powerful and easy to use iPhoto is, it will expand your digital photography options immensely. As you'll see from the environment discussion in this chapter and the numerous ways to share your digital memories that I'll explain in the chapters that follow, iPhoto does the digital darkroom just right.

The iPhoto environment has several major components: the Source list, the Workspace, the scrollbar, and various Window options, all of which are shown in Figure 1–1. I will cover these in detail in this chapter.

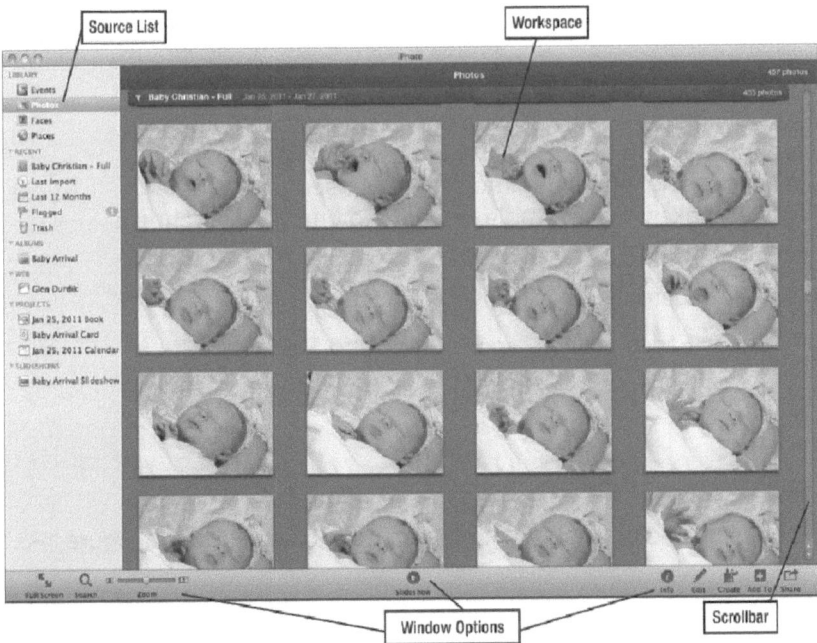

Figure 1–1. *Key work environment elements*

Source List

As you can see in Figure 1–1, the Source list is located all the way on the left side of the iPhoto work environment. Once opened, the Source list consists of the following six options:

- Library
- Recent
- Albums
- Web
- Projects
- Slideshow

The first section is called Library, and is shown in Figure 1–2. Notice that it is located below the three dots I covered in the Common Feature section of the Quick Start Guide of this manual.

Figure 1–2. *Library section of iPhoto sidebar*

In the Library section, you see the following options:

- **Events**: When you import photos, iPhoto imports them into Events. Events are grouped according to when photos were taken. You can import photos into a single Event or into several, based on the date and time they were taken. For example, a wedding one weekend and a birthday the next weekend.
- **Photos**: This is the master library of all your media.
- **Faces**: I will discuss Faces in Chapter 5: "Faces and Places."
- **Places**: I will also cover Places in Chapter 5: "Faces and Places."

Recent

The Recent section contains a helpful list of your recent activity, as shown in Figure 1–3.

Figure 1-3. *Recent section of iPhoto sidebar*

For example, each item in Figure 1–3 represents the following:

- **Baby Christian -- FULL**: This is showing that I created a album with that title.

- **Last Import**: If you click on this option, iPhoto will show you what media you just imported.

- **Last 12 Months**: This will show you what you imported over the last Year.

- **Flagged**: Please note the number "1" next to this option. This means that I tagged one photo in my Library. By flagging the photo, you can more easily locate it again, because it appears in this section. To flag a photo, click on it, and you will see a small grey flag in the upper left-hand corner. Click on the flag. When the photo has been flagged, it will have a small orange flag in the top left corner. This is shown in Figure 1–4.

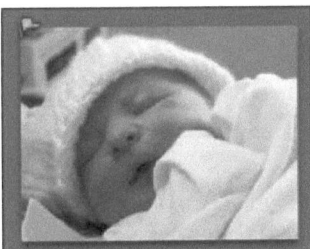

Figure 1-4. *Sample of a flagged photo*

- **Trash**: If you delete a photo, it goes into this trash can. You have to manually delete photos by clicking this icon.

Albums

Whenever you add a photo to your library, it is automatically put into an **Event** folder called Untitled. You can then create albums to better organize your photos.

To add photos to new album, do the following:

1. Highlight the photos you want to add.

2. Go to the **File** menu located at the top of your screen.

3. Click **New**, and then select Album.

That's all there is to it. You can give your album a title by changing the default text - "untitled album." Just type in the new title and the default text will disappear In the example shown in Figure 1–5, you see my album titled "Baby Arrival."

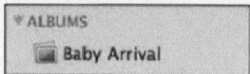

Figure 1–5. *Sample album*

> **NOTE:** To delete an album or other item from the sidebar, right-click the object you want to delete and select Delete in the window that appears.

Web

If you publish a photo or album to the available web services, an icon and the name of your account that you uploaded to will appear in this section. In Figure 1–6, you will notice that I have uploaded to my Facebook and MobileMe accounts. MobileMe is a service that provides many benefits to its users, including a great gallery for videos and photos that allows anyone to download your media.

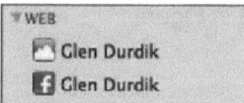

Figure 1–6. *Sample web access*

Projects

If you create calendars, cards, or books, each project you create will appear in the Projects section. In Figure 1–7, I created (1) Book, (1) Card, and (1) Calendar.

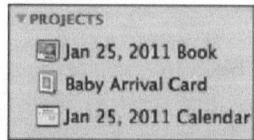

Figure 1–7. *Sample Projects section*

Slideshows

iPhoto allows you to create stunning slideshows of your photos. You can create one in a flash, or you can use the Create tool to save it for future use. Each one you create and save will show up in this section of the sidebar. An example is shown in Figure 1–8. I will also go into more detail about this tool later in the chapter.

Figure 1–8. *Slideshows section*

Well, that's it for the sidebar overview. From albums and events to calendars and slideshows, this is where you can access them all.

Workspace

The iPhoto workspace, shown in Figure 1–9, is where all the editing and creation of projects is done. I highlighted a few key areas in the figure. Here, you will see multiple pictures (if you have more than one photo). To edit a photo, double-click on it. This enlarges the photo so that it takes up the entire iPhoto workspace. Also in the Workspace, you see the name of the album that is currently being accessed. In this case, "Baby Christian—Full." In the center, you see that you are viewing your photos in the Photo section of the sidebar. Last, you can see how many photos are in this album in the upper right-hand corner.

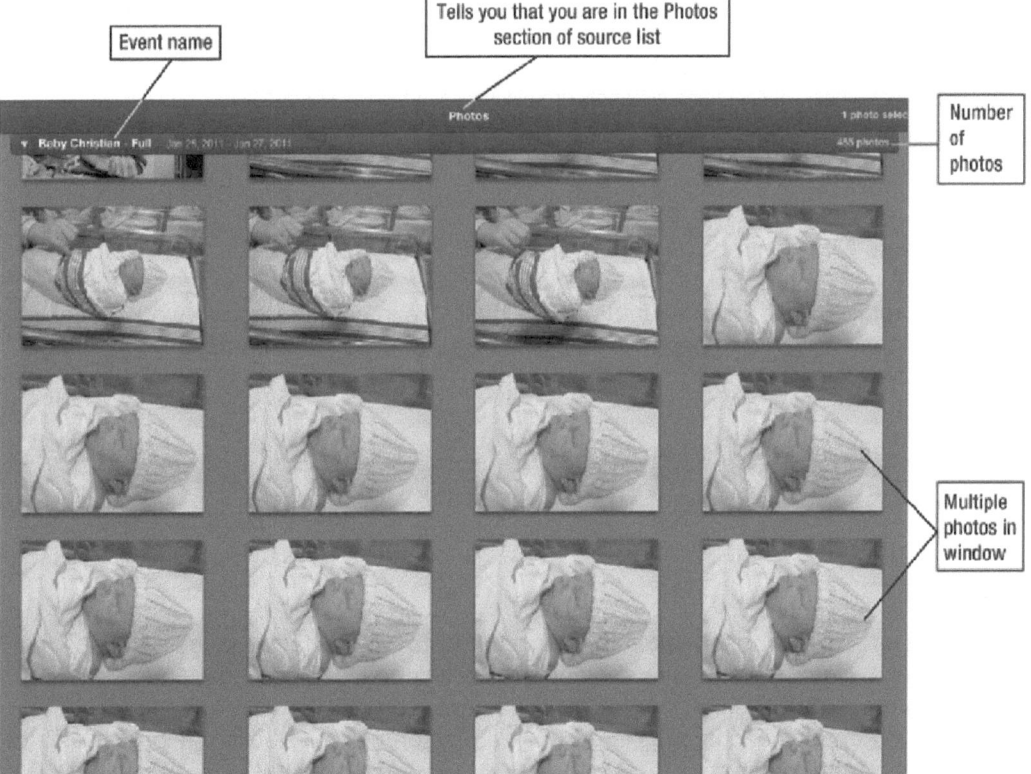

Figure 1–9. *Sample Workspace environment.*

If you are inside an Event and want to go back to the master list of Events, click the **All**

All Events

Events button at the top left of the Workspace.

If you are viewing a photo in the Photo section and want to go back to the main gallery

Photos

of photos, click the **Photos** button at the top left of the workspace.

Scrollbar

The scrollbar simply allows you to navigate through your photos. You can either drag the

toolbar tab up or down. Or you can click the up or down arrow found at the bottom of the scrollbar.

> **NOTE:** Remember, the common elements are discussed in the Quick Start Guide, so I will not cover them here.

Window Options

In all iLife applications, various functions are available in and around the workspace. These options allow you to perform simple tasks or access more complicated settings and functions.

Full Screen Mode Activator

Full Screen This option takes the current iPhoto window and makes it occupy the whole screen. No other items are shown. This means no Dock and no Menu System. This is a great feature, as you can better concentrate on your project at hand, and it makes all the options and images larger. If you plan on using iPhoto for a long stretch of time, you'll want to be aware of this option.

Search Tool

 The **Search** tool is available at the bottom left of your screen. You can search by date, keyword, rating, title, or description. If you click on this button, the **Search** box shown in Figure 1–10 appears.

Figure 1–10. *The Search field*

Zoom Slider

 By default, iPhoto displays your gallery photos at a certain size. The **Zoom** slider allows you to make these thumbnails larger by moving the circular button in the slider to the right, or to make them smaller by moving the circular button to the left. If you are viewing only one image, the **Zoom** slider is replaced with a preview bar, as shown in Figure 1–11.

Figure 1–11. *The photo preview bar*

Click on one of the small photos in this bar and you get a horizontal scrollbar. Move the grey oval button (located at the bottom, see Figure 1–12) left or right to navigate quickly through your precious memories.

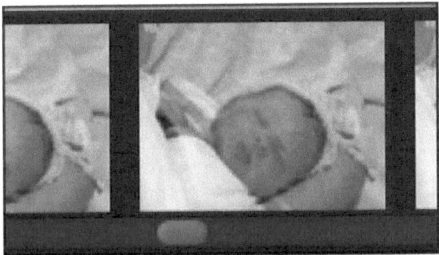

Figure 1–12. *Slide the oval button to move your preview bar forward and back*

Info Button

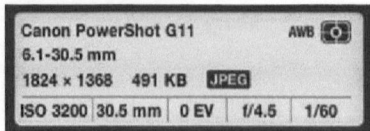

The **Info** button gives you access to important information about your photos. Click this button to reveal the info window shown in Figure 1–13.

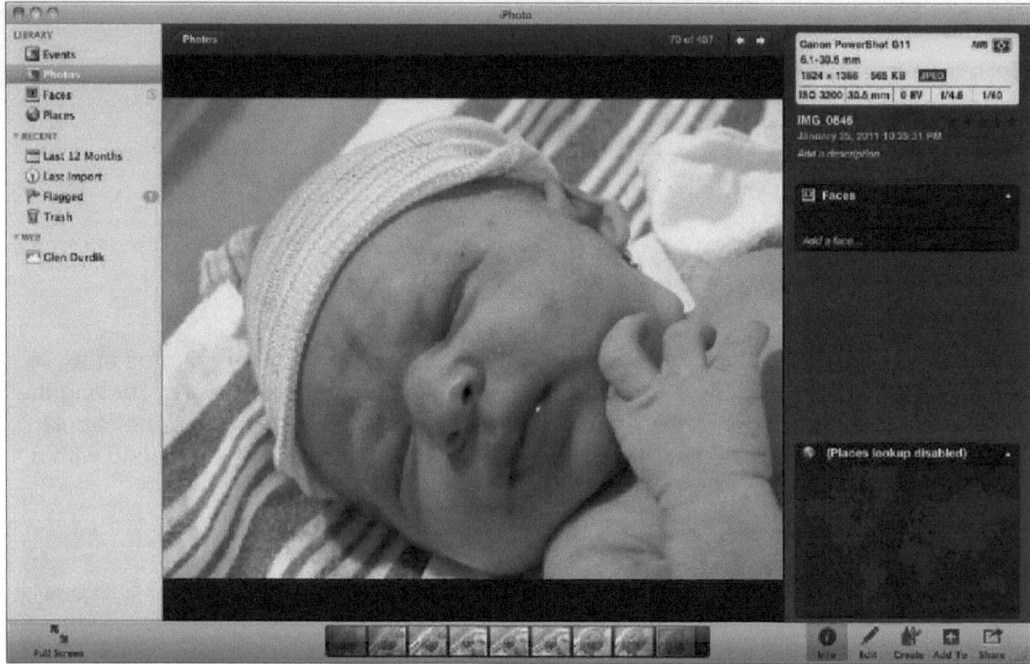

Figure 1–13. *Info window*

Figures 1–14 through 1–17 show the key sections of the info window.

Figure 1–14 shows you details about what camera was used and various other information you probably don't need to worry about, unless you are a professional photographer.

Canon PowerShot G11				AWB ⚙
6.1-30.5 mm				
1824 × 1368	491 KB	JPEG		
ISO 3200	30.5 mm	0 EV	f/4.5	1/60

Figure 1–14. *Camera settings*

Figure 1–15 contains a few important items. On the top left is the name of the file. To the right of this is a rating system. In this example, I gave the photo three out of five stars. You can have iPhoto sort your photos by various categories. This is useful if you want to find all "5 star" quality photos quickly, for example. To sort a photo based on your rating, you must go to the **View** menu and click **Sort Photos**, then select **Ratings**. You can also have iPhoto display the star rating under a photo. This is done by clicking on a photo and then going to the **View** menu and selecting **Ratings**. Below the name of the photo is the date and time the photo was taken. Below the date is a section to add your own comments. In this case, "baby has arrived!!!!"

Figure 1–15. *Name, date of photo, optional description, and rating system.*

Figure 1–16 shows you how you can add a face or show which person is assigned to a photo. I will go over Faces in more detail in Chapter: 5, "Faces and Places."

Figure 1–16. The *Faces section of info window*

Figure 1–17 shows you how to see what location the photo is associated with. At this point in iPhoto setup, I have not enabled Places. That's why you see "Places lookup disabled" in the figure. Faces and Places are simple concepts, but they take a while to explain fully. I will do so in Chapter: 5, "Faces and Places."

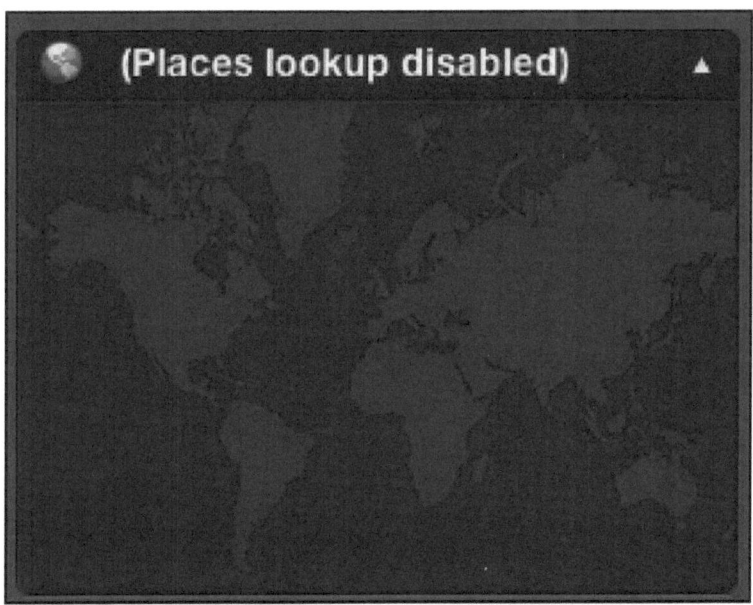

Figure 1–17. *Places section of info window*

Summary

Camera, check. Memory card, check. iPhoto, check. With these tools, you can record and store the visual treasures that make up your life. iPhoto will take these treasures and either enhance them or allow you to share them. In this chapter, you learned how to navigate the iPhoto Workspace. With this basic knowledge, you can start to take your photos to a new level and, because iPhoto is so easy to use, you can have a lot of fun.

Chapter 2

Setting Your Sights on iPhoto's Menus

Menus are found at the top of every Macintosh application. The **Apple** (symbol) menu is always farthest left. Next to it is the application menu. The title of this menu is always the name of the program you are using. As we see in Figure 2–1, if you are running iPhoto, you get the **iPhoto** menu. In this chapter, we'll explore each menu, beginning with **iPhoto**, and work our way to the last menu in every application, the **Help** menu. This will familiarize you with all the menu options you have at your fingertips. It's a crash course, so strap yourself in for a quick ride.

iPhoto Menu

The **iPhoto** menu, shown in Figure 2–1, provides a list of helpful items. Some of these— such as **Preferences...**—contain several noteworthy tabs, each with additional features designed to make your iPhoto experience a good one. In the following sections, I give an overview of each of these options.

Figure 2–1. *The complete iPhoto menu*

About iPhoto

The **About iPhoto** option, as I discussed in the "Common Features" section of the Quick Start guide of this manual, just shows you the version of the program you are running.

Preferences...

This is an important section for any application. Preferences are settings that affect how the application works. For iPhoto, there are five different tabs with many features to configure: **General**, **Appearance**, **Sharing**, **Accounts**, and **Advanced**. A description of each follows.

General Tab

The **General** tab is shown in Figure 2–2.

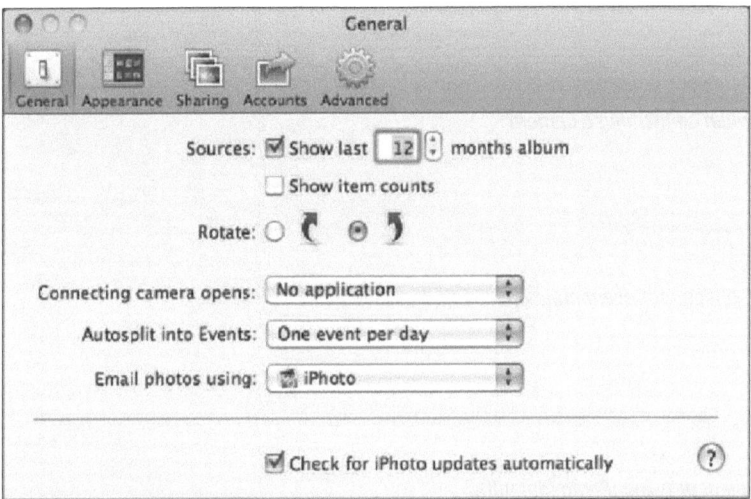

Figure 2–2. *General* tab of the menu choice *Preferences... found in the iPhoto* menu

The **General** tab's various options are as follows:

- **Sources:** The first line allows you to set how many months will appear for the **Last Import** section in the sidebar. The second line asks if you want to show the number of items in each sidebar section. For example, if you have 15 photos in the **Photos** section, by default it will not display 15. If you check this box, 15 will appear next to **Photos**.

- **Rotate:** This option determines if you want your photos to rotate clockwise or counter-clockwise (the default).

- **Connecting camera opens:** You are given the choices in Figure 2–3. If you remember, when you launched iPhoto for the first time, you were asked to decide what would happen when you attach a camera (via USB). By accessing this menu option, you can modify your original choice. Image Capture is an application supplied by Apple that can manage input devices such as cameras and scanners. iPhoto is a much more sophisticated application, so I feel that Image Capture is not the best choice.

- **Autosplit into Events**: When you import photos into iPhoto, by default it creates one event per day. With this setting, you can modify it to one event per week, or break it down into two-hour or eight-hour gaps. This is shown in Figure 2–4.

- **Email photos using**: You can choose between iPhoto and other email clients when you want to email a photo within iPhoto. This is shown in Figure 2–5.

- **Check for iPhoto updates automatically**: If you check the box next to this setting, iPhoto will check with Apple whenever it starts up and checks for updates.

Figure 2–3. *Options available when connecting a camera*

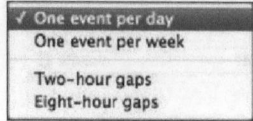

Figure 2–4. *Importing photos—options for event creation*

Figure 2–5. *Choices for email client or using iPhoto (default)*

Appearance Tab

The **Appearance** tab is shown in Figure 2–6.

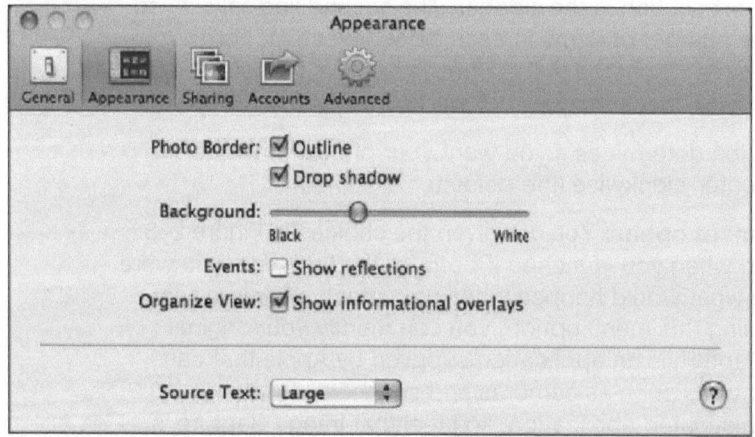

Figure 2–6. *Appearance tab of the menu choice **Preferences…** found in the **iPhoto** menu*

Its options are described in the following:

- **Photo Border**: This determines how your photo appears in iPhoto. By default, there is an outline and drop shadow around every photo.

- **Background**: This determines the color of the background behind your photos. Totally black is one extreme, and totally white is the other.

- **Events**: You can add a little more flair to your events by checking the box next to Show reflections. By default, this is turned off. See Figure 2–7 for an example of the reflection turned on.

- **Organize View**: You can choose to have informational overlays appear on the screen as you scroll through your library. The default is to show them. This will be a grey screen that contains appropriate info as you scroll (dates or ratings for example) that appears in the middle of window in the Photos view. Showing the date is the default, but you can also sort by ratings or titles.

- **Source Text**: This determines the size of the font in the Source List— or, as I call it, the sidebar. It can be large (default) or small.

Figure 2–7. *Example of Reflections turned on for events*

Sharing Tab

If there is more than one Mac on your network, you can share your photos (whole library or selected albums) or view photos from users that are sharing theirs. The **Sharing** tab is shown in Figure 2–8.

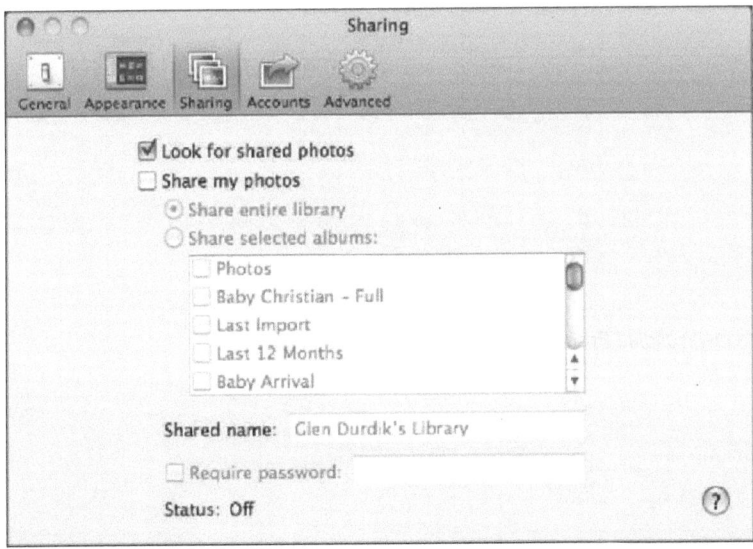

Figure 2–8. *Sharing* tab of the menu choice *Preferences...* found in the *iPhoto* menu

The options are described in the following:

- **Look for shared photos**: Check this box if you want to see shared photos. They will appear in the iPhoto sidebar.

- **Share my photos**: You can select your entire library or selected albums.

- **Shared name**: This is the name that others will see if you share your photos.

- **Require password**: Check this box if you want to keep your shared photos private. You must enter a password for this to function.

- **Status**: This just tells you if you are currently sharing your photos.

Accounts Tab

In Figure 2–9, the **Accounts** tab tells you what online accounts are currently being used in iPhoto. MobileMe is Apple's online service. I have two email accounts that I use, and my photos are shared via my Facebook account.

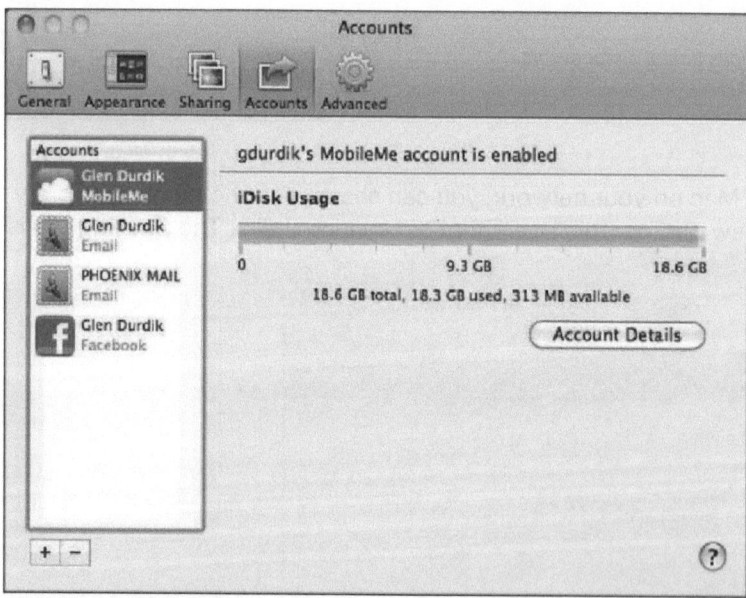

Figure 2–9. *Accounts* tab of the menu choice **Preferences...** found in the iPhoto menu

Advanced Tab

The **Advanced** tab is shown in Figure 2–10.

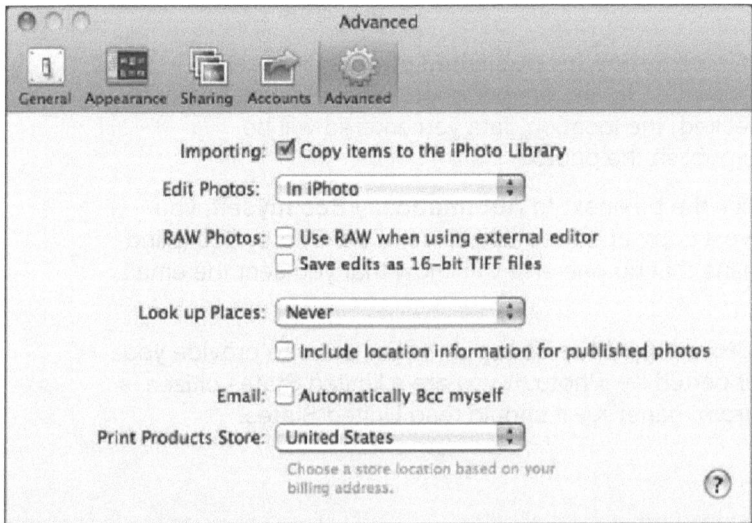

Figure 2–10. *Advanced tab of the menu choice **Preferences...** found in the **iPhoto** menu*

The following list explains the options in the **Advanced** tab:

- **Importing:** Decide if you want to actually add (duplicate) the photo into the iPhoto Library. If this is not checked, the item will not be duplicated, and iPhoto will use a pointer to the file. By default this is turned on.

> **NOTE:** If you decide not to copy the item, any changes to the photo will only take place in iPhoto; the original will not be changed. As I said earlier, if you make changes to photos (with this item checked), the change is permanent. Duplicate the photo if you want to experiment.

- **Edit Photos:** This may sound unusual, but you can actually have iPhoto edit photos in another application. You might have a more powerful photo editor and choose to use it instead.

- **RAW Photos:** RAW photos are the highest quality image a camera can take. Only high-end cameras can take RAW photos. These two options deal with these type of photos. The first line, when checked, will open the RAW copy of your photo as opposed to the JPEG or TIFF copy iPhoto made when it imported the photo. The second line allows you to save the file as a TIFF file. A TIFF file uses a much better compression technology, so it is recommended that you check this box if using RAW files.

- **Look up Places:** If your camera takes GPS data when a photo is taken, iPhoto can use the information to place the photos on the Places map. If your photo has this data, chose **Automatically** for this option. Most cameras do not record GPS data, so **Never** is the default.

- **Include location information for published photos:** You can manually add the location to any of your photos. If the check box next to this item is checked, the location data you entered will be transferred if you publish the photo.

- **Email:** If you check the box next to **Automatically Bcc myself**, you will always receive a copy of any email you send via iPhoto. Bcc (blind carbon copy) means that no one else will know that you sent the email to yourself.

- **Print Products Store:** Apple has set up an online store to provide you with products supported by iPhoto. If you are a United States citizen— not an evil alien from Planet X—it should read United States.

NOTE: The **Help** button appears in every section of the **Preferences...** window tabs. If you click on it, you can get more help on the section you are currently viewing. This guide gives you a great start to learning iPhoto, but this **Help** button or the Help menu can answer any other questions you might have.

Empty iPhoto Trash

When you delete a photo in iPhoto, it is not immediately deleted. You must click the **Empty iPhoto Trash** option to actually erase the item. When you do, a popup menu appears asking you to confirm that you want to permanently delete the selected files. An example of this is shown in Figure 2–11.

NOTE: To delete a photo, you can either click on the right-hand mouse button and chose **Trash** from the window that appears, or go to the **Photo** menu and chose **Move to Trash**.

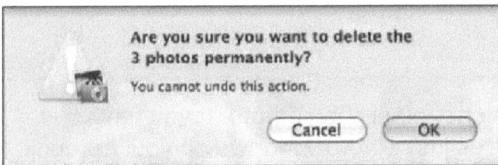

Figure 2–11. *Permanently deleting items in the iPhoto trash can*

Learn About Print Products

This option directs you to a website displaying descriptions of the projects you can create in iPhoto. This is includes books, card, calendars, and prints.

Learn About Aperture

Aperture is a more advanced photo management tool designed by Apple. It offers more selective retouching, more special effects, and produces more advanced slideshows, more advanced Faces and Places features, and a few more enhancements that make in more "professional" grade.

Provide iPhoto Feedback

I love it. Do you want new features? Here is your chance to let Apple know how you feel about iPhoto.

Register iPhoto

Basically, this is an option to fill out registration info for your application. Registration of this Apple product is not required for licensing purposes.

Check for Updates...

This subject was covered in detail in Part 1: "Quick Start Guide." Basically, it goes out to an Apple server and checks if the software you are running is up to date.

Services

Some applications have special add-ons called services. By default, iPhoto has none installed.

Hide iPhoto

Closes all the visible open windows of iPhoto. It does not quit the application.

Hide Others

Closes all the visible open windows of applications, other than iPhoto. If you have five applications open, this feature is nice, as it leaves just iPhoto windows on your screen. This feature works for all Mac applications, so you can hide iPhoto and other apps while working on another "main" application.

Show All

This allows you to bring back all of the windows you closed in the either of the previous two menu options.

Quit iPhoto

The studio has closed and it's time to close iPhoto. This option quits the application.

File Menu

The **File** menu (shown in Figure 2–12) contains a few very important options and some minor ones as well. Here you can create a new item that varies from a simple, new event to complex photo book. In this menu, you can export your work to a variety of standard image formats.

Figure 2–12. *File menu*

New

With the **New** command, you can create a variety of new items. As shown in Figure 2–13, you can create new projects such as a book, card, calendar, or slideshow. You can also create a new Empty Album, Smart Album, or Folder.

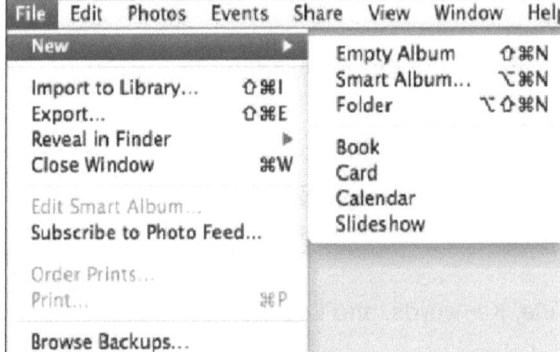

Figure 2–13. *New menu option found in the File menu*

A Smart Album is an album that you create that gives you the ability to have iPhoto automatically newly imported photos based on you criteria. Figure 2–14 shows just a handful of the conditions you can select.

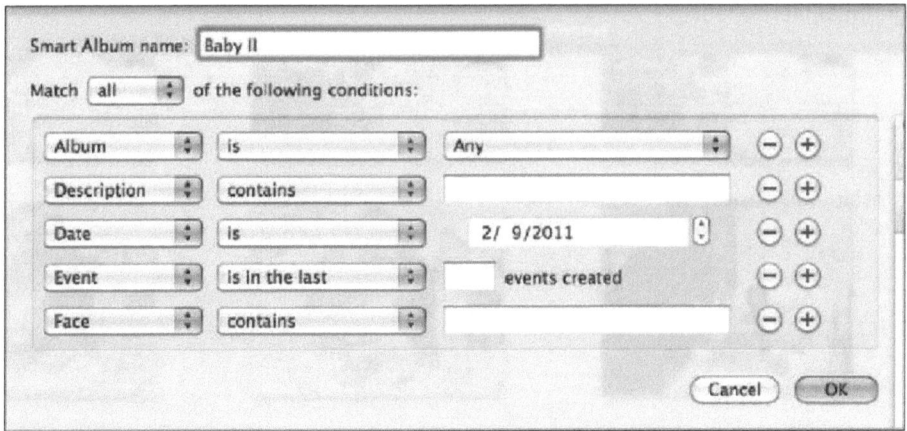

Figure 2–14. *Sampling of the criteria options available for a Smart Album*

Import to Library...

This was covered earlier in the chapter. It is used to add photos or videos to your iPhoto library.

Export...

You can export your photos into a vast number of formats through any one of four tabs: **File Export**, **Web Page**, **QuickTime**, or **Slideshow**.

File Export Tab

Figure 2–15 shows the **File Export** tab selected in the **Export** window. This window contains the following options:

- **Kind:** You can choose the type of file (JPEG or TIFF, for example).

- **JPEG Quality:** If you choose for JPEG files, you have the option to select the quality. Remember that higher quality means a larger file size.

- **Include:** You can chose to add Title, Keywords, and Location information.

- **File Size:** You change the file size if you wish (**Small** to **Full Size**).

- **File Name:** You are given options as to how iPhoto set its default name for a photo you want to export. **Use Filename** is the default, but you can also choose others. Below **File Name**, you can add a prefix to sequential filenames.

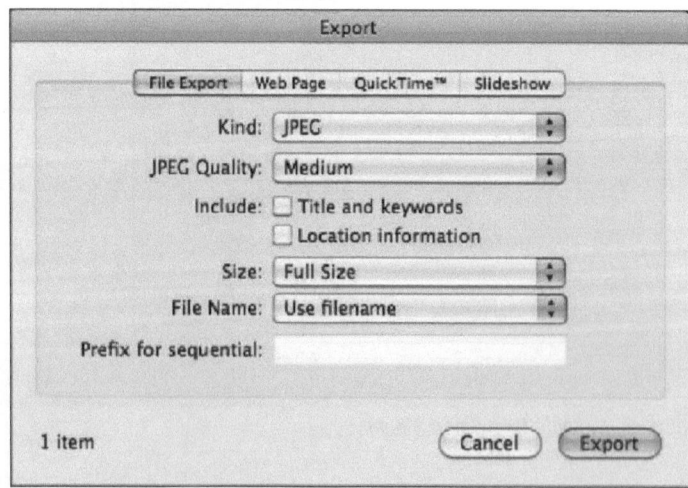

Figure 2–15. *File Export window of the **Export** menu option found in the **File** menu*

Web Page Tab

Figure 2–16 shows the **Web Page** tab selected. This window allows you to export your file as a web page for use in a web creation package with the following options:

- **Page:** Allows you to give the web page a title. Determine how you want the photos to appear on the page (how many rows and columns). Apply a **Plain** (default) or **Framed** template. Choose a background color for the web page and the texts color as well.

- **Thumbnail:** This is the small preview icon for the web page. In Figure 2–16, the maximum width and maximum height of 240 is the default. You are also given the option to add title and description info for the thumbnail.

- **Image:** Sets the image size for photos. The default is a maximum of 640 × 640. You can also add title, description, metadata, and location data.

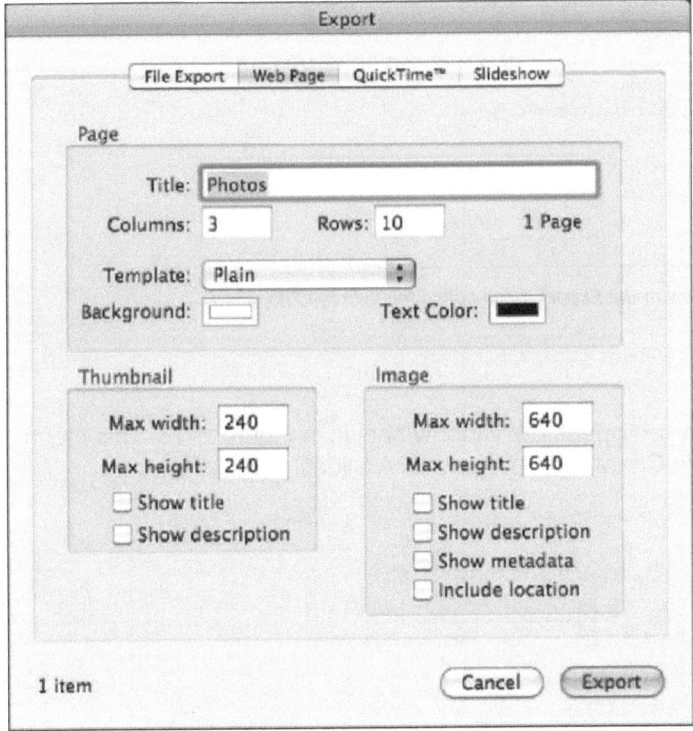

Figure 2–16. *Web Page Export* window of the *Export* menu option found in the *File* menu

QuickTime Tab

Figure 2–17 shows the **QuickTime** tab selected. You can set the width and height of the image to be exported, as well as how long it is going to be displayed. You can set the background color or image. Last, you have the option to add the currently selected slideshow music to the movie you want to export.

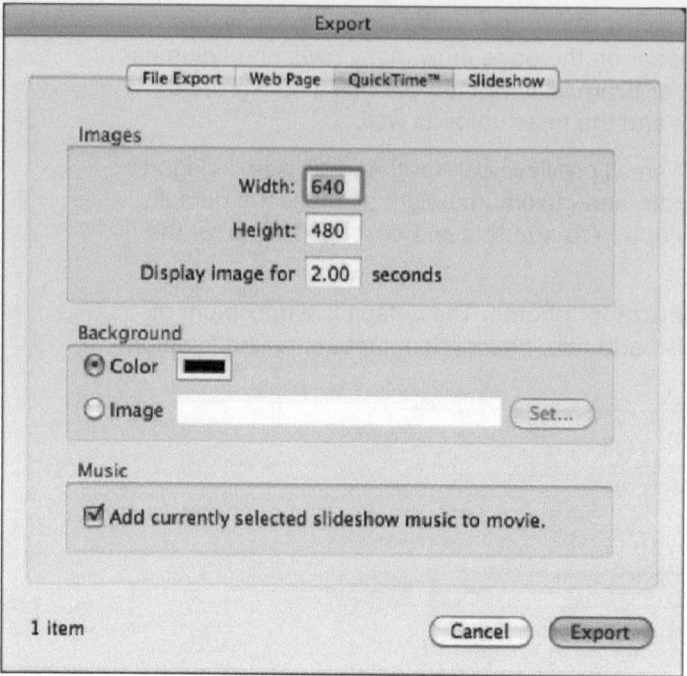

Figure 2–17. *QuickTime* export window of the *Export* menu option found in the *File* menu

Slideshow Tab

When selected, the **Slideshow** tab opens the window shown in Figure 2–18. This menu option will be discussed later in Chapter 6: And now ... A Slideshow"

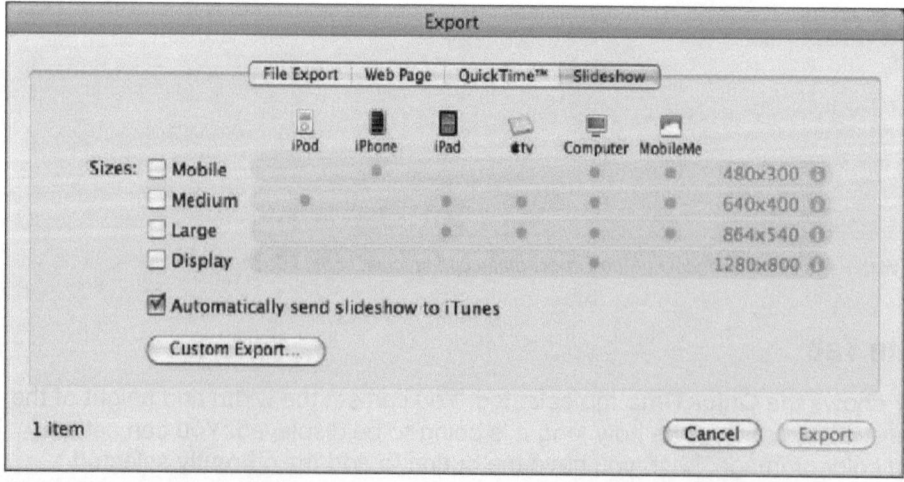

Figure 2–18. *Slideshow* export window of the *Export* menu option found in the *File* menu

Reveal in Finder

If you chose this option, iPhoto will bring up the actual location of the file you have selected on the hard drive on which it is saved.

Close Window

Closes the iPhoto window you are working in.

Edit Smart Album...

Allows you to modify the criteria you set originally when you created a Smart Album.

Subscribe to Photo Feed...

This brings up a window in which you can enter in a web address of a photo feed you are subscribing to.

Order Prints...

Here you can order high-quality hard copies of your photos.

Print...

This function allows you to print your photos to your attached printer.

Browse Backups . . .

Current Mac operating systems include a built-in backup utility called Time Machine. If you are using this application, you can browse previous backups for photos that might have been modified or deleted accidentally.

Edit Menu

The **Edit** menus for all iLife applications are very similar (see Figure 2–19). The commands to **Undo** an action or the very important tasks of **Cut**, **Copy**, and **Paste** are found in this menu. I will go over these commands and all of the others available in this menu in the following sections.

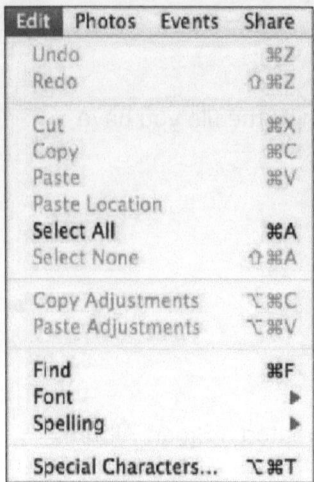

Edit	Photos	Events	Share
Undo			⌘Z
Redo			⇧⌘Z
Cut			⌘X
Copy			⌘C
Paste			⌘V
Paste Location			
Select All			⌘A
Select None			⇧⌘A
Copy Adjustments			⌥⌘C
Paste Adjustments			⌥⌘V
Find			⌘F
Font			▶
Spelling			▶
Special Characters...			⌥⌘T

Figure 2–19. *Edit menu*

- **Undo**: Undoes the last change you applied to your photo or project.

- **Redo**: Decided that you really want the change you just undid? Then use this button to redo the formatting change.

- **Cut**: Deletes the item you have highlighted.

- **Copy**: Puts the item you highlighted into the Mac memory so you can add to other locations.

- **Paste**: Takes the last item that you copied and "pastes" it in your current cursor location.

- **Paste Location**: If you have GPS info or manually added location data, you can use this command to copy this info to any other photo in your library.

- **Select All**: This selects all the items in the open window. This can be photos in an event or album or files on your hard drive.

- **Select None**: The opposite of Select All. Deselects what you just highlighted using Select All.

- **Copy Adjustments**: If you make adjustments using edit tools, this allows you to apply these formatting changes to any photo in your library. Very powerful, very convenient. You just perfect one photo to your liking and then apply the changes to any others. Great timesaver, don't you agree?

- **Paste Adjustment**: If you used the Copy Adjustment command, this pastes or duplicates the adjustments that were made to the photo you chose.

- **Find**: Brings you to the **Search** tool found in the **iPhoto** window.

- **Font**: Reveals the **Font** options available to modify text in your projects. This is shown in Figure 2–20.

- **Spelling**: This brings up the **Spelling** tool. The options available are shown in Figure 2–21.

- **Special Characters**: This is covered in Chapter 1: "Getting Around Your Digital Darkroom." Basically, a resource to find unique symbols.

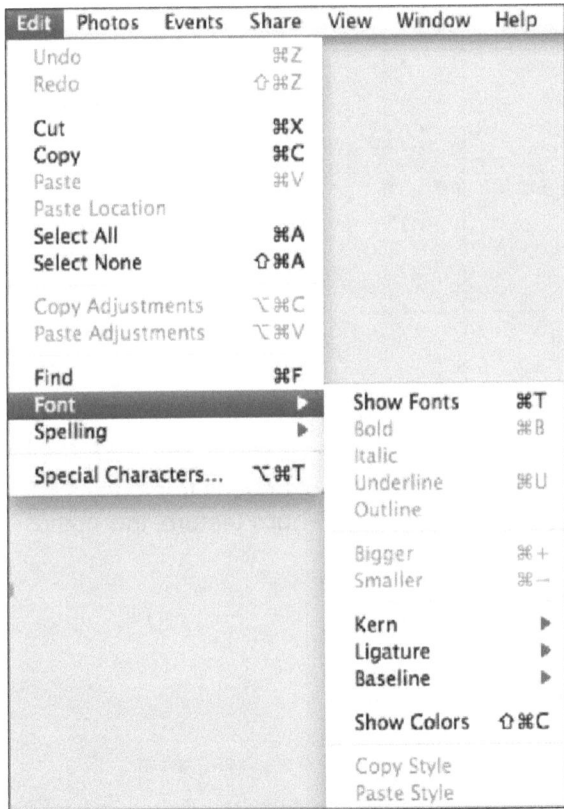

Figure 2–20. *Font options found in the **Edit** menu*

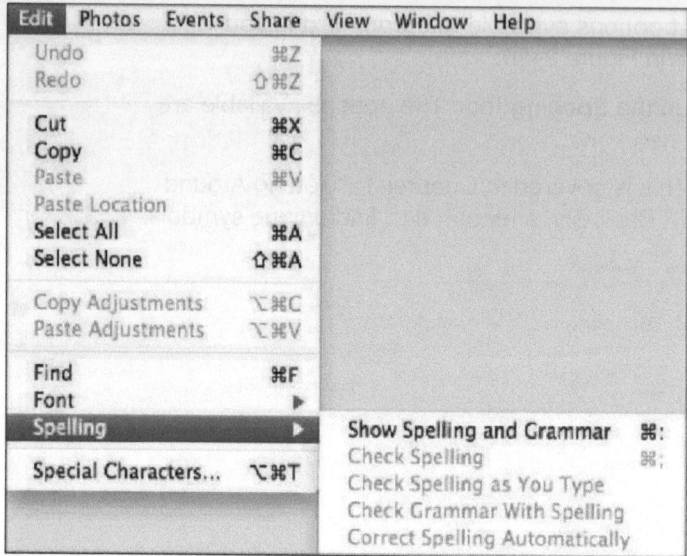

Figure 2–21. *Spelling options found in the **Edit** menu*

Photos Menu

With the **Photos** menu (shown in Figure 2–22), you have a lot of options to modify a photo. Whether it is a simple **Rotate** or a more complex **Edit Photo** feature, this menu means business.

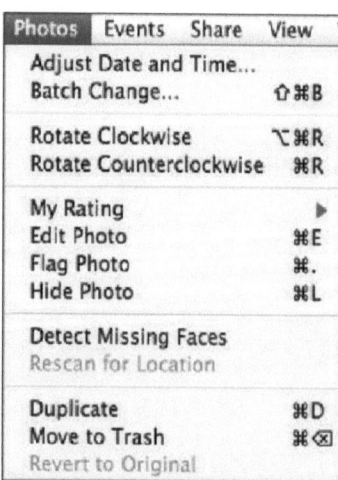

Figure 2–22. ***Photos** menu*

- **Adjust Date and Time...:** You can modify the date and time of the photo selected. Perhaps your camera's clock was set incorrectly; this option allows you to correct it.

- **Batch Change...:** You can change the title, date, or description of a selected group of photos.

- **Rotate Clockwise**: Does what it states: rotates your photos 90 degrees to the right.

- **Rotate Counterclockwise**: Rotates your photos 90 degrees to the left.

- **My Rating**: You can assign each photo a rating. iPhoto uses a five-star rating system. Figure 2–23 shows the full rating scale.

- **Edit Photo**: Brings up the **Edit** tool.

- **Flag Photo**: If you have gazillions of photos, tagging them makes it easier to find the specific photos you want. If you flag a photo, it appears in the **Flagged** section of the iPhoto sidebar.

- **Hide Photo**: Hides the currently selected photo from view. You must go to the **View** menu and select **Hidden Photos** to see the photo(s) again.

- **Detecting Missing Faces**: After iPhoto has a selection of detectable Faces to search through, you can use this tool to attach a face to a photo. I will cover Faces later.

- **Rescan for Location**: Rescans your library for photos that have location data in them. Helpful if your camera's GPS data is off.

- **Duplicate**: This simply makes a copy of your photo.

- **Move to Trash**: Takes the selected photo and moves it the iPhoto trash can, not the Macintosh trash can. You must go to the **iPhoto** menu and select **Empty iPhoto Trash** to permanently delete the file.

- **Revert to Original**: This menu option reverts your photo back to its original state.

Figure 2–23. *My Rating system found in the* **Photos** *menu*

Events Menu

Every photo in iPhoto must be in an event. If you want to create a new event for, say, trips to Florida, the **Edit** menu is where you do it (see Figure 2–24). I discussed flagging photos in the previous chapter. One of the benefits of flagging photos is that, if you have a ton of photos and only the best are flagged, you can gather them all and place them in one unified event.

Figure 2–24. *Events menu*

- **Create Event…:**This creates a blank event if no photo is selected. If you choose this option when one or more photos are selected, the photos will be removed from the event they are currently in and moved into the new event. A photo can only be in one event.

- **Create Event From Flagged Photos**: This is what most users are probably going to do. Select the photos you want to add to a new event and select this option. iPhoto will note that a photo can only be in one location and move the photo to its new location (the new event).

- **Merge With Above**: This simply merges two events.

- **Make Key Photo**: This is a little tool that is very important. Each Event has one photo that always appears as the front-most photo. If you select this option for any photo in your Event, it will make the new photo the top or "key" photo.

- **Add Flagged Photos To Selected Event**: Simply adds any flagged photos you have to the event you have selected.

- **Autosplit Selected Events**: You can split Events based on smaller amounts of time. First, you must set the event timeframe in iPhoto **Preferences...**. Then when you chose this command, the Event will be split into these new smaller timeframes.

Share Menu

I have to admit, the **Share** menu is one of the reasons I love applying technology to the already powerful art of photography (see Figure 2–25). Sharing ones precious memories with someone, or nowadays to the whole world via the web, is simply amazing. With this menu, a user can easily email a photo or make it available to the rest of the plugged-in society. I think you will agree that the options available in this menu are a lot more fun and powerful then going to a store and ordering extra prints!

Figure 2–25. *Share menu*

- **Email...:** You can send your photos via email to any of your friends or family.

- **MobileMe Gallery...:** As I mentioned earlier, MobileMe is a service from Apple, which you must pay for. It is great for sharing photos or videos, because it allows others to download your media if you wish.

- **Flickr...:** You can upload your photos to a Flickr account.

- **Facebook...:** You can upload your photos to a Facebook account.

- **iWeb**: I will start to discuss iWeb in Chapter 10: "Welcome to Web Creation the iWeb Way!" It is iLife's web page creation tool. It allows you to send it iWeb as a photo page or blog.

- **iDVD**: I will begin the discussion on iDVD starting in Chapter 7: "Beginner DVD Creation via iDVD. iDVD allows you to create amazing DVDs from your media library.

- **Burn**: You can "burn" (which means write) to a blank CD, CDR, or DVD. These are all optical disks that store large amounts of data.

■ **Set Desktop**: Absolutely love one of the newly imported photos? With this command, you can make any photo the desktop picture for your Macintosh.

View Menu

The **View** menu (see Figure 2–26) contains a few important features to help make your time using iPhoto much easier. You can make finding photos a snap by searching for titles, ratings, or keywords. Note that you have to enter in a custom title, rate a photo, or add keywords to all of your photos to make this possible. Once this data is entered, you can use the powerful **Sort** tool also found in this menu.

Figure 2–26. *View menu window*

■ **Titles, Ratings, Keywords**: All of these options can be shown when viewing a photo album or event. Just hover your mouse over the option you want and it will show underneath your photo.

■ **Event Titles**: This is turned on by default. Titles for each of the Events the photos are in will appear in the **Photos** section of the sidebar when activated.

■ **Hidden Photos**: If you previously hid photos being viewed on the screen, you can see them again by choosing this command.

■ **Sort Photos**: You can sort your photos in a number of ways. All of the available options are shown in Figure 2–27.

■ **Info**: This was covered earlier in the chapter when discussing the Info button.

■ **Design Options and Project Settings**: These two settings are only available when working on a project such as book or card.

■ **Photo Pane**: When in a project, this brings up the **Photos** sidebar.

■ **Photo Size**: This determines at what size the photos in the **Photos** sidebar will appear. Choose either small or large.

- **Full Screen**: This gives you the option of having iPhoto take up all of screen's real estate and hide all other items. If you are going to be doing a lot of work in iPhoto, this is a nice way to cut down on distractions.

Figure 2–27. *Options for sorting your photos (Date and **Ascending** are the defaults)*

Window Menu

Hmmm... I would describe the **Window** menu (see Figure 2–28) as one that performs a few tasks. **Minimize** and **Zoom** are found in every Apple application. New to this menu are the settings for **Manage My Keywords** and **Manage My Places**. Simple menu, but important nonetheless.

Figure 2–28. *Window menu*

- **Minimize**: This takes the current window and shrinks it down into the Dock. This is the same as the orange button found at the top left of every file or folder. To bring it back, select iPhoto from this menu or click on the small icon of the file in the Dock.

- **Zoom**: This makes the current window the largest it can be. This is the same as the green button found at the top left of every file or folder.

- **Manage My Keywords**: If you entered keywords into the photo's info section, this option will help manage them for you.

- **Manage My Places**: Here you can see all the Places you set in iPhoto. I will discuss Places and Faces after the **Help** menu is discussed.

- **Bring All to Front**: If you have more than just iPhoto open, you might have a lot of open windows. This command brings all of the open iPhoto windows to the front. If you are a power user, you will find this feature very helpful.

- **iPhoto**: This just tells you that iPhoto is running.

Help Menu

How do I create a calendar? If you have the **Help** menu handy (see Figure 2–29) you will learn how to create one in a snap. You can try to rely on the built-in Help system to get you on the right path to iPhoto nirvana; the Help system in iLife is filled with useful videos and step-by-step instructions. I have found, however, that some items are hard to find or are not covered at all. I think this is one of the best reasons to read this book. It covers every topic from A to Z.

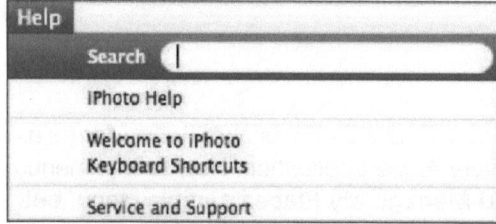

Figure 2–29. *Help menu*

- **Search**: In the **Search** field, enter a topic that you have a question about.

- **iPhoto Help:** This brings up the screen shown in Figure 2–30. You have two choices: **Get Started** and **Browse Help**. **Get Started** is a list of seven lessons to help you get familiar with the most common tasks users want to know about. This is shown in Figure 2–30. **Browse Help** gives you a more detailed list of help topics. This is shown in Figure 2–31.

- **Welcome to iPhoto:** This brings up the **Welcome Screen** when you first launch iPhoto.

- **Keyboard Shortcuts:** These are shortcuts that usually use the **Command** key (⌘) or **Option** key and perform a function. For example, hold down the ⌘ and the press the Q key to quit an application.

■ **Service and Support:** This brings you to an Apple site that covers tips and news about iPhoto.

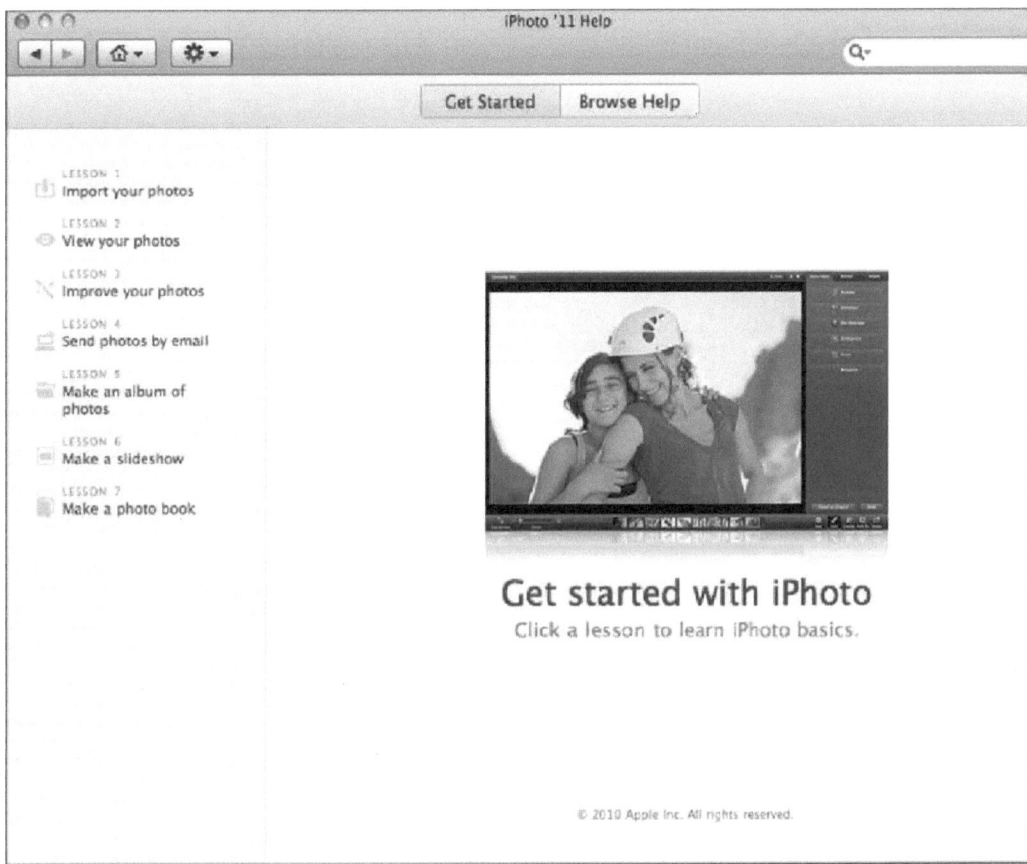

Figure 2–30. *Get Started section of the* ***iPhoto Help*** *window*

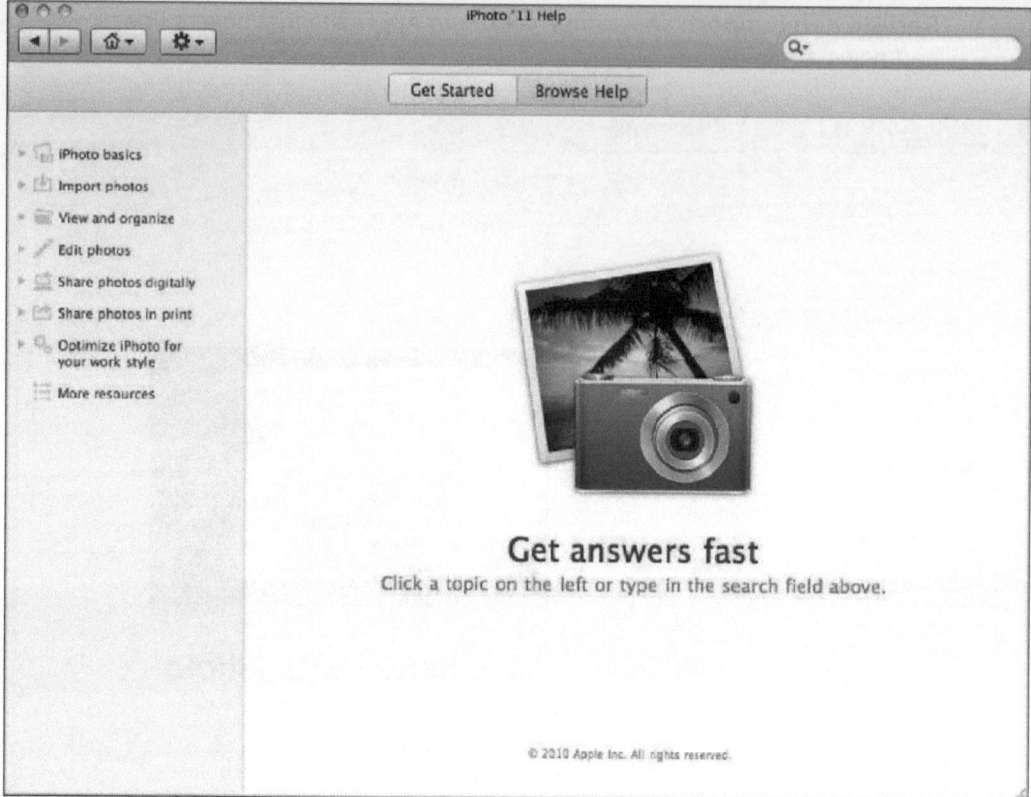

Figure 2–31. *Browse Help section of iPhoto Help*

Summary

With the previous chapter on navigating the iPhoto workspace and this chapter on menus, you should have a good idea of how to use iPhoto and become a digital darkroom master in no time. So get your creative juices flowing, because the next chapter shows you how to get your memories into the digital darkroom of iPhoto and to start using your knowledge to get you on the road to becoming a digital photo master, one click of the mouse at a time!

Chapter **3**

Getting Your Memories into the Digital Darkroom

Once your photos are in iPhoto, the fun really begins. In this chapter, you'll learn how to import your photos into iPhoto so you can get started editing and enhancing them to make them even more picture perfect.

Drag and Drop

The easiest way to get a photo into iPhoto is to drag it from your computer into the **iPhoto** window. Simply click and hold your mouse button on the photo and move it over the words **Event** or **Photo**. Your photo will now appear in the large area next to the source list.

> **NOTE:** You can also add your home videos to iPhoto. This is helpful because other iLife apps can find and use them when they are in the iPhoto Library.

Importing Photos Using iPhoto's File Menu

Another way to move your photos into iPhoto for editing is via the **File** menu. To do so, follow these steps:

1. Click **File ➤ Import to Library...** (see Figure 3–1).

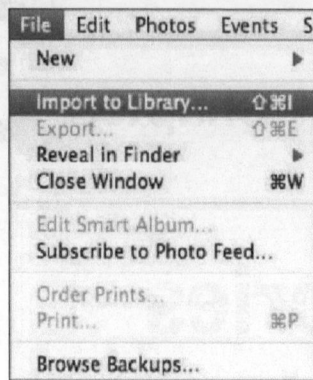

Figure 3–1. *The **Import to Library**... command found in the **File** menu*

2. You then need to locate the file(s) you want to add, as shown in Figure 3–2.
    Here, I selected the folder **Baby Highlights**, which contains a few of my
    photo files. They are in the commonly used JPG format.

Figure 3–2. *First step in locating your media*

> **NOTE:** If you are new to the Macintosh and the window in Figure 3–2 looks unfamiliar, please refer to a helpful section in the Quickstart Guide that covers this window in detail. Most Macintosh applications use the same window to access files.

3. Once you have navigated to the photo you want, click on the filename. A preview of the photo will appear. This is shown in Figure 3–3.

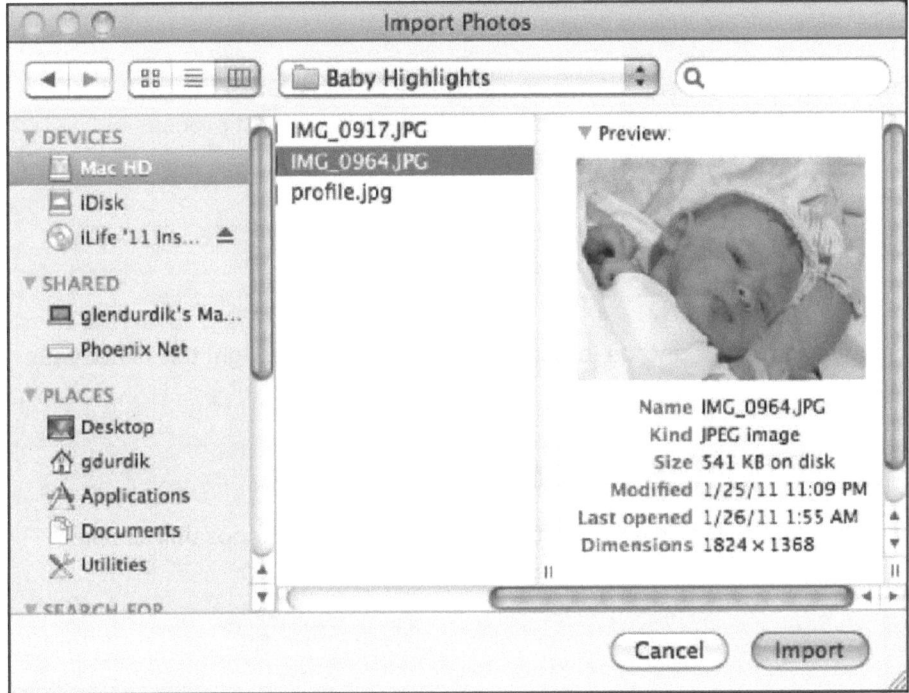

Figure 3–3. *A preview of file to be imported*

4. Click **Import** [Import] to add the photo to iPhoto. If you are importing a large number of photos, you will see the screen shown in Figure 3–4. Notice that it gives a countdown of how many photos are remaining to be imported. In the Source List, there is also an indicator that photos are being imported. This is shown in Figure 3–5.

> **NOTE:** If you want to add a large section of photos in sequence, you can hold down the Shift key (⇧). Click on the top photo and then on the last photo you want to import. If you want to add multiple photos, but not in sequence, hold down the Command key (⌘) while selecting the ones you want to add.

Figure 3–4. *Imports remaining*

Figure 3–5. *Sidebar status indicator of photos being imported*

5.   Notice that, on the right side of this screen, there is also a **Stop Import** button (Figure 3–6). Just click on this button to stop the import process when you have all the photos you want.

Figure 3–6. *The Stop Import button*

You're now ready shape your photos to perfection. Remember, though, this is not your father's darkroom.

Making Your Photos Picture Perfect

In the following pages, I will review the **Edit** button where the photo possibilities are endless and the final results are priceless.

Edit Button

This little button gives you the ability to make many enhancements to your photo. I will go over all the options available to you. The **Edit** button is located at the bottom of your workspace, on the right side. The first window that appears when you click on the **Edit** button is shown in Figure 3–7.

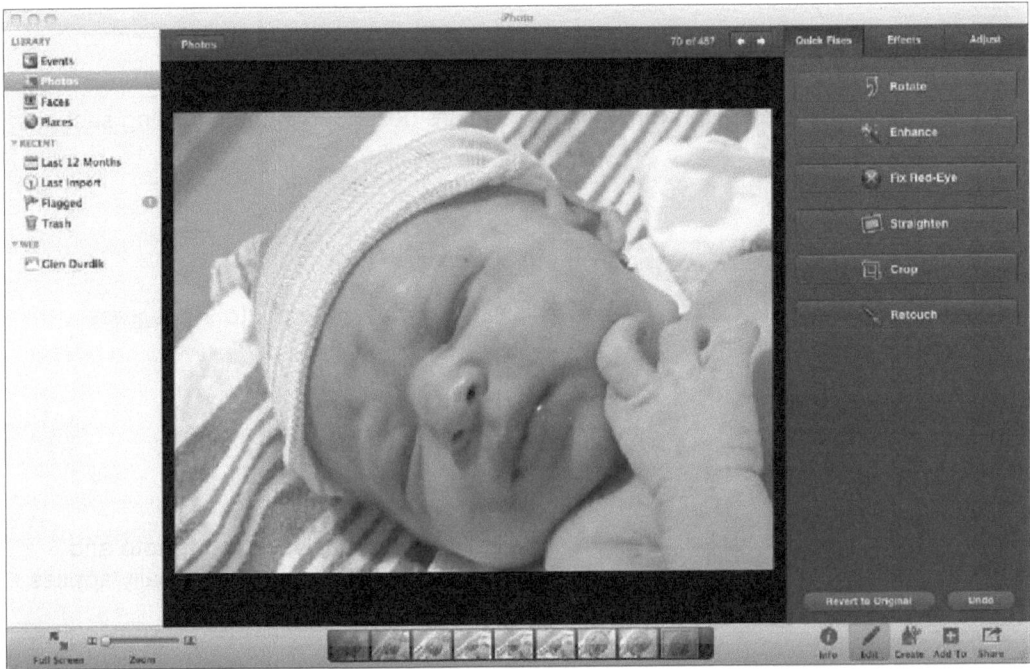

Figure 3–7. *Edit button—Quick Fixes tab*

Exploration of every feature is important, but if you make a mistake in this window and don't like the results, the following two buttons will save you.

Click on **Revert to Original**  to negate all changes made in this window, or

click on **Undo**  to negate the last action taken.

The **Edit** window has three sections: **Quick Fixes**, **Effects**, and **Adjust**. They are accessed via the corresponding tabs shown in the top right corner of Figure 3–7.

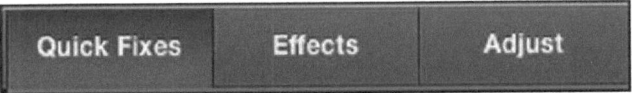

Quick Fixes

Quick Fixes contains many buttons, all of which are described in the following sections.

Rotate Button

 This simply rotates the photo 90 degrees counter-clockwise.

Enhance Button

Basically, iPhoto analyses your photo and does some photo magic mojo to it and tries to make it look its best. It basically applies an "edge-sharpening" effect.

Fix Red-Eye Button

The "red-eye" effect is a common problem caused by using a flash when taking photos. This tool allows you to rectify the issue. If you click on this button, you get the screen shown in Figure 3–8.

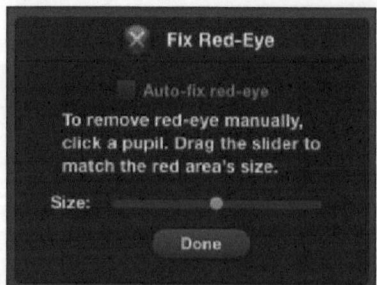

Figure 3–8. *Fix Red-Eye window*

You can check the box next to **Auto-fix red-eye** to have iPhoto fix it automatically, or you can do it manually. Just click on a pupil and match the size of it by moving the **Size** slider left to make it smaller or to the right to make it larger. Click on **Done** to implement the change, no matter which option you choose.

Straighten Button

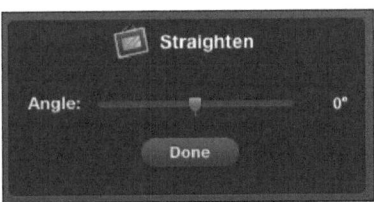 This allows you to straighten the photo to your liking. If you click on this button, you get the screen shown in Figure 3–9.

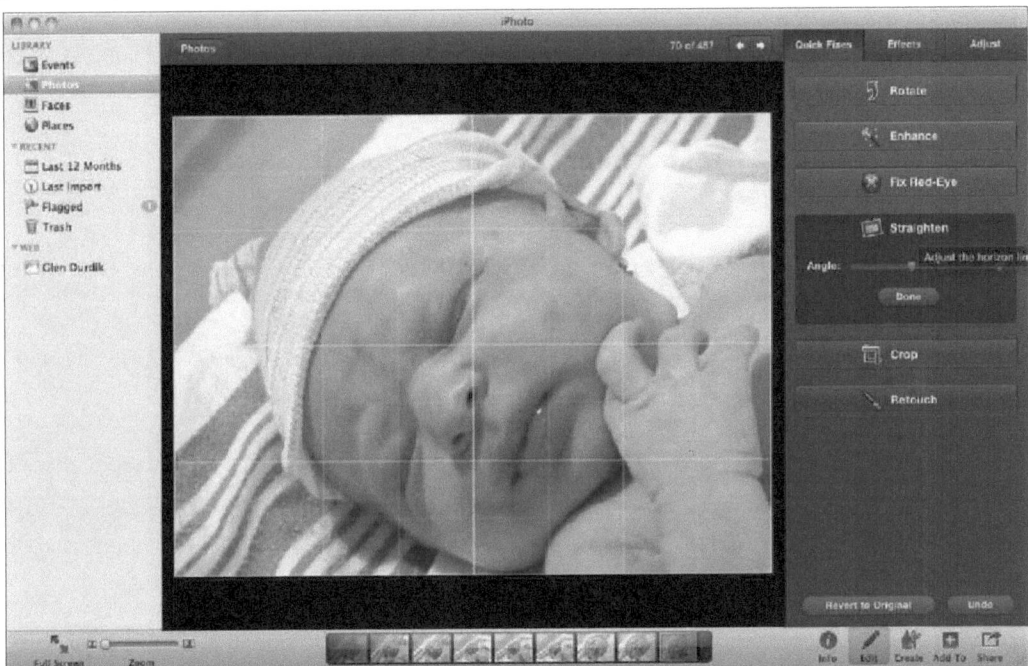

Figure 3–9. *The* ***Straighten*** *tool*

Notice that there are gridlines in your picture. Also notice that the **Straighten** button has changed to look like Figure 3–10.

You can change the angle of the photo to help straighten the image. This is shown in Figure 3–10. Then click on **Done** [Done].

Figure 3–10. *Changing the angle of a photo with the* ***Straighten*** *tool*

Crop Button

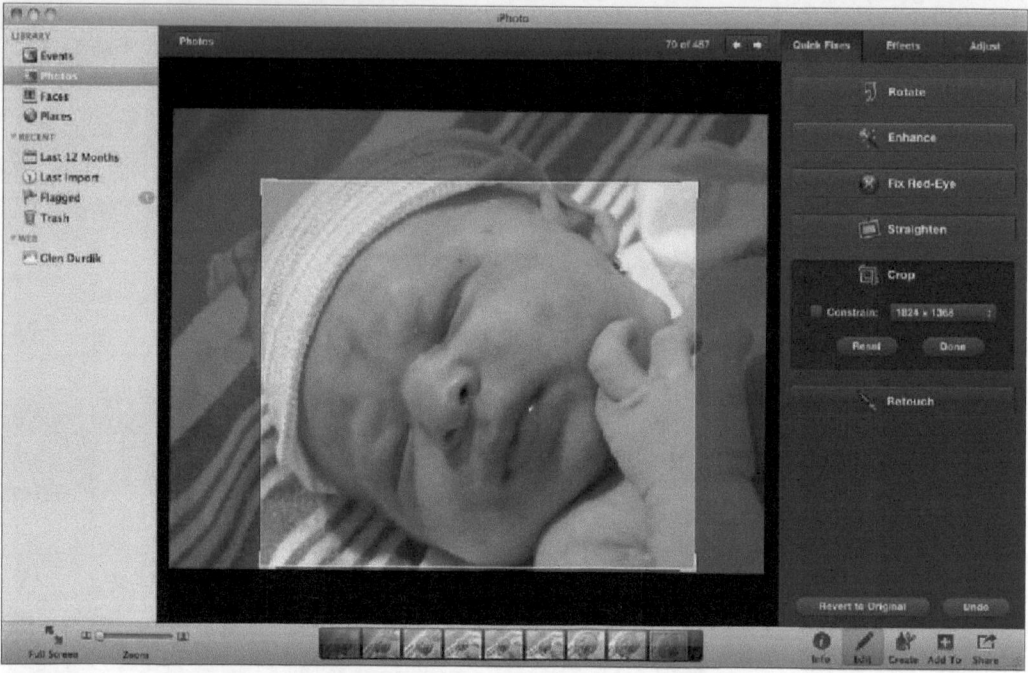

The **Crop** button simply allows you to remove parts of your photo by highlighting the part you want to keep. This is shown in Figure 3–11.

Figure 3–11. *The Crop tool—highlighting the section of the photo you want to keep*

Whatever is in the lighter area will be kept and whatever is in the darker area will be removed. You can manually select the area or crop the area to a certain size. Check the box next to **Constrain** and choose the size. This feature is shown in Figure 3–12.

Figure 3–12. *The Constrain tool*

Retouch allows you to remove blemishes in your photo. If you click on this button, you will see the screen shown in Figure 3–13.

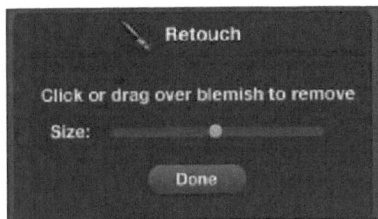

Figure 3–13. *Retouch tool—the Size slider*

You can resize the **Retouch** tool by moving the circular button left and right on the **Size** slider. If you approve of the changes, click on **Done** .

Effects

The **Effects** screen is shown in Figure 3–14.

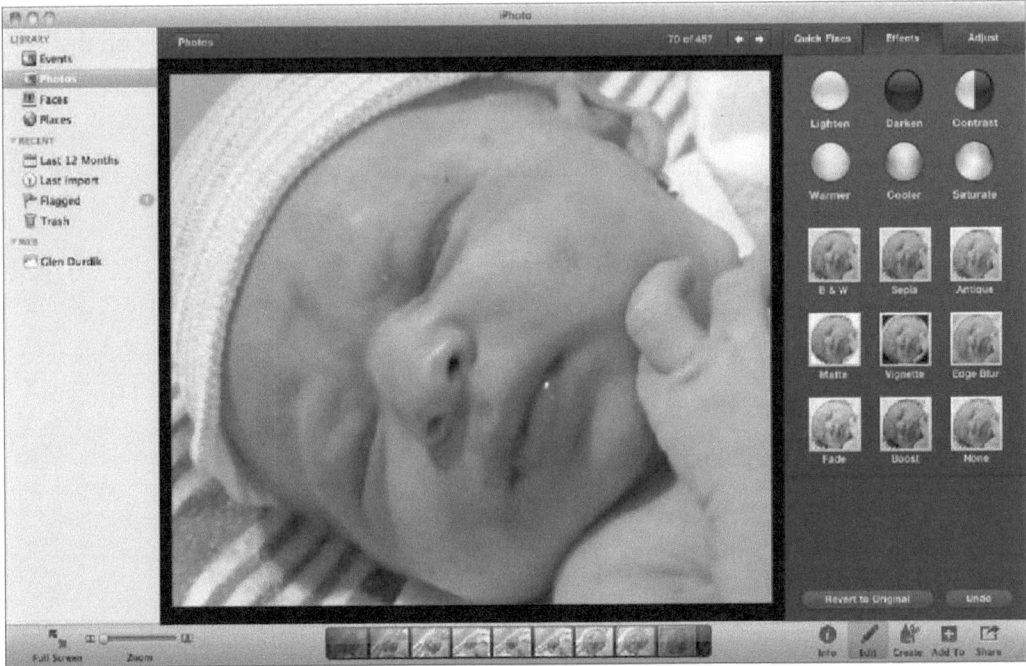

Figure 3–14. *The Effects screen*

Effects is broken down into two sections. The first is shown in Figure 3–15. Each circle performs a different task. For example, you can select to **Lighten** or **Darken** a photo, increase the **Contrast**, change certain color settings of the photo to give it a different appearance (**Warmer** or **Cooler**), or **Saturate** (enhance the brightness of all the colors).

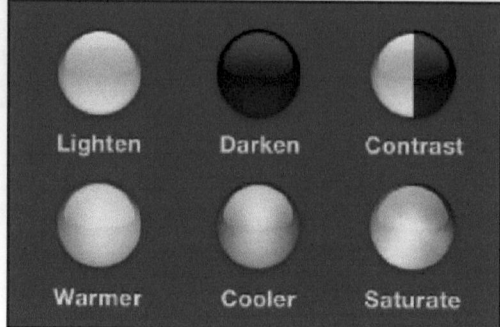

Figure 3–15. *Six circles that perform a certain color change to your photo*

The second section allows you perform special effects that can be applied to your photo. Figure 3–16 shows a visual sample of each effect. Each time you click on the effect you want to apply, the effect's change is increased.

The following is a description of the options:

- **B & W:** Changes a photo to black and white.

- **Sepia:** Applies a yellowish hue.

- **Antique:** Gives photo an aged appearance.

- **Matte:** Blurs edges and corner in an oval.

- **Vignette:** Darkens the photos corners.

- **Edge Blur:** Blurs the photos corners.

- **Fade:** Reduces color intensity.

- **Boost:** Increases color intensity.

- **None:** Removes all effects.

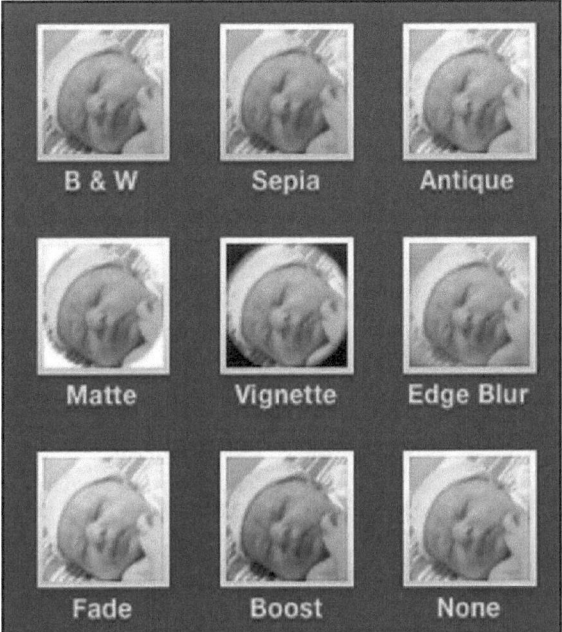

Figure 3–16. *Special effects that can be applied to your photo*

Adjust

The last tab is called **Adjust**. The full screen is shown in Figure 3–17. Notice that this tool consists of about 10 sliders that adjust certain aspects of your photo. This is more advanced than the other settings available via the **Edit** button. These settings should be familiar to professional photographers who manipulate photos daily. As with any creative program, you should explore all the options. Try out each adjustment to see if you like the result. Don't worry if you don't like it: that's what the **Undo** button is for.

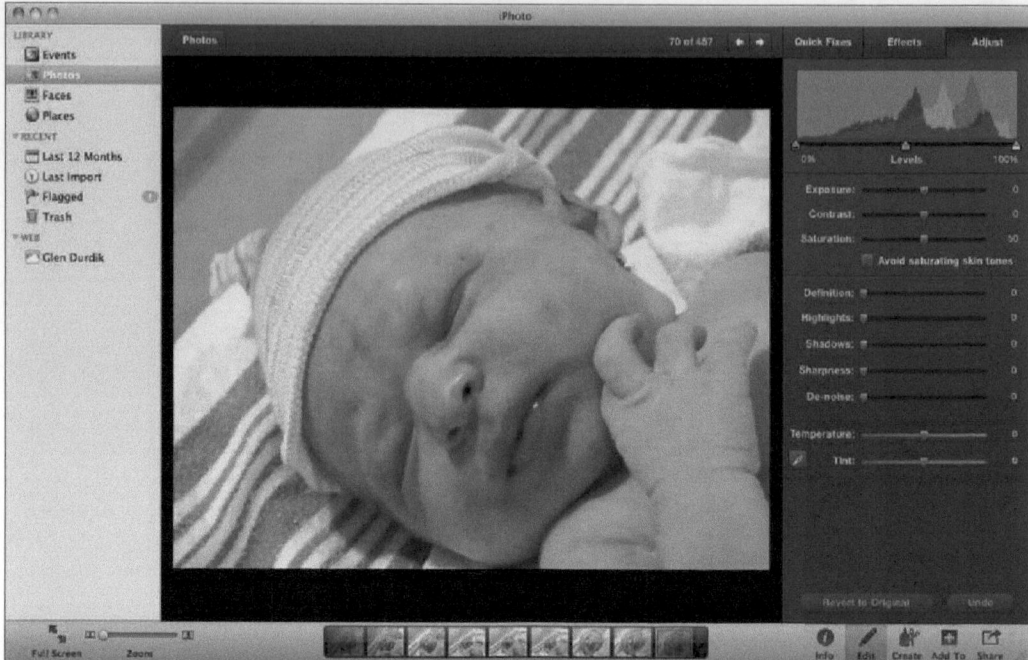

Figure 3–17. *The Adjust screen*

> **NOTE:** There is a checkbox allowing you to avoid saturating skin tones just below the **Saturation** slider.

Enhance Your Editing Experience

iPhoto has a pair of nifty tools to help make editing a breeze: the **Zoom** slider and the **Full Screen** view.

Zoom Slider

This slider is located at the bottom of your workspace on the left side. As you move the slider to the right, you enlarge the photo or "zoom in" on it. This makes it easier to see details in your photos. This is especially true in the case of red-eye reduction and blemish removal. Once the **Zoom** slider is activated, a mini **Navigation** window pops up and you may scroll around to get to the area for retouching easily.

Full Screen View

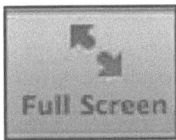

To activate this great feature, click on the **Full Screen** button located at the far left of your workspace on the bottom. When activated, your workspace takes up your complete screen. No other windows or distractions are shown. It allows you to fully concentrate on the current photo you are editing.

Summary

Your photos are imported in iPhoto. You have edited them to your liking so they look their best. Next, we will delve into the menus and workspaces. With the knowledge acquired in this and the next chapter, you can tweak your photos and enhance them in a variety of ways.

Chapter 4

Creating and Sharing Personalized Photo Keepsakes

The power of a photo is the ability to share with important people in your life your special moments. With iPhoto, you can do this in several great ways, from a comprehensive photo book about a vacation or a calendar of baby photos. You will love the options available.

Leveraging the Create Button

The **Create** button packs a wallop! With it, you can create amazing projects in just a few short steps. I will go over several projects in detail in this chapter. If you click on the **Create** button, you get the screen shown in Figure 4–1. I will work my way down all the options, from creating a book to creating a slideshow. You will notice in Figure 4–1 that I can also create an album. An album is a simple way to organize photos into different themes or events. An album also makes it easier to create other projects, because only the photos in the album will appear in the new project. Just select the photos you want and select **Album** from the **Create** button. That's it—you created a new Album. Now all you have to do is edit the title.

> **NOTE:** You can create also a slideshow with the **Create** button. I cover slideshows in Chapter 6: "And Now ... a Slideshow!"

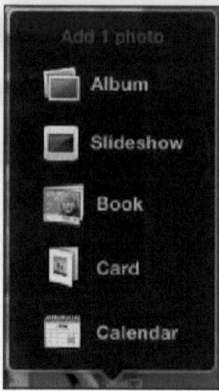

Figure 4–1. *All the great projects you can create in iPhoto*

Creating a Book

Follow these steps to create a book full of your precious memories:

1.   Choose a cover.

2.   Choose the color background of the cover.

3.   Determine how the book will be bound.

4.   Select the size of the book.

5.   Create the interior (most of your time is devoted to this).

6.   Purchase the book.

Choose a Cover

Figure 4–2 shows the first screen you will see after choosing to create a book. Please note that the cover is chosen by clicking the left or right arrow keys, or by clicking on the book cover that is *not* directly in front of you. There are choices to the left and to the right of the current cover.

Figure 4–2. *Select your cover in this window.*

Choose the Background Color for the cover

To the right of the current book cover, you will notice color swatches. If you click on a color, the background of the current cover will change. This is shown in Figure 4–3.

Figure 4–3. *Choosing a background color for your cover*

Determine How the Book Will Be Bound

You have three choices for your book's binding: hardcover, softcover, or wire-bound. You make a selection in the area of the screen shown in Figure 4–4. It is located at the top of the window in Figure 4–2.

Figure 4–4. *Choices for type of binding*

Select the Size of the Book

You have two choices when it comes to the size of the book. It can be Large (L)—which is the default—or Extra Large (XL). You make your selection in the bottom left side of the workspace (see Figure 4–5). Please notice that the one in the spotlight is the one that will be used.

Figure 4–5. *Selecting the size of the book*

Pricing Your Book

Once you have selected the book size, and before you create your interior pages, you get a price estimate of your book. This is shown in Figure 4–6. It is located in the bottom left-hand corner of the workspace. The price depends on the book's type, size, and number of pages. You will not know the final price until you have a final page count.

Figure 4–6. *Pricing estimate for a book*

Create the Interior

Once you have determined the size, cover, and type of book, you can start creating the interior. To begin, click on the **Create** button [Create] located at the bottom right-hand corner of your screen.

If you have too many pictures to fit into the default book size, the window shown in Figure 4–7 appears. You can add more pages or create an empty book. If you create an empty book, you pick the photos and layouts as you go.

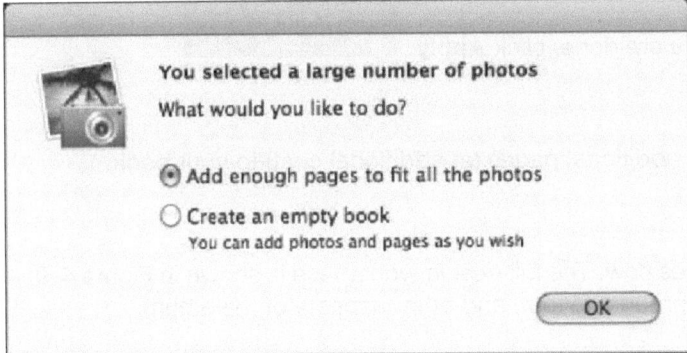

Figure 4–7. *There are too many photos to fit in the standard-sized book*

Book Workspace Elements

Figure 4–8 is an example of a book I created. It shows the options available to you while creating the interior of the book: **Add Page**, **Design (options)**, **Photos (selection)**, and **Change Theme**.

Figure 4–8. *Interior of a book workspace*

 With the **Change Theme** button, you can change the theme that you originally applied. After you are done, click **Apply.**

 Here you can add additional pages (at additional cost) to your book.

Let your creative juices flow. The full design workspace is shown in Figure 4–9. Here you can modify the background, layout, and other aspects of the album.

This button is covered in detail a little later in the chapter. I consider it a topic to be covered last, after going over the other features.

Figure 4–9. *Full design workspace*

To edit a page, double-click on it. There are then several changes you can make to each page of the book. The following sections detail them.

Background

In the book that I have chosen, I have nine choices for the background. This is shown in Figure 4–10. In Figure 4–11, please notice that the page being modified is highlighted with a thick outline, as well as the background I have chosen.

Figure 4–10. *Background choices*

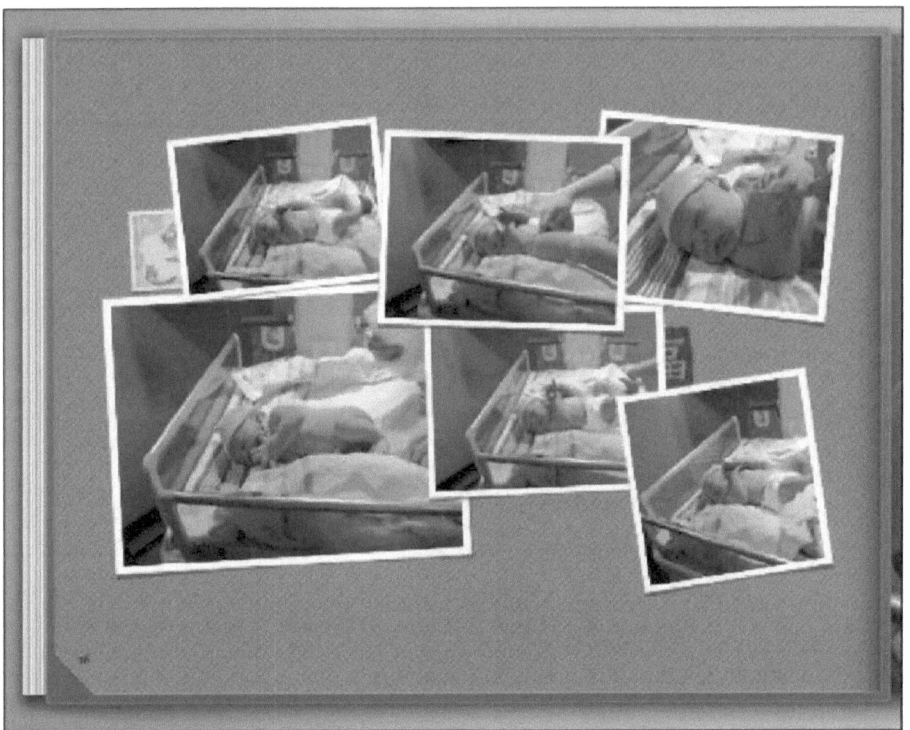

Figure 4–11. *The highlighted page (with the blue outline) is currently being worked on.*

Layout

You can choose to place between one and seven photos on each page. For each choice, iPhoto gives you a selection of options. In Figure 4–12, I have chosen to put two photos on the page. Also notice that you have the option of adding text to the page.

Figure 4–12. *Layout options*

You can also have the choice of the following four layouts (Figure 4–13):

- ■ **Text Page:** Choose between a selection of text-only layouts.

- ■ **Map:** Place a map as the background. Several layouts are available.

- ■ **Spread:** You can have one page spread over two pages.

- ■ **Blank:** An empty page.

You can select these other types of options by clicking on the text below **Layout**.

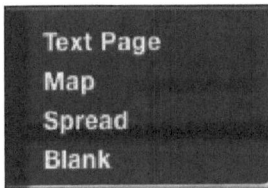

Figure 4–13. *Additional layouts available*

Photo Adjustment While Working on a Page

If you are editing a page for layout and background changes, you can also make an adjustment to each photo on the page. You can zoom in for a close up of the photo or zoom out. Just click on the photo and you'll see the **Zoom** bar appear above the photo. Move the circle to left to zoom out and to the right to zoom in (Figure 4–14).

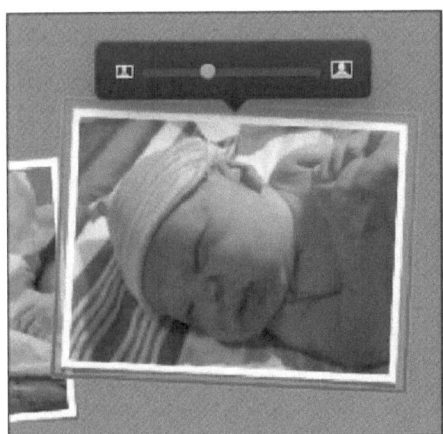

Figure 4–14. *Using the Zoom tool*

Text Editing While Working on a Page

Simply double-click on the text box. This will bring up a complete list of text options. This is shown in Figure 4–15. You can change the typeface, the color, the alignment, and a few other options.

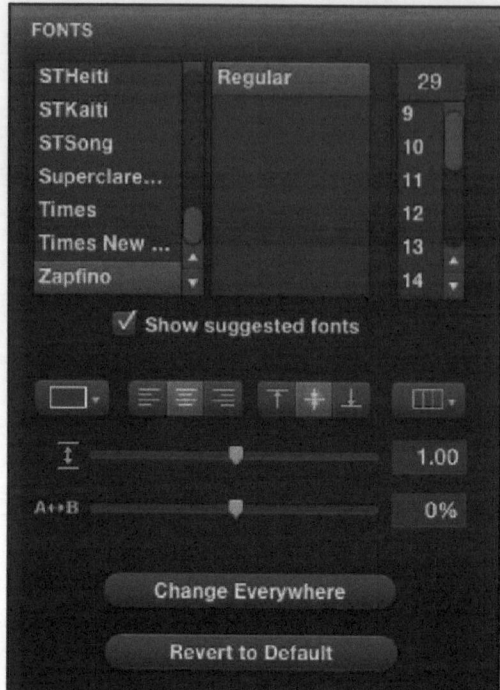

Figure 4–15. *Type options available while creating a book*

Navigator

When you are working on a single page, a **Navigator** window will appear (Figure 4–16). This allows you to easily navigate the book with small thumbnails of each page being shown in the window.

Figure 4–16. *The Navigator window*

This is where you have access to your Photo Library. This button gives you access to a sidebar attached to your main workspace(see Figure 4–17). This gives you a complete list of all the photos you can choose from.

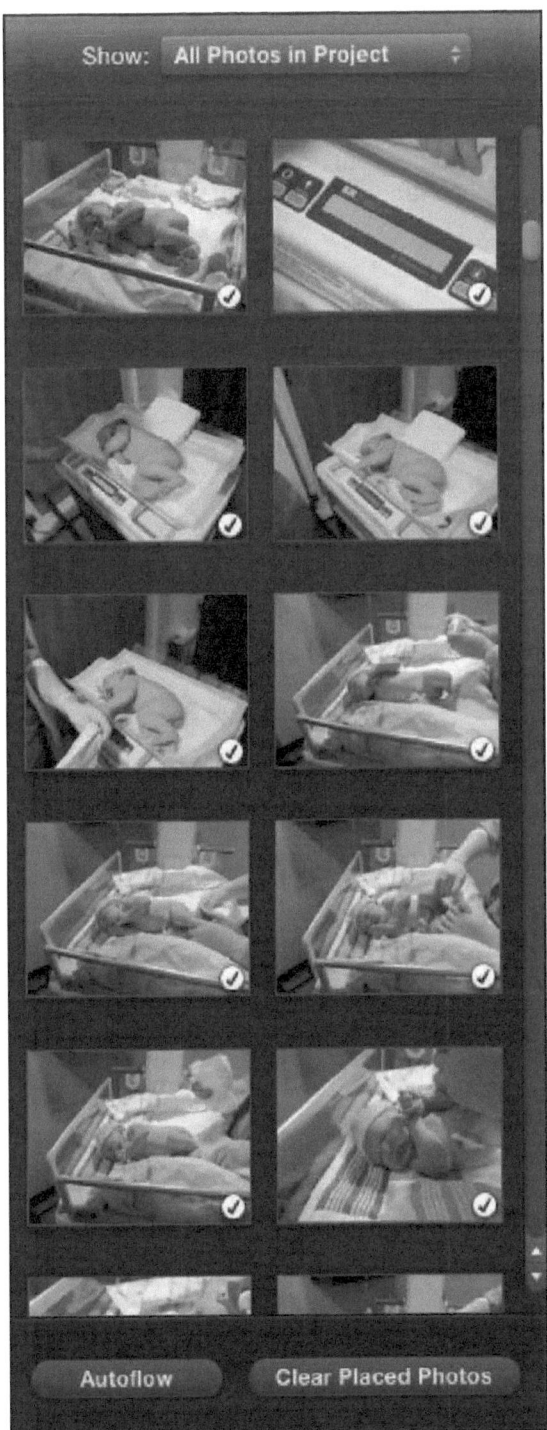

Figure 4–17. *Photo sidebar*

Note the check mark in each thumbnail. This means that the photos have been incorporated into the book. This will occur if you use the **Autoflow** button.

Autoflow Autoflow adds all the pictures that you have in your project and chooses its own layout for each page. It's simple to use, but no creativity is required. If you want more creative control, click on the **Clear Placed Photos** button.

Clear Placed Photos Now you can add photos and create different layouts at will.

If you click on **All Photos in Project** next to **Show:**, you get the window shown in Figure 4–18. Here you can see:

- **All Photos in Project:** Shows all available photos.

- **Placed Photos:** Shows only photos that you have used in the book so far.

- **Unplaced Photos:** Shows only the photos you have *not* used so far in the book.

- **Baby Christian—Full:** Shows the title of event.

- **Last Import:** Shows only the last photos you imported into iPhoto.

- **Last 14 Months:** Shows only the photos you imported over the past year.

- **Flagged:** Only shows the photos you have tagged.

Figure 4–18. *Options available to give you access to photos to add to your book*

Purchase Your Book

Buy Book

Okay, it's time to purchase your Pulitzer. Click on **Buy Book**. This is found in the middle of your book workspace, at the bottom. If there are any formatting errors, iPhoto will alert you. Otherwise, follow the steps and buy the book. You will need an Apple account to purchase it. If you buy music from iTunes, then you already have an account.

Creating a Card

Personalized holiday cards…nothing is more special. Whether it is just a plain-text card or a photo card, who knows more about saying something special than you? Simply follow these steps to create a card.

1. Choose the type of card. Creating a card is a little different from designing a book. The first step is to decide what type of card you prefer. For each type, there are different cover designs. The three choices are **Letterpress**, **Folded**, or **Flat**. See Figure 4–19. The choices are located at the top of the card cover design window.

Figure 4–19. *Choices of card type*

2. Choose a cover design. As with creating a book, the one in the front is the selected one. Clicking on the left or right arrow keys on the keyboard brings up the other designs. The **Cover Design** window is shown in Figure 4–20.

Figure 4–20. *Cover Design window*

3. To begin customization, click **Create**.

4. Edit the outside cover layout. You can modify the cover layout from the one you selected earlier. Click the picture on the cover. The result is shown in Figure 4–21.

Figure 4–21. *Editing the card cover layout*

5. Next, click on the small black box that appears over the top of the picture. For this card, we have four layout choices. This is shown in Figure 4–22.

Figure 4–22. *Layout choices for the front cover*

6. If you click on the **Design** button , you can further modify the photo on the front cover. There are two options available: **Effects** and **Edit Photo**. The **Effects** choices are **Black and White**, **Sepia**, **Antique**, and **Original** (if you want to leave it as is). This is shown in Figure 4–23.

    The **Edit Photo** button brings up all of the options found in the **Edit Button** section discussed in Chapter 3: "Getting Your Memories into the Digital Darkroom"

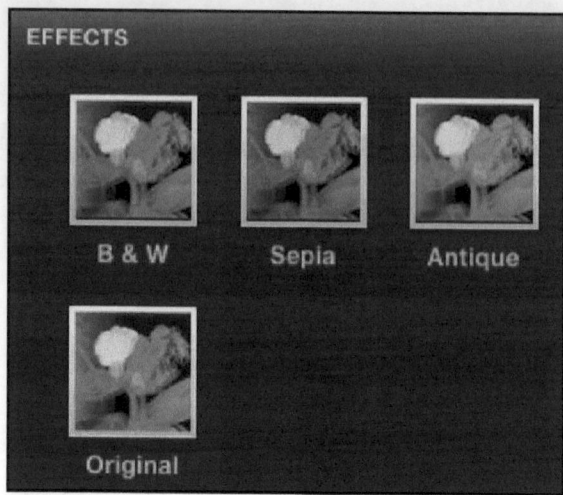

Figure 4–23. *Effects that can be applied to the photos used in the card*

7. The **Photos** button 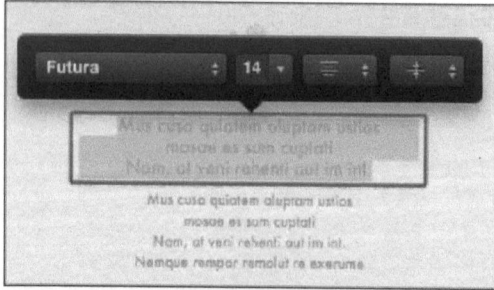 has the same functionality as the **Photos** button described in the "Creating a Book" section earlier in this chapter. Use this feature to add photos to your card.

8. After you are done with the cover, you can edit the inside of the card. To edit the text boxes, just click on them. You can edit the words in the card or adjust the font settings. The black box for formatting text is shown in Figure 4–24.

Figure 4–24. *Editing text in a card*

9. Purchase the card. Just click on the **Buy Card** button Buy Card . Follow the instructions to order them online. Again, you must have a valid Apple account. If you use iTunes to purchase music or videos, you are good to go.

Creating a Calendar

Creating a calendar based on a particular subject is quick and easy to do. In just five steps, outlined here, you can create great personalized gifts for all of the important people in your life.

1. Choose the cover of your calendar using the screen shown in Figure 4–25. As with creating a book or card, the layout in front is the selected one. Click on the choices to the left or right to see what other formats are available.

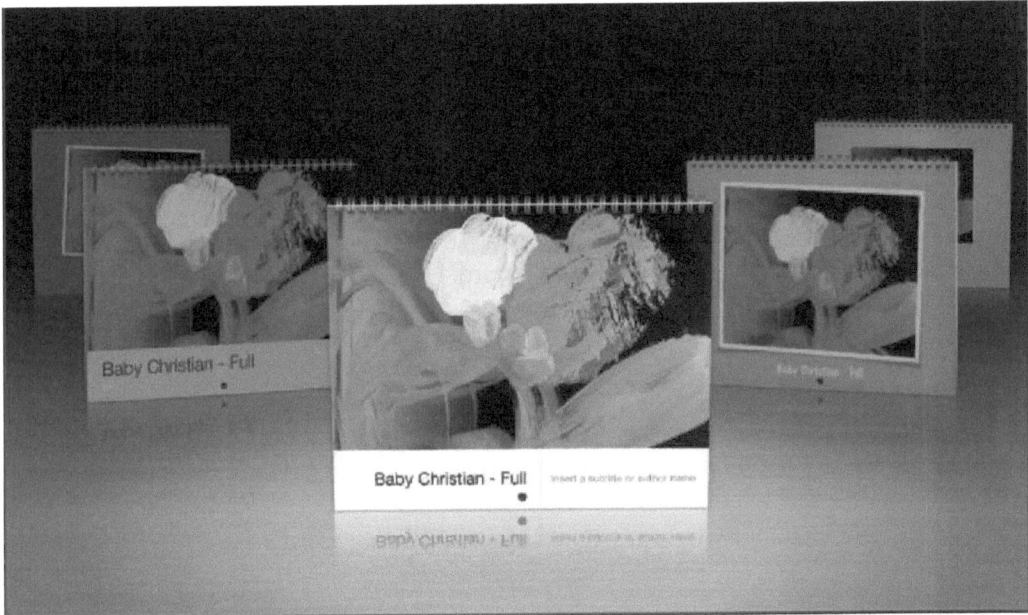

Figure 4–25. *Selecting your calendar's front cover*

2. Click the **Create** button.

3. Provide the requested information in the window that now appears on your screen (see Figure 4–26). This window is divided into two sections. The top section asks what the start date and month for your calendar should be. The second asks how many months you want the calendar to contain. You are also asked if you want to add national holidays. The default is not to include holidays (**None**), but if you want to include them, click **Show national holidays** and choose your country. It is possible to have all of the birthdays stored in your address book added as well. Finally, you can import important dates from your iCal application.

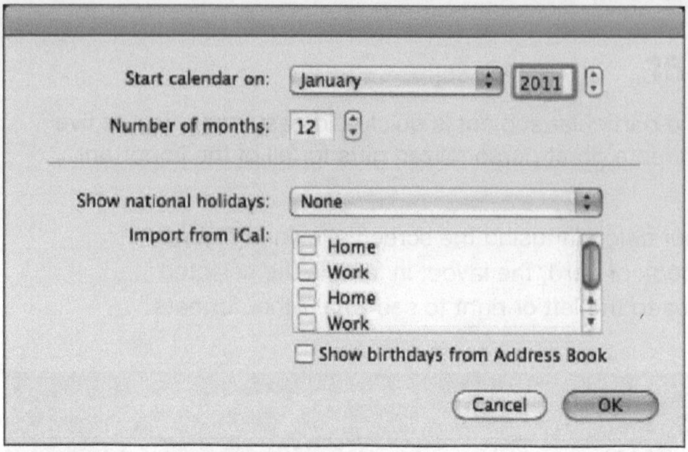

Figure 4–26. *Configuration window for creating calendars*

4. Customize your calendar using the **Design** button ![Design]. This is essentially the same as the book options. The two options are **Background color** and **Layout** (see Figure 4–27).

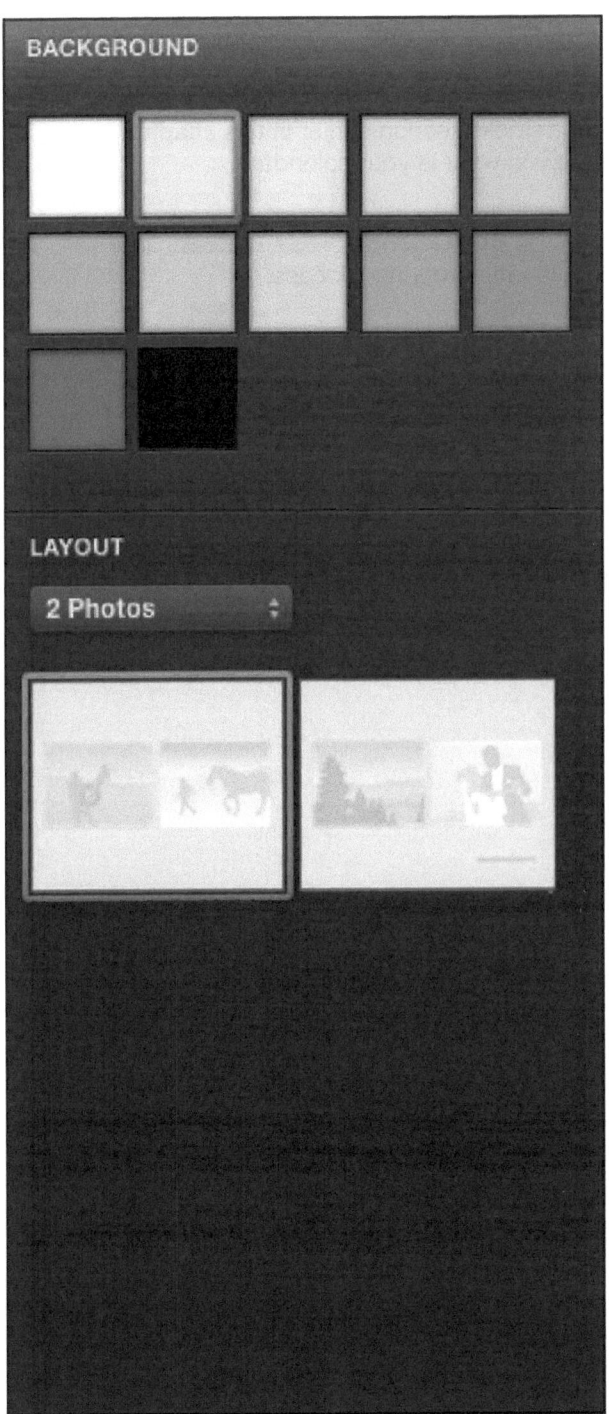

Figure 4–27. *Two options available when clicking the **Design** button while creating a calendar*

5.  The **Photos** button has the same functionality as the **Photos** button described in the "Creating a Book" section earlier in this chapter. It allows you to choose the photos you want in your calendar.

6. Purchase your calendar by clicking on **Buy Calendar** Buy Calendar and following the instructions to complete the ordering process.

Share Button

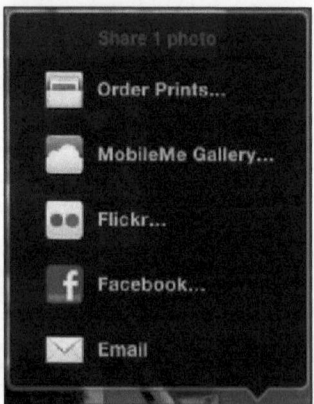

The **Share** button allows you to share your memories with other people via the Internet or by ordering prints. If you click on this button, you will see Figure 4–28 first.

Share 1 photo

Order Prints...

MobileMe Gallery...

Flickr...

Facebook...

Email

Figure 4–28. *Initial* **Share** *screen*

The first option is to order prints from Apple. You can choose the size and quantity for each photo you want to have printed (see Figure 4–29). Notice in the example that the two largest sizes (16 × 20 and 20 × 30) have a caution triangle next to them. This is telling you the quality of your photo is too low to be blown up to these big sizes.

Figure 4–29. *Purchasing prints from Apple*

The second choice is to upload it to a **MobileMe Gallery** (see Figure 4–30). This is a paid service from Apple. One of my favorite features is that items can be downloaded by people you give access to the **MobileMe Gallery**. Notice that you can create a new album with the photo(s) or add to an existing gallery.

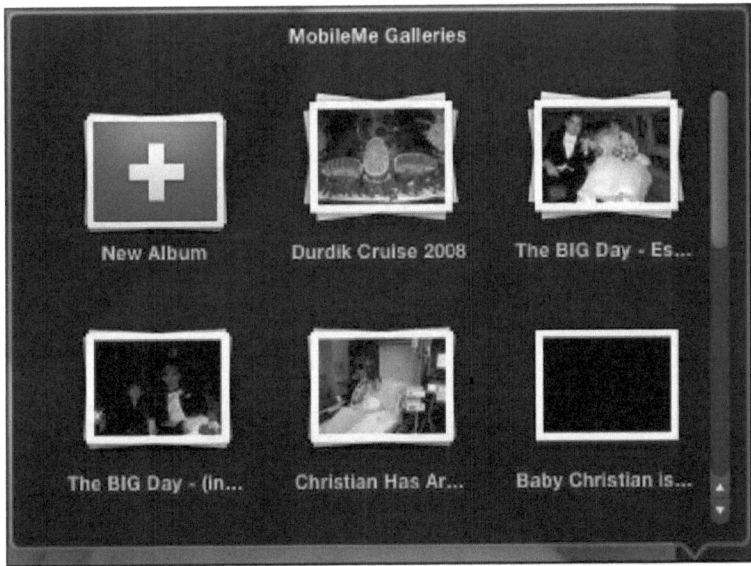

Figure 4–30. *Adding to a MobileMe gallery*

You can also upload it to a Flickr account. Flickr is a photo service provided by Yahoo. I do not have an account, but you easily create one for free. Facebook is another way in which you can share your photos (see Figure 4–31). Notice that you can add a photo to a new album, make it your profile picture, or post it to your wall.

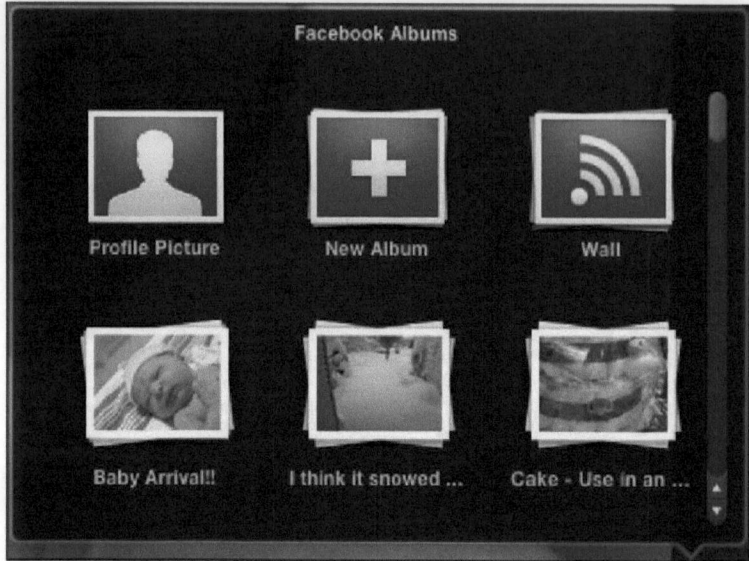

Figure 4–31. *Adding a photo to a Facebook account*

Last, you can send an e-mail to someone with the photo(s) you want to share. This is cool, because you can use one of ten custom backgrounds for the email itself (see Figure 4–32).

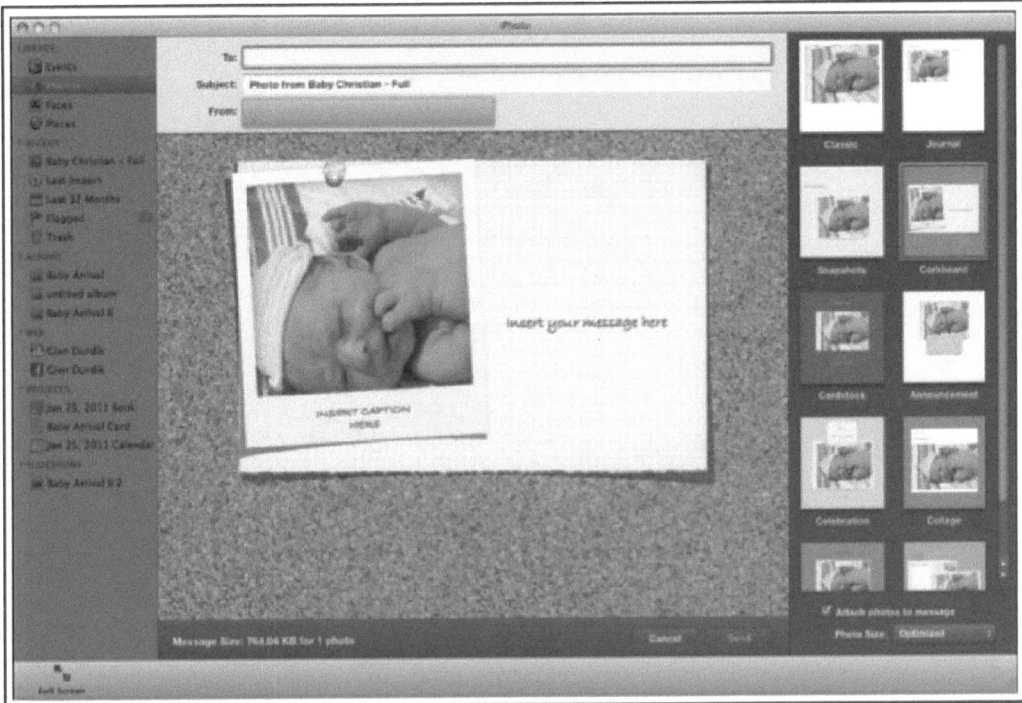

Figure 4–32. *Custom e-mail options available when choosing **Email** from the **Share** button*

Summary

With the power of iPhoto at your fingertips, you can create amazing keepsakes for you or anyone close to you. As you have seen, iPhoto has many simple and easy ways to share your precious memories with others, wherever they may be. Be creative. Whether you are sharing your memories on a piece of paper, via e-mail, or over the Internet...a picture is truly worth a thousand words or should I say, text messages?

Be warned: you can spend quite a bit of time creating your masterpiece.

Chapter 5

Faces and Places

Faces and Places are two great features of iPhoto. With **Faces**, you can have iPhoto find all the photos in your gallery that contain that Face (person). **Places** allows you to keep track of all the great locales you visited on your travels. Before you can avail of these two features, though, you have to set them up to work—so let's start with setting up Faces.

Exploring Faces

The first step is to get iPhoto to recognize faces and associate them with an individual. Here's how:

1.   Import your photos. Click on the photo that contains the face you want iPhoto to recognize.

2.   Click on the **Info** button on the bottom of your workspace.

3.   You will see a **Faces** box appear at about the middle of the screen. This is shown in Figure 5–1. If **Add a face...** does not appear, click the triangle located at the upper right-hand corner of window.

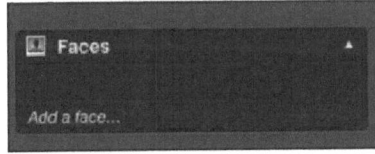

Figure 5–1. *Faces section of the Info window*

4.   Click **Add a face....**

5.   If iPhoto does not easily recognize a face, click and hold down the mouse button on one of the four small black boxes surrounding the white box. This is shown in Figure 5–2.

6. Continue to hold down the mouse button, and move the mouse
    diagonally until the whole face is surrounded by the white box.

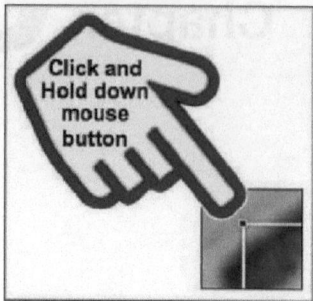

Figure 5–2. *Click and hold your mouse button down to enlarge the face recognition box*

The final result should look like Figure 5–3.

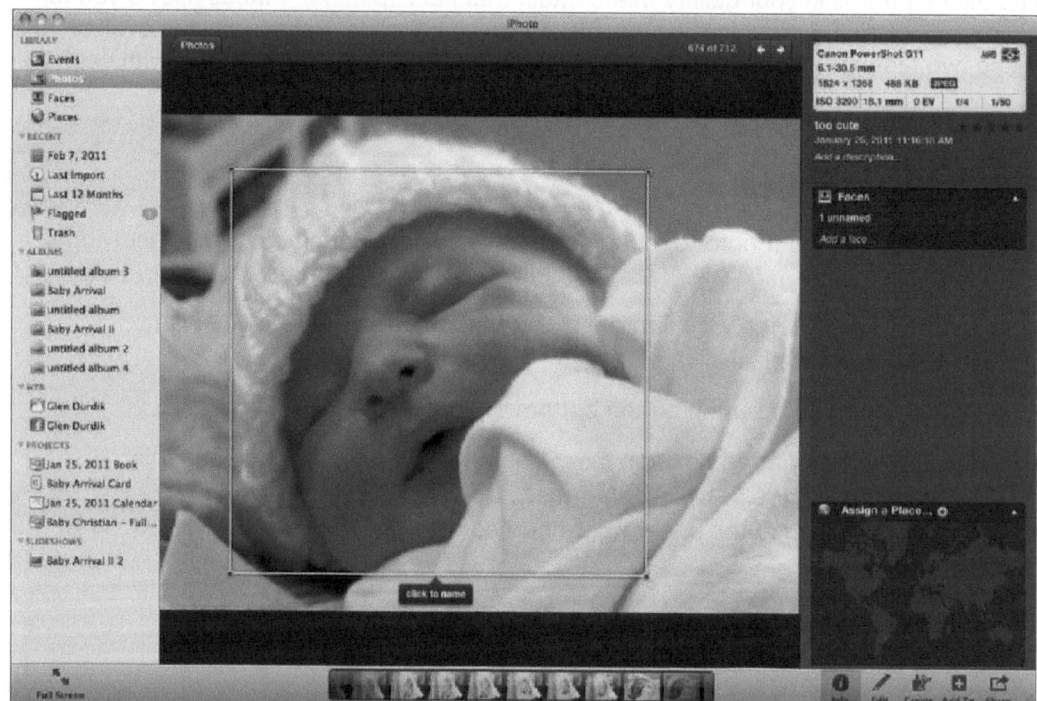

Figure 5–3. *The whole face must be highlighted for face recognition to work*

7. Identify the face by clicking on **Click to name**. This is also shown in
    Figure 5–3. I named the face "Baby Boy."

> **NOTE:** If iPhoto cannot recognize other photos, you will the message shown in Figure 5–4.

Figure 5–4. *No other face matches*

iPhoto has possibly found Elisa in 78 other photos in the example shown in Figure 5–5.

Figure 5–5. *Possible other photos with Elisa in them have been found*

8. Click on **Confirm Additional Faces....**

9. You are then presented with the screen shown in Figure 5–6. Click **Confirm** to approve this face. Continue until all of the photos are confirmed or denied. To deny a photo, press the **Option** button and then click on the photo to be rejected.

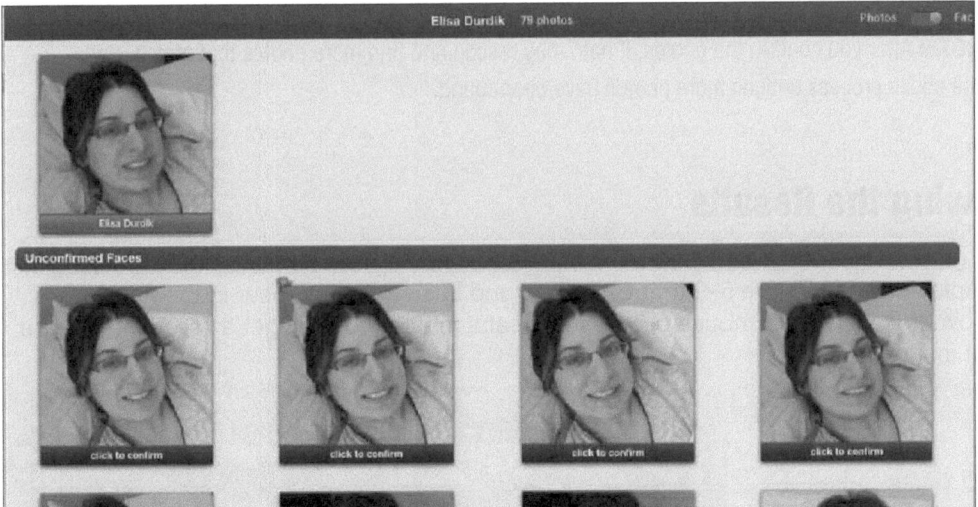

Figure 5–6. *Selecting the approved faces or rejecting faces that don't match*

Figure 5–7 shows a photo that was approved. Figure 5–8 shows a photo that was rejected.

Figure 5–7. *An approved face*

Figure 5–8. *A rejected face*

10. After you have approved or rejected the photos found, click **Done**.

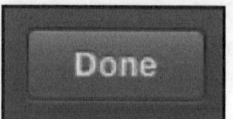

.

> **NOTE:** After you confirm the photos, iPhoto may rescan and find more photos that match. Redo the above process until no more photos have been found.

Viewing the Results

Now go to Faces and, in the source list, you will see the fruits of your labor. Notice in the example shown in Figure 5–9 that Baby Boy and Elisa Durdik appear in the **Faces** window. If you roll your mouse over a successful match, you will get a "slideshow" type effect inside the photo.

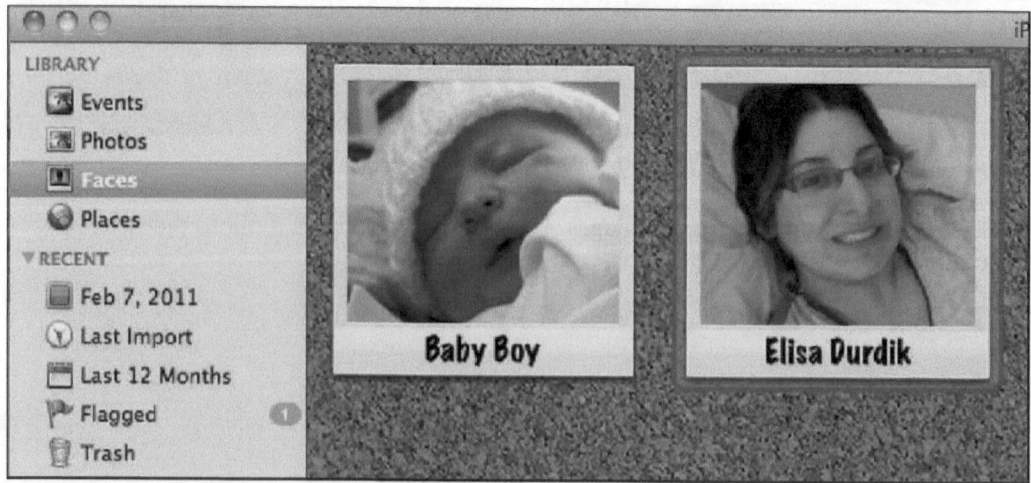

Figure 5–9. *The two faces we created in the example*

If we double-click on Elisa Durdik (remember Baby Boy found no matches), we get a window showing all the photos with her in it. On the top of the window, we have two items of interest: the first is her name with the number of photos found with her in it. This is shown in Figure 5–10.

Figure 5–10. *iPhoto found, and we confirmed, 103 photos of Elisa.*

Next, there is a toggle switch on top of the window that allows you to show either the full photo of Elisa or just her face. This is shown in Figure 5–11.

Figure 5–11. *Choose whether to show the full photo or just a face while viewing photos.*

To return to the full list of faces, click on **All Faces** button found at the top left section of the **Faces** workspace.

Exploring Places

Places is a great way of tracking where you have been. If your camera supports GPS (Global Positioning Satellite) data or you manually enter the data for each photo, once in the data is in – iPhoto will place a pin on every location that you have been. You can also start out with a home address. On the next few pages, I will get you started using this cool feature.

> **NOTE:** If your camera has GPS data, it will be added automatically when you import your photos.

Let's begin by getting iPhoto to recognize location data in photo.

1. Select a photo that you want to add location.

2. Click on the **Info** button.

2. Look for the **Assign a Place...** tab at the bottom right of your workspace. This is shown in Figure 10-12.

Figure 5–12. *Initial **Assign a Place...** section found in the **Info** window*

3. Click on **Assign a Place....** It should disappear and have a space to enter text. This is shown in Figure 5–13.

Figure 5–13. *The blank space in which you will type the location of the photo*

4. As you type the location, iPhoto will give suggestions. This is shown in Figure 5–14.

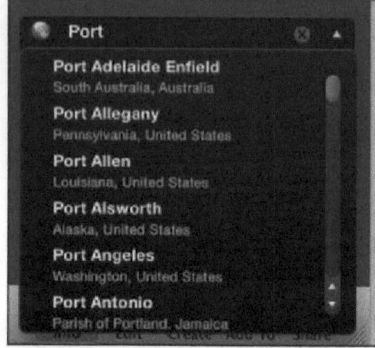

Figure 5–14. *iPhoto assisting in finding the exact location of your photo*

Fine-tuning Your Location

In the example found in Figure 5–15, I selected the New York Aquarium. Notice that a map has appeared showing the location with a pin at the exact location. You can view the map as Terrain, Satellite, or Hybrid (both Satellite and Terrain). Just click on the type of map you will like to see.

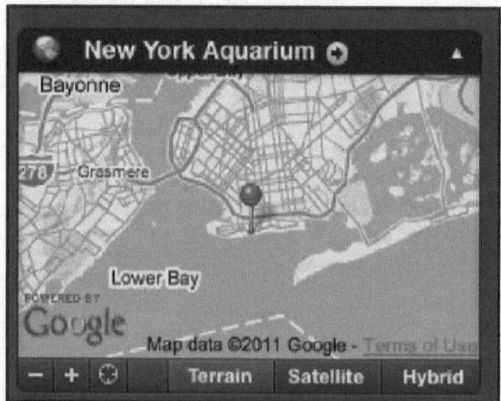

Figure 5–15. *Result of typing in the location for a photo*

 If you click on this button, iPhoto will zoom in on the location you selected.

 If you click on this button, iPhoto will zoom out from the location you selected.

When you go to the **Places** section of the source list, the bar shown in Figure 5–16 will appear. You can click on any of the grey triangles to get more details as to where the locations are that you have entered in. An example of **Places** is shown in Figure 5–17.

Figure 5–16. *Location bar on top Places workspace*

Figure 5–17. *Example of Places that I have marked on the map*

Figure 5–18 shows the full **Places** workspace with all the pins marking where I have been.

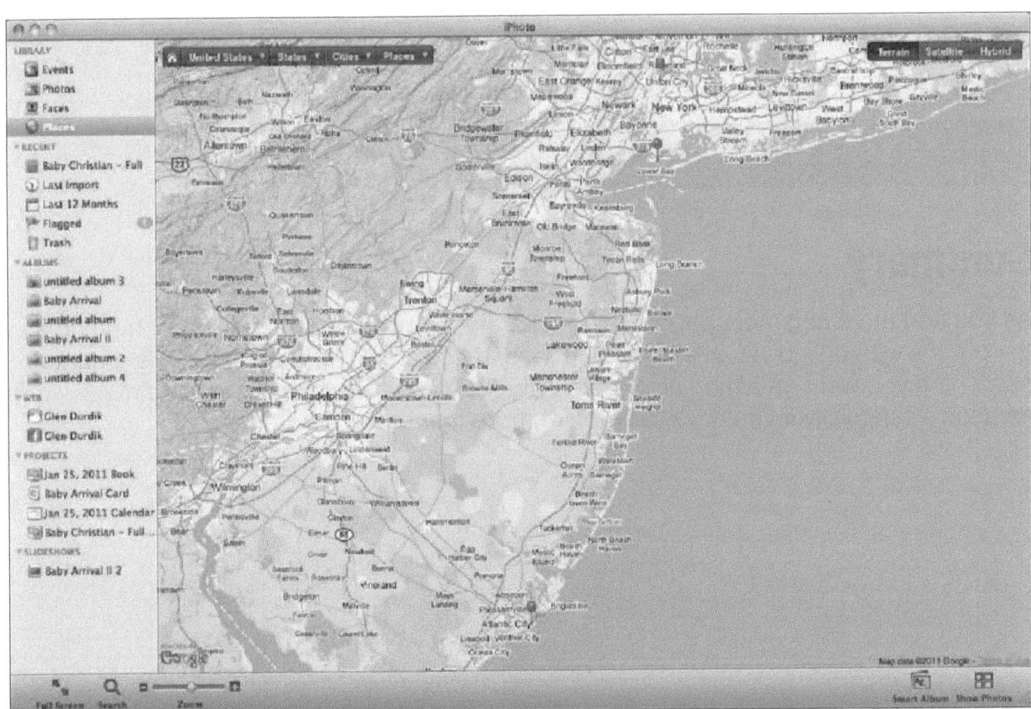

Figure 5–18. *Full Places workspace with three locations (three red pins) marked*

Last, in the bottom right of the **Places** workspace are two buttons. They are **Smart Album** and **Show Photos**.

This button creates a new Smart Album with just the photos that have been set with locations.

This button shows you all the photos that are marked with locations.

Removing Location Data

To forget or remove a location from your map, follow these steps:

1. Select the photo(s) or Events that include the data to be removed.

2. Click on the **Info** button on the toolbar locate at the bottom right of the workspace.

3. Select **Places** in the information pane.

4. At the right of the name, click on the **X** that appears.

Summary

As you add more and more photos to your library, you can see the benefit of tagging all the photos with an individual's name and face. If you are a world traveller, it is great to see where you went on a map and search for photos that were taken in certain location—especially if you have been there more than once.

Chapter 6

And Now ... a Slideshow!

The Slideshow button allows you to create amazing slideshows in no time. You can create a slideshow for current use on you Mac, use the **Create** button to save it for future use, or export it to other formats, such as a QuickTime movie or for use on an iPhone. In this chapter, I'll show you these options.

Themes

When you click on the **Slideshow** button, you are first presented with the option of selecting your theme. There are 12 themes available, as shown in Figure 6–1. You can preview each theme by hovering your mouse over it. After you select your theme, it will remain your theme until you select another from the Slideshow toolbar. This toolbar is discussed later in the chapter.

Figure 6–1. *The 12 available themes*

Notice that, on the bottom left-hand corner, you can make your theme choice your default. This is also shown in Figure 6–2. This will keep your selection for all new slideshows that you create, which is helpful if you create many slideshows and prefer one theme over all the others.

Figure 6–2. *Saving current settings as default settings*

After you have selected your theme, you can then move on to setting your music and other options. These choices are next to the **Themes** tab.

Music

The next step is to see what tunes you want to accompany your slideshow.

The **Music** tab is shown in Figure 6–3. Notice that it has a few sections to it, all of which are described here.

Figure 6–3. *The **Music** tab of the slideshows options window*

 Check this box if you want music to play when your slideshow is playing. If you uncheck this box, no music will play.

If you select **Theme Music** from the **Source** dropdown menu, you are presented with the options shown in Figure 6–4.

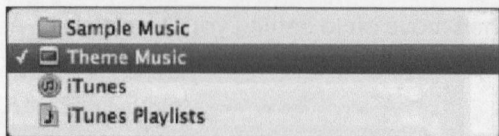

Figure 6–4. *The available locations for music to accompany your slideshow*

You can choose between **Sample Music** or **Theme Music** supplied in the application, or you can choose all music from iTunes or iTunes Playlists. You can sample the song

by clicking this **Play** button.

This is a search tool that allows you to (hopefully) find the songs you are looking for. If you want total control over the music, make sure to check the box next to **Custom Playlist for Slideshow**. This is shown in Figure 6–5. Drag your songs into the box shown above and then you can rearrange them however you like.

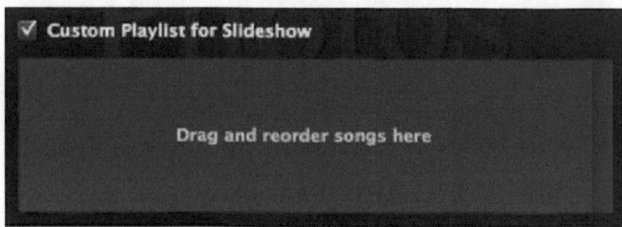

Figure 6–5. *Custom Playlist for Slideshow window, when checked off*

Settings

The last tab is also broken down into sections. The complete **Settings** tab is shown in Figure 6–6.

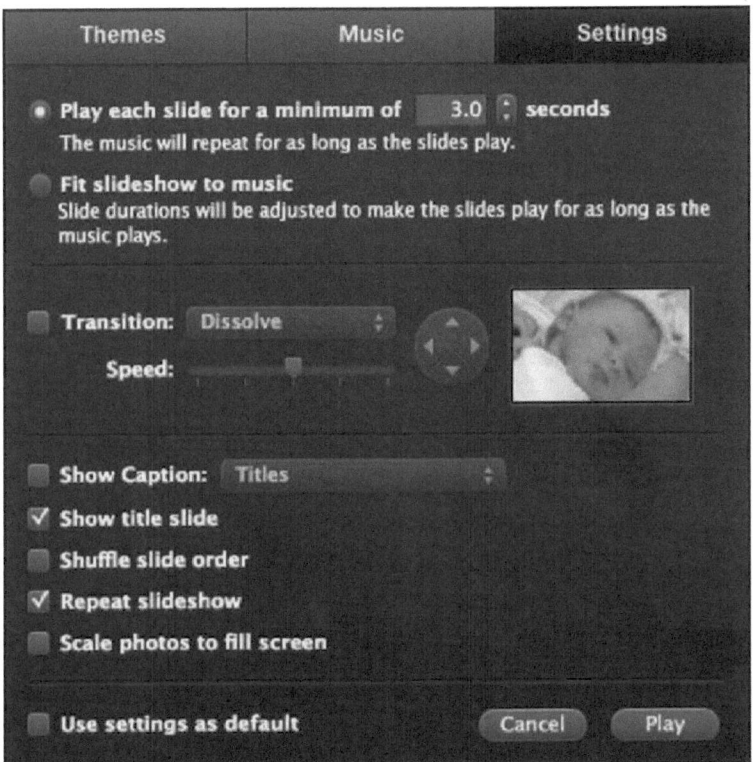

Figure 6–6. *The complete Settings tab*

Play each slide for a minimum of `3.0` ↕ **seconds**
The music will repeat for as long as the slides play.

This is where you decide how long you want each slide (photo) to appear. In this example, it is 3.0 seconds.

Fit slideshow to music
Slide durations will be adjusted to make the slides play for as long as the music plays.

If you want the slideshow length to automatically fit the music track you have selected, click the grey circle next to **Fit slideshow to music**.

Transition: This determines which special effects you want iPhoto to use when transitioning between slides. The choices available to you are shown in Figure 6–7. You can also change the speed of the transition. Note that not all themes have transition options. Also, if you change your theme, your transition settings will be reset each time.

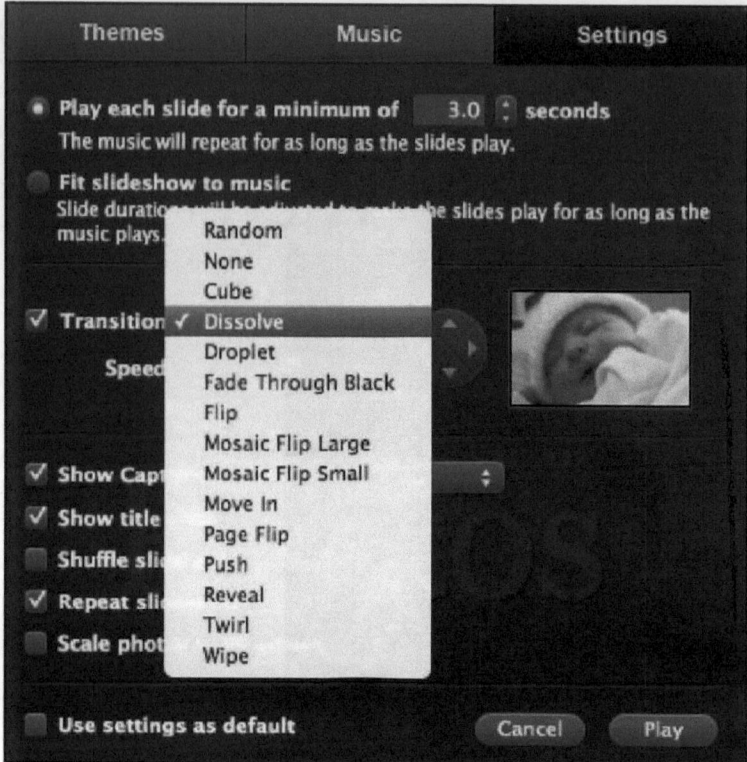

Figure 6–7. *Transitions options*

Show Caption: This determines (if checked) what info you want displayed during the slideshow. The choices available are shown in Figure 6–8.

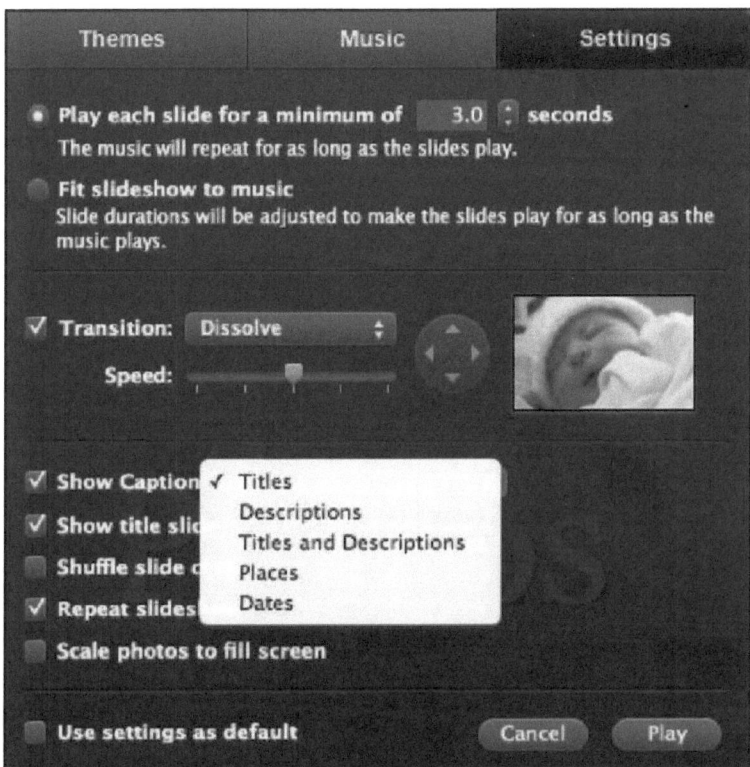

Figure 6–8. *Options available for the Show Caption option*

Show title slide: Simply asks if you want to show a title slide at the beginning of your slideshow.

Shuffle slide order: If you want to mix things up a bit, chose this option. iPhoto will randomly select pictures from your album.

Repeat slideshow: If this is checked, the slideshow will automatically repeat until you cancel it.

Scale photos to fill screen: By default, this is turned off. If you select this option, your photos will be enlarged to fit the entire screen. This may or may not distort your images; try it and see if you like the results.

Use settings as default: This will keep your settings for every subsequent theme you select.

Slideshow Toolbar

The Slideshow toolbar is activated when you are viewing a slideshow and move your mouse in the Running Slideshow window. The full toolbar is shown in Figure 6–9.

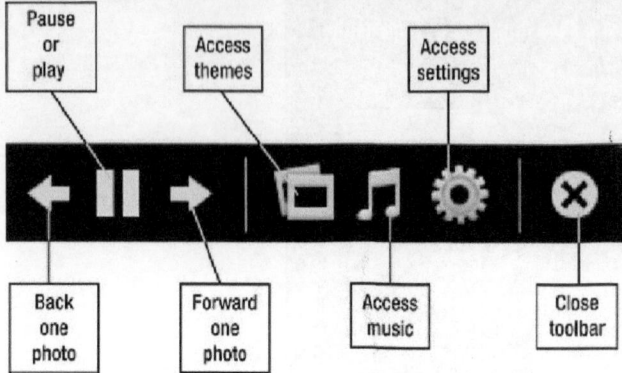

Figure 6–9. *The Slideshow Toolbar and its functions*

You can move forward by clicking on the arrow pointing to the right. You can move back one photo by clicking on the arrow pointing to the left. You can pause the slideshow by clicking on the two vertical lines. You can resume play by clicking on the **Play** button, which replaces the pause button.

> **NOTE:** To stop a slideshow, press the ESC key on your keyboard.

Creating a Slideshow to Save for Future Use

Creating a slideshow using the **Create** tool is similar to creating a slideshow the way I just showed you. Doing it this way provides you the option of exporting the slideshow to another format. The **Create** button Create is located at the bottom of your screen, at the far right. The slideshow you create can be either a standalone QuickTime movie that you can play on other devices such as an iPhone or, if you have no other choice, a Windows machine.

1. Determine what photos you want in the slideshow.

2. Go to the **Create** button Create and select **Slideshow**. You will get the screen shown in Figure 6–10.

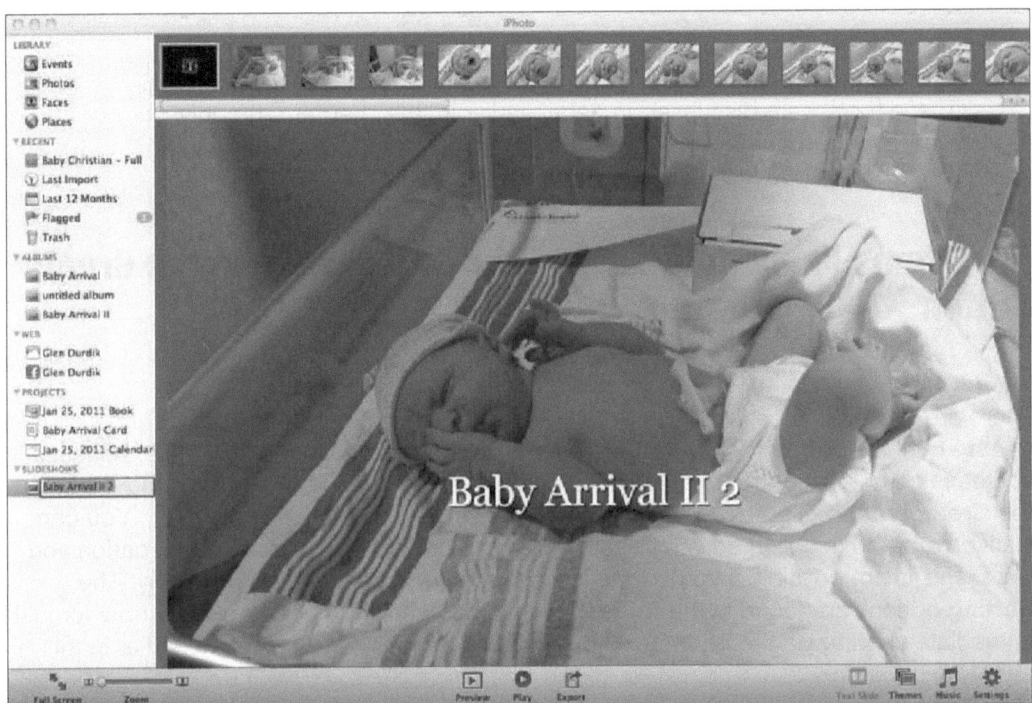

Figure 6–10. *Complete slideshow workspace*

3. Notice in Figure 6–11 that you can name the slideshow in the iPhoto sidebar, and that the default title appears on top of the first picture. To edit this title, click on the words in the title. In this example, "Baby Arrival II 2." This is shown in Figure 6–11. Notice that the text is now highlighted in a blue box.

Figure 6–11. *Changing the title of the slideshow*

4. Click on **Preview** or **Play** to see what the default settings are in case you'd like to make changes. **Preview** will show the slideshow inside the iPhoto workspace. **Play** will show the slideshow in full screen mode.

5. Change the **Themes**  and **Music** settings to your liking. These tools were discussed in detail earlier in this chapter. The only difference is that they were two tabs in the **Settings** window and they are separate buttons here.

New Items Found in Creation of a Slideshow via the Create Button

There are two differences with the **Settings** button when you choose the **Create** method. First, the **Shuffle Slide Order** is removed. This makes sense, because you have complete control over all the aspects of the slide order while creating it using the **Create** button. Figure 6–12 shows the **Slideshow** photo preview window. You can click on a photo (highlighted with a yellow box) and move the photo to any location you wish. This is not possible if you create a slideshow for immediate viewing only. The **Setting** options are found in the **Slideshow** toolbar when you create a slideshow for just immediate viewing via the **Slideshow** button. The toolbar was discussed earlier in this chapter.

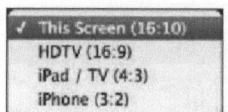

Figure 6–12. Slideshow photo preview window, which is located at the top of the workspace

Second, there is a new option, **Aspect Ratio.**

You can export your slideshow to different devices, but not all of them have the same aspect ratio. You can change the aspect ratios settings here. The choices are shown in Figure 6–13.

✓ This Screen (16:10)
  HDTV (16:9)
  iPad / TV (4:3)
  iPhone (3:2)

Figure 6–13. Choices of aspect ratios

This Slide Tab

You can now make changes to individual slides. This is the second tab in the **Settings** window. The first tab is called **All Slides**. It contains all of the options I discussed earlier. The second is called **This Slide**. Both are shown in Figure 6–14. You can change the color of the slide to **Black & White**, **Sepia**, or **Antique**. You can set a custom time duration or transition for the slide. Last, you can activate the **Ken Burns** effect. This effect basically looks like a video camera zooming in or out or left or right above the photo.

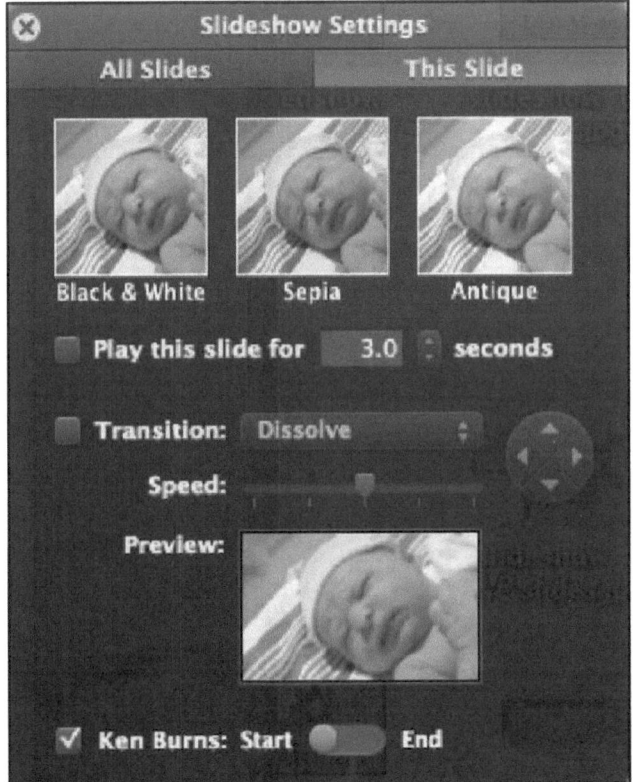

Figure 6–14. *This Slide tab of the Slideshow settings window*

If you look closely at Figure 6–12, you will notice the highlighted box is a completely black box with a grey letter "T" in it. This is a text slide. While creating a slideshow in this fashion, you can add text slides wherever you want. Click on the slide location to the left of the slide to which you want to add text, and then click on the **Text** slide button. The text will appear on top of the picture to the right of the text slide. To

edit the text, just click on **Subtitle Text Here**  and then
type what you wish.

Exporting Your Slideshow

You can export you slideshow to a variety of Apple devices as a QuickTime movie. To
begin this process, click on the **Export** button ![Export] (next to the **Play** button). You are
then presented with the screen shown in Figure 6–15. Note the blue checkmarks next to
the sizes (**Mobile**, **Medium**, **Large**, and **Display**). These are the sizes I will export the
slideshow in. Also, note that on the top of the window, it explains what devices these
sizes will play on (**iPod**, **iPhone**, **iPad**, **Apple TV**, **Computer**, or **MobileMe**). Finally,
notice the option to **Automatically send slideshow to iTunes.** This is great, as these
are the devices you connect to your Mac via iTunes.

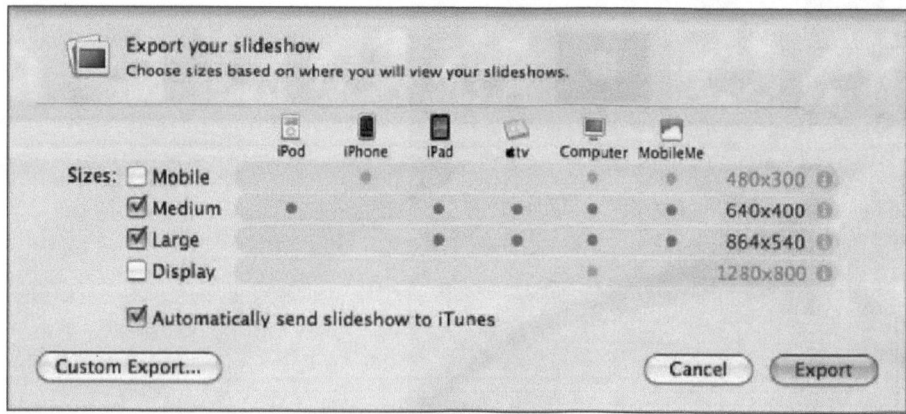

Figure 6–15. *Example of the default Export screen*

If this is fine, just click on **Export** ![Export]. The size of the slideshow determines
how long it will take to create the movie.

![Custom Export...] If you want to customize the way iPhoto renders (creates the
movie file), then you can click on **Custom Export**. You probably will never use this, but I
will go over the basics of what is involved.

The first screen that appears is shown in Figure 6–16. Notice that you can name the
slideshow next to **Save As:**. You can set where the slideshow is going to be saved next
to **Where:**, and select what type of file you want to export the movie as. The export
options are shown in Figure 6–17.

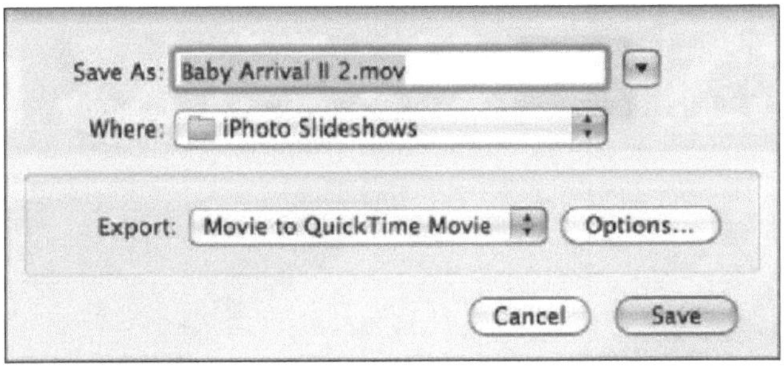

Figure 6–16. *Initial screen of* **Custom Export**

Movie to 3G
Movie to Apple TV
Movie to iPhone
Movie to iPhone (Cellular)
Movie to iPod
Movie to MPEG-4
✓ Movie to QuickTime Movie

Figure 6–17. *Different type of movie formats available*

You will notice in Figure 6–17 that **MPEG-4** and **QuickTime** Movie are the only two universal formats. They should work on any computer.

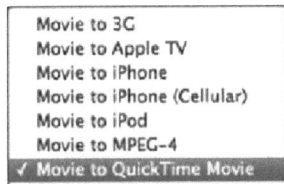 When you are exporting a movie this way, you also have control over other settings in the movie. Click on **Options...** to get another customization screen. This is shown in Figure 6–18. Again, these settings should be fine for the normal user. If you are unhappy with how the video turned out, you can go to this screen and modify the settings. For video, you can change **Frame Rate**, **Compressor** type, and **Quality** (the higher the quality, the larger the file). You can also add a filter such as **Blur**, **Emboss**, **Sharpen,** or **Lens Flare**. You can set the dimensions of the video as well. For audio, you can make it **Stereo** or **Mono** or change the compressor. Last, you can set the video to be prepared for Internet streaming.

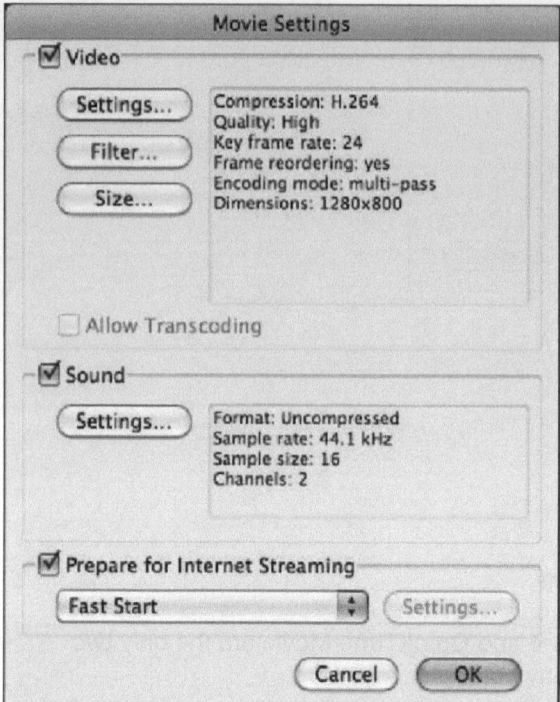

Figure 6–18. *Movie settings available when clicking on **Options** in the **Custom Export** window*

Summary

A slideshow is a great way to present your photos. It can be seen on any computer screen or on Apple's iOS devices. iPhoto makes creating a stunning slideshow and then sharing it with the world possible with just a few clicks of the mouse.

iDVD

Do you prefer to share special occasions by giving physical media to friends or family?

If you are someone who feels sharing memories on the Internet is not for you, then iDVD is a great solution. Create a truly personal DVD for any family event with ease by using iDVD. As you will see, iDVD allows you to create a DVD with a few mouse clicks—while also giving you the ability to create a movie masterpiece with amazing effects.

Part V

iDVD

Chapter 7

Beginner DVD Creation via iDVD

iDVD is a great application for creating awesome DVDs. You can create professional looking DVDs in a few easy steps via **Magic iDVD**, create a DVD from scratch, or just attach a video camera and use **OneStep iDVD** and be done in a snap. Figure 7–1 shows the startup screen for iDVD. In this first chapter on iDVD, I will cover what these choices entail, along with which options are available in each one. The next chapter will cover the **Create a New Project** option and the steps necessary to create a DVD from scratch. This is a much more involved process, but gives you more flexibility.

Figure 7–1. *Initial Startup screen for iDVD*

Before we begin, you might be wondering about the two buttons at the bottom left side of the screen.

The **Help** button simply brings up the **Help** section of iDVD.

Click the **View Tutorials** button to bring up an Apple website that contains videos highlighting several important tasks in the iDVD program. This is shown in Figure 7–2.

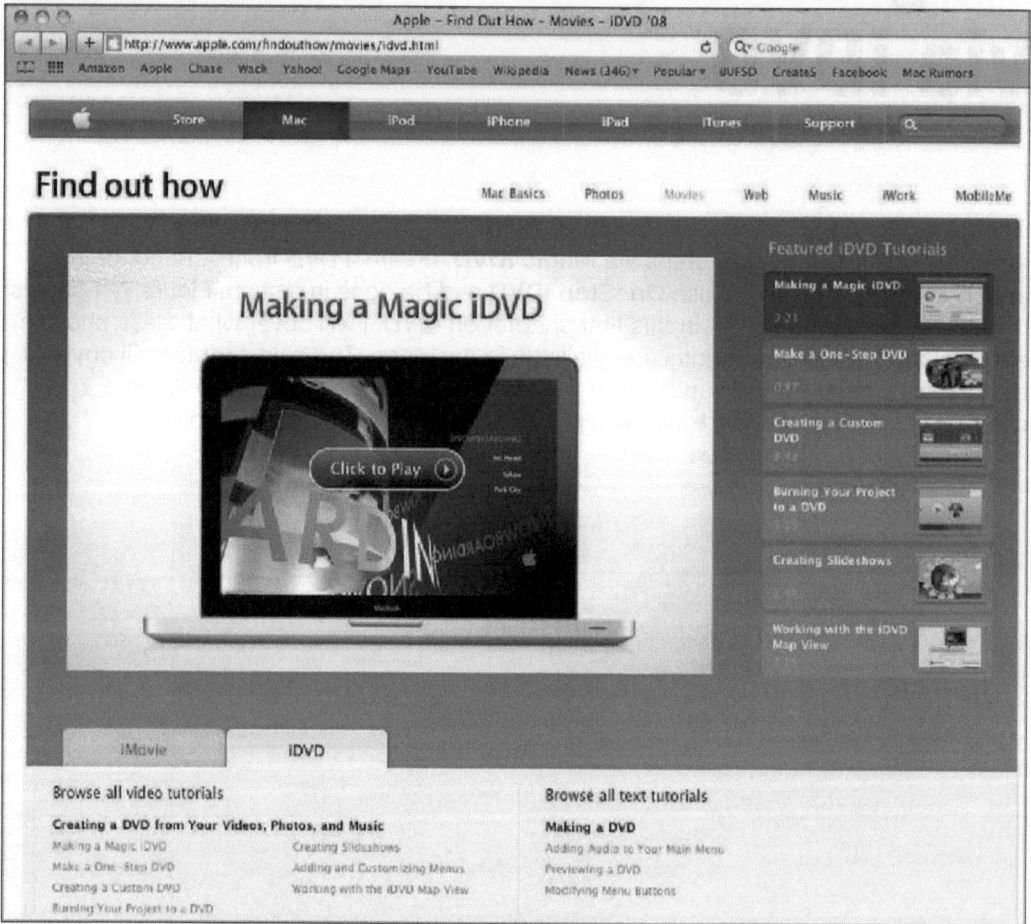

Figure 7–2. *Apple's website that contains several iDVD video tutorials*

OneStep DVD

Let's start at the bottom of the list, which is the simplest way of creating a DVD: the **OneStep DVD** creation process.

1. Attach your video camera and make sure it is set to VCR Mode.

2. After you click on the **OneStep DVD** button , you are presented with the screen shown in Figure 7–3.

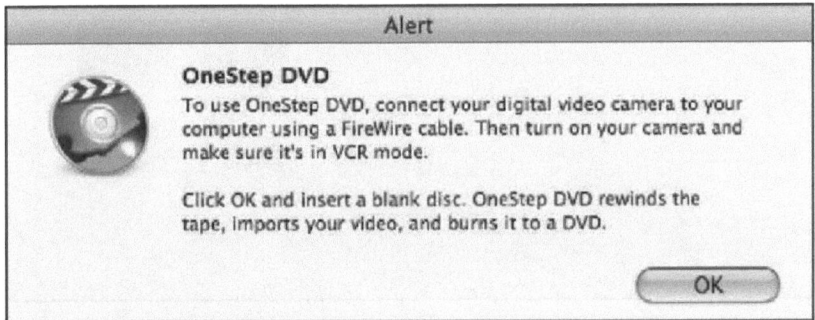

Figure 7–3. *The OneStep DVD creation screen*

3. Click **OK** and then insert a blank DVD. OneStep DVD will rewind the tape or memory card, import the video, and then burn it to a DVD.

That's it! No frills, but a sharable DVD in no time.

Magic iDVD

The **Magic iDVD** process is more involved than OneStep DVD, and it gives you the chance to customize some aspects of the DVD.

1. Click on the **Magic iDVD** button to begin the process.

You are then presented with the screen shown in Figure 7–4.

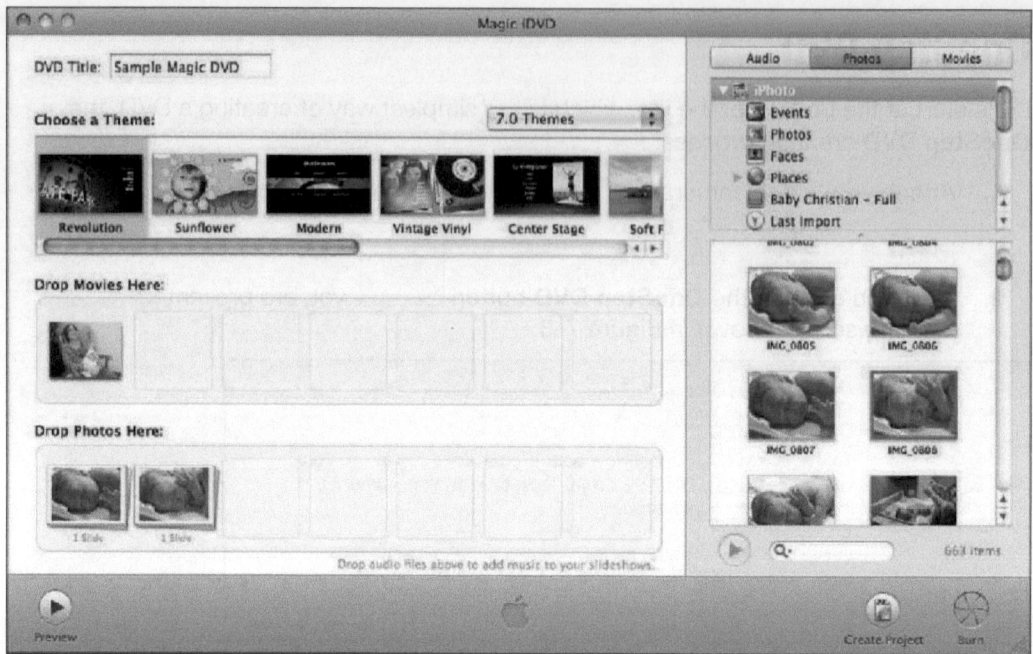

Figure 7–4. *The Magic iDVD Creation screen*

At the top left of the Magic IDVD workspace, next to DVD Title, type in a name for your DVD project. In the example in Figure 7–3, I named it Sample Magic DVD.

2. Choose a theme. This option is just below the DVD title option. Slide the long blue button left or right to see all of the version 7.0 themes. You have to 10 to choose from. If you click on 7.0 Themes, you can choose version 6.0 themes. This gives you another 10 choices.

3. Locate all the movies you want to add to the DVD. They must be in your **Movies** folder or in you iPhoto library. iDVD will not recognize movies from other locations. Drag the ones you want into the section called **Drop Movies Here:**. Add as many as you want. In Figure 7–3, you can see that I added only one video so far.

4. Add any photos you want in this project. They must be from your iPhoto library. In Figure 7–3, you can see that I added two photos.

5. You can add music to accompany the slideshow Magic IDVD will create from the photos you inserted. The music must come from iTunes. Just drag the songs into the workspace.

6. Click on the **Preview** button Preview to see how the final DVD will look. Make any changes to finalize your project.

7. If you are pleased with the results, click on the **Burn** button. This will create the project and then copy it onto a blank DVD.

8. If you are mostly pleased with the results, but want to tweak it a bit, click on the **Create Project** button. This will create a DVD project based on your input so far. Once it is completed, you are brought into the main iDVD workspace. Here, you have full control over every detail of your project. The tools available in these workspace will be discussed in Chapter 8: "iDVD Workspace: The Widescreen Edition."

Open an Existing Project

If you already created a project, this option allows you to open it and continue to work on it. This is shown in Figure 7–5. The application defaults to your Documents folder, but you can navigate to any location where your work is saved.

Figure 7–5. *Example of opening an existing project from your hard drive*

Summary

In this chapter, you were introduced to iDVD, Apple's powerful DVD-creation tool. With it, you can create a personal DVD in just a few steps. As you have just seen, Apple continues to provide excellent tools—either within iDVD or on the Internet—to get you on the way to becoming a great DVD creator. In the next chapter, I will go further in depth into all options available to truly customize your project.

iDVD Workspace: The Widescreen Edition

In the previous chapter, we discussed two easy ways of creating DVDs. The workspace environment I will discuss in this chapter is not available via the **Magic iDVD** or **OneStep DVD** creation options. In this chapter, I will go over all the options and settings that you can modify to completely customize your DVD.

Starting from Scratch

To start from scratch, click on the **Create a New Project** icon found in the initial iDVD startup window.

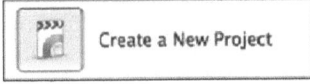

Next, you are asked three questions. The window that appears is shown in Figure 8–1.

1. What do you want to name your DVD? Type in your title next to the words **Save As:**.

2. Where do you want to save your project? The default is your

   Documents folder. If you click on the blue downpointing arrow ▼, you are presented with full access to all your possible saving locations.

3. What **Aspect Ratio** do you want to use? The standard will make your DVD the size of a non-widescreen screen. They are square rather than rectangular. If you choose widescreen, your DVD will be the size of widescreen TV or monitor.

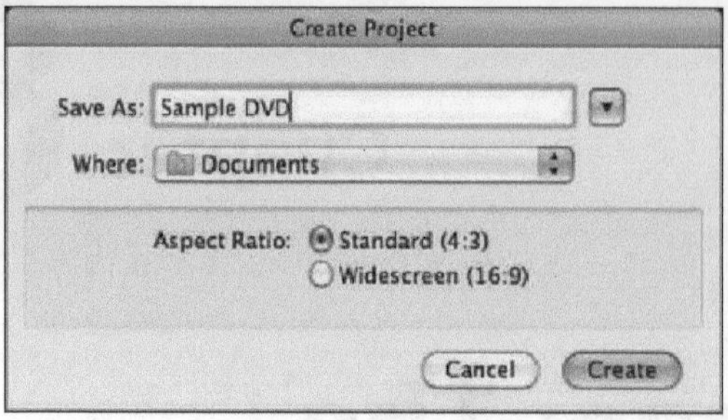

Figure 8–1. *Initial screen to create a DVD from scratch*

Once you have named your DVD and set the save location and aspect ratio, you are ready to learn how to become the next famous Hollywood producer and create the next straight-to-DVD mega-hit.

iDVD's main workspace

The main iDVD workspace is shown in Figure 8–2. It gives you a simple yet elegant interface with which to customize your iDVD project. By using the powerful **Add** button or choosing the perfect theme, iDVD makes it simple to create a beautiful, professional-quality DVD.

Figure 8–2. *iDVD main workspace environment*

NOTE: Notice the three icons at the bottom of the workspace environment. If an icon is blue, as are the center arrows in this example, that means its function is currently in use. If it is black, then it is not being accessed.

Add Button

The **Add** button, located at the bottom of your workspace, at the far left, allows you to add one of three things to your project. They are:

- **Submenu:** When clicked on a playing DVD, it brings you to a new window. It could be a second page of videos or a page with a slideshow of photos. You can create as many as you wish.

- **Movie:** Creates a placeholder in your iDVD workspace for a movie. You can choose one from the iDVD media tray or one from anywhere else on your hard drive.

NOTE: It is very important to keep all of your files used for your project on one storage device. Once you add media to your project, it should not be removed. If you remove movies or photos, iDVD will not find them, and they will not be in your final project.

- **Slideshow:** Allows you create a slideshow of photographs of your choosing. The slideshow creation window is shown in Figure 8–4. You can select your photos from the **Media** tab at the right side of your screen, or drag them from any other location into the **Slideshow** window. You can set the slide duration, assign transitions between slides, and change the volume of the music you have selected. A list of all available transitions is shown in Figure 8–5. The last set of options are found when you click on the **Settings** button. This is shown in Figure 8–6. You can choose to:
  - Loop the slideshow (play it over and over again).
  - Display navigation arrows (to move one photo forward or back).
  - Add image files to the DVD (recommended) or show titles and comments (only good if you manually changed the photos names from the generic ones created when your camera took the photo).
  - Duck audio while playing movies. This lowers the volume of the DVD soundtrack while your slideshow plays.

- If you want to get back to edit your slideshow, you must double-click on the name of your slideshow.

The screen that pops up when you click the **Add** button is shown in Figure 8–3.

Figure 8–3. *Choices available when you click on the **Add** button*

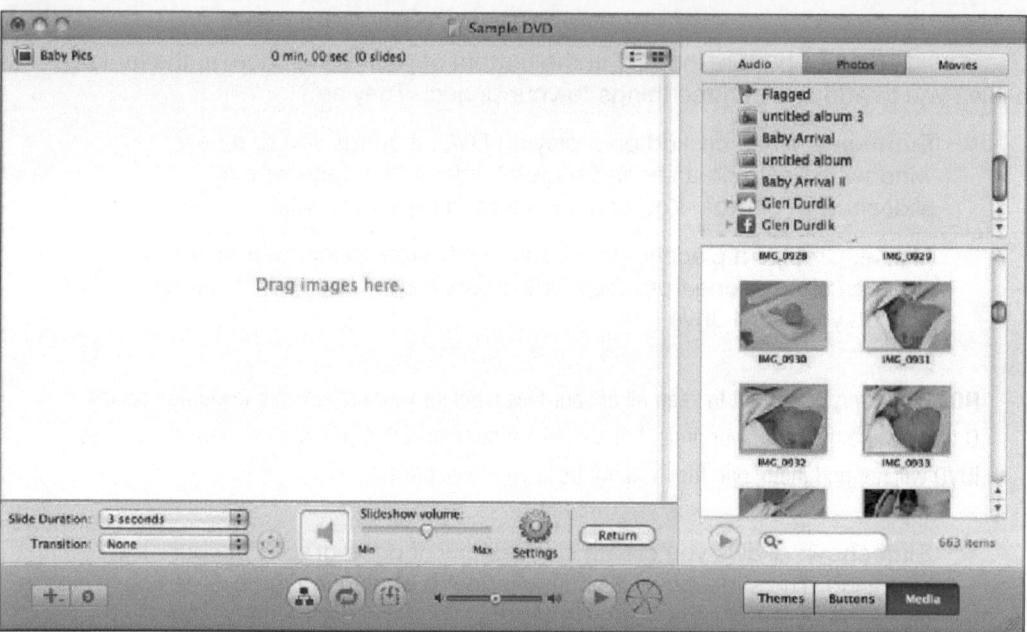

Figure 8–4. *Slideshow creation window*

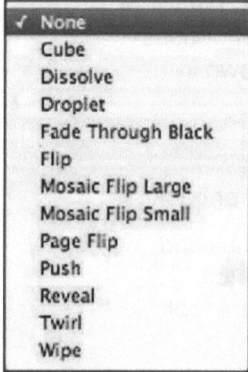

Figure 8–5. *List of all available transitions*

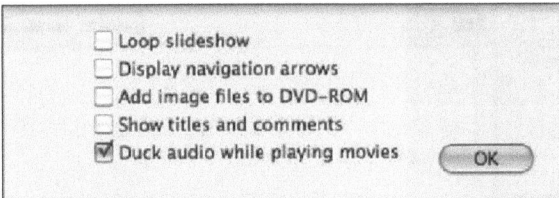

Figure 8–6. *Slideshow setting options*

Inspector Button

This button gives you info on several aspects of your currently active iDVD window. The window is broken down into several options, as shown Figure 8–7.

- **Customizing your background animation**

    - You can include an intro set and an outro set. By default, the loop duration of the music is 30 seconds. When the loop is set for that long, the outro portion kicks in and fades the music. If you reduce the loop duration, the sound will not fade.

    - **Loop Duration:** This sets the duration of the animation and sound. As just discussed, it can be set to between 0 and 30 seconds.

- **Audio**

    - This simply adjusts the volume for each project window you are working on. Each new section can have its own volume.

- **Buttons**

    - **Snap to grid**: Keeps all recently added items to the current iDVD window in a neat row.

    - **Free positioning**: Allows you to arrange the titles of added items in any order or fashion you wish.

    - **Highlight**: Determines the color of the text when you move over it during a playing DVD. For example, the default normal titles are white in the theme I am using in this chapter. When previewing it or after it is burned, the titles will turn orange when I move my mouse over them.

- **Drop Zones**

    - **Show drop zones and related graphics**: In each of the themes, there are locations were you can add, or "drop," graphics into them. This is turned on by default and the drop zones will be clearly marked in each them.

Figure 8–7. *Info window of an active iDVD Window*

DVD Map Button

This is key if you are going to be creating a large and complex DVD with many items. It is a simple visual roadmap as to what button leads to what screen. A sample DVD map is shown in Figure 8–8.

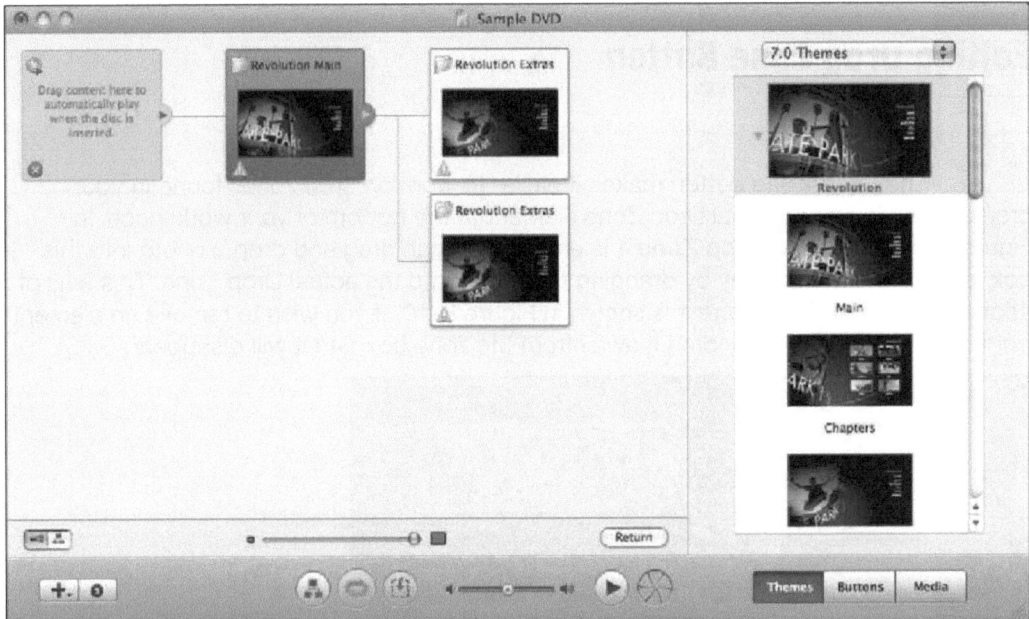

Figure 8–8. *Example of the DVD map*

Please notice the following new items in this window.

- This is the **Orientation** button found in this workspace. This allows you to see the map vertically or horizontally.

- The slider in the middle of the window determines the size of the preview windows in the workspace. Move it to the left to shrink the previews and to the right to make them bigger.

- The **Return** button returns you to the regular iDVD working environment.

Motion Button

The **Motion** button starts or stops the preview of the animations in you DVD. It might get annoying hearing the same soundtrack over and over and over again. This will make things nice and peaceful as you work on your next big DVD.

Editing Drop Zone Button

The **Drop Zone** button makes it easier to work on drop zones found in your project. It adds an additional Drop Zone element at the bottom of your workspace. In Figure 8–9, we see that **Drop Zone 1** is empty. You can drag and drop a photo into this box, or do it the normal way by dragging the photo into the actual Drop Zone. This way of adding a photo to **Drop Zone 1** is shown in Figure 8–10. If you wish to remove an element from the Drop Zone, simply drag it away from the zone box and it will disappear.

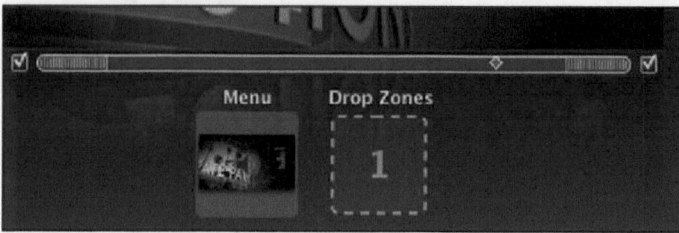

Figure 8–9. *Added element to Drop Zone*

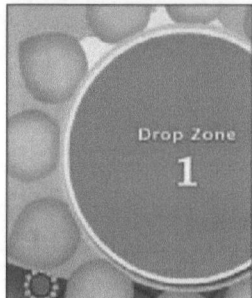

Figure 8–10. *Example of a Drop Zone*

The **Volume Slider** simply adjusts the volume of the music or video being played.

Play button

The **Play** button plays the DVD as if it is actually running in a DVD player. The window is just the project screen; no iDVD buttons or options are shown. In Figure 8–11, we see a new window that appears when accessing the **Play** command. It is a simple DVD player interface, so that you can see how to navigate your project when being used in a player.

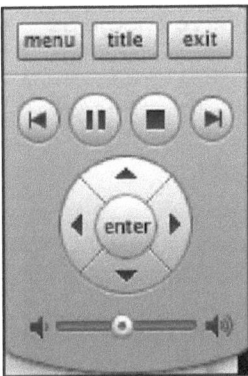

Figure 8–11. *Simple DVD player interface that appears when viewing with the **Play** button*

Burn Button

The **Burn** button is the last button you click when you are ready to actually create a physical DVD. Once clicked, the button turns into this . iDVD is a very mindful program. If it finds missing items or other oddities in your project, it will warn you. A warning is shown in Figure 8–12. You are given the choice of canceling the process, continuing to burn the DVD with the errors, or opening the DVD map to further investigate the problem.

Figure 8–12. *Sample caution message warning of problems found in your project*

Themes Button

The **Themes** is located at the bottom right of your project workspace. A theme contains different animations, soundtracks, and backgrounds. iDVD comes with many different ones. In Figure 8–13, we see a partial list of the themes found in the latest version, 7.0. If you click on **7.0 Themes**, you can access **All Themes**, **6.0 Themes** only, **Old Themes** only and finally, you can choose from a list of you **Favorites**. This is shown in Figure 8–14. This is done by going to the **File** menu and selecting **Save Theme as Favorite…**. This is shown in Figure 8–15. The next step is to name this new favorite. This is shown in Figure 8–16.

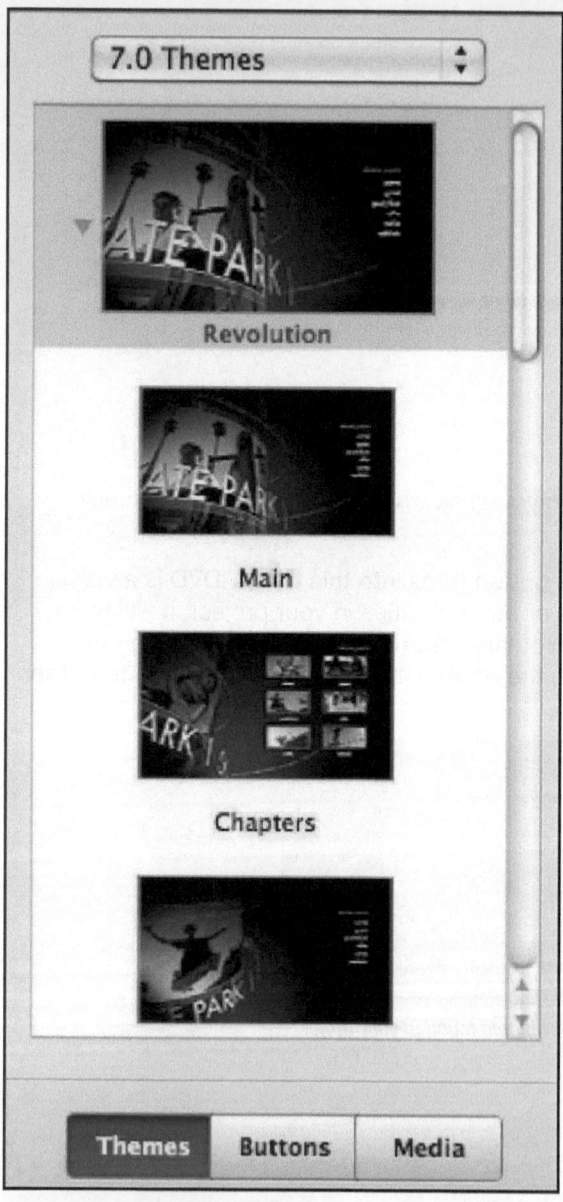

Figure 8–13. *Themes button of iDVD*

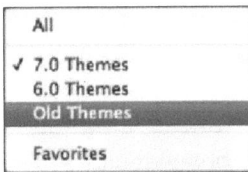

Figure 8–14. *Categories for choosing a DVD theme*

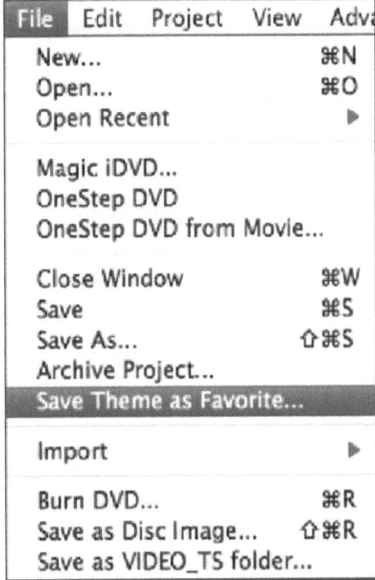

Figure 8–15. *Step 1: saving a **Favorite** to your **Favorites** folder*

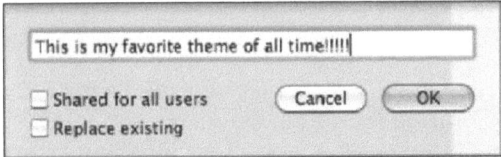

Figure 8–16. *Step 2: saving a **Favorite** to your **Favorites** folder*

Notice that you can make this **Favorite** available to all the users on your Mac by checking the box next to **Shared for all users**. Also notice that you can replace the existing theme with the one you are creating. In the example in Figure 8–16, my theme is not to be shared with others and is not replacing the existing theme.

Buttons Button

Buttons The **Buttons** button gives you access to a variety of buttons that can be used within your project. Buttons may be repositioned on the page to align with other buttons and titles or to balance your page design. A yellow line will appear when two objects are in alignment.

> **NOTE:** Some button shapes may actually move the image, change the button size and will need repositioning.

An example of the shapes that can be applied behind titles is shown in Figure 8–17.

Figure 8–17. *Sample of Shapes available to be used behind titles*

You are given other choices as well. This is shown in Figure 8–18.

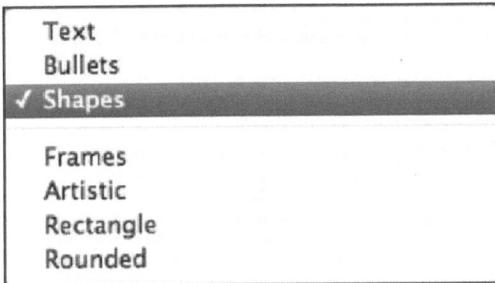

Figure 8–18. *All of the button choices available to be added to you project*

You can really experiment for a long time as there are so many options. For example, in Figure 8–19, I added a cool frame around a movie embedded in my project. Looks a lot better that a plain title, don't you agree?

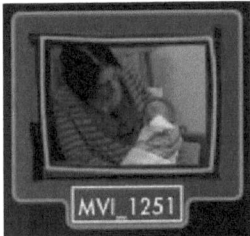

Figure 8–19. *Example of a frame added around a movie element in my project*

Media Button

At the far right of you project workspace, lies the **Media** sidebar. In iDVD, this consists of the **Audio**, **Photos**, and **Movies** tabs. In Figure 8–20, we see the **Audio** and **Photos** section of this button. **Audio** defaults to your iTunes library or GarageBand songs, and Photos defaults to your iPhoto library. You can drag other media from any other location into your project. In Figure 8–21, we see the **Movies** section of the **Media** button. The three choices in this window are iMovie movies, videos in your **Videos** folder, and your iPhoto library.

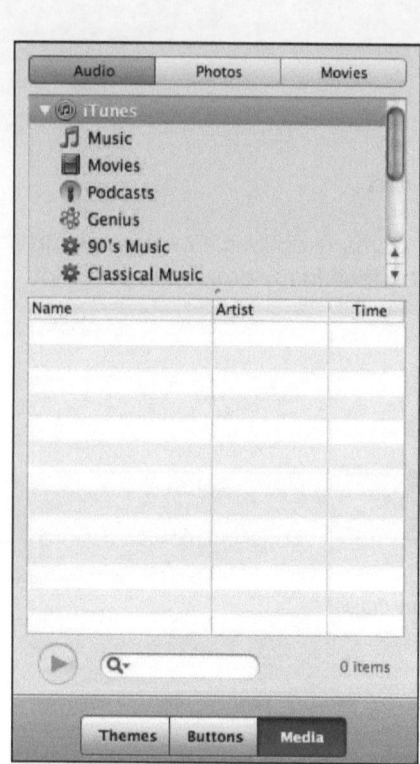

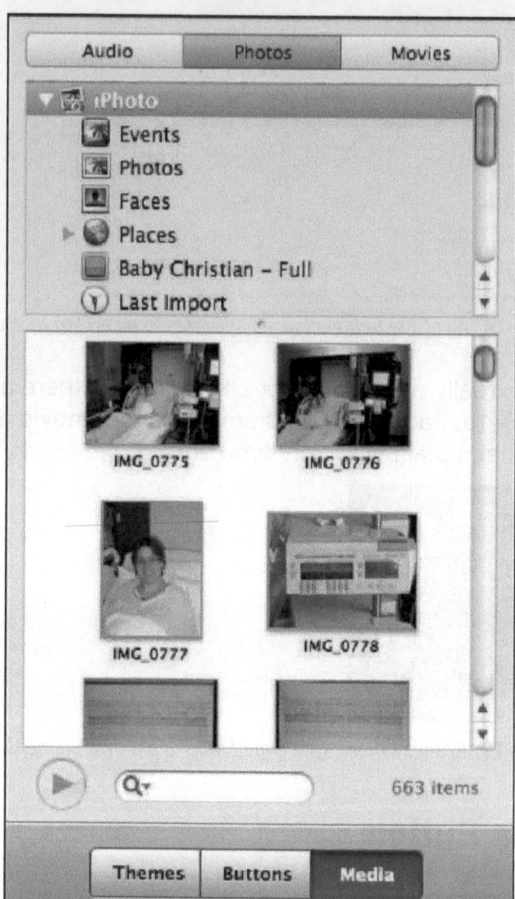

Figure 8–20. *The Audio and Photos section of the Media button*

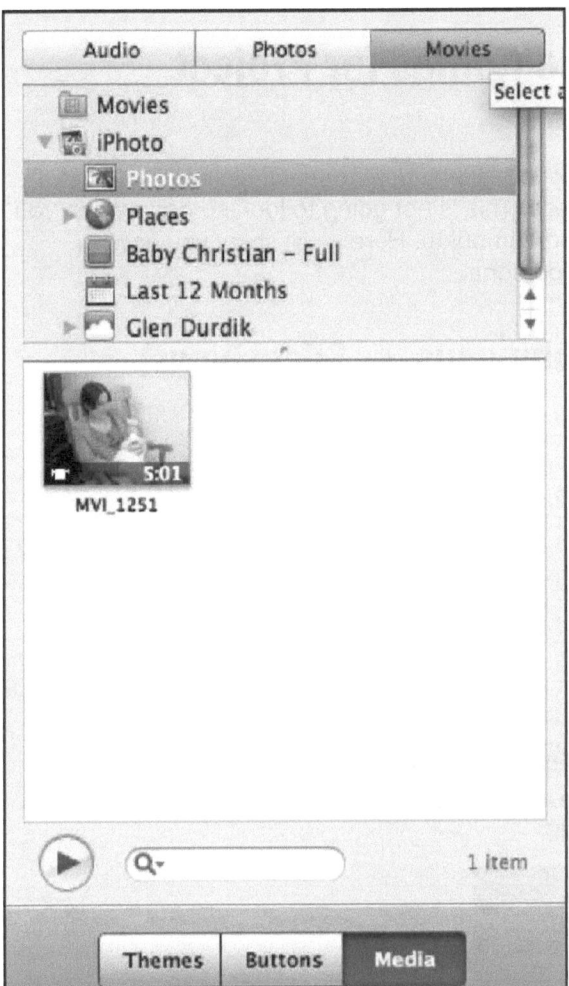

Figure 8–21. *The **Movie** section of the **Media** button*

Play Button and Search Tool

In every section of the **Media** button, there is a **Play** button (triangle pointing to the right) and a search tool (magnifying glass and a space to type text). The **Play** button is great, as you can hear or see the media in order to make a more informed decision if you want it in your project. And if you have hundreds or thousands or songs in iTunes, a search tool is an absolute must.

Getting Rid of the Generic Names for Project Elements

As you probably noticed, iDVD adds generic placeholders for each element you add, such as **My Slideshow** or **Add Movie Here**. This is not going to look so good when you show it to your second cousin visiting from Timbuktu. Here, I will show you how to modify these to make your project more personal.

Editing Titles (of Movies, Submenus, or Slideshows)

To edit a title, follow these steps:

1. Click on the title. Your item should now be highlighted with a blue outline. This is shown in Figure 8–22.

Figure 8–22. *Step 1: changing a title's entry*

2. Click on the text in the title. Your title should have a blue background. This is shown in Figure 8–23. Type in the new title. Notice that you can change the font and its size as well.

Figure 8–23. *Step 2: changing a title's entry*

Summary

In this chapter, I covered all of the elements needed to get around the iDVD workspace. With this knowledge in hand, you are on your way to making a truly memorable DVD to share your precious memories with others. Oh, one last thing: I recommend scheduling a nice dinner and movie after hitting the **Burn** button ![burn icon]. It takes forever to burn a DVD. But, the final results will wow everyone, so the time is well spent.

Chapter 9

Burning Questions About iDVD Menus

The iDVD menus are found at the top of your Mac's screen. You'll notice that a lot of the options are the same as with iPhoto, and all the other applications in the iLife suite. However, each app serves a different purpose and contains menus that are specific to that app. I covered the creation process and workspace environment in the previous two chapters. In this chapter, you will see that a few options that we've already discussed can also be achieved via a menu. More important, this chapter will cover new options not found elsewhere in the program. On the following pages, I will cover each menu in detail. So...get ready to master the menus, one option at a time.

iDVD Menu

Let's start with the **iDVD** menu, shown in Figure 9–1. At a glance, it might be hard to distinguish this menu from the other iLife app menus. As with the other menus, the most important option found here is the **Preferences...** option.

Figure 9–1. *iDVD menu*

About iDVD

This menu item tells you which version of iDVD you are currently running.

Preferences...

This menu item contains several tabs that provide the options to configure how the iDVD functions: **General**, **Appearance**, **Sharing**, **Accounts**, and **Advanced**.

General Tab

The **General** tab is shown in Figure 9–2. A description of each option follows the figure.

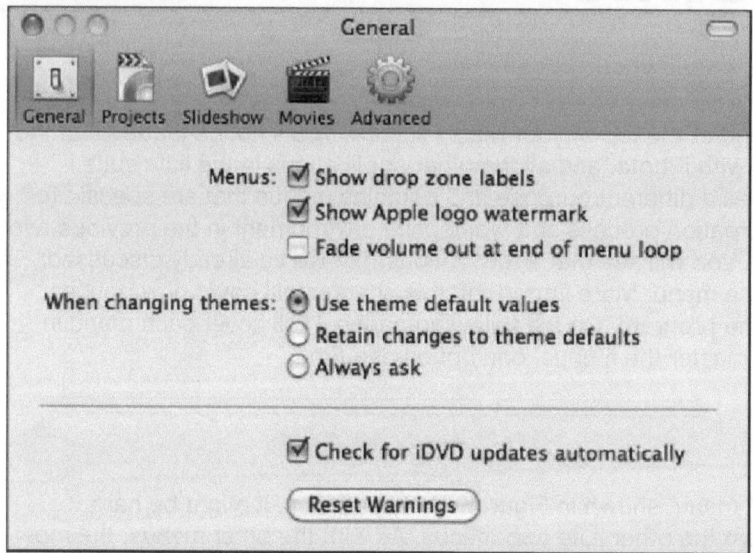

Figure 9–2. *General* tab of the *Preferences...* menu option found in the *iDVD* menu

The **Menus** section contains the following three options:

- **Show drop zone labels:** These are the areas to which you can add photos for backdrops.

- **Show the Apple logo watermark:** Be proud and show the world you used a Mac to create your project. This option places a small Apple logo inside your project.

- **Fade volume out at end of menu loop:** If this item is checked, the music selected for a menu will gradually decrease in volume as it ends the loop. I think it makes it sound a little more professional.

The **When changing themes** section offers the following options:

- **Use theme default values:** You can change the settings for each theme supplied in IDVD. This simply opens the unmodified version.

- **Retain changes to theme defaults:** This would allow you to automatically save any changes to the default themes. I would recommend leaving it off, as you would have to reinstall the application if anything gets overwritten by accident.

- **Always ask:** iDVD simply wants to make sure you want to change the current theme.

If you check the box next to **Check for iDVD updates automatically**, iDVD will connect to an Apple server to see if there are any software updates.

Projects Tab

The **Projects** tab is shown in Figure 9–3. A description of each option follows the figure.

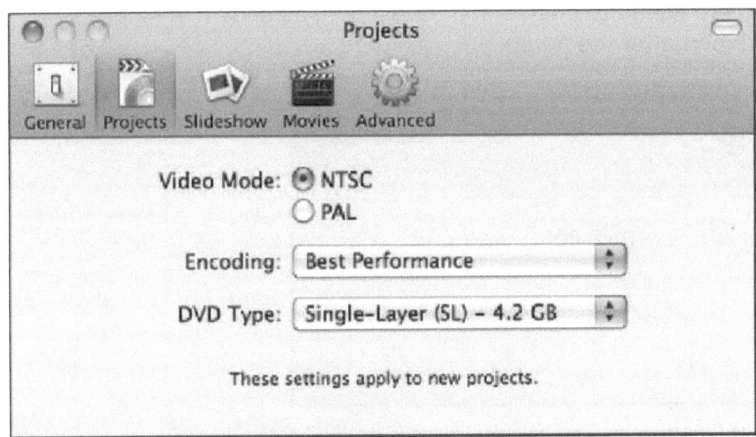

Figure 9–3. *Projects tab of the Preference... menu option found in the iDVD menu*

- **Video Mode:** Choose between NTSC or PAL video encoding. Depending on what country you are in, the video standards may be different. NTSC is the standard used in the United States.

- **Encoding:** This determines the quality of the final DVD. It can be **Best Performance**, **High Quality**, or **Professional Quality**. **Best Performance** takes the least amount of time to burn, and **Professional Quality** takes the longest. To help you decide which method is best for your project, consider how long your video is. If it is about an hour long, you should choose **Best Performance**. If it ranges from one hour to two hours, you should choose **High Quality**. If you want the absolute best final result and the video is more than two hours, choose **Professional Quality**.

  To determine the length of video in your project, select the **Project Info...** option from the **Project** menu. You will see a capacity meter. This meter will be constantly updated when you add new videos or other media.

- **DVD Type.** This could be either **Single-Layer** (most common), which holds 4.2 GB of data, or **Double-Layer**, which holds 7.7 GB of data.

Slideshow Tab

In the **Slideshow** tab, you are asked to answer four questions, as shown in Figure 9–4. These questions are described after the figure.

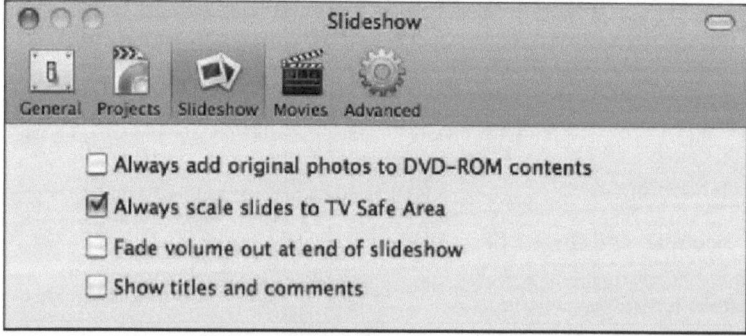

Figure 9–4. *Slideshow* tab of the *Preferences...* menu option found in the *iDVD* menu

- **Always add original photos to DVD-ROM contents:** Simply adds original photos to your final DVD. I believe this should be on by default. Why? If it is checked, whomever has a copy of your DVD can have access to this media and copy it to their computer if they wish.

- **Always scale slides to TV Safe Area:** This is on by default. It adjusts the size of your photos so that they always fit in the slideshow screen space and nothing is cut out.

- **Fade volume out at end of slideshow:** Simply fades the music when the slideshow ends.

■ **Show titles and comments:** If you named your photos a unique name like Hawaii 2009 or added comments, you might want iDVD to show these names and comments at the bottom of the photos during the slideshow.

Movies Tab

The **Movies** tab is shown in Figure 9–5. A description of each option follows the figure.

> **NOTE:** It is important to keep any media you are using in one central location. If you move or delete media from its original location, iDVD won't find it, and it will have to be added back into your project.

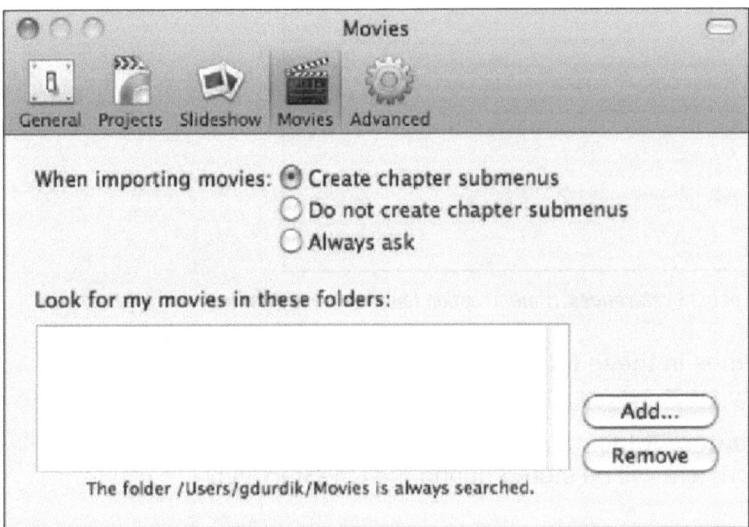

Figure 9–5. *The **Movies** tab of the **Preferences...** menu option found in the **iDVD** menu*

■ **When importing movies:** This option determines what happens when you import a movie. The default is to use the **Create chapter submenu** option. This is perfect for most users, although it could be either of the other two options:

   ■ **Do not create chapter submenus**

   ■ **Always ask**

■ **Look for my movies in these folders:** Here you can add other locations in which iDVD will look for videos that can be imported. It already looks in your **Movies** folder, iMovie movies, and iPhoto.

Advanced Tab

The **Advanced** tab is shown in Figure 9–6. A description of each option follows the figure.

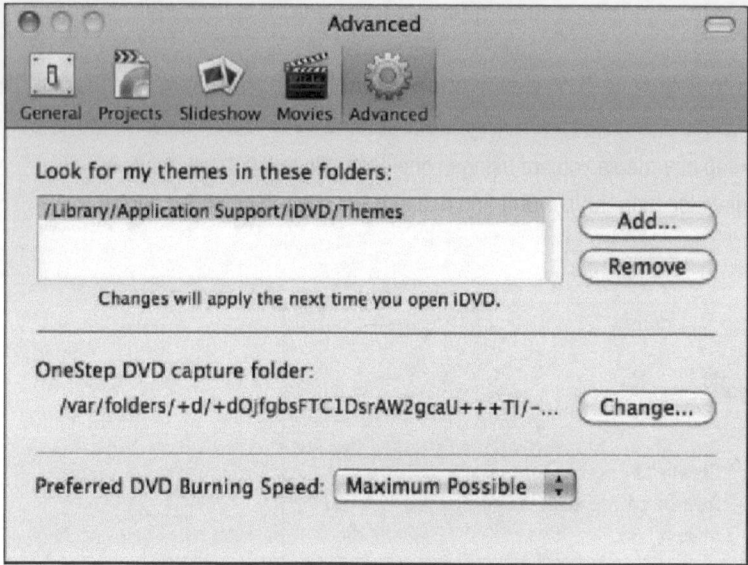

Figure 9–6. *The **Advanced** tab of the **Preferences...** menu option found in the **iDVD** menu*

- **Look for my themes in these folders:** Here you can add locations in which you want to store new or modified themes for iDVD to use.

- **OneStep DVD capture folder:** Simply determines where the video from your video camera will be stored during the OneStep DVD creation process.

- **Preferred DVD Burning Speed:** Allows you to change the speed at which the DVD is to be burned. **Maximum Possible** is the default. However, you might experience issues burning at the maximum speed. Please match the speed with the maximum speed the manufacturer states it can be burned. It could be 1x, 2x, 4x, or 8x. Usually, the higher the speed of the disk, the higher the price.

Shop for iDVD Products

This option brings you to a website that sells items for iDVD use. At last check, the site only has blank DVDS for sale.

Provide iDVD Feedback

This brings you to a website that allows you to provide feedback about iDVD. You are given the opportunity to choose from a long list of possible issues. The site also contains a sidebar of helpful hints for iDVD.

Register iDVD

This brings you to a website to register iDVD. This is not required for the app to run.

Check for Updates...

Goes to Apple to make sure iDVD is up to date.

Services

If there are any installed, this is where they can be accessed. By default, there are none.

Hide iDVD

Hides all of the open windows of iDVD.

Hide Others

Hides all of the open windows of all open programs except iDVD.

Show All

Shows all open windows for all of the applications that are open.

Quit iDVD

This will shut down iDVD.

File Menu

I guess you could also call the **File** menu, shown in Figure 9–7, the **Creation** menu, as most of the following options create new projects or finish the process by actually creating the physical DVD with your project on it.

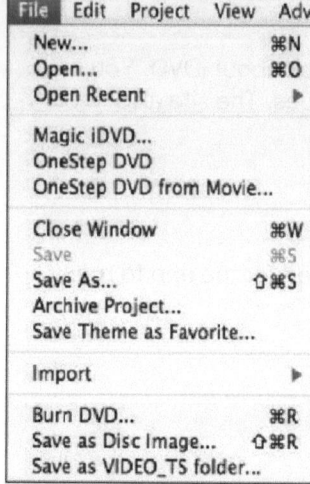

Figure 9–7. *File menu*

- **New...:** Brings up a window to create a new DVD project.

- **Open...:** Allows you to open a project that is in progress.

- **Open Recent:** Gives you a list of the most recently worked upon projects to choose from.

- **Magic iDVD...:** Brings up the window to begin the Magic iDVD DVD creation process. This was covered in Chapter 7: "Beginner DVD Creation via iDVD."

- **OneStep DVD:** Brings up the OneStep window to begin the OneStep DVD creation process. OneStep allows you to attach a video camcorder and create a DVD in just a few clicks. This was covered in Chapter 7: "Beginner DVD Creation via iDVD."

- **OneStep DVD from Movie...:** Brings up the OneStep window to begin the OneStep DVD creation process by using a video on your hard drive as opposed to an attached camcorder.

- **Close Window:** This closes the current open window.

- **Save:** Allows you to save your project.

- **Save As...:** Allows you to save your project with a different name. This is helpful if you want to save more than one version of your project.

- **Archive Project...:** Allows you to save you project into a complete package. This is useful if you want to move or back up your project to a different Mac. The **Archive Project Save** window is shown in Figure 9–8.

Figure 9–8. *Archive your project with this window.*

- **Save Theme as Favorite...:** Allows you to make the current theme you are working on a "favorite." This adds it the Favorites list when you go change a theme.

- **Import:** This allows you to bring in Video, Audio, Images, or Background Videos.

- **Burn DVD...:** This brings up the window to start the burning process. If there are any problems that iDVD has found, it will alert you before starting the actual burn.

- **Save as Disc Image...:** A disk image is an exact copy of a completed DVD, but it has not yet been burned to a DVD. Mac's Disk Utility can take this image file and create a DVD from it.

NOTE: If you burn your project to a double-layer disc, you should burn directly from iDVD rather than from a disc image. Burning from a disc image may cause the DVD to freeze on some DVD players.

- **Save as VIDEO_TS folder...:** This option also allows you to create a file that can be played on your Mac without actually burning it. It is similar to creating a disk image in that it takes about the same time to create. It differs in that you cannot use it to burn a DVD from it.

Edit Menu

After looking at Figure 9–9, you will see again that many Macintosh apps follow a common menu system and each menu has the same or similar options. The **Edit** menu contains the very important features of **Undoing** your last action or using the ever-present **Cut**, **Copy**, or **Paste** options to make changes to your project.

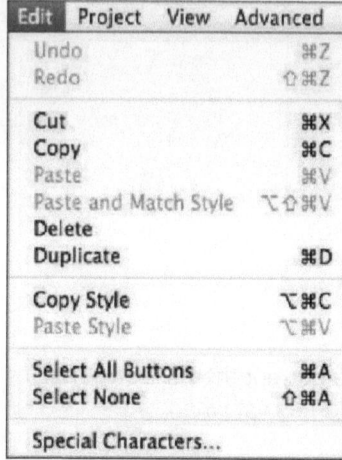

Figure 9–9. *Edit menu*

- **Undo:** Undoes your last action.

- **Redo:** If you decide after performing an **Undo** that you want the change reinstated, choose this option.

- **Cut:** Deletes the highlighted item from your project.

- **Copy:** Takes what you have highlighted and puts it into the Mac's memory so that you can add it elsewhere in your project.

- **Paste:** After using the **Copy** command to copy and item, this command "pastes" what was copied at your cursor's location.

- **Paste and Match Style:** This option takes whatever type you copied from whatever location and pastes it with the same style as the one you are using in your application. For example, if you copy some text from a website, the fonts and sizes are probably different than what you are using in your project. If you choose this option, the pasted text is formatted to match your current project's styles.

- **Delete:** The removes whatever elements you have highlighted from you project.

- **Duplicate:** This copies and then inserts a second copy of whatever element is highlighted.

- **Copy Style:** This simply copies the formatting of the text you have highlighted.

- **Paste Style:** This pastes the style you have just copied onto the highlighted text you want to change.

- **Select All Buttons:** This simply highlights all of the button elements found in your current window. This is helpful if you want to move all of the elements in one group, for example.

- **Select None:** This simply un-highlights what you have just highlighted by clicking on an object(s) or using the **Select All Buttons** option.

- **Special Characters:** If you want to add a special symbol or text item, this tool allows you to find them easily and then add them to your project.

Project Menu

Need to add an element to your project? Look no further than the **Project** menu (Figure 9–10). **Customizing drop zones to adding titles...** this menu's got you covered. However, the most important option in this menu is the **Project Info...** option. This gives you the heads-up on what is in your project and your settings for burning the disk. It's always good to check this window often to see how you are doing on disk space for the final project.

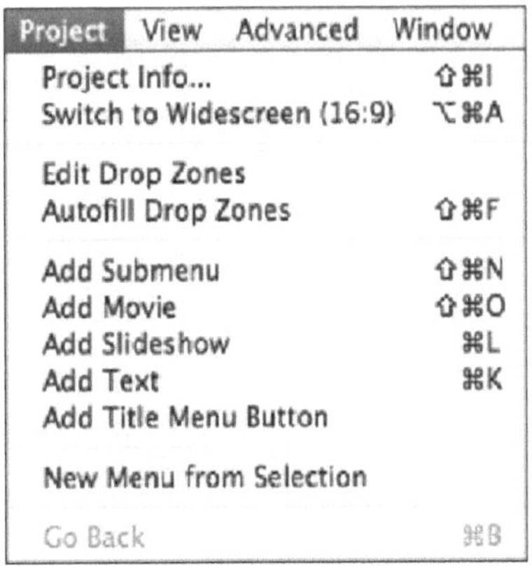

Project	View	Advanced	Window

Project Info...	⇧⌘I
Switch to Widescreen (16:9)	⌥⌘A
Edit Drop Zones	
Autofill Drop Zones	⇧⌘F
Add Submenu	⇧⌘N
Add Movie	⇧⌘O
Add Slideshow	⌘L
Add Text	⌘K
Add Title Menu Button	
New Menu from Selection	
Go Back	⌘B

Figure 9–10. *Project* menu

Project Info... is an awesome resource! This option gives the complete low-down on your project (Figure 9–11). A description of all of the elements follows the figure.

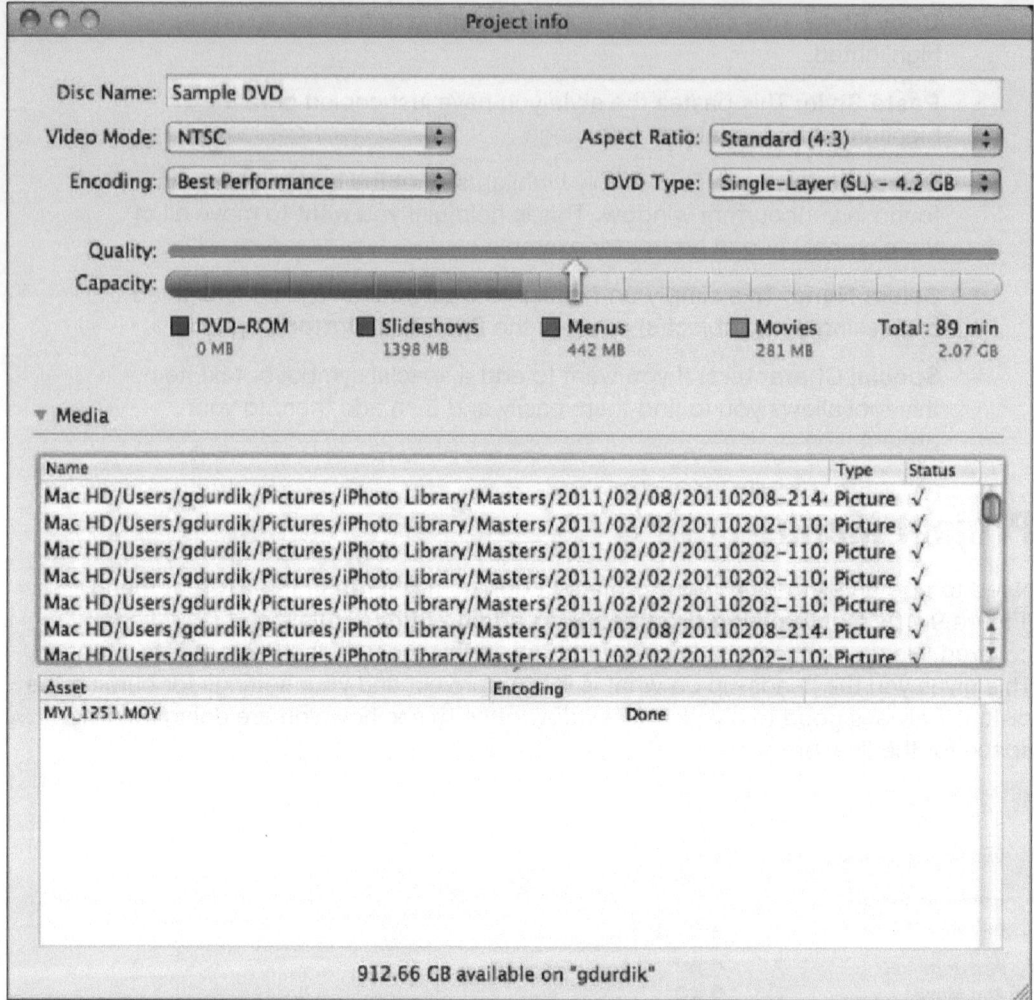

Figure 9–11. *The Project Info... window found in the Project menu*

The first five items discussed (found in the top section of this window) contain options found at other locations in iDVD as well.

- **Disc Name:** Allows you to change the disc name of the DVD you are going to burn.

- **Video Mode:** As I mentioned, it could be NTSC (United States and other countries) or PAL.

- **Aspect Ratio:** As I mentioned, **Standard** will give you a square image as a final result, and **Widescreen** will give you a rectangular image, which is pretty much the norm nowadays. But always be aware of where the DVD is going to be viewed and choose the right option

- **Encoding:** It could be **Best Performance**, **High Quality**, or **Professional Quality**. **Best Performance** takes the least amount of time, and **Professional Quality** gives you the best image quality, but takes the longest to burn.

- **DVD Type:** It could be either a **Single Layer** (most common) or a **Double-Layer** disc. A **Double-Layer** holds about twice as much data than a **Single-Layer**.

- **Quality:** This gives you a graphic line of how much space each encoding will take.

- **Capacity:** This shows a line graph of how much space each element on your DVD will take in the final project. In Figure 9–11, we see that my huge **Slideshow** takes about 1.3 GB of space, **Menus** take about 450 MB of space, and **Movies** take up about 280 MB of space. This line also tells you how long the DVD is and the total space required. In the example I used, the total time was 89 minutes and about 2 GB of space. That's just about half the size of a single-layer disc. Please check this line occasionally. You must be mindful of the size of your project and whether it will fit onto a DVD. If the project is too large, you might want to not include original photos or reduce the quality by changing to **Best Performance** or **High Quality**. If you feel that everything must be included, you have the option of purchasing double-layer DVDs, which hold a little less then double of a single-layer DVD.

- **Media:** Lists all the photos going to be added to the DVD.

- **Assets:** Shows all the items that are encoded onto the DVD. In my example, I have one movie (the .MOV file).

Now I'll go over the remaining options in the **Project** menu.

- **Switch to Widescreen:** Gives you the option to switch to the other size available. It would say **Switch to Standard** if the project you are working on was currently set to **Widescreen**.

- **Edit Drop Zones:** Brings up a small window at the bottom of your workspace that shows all drop zones in your current window. Sometimes it is difficult to see what zones are available in a theme. This makes all readily visible.

- **Autofill Drop Zones:** This option randomly selects photos from your iPhoto Library and uses them to fill your drop zones.

- **Add Submenu, Add Movie, Add Slideshow:** These add the selected element to your project.

- **Add Text:** Allows you to add just plain text to anywhere on your workspace.

- **Add Title Menu Button:** Allows you to add a **Title Menu** button, which brings back to the main menu.

- **New Menu from Selection:** Creates a new menu from the item you have highlighted.

- **Go Back:** Brings you back to the previous window you were working on.

View Menu

The **View** menu, shown in Figure 9–12, knows all...I mean shows all. For example, the **Show Map** and **Show Inspector** options are essential to creating great DVDs. The Map provides a great visual guideline to help organize your project. The Inspector gives you a ton of options to customize your DVD.

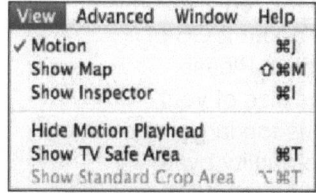

Figure 9–12. *View menu*

- **Motion:** iDVD has animations in most themes. You might get tired of seeing the same thing over and over again—as well as hearing the same music. This option stops all actions in the background.

- **Show Map:** This brings up the map of your project (Figure 9–13.). The map shows all of you windows and how they are interconnected. If you are creating a huge DVD, this is a must!

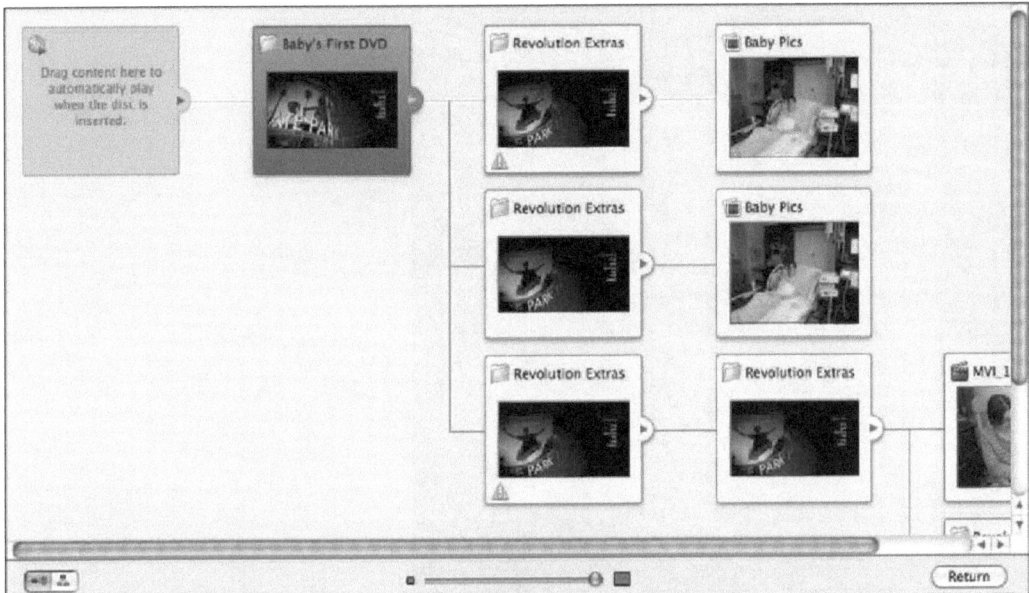

Figure 9-13. *Sample project map*

> **NOTE:** This is a good point to bring up two options that might be missed by a casual user.
>
> **1.** The grey screen in the upper left-hand corner of the project map states that you can drag any media onto it and that media will automatically play when the DVD is inserted into a player or computer.
>
> **2.** You can drop photos onto the background of your theme. This means you can add a special photo as a backdrop, thereby not being limited to the backdrops of your chosen theme. Each theme will add the photo in a unique way.

- **Show Inspector:** This is shown in Figure 9-14. It is covered in detail in Chapter 8: "iDVD Workspace: The Widescreen Edition." You can see in the figure that it allows you to modify quite a few items.

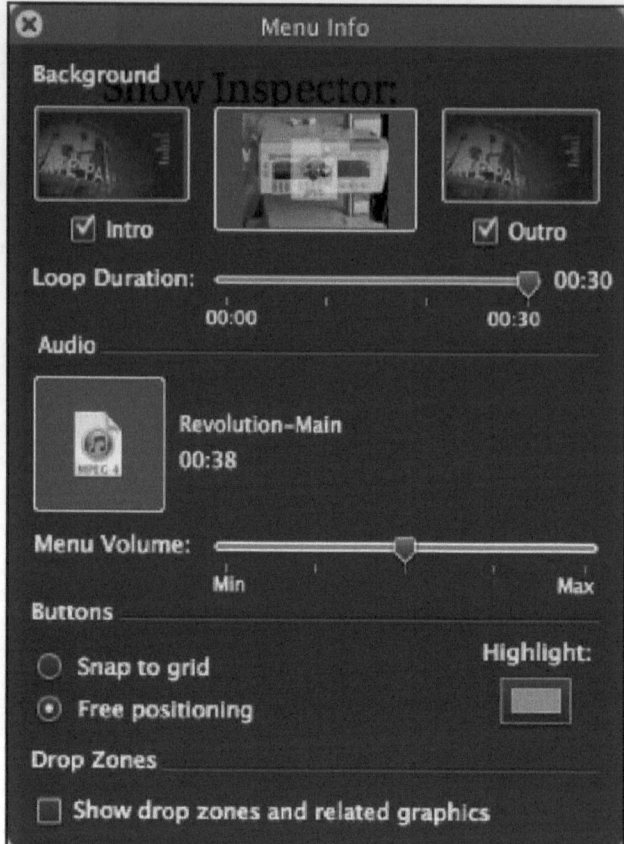

Figure 9–14. *Inspector window*

- **Hide (Show) Motion Playhead:** This is shown in Figure 9–15. It is a graphical timeline of the animations and fade-ins and fade-outs of the music in your current window.

Figure 9–15. *Sample motion playhead*

- **Show TV Safe Area:** This puts a red box inside your workspace. Anything inside the red box is guaranteed to be visible on the majority of TVs. As per iDVD, this is an approximation.

- **Show Standard Crop Area:** This goes hand in hand with **Show TV Safe Area**. Make sure all buttons and menus are within the red guidelines for both options to be 99 percent sure they will not be cut off on a TV screen. Figure 9–16 shows a workspace with both safe areas applied.

Figure 9–16. *TV Safe Area* and *Standard Crop Area* example

Advanced Menu

This menu contains items that impact the way themes can be applied and determines how your DVD is to be set up for the final burn (see Figure 9–17).

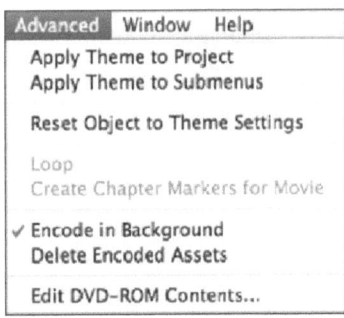

Figure 9–17. *Advanced* menu

- **Apply Theme to Project** and **Apply Theme to Submenus:** These are very useful if your project has a movie with chapter markers. If you have multiple chapter markers, you have more than one menu option on the screen. When you click on a theme thumbnail, iDVD asks if you want to apply your chosen theme to the entire project. This will make the theme choice on all menu options to be the same. If you want to do this task later, you can choose the **Apply theme to Project** option. If you want to apply the theme just to the submenus, you can choose the **Apply Theme to Submenus** option.

- **Reset Object to Theme Settings:** This is similar to the above to items, but applies to individual items. This could be changing one submenu instead of changing the whole workspace.

- **Loop (Slideshow or Movie):** You can have iDVD constantly looping a Slideshow or Movie in your finished DVD.

- **Create Chapter Markers for Movie:** If you are inserting a long movie, you can have iDVD put "markers" at specified points (every 5 minutes, for example) so that users can jump to any marked-off point in the movie.

- **Encode in Background:** It takes quite awhile for iDVD to get media ready for DVD creation. This encoding process can be done in the background (the default) so that you can work on other items at the same time.

- **Delete Encoded Assets:** This deletes any final encoded assets that were added to your project.

- **Edit DVD-ROM Contents...:** This brings up a window to add any additional items you want to add to your final DVD (Figure 9–18). Click on **New Folder** to add a folder, or click on **Add Files** to add new items.

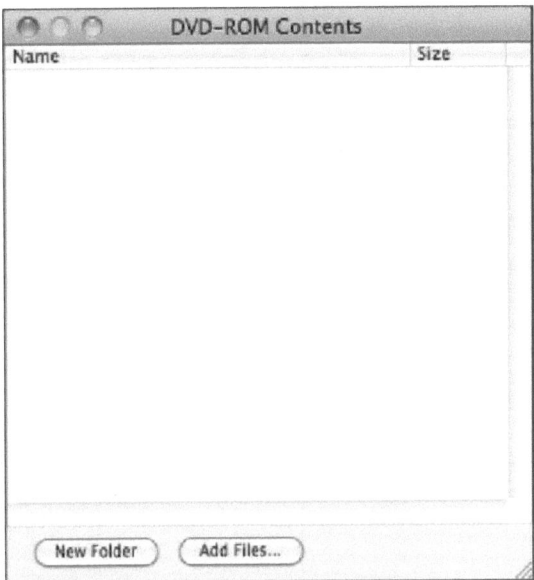

Figure 9–18. *Adding extra files to your DVD*

Window Menu

As you can see from Figure 9–19, the menu is similar to menus in other apps. The key two items are **Actual Size and Fit to screen**. These two options determine the amount of monitor real estate your project will take up.

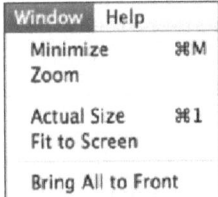

Figure 9–19. *Window menu*

- **Minimize:** Shrinks the current application's window down into the dock. You must click on the dock icon to return it to the original state.

- **Zoom:** Does not really do anything on my 24" iMac. If I expand the iDVD workspace, it only slightly adjusts my workspace.

- **Actual Size:** This performs a reverse to normal zoom. When applied, it shrinks my workspace to the smallest it can be.

- **Fit to Screen:** This expands your workspace to the largest it can be.

- **Bring All to Front:** Brings all of iDVD's menus to the front.

Help Menu

How do I add a movie? Burn a disc? iDVD's **Help** menu is there to guide you through some common tasks. You can also search for a specific topic within iDVD (Figure 9–20).

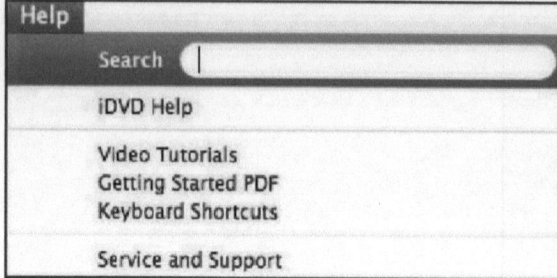

Figure 9–20. *Help* menu

Search

Type in any topic you have a question about. I have to be honest: the built-in Help for iDVD is pretty skimpy. Some topics I looked up were not there are all. Not good, Apple. I hope this manual has filled in many of the blanks.

iDVD Help Window

This is a quite a bit more helpful than **Search**. This window is broken down into three parts. iDVD Help is shown in Figure 9–21. It contains several topics, each showing you how to perform a certain task or providing general info on iDVD and DVDs. The second and third sections are shown in Figure 9–22. The second section, **New to iDVD?**, is the best place to find answers when you are getting started.

I tried to cover the A to Z of iDVD in these three chapters, but you can reinforce this knowledge or look for items that you want to learn a lot more about. This section contains three items. **What is iDVD?** is a basic guide to the program. The **Getting Started PDF** is a great resource that you can print out and refer to. The last section sends you to an Apple site to view tutorials on the web. This primarily deals with problems when using iWeb. Most users will never have to go to this support website, as most Apple applications are stable or there is fix available shortly (most of the time).

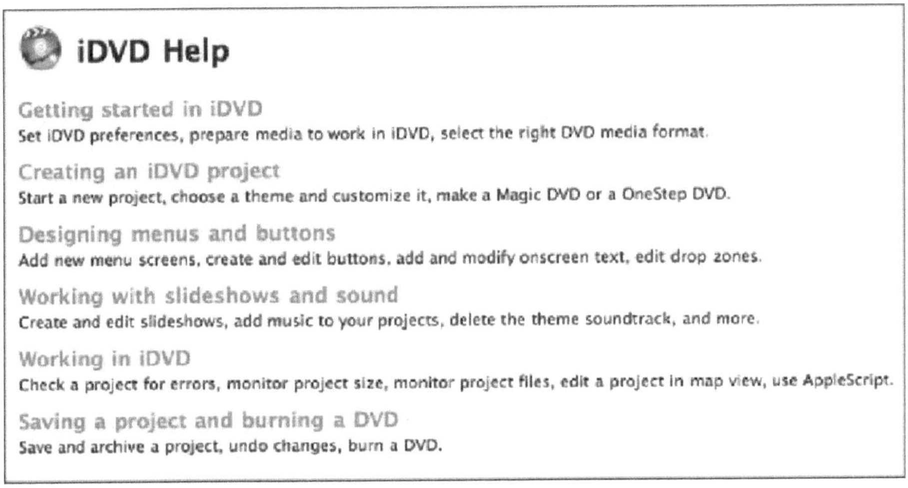

iDVD Help

Getting started in iDVD
Set iDVD preferences, prepare media to work in iDVD, select the right DVD media format.

Creating an iDVD project
Start a new project, choose a theme and customize it, make a Magic DVD or a OneStep DVD.

Designing menus and buttons
Add new menu screens, create and edit buttons, add and modify onscreen text, edit drop zones.

Working with slideshows and sound
Create and edit slideshows, add music to your projects, delete the theme soundtrack, and more.

Working in iDVD
Check a project for errors, monitor project size, monitor project files, edit a project in map view, use AppleScript.

Saving a project and burning a DVD
Save and archive a project, undo changes, burn a DVD.

Figure 9–21. *iDVD Help* section of *iDVD Help* window

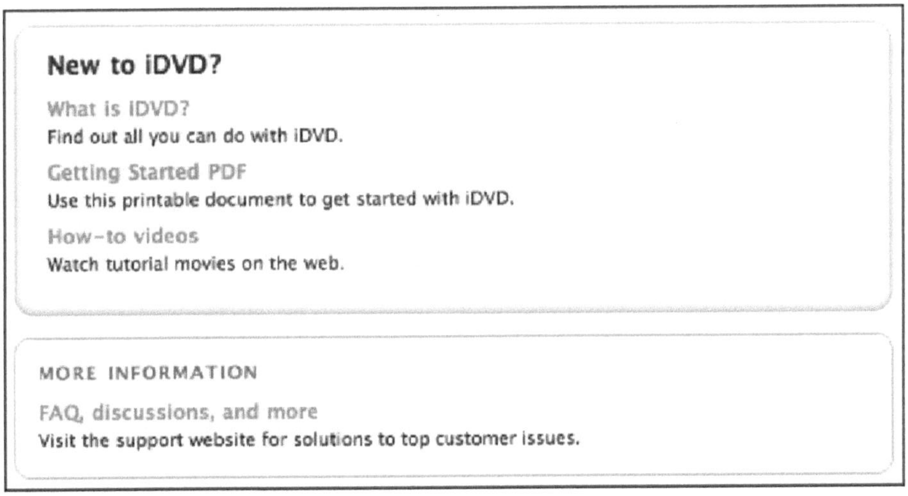

New to iDVD?

What is iDVD?
Find out all you can do with iDVD.

Getting Started PDF
Use this printable document to get started with iDVD.

How–to videos
Watch tutorial movies on the web.

MORE INFORMATION

FAQ, discussions, and more
Visit the support website for solutions to top customer issues.

Figure 9–22. *New to iDVD* section and *More Information* section of the *iDVD Help* window

Video Tutorials

As mentioned above, this sends you to an Apple site with a few tutorials to get you started.

Getting Started PDF

This is a handy, 35-page mini-guide that you can print out to help you get on the right track and start using iDVD.

Keyboard Shortcuts

With the use of certain keys on the keyboard, you can perform many tasks without using your mouse. The most common key is the Command key (⌘), found next to the space bar, or the Shift key (⇧). To create a new project for example, hold down the Command key (⌘) and then press the N key.

Summary

I hope that with the help of these three chapters on iDVD, you feel confident getting around the workspace and menus. As with any multimedia project, you can spend a short amount of time and create a simple DVD or spend hours or days perfecting your DVD treasure. iDVD is designed to help you with getting simple projects done with just a few clicks here and there, but it can also give you the power to fully unleash your creative side and have a final result to rival *Titanic*! Well, maybe not, but I am sure you are going to find it fun and exciting creating your own personal blockbuster.

iWeb

Designing a great looking web page can take quite some time to accomplish. Fortunately, Apple created iWeb to take the "heavy lifting" out of creating web pages. This program provides great templates, easy to use web page–creation tools, and simple-to-follow publishing procedures to help you get your new site onto the Internet quickly and easily. This combination makes it ideal for anyone who wants to get started with web design.

Chapter 10

Welcome to Web Creation the iWeb Way!

iWeb is a great tool for sharing your thoughts and memories on the Internet. It contains many tools to get you started on your journey to becoming a web master. In this chapter, we will see how iWeb provides useful templates for most situations, how it provides an easy to understand user environment, and most important, it makes getting your site online easy.

The real power of iWeb, however, is not what you see; it is what you do not see. It does all the grunt work behind the scenes to make your site "web compliant," and leaves you to just worry about design, rather than learning complex web coding.

This chapter will guide you through the site creation and uploading process. As with other iLife apps, your journey begins with a Welcome Screen that provides links to resources that will help get you started in iWeb. iWeb, as with many other apps, provides you with the building blocks to help get your project started, such as Themes created by Apple that are tailored to fit the many reasons why a person wants to create a website. Once you have the starting point set, iWeb's workspace is designed to let the beginner customize and enhance their new site with ease. And more importantly, when you are ready to upload and make your site live to the world, iWeb takes this complex task and simplifies what needs to be done, making the process of going live with a site a lot less daunting.

> **NOTE:** If you have MobileMe, the first screen you will see is the one shown in Figure 10–1. By default, iWeb wants to upload your web site(s) to MobileMe. The first screen you see asks if it is okay if iWeb stores your MobileMe password so you are not asked for it each time you make changes to your site or add a new site.

There are other ways to get your site published on the Web, and I discuss them later in this chapter.

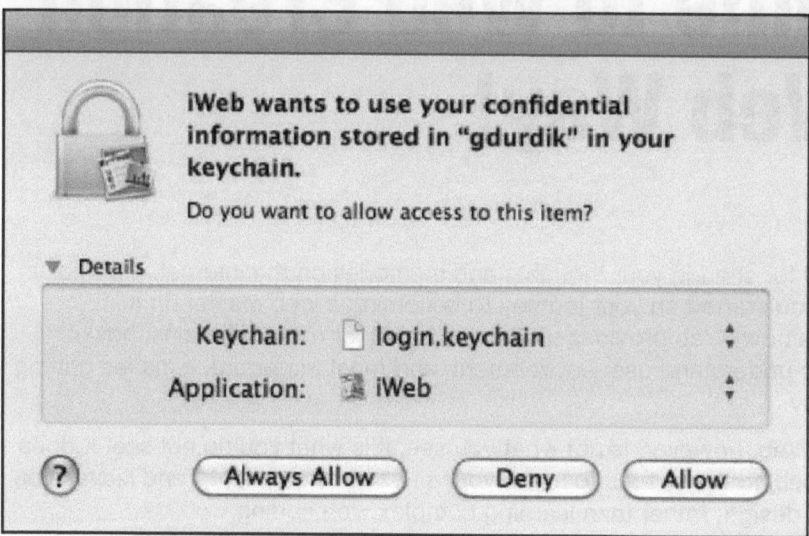

Figure 10–1. *Allowing iWeb to access and store your password info*

Welcome Screen

In Figure 10–2, we see the initial **Welcome** screen. The first item of interest in this window is the **Click to Play** button, which shows a short Getting Started video. Click **Close** to close this window. Clicking the **Learn more** button gives you access to video tutorials on the updated iLife applications only (GarageBand, iMovie, and iPhoto). It also gives you access to the **Hands-on Help** section, which brings you to an Apple web site to learn about support found in their retail stores.

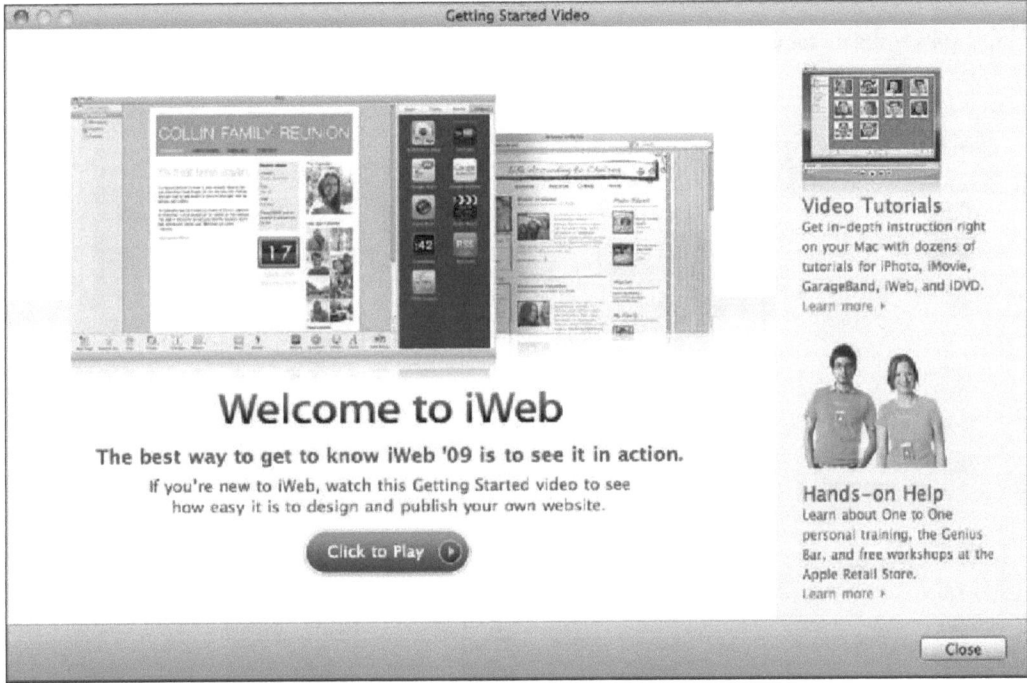

Figure 10–2. *Welcome screen of iWeb*

Choosing a Theme

The first step of creating a stellar web site is to choose a theme. Click on the **Close** button to get started. The next screen that appears is shown in Figure 10–3. There are 28 theme templates to choose from. By default, all templates are shown. However, you can choose to see just the templates for each version of iWeb. Click on **All** to select this option and you'll get the screen shown in Figure 10–4. A full graphic showing all of the templates available is shown in Figure 10–5.

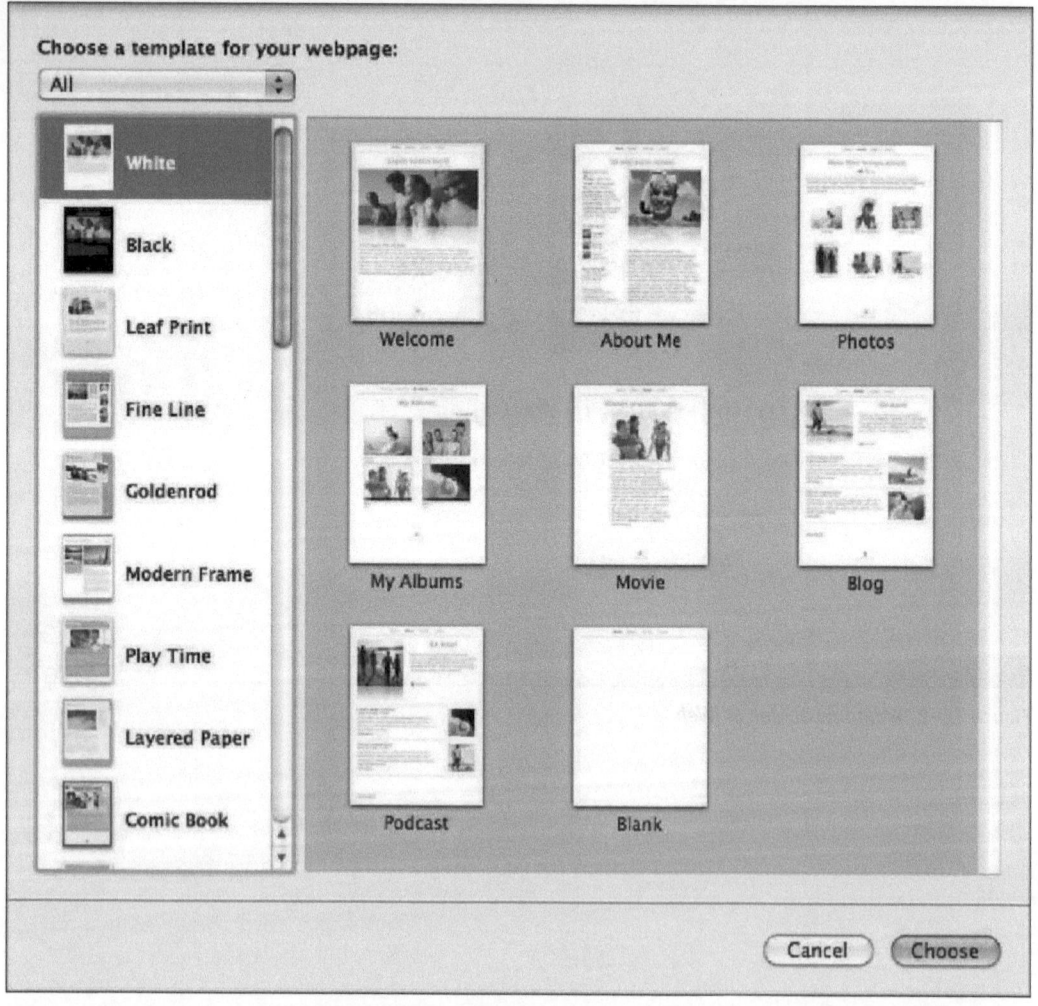

Figure 10–3. *Choosing a theme template for your site*

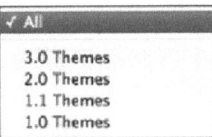

Figure 10–4. *Choosing a template by iWeb version*

Figure 10–5. *The 28 templates in iWeb*

NOTE: You can search online to purchase additional templates for iWeb.

When you are choosing the template, please notice the screen to the right of the template list shown in Figure 10–3. This lists the types of pages you can include in your site (see Figure 10–6), which are listed here:

- Welcome
- About Me
- Photos
- My albums
- Movie
- Blog
- Podcast
- Blank

Note that each page type has a different default layout and each has a different purpose. You can modify these default settings to your liking. You can also choose **Blank** if you want to create a page from the ground up.

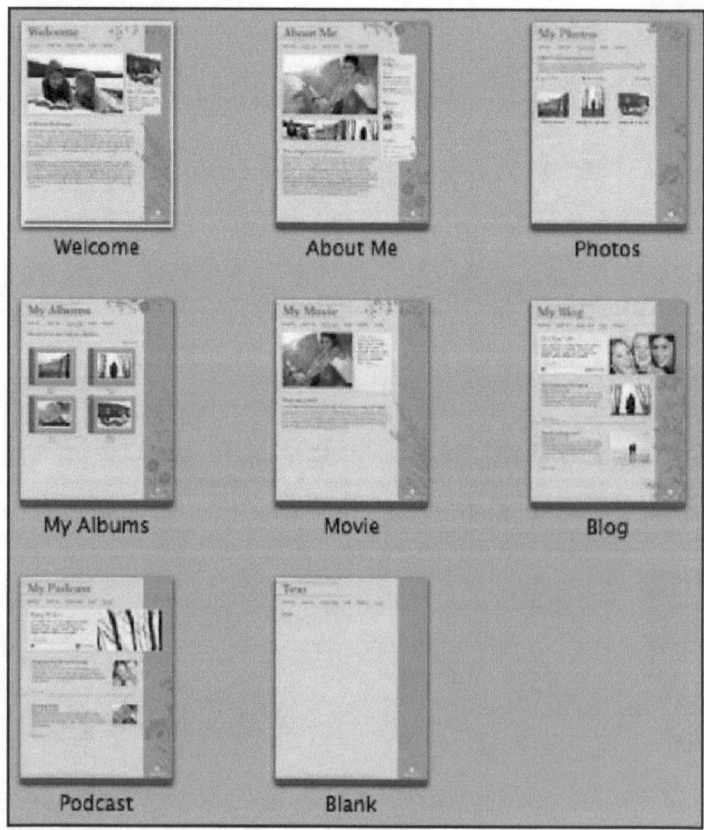

Figure 10–6. *Types of pages available in every template*

iWeb Work Environment

Figure 10–7 shows the main iWeb workspace after you have chosen a template. It basically is broken down into four sections: **Site Sidebar**, **Workspace**, **Toolbar Tools**, and **Media Sidebar**.

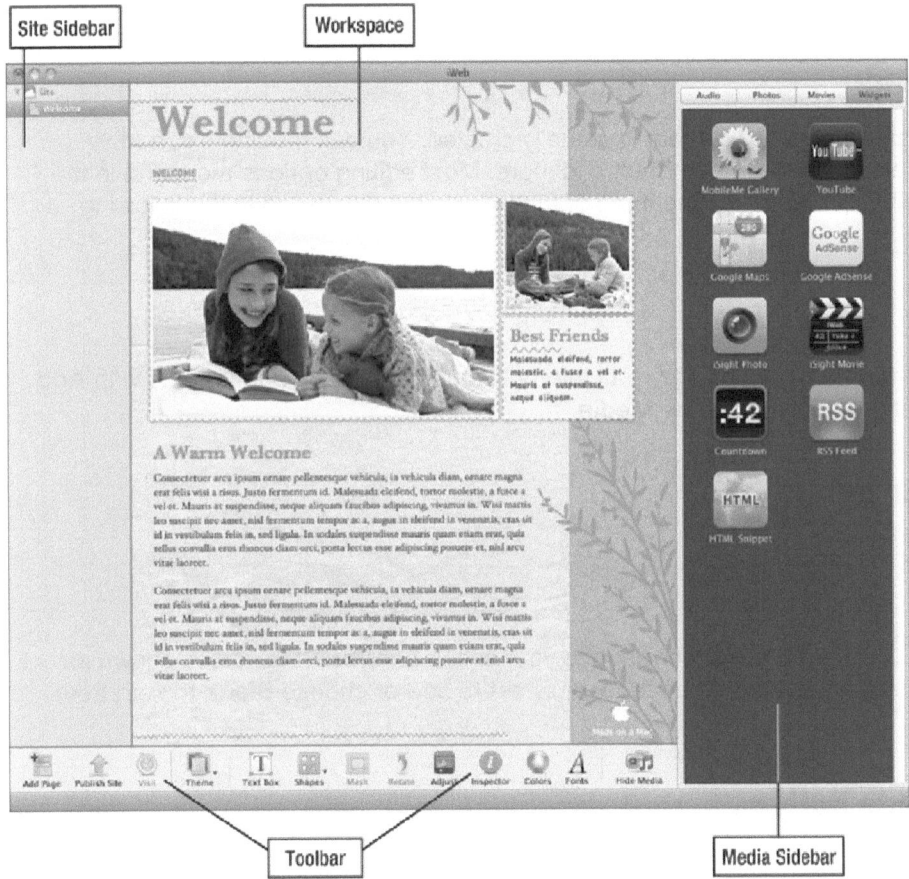

Figure 10–7. *iWeb working environment*

Site Sidebar

This section keeps track of your site or sites. Figure 10–8 shows a site that is not yet named and the two pages in the site. If we click on the default page names (**Welcome**, **Blank**, **About Me**, and so on) we can name them to our liking. In Figure 10–8, I named the blank page **Baby**.

Figure 10–8. *Site toolbar*

Workspace

This is the area where the content is actually created. You can modify text, add graphics, upload videos and photos, and more. Most editing options are found in the toolbar section of the environment. All of these tools are discussed in the following sections.

Toolbar Tools

You can perform a lot of editing via all the tools found in this toolbar. It starts with **Add Page** and ends with **Hide/Show Media**.

Add Page Button

 This adds another page to your site. It brings up the screen shown in Figure 10–6. Choose the type of page you want to add or choose **Blank** to start from scratch.

Publish Site Button

After you are done with your page, clicking this button will publish it to the web.

> **NOTE:** When you publish a new site or page with the same name, the new version will overwrite the old. Please keep this in mind before proceeding.

The first screen you will see is the one shown in Figure 10–9. This is a warning not to use material for which you do not have the copyright. I would check the box next to **Don't show again** so this warning never appears again.

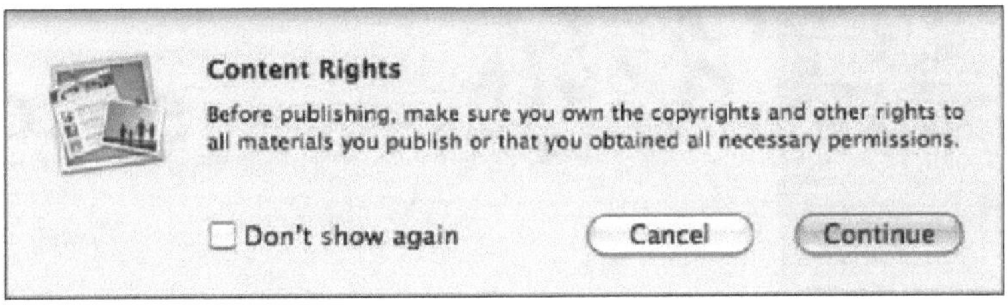

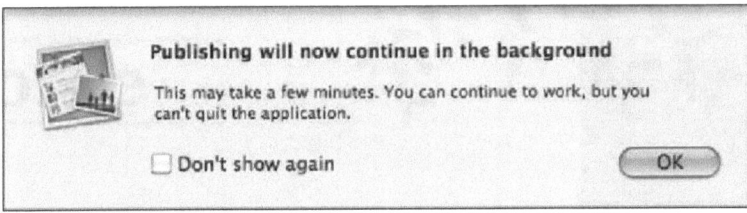

Content Rights

Before publishing, make sure you own the copyrights and other rights to all materials you publish or that you obtained all necessary permissions.

☐ Don't show again   Cancel   Continue

Figure 10–9. *Copyright warning*

The next screen (Figure 10–10) notifies you that the publishing of your site will take place in the background. This means you can work on other items on your Mac while this is being done. Again, you can check the box next to **Don't show again** to have this message not appear whenever you add pages or just update your site.

Publishing will now continue in the background

This may take a few minutes. You can continue to work, but you can't quit the application.

☐ Don't show again   OK

Figure 10–10. *Publishing will occur in background message*

After the site has been successfully published, you get the screen shown in Figure 10–11. Notice that you have three choices. Clicking **OK** just closes the window. **Visit the Site Now** takes you to your published site. The third option, **Announce**, is cool. You can have iWeb announce your new site via e-mail to whomever you wish. This is shown in Figure 10–12.

Your site has been published.

Your site is located at:

http://web.me.com/gdurdik/Site

You can announce your website with an email message containing your website address, or view the website in your browser.

Announce   Visit Site Now   OK

Figure 10–11. *Site has been successfully published*

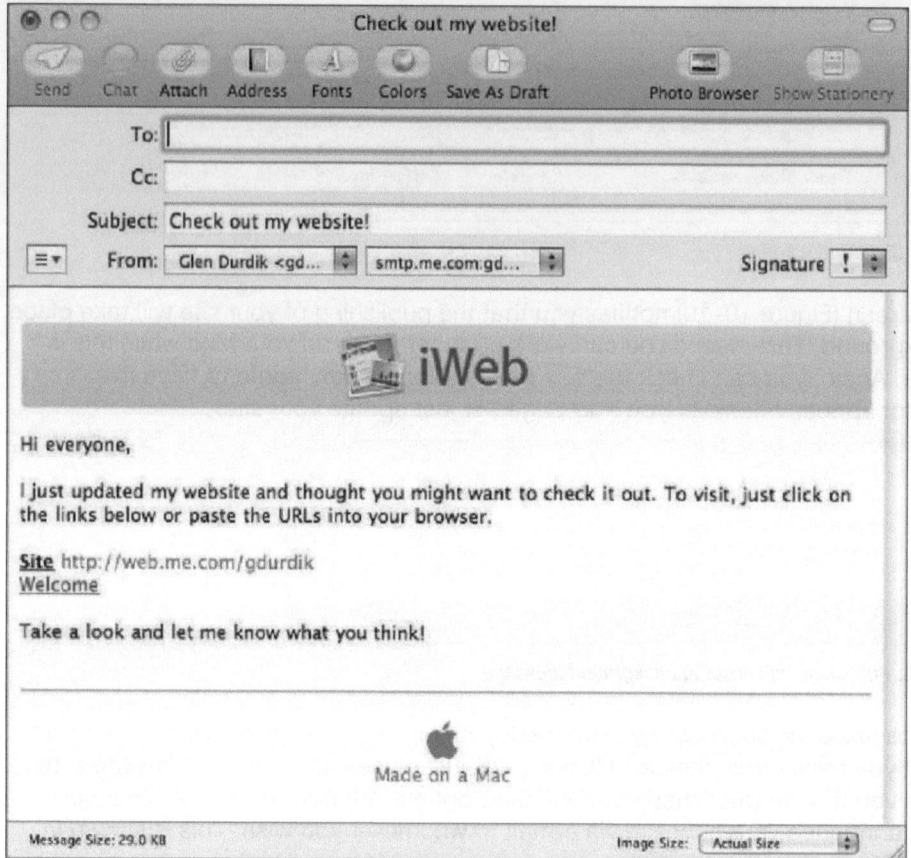

Figure 10–12. *Announcing your new site via e-mail*

Visit Button

 This simply takes you to your "live" site in a browser such as Safari or Firefox.

Theme Button

During the initial creation of your site, you chose a theme. This button allows you to change your theme selection. The choices available are shown in Figure 10–5.

Text Box Button

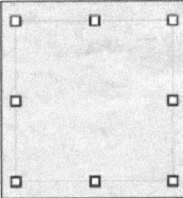 This allows you to add a text box to your page. You can then move it or change the font size. As you add text, the box automatically grows downward. You have to manually make the box wider by clicking on one of the white boxes around the text box. This is shown in Figure 10–13. To insert text, click on the box twice. You can see a blank text box in Figure 10–14.

Figure 10–13. *Drag the white boxes to manually adjust the size of the text box*

Figure 10–14. *A text box ready to accept text*

Shape Button

This allows you to add various types of shapes into your web page. The complete list of choices is shown in Figure 10–15.

Figure 10–15. *Types of shapes that can be added to a web page*

Mask Button

This button allows you to hide parts of your picture. You must click on the picture you want to mask for this function to work. In Figure 10–16, we see a sample mask in process. The full yellow box is the complete picture. The item inside the box with the white boxes around it is the area that will be seen after the mask is applied. As with text boxes, you can enlarge or shrink the box by dragging these white boxes.

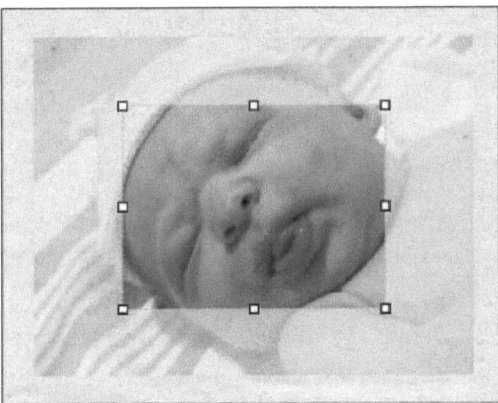

Figure 10–16. *Example of mask being applied*

Below the mask box, we see the slider shown in Figure 10–17. This slider either enlarges or shrinks the photo inside the masking area.

Figure 10–17. *Mask slider*

Rotate Button

 This rotates a photo 90 degrees counter-clockwise.

Adjust Button

This brings up a comprehensive list of potential adjustments to a photo on your page. The available adjustments are shown in Figure 10–18.

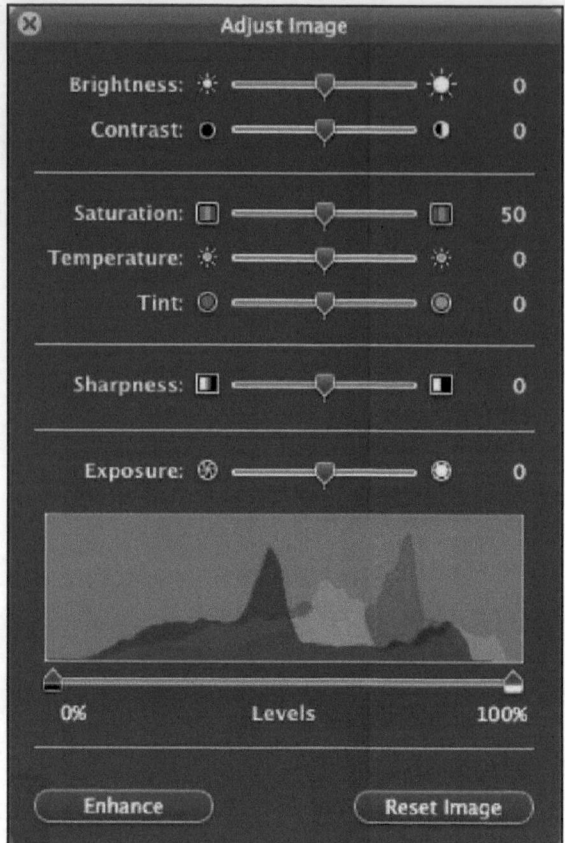

Figure 10–18. *Adjust Image tool*

Colors Button

This brings up a color selection tool. This is shown in Figure 10–19. Please note that you have five choices of color selection. The first option (the color wheel) is shown in Figure 10–19. The other options are on the top of the window. These options are: color sliders, color palettes, image palettes, or crayons. This is shown in Figure 10–20.

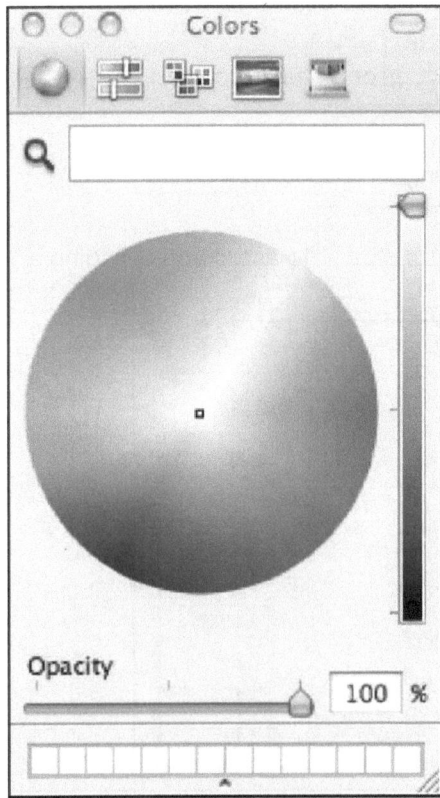

Figure 10–19. *Color wheel—the default selection tool*

Figure 10–20. *Other color selection tools*

Fonts Button

NOTE: Not all fonts work well with all browsers. As with layout and graphic choices, always test, test, test to see how your web page will appear in different browsers.

The Fonts button options are shown in Figure 10–21. You change the font, adjust the size, or change the color. The vertical slider next to the numerical font sizes will increase your font size when you slide it up and decrease the size when you slide it down. You can add an underline  or a strikethrough

(line going through text). You can change the document color

. Last, there is a search tool 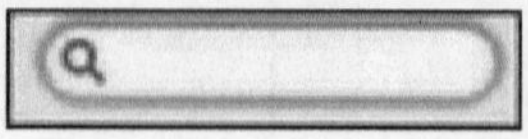 to assist you in finding a
particular font.

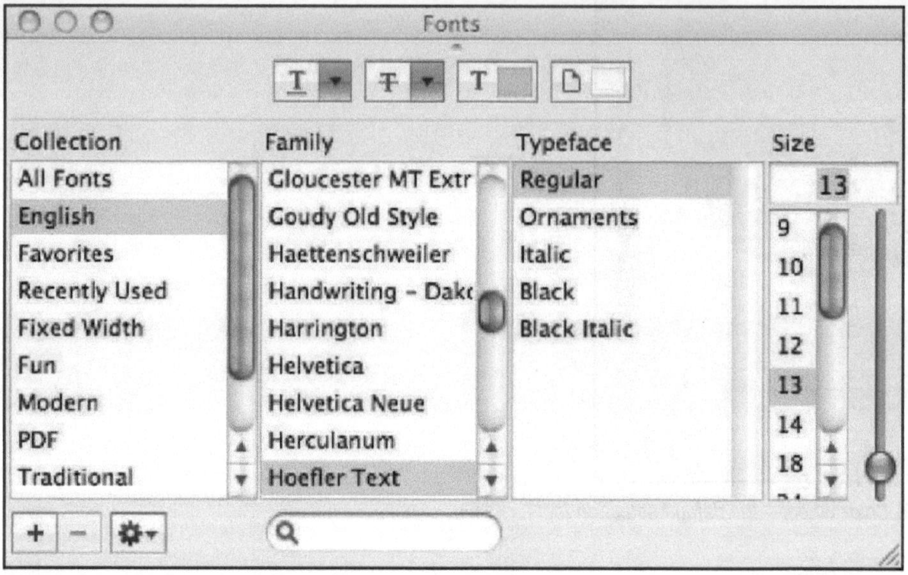

Figure 10–21. *Font options, accessible via the* **Fonts** *button*

Hide Media Button

 This hides the media sidebar from your main workspace. There are four types of media: **Audio**, **Photos**, **Movies**, and **Widgets**. **Audio** is shown in Figure 10–22. Notice that it looks for audio files created by GarageBand or stored in the iTunes Library.

Figure 10–22. *Audio* tab of the *Media* sidebar

Photos is shown in Figure 10–23. It is not shown in the screenshot, but iWeb can access your MobileMe or Facebook photos, too.

Figure 10–23. *Photos* tab of the *Media* sidebar

The Movies tab is shown in Figure 10–24. Please note that it looks for movies in your Movies folder, in iPhoto, or in iMovie.

Figure 10–24. *Movies tab of the Media sidebar*

The **Widgets** screen is shown in Figure 10–25. A widget is basically a tiny application inserted to your web page. To add one of the following to your page, click and hold down your mouse button and drag the icon of the widget you want onto your workspace, or just double-click on the widget.

Figure 10–25. *Widget tab in the* **Media** *sidebar*

- **MobileMe Gallery:** Provides access to any of the photo galleries or videos you have stored in your MobileMe online gallery.

- **YouTube:** Allows you to add a hyperlink to YouTube videos. This screen is shown in Figure 10–26.

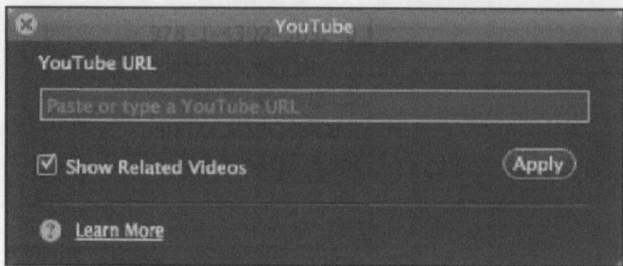

Figure 10–26. *Inserting YouTube videos into your web page*

- **Google Maps:** Allows you to insert a Google map into your web page. All you have to do is type in the address and click on **Apply**. Please notice that you have the option to show the **Zoom Controls**, **Search Bar**, and **Address Bubble**. This is shown in Figure 10–27.

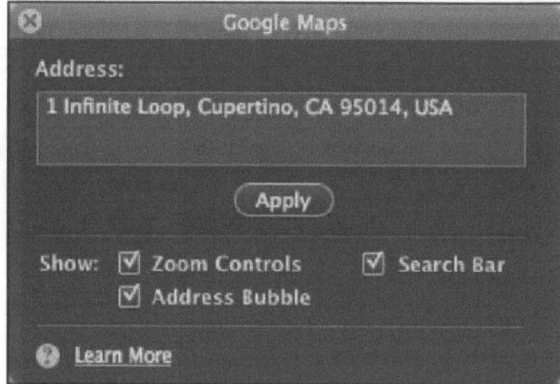

Figure 10–27. *Inserting Google Maps*

- **Google Adsense:** If you set up an Adsense account, you can add this into your web page and earn money every time someone clicks on the online add being sent to your site via Google.

- **iSight Photo:** Most Macs nowadays have a built-in camera on the front top of their screen. This accesses the camera and allows you to add a new photo from the camera.

- **iSight Movie:** As with the **iSight Photo** option, this accesses the built-in camera and then imports the video and places it on your page.

- **Countdown:** This allows you to add a countdown timer to you site. You have the option of customizing what is displayed. You have three choices as to the loop of the timer. Click on the numbers in this window to see your choices. Next, you can decide if you want the year to be displayed. Move the slider next to **Years** to activate it or deactivate it. You set the date you want to count down to at the bottom of the screen. This window is shown in Figure 10–28.

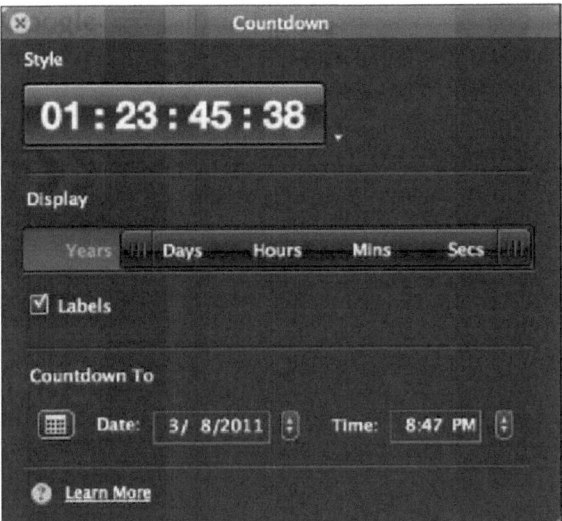

Figure 10–28. *Countdown widget*

■ **RSS Feed:** This allows you to add an RSS feed to your web page. You just have to enter the subscription URL and then click on **Apply**. Then you can choose from eight different layouts. You can also modify the number of entries at the bottom of the window. You can also choose whether to show the date and determine the length of the article to be displayed, the photo size, and the photo orientation. This is shown in Figure 10–29.

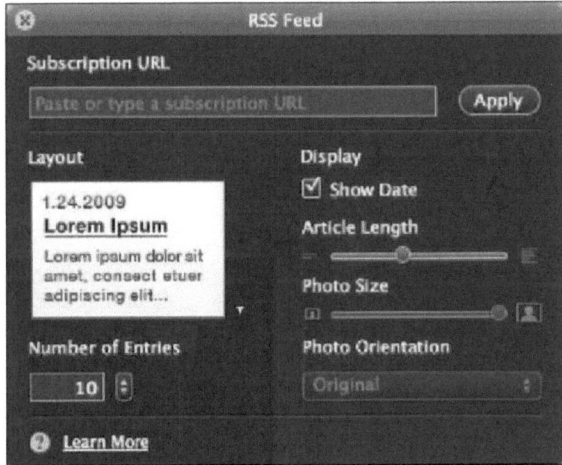

Figure 10–29. *RSS widget*

- **HTML Snippet:** This allows you to embed a web page as the actual web page in your site (www.apple.com's graphics and other elements will show up inside this widget box—not a clickable text link). This is shown in Figure 10–30. Just type the URL in the box and click on **Apply**.

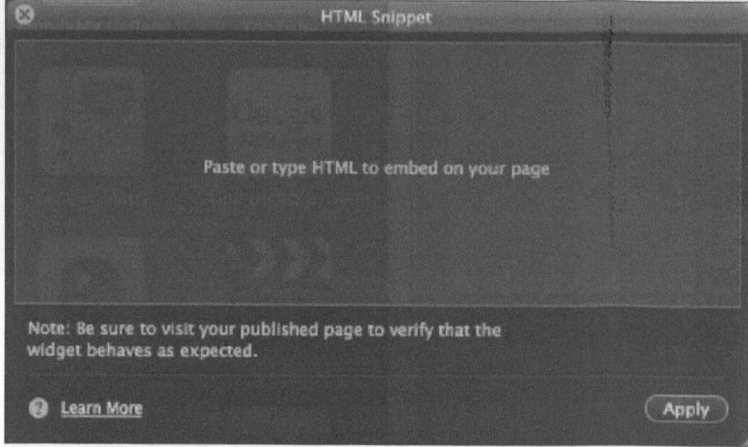

Figure 10–30. *An HTML snippet widget*

Three Ways to Publish Your Site

If you click the word **Site**, you can select to publish your site via MobileMe, FTP, or from a local folder. You can also rename the site to anything you like.

MobileMe Publishing

MobileMe is a paid service that provides you an e-mail account, your own web pages, and other services. The setup page is shown in Figure 10–31. It is broken down into the following three sections:

- **Publishing:** The **Publishing** section has the following three subsections:

  - **Publish to:** This is where you select the publishing method. Figure 10–31 shows the MobileMe option.

  - **Site Name:** This is another way of naming your site. The default name is **Site**. Renaming it will make it easier to search for it online.

  - **Contact e-mail:** This is not required for publishing to take place.

  - **MobileMe account:** This is the admin e-mail address for your MobileMe account.

■ **Privacy:** By default, your published web page is visible to all World Wide Web users. If you check the box next to **Make my published site private**, your web site will be password-protected. This is great if you want to show private pictures to only select visitors.

■ **Facebook:** If you check the box next to **Update my Facebook profile when I publish this site**, iWeb will post this update to your Facebook account.

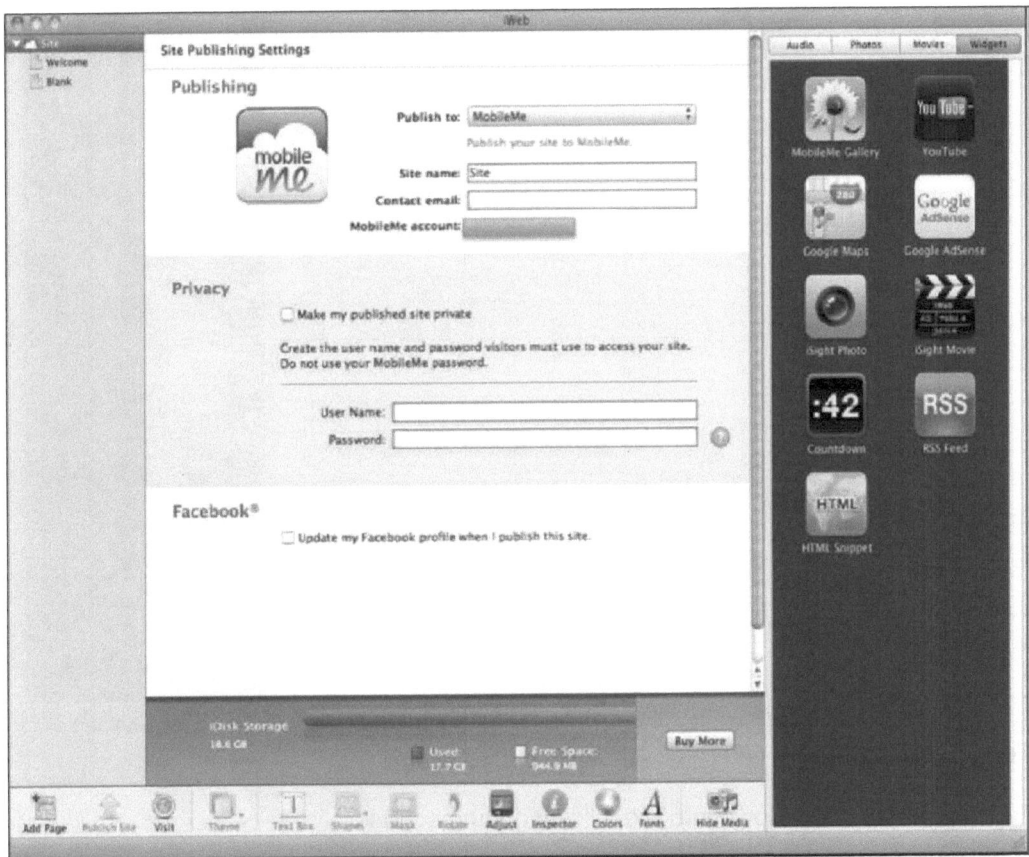

Figure 10–31. *Publishing with a MobileMe account*

Publishing via FTP Server

Figure 10–32 shows the FTP publishing option.

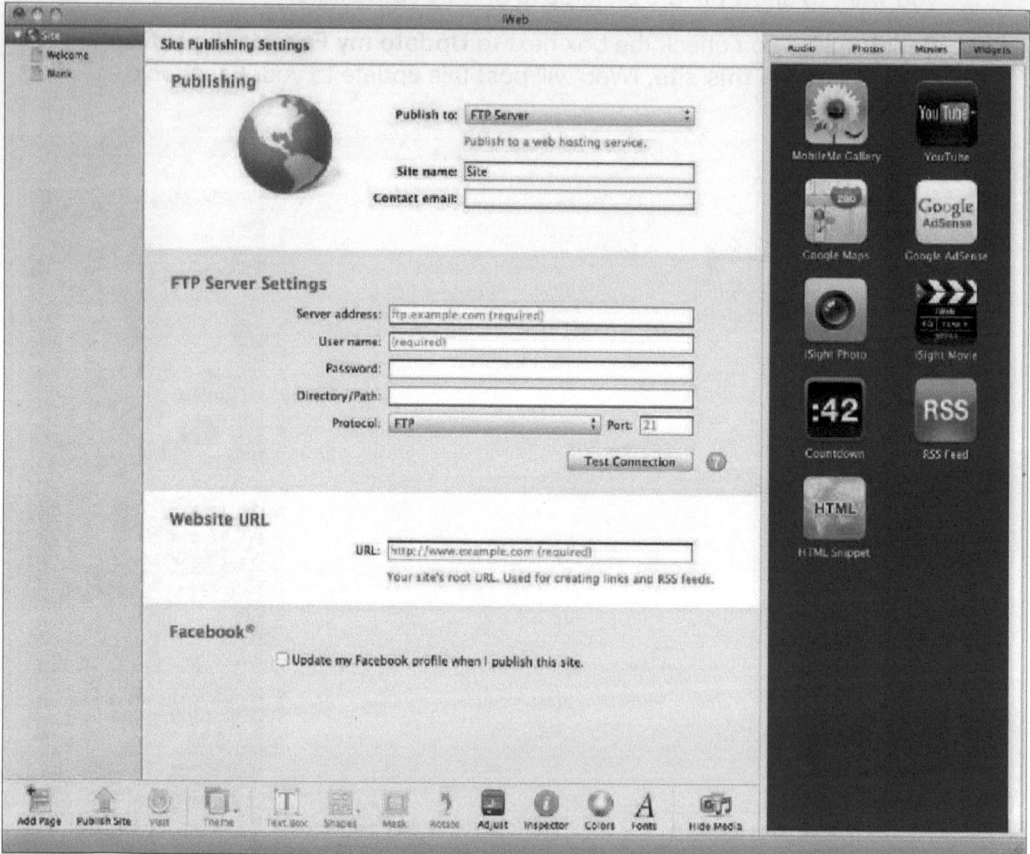

Figure 10–32. *Publishing via FTP*

This screen is broken down into the following four sections:

- **Publishing**: This has the same setup issues as a MobileMe account, but FTP is chosen by clicking on **MobileMe** and selecting **FTP Server**.

- **FTP Server Settings:** You must have several pieces of vital information to upload a site via FTP. These are:

    - **Server address:** This usually starts with `ftp.` and usually ends in `.com` (for a business server) or `.edu` (for a school server). The middle section is specific to you.

    - **Username and password:** An ftp server usually requires authentication so that uninvited "baddies" can't access your private files.

- **Directory/Path:** This is the location on the server. It usually follows the format: /Enterlocationhere/.

- **Protocol:** This is the method used to upload your site to the ftp server. This could be: **FTP, FTP with Implicit SSL, FTP with TLS/SSL,** or **SFTP.**I have no idea what the differences are between these. Just know that whatever company or school's server you are using, the network administrator will tell you which one to use.

- **Port:** Every type of Internet communication requires a different port. In the example in Figure 10–32, we see that the FTP port default is port 21.

- **Test Connection:** This is great.—if you click on this button, you can verify that all of your settings will work and the web site will be uploaded successfully.

> **NOTE:** Test connection will not determine that the directory path you entered is the correct one. It will just tell you that that path exists.

Website URL

This is the site's root URL—its home base. It is required.

Facebook

This option means that your Facebook account will be automatically updated when the site is published.

> **NOTE:** The following items will not work if you publish via FTP or a folder:
>
> - Hit counter
>
> - Password protection
>
> - Search feature in blogs
>
> - Comments and attachments
>
> - RSS feeds (unless you specify the URL when publishing)
>
> There are ways of getting around these limitations, but covering them is beyond the scope of this book.

Publishing to a Local Folder

This method, which you perform with the options in the screen shown in Figure 10–33, is useful if you want to use a third-party program to upload your site. Other programs might have features not available in iWeb's FTP uploading option.

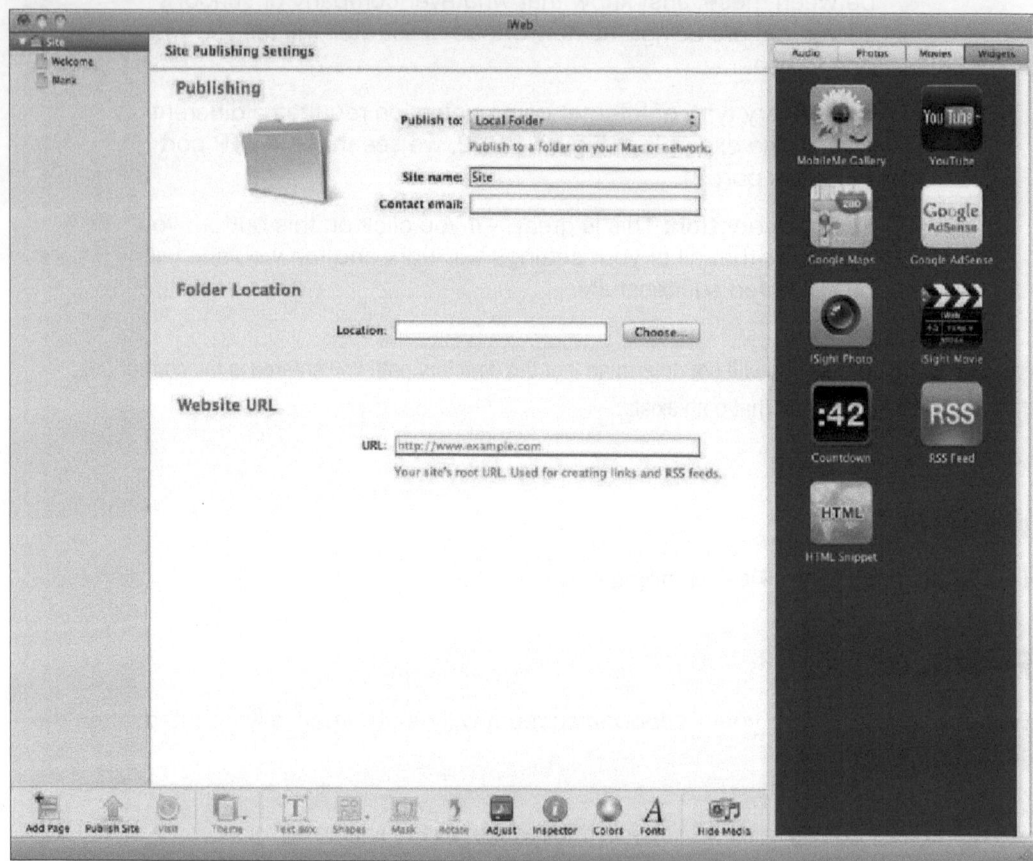

Figure 10–33. *Saving your web site to a local folder (on your hard drive.)*

- **Publishing:** This is essentially the same as the FTP publishing section. You just have to choose **Local folder** next to **Publish to:**.

- **Folder Location:** Click **Choose...** to assign a location to your web site on your hard drive.

- **Website URL:** This is the site's root URL—its home base. It is required.

Summary

In this chapter, I covered all of the tools available in iWeb, except the **Inspector** button, which I cover in Chapter 11: "When in doubt in iWeb...go to the Inspector!"

I ended this chapter by explaining the ways available to publish your site or save it to your hard drive for use with other Internet applications. After reading this chapter, you are on the path to creating web site wonders, from a simple photo page to a site that includes a wider variety of your chosen media.

When in Doubt in iWeb, Go to the Inspector!

The **Inspector** button is an important tool to learn about, because with it, you can accomplish many, many tasks. This nifty tool consists of eight different tabs, or, to use the iWeb lingo, Inspectors, each of which performs a different function within iWeb. These functions modify the following elements:

- Page
- Photos
- Blog and Podcast
- Text
- Graphic
- Metrics
- Link
- QuickTime

This chapter will go over all of these options in detail.

How Do I Access the Inspector Function?

The **Inspector** button is located at the bottom of your screen—roughly in the middle of the options you see available. Clicking this button brings you to the **Inspector** window, shown in Figure 11–1. You can also access this window by selecting **Show Inspector** from the **View** menu.

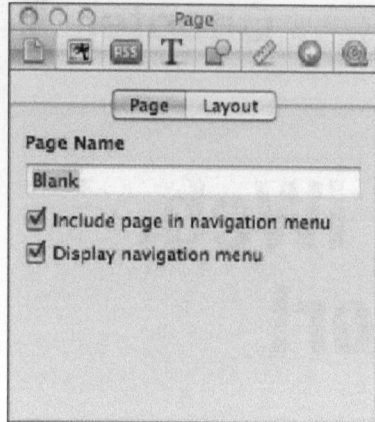

Figure 11–1. *Inspector window*

At the top of Figure 11–1, you see eight buttons, which represent the eight Inspectors. I'll explain each in detail, moving left to right, starting with the **Page Inspector**.

Page Inspector

The **Page Inspector** makes layout and background changes a snap—from changing the page name to the page size to changing the page background to the browser background. To begin using this tool, click the **Page** icon. You then see the **Page** tab and the **Layout** tab. Click the appropriate tab to work with either the **Page** section or the **Layout** section.

The **Page** section is shown in Figure 11–1. Here you can name your page by entering a name in the **Page Name** field. It will make navigating your site much easier if every page has a unique name. You can also decide if you want to include the page in the **Navigation** menu by clicking on the check box next to **Include page in navigation menu**. The **Navigation** menu appears at the top of your page if you choose this option. An example is shown in Figure 11–2. Please note the curvy line below the title **Baby**. This line signifies the page that is currently being viewed. **Welcome** is the only other page so far in my example. To show the **Navigation** window on your page, make sure the check box next to **Display navigation menu** is checked.

Figure 11–2. *Navigation window of a website*

The **Layout** section is shown in Figure 11–3. It consists of the following three sections:

■ **Page Size**: Here you can set certain aspects of your page size:

    ■ **Top and Bottom Padding** puts more or less blank space at the top and bottom of your page.

    ■ **Content Width** can make the page wider.

    ■ **Content Height** can make the page longer.

    ■ **Header and Footer Height** moves the area that contains the buttons at the top of the page down lower on the page, adding space above the buttons.

■ **Page Background:** If you click on **Image Fill** (default if you choose a theme template) you are given the following choices for a background: **None, Color Fill, Gradient Fill, Image Fill,** or **Tinted Image Fill.** Below **Image Fill** you can choose from the following options:

    ■ **Scale to Fit**

    ■ **Scale to Fill**

    ■ **Stretch**

    ■ **Original Size**

    ■ **Tile**

Last, if you click on **Choose...** you can select your own photo as a background. The other options for a background are the following:

    ■ **Color Fill**: If you choose **Color Fill**, you are given to the option to select any color you want for a background.

    ■ **Gradient Fill**: If you choose **Gradient Fill**, you are given the chance to create your own custom gradient background. A gradient takes two colors—which you choose. It then puts one color on top of the other, melding the colors. You can also change the angle of the meld as well.

    ■ **Tinted Image:** If you select this option, you can choose the color to tint the image.

■ **Browser Background**: This determines the color around the page. It can be either a **Color Fill** or an **Image Fill**. If you choose **Color Fill**, you have the option of adding any color in your page to the color palette. To do this, click on the rectangular box below the **Color Fill** option. This will bring up the color palette.

Click on the magnifying glass icon to begin the color selection process. Simply move the magnifying glass icon over the area that you want to save the color. Click the mouse button. This will add the color to the palette. To save this color for future use in your site, simply click your mouse on the color bar next to the magnifying glass icon and drag the color to the row of small rectangles at the bottom of the screen. This will put the new color in a rectangle and save it for use anywhere else in your project.

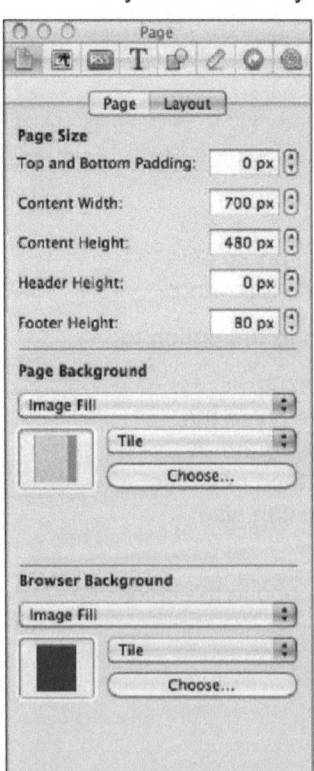

Figure 11–3. *Layout section of the* **Page** *tab*

Photos Inspector

The **Photos Inspector** deals with photo interaction in iWeb. You can set sharing settings or determine how slideshows are to be viewed on the web. This tab is broken down into the following two sections:

- **Photos**: This section is shown in Figure 11–4. This is further broken down into two parts:

  - **Photo Sharing**: This asks how you want to share your photos. If you use a **Photos** page, which contains a **Photo** grid, you can choose the quality of the download size of a photo. The choices are: **Small (fast download)**, **Medium, Large (Higher quality), or Original (Full Quality)**. Below that, you can check the box next to **Allow visitors to subscribe to your photos**. If this is checked, the latest photos to be added to your site are automatically downloaded to the visitor's computer in iPhoto. If the unfortunate user is not using a Mac and iPhoto, they will see the updates in their RSS reader.

  - **Comments**: The bottom section of this tab involves adding comments to photos. If checked, you allow visitors to add comments to your page. You can allow visitors to add attachments by checking the box next to **Allow attachments**. The last item asks if you want to display a comment indicator.

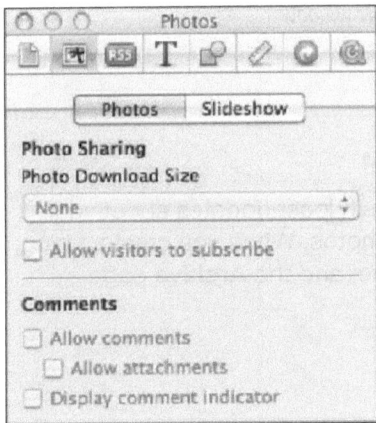

Figure 11–4. *Photos tab of Inspector window*

- **Slideshow**: This section is shown in Figure 11–5. This is also only available when you use a **Photos** page that contains a **Photo** grid. It is broken down into four sections:

  - **Enable Slideshow**: The first option asks if you want to enable a slideshow by checking the box next to **Enable slideshow**.

- **Transitions**: The next option is what transition you want to use between photos. You can choose between **None**, **Dissolve**, **Random**, **Reveal**, **Push**, or **Fade Through Background**.

- **Appearance**: The third option determines the appearance of the photos. You have three options: **Show a reflection of the photo**, **Show captions for the photo**, or **Display the photo full screen**.

- **Page Background**: The last option in this section involves the **Page** background of the slideshow. Click on the color box select a color.

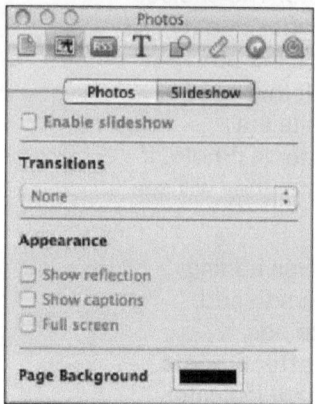

Figure 11–5. *Slideshow section of the Photos tab found in the Inspector window*

Blog and Podcast Inspector

This is broken down into two sections: **Blog** and **Podcast**.

A blog is often a personal webpage that allows you to easily post updates about your current status in no time and to share and archive your photos. When you create a blog, three pages are created: The **Blog** page, the **Entries** page, and the **Archive** page. A sample **Blog** page is shown in Figure 11–6.

Figure 11–6. *Sample **Blog** page*

In iWeb, you can add or delete blog posts easily in the **Entries** page, which is shown in Figure 11–7.

Figure 11–7. *Entry page*

The **Archive** page is shown in Figure 11–8.

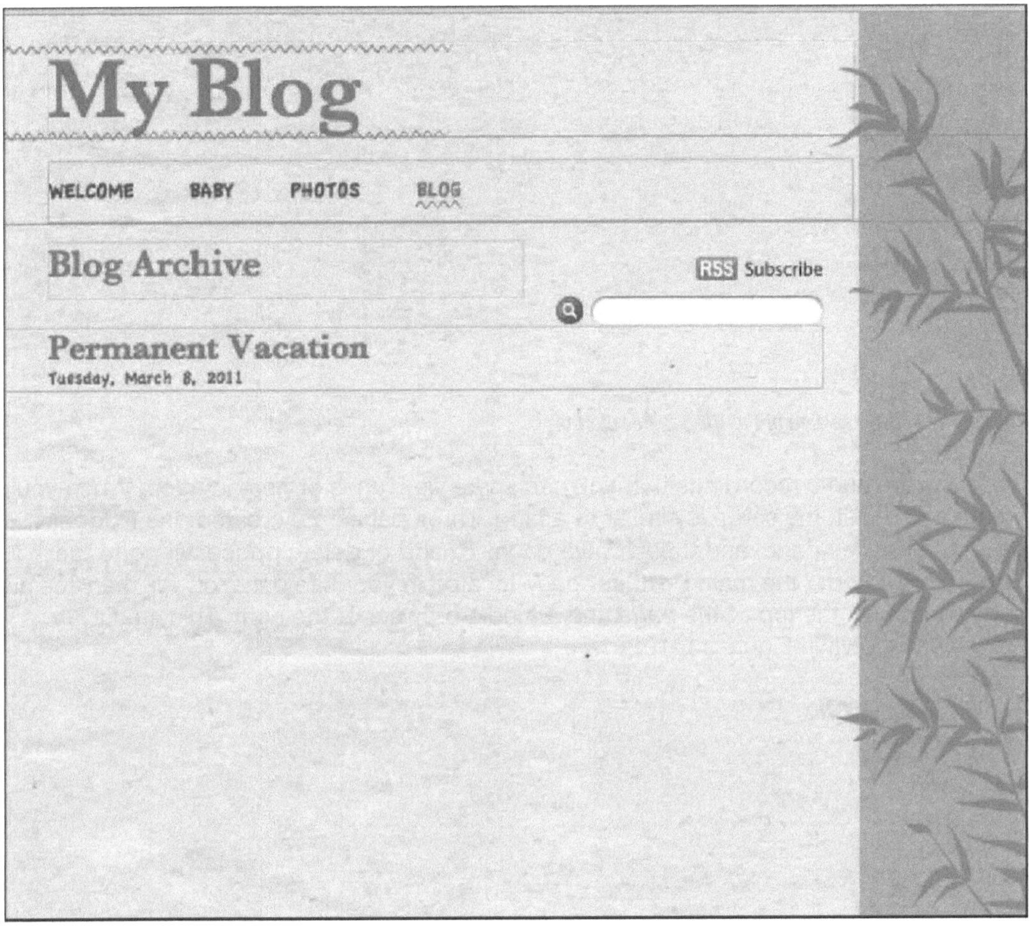

Figure 11–8. *Archive page*

The **Blog** section of the **Blog & Podcast** tab, shown in Figure 11–9, is broken into three parts:

- **Blog Main Page:** Here, you to set the number of excerpts shown (up to 50) and the length of each excerpt to be shown via a slider. Move it to the left for fewer lines and to the right for more lines.

- **Comments:** The second option asks if you want to **Allow comments** or **Allow attachments**.

- **Search:** The last option asks if you want to **Display (a) search field**.

Figure 11–9. *Blog section of the Blog & Podcast tab*

Podcasts are audio recordings that you can share via iTunes or here in iWeb. When you create a podcast, the setup is similar to a blog. Three pages are created: the **Podcast** page, the **Entries** page, and the **Archive** page. To add or delete podcasts, go to the **Entries** page under the main **Podcast** page located in your site bar. You will then see an entry window at the top of the page and a media browser at the right. This media browser is shown in Figure 11–10.

Figure 11–10. *Media browser*

Your podcasts will appear at the bottom of your screen. This is also shown in Figure 11–10.

The Podcast section is shown in Figure 11–11. It is broken down into two sections:

- **Podcast Series**: You provide various information about your podcast here. First, you provide the **Series Artist** and **Contact email** of the maker of the Podcast. Next, you have to determine what will be the **Parental Advisory** for the Podcast. This could be: **Clean, Explicit, or None**. You then decide if you want the podcast to be available in the iTunes store. Click the check box next to **Allow Podcast in iTunes Store** if you do.

- **Podcast Episodes**: The second section deals with podcast episodes. It asks for an **Episode Artist** and you have to set the **Parental Advisory** and decide whether to make your series available on iTunes.

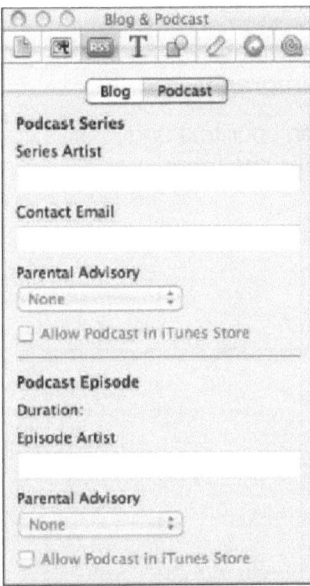

Figure 11–11. *Podcast section of the Blog & Podcast tab*

Text Inspector

The **Text Inspector** is your friend. A good web page is polished in its look and organization. This Inspector allows you carefully align your text and give your site that user-friendly, professional look. This tab is broken down into three separate sections:

- **Text**: This section is shown in Figure 11–12. It is broken down into three sections: **Color & Alignment**, **Spacing**, and **Inset Margin**.

    - **Color & Alignment**: You can assign a color by clicking on the small rectangular box [image] and choosing a new color. You can change the alignment [image] (left, centered, right, or justified) by clicking the graphic to match the alignment you want. The next three buttons next to alignment allows you to either align the text to the **Top of text box or shape**, **to the Center of the text box or shape**, or **the bottom of the text box or shape** [image].

Background Fill: You can choose a separate background fill for the text in the text box. For example, black text with a red background around the text and the main page background is blue.

■ **Spacing**: You can change the following spacing options: **Character**, **Line**, **Before Paragraph**, or **After Paragraph**.

■ **Inset Margin**: The **Inset Margin** is space between your text and the border around your text. The larger the number, the more "white space" will appear around your text.

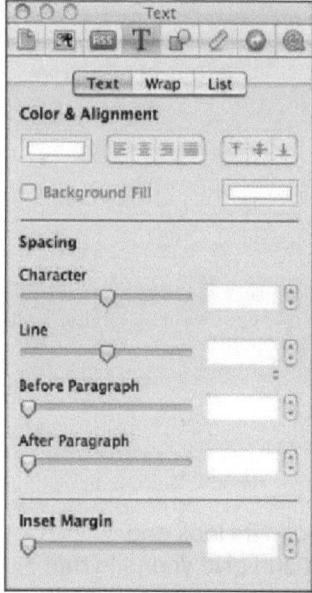

Figure 11–12. *Text section of the Text tab*

■ **Wrap**: The next section is called **Wrap**. This is shown in Figure 11–13. When you check the box next to **Object causes wrap**, text will wrap around the objects in the web page.

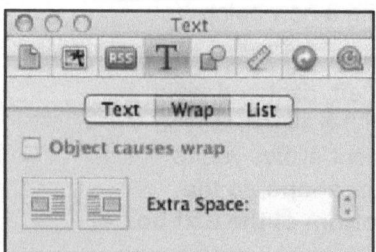

Figure 11–13. *Wrap section of the Text tab*

- **List**: This is shown in Figure 11–14. You can create a list with the following options: **No Bullets**, **Text Bullets**, **Image Bullets**, **Custom Image...**, or **Numbers**.

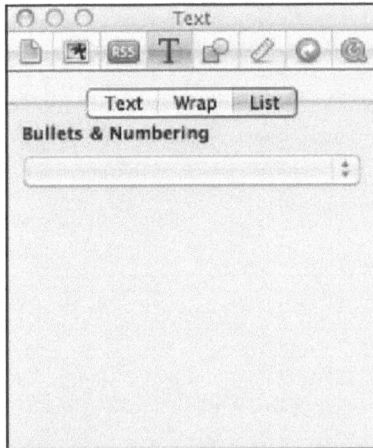

Figure 11–14. *List section of the Font tab*

Graphic Inspector

Graphics are what make a web page stand out. The **Graphic Inspector** gives you the opportunity to customize your graphics and give them more pizzazz. This tab, which is shown in Figure 11–15, is broken down into five sections:

- **Fill**: The first section is the **Fill** option. If you select a text box, you can fill with either: **None (no fill)**, **Color Fill**, **Gradient Fill**, **Advanced Gradient Fill**, **Image Fill**, **or Tinted Image Fill**.

- **Stroke**: This determines the border around an object. It can be **None**, **a line**, or **a Picture Frame**. You can choose from 21 different frames. A small graphic of all the available frames is shown in Figure 11–16.

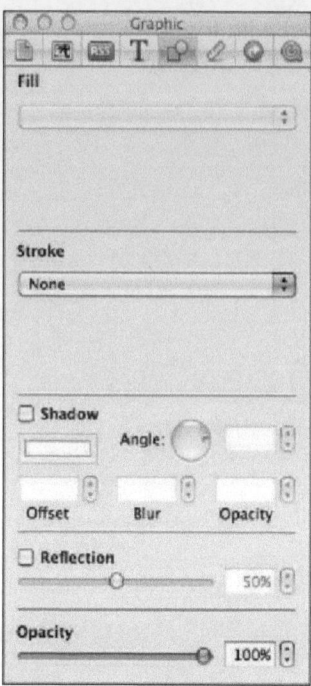

Figure 11–15. *Graphics tab of the Inspector window.*

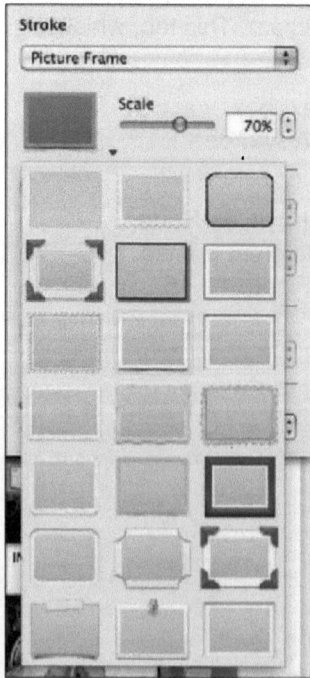

Figure 11–16. *Stroke option, showing available frames to go around objects*

- **Shadow**: Allows you to add a customizable shadow around your objects. **Reflection** adds a short reflection to your photo. Your **Dock**, by default, has a shadow below it as well.

- **Opacity**: The default is 100%. If you move the slider to the left, your photo fades and the background colors behind it become more visible.

Metrics Inspector

The **Metrics Inspector** also deals with graphics. The size or position can be set to exact numbers to give you full say as to how big or where the graphic should be. The **Metrics** tab is shown in Figure 11–17.

- **Size**: This modifies the size of the photo you have selected. You can increase the width or height. By default, **Constrain proportions** is checked. This will match the increase you make to the other variable. If you increase the height, the width will be adjusted to keep the original proportions. The original size button will display you photo at its actual size. If you took a relatively high-resolution photo, this will make your photo HUGE in your web page.

- **Position**: You can precisely maneuver your photo to an exact location by modifying the X and Y variables in the **Position** section of this window.

- **Rotate**: You can modify the object by **Free** rotating it by using the circular spin wheel, by changing its angle, or by clicking on the two **Flip** options.

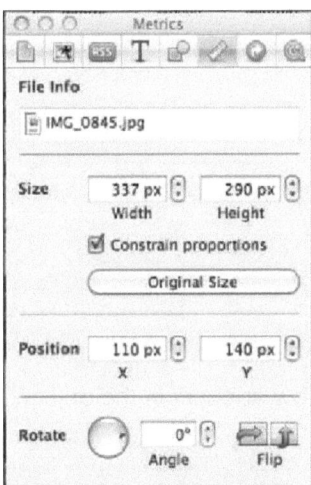

Figure 11–17. *Metrics* tab of the *Inspector* window

Link Inspector

This is a very important tab. This is where you can add hyperlinks to objects so they link to another web page or other items.

- **Hyperlink**: The **Hyperlink** section of this tab is shown in Figure 11–18. Click on the object you want to make "linkable" and check **Enable as a hyperlink** to make start the process. Next, choose what you want to link to. Here are your options next to **Link To:**

    - **One of My Pages**: If you choose **One of My Pages**, a list of all your site's pages appears.

    - **An External page** (shown in Figure 11–14): If you choose this option, you must insert the web address or URL for the page you want to link to. You are also given the choice to open the hyperlink in a new window by checking off the box next to Open link in new window.

    - **A File:** If you choose a file, a screen appears, allowing you to navigate your hard drive to find the file you want to link to.

    - **An Email Message**: If you choose this option, you are asked to enter a valid e-mail address and, if you like, a subject line.

- **Make hyperlinks active**: When this option is checked—you cannot edit the object when it selected—the web page you choose appears.

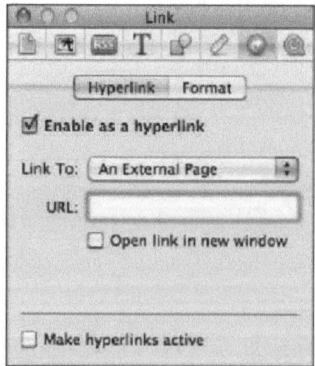

Figure 11–18. *Hyperlink section of the Link tab*

After you attach a hyperlink, a small blue circle with a white arrow appears in the object. This is shown in Figure 11–19.

Figure 11–19. *Example of an object that has a hyperlink attached to it*

Once you attach a hyperlink to an object, you can customize the appearance and functionality of that hyperlink with the following options:

- **Format:** This is shown in Figure 11–20. This only applies to text-based hyperlinks.

    - **Normal**: This determines the text color for hyperlinks. Click on the rectangular box to choose a color. If you click on the letter U with an underline, the link will have an underline below it when selected in your page. For **Normal**, no underline is the default.

    - **Rollover**: This determines the text color of hyperlinks when the visitor moves a pointer over them. Click on the rectangular box to choose a color. If you click on the U with an underline, the link will have an underline below it when selected in your page.

    - **Visited**: This determines the text color after a hyperlink has been clicked. Click on the rectangular box to choose a color. If you click on the U with an underline, the link will have an underline below it when selected in your page.

    - **Disabled**: This indicates the text color of a hyperlink that can't be clicked. Click on the rectangular box to choose a color. If you click on the U with an underline, the link will have an underline below it when selected in your page.

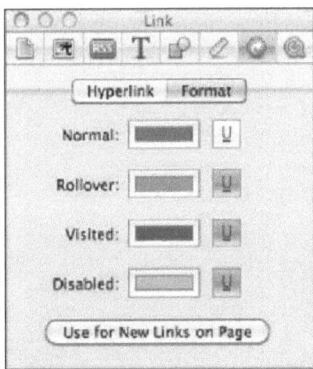

Figure 11–20. *Format section of the* **Link** *tab*

QuickTime Inspector

If you added a QuickTime-capable movie in your website, this tab allows you to modify key settings for it. It is shown in Figure 11–21.

- **Start and Stop**: Allows you to set at exactly which points the video will start and end play.

- **Poster Frame**: This is the frame you want to be shown before the video is ready to viewed on your web page.

- **Autoplay:** Automatically plays when page is accessed.

- **Loop**: Plays over and over again.

- **Show the movie controller**: This is nice as it allows visitors to adjust settings or easily play and pause the video. Just click the check box next to any of the previously mentioned items to activate them.

Figure 11–21. *QuickTime tab of the Inspector window*

Summary

The **Inspector** button has a gazillion options within. Most elements in your web page can be modified by an option found in the **Inspector** tool. It might take a while to get the ins and outs of this powerful feature, but as you explore and see how nicely iWeb has laid it out, you'll soon find it easy to use.

Chapter 12

Bookmark This Chapter on iWeb Menus!

Let's end our discussion on iWeb with a rundown of its menus. As I stated before, menus are located at the top of every Macintosh window. I will start with the **iWeb** menu and end with the **Help** menu. From creating or editing your project to finding help, knowing where the different menu options are is key.

iWeb Menu

The iWeb Menu is fairly straightforward. You will notice that the app-named menu in each application contain the same choices. The most important option in each app is **Preferences...**. Here you can customize the actual working environment of the app. See Figure 12–1.

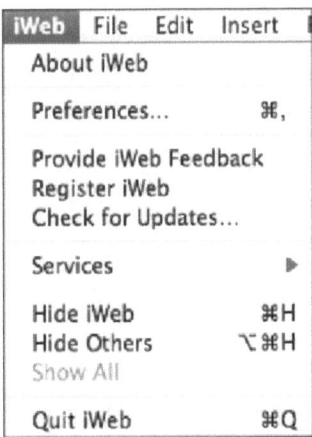

Figure 12–1. *iWeb menu*

- **About iWeb**: This tells you what version you are currently running.

- **Preferences...**: The screen that appears when you choose this menu is shown in Figure 12–2. Here, you can modify the working environment of iWeb.

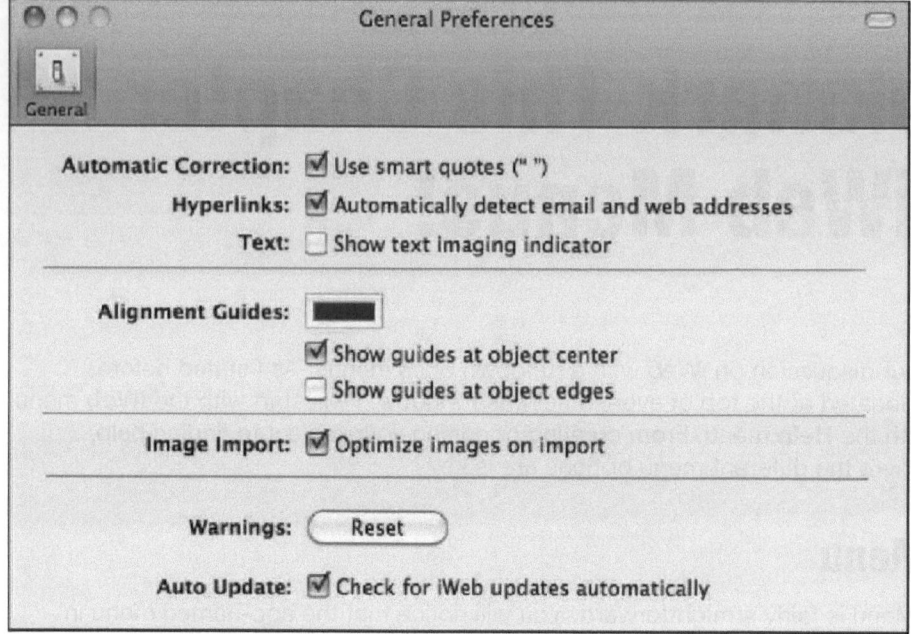

Figure 12–2. *General Preferences* *window of the* *iWeb* *menu*

- **Automatic Correction:** Just asks if you want iWeb to replace normal quotes "" with smart quotes "".

- **Hyperlinks:** If this option is checked, e-mail addresses (glen@server.com) and web addresses (www.apple.com) are automatically turned into hyperlinks. No other action is required to have these types of data linked to the web or an e-mail account.

- **Text:** Certain text boxes in iWeb are converted to images so that they appear more uniform on different browsers. If a text box has been converted, it will have this graphic attached to it [▣].

- **Alignment Guides:** These are provided to help you align objects placed in your web page. If you click on the rectangle next to **Alignment Guides**, you can change the color of these guides. The default is **Show guides at object center.** You can also choose **Show guides at object edges**.

- **Image Import:** Most cameras take pictures that are large in file size (megabytes). This option should always be left on, as it takes the photo and makes it more suitable for a web page by making it easier for your web browser to display it.

- **Warnings:** Certain actions may trigger alerts in iWeb. If you have disabled alerts from appearing again, this option resets the alert system and you'll receive alerts again.

- **Auto Update:** If this is selected, your Mac will check to see if there are any updates to the program.

- **Provide iWeb Feedback:** This brings you to the Apple website, where you can critique the program.

- **Register iWeb:** Here you can register the program. This is not required.

- **Check for Updates...:** This will also send a message to an Apple server to see if there is a new version available for download.

- **Services:** If there are any special add-ins to the default services available on your Mac, it will show up here. By default, there are none.

- **Hide iWeb:** This makes all visible iWeb windows disappear. They are still open—just not on the screen. You have to click on the application icon in the dock to bring back the screens. In this case, the iWeb icon.

- **Hide Others:** This hides all other applications when running iWeb. If you suddenly notice that you have 50 open windows and can't find something, this will clear all other windows except iWeb windows.

File Menu

Want to create a new page or site while working in iWeb? Want to upload changes to your site and make them "live" on the Internet? Or save your work for later?

This menu gives you all of these options, plus some advanced features, such as setting up your domain, setting up Google Adsense, checking for new comments on your site, or submitting a podcast to iTunes. See Figure 12–3.

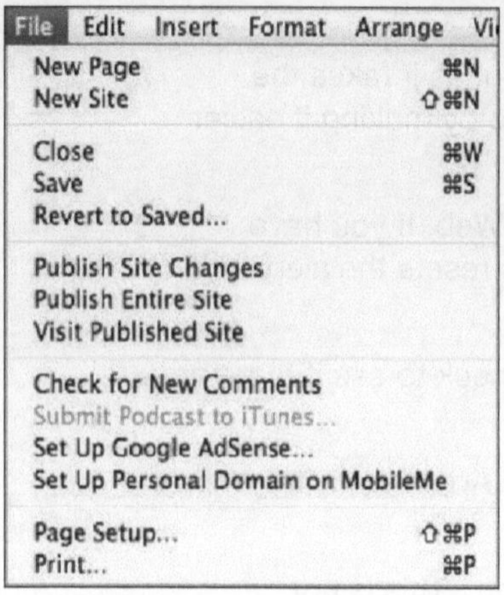

File	Edit	Insert	Format	Arrange	Vi

New Page	⌘N
New Site	⇧⌘N
Close	⌘W
Save	⌘S
Revert to Saved...	
Publish Site Changes	
Publish Entire Site	
Visit Published Site	
Check for New Comments	
Submit Podcast to iTunes...	
Set Up Google AdSense...	
Set Up Personal Domain on MobileMe	
Page Setup...	⇧⌘P
Print...	⌘P

Figure 12–3. *File menu of iWeb*

- **New Page:** Adds a new page to your website. Clicking this brings you to a page where you choose the template for the type of page you want to add. It can be a photos page or blank page, for example.

- **New Site:** You can have multiple sites in one workspace. But, as I mentioned, you can only have one workspace in iWeb. This adds a new site (Site 2 by default) and also brings up the template selection screen.

- **Close:** This closes the screen you are working in, but not before iWeb asks you if you want to save your work.

> **NOTE:** I am a computer tech by trade, and I just want to add: SAVE YOUR WORK OFTEN. There is always a chance that something may crash.

- **Save:** This saves your current work. Notice there is no **Save As...** option below **Save**. As I said, you can only have one workspace. When you return to iWeb and launch it, the one and only workspace will automatically open.

- **Revert to Saved...:** A window will appear asking if you want to roll back any changes you made in this session to the last saved version. One major undo.

- **Publish Site Changes:** This will upload any changes you made since the last time you uploaded and published your site.

- **Publish Entire Site:** This will publish or re-publish your entire site.

- **Visit Published Site:** See what all of your hard work looks like live. It opens your published site in your default web browser.

- **Check for New Comments:** If you have a photo in your web page, and you used the **Inspector** button to allow comments to be made to the photo, this is where you can see the comments.

- **Submit Podcast to iTunes…:** This allows you to add podcasts (imported into iWeb from GarageBand, for example) to iTunes.

- **Set Up Google Adsense…:** Google Adsense allows you to make money by placing ads in your site. You must create a free account to get started.

- **Set Up Personal Domain on MobileMe:** If you own your own personal domain (www.yourname.com, for example), you can have MobileMe use this instead of Apple's MobileMe servers. This is accessed by going online and adding the domain. The first screen involved is shown in Figure 12–4.

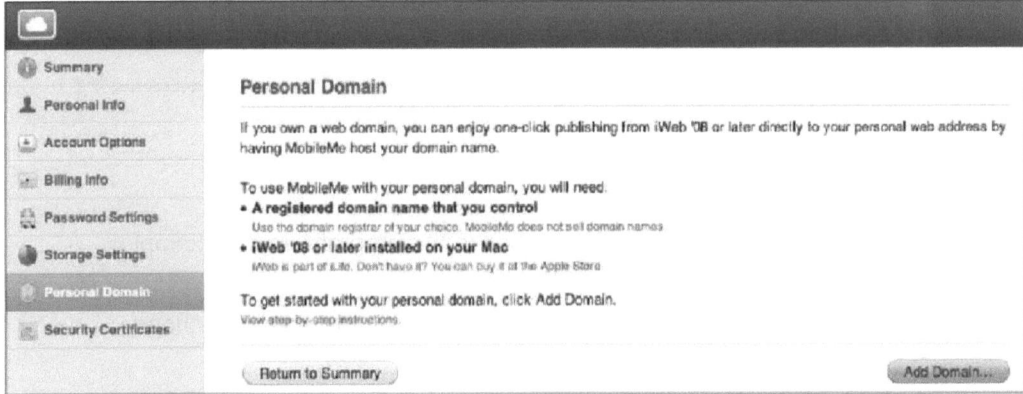

Figure 12–4. *Setting up a personal domain in MobileMe*

- **Page Setup…:** This is where you choose the settings for a printed document.

- **Print:** This allows you to print your web page.

Edit Menu

From the **Edit** menu, you can access the **Cut**, **Copy**, **Paste**, and **Undo** features. To select all items at once, you can also use the **Select All** command.

Figure 12–5. *Edit menu of iWeb*

- **Undo (Action):** Undoes your last action in the program. In the example shown in Figure 12–5, it is to undo a **Rotate** action.

- **Redo (action):** If you decide that you actually want to keep the change you just undid, click **Redo**.

- **Cut:** Deletes selected items.

- **Copy:** Takes the item you have highlighted and puts it into the Mac's memory.

- **Paste:** Takes what is in the Mac's memory and places or "pastes" the item at your cursor's location on the screen.

- **Paste and Match Style:** This takes what you copied and then pastes it into your document with the original formatting still applied.

- **Delete:** Deletes an item from your workspace.

- **Delete Page:** Deletes an entire page from your site's toolbar.

- **Duplicate:** Takes what you highlighted and automatically pastes it right back into your workspace.

- **Select All:** Highlights all elements in your workspace.

- **Deselect All:** Changed your mind after using the **Select All** command? Use this to undo that action.

- **Find:** This allows you to find text in your web page. You can then replace the item or all the items with a new text entry.

- **Spelling**: This activates the spelling tool.

- **Special Characters:** This is great for web pages. Want to a special symbol to your page, such as a trademark symbol? Look here to find it.

Insert Menu

A web page with just text is not very interesting. With this menu, you can spice up your page and insert live hyperlinks, shapes, buttons, and advanced widgets. The tools are all here—explore and make your page stand out.

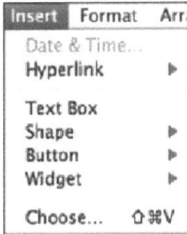

Figure 12–6. *Insert menu of iWeb*

- **Date & Time:** This allows you to add the date and time to a newly created text box. The screen that appears is shown in Figure 12–7. Please notice that you can choose the format of the text to be placed in your web page. Also, notice that you can have iWeb constantly update this special text box by selecting to **Automatically update the date and time when iWeb is opened**. Click **Insert** to complete the process.

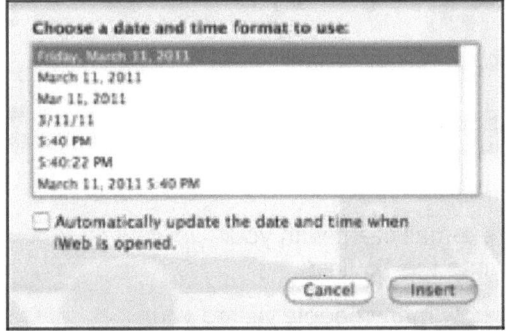

Figure 12–7. *Inserting the date and time to your web page*

- **Hyperlink:** You can insert a hyperlink to a separate web page, e-mail address, or to a separate file. This is shown in Figure 12–8.

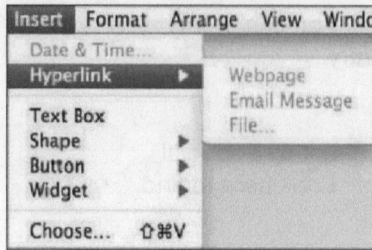

Figure 12–8. *Inserting a hyperlink into iWeb*

- **Text Box:** Inserts a blank text box onto your web page.
- **Shape:** This allows you to add a shape to your web page. If you access shapes from this menu, each item is described in words. This is shown in Figure 12–9. If you insert a shape from the **Shape** button in the **Tools** toolbar, the item is a picture of the shape.

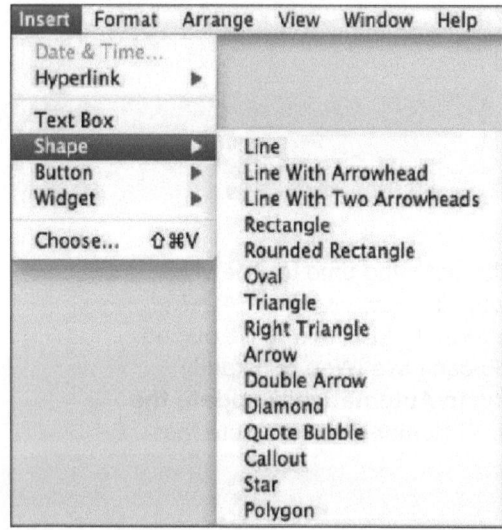

Figure 12–9. *Inserting a shape with the **Shape** command found in the **Insert** menu*

- **Button:** Here you can subscribe via a button action—RSS Feed, Podcast, or Photocast (Figure 12–10). You can also add a button for the following:
  - **E-mail Me**: Brings up the visitor's e-mail client with your selected e-mail address inserted into the **To** field.
  - **Hit Counter**: This keeps track of how many people visited your site. The law of "the more the merrier" applies.
  - **Made on a Mac**: If you add this, a small badge will be placed in your web page that states Made on a Mac.

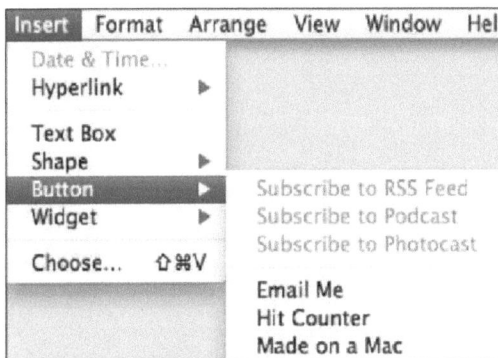

Figure 12–10. *Insert* button command found in the *Insert* menu

- **Widget:** This inserts one of nine widgets into your web page. This menu item is shown in Figure 12–11. Widgets are discussed in detail in Chapter 10: "Welcome to Web Creation the iWeb Way!"

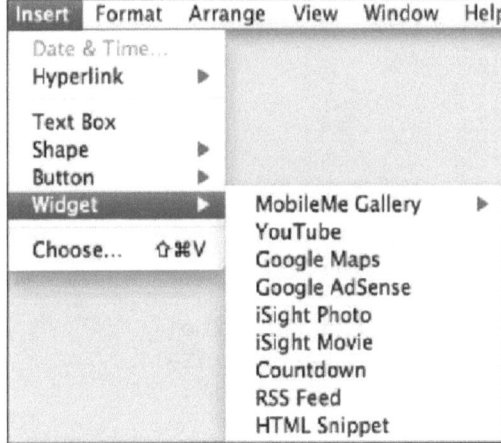

Figure 12–11. *Inserting a widget via the **Insert** menu*

- **Choose...:** This allows you to add media files on your hard drive that are not found while going to the media sidebar for audio, video, or photos.

Format Menu

This menu allows you to modify your font style and alignment, copy, and paste styles (great for making changes to multiple sections of a project) or to perform the more advanced tasks of masking or adding an Instant Alpha.

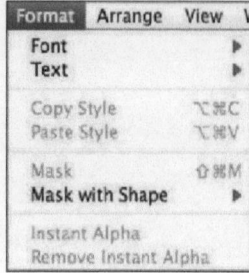

Figure 12–12. *Format menu of iWeb*

■ **Font:** This allows you to format various aspects of the font you are
using in text boxes or other text items. The options available are
shown in Figure 12–13.

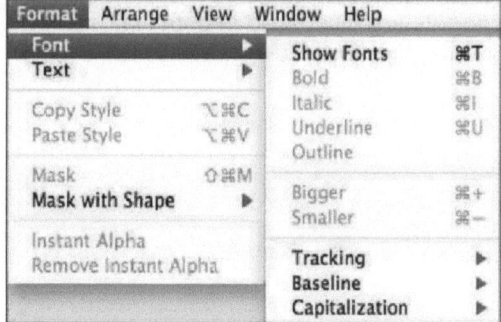

Figure 12–13. *Options available via the **Font** menu option found in the **Format** menu*

■ **Text:** This allows you to set the alignment of your text. It could be
aligned left, right, centered, or justified. This is shown in Figure 12–14.

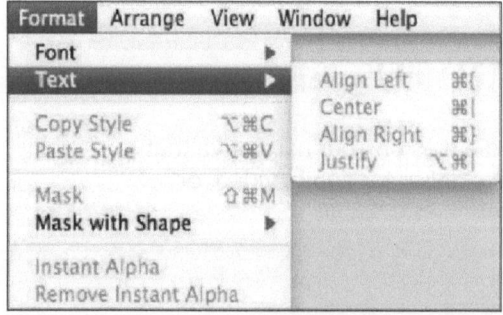

Figure 12–14. *Justification options available via the **Text** menu option found in the **Format** menu*

■ **Copy Style:** If you have a very large website, it might be useful to copy
the style of text boxes and apply them to other newer text boxes. This
is what this tool does.

- **Paste Style:** After you have copied a chosen style, use this command to reformat the text to the style you copied. I just love how technology makes tedious tasks easy.

- **Mask:** "Masking" is basically taking a photo and hiding parts you don't want to be shown in the final web page. Just select what you want to be seen and all other sections of the photo will disappear from view. It is still there, it just can't be seen.

- **Mask with Shape:** This allows you to perform a mask, which is normally applied with a square box, with a different shape. The choices are shown in Figure 12–15.

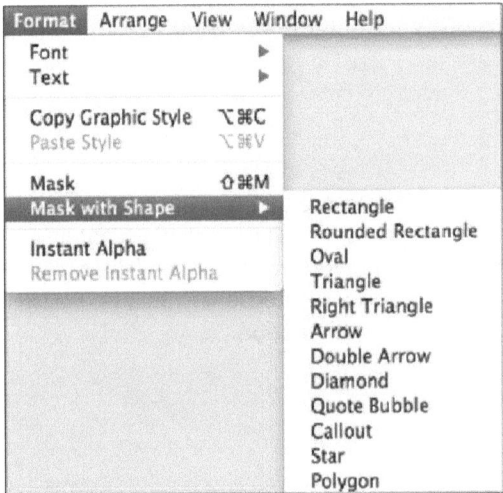

Figure 12–15. *Shapes available for masking*

In the example in Figure 12–16, I applied a mask of a diamond shape to a picture of a baby.

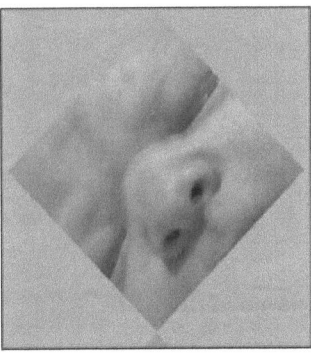

Figure 12–16. *Mask applied—Diamond shape*

- **Instant Alpha:** This is not a quick breakfast item. I can't describe it better than the screen that comes up when you choose it. This is shown in Figure 12–17.

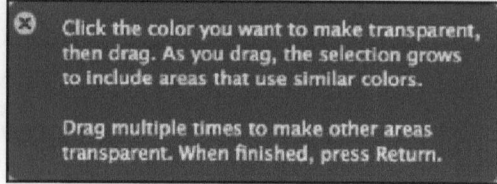

Click the color you want to make transparent, then drag. As you drag, the selection grows to include areas that use similar colors.

Drag multiple times to make other areas transparent. When finished, press Return.

Figure 12–17. *What Instant Alpha does*

- **Remove Instant Alpha:** Basically, a separate undo for unapplying the **Instant Alpha** effect.

Arrange Menu

Think of iWeb as a bed. Your text boxes, photos, and so on are all blankets on the bed. With the **Arrange** commands shown in Figure 12–18, you can decide exactly what lies directly on the bed and on each layer on top. For example, you might have a text box in the middle of your web page. You decide you want to add a photo behind this text box. With these commands at your fingertips, you can perform this action.

Figure 12–18. *Arrange menu of iWeb*

- **Bring Forward:** Takes the object "up" one level. Can be applied as needed.

- **Bring to Front:** Takes the selected object and place it on top of all of the other objects. The "teddy bear" on the bed.

- **Send Backward:** Sends the object "down" one level. Can be applied as needed.

- **Send to Back:** Sends the object to the very bottom of the stack.

NOTE: If you right-click on an object, a pop-up window appears, allowing you to perform the above four options without going to the **Arrange** menu.

- **Align Objects:** This takes a selected item and aligns it to the web page. If you chose **Align Objects—Center...** it will center the item on the web page. The available options are shown in Figure 12–19.

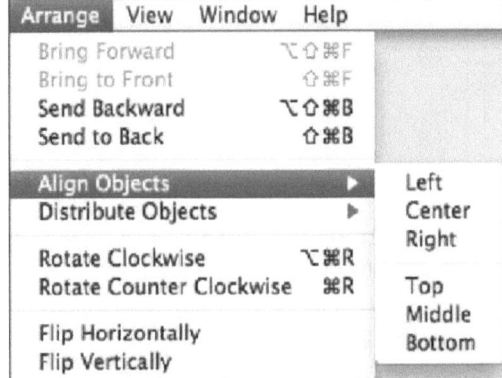

Figure 12–19. *Options available for aligning objects on your web page*

- **Distribute Objects:** This saves you a lot of time by taking all of the items you selected and spacing them evenly—horizontally or vertically. Please note that the items are aligned based on the first object you select.

- **Rotate Clockwise:** Rotates the object selected 90 degrees to the right.

- **Rotate Counter Clockwise:** Rotates the object selected 90 degrees to the left.

- **Flip Horizontally:** Takes the object selected and flips it horizontally.

- **Flip Vertically:** Takes the object selected and flips it vertically.

View Menu

A web page contains many elements. The **View** menu allows you to further customize your page. The **Inspector** window contains a lot of features, which are all covered in Chapter 11: "When in Doubt in iWeb, Go to the Inspector!"

Figure 12–20. *View menu of iWeb*

- **Show Layout:** When chosen, this will display all of the text boxes' borders and other guidelines at the top and bottom of the page, such as the **Navigation** menu.

- **Show Inspector:** This is not a CSI detective. The **Inspector** window contains a ton of useful options for modifying objects in your page. I devoted the previous chapter to this wonder of modern technology. It can also be accessed by clicking the **Inspector** button 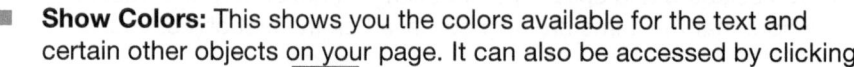.

- **Show Colors:** This shows you the colors available for the text and certain other objects on your page. It can also be accessed by clicking on the **Colors** button. A brief discussion on this tool is found in Chapter 10, "Welcome to Web Creation the iWeb Way!"

- **Show Adjust Image:** This brings up the **Adjust Image** tool. It allows you to perform many adjusts to your image. This includes slider adjustments for:
    - Brightness
    - Contrast
    - Saturation
    - Temperature
    - Tint
    - Sharpness
    - Exposure

- **Enhance button:** This performs mysterious and magical enhancements to improve your image.

  - **Reset Image**: Brings you back to your original, untouched image.

- **Hide Media/Show Media:** This either hides the media sidebar or brings it back.

Window Menu

This is a very simple menu with really only three options. You can enlarge a window via **Zoom** or shrink the workspace window to the dock via the **Minimize** button. Finally, you can bring all iWeb windows to the front of the screen if you have other apps and their workspace windows open.

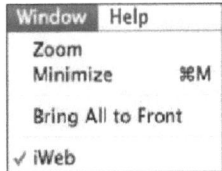

Figure 12–21. *Window menu of iWeb*

- **Zoom:** This toggles your web page from showing your current workspace environment to showing the complete page.

- **Minimize:** This takes the iWeb workspace and zips off your screen and into the dock. To get your project back on the screen, you have to click on the tiny icon for your work in the dock.

- **Bring All to Front:** This brings all iWeb windows to the front of your screen..

- **iWeb:** Just lets you know that you are currently working in iWeb.

Help Menu

New to web page design? As with other iLife apps, the **Help** menu in iWeb assists you in finding answers to questions about the program. It also contains a useful glossary of terms to help you better understand the features and technologies involved in web page creation.

Figure 12-22. *Help menu of iWeb*

- **Search:** Type in the subject you have a question about and hit return to see if iWeb's help system has the information you need. Or you can refer to the iWeb chapters in this book and get your answer while working on a website, or offline reading it in comfy chair.

- **iWeb Help:** This is a handy place to go for instructions on performing certain tasks in iWeb. It also includes a brief overview of iWeb.

- **Glossary:** A must read for every novice web designer. All of the terms I have mentioned that relate to web creation are clearly described in this glossary, from *blog* to *widget*.

- **Getting Started Video**: Brings you back to the **Welcome** screen, which contains a short introductory video to iWeb.

- **Keyboard Shortcuts:** Learn keyboard shortcuts for this application and any other and you will become a power user in no time. Save time by not using your mouse for every action you make.

- **Service and Support:** This is another helpful resource for learning about iWeb. The key new elements are links at the bottom to access downloads, manuals, see its System Requirements, and even access video tutorials. The top of this webpage is shown in Figure 12-23.

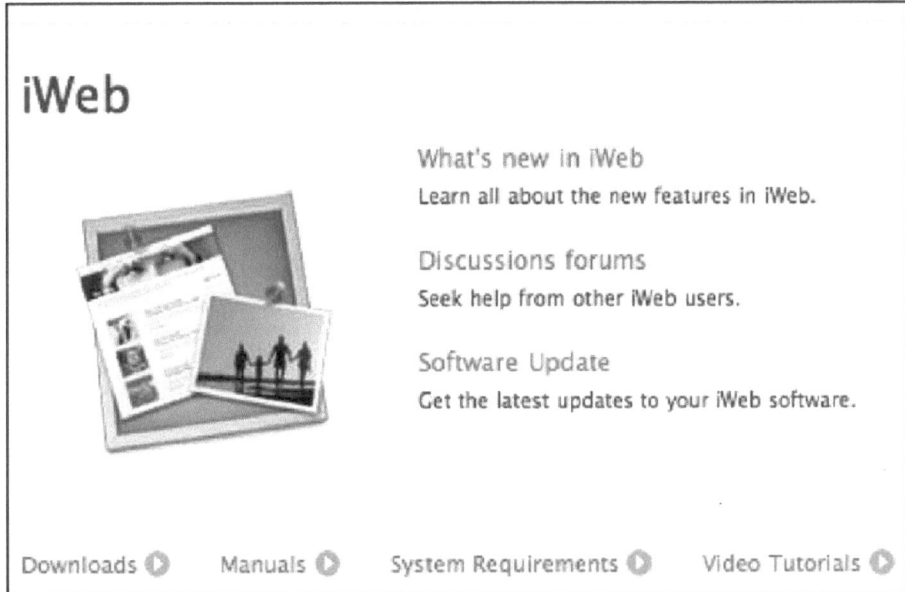

Figure 12-23. *Top portion of the **Service and Support** web page for iWeb*

Summary

That's a wrap for iWeb—we've covered everything from creating tools to finding help. Once again, Apple has taken a relatively complex process and made it simple and easy to do. So, start creating your web pages and share your life on the Internet. Just don't spend too much time surfing—there's no end to what you can find on the Internet.

iMovie

So… got any home videos?

iMovie is the perfect application to take your precious moving moments and give them the look of a Hollywood release. This program includes all the basic tools you need to begin learning how to edit video. Plus, this program also includes quite a few advanced features that will keep you learning and growing until you are well down the path of becoming the next great director!

Chapter 13

Lights...Camera...Themes ...iMovie Workspaces!

Before I delve into the movie-creation process, there are several terms that are used in this program that you should understand and know how they apply to iMovie.

IMOVIE GLOSSARY

FPS: This stands for *frames per second*. Each frame consists of one static recorded image. A sequence of these images or frames makes you feel the sense of motion. The number of these static images recorded in a second is called the frame rate. The video camera that you use will determine how many frames per second it will record. Also, when you first create a movie, you are asked to define an ending frame rate. Thirty is the default for most users, but you can choose 24 for a more cinematic feel.

TRAILER: A trailer is short video that contains key elements of a larger movie to help promote the longer movie. It's a preview, like you see at the movies.

TRANSITIONS: To make the segue between film clips more smooth, you can add animations to go-between clips. iMovie allows you to adjust the default settings of these animations or "transitions" to achieve the desired effect.

AUDIO WAVEFORMS: iMovie separates your audio data from your video data. These audio files, or "waveforms," can then be edited in iMovie.

STORYBOARD: It is good practice to map out how you want your film to flow. A storyboard is a guideline as to the order in which your clips will appear in your film. A storyboard assistant is part of the trailer-creation process.

> **TIMELINE:** A movie clip is comprised of a series of frames. These frames then take a second to be displayed. The iMovie Timeline allows you to carefully edit your clips, effects, and transitions so that everything appears for just the amount of time you want it to.
>
> **EVENT:** These are the video clips imported into iMovie.
>
> **PROJECT:** This is main working area of iMovie. All elements—such as event clips, animations, and photos—are combined into one comprehensive project file.

Theme Selection

When you first start iMovie, you are presented with a few different options: you can begin from scratch, choose one of several themes provided by iMovie, or select a really cool trailer-style movie (new to this version).

When you select **New Project...** from the **File** menu, you see the screen shown in Figure 13–1. The left side of this window is broken down into two segments. The top section provides you the option to start from scratch (**No Theme**) or the choice of seven preset themes: **Photo Album**, **Bulletin Board**, **Comic Book**, **Scrapbook**, **Filmstrip**, **News**, or **Sports**. Each theme has unique characteristics. From creating movies that look like digital photo albums to creating videos of your child's soccer game that look like television sports programs, iMovie has a theme for all your needs. The bottom section of the screen provides you a group of trailer options to choose from (discussed in the following section).

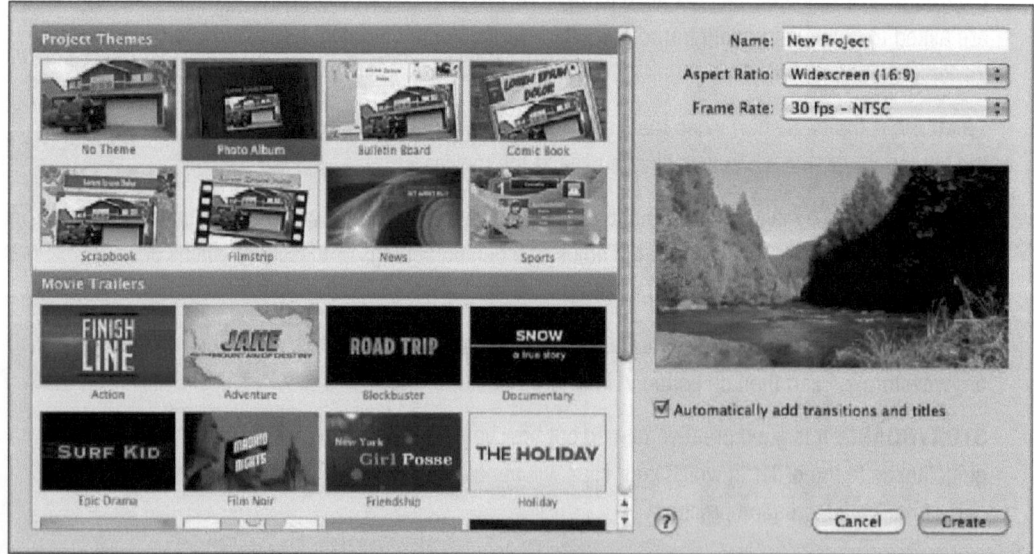

Figure 13–1. *Creating a new project in iMovie*

To the right of the theme choices, you must complete the following fields:

- Enter a name next to **Name:** (if you don't want it to be named New Project).

- Set the aspect ratio next to **Aspect Ratio:** You can choose from **Widescreen** or **Standard**. If you want your movie to play on a rectangular television, as most new televisions are, choose **Widescreen**. It is the default.

Set the frame rate next to **Frame Rate:**. The default is **30 fps**. You can also choose **25 fps** for PAL televisions. These are not used in the United States, but if you want your movie to be seen in another country that does use the PAL system, choose this setting. Finally, you can choose **24 fps—Cinema**. This will give your movie a motion-picture look and feel.

You can preview each theme just below these settings. In Figure 13–1, the Photo Album theme is selected and a short video preview of the elements it includes will be played in this screen. In this example, I took a picture of the video when it is showing a picture of a stream.

Below this window is an option to automatically add transitions and titles. If you want the movie-making process to be more automated this is a good option. Click **Create**

to start the process rolling...

Creating a Trailer from Your Video Clips in a Flash

The latest version of iMovie allows you to create an amazing trailer out of your video clips. Figure 13–2 shows the various trailer themes: **Action, Adventure, Blockbuster, Documentary, Epic Drama, Film Noir, Friendship, Holiday, Love Story, Pets, Romantic Comedy, Sports, Spy, Supernatural**, or **Travel**. That pretty much covers all the genres!

Figure 13–2. *Available trailer themes*

To create a trailer, follow these steps:

1. For best results, a lot of clips provides the best final project. It is recommended to have at least 15 -20 short clips to add to the Trailer.

2. Choose your trailer theme. The **Preview** section will display a sample of each theme.

3. Name the trailer and set the other preferences as discussed previously.

4. Click **Create** [Create] to start the process rolling.

5. Fill out all of the information requested in the **Outline** section. The top of this section is shown in Figure 13–3. The fields you have to fill out are **Movie Name**, **Release Date**, **Cast** (star's name and gender), **Studio Info** (be creative), and **Credits**. Notice that there is a **Preview** window next to these fields. Any change you make will be reflected in this window.

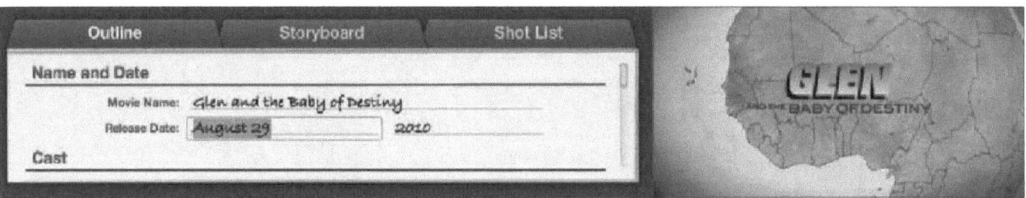

Figure 13–3. *Top of the Outline section of a trailer*

6. Fill in the blanks for all the empty spaces in the storyboard. The **Storyboard** screen is shown in Figure 13–4. Designing a trailer via the Storyboard tab makes the flow of the trailer come to life and each theme's Storyboard is created to help you create the best "promo" from your work. Please notice that iMovie uses pictures to indicate what type of clip would look best in each section of the trailer. In Figure 13–4, it asks for a video of a person, then a landscape, and then a person again. For the trailer theme I am demonstrating, there are 22 slots to fill in. It sounds like a lot of work, I know, but trust me: it's worth the time and effort. iMovie highlights the sections to be filled out with a yellow outline.

7. Drag the section of video that you want to add and iMovie automatically adds the video. iMovie then moves on to the next section, which is again highlighted. Repeat until all slots are filled. The clips you can use are found in your **Event—Preview** window. This workspace and all other iMovie workspaces are discussed next in this chapter.

Figure 13–4. *Creating your trailer storyboard*

8. Fill in your shot list. This might be easier to fill in than the storyboard. The shot list groups all type of shots into their own sections. In Figure 13–5, we see that it grouped all **Action** clips into one section. It is easier to use, I believe, because you plan how many of each type of shot you will need.

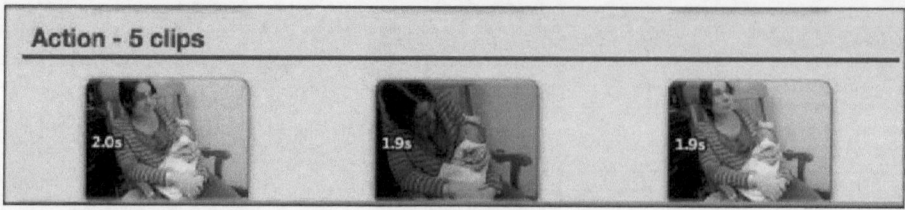

Figure 13–5. *The Shot List feature*

9. Click the **Full Screen Preview** button ▶ or preview the video in the **Preview** window by clicking on ▶. These two buttons are located at the top right of the **Project** window.

10. After everything is set, go to the **File** menu and select **Finalize Project**. Then go out to dinner. This is going to take a long, long time. I will cover the menu options in more detail in Chapter 15: "Calling the Shots with the iMovie Menus."

You have now seen how to start the movie-creation process and create a complete trailer. Now I will go over what makes creating movies in iMovie so simple to do. There are a lot elements, but as you will see, they are easy to use and give you a lot of functionality to play with.

iMovie Workspaces

The iMovie workspace is the heart of the program. Each section plays a key role in creating your project. Over the following pages, I will cover all of the different workspaces—the defaults and the ones opened via an iMovie tool. Figure 13–6 is a breakdown of the major elements found in the iMovie workspace.

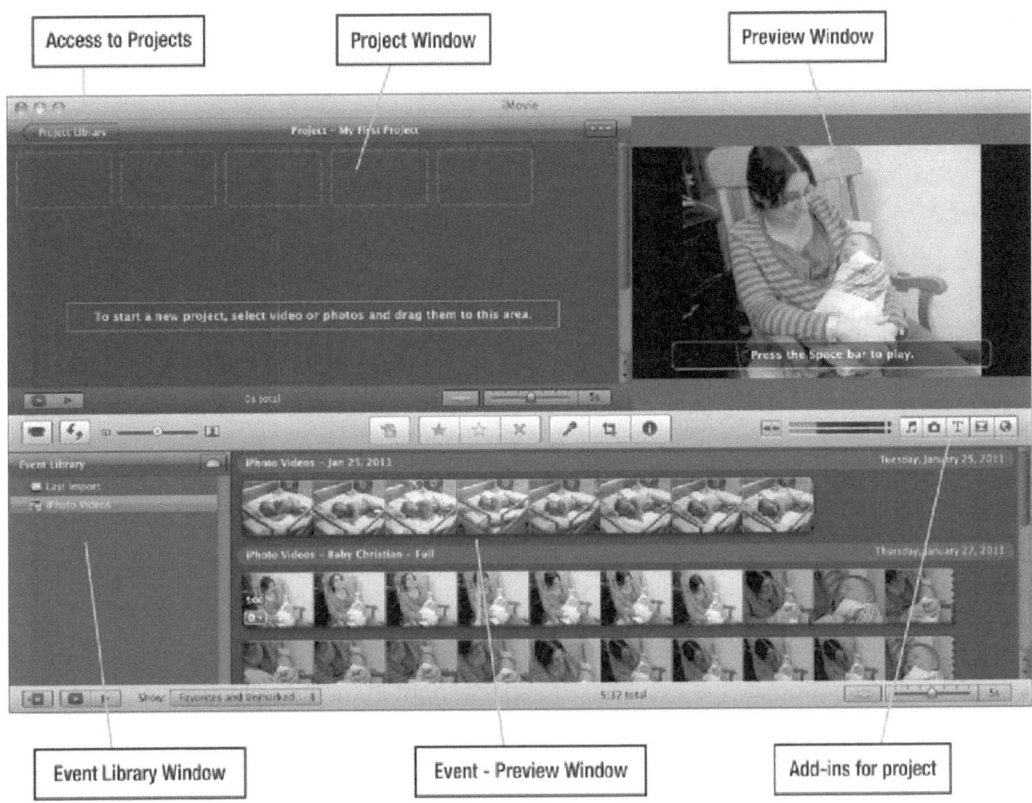

Figure 13–6. *Major elements of the iMovie workspace*

Project Window

This section is where all of your video editing takes place. In Figure 13–1, I had not yet added any movie clips into my new project. Notice that, inside the **Project** window shown in Figure 13–6, it tells me to drag any video or photos into this screen to get started.

> **NOTE:** I could not get videos from my hard drive to automatically drag into the **Project** window. You must import the movies via the **Import Movies** command from the **File** menu. This places the clip into the **Event Library**, not the **Project** window.

To add clips to the **Project** window, highlight the section of a video you want from the **Event—Preview** window and the section is then designated by a rectangular border. Moving this border to the left or right will determine how many frames and the amount of time you want to import. This is shown in Figure 13–7. Either drag the selected clip into the **Project** window or just click on the **Add to Project** button ![] located between the **Project** window and the **Event—Preview** window.

Figure 13–7. *Selecting a section of video that you want to add to the **Project** window from the **Event - Preview** window*

Other Elements Around the Project Window Workspace

There are quite a few other options found around this workspace, from previewing your project clip and showing the audio portion of your video to changing the size of the video snapshot. These items are described here:

10s total On the bottom of the **Project** workspace, right in the middle, is a clock displaying how long your video runs.

This button at the very top right-hand corner toggles between two timelines. One is single row and the second is multiple rows. Multiple rows cuts the timeline into sections going down your workspace instead of across your screen.

This starts the action in the timeline. A red bar moves along the timeline and indicates which location in the clip is currently playing.

This previews the movie in full-screen mode.

This button shows or hides the audio waveforms. It makes the different elements more pronounced in your project.

2s This changes the number of thumbnails displayed in the **Project** window. Slide it to the right to see more thumbnails and slide it to the left to see fewer.

This buttons allows you to switch the default locations of the **Project** window and **Events**. This is useful if you are creating a long video, as the bottom section (**Event Library** and **Event—Preview** window) is longer than the top section. This is because the **Preview** window takes up part of the top section of the iMovie workspace.

This slider allows you to increase the size or decrease the size of the video snapshots in your project.

Access to Projects—Project Library

By clicking on the **Projects Library** button at the very top of your **Project** window, you bring up a sidebar showing all of your projects. This is shown in Figure 13–8. Notice that it gives a visual preview of the project, the name(s) of your projects, the length of the project in minutes and seconds, and finally, tells you when your project was last modified. Highlight the project you want to use and click on the **Edit Project** button found in the upper left-hand corner of this window.

Figure 13–8. *Project Library* window

Preview Window

This is a small window that shows the results of all your editing. To start a preview in this window only, click on the black triangle pointing to right found at the bottom of the project window.

If you want to preview the end result in a full screen environment, click on the grey arrow pointing to right surrounded by a black oval . The Crop tool options only shows up in the Preview window. The options available with the tool are found in the next chapter as some items are more advanced then material covered in this introductory chapter.

Event Library Window

This window shows all of the videos imported in iPhoto. If you import the movie via the **File ➤ Import Video** command, the video will appear inside this window below the year it was made. By default, it is called **New Event**. If you double-click on the title, you can rename it. This is recommended if you are going to add many videos into iMovie. This screen is shown in Figure 13–9.

Figure 13–9. *Adding a video via the File ➤ Import command*

At the bottom right of this workspace are three important buttons. The first two deal with previewing your clips and the third allows you to hide or show this window.

 This **Preview** button in the **Preview** window is also found at the bottom of the **Event Library** window. However, this previews all of your clips in the **Event—Preview** window.

If you want to preview the end result in a full-screen environment, click on the grey arrow surrounded by a black oval .

 This button hides or displays the **Event Library** window.

Event—Preview Window

In the example shown in Figure 13–1, the videos in this section are from iPhoto. iPhoto does not perform video editing, but it is a good place to store videos, because other iLife applications can see them in it. If you have already added videos into iPhoto, the screen shown in Figure 13–10 will appear. iMovie creates thumbnails or "snapshots" at various moments of your videos. This screen is just telling you that iMovie will create these snapshots for all of your videos in iPhoto.

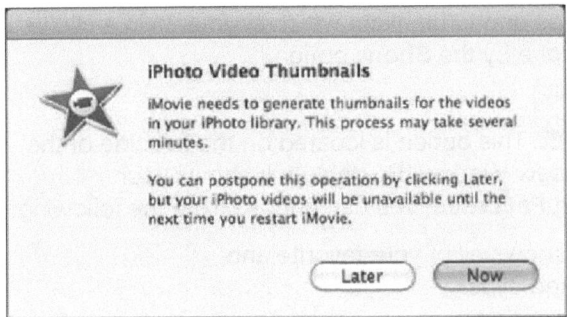

Figure 13–10. *Creating thumbnails for all of your videos found in your **iPhoto** library*

Figure 13–11 shows a sample of the **Event—Preview** window. In this example, I have two different iPhoto elements: **Jan 25, 2011** and **Baby Christian—Full**.

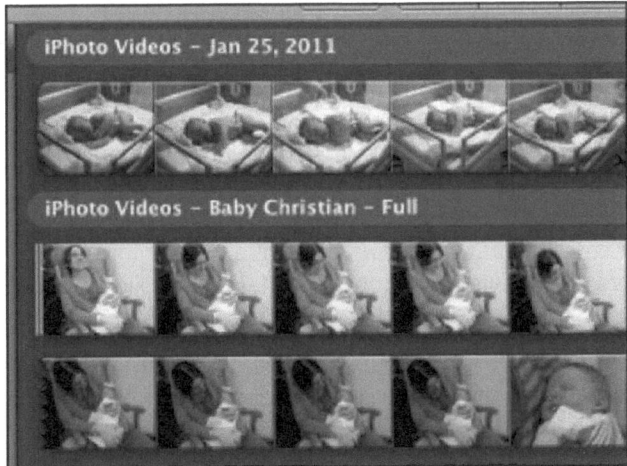

Figure 13–11. *Example of videos in the **Event—Preview** window*

Knowing Which clips from the Event—Preview window are in Your Project

After you have added the section you want to the **Project** window, you will see an orange line at the bottom of the clip (see Figure 13–12). (Note that in the screenshot this line appears black.)

Figure 13–12. *Example of the orange line signifying that the clip is your **Project** window*

iMovie makes it easy to organize your clips and to highlight which segments in a clip you are sure to use or not to use. This is all done by the **Show:** option.

 This option is located on the left side of the screen at the bottom of the **Event—Preview** window. By default, it shows your **Favorites and Unmarked**. If you click on **Favorites**, you can choose from the following:

- **Favorites and Unmarked:** This shows all of your favorite and unmarked clips, except for rejected clips.

- **Favorites Only:** This shows only the clips you chose as favorites. This is very useful if you have hours of video and only small sections are worthy of adding to your final project. When you choose this option, only your favorites will appear in the **Event—Preview** window.

- **All Clips:** This shows every second of every video in every event you added. This is useful if you want to see everything.

- **Rejected Clips:** This only shows the clips you selected and marked as **Rejected**. This is useful, as it allows seeing the items again; they are not deleted, they are just not shown. These clips are also included if you select the **All Clips** option.

This information bar is shown at the bottom of the **Event—Preview** window. It contains the following four items:

- **Time of all media in this window:** In the previous example, the total time of all my clips is 5:37. That is five minutes and 37 seconds.

- **View Audio Waveforms** : This displays a graphical representation of the audio found in your clips.

- **Frames Per Thumbnail** : This changes the amount of frames that are previewed in your workspace.

- This corner handle is new, but I mentioned it in previous chapters. You use it to make your complete iMovie environment larger or smaller by clicking and holding your mouse on its handle.

Marking/Unmarking Clips As Favorites or Rejecting a Clip

Marking clips makes editing your project much easier—especially if you have a lot of video clips. You can highlight favorites you know you want to use or reject video that just did not cut it.

 Highlight the section of the video that you want to mark as a favorite. Click on the black star button located below the **Project** window. A green line at the top of the clip will appear in your video signifying what portion is a favorite. This is shown in Figure 13–13 (although in the screenshot the line appears black).

Figure 13–13. *The green line that appears showing sections selected as favorites*

This button—a grey star—deselects a segment as a favorite. You do not have to select the exact beginning and exact ending—just highlight the area around the favorite.

Want to make a ton of video that you don't presently need disappear from the screen? Highlight the sections that are not needed and click on this button. Then make sure that you choose **Favorites and Unmarked** or just **Favorites** next to **Show:**. Two or three hours of unwanted video will be gone from your screen. This is very useful as you use more and more videos for your projects. A red line at the top of the clip signifies the unwanted clip if you choose an option that shows rejected clips. This is shown in Figure 13–14.

Figure 13–14. *Example of the red line that appears showing what video is rejected*

Add-ins for your Movies

There are five items in this section of the iMovie workspace: **Music and Sound Effects**, **Photo Browser**, **Title Browser**, **Transition Browser**, and last - **Maps, Background and Animatics**. I will cover each over the following pages.

■ **Music and Sound Effects** is shown Figure 13–15.

Figure 13–15. *Music and Sound Effects* add-in

To add an item, drag it to the location you want in the **Project** window. This is shown in Figure 13–16.

Figure 13–16. *Example of a sound effect being added to your movie*

Please notice that I added the sound effect **Big Waterfall** and that it lasts for six seconds (**6s**). It was originally longer. To edit the length of sound effects, click on the end of the clip and drag it to the length of your choice.

■   The **Photo Browser** is shown Figure 13–17.

Figure 13–17. *Photo Browser add-in*

With this tool, you can add photos to your movie. It contains your iPhoto library, MobileMe galleries, and Facebook galleries. As with audio, drag the selected item to the location of your choice. In Figure 13–18, I inserted a photo into my movie clip. It is a picture of a flower on a window. Please notice that iMovie separated it from the video by placing a wide gap between the photo and video clips.

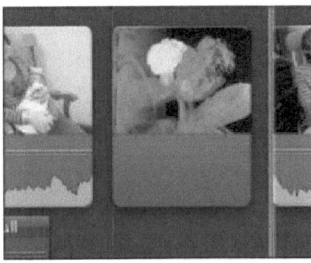

Figure 13–18. *Example of a photo inserted between two video clips*

NOTE: I have **Show Audio Waveforms** turned on. This is done by clicking on the **Waveform** button [image] found on the bottom right-hand corner of the **Project** window. This makes it easier to determine which elements are movies and which elements are photos. It will turn blue if it is on [image].

■   The **Title Browser** [T] is Figure 13–19.

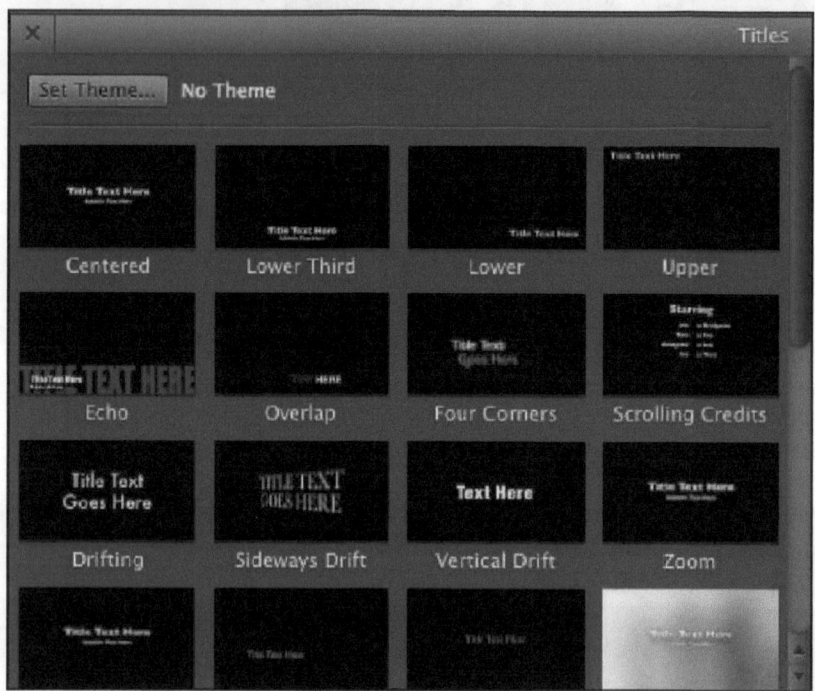

Figure 13–19. *Title Browser* add-in

You can add a title anywhere in your video. Just drag a selected theme to the location of your choice. You have 32 options to choose from. I have to say it again: explore the options and have fun trying each one.

■   The **Transition Browser** [image] is shown in Figure 13–20.

You can add transitions between elements in your movie. You can fade to black between two scenes, for example. Again, you can add transitions anywhere you like. You have 24 to choose from. As you can see by now, adding elements is pretty easy...choosing the best element for the job is the hard part, and that's up to you.

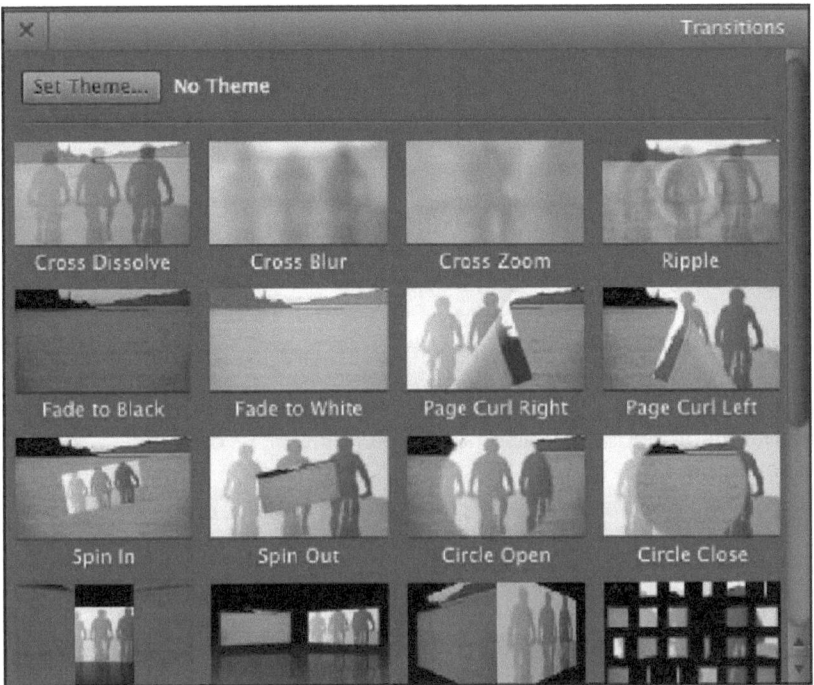

Figure 13-20. *Transition Browser add-in*

Maps, Background, and Animatics 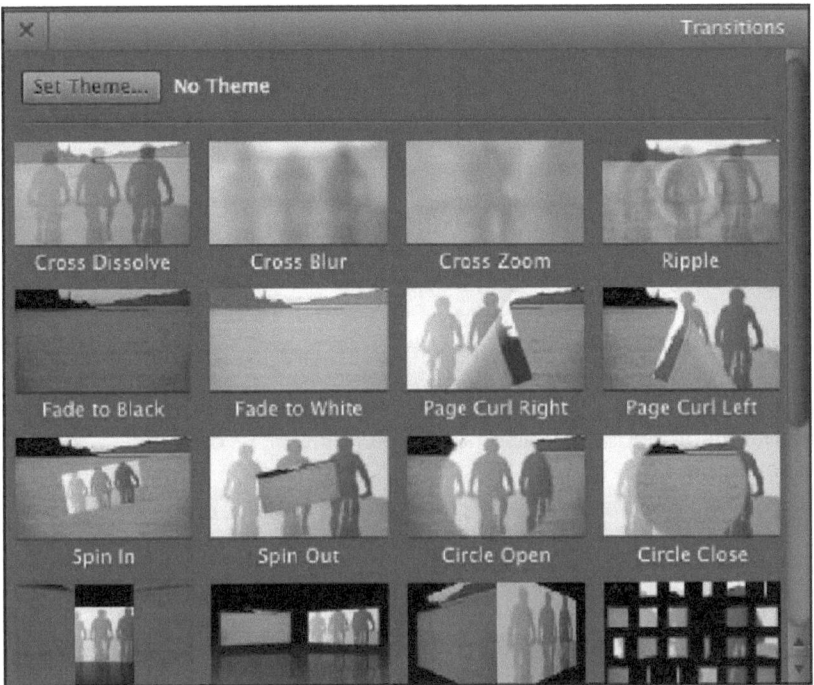 also includes **Globes**. These are useful as elements behind titles. They allow you to provide stunning animation or an appropriate graphic to go behind an otherwise boring title page in your movie.

- **Globes and Maps:** You can choose between eight animated objects or four stills (see Figure 13-21).

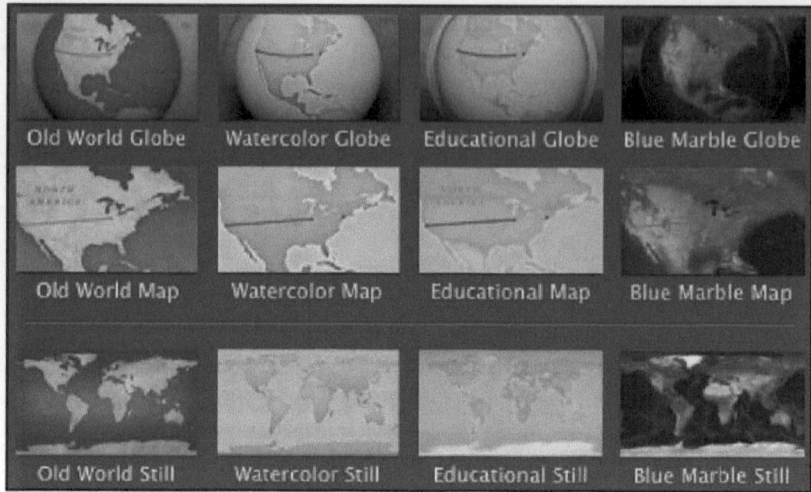

Figure 13–21. *Animated globes, maps, and stills*

■ **Backgrounds: Curtain**, **Organic**, **Blobs**, and **Underwater** are animated backgrounds. You also have the choice of 12 colored stills (see Figure 13–22).

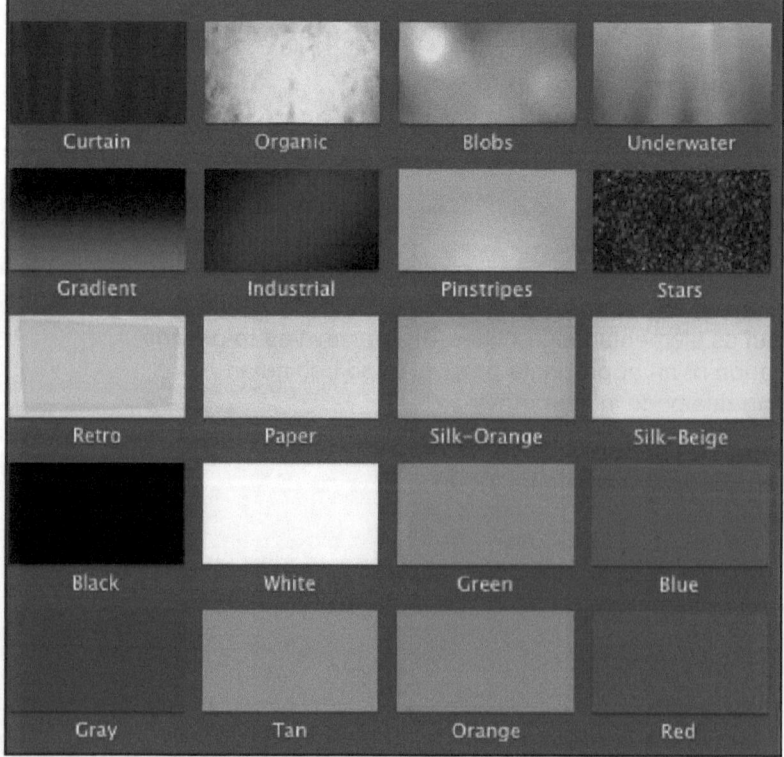

Figure 13–22. *Available backgrounds*

■ **Animatics:** These simply allow you to plan your final video by adding a sample representation of a person, group, or animal to be replaced later by the actual item—a specific person group or animal (see Figure 13–23). Consider it a digital placeholder.

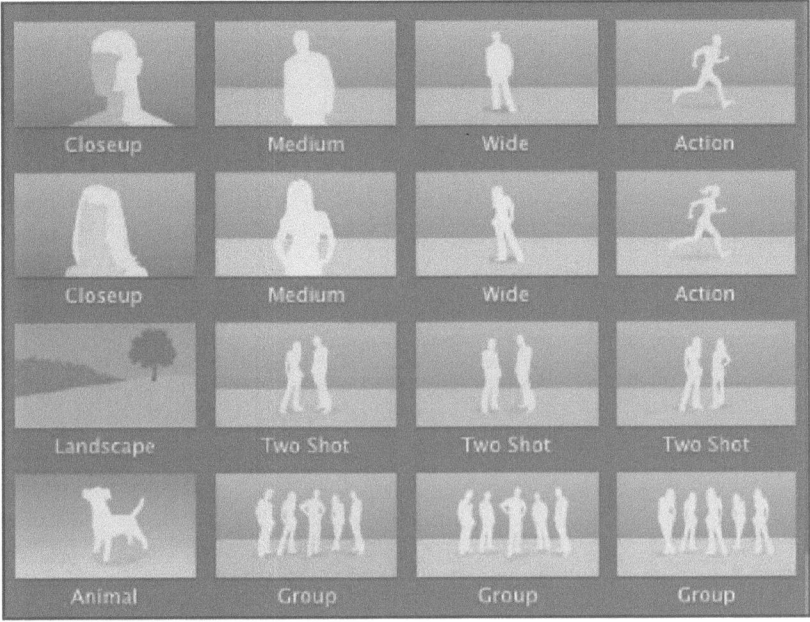

Figure 13–23. *Animatics add-ins*

That about covers the major elements of all of the iMovie workspaces. Now, I want to cover a couple of items not yet mentioned: the Camera button, and the Voiceover button. More advanced features will be covered in Chapter 14: "The Inspector, Ken Burns, the Gear Button, and Other Useful Advanced Tools of iMovie."

Importing Live Video or Accessing a Video Camera

The **Camera Import** button allows you to use your built-in iSight camera (all newer Macs and Apple laptops have one at the top center section of your unit).This button is located in the middle of your workspace—at the far left.

To insert a video from an iSight camera, follow these steps:

1. Click the **Camera Import** button .

2. You will then see the screen shown in Figure 13–24.

Figure 13–24. *Initial video capture screen of iMovie*

Please notice the following items on the screen:

- **Video Size:** You can change the video size from the default of 640 × 480 to 1024 × 576 via the dropdown menu next to **Video Size**. This is located toward the middle at the bottom of this screen.

- There is a large timeframe counter directly below your video being shot. This will start at zero and increase as the video is being recorded. Please also notice the tiny letters **REC** and the red dot are two other visual clues that you are actually recording video. An example of video being captured is shown in Figure 13–25.

Figure 13–25. *Example of timeframe counter while recording, and the **Stop** button*

- **Capture...**: Click on this to start the recording process.

- **Stop** (shown in Figure 13–25: This will cease the video recording.

- **Done**: This closes the video capture screen.

■ **Camera**: The default is your built-in camera. If you attach an external camera, that camera will become a choice in dropdown menu next to **Camera**.

3. Click **Capture...**: This will bring up the screen shown in Figure 13–26.

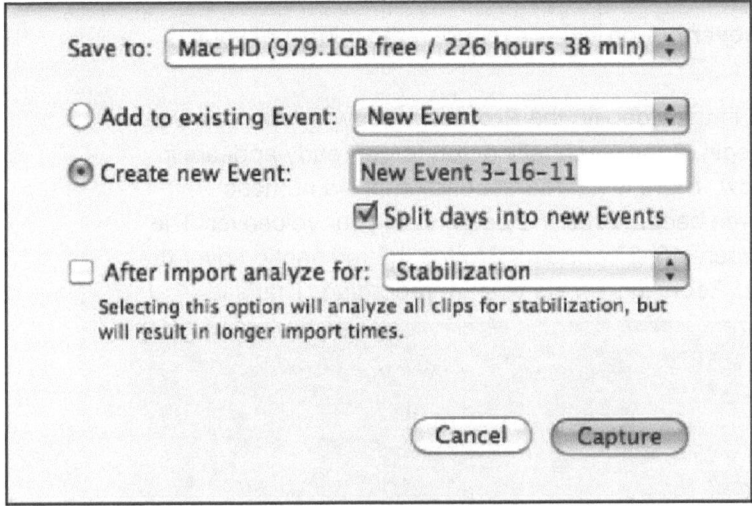

Figure 13–26. *Capture options available recording video via an iSight camera or external camera*

Fill in the following fields:

■ **Save to:** This is where your Mac will save the imported video. Notice that it also gives the amount of free space available (movie files can be massive) to save your movie and the amount of time this space gives you (226 hours and 38 min, in this example).

■ **Add to existing Event:** This will add the newly recorded video to an event you already created in iMovie. If you have more than one event, click on the event name shown and choose it from the pop-up menu.

■ **Create new Event:** This will create a brand new event. You can name the event next to this option and decide if you want to split days into new events.

■ **After import analyze for:** Choose from **Stabilization** (default), **Stabilization and People**, or just **People**. Notice that it is not on by default and that import times will increase if selected.

4. After you made your choices, click on **Capture** [Capture] to begin the actual recording.

5. Click on **Stop** [Stop] to end the recording process.

Adding a Voiceover to Your Video

Follow these two simple steps process to add a voiceover:

1. Click on the **Voiceover** button [icon] found in the middle of your screen.

2. Click on the frame in the video (in the **Project** window) where you want the voiceover to begin. A message telling you to get ready appears in the **Preview** window. There is a three-second timer—a numeric countdown and three beeps. After the beep, start your voiceover. The screen shown in Figure 13–27 appears. Notice the red section over the video and the word **Recording** while you are recording. That's it.

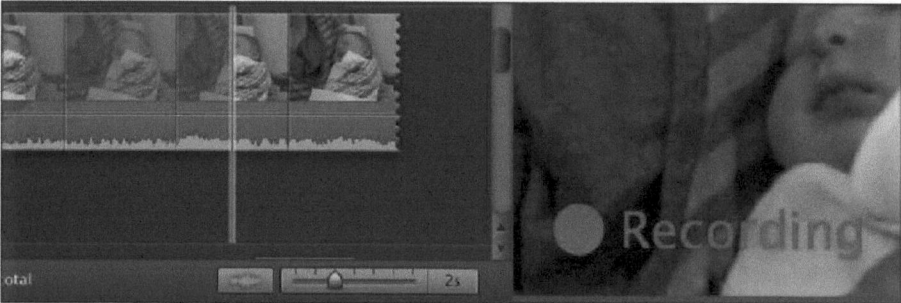

Figure 13–27. *Example of visual cues showing you are recording a voiceover*

To stop recording, click the spacebar on your keyboard.

Figure 13–28 shows the options you need to select from before you record.

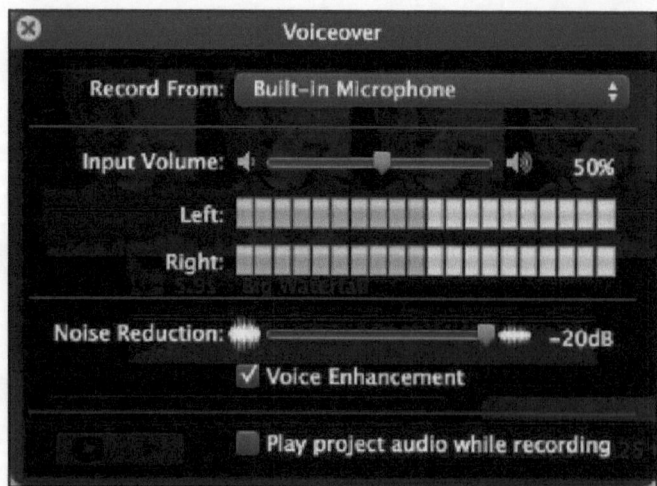

Figure 13–28. *Audio options for adding a voiceover*

These options are:

- **Record From:** This can be your built-in microphone or an external device.

- **Input Volume:** Depending on where or what you are recording, you might have to adjust the input volume in order to get a higher quality voiceover.

- **Left: / Right:** This shows you the volume for the left and right side.

- **Noise Reduction:** If you have the **Voice Enhancement** checkbox checked (the default), this will enhance voice recordings. You can adjust the enhancement by sliding the grey object in the slider next to **Noise Reduction** to the left or right.

- **Play project audio while recording:** Check the box next to this option if you want the audio previously added or found in your clip to play when you record your voiceover.

Sharing Your Movie

You have many options for sharing your work with iMovie, all of which are found in the **Share** menu. This is covered in detail in Chapter 15: "Calling the Shots with the iMovie Menus."

Summary

I started this chapter by explaining that you can create movies or trailers either by using presets or by starting from scratch. I then moved on to introduce the key workspaces and several supporting buttons around these workspaces. This chapter was a good overview to get you started exploring this powerful and easy to use program. As you will see in coming chapters, iMovie has a plethora of advanced features to help you turn your home movies into professional quality films.

iMovie Advanced Features: The Inspector, Ken Burns Effect, and More

In the previous chapter, I discussed the various workspaces of iMovie and the tools that support each. That was a good starting point from which we will now delve deeper into the more complex built-in features of iMovie, such as the **Inspector**, **Ken Burns Effect**, **Gear** button, and other tools. Becoming a master editor can take some time. iMovie has the features you need, but be patient while learning all that it available to edit your project. It will be worth it. Spielberg started small as well! Let's start with the **Inspector** tool.

The Inspector

The Inspector tool can be accessed two ways. The first is to click on the **Inspector** button located in the middle of the screen, just below the **Preview** window. The second way is to access it via the **Gear** button.

That's right: the Inspector and Gear tool do almost the same thing. The **Gear** button includes the Inspector features plus other items, like the **Cropping & rotation** option or the **Precision Editor**, depending when you access it. The **Gear** button appears on the left side of any clip you click on. Toward the end of this chapter, I will go over the other functions of the Gear tool.

The Inspector tool has three sections: **Clip**, **Video**, and **Audio**. In the following sections, I will cover these three tabs, followed by the options included within each.

Clip Tab of the Inspector Button

The **Clip** section is shown in Figure 14–1. As you can see, this one little tab contains many options that can be applied to your clip. These options include adding video or audio effects or using advanced tools to change the video image or enhancing the audio. This little button does quite a lot!

Figure 14–1. *Inspector tool—the Clip tab*

Duration

This shows how long the clip is going to play. You can adjust this by changing the time next to word **Duration**. In Figure 14–1, the duration is 7.7 seconds.

Source Duration

This displays the length of the total of all the clips found in the **Event—Preview** window. In Figure 14–1, the total length of the source was 5 minutes and .9 seconds.

Video Effect

You can add 20 different video effects to a highlighted video segment: **None, Flipped, Raster, Cartoon, Aged Film, Film Grain, Hard Light, Day Into Night, Glow, Dream, Romantic, Vignette, Bleach Bypass, Old World, Heat Wave, Sci-Fi, Black & White, Sepia, Negative,** or **X-Ray**. A small example of each is shown in Figure 14–2. A sample of the effect is shown in the **Preview** window when you drag the red timeline indicator over the effect in the effect preview window. The effect only shows up in the **Preview**.

However, a small "I" appears at the far left of the **Project** window when you move the red timeline indicator across the project. This is only way besides watching a preview do you know an effect has been applied.

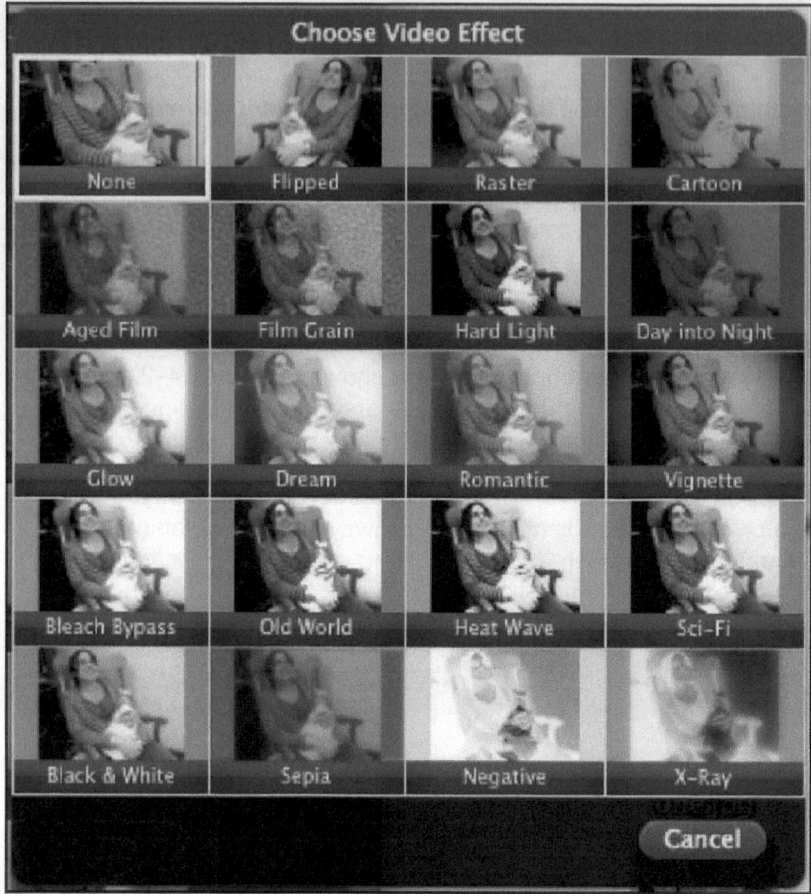

Figure 14–2. *The 20 video effects that can be applied to your video clips*

Audio Effect

Not only can you apply amazing video enhancements to your project, you can also modify the sound. You have 20 choices to choose from. They are: **None, Muffled, Robot, Cosmic, Echo, Telephone, Shortwave Radio, Multi-tune, Small Room, Medium Room, Large Room, Cathedral, Pitch Down (1 — 4),** and **Pitch Up (1-4).** In Figure 14–3, we see all these choices and a nifty little picture showing what each effect does.

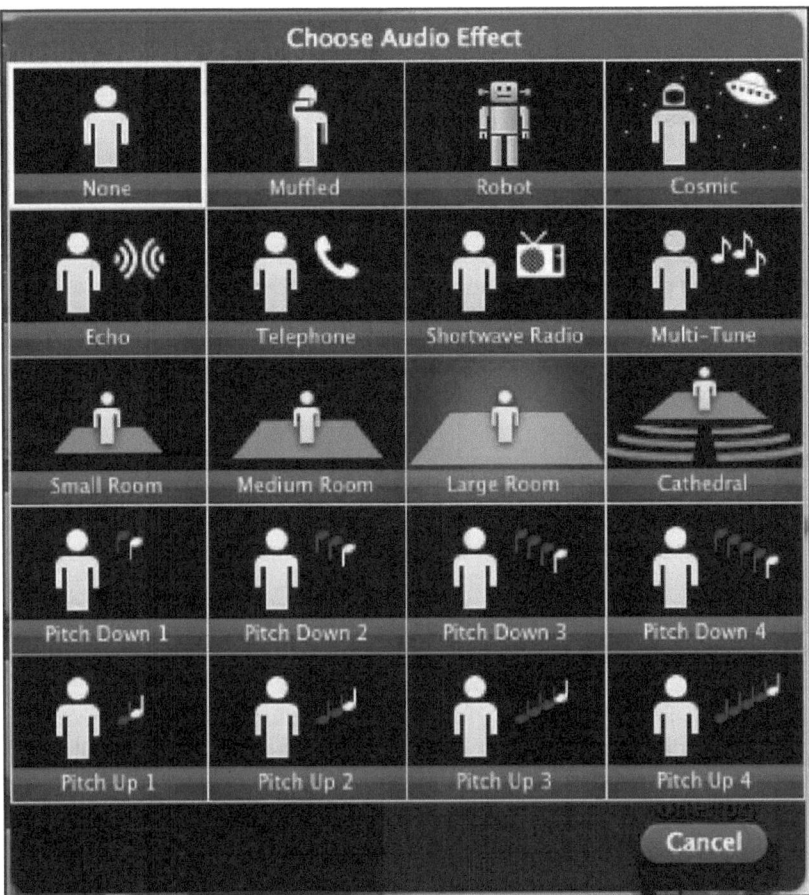

Figure 14–3. *The 20 audio effects that can be applied to your video clips*

Once again, I encourage you to explore all the options. You are only limited by your imagination…(and time you have to experiment).

Speed

You can speed up or slow down the speed of your clip or even play it in reverse. In Figure 14–1, we see that we first must convert this clip for this tool to be applied. After it has been coverted, the screen in Figure 14–4 then appears inside the Inspector window.

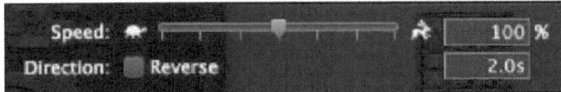

Figure 14–4. *Speed options found in the **Clip** tab of the **Inspector** button. (Clip has been converted.)*

Move the slider toward the turtle (left) to slow it down, or toward the Rabbit (right) to speed it up. To the left of the Rabbit is an indicator of the change being applied (400 x for increased speed, or 50% for slower speed for example). Below that is the amount of time the clip is now (2.0s in this example). It would increase if you slow it down and decrease if you speed it up. A small Turtle or Rabbit icon will appear on the far left of the clip in the Project window if this is applied.

Stabilization

This is a technique to help you remove unwanted shaking that occurred during the filming of your clips. A red squiggly line will appear in the clip if this is applied.

Maximum Zoom

This allows you to zoom in or zoom out on the video clip.

Rolling Shutter

If the box next to **Reduce motion distortion** is unchecked, you also reduce the shaking of video taken. There is a drop-down menu below this check box. It determines how the correction is going to applied. The choices are **None**, **Low**, **Medium**, **High**, and **Extra High**. Apple recommends **Medium** for most consumer camcorders and **Extra High** for flip-type camcorders or video taken from a phone.

Done

Click on this after you have made (or not made) any changes.

Video Tab of the Inspector Button

The **Video** tab (see Figure 14–5) is another reason I love iMovie and iLife. With it, an amazing project can be done in no time (with a little background supplied by this manual) or taken to perfection by giving the user tools to really customize and enhance everything in the project.

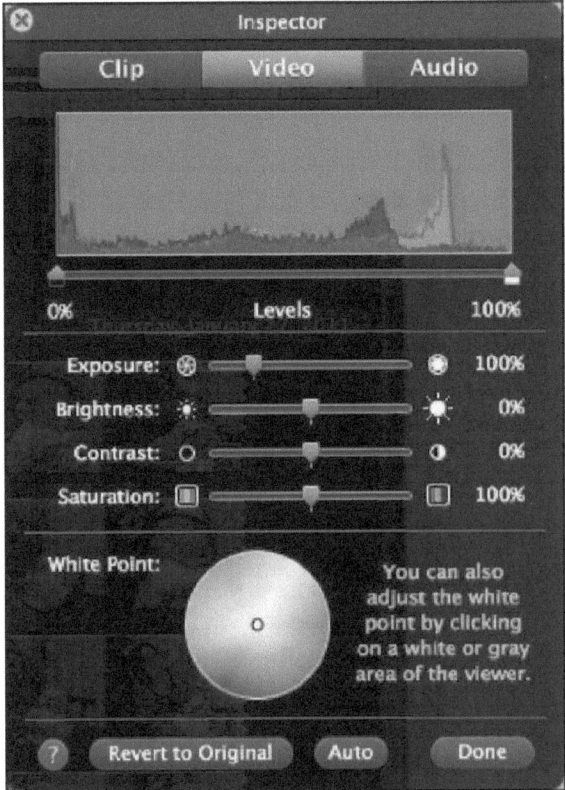

Figure 14–5. *Video tab of the Inspector button*

The **Video** tab is not for the general, casual user, but it might come in handy some day. The first item is a visual graph. This graph helps you determine and change, if you wish, the black and white in your clip. To adjust this, move the slider labeled **Levels** to the left increase black and to the right to increase white in your clip. If you apply a video

adjustment, a little star icon ![icon] will appear on the far left of the selected clip in the Project window.

The next section, you are given the following four variables to adjust via a slider:

- **Exposure:** Changes the shadows and highlights. Moving the slider to the right intensifies the highlights.

- **Brightness:** Changes the overall light level. Moving the slider to the right makes the image lighter.

- **Contrast:** Changes the relative contrast of light and dark tones. Moving the slider to the right makes edges between light and dark areas more robust.

- **Saturation:** Changes the color intensity. Dragging the slider to the right makes the colors deeper and dragging the slider all the way to the left makes the image black and white.

> **TIP:** If you turn on **Advanced** tools in the **General** tab of the **Preferences...** window found in the **iMovie** menu, you are given three more choices. These are shown in Figure 14–6. Moving the sliders to the right makes each selected color more intense.

Figure 14–6. *Additional items to modify if you turned on **Advanced** tools*

Other options include:

- **White Point**: This is the other way of changing the colors in your project. This is done by changing the color white (called the white balance). You can either click on different spots inside the circle  to effect a change or by clicking on a white or grey area in the **Preview** window, which also resets the white point.

- **Purple Question Mark** (bottom Left of window): This brings up the help section for this window from the **iMovie** help tool.

- **Revert to Original**: Don't like the changes you made? Click on this button and all changes made are cancelled.

- **Auto**: This also brings it back to the way iMovie originally displayed your clip.

- **Done**: Click on this after you have made (or not made) any changes.

Audio Tab of the Inspector Button

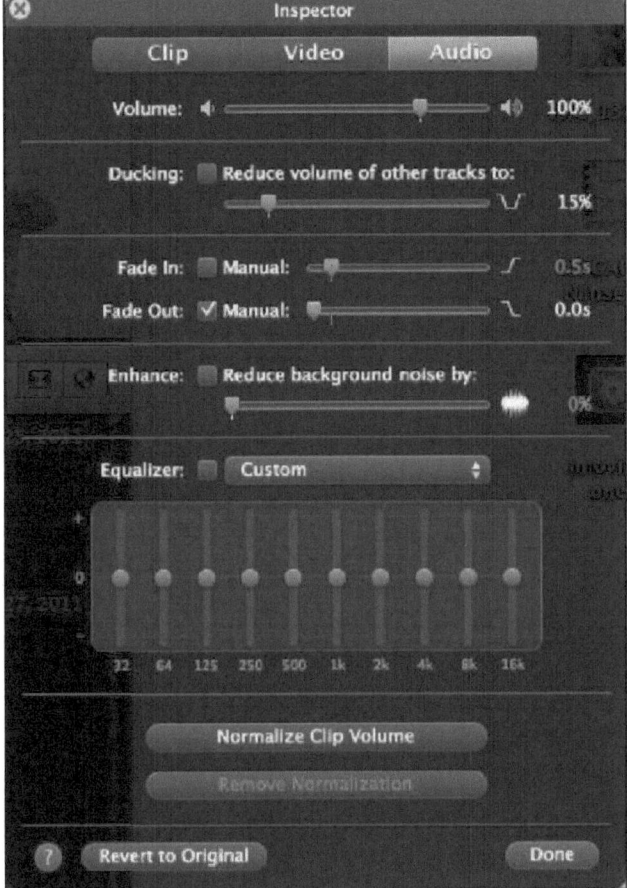

Figure 14–7. *Audio* tab of the *Inspector* button

- **Volume:** This determines the overall sound volume of your clip. It is adjusted by a slider. The default is 100%.

- **Ducking:** Ducking allows you to reduce the volume of other audio items in your project. To turn it on, you must check the box next to **Reduce volume of other tracks to:**. The default is 15%, but it can as high at 100% (no other sounds).

- **Fade In:** This is off by default. It allows you to gradually add the selected sound item into your clip. Click the check box next to **manual** and then select the time frame for the **Fade IN**. The default is .5 seconds. It is adjusted by moving a slider control to the left and right.

- **Fade Out:** This is the opposite of **Fade In**. This determines how the sound selected ends in your selected clip. It is also off by default. You can also adjust it with a slider.

- **Enhance:** This item attempts to make your primary audio in your clip (usually voices) by reducing background noise. To adjust this, you must check the box next to **Reduce background noise by:**. You adjust this setting by moving a slider to the left (down to 0%) or up to no background noise (100%).

- **Equalizer:** This allows you to customize certain audio frequencies to one of several sets included. It is off by default. You can choose Custom or one of the following, shown in Figure 14–8.

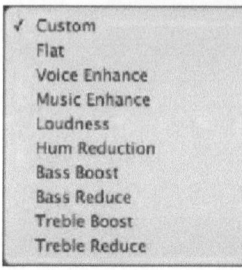

Figure 14–8. *Available equalizer settings*

- **Normalize Clip Volume / Remove Normalization:**. When you click on the **Normalize Clip Volume** button, iMovie calculates the volume change required to make the loudest part of the selected clip to its maximum listening volumes without causing distortion. All other audio is then adjusted to match this calculated level.

- **Purple Question Mark** (bottom Left of window): This brings up the help section for this window from the iMovie help tool.

- **Revert to Original:** Don't like the changes you made? Click on this button and all changes made are cancelled.

- **Done:** Click on this after you have made (or not made) any changes.

Ken Burns Effect

The Ken Burns Effect is a simple but stunning addition to your video. This effect is named after Ken Burns, who is a director and producer of documentary films. His projects were innovative in the way they showed archival material. One of his effects in these films became so famous they named it after him. It can be applied to basically any item you add to your project. I personally think it looks the best on photos only. It allows you to pan and zoom around a selected object.

The steps to add a Ken Burns Effect are as follows:

1. Click on the **Crop** button 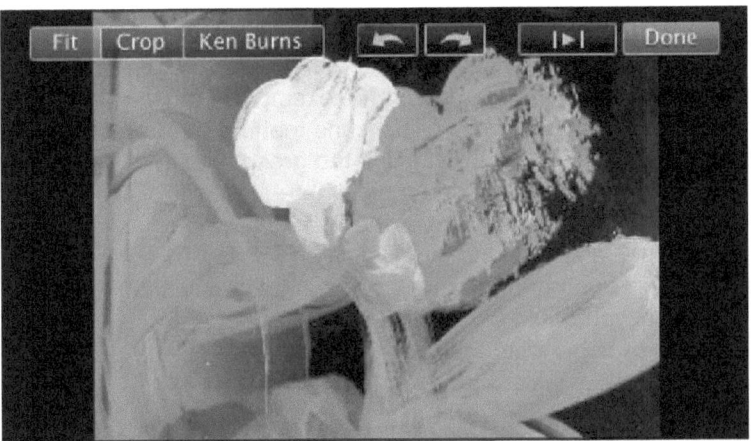. This is located just below the **Preview** window (toward the left.)

2. All other actions take place within the **Preview** window. Your **Preview** screen will now look like Figure 14–9.

Figure 14–9. *Preview window after clicking on the Crop button*

3. Click on the words **Ken Burns**. You will then be given the screen shown in Figure 14–10.

Figure 14–10. *Applying the Ken Burns effect*

You have three decisions to make.

- The first is to decide what the starting screen of the event will be. In Figure 14–10, we see the **Start** area highlighted in green. The arrow pointing to a red X is the center of the image. It might be hard to see, but there are two arrows next to **Start** in this window. If you click on this button, the **Start** and **End** screens are reversed.

- Second, what will the ending screen look like? After you have selected the beginning area, in green, select the ending area, which is in red. Notice that the red area in the example is much larger than the starting (green) area. This means that the photo will first appear centered around the highlighted green area and pan out slowly to the final ending screen highlighted in red. To move either area, move your cursor over the area you want to move and you will see a small hand icon. Click and hold down the mouse button until you find the place you want. If you want to resize either area, you could either click on the four corners and drag it smaller or larger diagonally or click on one the sides to make it taller/shorter or wider/narrower.

- The third option is **Allow Black**. This allows or disallows black borders on the cropped objects in this screen. It is on by default. If you click on it, **Disallow Black** will appear on your screen and the available screen real estate is much larger, as the black area around you item is now included.

4. Click on the **Preview** button ▐►▌ inside the **Preview** window to test out the results.

5. Click on the **Fit** icon ▐ Fit ▌ to disable the Ken Burns Effect you just set. The **Fit** icon makes sure that all of the media in the **Preview** window will be visible in your final movie. The Ken Burns Effect will take your photo or video and potentially cut off the edges of the item the effect is being applied to.

6. Click on **Done** ▐ Done ▌ to apply the effect.

> **NOTE:** You can only adjust the size of the start and end screens to a certain degree. The Ken Burns Effect requires that they be a within certain limits to make the effect look as advertised.

Cropping an Object via the Preview Window

Click on the **Crop** button ⬚. This is located just below the **Preview** window (toward the left). All other actions take place within the **Preview** window. Your **Preview** screen will now look like Figure 14–9.

1. Click on the word **Crop** ⬚ inside the **Preview** window. It is on the top left hand side of the window. You are then presented with the screen shown in Figure 14–11.

Figure 14–11. *Example of the* **Crop** *tool of the* **Crop** *button being used*

2. Whatever is inside the green box shown in Figure 14–11 will be shown in the final project. All other sections will not be shown. You can expand or decrease this area to your liking. As with the Ken Burns Effect, you can only modify to a set minimal and a set maximum area. Also, the option to **Allow Black** is available at the top left of the screen. This expands your workspace as you can now add the black area around the media you are currently working on.

3. Click on the **Preview** button ⬚ inside the **Preview** window to test out the results.

4. Click on the **Fit** icon ⬚ to disable the crop area you just set.

5. Click on Done ⬚ to apply the effect.

Rotating Your Media

You can rotate any item via the **Crop** tool. In the **Preview** window, you can rotate your selected item 90 degrees counter-clockwise by clicking on the arrow pointing to the left ⬅. You can rotate your item 90 degrees clockwise by clicking on the arrow pointing to the right ➡. These arrows are located just about the middle at the top of the **Preview** window. Click on **Done** [Done] to apply the change.

Gear Button

The **Gear** tool gives you access to the three **Inspector** tabs and the **Cropping and Rotation** tools just discussed. It also gives you access to other more advanced workspaces, such as **Precision Editor** and **Clip Trimmer**. I will cover each new workspace next. The key thing to remember is that the Gear options change depending on which object you are working on; a movie, background, or photo. Let's start with a movie.

If you select a clip and click on the **Gear** button (far left of the object's timeline) you are presented with the screen shown in Figure 14–12.

Figure 14–12. *Example of the options available using the Gear tool on a movie clip*

First, notice that the Inspector tabs (**Clip, Video,** and **Audio**) and **Cropping & Rotation** can be accessed here and are located at the bottom of this tool, as well as access to two new workspaces on top (**Precision Editor** and **Clip Trimmer**).

Precision Editor: Video Clips

The **Precision** editor is a powerful tool to help make it easier to modify the points at which one clip transitions into the next object in your project. It can be applied to different elements, such as video clips and transitions.

You can trim or extend frames at the end of one or the beginning of the next object. While using this editor, you can see the clips at either side of the transition, and also see and work with the unused frames of both clips. It allows you to reposition and trim other elements in your project, such as transition animation added between clips, audio elements, titles, voiceovers, and the like. The **Precision** editor takes over the space normally occupied by the **Event Library** and **Event—Preview** windows. This makes removing unwanted video before or after your selected clip a lot easier.

Figure 14–13 shows an example of the **Precision** editor with additional items turned on. To access the add-ons and have them visible, the icons are shown at the top right of the workspace. The line between the two clips is designated by narrow blue line. The shaded areas are frames you are not using.

To change the location where the transition begins and ends after the transition point, click on the clip you want to change. You will then see a small hand. While the mouse button is held, move the clip to the left or right until you reach the new point of transition. If you move the timeframe at top, you change the transition before the transition. If you move the timeframe at the bottom, you change the transition after the transition point.

To reposition the actual transition point, click on the small blue dot between the top and bottom timeframes.

Figure 14–13. *The* **Precision Editor** *window*

When this button is chosen (turns blue), the editor will show all the extras in your project. In the example shown in Figure 14–13, I have one additional item—the title, "Baby Boy."

When this button is chosen (turns blue), the editor will show or hide audio waveforms.

This button will bring you to the previous edit in your project.

This button will bring you to the Next edit in your project.

[▶|] This button will play the current edit in the preview window.

[Done] Click on this button to close the Precision editor and return to the normal workspace environment.

Clip Trimmer: Video Clips

In the example shown in Figure 14–14, we see a large video clip with a small section highlighted with a border. The area in yellow is the section of the video in your project. You can change the starting and ending points of the clip by just clicking then holding your mouse button on edge of the beginning or ending section. Drag it one way to increase or another to decrease the size of the clip. You can also change the whole clip and keep the same amount of time by click and holding your mouse button in the yellow section and then moving the entire yellow area to its new better location.

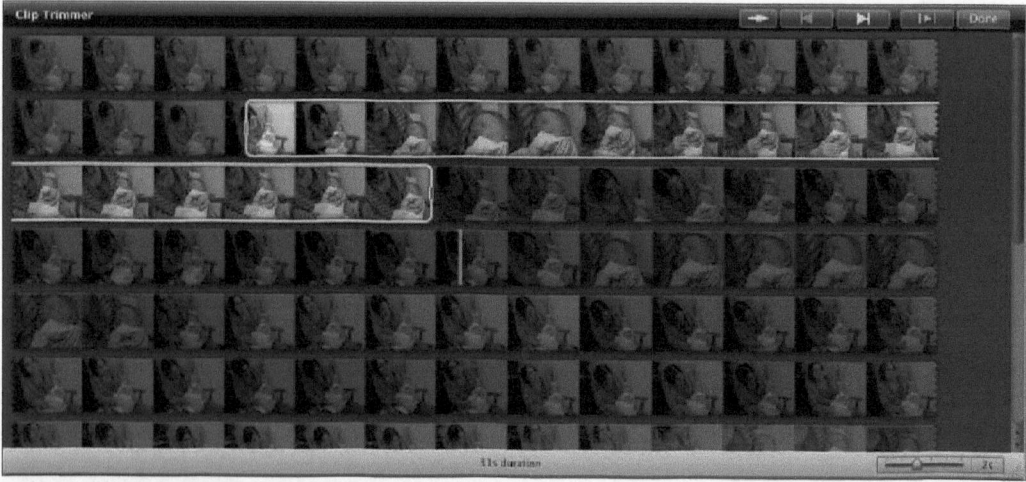

Figure 14–14. Clip trimmer (videos only)

Precision Editor: Transitions

You can also access the **Precision** editor for transitions between project elements. This is also done by clicking on the **Gear** button, but this **Gear** button appears inside the transition clip in your project. This workspace is shown in Figure 14–15. You can adjust the length of the transition by moving the horizontal blues lines in either direction. If you move the left-hand line further to left or move the right-hand line to the right, the transition time will increase. Please note that you can only increase the time of the transition to a set maximum as the actual transition you use can be only set within a certain set of times. As with the precision editor for movies, the grey areas in this workspace represent frames not being utilized.

Figure 14–15. *Example of the **Precision** editor for transitions*

Transition Inspector Window

Figure 14–16. *Inspector window accessed via the **Transition** adjustment feature of the **Gear** button*

You are given several options to customize. They are as follows:

- **Duration:** Set how long the transition is going to be.

- **Applies to all Transitions (check Box):** If you want to apply a new time to all of your transitions at once, check this box.

- **Overlap:** It is set to **All—Maintain Clip Range**. It can also be set to **Half—Maintain Project Duration**.

- **Transition:** Here you can select any one of the available transitions found in iMovie.

The **Gear** button applies to other items as well. This includes backgrounds, photos, and audio. The options available for each item is different. Following is a summary of each.

- **Gear** button options available for **Backgrounds**:

  - **Precision Editor:** Same workspace environment as other elements. Move the Small blue dot in the middle of the screen to the new duration.

- **Clip Adjustments:** Here you can set the duration and choose a new background.

- **Cropping & Rotation:** This brings up all of the tools discussed earlier in the chapter with regards to the **Crop** tool.

- **Gear** button options available for **Photos**:

  - **Precision Editor:** Same workspace environment as other elements. Move the small blue dot in the middle of the screen to the new duration.

  - **Clip Adjustments:** Here you can clip duration and apply it to all stills in your project and add or change a video effect. You also have access to **Video Inspector** via a second tab.

  - **Video Adjustments:** This brings you directly to the **Video Inspector** tool.

  - **Cropping, Ken Burns & Rotation:** Same features as discussed earlier in this chapter.

- **Gear** button options available for **Audio**:

  - **Clip Adjustments:** This brings up a specialized workspace to customize the audio. This is shown in Figure 14–17. It contains all of the elements previously discussed except for the musical note in middle top of the screen. This allows you to add "beat markers" to help to match the audio to the video. Move your mouse over the musical note icon, hold down the mouse button, and drag your cursor to the location you want to add a marker. An example of a beat marker is shown here.

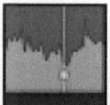

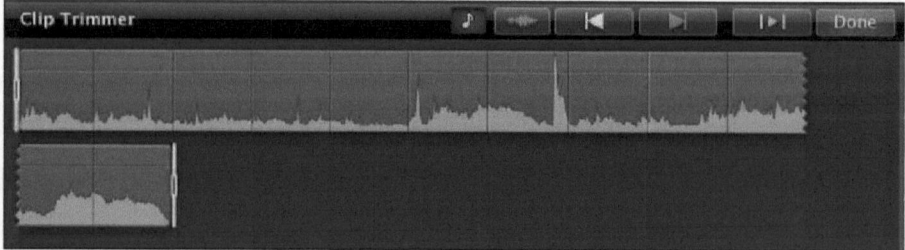

Figure 14–17. *Clip Adjustment workspace for audio*

- **Clip Adjustments:** This brings up the **Audio** and **Clip** tabs of the **Inspector** tool.

■ **Audio Adjustments:** This brings you directly to the **Audio** tab of the **Inspector** tool.

That's it for the new workspaces: the Crop tool, the Ken Burns Effect, and the great **Gear** tool. A lot of options…don't you agree?

Even More Advanced Features Await You

You actually have a lot more to chose from if you activate the Advanced tools. If you go to the **iMovie** menu and choose **Preferences** from the dropdown menu, you can activate via a check box these tools. Here is a brief run-down of what it added to the iMovie experience:

■ Add video to the end of a project just by selecting it in the **Event** browser.

■ Mark video as "favorite," "rejected," or "unmarked" just by selecting it.

■ Tag and filter your video with keywords.

This is done by the magnifying glass icon ▄▄▄ now found next to the **Preview** button under the **Event Library** window. Figure 14–18 shows the new workspace that appears. It shows up between the **Event Library** workspace and the **Event–Preview** window workspace.

Figure 14–18. *Filter by **Keyword** window, available when **Advanced** tools is activated*

To add a keyword, you must first click on the little key icon 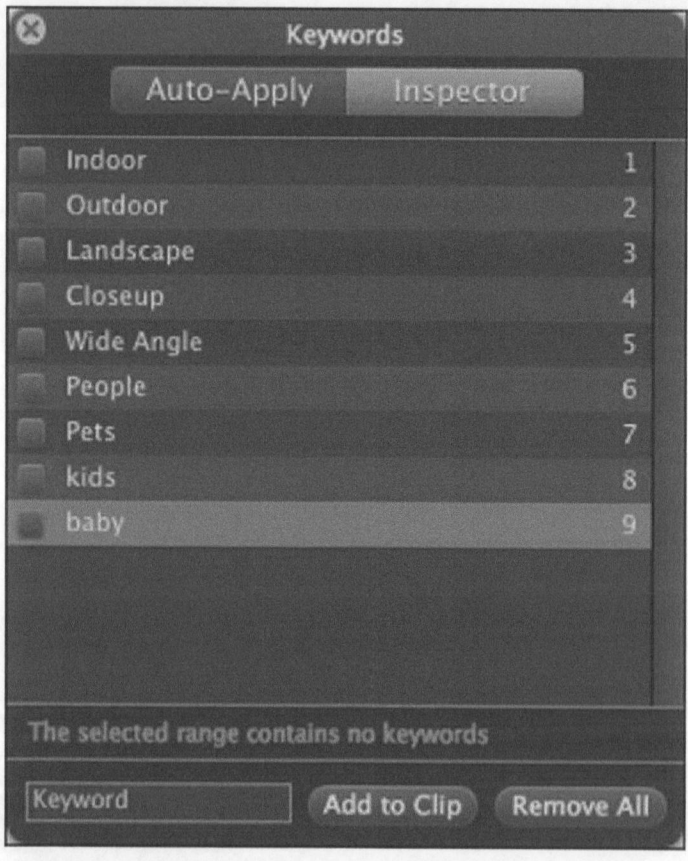,
which is located just left to the **Voiceover** button . If you click on
it, you will see the screen shown in Figure 14–19.

You can click on one of the preset names (**Indoor**, **Outdoor**,
Landscape, and so on) or add your own by clicking your mouse inside
the box that states **New Keyword**. After you have made your
selection, click on **Add** . You are also given the option to
remove a keyword already applied by clicking on **Remove**
in this window.

Figure 14–19. *Adding a keyword to a selected object in your Project*

- Easily replace a clip in your project with an equal length of video from
  a selected Event clip.

- Add chapter markers and comments to your movie projects. These two icons now appear inside the Project window at the top right-hand corner. **Commments** and **Chapter Markers** are added by clicking and holding your mouse on either icon and then dragging your mouse to the spot in your timeline where you want the new element.

> **NOTE:** Chapter Markers are highly useful if you transfer your project to iDVD to create a DVD. With these markers, you can have users "jump" to any marker in your video while viewing your DVD, just like with the commercial DVDs.

- Add cutaway, picture-in-picture, and split-screen (side-by-side) clips.

    - **Cutaway:** This is a clip that you paste on top of another—usually to show two different sides of a single event. Cutaway clips are great for covering parts of unwanted frames, because it covers an equal portion of the video clip you added it to. This means that the entire duration of the final clip doesn't change.

        To add a cutaway, select a video clip from the **Event—Preview** window and drag it over the clip you want it added to. You will then see a white (+) symbol inside a green circle. Release the mouse button at the location you want to add the cutaway. You will then see a window with a ton of choices. This is seen in Figure 14–20.

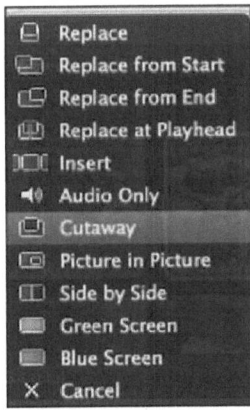

Figure 14–20. *New Insert menu when Advanced tools are turned on. Select Cutaway to add the cutaway segment.*

This is the new **Insert** menu. Remember in the last chapter that this menu just had a few choices. Your timeline will now look like Figure 14–21. The **Cutaway** section is above the original clip and the greyed out areas in the old section is the portion that now will not be seen.

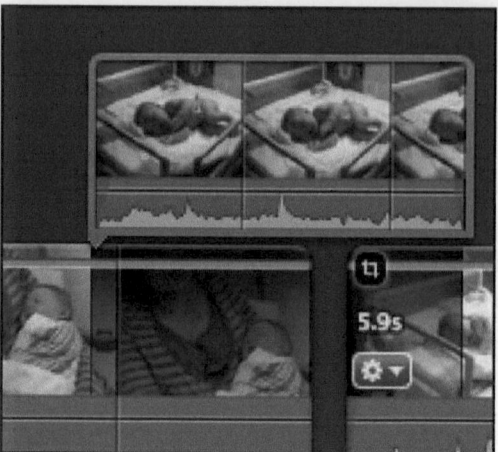

Figure 14-21. *Example of a cutaway added to a video clip*

- **Picture in Picture:** This is also part of the new **Insert** menu. Basically, follow the same procedure as with a cutaway, but select **Picture in Picture** from the **Insert** menu instead. In Figure 14-22, you see the **Preview** window after I have added a second video to be seen at the same time. You can click and hold the mouse button on any of the white corners to make the second embedded or **Second** video smaller or larger. This added video can also be moved in your workspace. Figure 14-23 shows what the timeline looks like in the **Project** window with a **Picture in Picture** inserted. Please notice that is just on top of the original timeline; no frames have been removed in this process.

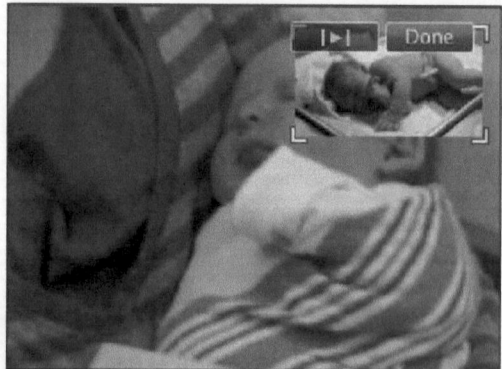

Figure 14-22. *Preview window showing newly added second video embedded in a video clip*

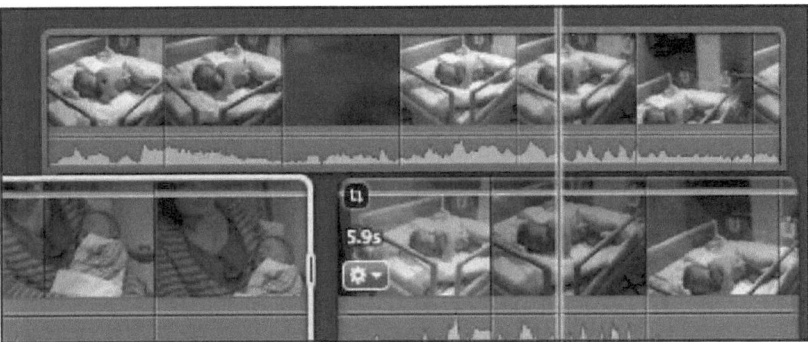

Figure 14–23. *Timeline after* ***Picture in Picture's*** *second video has been added*

- **Side by Side:** As with the first two new insert features, you select the video segment you want to add by dragging to the point in the **Project** window you wish to apply the **Side by Side** effect. Then select **Side by Side** from the new **Insert** menu. Your newly added clip will appear on top of the original clip in the **Project** window. No frames will be removed. In Figure 14–24, we see the **Preview** window with the two video clip playing at the same time—next to each other. I think this really cool. Then again, I think everything Apple makes is really cool.

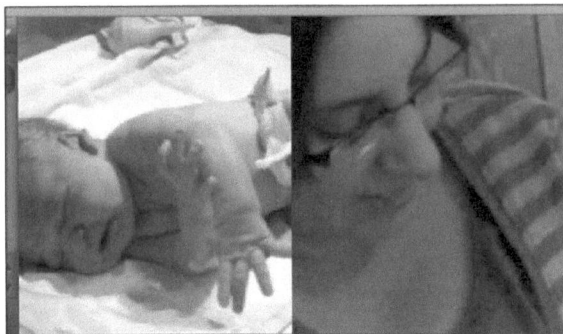

Figure 14–24. ***Preview*** *window showing two video clips playing side by side*

- **Green-screen or Blue-screen effects:** You can use these effects to superimpose video over other video segments or one of iMovies backgrounds. The people or object in the clip must be shot with a green or blue background behind them—nothing else in your video. This option is also available via the newly expanded **Insert** menu. When the original *Superman* movie came out years and years ago, this then-groundbreaking technique was used for all of the flying scenes.

New Replace Options in New Insert Menu

When you activate the **Advanced** tools in iMovie, you are also given three new "replace" commands in the Insert Menu: **Replace from Start**, **Replace from End**, and **Replace at Playhead** (see Figure 14–25).

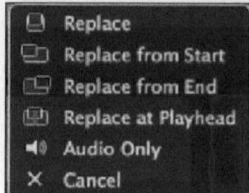

Figure 14–25. *New Replace options in new Insert menu.*

Using the Right-Hand Mouse Button in iMovie

In iMovie, if you right-click on an object, you are presented with a lot choices. All of the options are available via different tools or menus. The right-click just brings a lot them together in one big menu. Figure 14–26 shows the result of right-clicking on a video segment in the **Project** window. The right-click menu is available in many Macintosh programs, but iMovie gives you a lot more options via this step then other applications do.

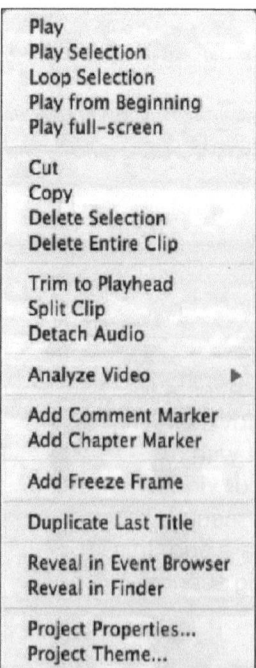

Figure 14–26. *Right-clicking on a video segment in the Project window.*

Summary

The last two chapters should have you well on the way to creating Hollywood's latest blockbuster, and with the skills you've learned you can even make the trailer for it, too. From the simple act of adding video to the Project Window to recording voiceovers to enhance your video, iMovie does not disappoint. There is one piece missing, the menus of iMovie, the coverage of which is coming up in chapter 15 and will conclude this iMovie trilogy. Grab some popcorn and have fun with your new favorite video editing software!

Calling the Shots on the iMovie Menus

In the previous two chapters, we've reviewed many features of iMovie. The final piece of the iMovie trilogy is a discussion of its menus, which contain quite a few important tools not yet discussed, along with others that have been mentioned in passing. As before, let's cover each menu option, moving from left to right across the menu interface.

iMovie Menu

The **iMovie** menu is shown in Figure 15–1. It contains several options, which are discussed in the following sections.

Figure 15–1. iMovie's **File** menu

About iMovie

This is pretty straightforward. It tells you which version of the application you are using.

Preferences…

Preferences… is broken down into four tabs: **General**, **Browser**, **Video**, and **Fonts**.

General Tab

The **General** tab, shown in Figure 15–2, contains items that affect various aspects of the iMovie workspace. As you explore iMovie, please remember that you can access more advanced tools in this tab when you check the **Show Advanced Tools** box.

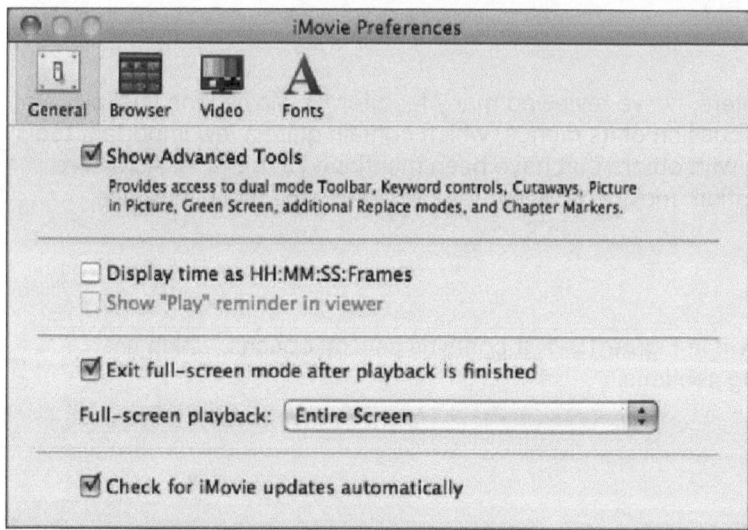

Figure 15–2. *General tab of the Preferences… window*

- **Show Advanced tools:** The new features added to iMovie were discussed in detail in Chapter 14: "iMovie Advanced Features: The Inspector, Ken Burns Effect, and More."

- **Display time as HH:MM:SS:Frames:** This enables more accurate editing because the actual frame you are editing is shown. Remember, there are usually 30 frames per second. Now you can access each of them individually.

- **Show "Play" reminder in viewer:** This feature is supposed to turn on or off the play reminder in the viewer. However, it appears to be disabled and is not available in the current version of iMovie.

- **Exit full-screen mode after playback is finished:** This just returns you to the standard iMovie workspace environment after the movie is previewed in full-screen mode.

- **Full screen playback:** Choose from **Entire Screen** (the default), **Entire screen—Reduced resolution**, **Actual Size**, or **Half Size**.

- **Check for iMovie updates automatically** (the default)**:** When checked, iMovie will search an Apple server for any updates to the program.

Browser Tab

This tab is broken down into four sections. The first and largest section deals with items that either show added information in your project, an option to use project crop settings, or tells you what happens after your imported clip has been analyzed. The other three sections deal with setting keyboard controls in iMovie.

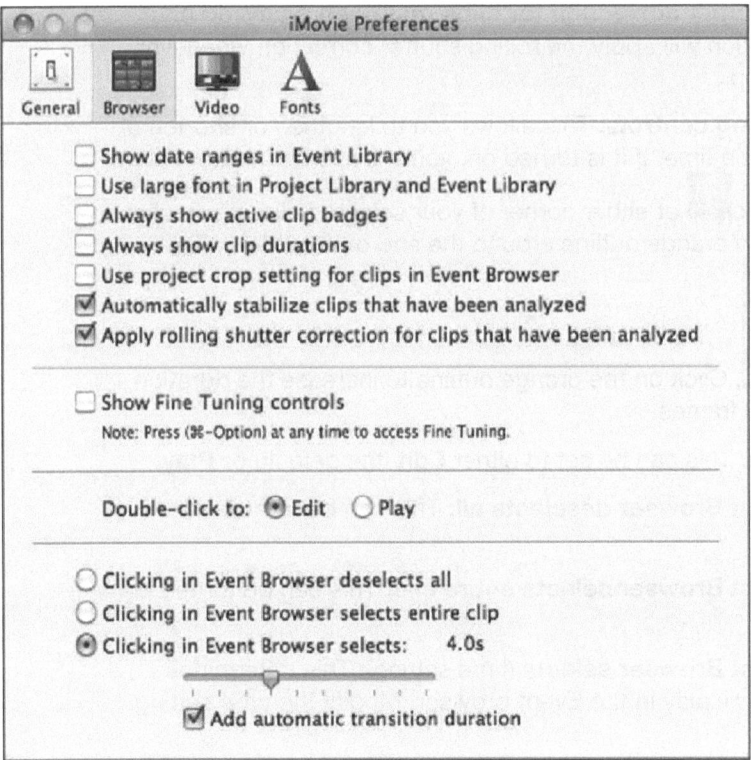

Figure 15–3. *Browser* tab of the *Preferences...* window

- **Show date ranges in Event Library:** This adds the date the video clips were shot below the name of the clip.

- **Use large font in Project Library and Event Library:** This option increases the font size of the text used in these libraries.

- **Always show active clip badges:** Normally, the actions taken or to be taken (gear button) do not show until you select the clip. If you activate this action, you will always see these badges in your clip.

- **Always show clip durations:** If you select this option, the length of each video segment will appear in the left corner of your video clip.

- **Use project crop setting for clips in Event Browser:** This option will set a default project crop setting that will always be applied in the Event Browser.

- **Automatically stabilize clips that have been analyzed** (the default): This option will stabilize your clips whenever you analyze a clip via the **File** menu option. This feature may have unwanted side-effects, such as blurring.

- **Apply rolling shutter correction for clips that been analyzed** (the default): This option will apply the rolling shutter correction whenever you analyze a clip.

- **Show Fine Tuning controls:** This allows you to lengthen or shorten a clip one frame at a time. If it is turned on, you will see two white arrows inside a blue box at either corner of your selected clip. If you click on the arrows, an orange outline around the end of the video will appear . Click on the orange outline to increase the duration plus or minus 30 frames.

- **Double-click to:** This can be set to either **Edit** (the default) or **Play**.

- **Clicking in Event Browser deselects all:** This can be turned on or off.

- **Clicking in Event Browser selects entire clip:** This can be turned on or off.

- **Clicking in Event Browser selects** (time setting)**:** This determines how long a clip will play in the Event browser. Modify the time setting using the slider.

- **Add automatic transition duration** (the default)**:** This can be turned on or off. When it is turned on, each transition you add will be the same length of time.

Video Tab

The **Video** tab only provides you with one option, which is to decide how to import HD video. It is set to **Large** by default (see Figure 15–4), but can also be **Full—Original Size**. Please notice that this setting does not apply to DV or MPEG-2 videos.

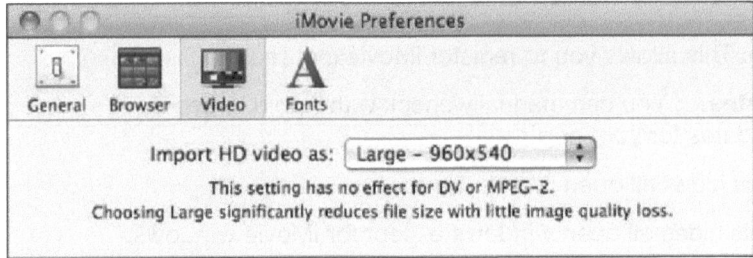

Figure 15–4. *Video tab of the Preferences... window*

Fonts Tab

When you insert a title (at the beginning of your movie for example), you are given the nine default font choices shown in Figure 15–5. The **Fonts** window allows you to customize what fonts and colors you want to use. Click on a font name to apply a font color.

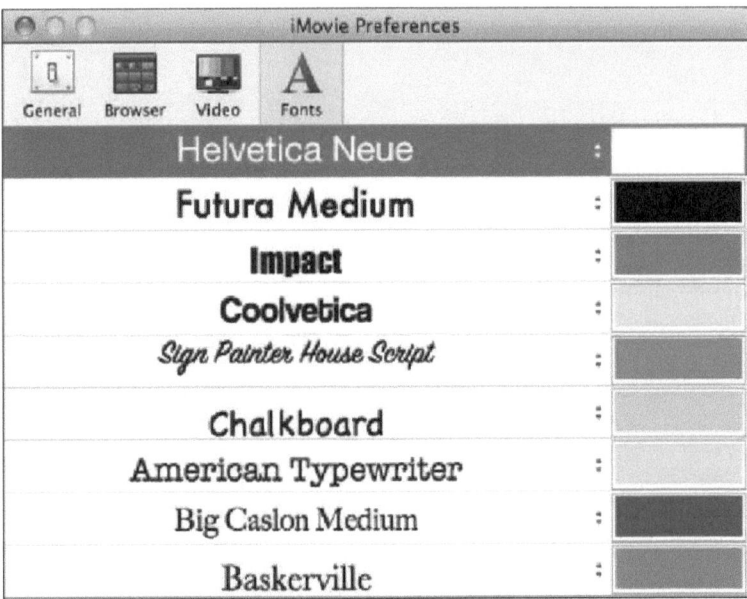

Figure 15–5. *Fonts tab of the Preferences... window*

Remaining iMovie Menu Options

There are a few more items in the **iMovie** menu. These commands are found in the app-named menus of all other iLife apps as well.

- **Provide iMovie Feedback:** This allows you to send feedback to Apple about iMovie.

- **Register iMovie:** This allows you to register iMovie (not required).

- **Check for Updates...:** You can manually check with Apple to see if there are any updates for your app.

- **Hide iMovie:** This hides all open iMovie windows.

- **Hide Others:** This hides all open windows except for iMovie windows.

- **Show All:** This shows all open windows.

- **Quit iMovie:** This shuts down iMovie. It automatically saves any changes.

File Menu

This menu, shown in Figure 15–6, contains many options. With it, you can create a new project, folder, or event. You can import media, adjust project properties, or change your project theme. You can move unwanted clips to the trash, and analyze or optimize your video.

Figure 15–6. *File menu*

New Project...

The **New Project...** window is shown in Figure 15–7. You can choose to start from scratch by selecting No Theme in the upper left-hand corner, or choose from one of seven template themes. You can also decide to create a trailer. The settings that need to be addressed are discussed at the beginning of Chapter 13: "Lights...Camera...Themes...iMovie Workspaces!"

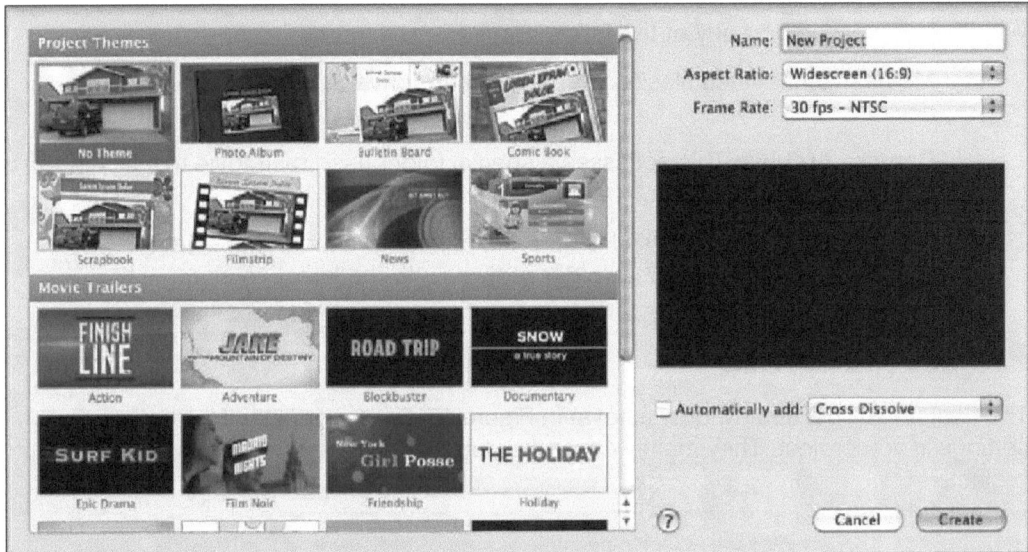

Figure 15–7. *The New Project... window*

New Folder...

This menu is helpful for organizing your projects that are in the **Project Library**. For example, you can create a folder called **Baby Videos** and put all of you baby videos in it.

New Event

This creates a new empty event. This empty event is created in the **Event Library** with its name containing the date you created it.

Duplicate Project

If you want to experiment on a project, but want to keep an original—this is perfect. Click on a project in the Project Library and then select this command. You will then have two copies of the same project. The new project has the same name plus a "1" added to it.

Import from Camera...

Covered in Chapter 14: "iMovie Advanced Features: The Inspector, Ken Burns Effect, and More," this is where you can add video via a built-in or external camera.

Import

With this, you can import any of the following:

- **Movies:** Other video files found on your hard drive or other storage device.

- **Camera Archive:** This accesses a special folder used by iMovie to store camera media data.

- **iMovie HD Project:** iMovie HD was the previous version of iMovie. This allows you to add these older projects into the latest version.

Project Properties

The **Project Properties** window (shown in Figure 15–8) sets defaults for another of settings in you project. They mainly cover the duration of certain elements in your project.

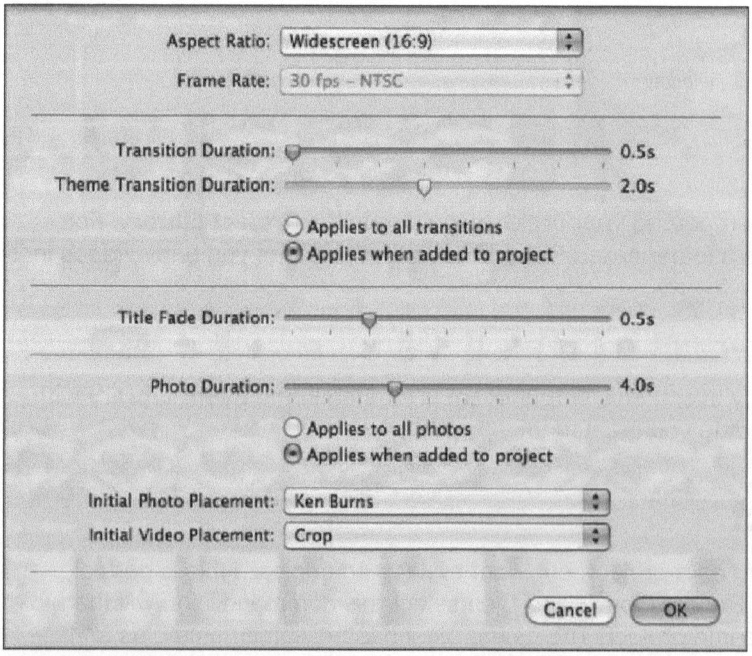

Figure 15–8. *Project Properties* accessed via the *File* menu

- **Aspect ratio:** Here you change the video dimensions of your project. When you first create a project, you must choose from **Widescreen** (rectangular image) or **Standard** (square image). This option allows you to change your original selection.

- **Frame Rate:** This lets you know at what frame rate your video was shot. It cannot be modified in this menu.

- **Transition Duration:** This sets the default length of the transitions you add to your project. The default is 15 seconds. It is modified by a slider and can go up to four minutes.

- **Theme Transition Duration:** This sets the default length of the theme transitions. The default is two minutes, but it can go as low as 15 seconds and as high as four minutes. This is only available if you choose a theme for your project. Below the slider to set the time duration, you can decide to either set the time to apply to all transitions or applied when you add one to a project. Just click on the button next to the choice you prefer.

- **Title Fade Duration:** This sets the length of the title fade for all of the titles in your project. The default again is 15 seconds.

- **Photo Duration:** This sets the length of time a photo is to appear in your project. The default is four seconds, but you can adjust it with a slider. As with **Theme Transition Duration**, you can have it apply to all of your photos or just as they are added to your project.

- **Initial Photo Placement:** This determines which crop tool option will be applied when a photo is imported. The **Ken Burns effect** is the default, but it can also be **Fit** or **Crop**. These options were discussed in Chapter 14: "iMovie Advanced Features: The Inspector, Ken Burns Effect, and More."

- **Initial Video Placement:** This determines which crop tool will be applied when a video is imported. The default is **Crop**. It can also be **Fit in Frame**.

Project Theme

Not happy with the theme you originally picked? This is where you can change the theme to another or remove it completely.

Convert to Project

If you started out creating a tantalizing trailer but decided to make it a magnificent movie instead, use this option to convert the trailer to full-fledged video project.

Finalize Project

This is not exactly what you would expect, but it's very useful. When you choose this option, iMovie renders your project (at this time) in all available sizes (**Mobile**, **Medium**, **Large**, **HD 720p**, and **HD 1080p**). The render process or preparing stage uses these files when you share your project via one of many Internet options. Doing this now saves time later when you finally share the video. Please note that iMovie can't see these files and the size rendered depends on the media in your project.

Move to Trash

This option will take an item you have highlighted and send it to the trashcan.

Move Rejected Clips to Trash

As I mentioned in Chapter 13: "Lights...Camera...Themes...iMovie Workspaces!" you can mark clips as favorites or rejected clips. This option takes all of your video segments marked as **Rejected** and moves them to the trashcan.

Space Saver

Video clips can take huge amounts of space on your hard drive. **Space Saver** (see Figure 15–9) allows you to permanently remove certain files in your project. The first choice, which is the default, is **Not added to any project**. You can also select clips that are **Not marked as Favorite** or **Not marked with a keyword**.

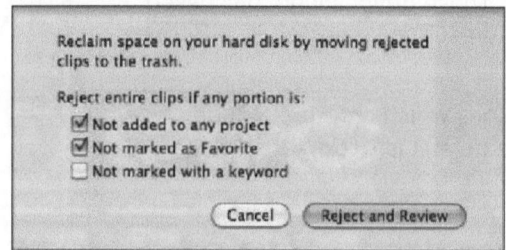

Figure 15–9. *Space Saver option found in the File menu*

To delete these files, click the **Reject and Review** button [Reject and Review]. Figure 15–10 shows the final review process and the button to actually move the clips to the trash. A rejected clip has a red line going through the top of it. This option appears the **Event—Preview** window.

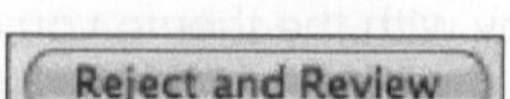

Rejected Clips   Move Rejected to Trash   Hide Rejected

Figure 15–10. *Final review window when applying the Space Saver option*

Consolidate Media...

This is a nice feature, as it grabs all of the media you used in your project into one location (see Figure 15–11). This way, you can make sure all items are in one spot and not on devices that can be removed.

Figure 15–11. *Consolidating media*

Additional File Menu Options

The remaining options found in this menu are fairly straightforward. They are:

- **Merge Events...:** This allows you to combine selected events into one event.

- **Split Event Before Selected Clip:** It might be easier to work with smaller events. This command splits a selected event into two new smaller clips.

- **Adjust Clip Date and Time...:** The video camera you used might have had the wrong time on it. When iMovie imports the video, the time and date are used. This tool allows you to change and correct the time so that it appears correctly in the Event Library.

■ **Analyze Video:** This option, shown in Figure 15–12, checks your video for **Stabilization and People, Stabilization or just People. Stabilization and People or Stabilization** attempts to reduce the camera shaking in your video. If you select on option to analyze for People—iMovie will scan the video and attempt to differentiate all the unique individuals in it. This way, you can easily find clips later on that contain a certain person. Be warned - these options take a long time to render. You can also select to **Mark Camera Pans**. If you already analyzed the clip for Stabilization—Mark Camera Pans will note in the clip when the camera moves left or right. You can use this added info when editing your movie as you can filter for these changes and use it when needed.

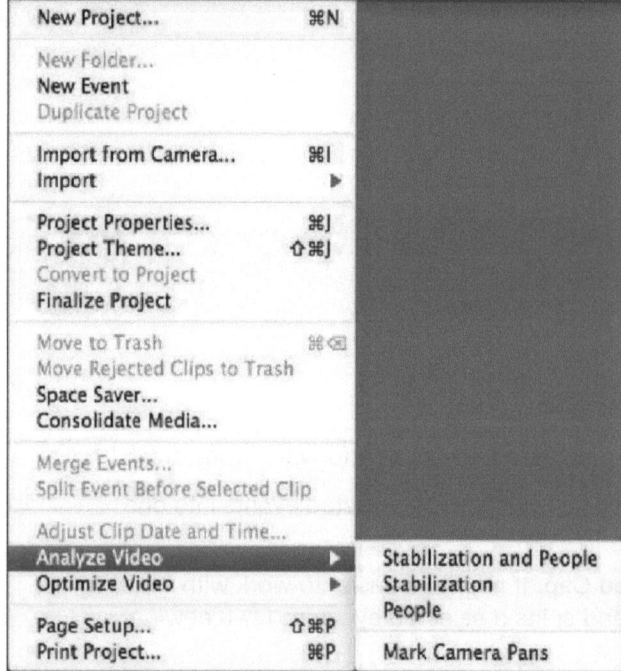

Figure 15–12. *Analyze Video options*

■ **Optimize Video:** This has to be done if you are going to perform certain special effects, such as replay and rewind.

■ **Page Setup...:** The page setup options for printing your project.

■ **Print Project...:** This allows you to print your project.

Edit Menu

This menu is shown in Figure 15–13. As you can see, most of its options are found in Edit menus of the other iLife apps. The one truly new item is the **Transition Overlay**, which determines how the transition interacts with the video clip next to it.

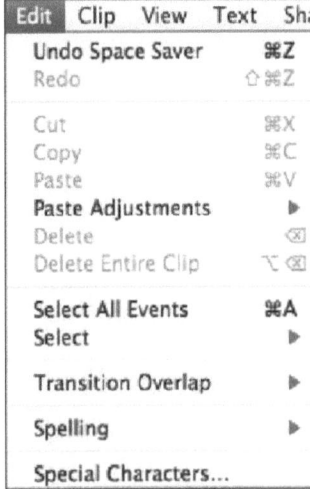

Figure 15–13. *Edit menu*

- **Undo (action):** This will undo your most recent action.

- **Redo:** This will reapply an action you just "undid."

- **Cut:** This will remove any selected item from your project.

- **Copy:** This will take an item you have highlighted and put it into the Mac's memory.

- **Paste:** This will insert the item you just copied back into your project, wherever your mouse pointer is.

■ **Paste Adjustments:** The **Paste Adjustment** command is found in many applications. Instead of pasting the actual item, it pastes the formatting on the item. In Figure 15–14, we can see that adjustments can be applied to ten different elements separately or all elements at once.

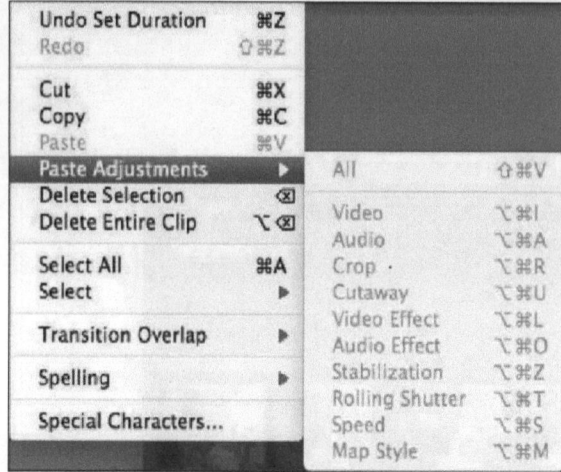

Undo Set Duration	⌘Z		
Redo	⇧⌘Z		
Cut	⌘X		
Copy	⌘C		
Paste	⌘V		
Paste Adjustments	▶	All	⇧⌘V
Delete Selection	⌫	Video	⌥⌘I
Delete Entire Clip	⌥⌫	Audio	⌥⌘A
Select All	⌘A	Crop ·	⌥⌘R
Select	▶	Cutaway	⌥⌘U
		Video Effect	⌥⌘L
Transition Overlap	▶	Audio Effect	⌥⌘O
Spelling	▶	Stabilization	⌥⌘Z
		Rolling Shutter	⌥⌘T
Special Characters...		Speed	⌥⌘S
		Map Style	⌥⌘M

Figure 15–14. *Paste Adjustment options in the Edit menu*

■ **Delete Selection:** This deletes highlighted items from your project.

■ **Delete Entire Clip:** This will delete the entire clip if only a portion of a clip is highlighted.

■ **Reject Selection/Reject Entire Clip:** These two options appear in the **Edit** menu when you are highlighting video in the **Event—Preview** window. They will reject the item instead of delete it. This is more useful as the material is not erased—just marked as rejected.

■ **Select All:** This will select all clips in the **Project** window.

■ **Select Entire Clip:** This is not shown in Figure 15–14, as it will only appear when your timeline is inside a video clip and you need to select the entire clip. This will then highlight the entire clip in the **Event— Preview** window.

■ **Select:** As we can see in Figure 15–15, the **Select** command makes it easy to select a certain element type in your project. For example, this option will select all transitions if you chose **Transitions** from the menu.

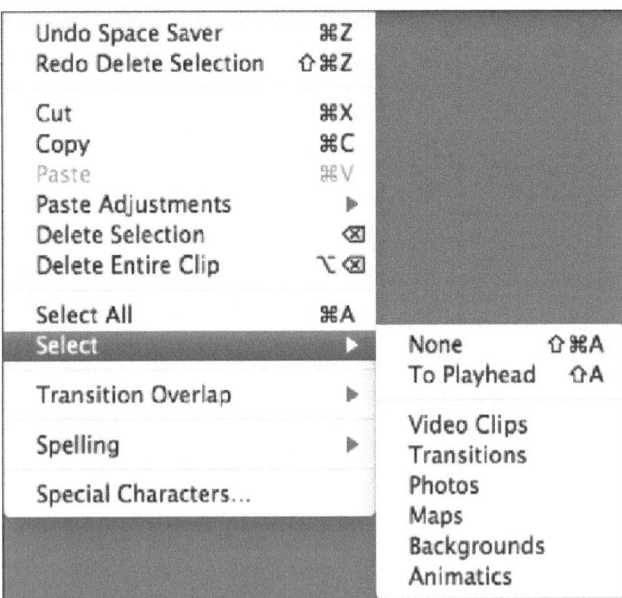

Figure 15–15. *Select option of the Edit menu*

- **Transition Overlap:** You are given the following two choices:
  - **All—Maintain Clip Range:** This combines two clips with an overlap defined by the length of the transition and is placed over the overlapping region. This means that no additional content from the two ends are added.
  - **Half—Maintain Project Duration:** The transition spans the two clips. One half of the transition overlaps each clip. This means that additional content from each adjoining end is added to fill out the transition. The total time of your project remains the same.
- **Spelling:** This accesses the spelling tool.
- **Special Characters…:** Want to add a special symbol, but not sure where to find it? Click here.

Clip Menu

The **Clip** menu contains many useful features (see Figure 15–16). The first few items allow you to apply special effects like **Slow Motion**. You can join or split clips in this menu as well.

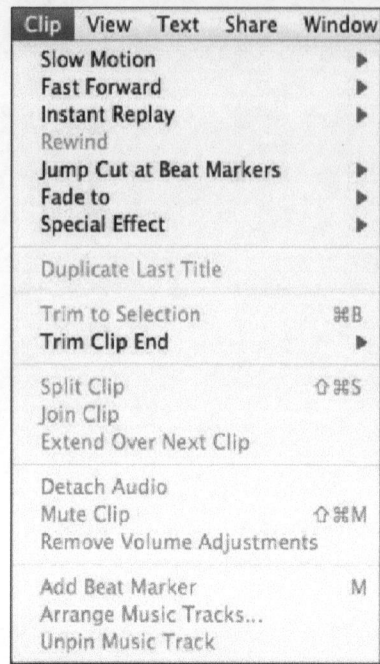

Figure 15–16. *Clip menu*

Slow Motion

This allows you to modify the speed of a clip by applying a slow motion effect. You can choose between **10%**, **25%**, or **50%**. If you apply this effect, the motion in the clip will be slower and the length of the video clip will increase.

Fast Forward

This allows you to modify the speed of the clip by applying a fast forward effect. You can choose between **2x**, **4x**, **8x**, or **20x**. The motion in your video will appear to be sped up and the length of the video clip will decrease.

Instant Replay

This option will take your selected clip, duplicate it, and then add a slower version of it next to your selected clip. The words **Instant Replay** also appear in this newly added clip. You can choose between **10%**, **25%**, or **50%**.

Rewind

This will take a selected clip, duplicate it, and play it in reverse.

Jump Cut At Beat Markers

This will "jump" your video ahead by the number of frames you select. You must first have added beat markers to use this feature. You can choose between 3 frames, 5 frames, 10 frames, 20 frames, or 30 frames.

Fade to

This allows you to apply one of three effects to a selected range in your video clip found in the **Project** window. They are**: Black and White**, **Sepia**, and **Dream**.

Special Effect

This allows you to accomplish three different effects. The first, which I love, is **Flash and Hold Last Frame**. This will take the last frame of your selected clip and add it next to your clip and hold it for a few seconds. Before the original clip and the added still of the last frame, iMovie will present a white flash between the two. Very dramatic, no? The next two effects only apply if you added beat markers. The first splits the video at the beat markers and the second flips the video at the beat markers.

Duplicate Last Title

If you already added a title in your project, this will copy the last one and add it to the new clip you have selected.

Trim to Selection

The length of the complete video clip you have selected will be trimmed to the section of the clip you have highlighted in yellow.

Trim Clip End

This option will allow you to trim a video clip by moving the timeline to the left or right.

Split Clip

This will split the clip that the red timeline bar is in at the point of the red bar.

Join Clip

This will only join clips that were just split via the **Split Clip** command.

Extend Over Next Clip

Use this if you want to join two clips that are next to each other in the **Project** window.

Detach Audio

This will separate the audio portion from your video clip and place it in a separate window. This is shown in Figure 15–17. Please notice that now the audio clip has its own **Gear** button that you can use to adjust audio.

Figure 15–17. *The audio portion of a video clip being detached from the video element*

Mute Clip

This will turn off the sound in your selected clip.

Remove Volume Adjustments

This removes all custom adjustments made to the audio segment you have highlighted.

Add Beat Marker

Beat markers are your friends. You need to add them to sync music or other audio clips with visual items. This includes video clips, titles, photos, and so on. After you add a beat marker, you can drag audio clips to the exact location you want in the visual element.

Arrange Music Tracks...

If you have more than one background audio clips, with this tool you can change the order in which they play in your project.

Unpin Music Track

This is useful if you want to keep the music "pinned," or stuck to a particular spot in your clip. To pin a clip, drag the audio track until the audio file turns purple. Move the audio to the location you want. You will see a small pin appear at the top far left corner of the audio element.

View Menu

Quite simply, this menu determines what is to be shown in your workspace or viewing options. See Figure 15–18.

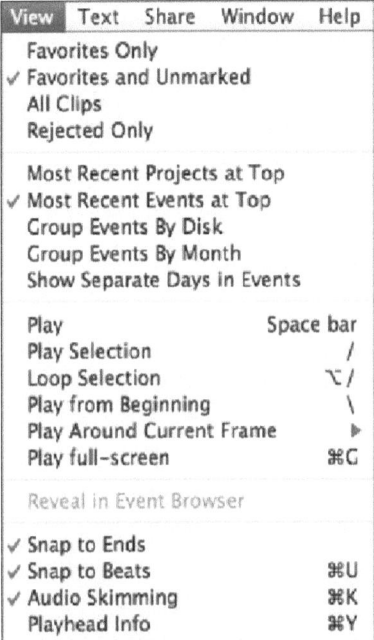

Figure 15–18. *View menu*

- ▣ **Favorites Only**

- ▣ **Favorites and Unmarked (Default setting)**

- ▣ **All Clips**

- ▣ **Rejected only:** You can designate clips as favorites or rejected.

These four above options determine what you want to see.

- ▣ **Most Recent Projects at Top:** This option will list the latest project at the top of the Project Library window.

- ▣ **Most Recent Events at Top (default setting)**

- ▣ **Group Events by Disk (disk = your hard drives)**

- ▣ **Group Events by Month**

- ▣ **Show separate Days in Event:** These four items deal with how your events are shown in the **Event—Preview** window.

- **Play:** This plays your project from the point where the red timeline marker is located.

- **Play Selection:** This plays the section of video you have highlighted.

- **Loop Selection:** This will play the video segment you have highlighted over and over again until you stop it.

- **Play from Beginning:** This will play your project from the very beginning.

- **Play Around Current Frame:** If you select this option, the video will play one or three seconds around the red timeline marker (you choose).

- **Play full-screen:** This will play the video full-screen size. This is useful, as the **Preview** window sometimes does not do your video or video effects justice, and makes editing a lot easier.

- **Reveal in Event Browser (Event—Preview window):** This will highlight in yellow the section of video you highlighted in yellow in the **Project** window.

- **Snap to Ends:** If this is selected (it is by default), when you move a title—the beginning of the title will align with the beginning or end of the clip as you move the title bar. A yellow line will appear indicating the title has been "snapped" to an end.

- **Snap to Beats:** If this is selected (it is by default) selected items will align with beat markers.

- **Audio Skimming:** This is turned on by default and simply allows you to hear the audio portion of your video segment.

- **Playhead Info:** If this is turned, the creation date and time will appear at the very top of the project window. This is shown in Figure 15–19.

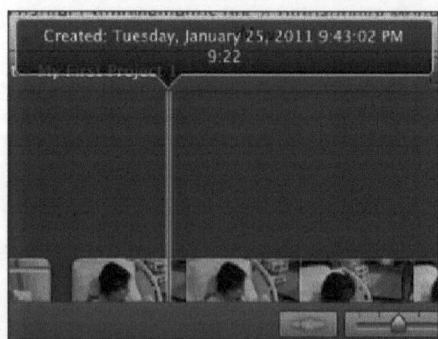

Figure 15–19. *Playhead info being displayed in a project*

Text Menu

The **Text** menu deals with all things text. If you want to change the font, font size, alignment, or other text-related items, you can do it all here.

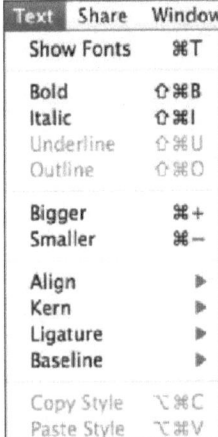

Figure 15–20. *Text menu*

- **Show Fonts:** This brings up the window shown in Figure 15–21. Here you can choose between any font installed on your machine, choose its typeface, or its size.

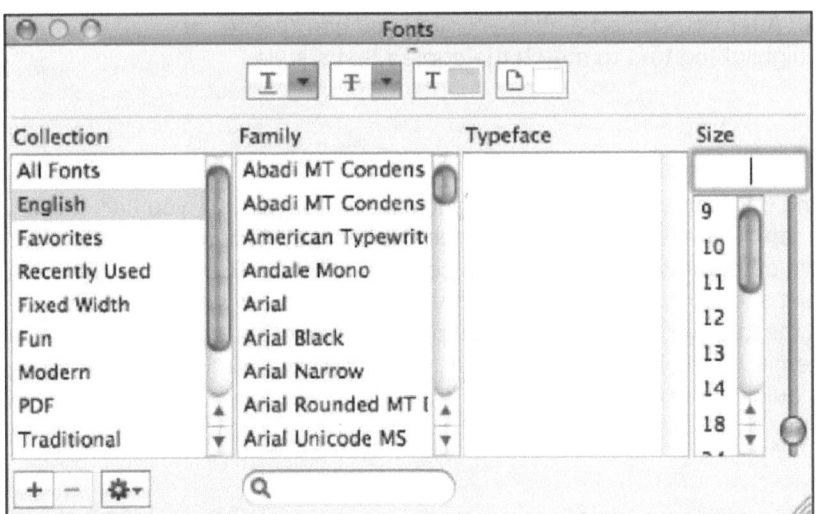

Figure 15–21. *Show Fonts window of the Text menu*

- **Bold:** Makes the text **bold**.

- **Italic:** Makes the text *italic*.

- **Underline:** Underlines the selected text.

- **Outline:** Makes the font appear to have an **outline**.

- **Bigger:** Makes the selected font bigger by a small amount each time you select it.

- **Smaller:** Makes the selected font smaller by a small amount each time you select it.

- **Align:** Can be **Left**, **Center**, **Justify**, or **Right**.

- **Kern:** Kerning determines the space between text characters. Choose from **Use default**, **Use None**, **Tighten**, or **Loosen**.

- **Ligature:** Ligature occurs when two or more graphemes are joined as a single glyph. Basically, in English, this means that ligatures replace consecutive characters. You can choose between: **Use default**, **Use None**, or **Use all**.

- **Baseline:** This can be **Use default**, **Superscript** (raises text above its normal location), **Subscript** (lowers the text from its normal location), **Raise or Lower** (allows you to customize further where you want the text to be).

- **Copy Style:** If you are making a long movie about a nice ten-day cruise with the family, you might have a few titles in the project. This just copies the style of the title—not the actual words.

- **Paste Style:** After you copied a style you like, you can "paste" or modify the highlighted text to match the copied text's style.

Share Menu

Ah…the Power of the Internet! With the **Share** menu (see Figure 15–22), you can share your memories in a ton of different ways…mostly on the Internet. This menu is broken down into three main categories. The top section containing Media Browser…, iTunes and iDVD and the last section containing export options do not allow you to directly share your work on the Internet. However, they all produce work that can be later uploaded to the Internet. The middle section of this menu contains six ways to get your project on the Web quickly and easily.

Figure 15–22. *Share* menu

After you have chosen the way you want to share your project on the Internet, click on the **Publish** button located at the bottom right-hand corner of the window.

Media browser

If you chose **Share via Media Browser** (see Figure 15–23), your work will be available in other applications, such as iDVD or iWeb. I discussed these great little powerful apps earlier in this guide. iDVD is covered in chapters 7 - 9 and iWeb is explained in chapters 10–12.

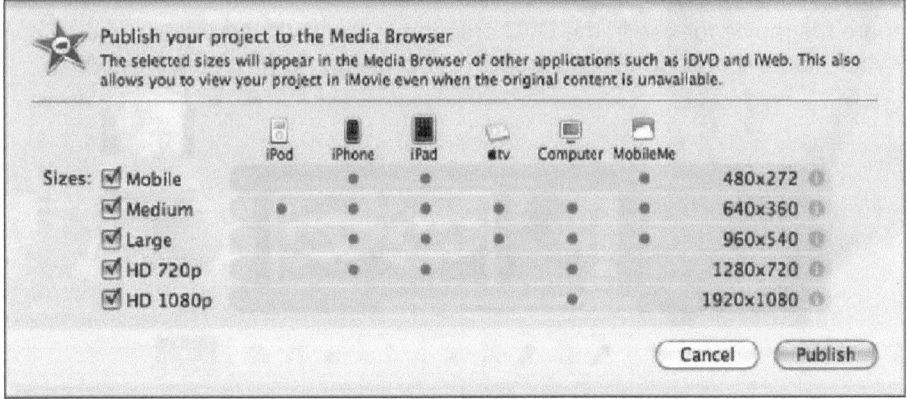

Figure 15–23. *Publishing your project to the media browser*

Please notice the little table at the bottom of this window. Here you decide in what size(s) you want the video to be rendered. Each size will play on certain Apple devices or be able to viewed in MobileMe. As you move up from mobile to HD the size of the file gets larger and larger. So, check carefully what sizes you want iMovie to publish. This little table appears on most of the other sharing options.

iTunes

iTunes is a great way to store your media and, more important, iTunes allows you copy your media to an iOS device. Again, iTunes is an essential gear in the framework of getting the most out of iLife.

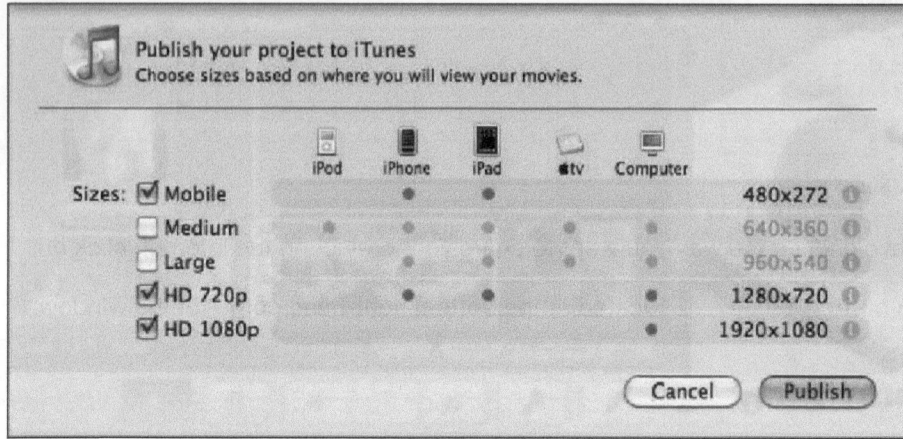

Figure 15–24. *Publishing to iTunes*

iDVD

This will prepare the movie for use in the DVD creation tool—iDVD. After it is done processing, your Mac will open iDVD and insert your project into your current iDVD project.

MobileMe

MobileMe is a service you pay annually for provided by Apple. This window is essentially the same as the other share options except for **Viewable by: Section** at the bottom of the window.

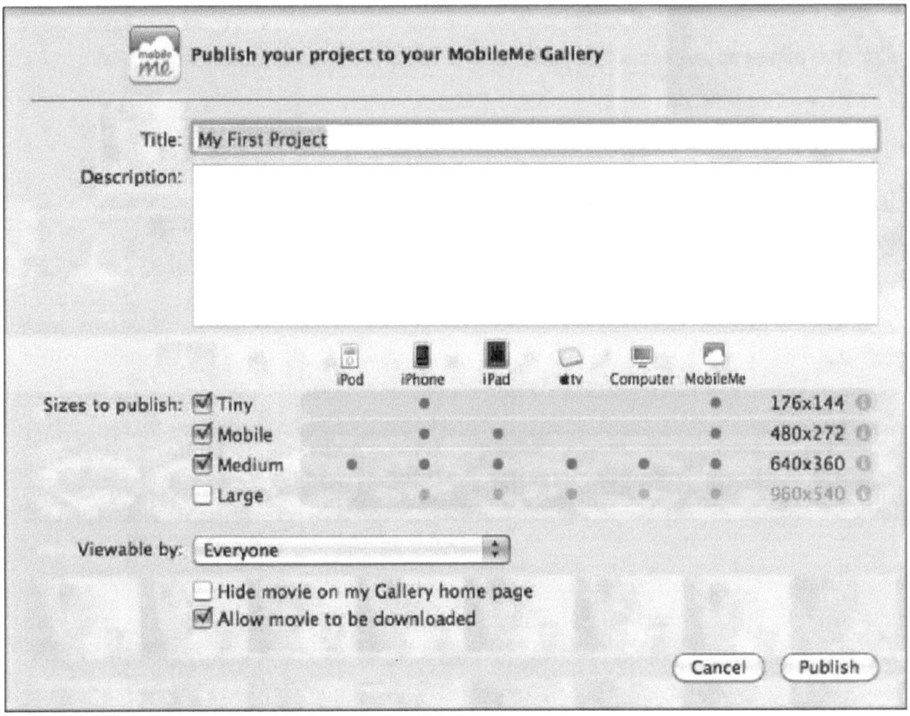

Figure 15–25. *Publishing to MobileMe*

You can have your project viewed by **Everyone** (the default), **Only Me**, or **Create Unique Names and Passwords** so that only authorized people can see your precious memories. If you choose **Only Me**, the **Hide movie on my Gallery home page** is automatically checked. Here is the best feature of MobileMe: you can check the box next to **Allow movie to be downloaded**. This means that whoever has access to your gallery can download the video(s) to their own computer.

YouTube

YouTube is simply awesome. Anyone can upload (copy to their site) any video they wish for free. (Note: it can't be copyrighted material). With this feature, getting your movies on YouTube is a snap.

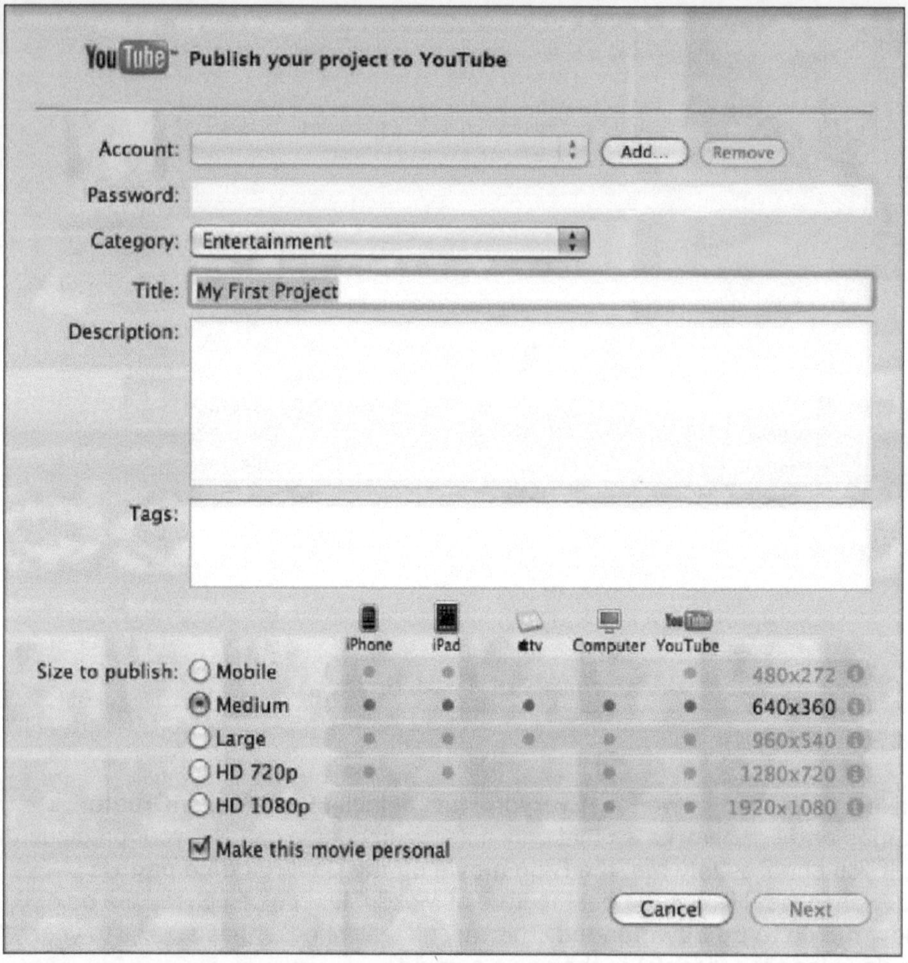

Figure 15–26. *Publishing your project to YouTube*

Please notice that you can only upload your movie in one size. Smaller sizes like **Mobile** or **Medium** are best, as they are viewable faster. Higher quality sizes take longer to upload, but the quality of the video will be better in YouTube. Also, you must already

have a YouTube account to use this feature. Click on the **Add** button  located at top right corner to add an account. You must uncheck **Make this movie personal** if you want other visitors to see your videos. This check box is located at the bottom of the YouTube publishing window.

Facebook

Come on, admit it, you spend too much time on it. As with YouTube, you must first have a valid Facebook account to use this feature.

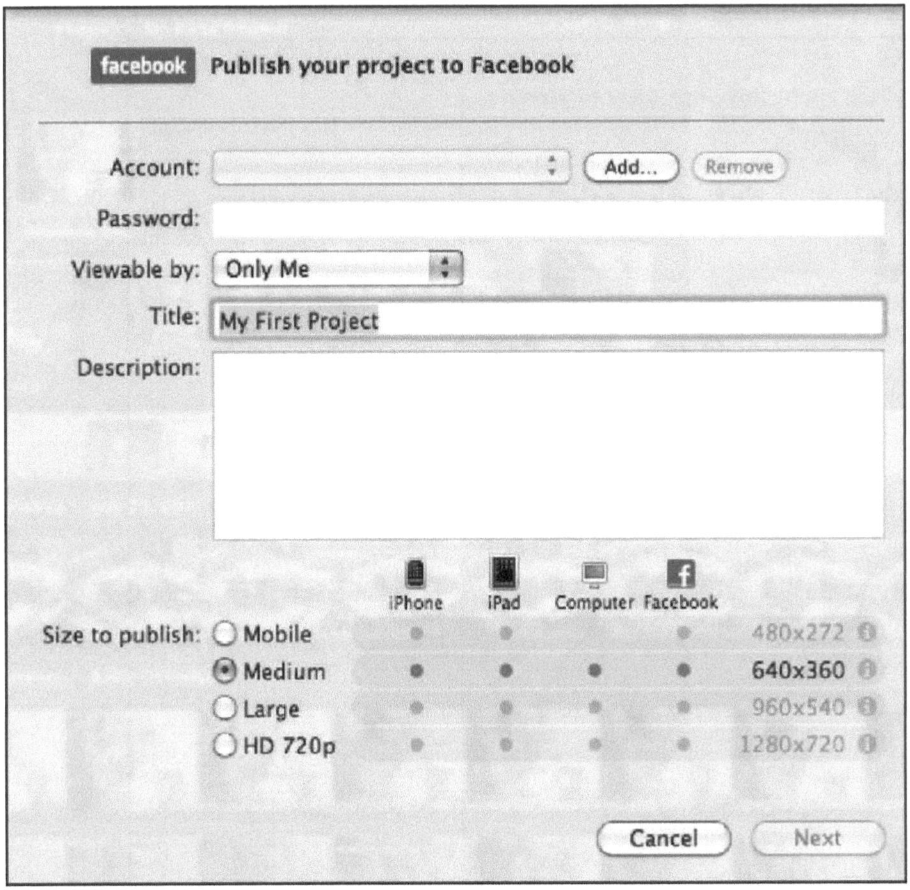

Figure 15–27. *Publishing your video to Facebook*

Again, click on the **Add**  button to add your account to this window. You decide who can view the videos by selecting **Everyone**, **Friends of Friends**, **Only Friends**, or **Only Me**. As with YouTube, you can only upload one size and the smaller sizes upload faster and view faster on the site.

Vimeo

Vimeo is another site that you can publish your videos to. The only difference in publishing your video to it is the options next **to Viewable by:**. They are **Anyone**, **My Contacts**, or **Nobody Else** (the default).

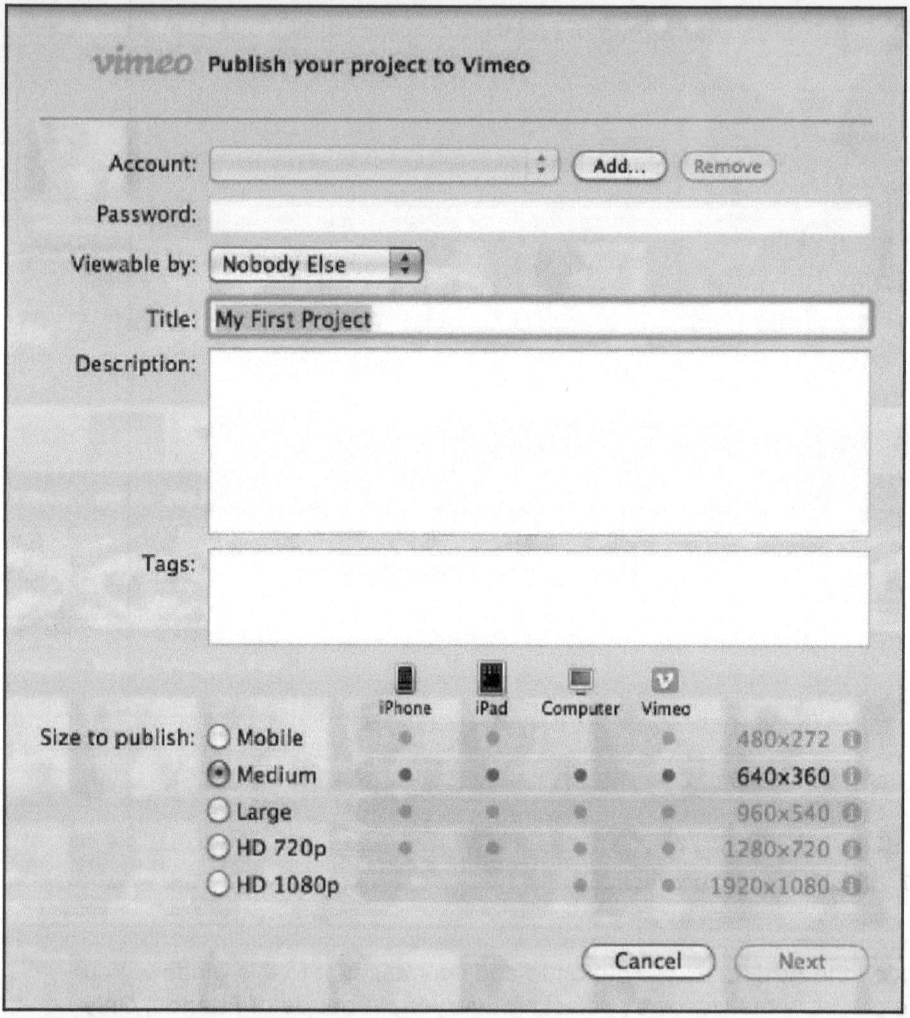

Figure 15–28. *Publishing your video to Vimeo*

CNN iReport

Nothing really new in this window as far as options needed to be filled out. I have to say it though: "This is CNN."

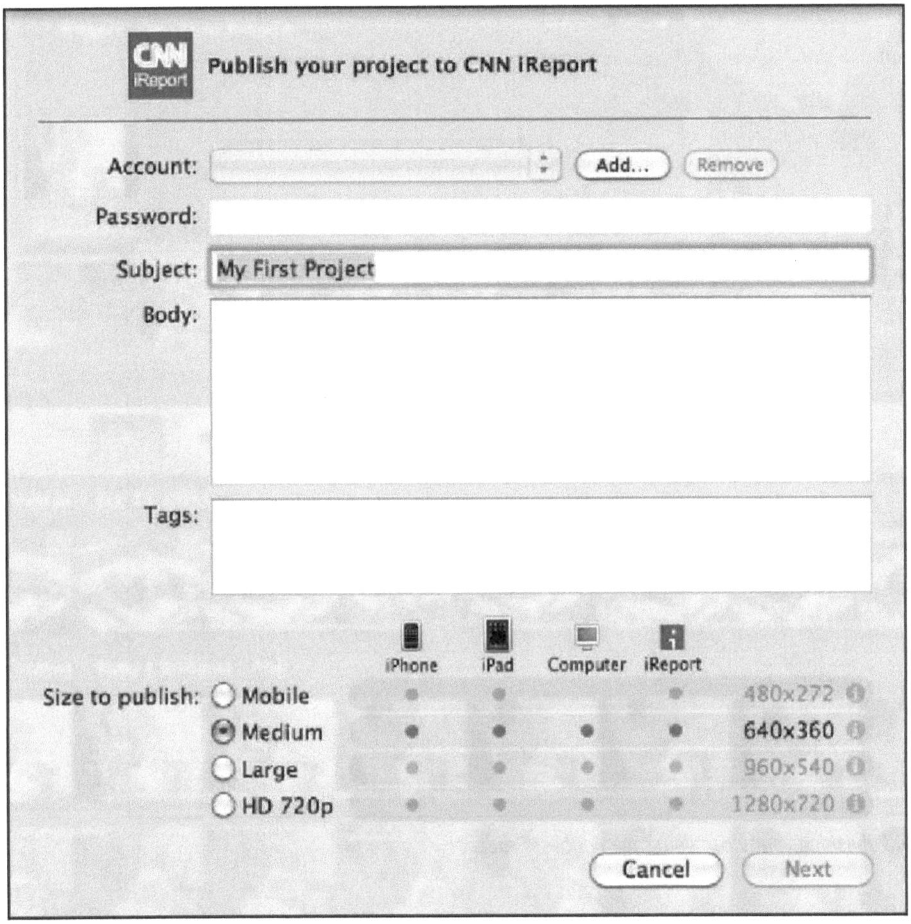

Figure 15–29. *Publishing your video to CNN iReport…*

Podcast Producer

Podcasts are episodes of voice or video that people can subscribe to see or hear. You must have a server location to fill out the **Account** section of this window.

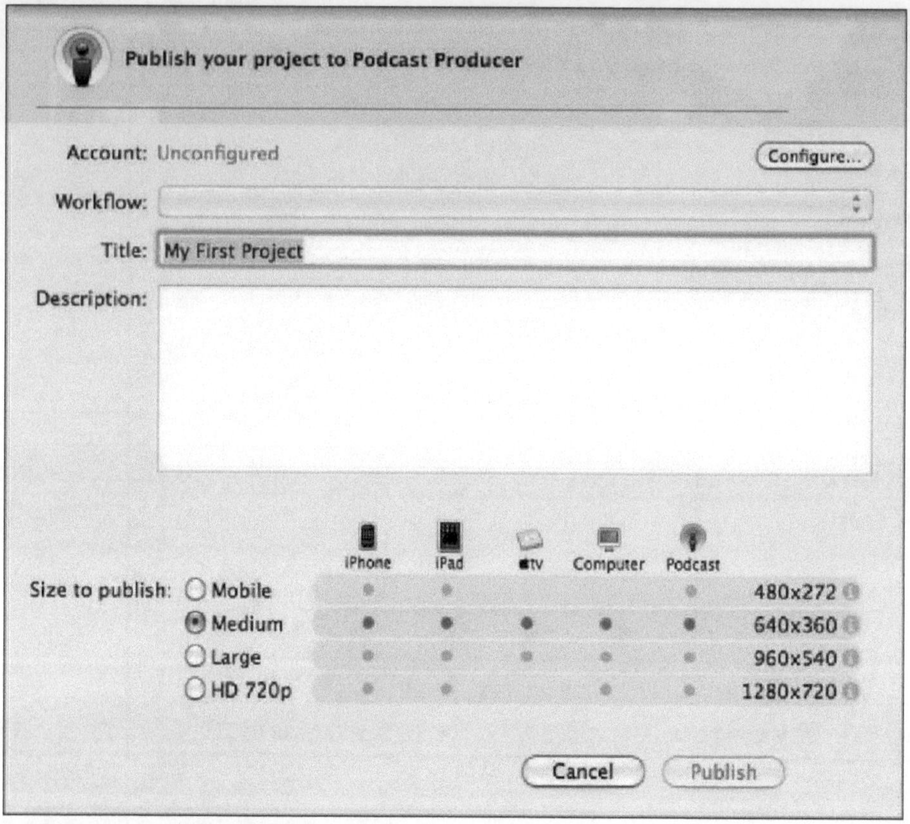

Figure 15–30. *Publishing your video using the Podcast Producer*

Export Video

If you select **Export Video...**, you just have to choose the filename, where you want to save it, and what size to export it as. You can't change the format of the video with this option. If you do want to customize the video and audio settings, you must use **Export Using QuickTime**, which is discussed next. See Figure 15–31.

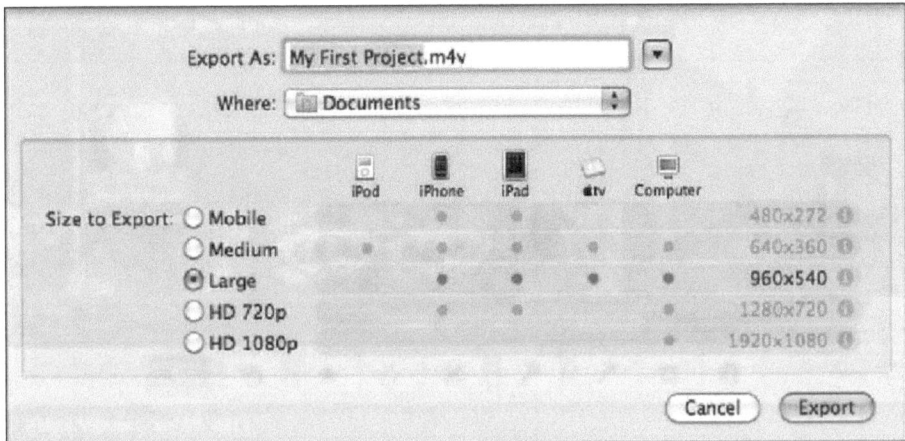

Figure 15–31. *Exporting your video using the **Export Video** option*

Export Using QuickTime...

This is a very complex procedure to perform if you want to really customize every aspect of the final video output of your project. Figure 15–32 shows the initial screen in the process.

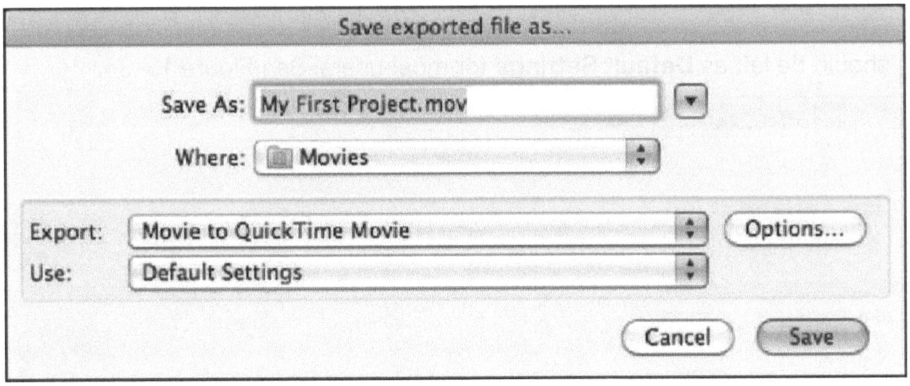

Figure 15–32. *Exporting a video via QuickTime.*

Please note that you can just click on **Save** ⌊Save⌋ and not change anything. Your movie will be exported as a fully functional QuickTime video. You have three major options to configure if you wish customize the export. They are: the **Export** dropdown menu, the **Use** dropdown menu, and the **Options** button. They are clustered just below the top section of this window. This top section is where you can name the movie and decide where you want to save.

Export

As we see in Figure 15–33, we are not limited to exporting a video as a QuickTime movie.

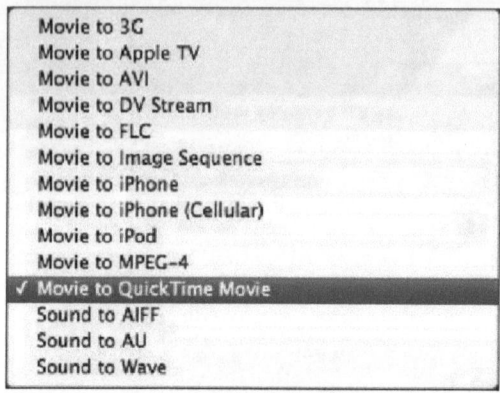

Figure 15–33. *All available formats that you can convert your movie into*

You can choose formats for specific Apple iOS devices (Apple TV, iPhone, iPod), other standard video formats used by computers (AVI, MPEG-4), audio files (AIFF, AU, WAVE), and a few other specialized formats (DV Stream, FLC, Image Sequence). I think Apple has pretty much covered all the bases here.

Use

This setting should be left as **Default Settings** for most users. See Figure 15–34.

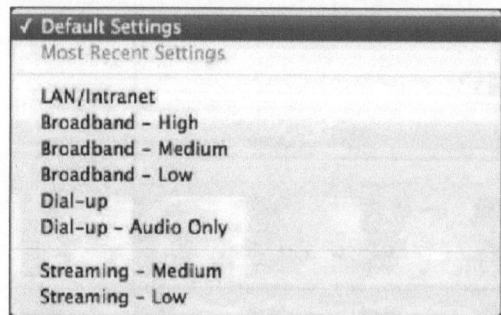

Figure 15–34. *Options available to decide how the Internet will use the video*

All of the other options listed under Use determine how the file is to interpreted on the Internet.

- **LAN/Intranet:** This is the fastest connection you can have and should be chosen if your video is only going to be seen in this environment.

- **Broadband:** This is what most users have with their Internet connection at home.

- **Dial-up:** This uses much older technology and probably will never be used by most current computer users.

- **Streaming:** This is a technology that streams you video in a unique way. This is useful for large movies because your web browser will download a section of your video before starting to play the movie.

Options...

The **Options...** window is shown in Figure 15–35. It is brought up when you click on **Options** directly across from the **Export** line.

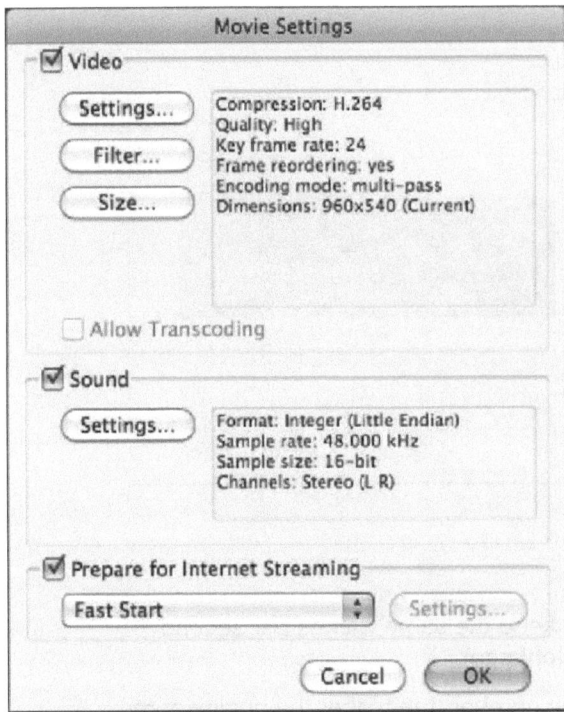

Figure 15–35. *Initial screen of the **Options...** button.*

This window is broken down into the following three sections: **Video**, **Sound**, and **Prepare for Internet Streaming**.

Video

This is the first option located at the top of this window. This is further broken down into three sections. They are: **Settings**, **Filter**, and **Size**.

Settings

The **Settings** page is shown in Figure 15–36.

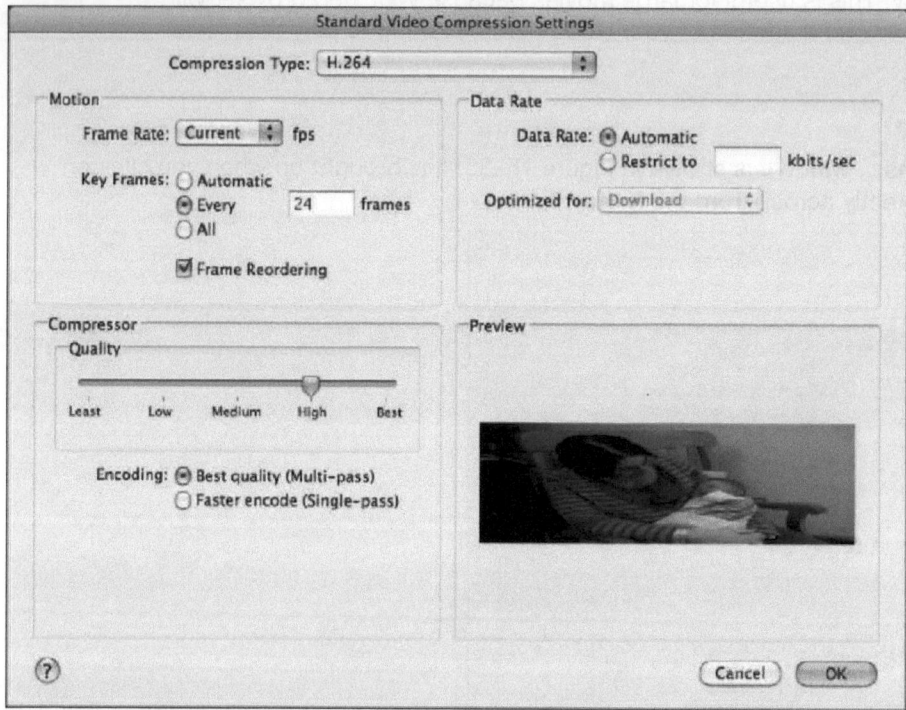

Figure 15–36. *Video compressing settings*

- ■ **Motion**

    - ■ **Frame Rate:** Here you can keep the same frames per second (default, usually no need to change).

    - ■ **Key Frames:** The higher the number, the higher the quality of the video and larger the final size of file.

- ■ **Data Rate:** This normally does not have to be changed and can be left as automatic. You have the option in this section to **Optimize the video for: CD/DVD-ROM**, **Download**, and **Streaming**. This option is only available if you enter in a custom data Rate inside the box between **Restrict to** and **kbits/sec**.

- **Compressor:** This has two options. The first is a slider to determine the quality of the compression. **Least** will give you the smallest file in size and worst quality video image. You can move the slider to anywhere in between and the highest option is **Best**. This will give you the best image quality and the largest file size. You also have the choice of **Best quality** or **Faster encode**. Best quality will give you the best image and is the default.

Filter

As shown in Figure 15–37, there are several different filters or adjustments that you can apply.

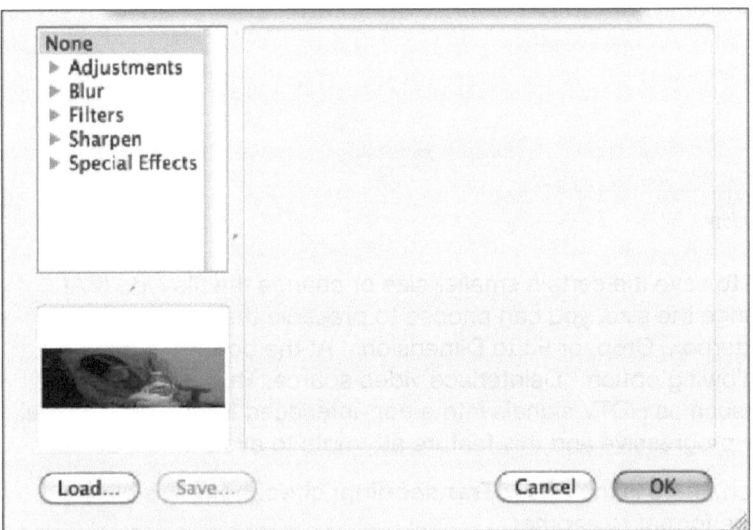

Figure 15–37. *Filter adjustments available to apply to final video output*

They are:

- **Adjustments:** There are five different settings to customize. These are only really needed by pros who know what each setting does.

- **Blur:** You can add a blur effect. You can go from "1" which is the least amount of blur, up to "7" for the largest amount of blur.

- **Filters:** You can chose between: **Edge detection**, **Emboss** (pretty cool), or **Convolution Kernel**. Convolu....what? Again, some of these settings are very advanced and not for most casual users who create family movies.

- **Sharpen:** This will attempt to sharpen the images in your video. Again, "1" is the least and "7" is the highest adjustment.

- **Special Effects:** Here you can change the **Color Style**, **Color Tint**, **Film Noise** (useful to make videos appear like they were made many years ago and see aging effects in it), and **Lens Flare**.

Size

Here you are given a ton of different dimensions to choose from for your final project. This is shown in Figure 15–38.

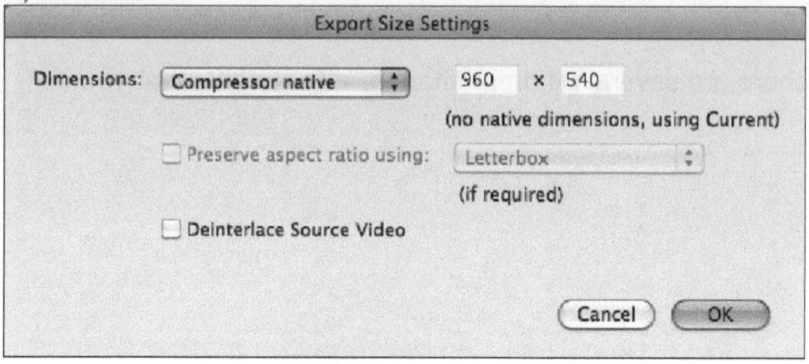

Figure 15–38. *Export Size Window*

This is useful if you want to save it a certain smaller size or change the file type (PAL, HD, or NTSC). If you change the size, you can choose to preserve the aspect ratio by one of three choices: Letterbox, Crop, or Fit to Dimensions. At the bottom of this window, you have the following option - Deinterlace video source: This allows you to convert interlaced video such as HDTV signals into a non-interlaced form. This is useful, as most devices are now progressive and this feature attempts to avoid visual defects.

Just below the Size button, there is the **Allow Transcoding: checkbox.** This allows direct conversion from one format to another.

Sound

Here you can change the audio format (nine choices), channels (stereo, mono and a few more lesser known formats), and rate (the higher the number the better the final audio quality will be). See Figure 15–39.

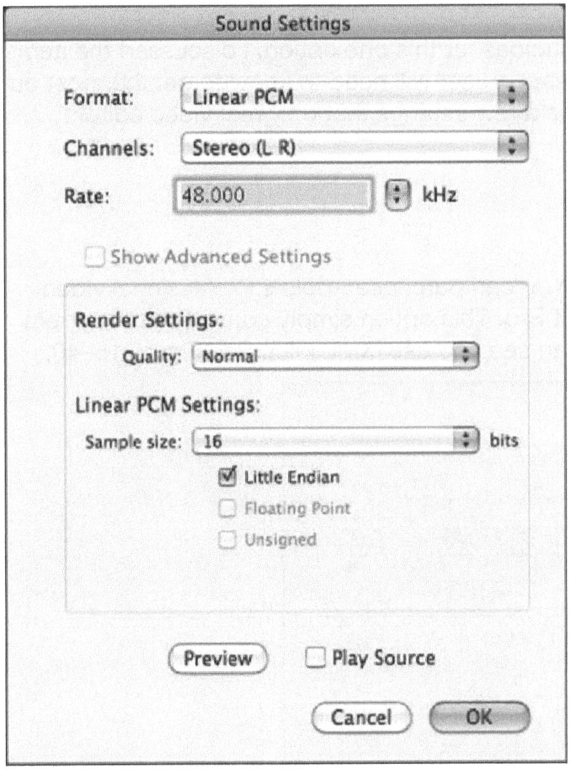

Figure 15–39. *Audio options found in the **Export to QuickTime...**window*

Render settings can be either: **Normal** (default) or a range from **Faster** to **Best**.

- **Linear PCM Settings:** Your guess is good as mine... I would leave it as is unless you are an audio engineer and know what the options do.

- **Preview:** This will preview your audio settings.

- **Play Source:** This will play your source music through the speakers.

Prepare for Internet Streaming

This makes the video more suitable for web sites as streaming a video performs better than a video that was not set to stream. You can choose from: **Fast Start**, **Fast Start— Compressed Header**, and **Hinted Streaming**. If you choose **Hinted Streaming**, the **Settings** button comes alive and you can configure this feature.

I think you can see that are a myriad of choices for this one option. I discussed the items I feel a first-time user and a more experienced user will need to know to get the most out of iMovie. But, as we have seen, there are a few settings that only real video editors know how to use and modify.

Export Final Cut XML

iMovie getting a little too basic for you? You can purchase Apple's Professional video editing software package called Final Cut Pro. This option simply converts your current project into a format that Final Cut pro can see and use (XML File). See Figure 15–40.

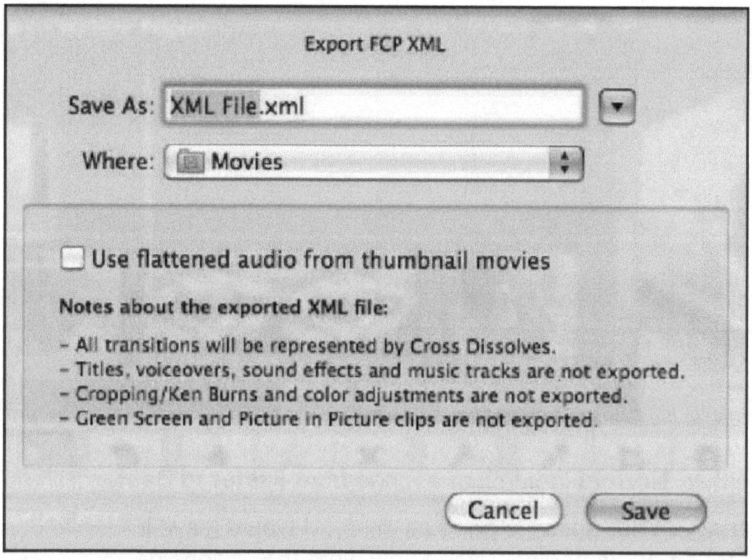

Figure 15–40. *Exporting to Final Cut Pro*

Remove From

Oops! The video you uploaded has a major flaw, needs to be revised for new content, or you just want it off the Internet. This option is here to your rescue. It removes your project from any of the shared places I discussed on the previous pages. See Figure 15–41.

Figure 15–41. *Removing items from a shared location*

Window Menu

For the most part, the **Window** menu (Figure 15–42) gives you access to any of the elements already discussed in this book; from viewing the precision editor to displaying the transitions workspace, so I will not rehash them here. This is just another way of accessing all of these items.

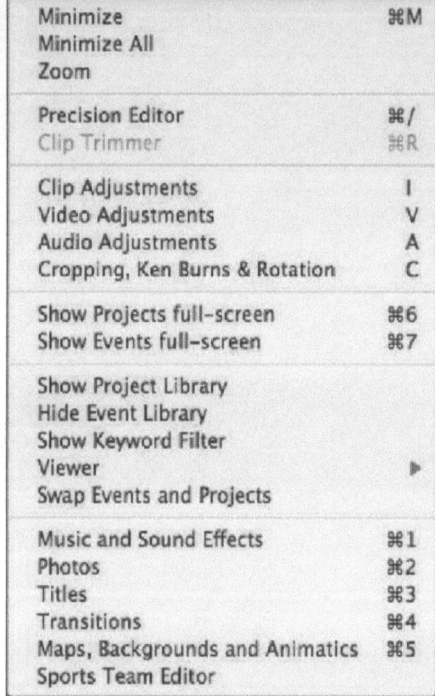

Minimize	⌘M
Minimize All	
Zoom	
Precision Editor	⌘/
Clip Trimmer	⌘R
Clip Adjustments	I
Video Adjustments	V
Audio Adjustments	A
Cropping, Ken Burns & Rotation	C
Show Projects full-screen	⌘6
Show Events full-screen	⌘7
Show Project Library	
Hide Event Library	
Show Keyword Filter	
Viewer	▶
Swap Events and Projects	
Music and Sound Effects	⌘1
Photos	⌘2
Titles	⌘3
Transitions	⌘4
Maps, Backgrounds and Animatics	⌘5
Sports Team Editor	

Figure 15–42. *Window menu*

- **Minimize:** Takes your current window and places it in the dock. You must access this window again by clicking on the icon in the dock.

- **Minimize All:** Same as above, but does all windows.

- **Zoom:** Makes your iMovie workspace take up your entire screen real estate.

- **Show Projects full screen:** This is very useful, as the **Project** window by itself takes up the whole screen. The new interface is shown in Figure 15–43. There is a **Play** button and show events button on the far left. Each video segment is separated and showed individually at the bottom of this window and at the far right, we have the **Show Cover** flow effect and **Show/Hide Filmstrip** button.

Figure 15–43. *Bottom of full-screen mode—Projects*

- **Show Events full-screen:** This is basically the same as viewing Projects full-screen; it's just applied to events.

    These two items make you life a lot easier as you can really see the video in all its detail in this larger environment.

- **Viewer:** This allows you to adjust the size of the **Preview** window.

- **Sports Team Editor:** This is essential to any coach who wants to make videos about his team. This editor is shown in Figure 15–44. With this feature, you can keep track of all your players' names, their photos, and have a spot to place your team logo.

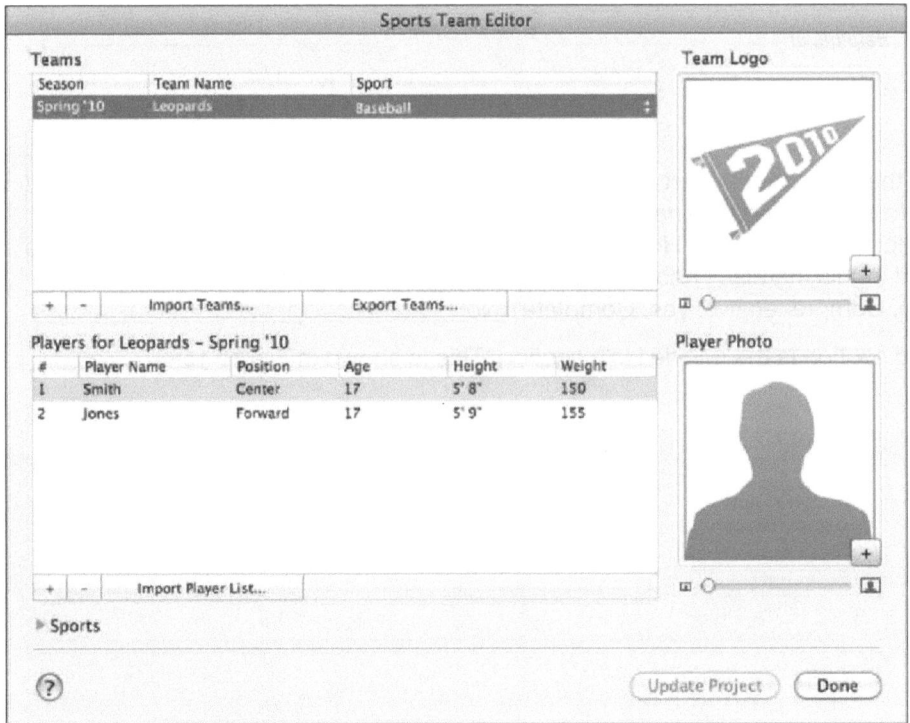

Figure 15–44. *Sports Team editor window*

You can also import a team list from a text file. Please follow the instructions in Figure 15–45 to properly create the text file.

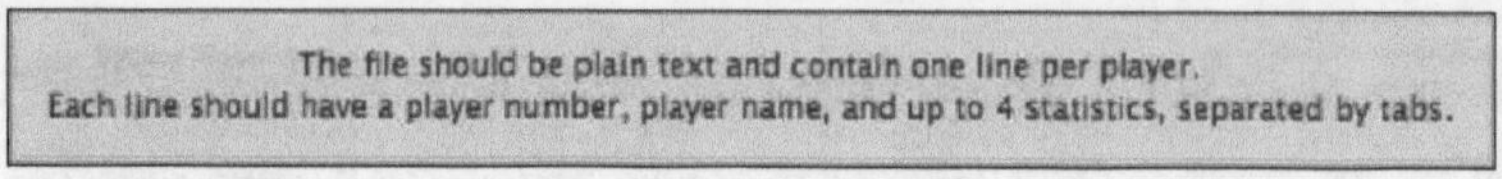

The file should be plain text and contain one line per player.
Each line should have a player number, player name, and up to 4 statistics, separated by tabs.

Figure 15–45. *Format requirements for plain text document to be used to import player's info*

Help Menu

Lights...Camera...Launch iMovie...now what? As with other Macintosh apps this menu is there to guide you through various topics or search for a specific item. This is last menu for iMovie. It contains several sections. See Figure 15–46.

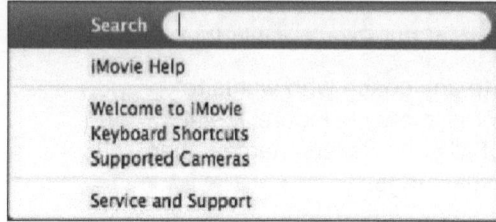

Figure 15–46. *Help menu*

Search

The first is the search tool. Next to **Search**, type in a topic you have a question about. I would like to say it again: The help system for iLife's applications is advanced and contains a lot of help options. However, I have found it hard to find advice on some the items found in this manual. I had to search the Internet to help understand what some features do. Comprehensive, yes. Complete? No!

The second section is the iMovie Help section. This is shown in Figure 15–47.

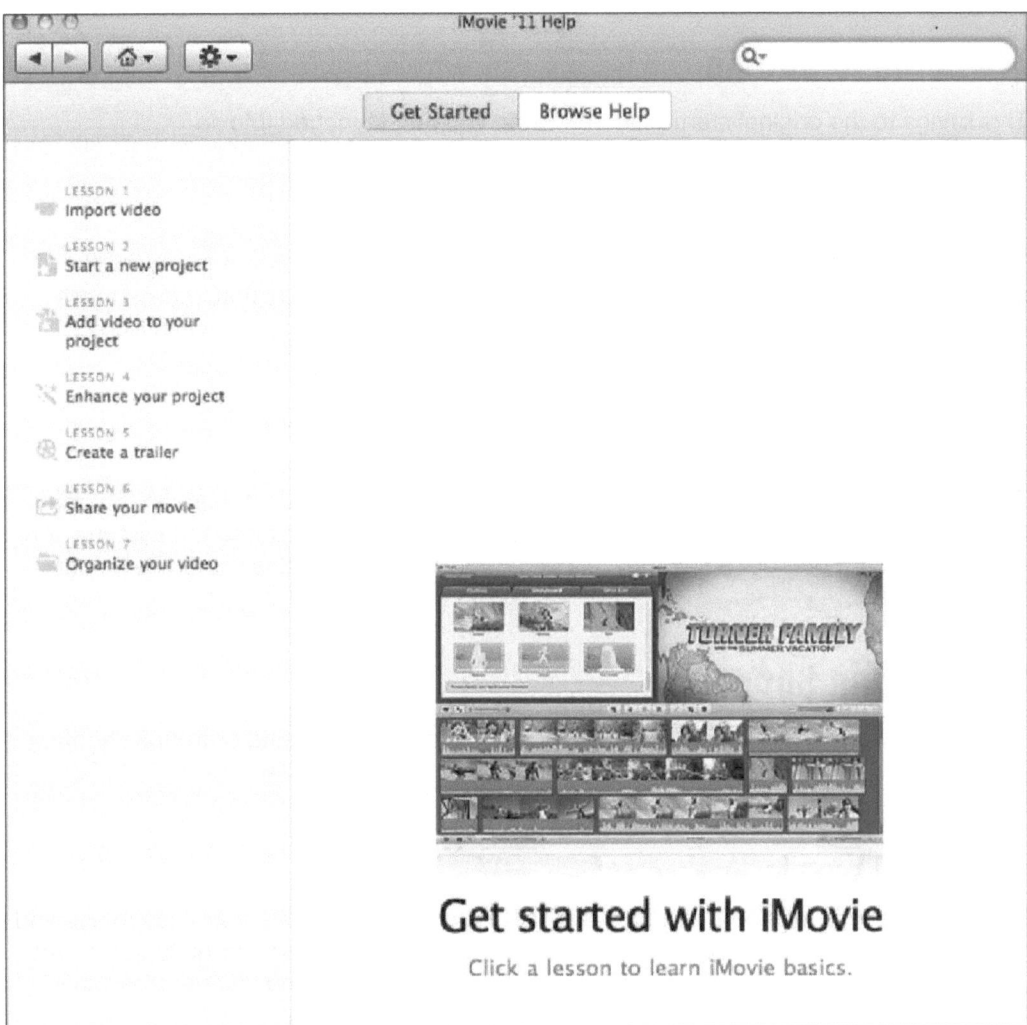

Figure 15–47. *iMovie Help Window*

This window follows the same format as other iLife apps. That is, there is a **Get Started** button (shown in Figure 15–47) that guides you through several key items all iMovie users should know how to do. The second section called **Browse Help** gives you further guidance by covering certain topics such as **Share your video project**, **Create an iMovie Project**, and **Organize video**.

Welcome to iMovie

This brings to the original startup screen when you first launched iMovie.

Keyboard Shortcuts

There are a lot of features found in iMovie. If you get hooked on it and you want to navigate the menus or tools faster, there are keyboard commands that access these items without having to use your mouse constantly. This feature gives you a list of of the ones available in iMovie.

Supported Cameras

This is highly important because Apple has to add every camera out there so that they can be used with iMovie. Apple has done a great job and has included the vast majority of cameras out there, but a few may still be missing. Check out this list to see if your camera appears.

Service and Support

This brings you to a site maintained by Apple to help you with using or troubleshooting iMovie.

Summary

And so the curtain falls on this trilogy of chapters about iMovie. It's way easy to use and yet powerful enough to keep you engaged and learning new things for quite some time. The only limitations are your creativity and the amount of free time you get to explore this stunning and elegant video editing program.

Part VIII

GarageBand

Does music move you?

GarageBand is divided into two different roles. Its first role is to teach you how to play the guitar or piano—it even gives you access to a store to purchase lessons from legends in the industry. Its second role is to enable you to write your own musical compositions. You can attach and record your own instruments, or you can compose a song note-by-note using one of GarageBand's software instruments. If there is a little Elvis in you, GarageBand makes it easy to let it out.

Chapter 16

Rockin' Around the GarageBand Sidebar

Ever dreamed of learning to play the piano or guitar? Have a song in your head that you know might be a top-ten hit? GarageBand delivers.

As with iMovie, a lot of GarageBand's features are geared toward someone new to the focus of the app. In this case, GarageBand can help you learn how to use a certain instrument, or you can spend hours fine-tuning your song with multiple instruments and other elements. This chapter provides an overview of the sidebar options of the program. Chapter 17: "Fiddlin' with the Functions Around the GarageBand Workspace" will go into more detail of all of the elements and options found in the various workspaces.

So, turn up the volume—let's get ready to jam with GarageBand!

Pump up the Jam . . .

When you first start GarageBand, you're greeted with the **Welcome** Screen. This is essentially the same as the other iLife **Welcome** screens; it just notes that there are sections in the app to help get your started or find help on particular elements of it.

After you click **Close**, you are presented with the screen shown in Figure 16–1. This screen lays out all of the project options available to you in GarageBand: **New Project**, **Learn to Play**, **Lesson Store**, **Magic GarageBand**, **iPhone Ringtone**, and **Recent Projects**. Let's run through each of them now.

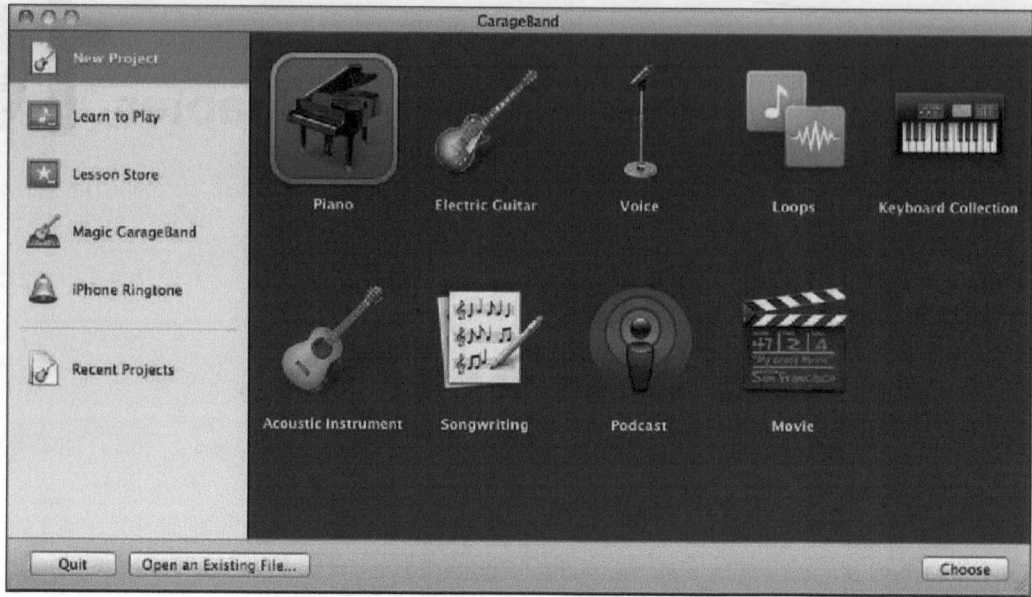

Figure 16–1. *Project options available in GarageBand*

New Project

This is the most involved project option you can choose. This option allows you to channel your inner Beethoven or Lennon. Whether you are experienced in songwriting or just starting out, GarageBand makes writing music easy and fun. The GarageBand workspace is the same for each option. I will cover the workspace in detail in the next chapter. As you can see from Figure 16–1, there are nine different new projects you can choose from: **Piano Electric Guitar**, **Voice**, **Loops**, **Keyboard Collection**, **Acoustic Instrument**, **Songwriting**, **Podcast**, and **Movie**.

A brief description of each follows.

Piano

This creates a new song with the piano as the default instrument. You can add more instruments if you wish. I will cover a new project workspace in more detail in the next chapter.

Electric Guitar

This creates a new song with an electric guitar as the default instrument. One of the cool features of GarageBand is that you can also choose what amplifier you want to "attach" the guitar to. You have over 40 to choose from. You can easily spend a few hours of experimenting with this.

Voice

This option gives you two default elements: **Male Basic** and **Female Basic**. GarageBand provides 20 effects that can be applied to the voice being recorded, including **Gospel Choir**, **Helium Breath**, **Live Performance**, **Male Rock Vocals**, and **Radio**. I think GarageBand has enough options here to satisfy everyone.

Loops

A loop is snippet of music that can be easily added to your project whenever you need it. Apple includes dozens of prerecorded loops in GarageBand. When you select **Loops** as a new project, you can create your own loop and have it also available for other sections of your project. You can create a loop with a real instrument. These are audio recordings. You can also create one with a software instrument that uses one of the many digital instruments included in GarageBand. A real instrument loop can be edited and added to either a real instrument or electric guitar tracks. A software loop can be edited note by note and can be viewed in **Piano Roll** or **Score** view.

Keyboard Collection

This starts you out with a sample of available keyboard instruments in GarageBand. The sample includes **Grand Piano**, **Electric Piano**, **Classic Organ**, **Smokey Clav**, **Solo Star**, **Falling Star**, and **Syncho Nice**. There are a number of other choices as well.

Acoustic Instrument

This allows you to record via the microphone various instruments. Depending on the instrument you are using, GarageBand might have a filter to enhance the recording. You can also apply effects such as **Celestial Spring**, **Double Filter**, **Lunar Bounce**, **Telephone Lines**, and **Zapper**.

Songwriting

This project starts out with a voice track, acoustic guitar, piano, muted bass, and drums. The drums track already has beats entered into this environment. As with the other types of projects, this is just a starting point defined by GarageBand. You can add or remove any element as you see fit.

Podcast

This sets up your project to create a podcast. It includes a male voice, female voice, jingles, and a special podcast track. GarageBand has special voice filters available just for podcasts. They include **Male Narrator**, **Male Radio Noisy**, and **Male Radio**. The podcast track allows you to add episode artwork, mark sections of the track as chapters, or display a URL.

Movie

Want to add a soundtrack to a movie? With this feature, you can add a movie by dragging it into its workspace and setting the music to the movie second by second. GarageBand separates the audio from the video so it is fully editable in GarageBand.

Learn to Play

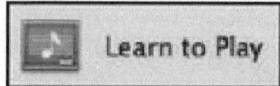

Want to learn the basics of playing a guitar? Learn the secrets of rock guitarists? How about learning the piano?

If you choose this option, you are given three main choices located at the top of the screen: **Guitar Lessons**, **Piano Lessons**, or **Artist Lessons** (see Figure 16–2).

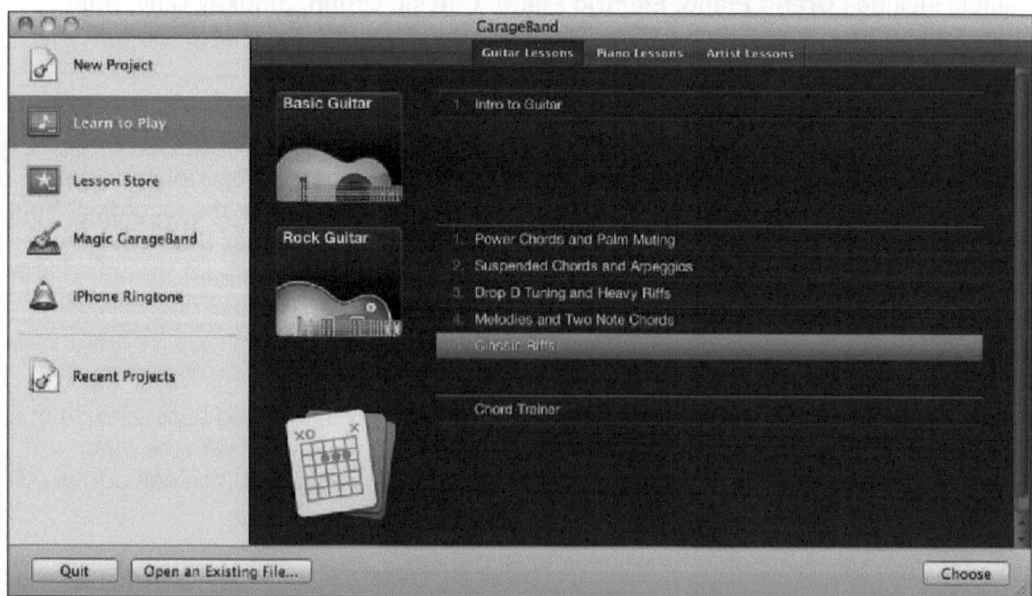

Figure 16–2. *Options for learning how to play the guitar*

Guitar Lessons

Notice in Figure 16–2 that I have selected **Guitar Lessons**.

You can select from **Basic Guitar**, **Rock Guitar**, or **Chord Trainer**. When you select any of the options, you are presented with a tutor that will help you learn the topic you have chosen. Click **Choose** Choose to select an item. Let's pick the **Intro to Guitar** option to sample these powerful and easy-to-follow lessons.

The first screen that appears is shown in Figure 16–3. Here we see the tutor as he starts introducing the topic. If you have a guitar, you can attach it and play alongside the tutor.

Figure 16–3. *Learning to play guitar*

Toward the bottom of the screen, there is a timeline that tells you at what stage of the tutorial you are. This is shown in Figure 16–4.

Figure 16–4. *Timeline of the tutorial video*

You can move the timeline marker to any location if you want to skip ahead or go back. The sections covered in the video are **Acoustic Guitar**, **Electric Guitar**, **Holding the Guitar**, **Tuning**, **Picking and Strumming,** and **Strumming an E Chord**.

If you have a guitar, you can follow along with the trainer and record the results. The options available are shown in Figure 16–5.

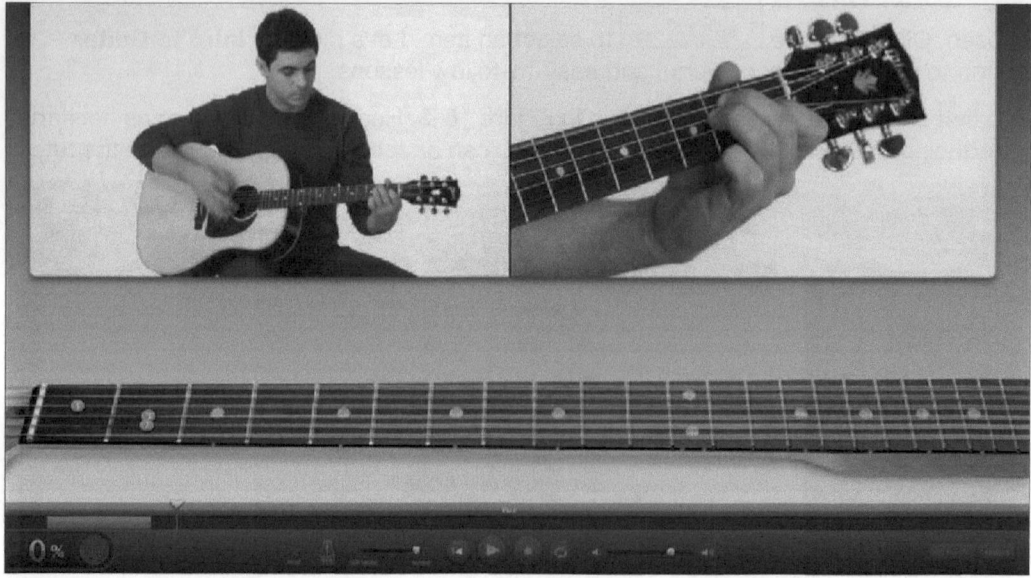

Figure 16–5. *Playing with Trainer window*

In Figure 16–5, the options are as follows:

Input: By default, this is your built-in microphone.

Metronome: This will play a constant tic at user-adjustable lengths of time.

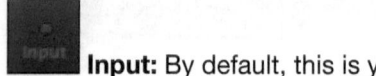 **Playback Speed:** This option allows you to slow down the lesson being played. You can move the slider all the way to the left, which plays the lesson at half speed.

Go Back to the Beginning: This button returns you back to the beginning of the lesson.

Play: This will start or stop playback.

Record: This will record your audio as you match the trainer's notes. The notes will be displayed in the screen with numbers stating which strings have to be played and in what order. This is shown in Figure 16–6. You can also change the view angle of the guitar neck from flat on to ¾, as well as to left-handed playing.

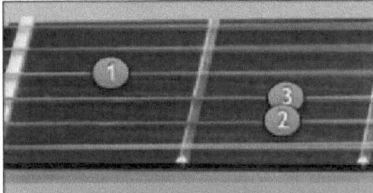

Figure 16–6. *Example of the strings that must be played while trying to match the trainer*

Cycle Region: This will turn the cycle region on or off.

Audio Volume: This slider will adjust the volume of audio while listening to the lesson or playing along with the trainer.

My Results: This will display the accuracy of how well you match the trainer. If this is turned on (the default), you will see a line just below the window displaying the accuracy. Because I do not have a guitar, I will never get a match and the redline will reflect this at bottom of tutorial window. This is shown in Figure 16–7. You also have percentage indicator at the far left of this window.

Figure 16–7. *Example of not matching the trainer note for note*

Click the **History** button and Figure 16–8 will appear. This window keeps track of your progress. Please note that the graph appears blank because I do not own a guitar to plug into my Mac. Therefore, GarageBand is telling me that I am not (and cannot at this time) match the notes played to me. There is also an option to reset the lesson. This button is located at the far left bottom of the screen. You can also open this lesson in a full-featured GarageBand window. Click the **Open in GarageBand** button, which is also located at the far left bottom of the screen.

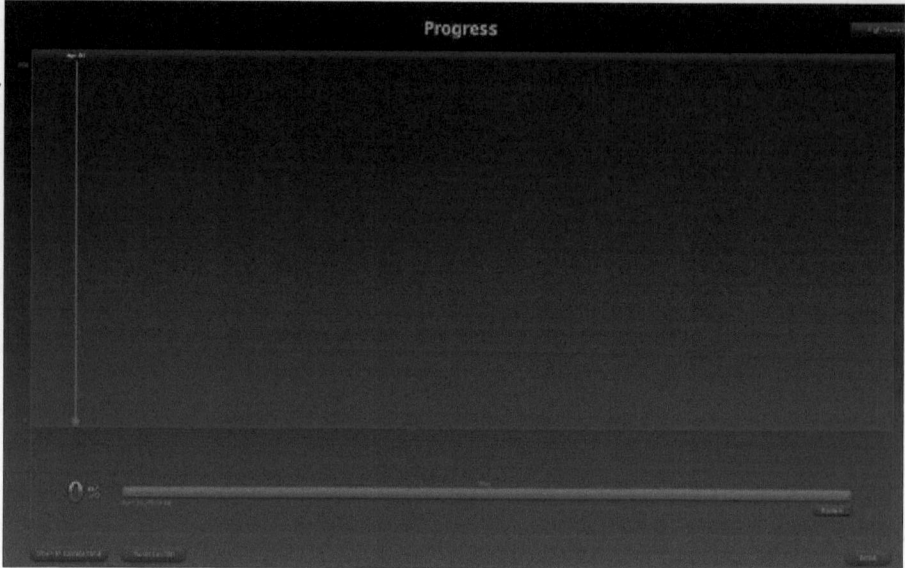

Figure 16–8. *Progress window that appears when clicking on the **History** button*

At the top right-hand corner of this window is another set of useful tools. This section is shown in Figure 16–9. The first choice located at the far left is the **Glossary**.

Figure 16–9. *Top corner of guitar lesson workspace*

Glossary: If you click this button, a very useful list of musical terms is brought up. The items in the **Glossary** are shown in Figure 16–10.

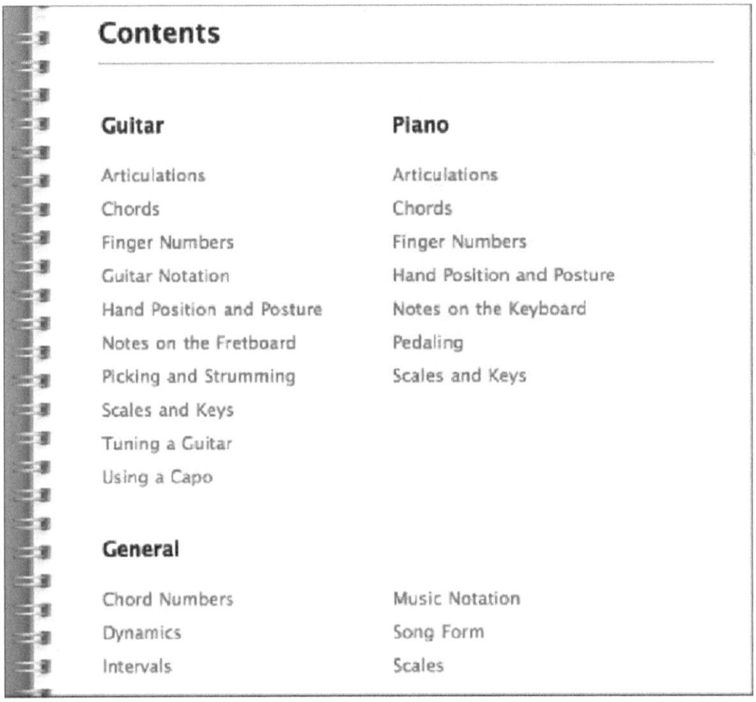

Contents
Guitar
Articulations
Chords
Finger Numbers
Guitar Notation
Hand Position and Posture
Notes on the Fretboard
Picking and Strumming
Scales and Keys
Tuning a Guitar
Using a Capo
Piano
Articulations
Chords
Finger Numbers
Hand Position and Posture
Notes on the Keyboard
Pedaling
Scales and Keys
General
Chord Numbers
Dynamics
Intervals
Music Notation
Song Form
Scales

Figure 16–10. *Glossary terms*

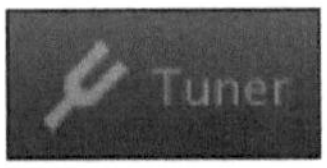

Tuner
The **Tuner** button allows you to tune your guitar. If this option is chosen, the screen in Figure 16–11 will appear. I just whistled into the mic to demonstrate how the program reads the sounds as notes.

Standard Tuning
E-A-D-G-B-E
50-
+50
D
Click on the string you want to tune...

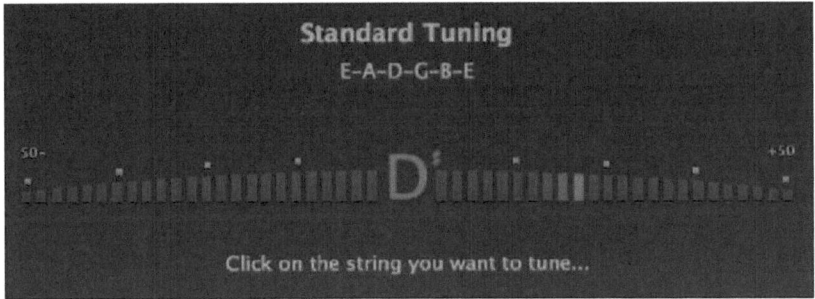

Figure 16–11. *Example of the tuner function while using the Play option in guitar lesson*

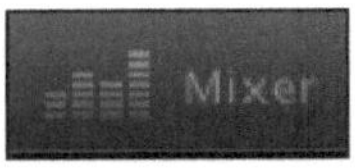

Mixer
The **Mixer** button allows you to customize the way elements are used in this option. This is shown in Figure 16–12.

Figure 16–12. *The **Mixer** window*

The following buttons are found in this window:

- This will mute or unmute a track.

- This will solo or unsolo a track. (Play only the selected track.)

- This slider determines the volume of the track.

This allows you to change the environment of the Guitar workspace when playing in this option. This is shown in Figure 16–13.

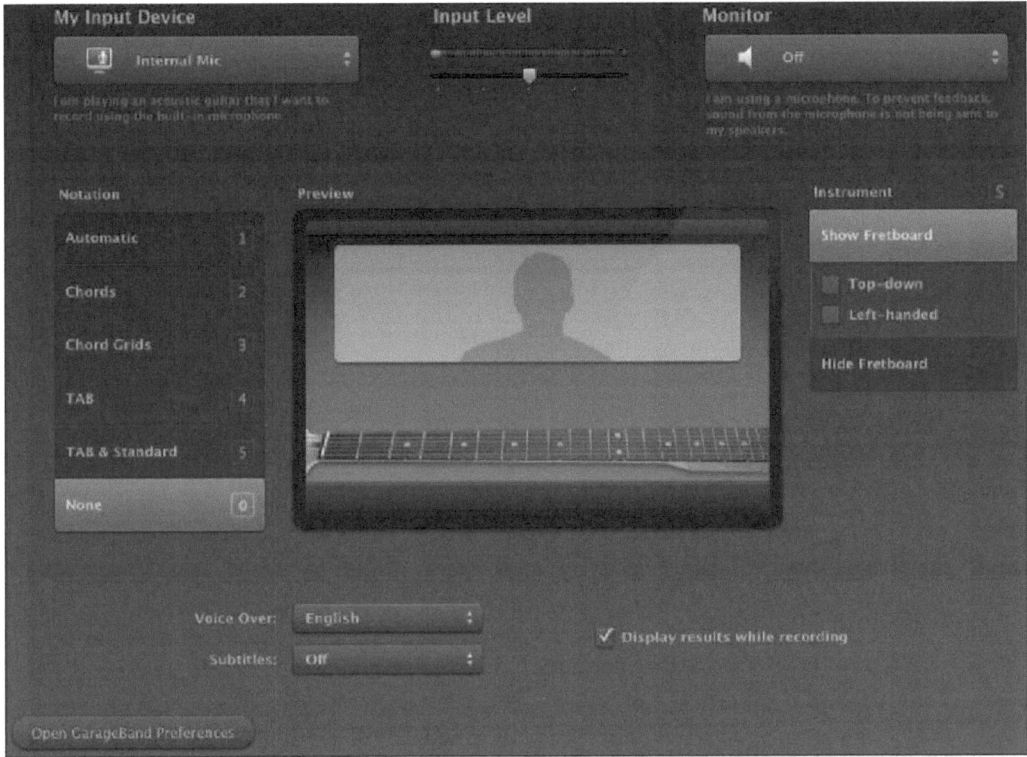

Figure 16–13. *Setup window*

The options available are as follows:

- **My Input Device:** Can be **Internal Mic** or **Line In** (guitar attached to Mac).

- **Input Level:** This allows you to adjust the volume.

- **Monitor:** This can be **OFF** (the default, to avoid feedback; music is not played back on your speakers), **ON** (this plays your music through your speakers or headphones, or **ON with No Feedback Protection**.

- **Notation:** If you choose one of the options listed—**Automatic**, **Chords**, **Chord Grids**, **TAB**, **TAB & Standard**, or **None (Default)**—the selected item will appear in the playing workspace. An example of having Cord Grids turned on it shown in Figure 16–14.

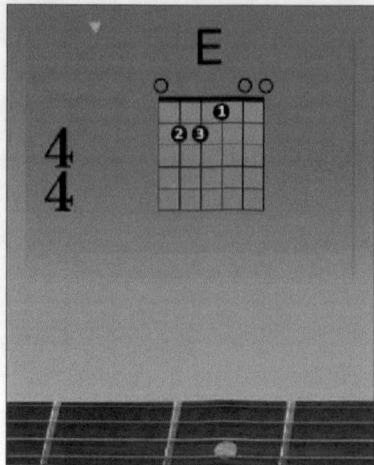

Figure 16–14. *Example of Chord Grids turned on*

- **Preview:** This gives you a small preview of how the guitar workspace will look with any of the notation settings or how you choose to have the guitar positioned.

- **Instrument—** This determines how the guitar is displayed in the workspace. It can be either: Show Fretboard (default) or Hide Fretboard. If you choose Show Fretboard the guitar can also be shown Top-down or Left-handed.

- **Voiceover:** This can be either: **English (Default)**, **French**, **German**, **Japanese**, or **Spanish**.

- **Subtitles:** This allows you to add subtitles for 14 different languages.

Display Results While Recording: This is on by default. It displays the notes when you are playing.

Open GarageBand Preferences: This opens the **GarageBand Preferences** window. You can modify several settings in this window. This will be discussed in detail in the next chapter.

This will also bring up musical notation on your screen. The choices available are **Automatic**, **Chords**, **Chord Grids**, **TAB**, **TAB & Standard**, **None**, or—new to the mix—**Full Page**. **Full Page** displays all of the notes of the song you are trying to match in one page.

Lesson Store

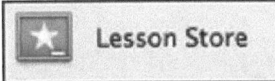

Would you like to further you knowledge by using more advanced lessons, or learn from a famous artist? GarageBand allows you to individually download new lessons, or gives you the choice of quite a few artists to help you master your skills.

The first screen that appears is shown in Figure 16–15. Here you can choose between new **Guitar Lessons**, **Piano Lessons**, or **Artist Lessons**. You can return to this screen at anytime by clicking on the small **Home** button at the top of the window.

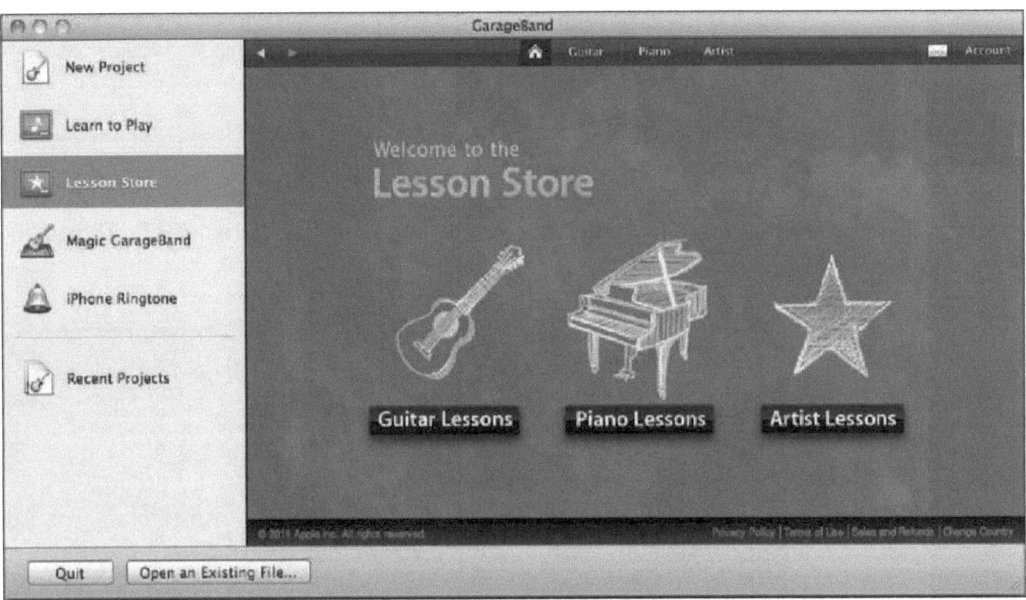

Figure 16–15. *Initial **Lesson Store** screen*

If you click **Guitar Lessons**, you are brought to the screen shown in Figure 16–16. At the top of the screen, you can chose between three famous artists. If you click on an artist, you will see a small description of the lesson and a short video clip of the lesson. Each lesson costs $4.99. I know—I thought they were free, too.

You can also download eight more **Basic Guitar** lessons, five **Rock Guitar** lessons, or seven lessons on the **Blues Guitar**.

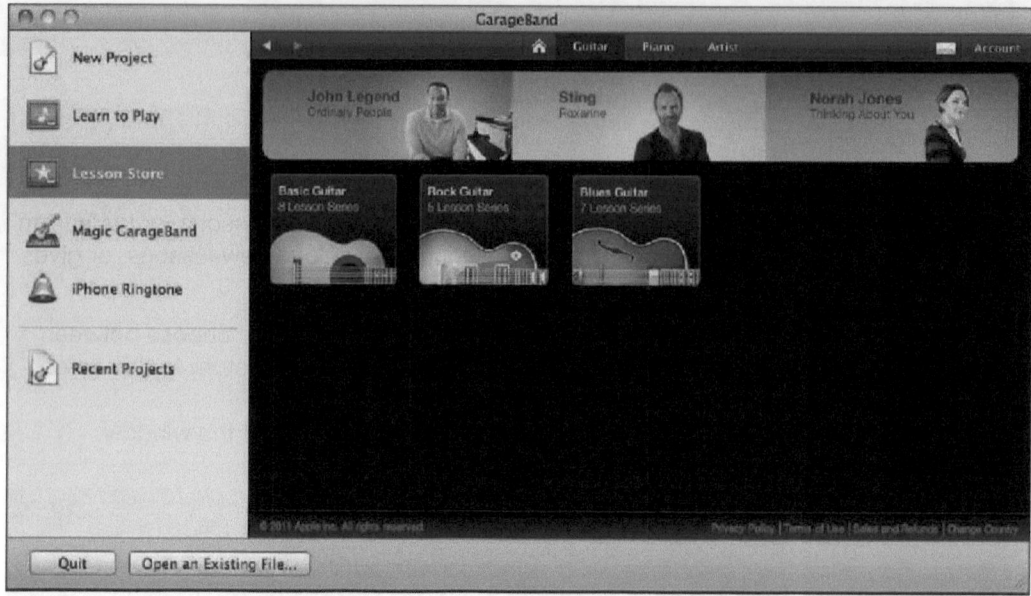

Figure 16–16. *Choices of guitar lessons*

If you pick **Basic Guitar,** you can see what each lesson entails (Figure 16–17). These downloads are free.

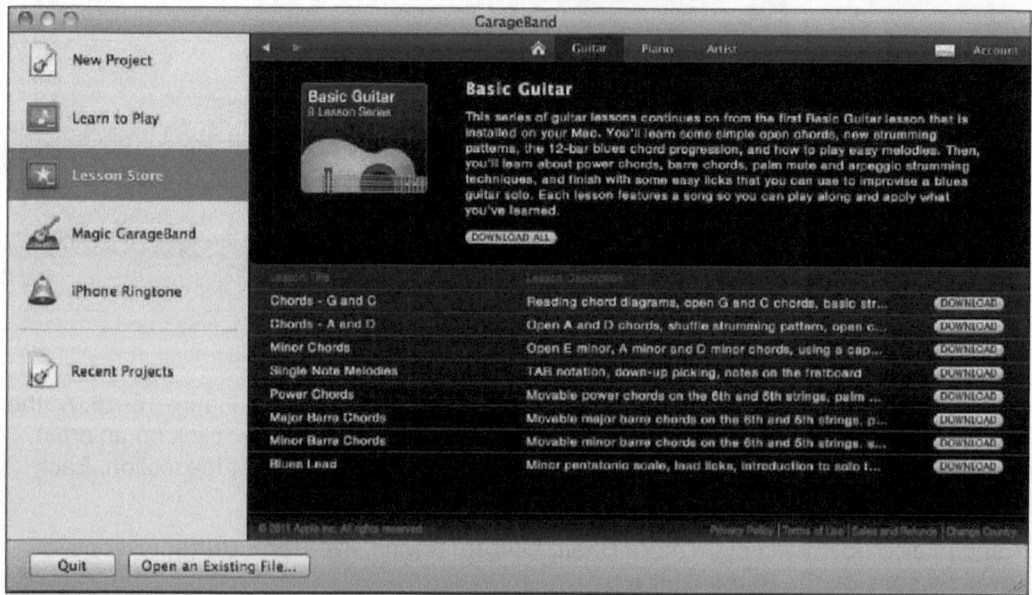

Figure 16–17. *Basic Guitar lessons available from the Lesson Store*

You can pick individually what lessons you want to use and download them one by one by clicking the **Download** button DOWNLOAD next to lesson description. You can choose **Download All**  after the intro paragraph at the top of the window. After you download one or all, these lessons will appear the **Learn to Play** section.

The **Piano Section** is essentially the same, but offers piano lessons. It contains eight more basic piano lessons, six pop piano lessons, and four classical piano lessons. The artist lessons at the top of the screen remain the same.

The **Artist Lessons** section contains 15 guitar lessons and 8 piano lessons for purchase.

There are two important buttons located at the top right of your screen.

Envelope: This button is located at the top of your screen, to the far right. If you click on it, you can have Apple e-mail you whenever new lessons are added.

Account: You must have an Apple ID to purchase artist lessons. This button will allow you to log in to your account or create a new account if you need it.

Magic GarageBand

Ever want to jam with a band? With this cool feature, GarageBand creates nine different groups to jam with: **Blues, Rock, Jazz, Country, Reggae, Funk, Latin, Roots Rock**, or **Slow Blues**. The initial selection screen is shown in Figure 16–18.

Figure 16–18. *Choice of bands to jam with*

If you move your mouse over a selection, a small **Preview** button will appear and, when you click on it, you can hear a sample of the music that the band plays.

Reviewing the Options . . .

Let's demonstrate **Magic GarageBand**'s awesomeness by selecting the **Rock Band**. To choose a band, double-click it. The screen shown in Figure 16–19 will appear.

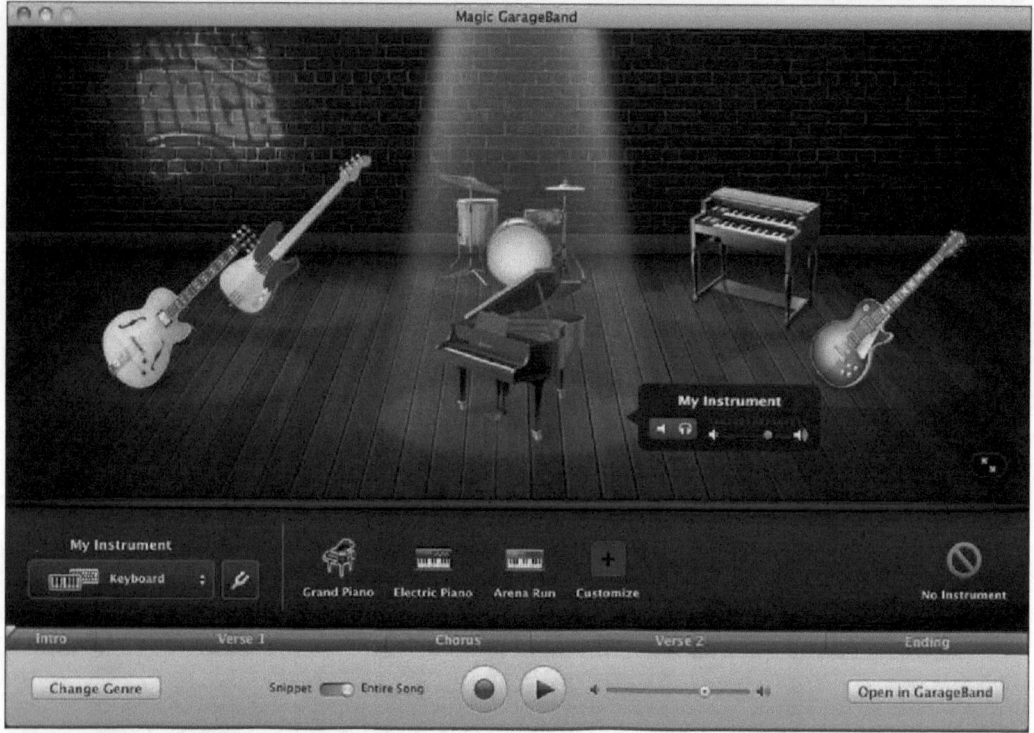

Figure 16–19. *The Magic GarageBand workspace: Rock Band*

There are quite a few things to go over in this screen. Let's begin with **My Instrument**.

The instrument currently being accessed is highlighted in a yellowish spotlight.

My Instrument: It could be **Keyboard** (on by default in this group setting), **Internal Mic**, or **Line In**. You can also modify the monitor settings in this dropdown menu. Please notice the selection of pianos next to my instrument. Depending on what instrument you select, a list of different instruments will appear for each item. Also, please notice that you will see a small **My Instrument** setting window appear next to the instrument you have chosen. This is seen in Figure 16–20. Here you can change the volume of the instrument via the volume slider, mute the sound completely for this instrument by clicking on the speaker icon  or solo the instrument by clicking on the headphone icon .

Figure 16–20. *Example of the* **My Instrument** *setting window*

Tuning Fork: This will help you tune your instrument if you are using the internal mic or line in. You need a special adapter to plug your instrument into the line-in port of your Mac.

Change Genre Don't want to be a rock star? Here you can go back and change the band you will jam with.

Audition After you have selected your new band (or decided not to fire your current band), click on **Audition** to return to the main **Jam Session** window.

Snippet ○ Entire Song You can jam to an entire song (default) or just a snippet (a short piece of the song).

This button will record your jam session.

This button will get the band ready and start the jam session.

This slider adjusts the volume of your session.

Open in GarageBand This will take the track you are jamming to and open it in the main GarageBand workspace so that you can edit each instrument individually.

This button, found in the **Jam** workspace in the lower right-hand corner, will make the session take over the your whole screen.

Verse 1 This is the timeline indicator for the song. You can manually move to any location in the song. It is located below the instrument selection line.

No Instrument If you click on this button, the currently selected instrument will be taken out of the band. You must click on an instrument to replace it.

iPhone Ringtone

iPhone Ringtone starts you off with three default workspaces to create a custom iPhone ringtone: **Example Ringtone**, **Loops**, or **Voice** (see Figure 16–20). You can then modify any one of these options and create your own personalized ringtone.

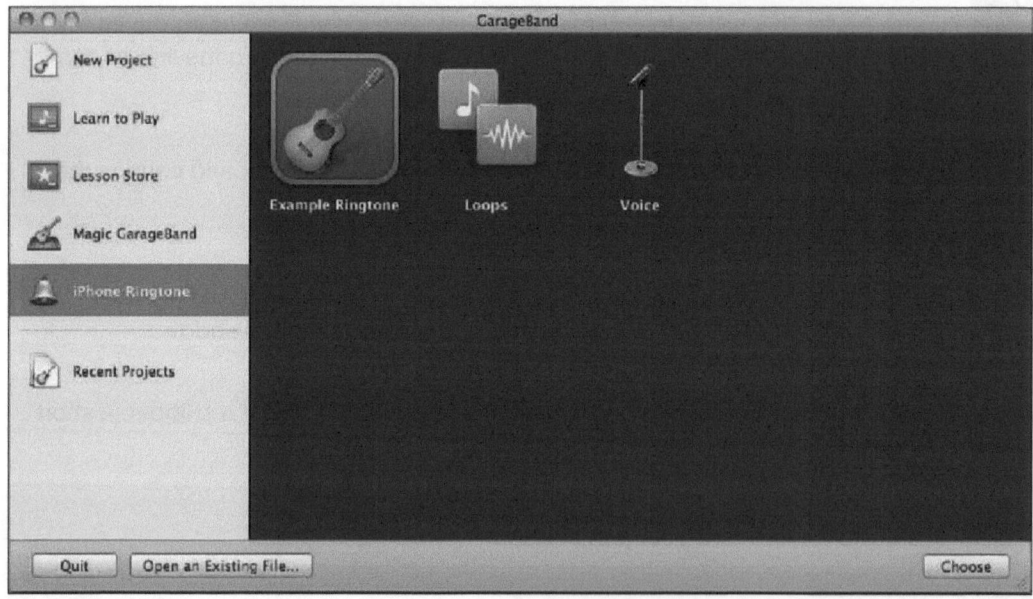

Figure 16–21. *Choices to start the process of creating a custom iPhone ringtone*

The next two sections are fairly straightforward. They both allow you to access previous work done in GarageBand.

Recent Projects

This option lists all of your current songs you are working in. An example is shown in Figure 16–21.

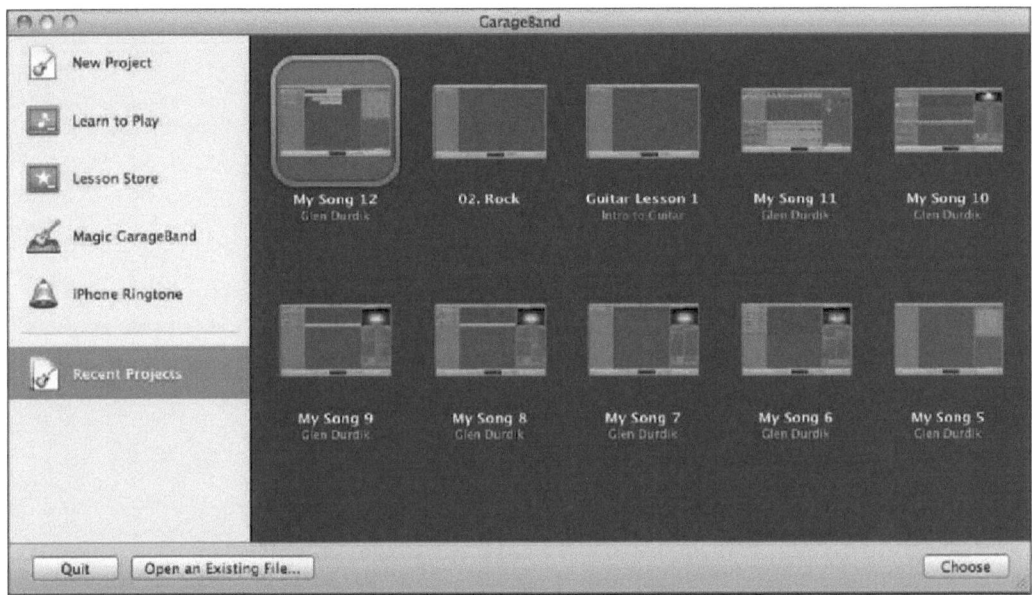

Figure 16–22. *The* ***Recent Projects*** *window*

 **Click Open an Existing File . . .** to bring up a finder window showing all of projects you have been working on. Your projects are stored in the GarageBand folder located in your Music folder.

Quit This will quit your current session in the GarageBand studio.

Summary

This wraps up my discussion on the sidebar of GarageBand. As we have seen, you have a lot of options to choose from. With GarageBand, you can create the next biggest hit from scratch or learn how to play the piano or guitar. GarageBand tops the charts when it comes to music creation for home use or learning how to be a better guitarist or pianist.

Chapter 17

Fiddlin' with the Functions Around the GarageBand Workspace

In the previous chapter, we saw the many ways you can create music in GarageBand via the sidebar options. In this chapter, I will explain the main workspace of GarageBand, and all the functions around it. So, let's get started with learning about the workspace and writing our first note in GarageBand. Grammy's, here we come.

Creating a New Piano Project

Recall from the last chapter that when you first start GarageBand, you're greeted with the **Welcome** Screen. After you click **Close**, you are presented with all of the project options available to you in GarageBand. I'll start our journey by creating a new project with a piano as the default instrument. The first item that appears is the **Save** window. This is shown in Figure 17–1.

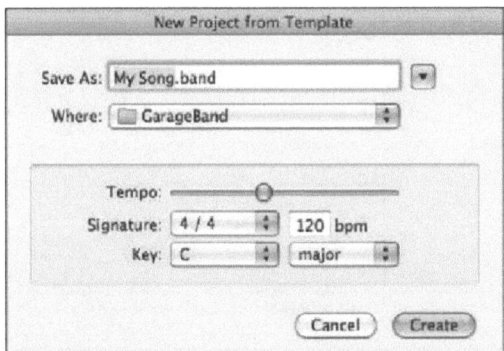

Figure 17–1. *Save window in GarageBand*

In this window, you must enter a name next to **Save As:** (glenrocks.band, in this example) and indicate where you want to save it (in this case, the GarageBand folder located in your music folder). The next section in this window deals with the musical aspects of your file.

The options are:

- **Tempo:** This determines at what speed your song is going to play.

- **Bpm:** This stands for "beats per minute." As you move the slider next to **Tempo**, this number either increases or decreases. You can also enter a number manually.

- **Signature:** This defines how musical time is divided into measures and beats. In the example in Figure 17–1, we see it is 4/4. The first number determines the number of beats in each measure. The second number determines the beat value. Beat value is the length of the note that gets one beat. 4/4 is the most commonly used signature.

- **Key:** This defines the central note to which other notes relate.

- **Major or Minor:** A key can be either major or minor. If you change the scale, the key might be changed to follow the common practice of printed music.

I am not a trained musician and a lot of people reading this manual are probably not either. I usually just leave this section as is. As you learn more about writing music and what sounds good to you, you will learn if these settings need to be customized to better match the song you are about to write.

Examining the GarageBand Workspace

After you've named your file, determined where you want to save it, and which musical settings to use, click **Create** [Create].

This will bring up the main GarageBand workspace, which is shown in Figure 17–2. The following sections describe the areas highlighted in the figure.

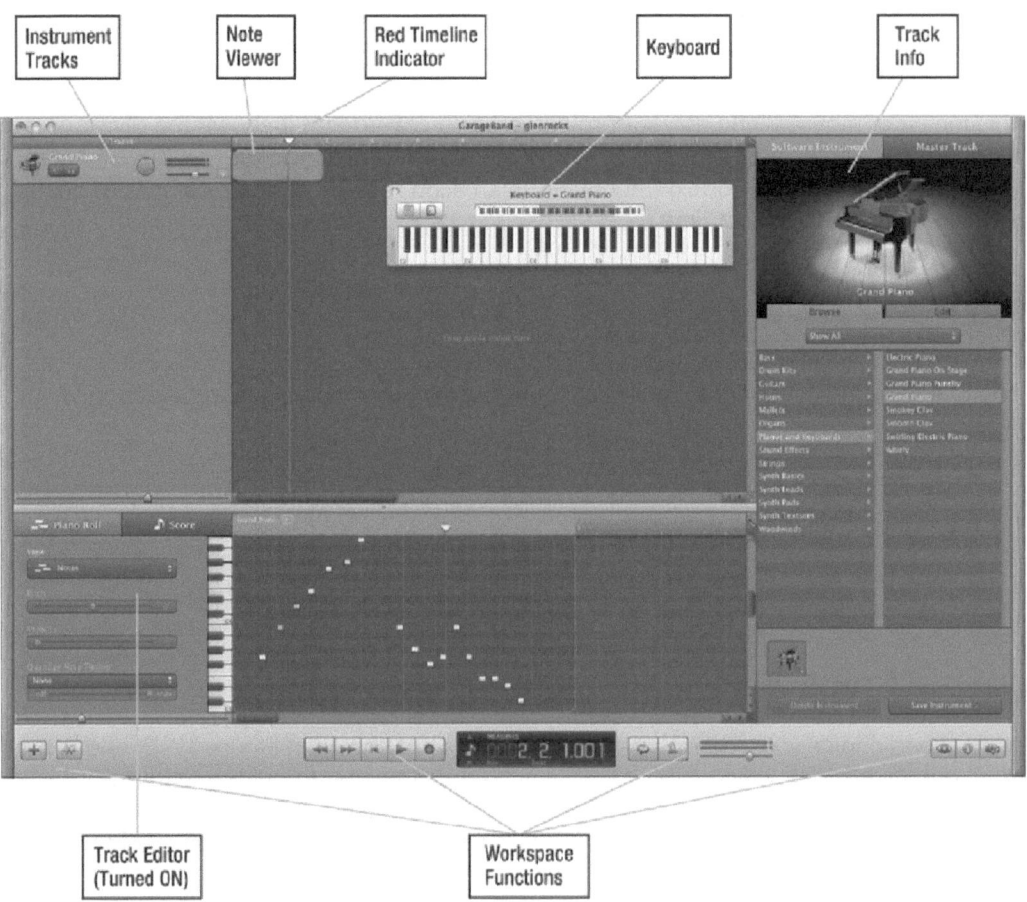

Figure 17–2. *Main GarageBand workspace*

Instrument Tracks

This shows you which instruments (and voices) you have in your song. As I discussed in the previous chapter, the type of new project you select determines the default instruments to be in the workspace. In this example, I chose the **Piano** option, and only the piano shows up in the **Instrument** track section.

Note Viewer

This displays the notes recorded in your song in a simple, non-labeled graph. As you record, each newly recorded segment is called a region. Regions are denoted as rounded rectangles in your timeline. You can later move, copy, or split regions. To get a more comprehensive layout that makes it easier to determine a note you have recorded, you must turn on the track editor. This is discussed a bit later in this chapter.

Red Timeline Indicator

This indicator moves along as your project is being played and it shows the divisions of time in either beats and measures or minutes and seconds. If you turn on the alignment guides (activated in the **Control** menu), you can align regions or other items with beats, measures, or other units of time.

Keyboard

This is one of the methods for recording notes via GarageBand's software instruments. You can view the keyboard by going to the **Window** menu and selecting **Keyboard**.

Musical Typing

The second choice is called musical typing. This is not shown in Figure 17–2, and is a more detailed layout, which should help any beginning writer to quickly learn the different notes. To view the musical typing method of musical input, you too have to go to the **Window** menu and select **Musical Typing**. As you play around with GarageBand, you will see which method of note input you prefer.

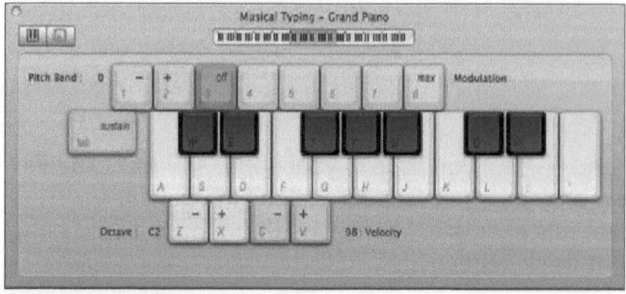

Notice these two buttons in the upper right-hand corner of the **Musical Typing** interface. The button on the left will convert the **Musical Typing** layout to the standard **Keyboard** interface. If you are in the **Keyboard** mode, you can click on the button on the right to return to the **Musical Typing** interface. Please note that these buttons do not appear in the **Keyboard** window until you have accessed the **Musical Typing** layout at least once.

Audio Input

You can also record music via your built-in microphone or line-in. The line-in port allows you to connect (with a special cable) your musical instrument directly into GarageBand for recording. The audio input is determined by a setting found in the **Preferences...** section of the **GarageBand** menu. This is further discussed in Chapter 18: "Help Composing Your Song with Notes on GarageBand Menus."

Track Info

This contains two sections and can be removed from the workspace to allow more room for the **Note Viewer** window. This can be accessed at any time by clicking on the **Track Info** button at the bottom of your workspace at the far right.

Software Instrument Section: Browse Tab

This displays all of the software instruments that you can choose from. If you want to change the default piano instrument to another instrument, just select an instrument in the **Instrument Track** window and then choose from one of the many keyboard instruments under the **Browse** tab or select a totally different instrument. The instrument will automatically change in the **Instrument Track** window. I started out with a basic piano at the beginning of this chapter. Now, armed with the knowledge of how to change my instrument, I have seven more keyboard instruments to choose from. And when you are ready to add more instruments to your song, you have a ton of software instruments to choose from. Start with the basics, learn what sounds good to you, and then the sky is the limit.

Be warned: as with other iLife creation tools, your free time might suddenly be all booked up as you discover new ways to perfect your project.

The **Browse** tab is shown in Figure 17–3.

Figure 17–3. *Browse tab of the Software Instrument section*

Software Instrument Section: Edit Tab

This section allows you to set various aspects of the instrument you have chosen. In the example shown in Figure 17–4, I have chosen the Smokey Clav keyboard instrument. You can change the **Sound Generator** settings, **Effects** settings (three different ones for this instrument), the **Visual EQ** (equalizer), **Master Echo**, and **Master Reverb**. At the bottom right of this window, you can save your changes by clicking on the **Save Instrument...** button. Everyone has a mental snapshot of what his or her song should be. This option gives you even more ways to explore and narrow down just exactly what those notes floating in your head will sound like in the real world.

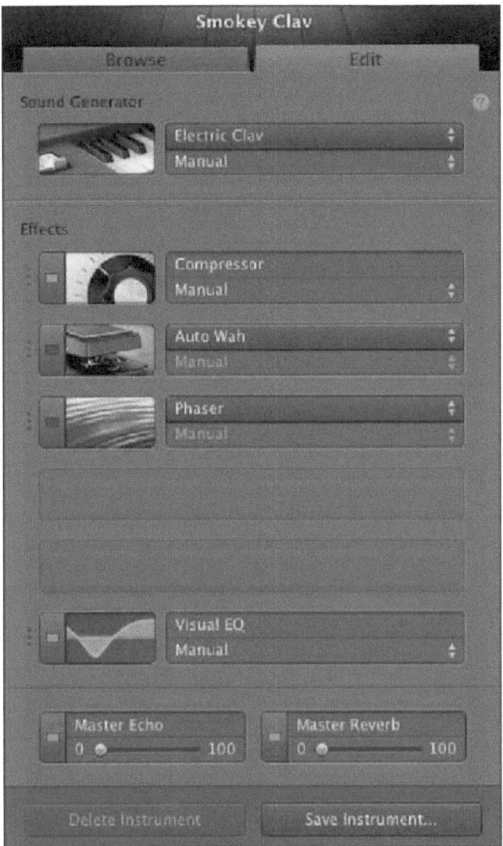

Figure 17–4. *Edit tab of the **Software Instrument** section*

Master Track Section: Browse Tab

This tab allows you to change master effects presets you want to be shown in the **Track Info** menus. The list of effects that are available are shown in |Figure 17–5.

Figure 17–5. *List of effects that can be shown in the **Track Info** menus*

Master Track Section: Edit Tab

Within this tab, you can change **Track Effects** (**Echo** and **Reverb**) and **Master Effects** (**Visual EQ**, **Compressor**, and **Ducker**). The complete **Edit** tab is shown in Figure 17–6.

If you make changes to these settings, you can save it as a new master. You can save it by clicking on the **Save Master...** Save Master... button at the bottom right of the tab.

Figure 17–6. *Master Track section of the Track Info window, Edit tab*

Add New Track Button

The **Add New Track button** is located along the bottom of the GarageBand workspace, all the way on the left. This is shown Figure 17–2. Click this button to access the three options for adding a new track shown in Figure 17–7. The options include: **Software Instrument**, **Real Instrument**, or **Electric Guitar**. **Instrument Setup** allows you to access how the instrument is connected (not the software instrument). It can be **System Setting**, **Built-in Microphone**, or **Built-in Input**. You can also change how you want to hear sound. It can be **System Setting** or **Built-in Output**.

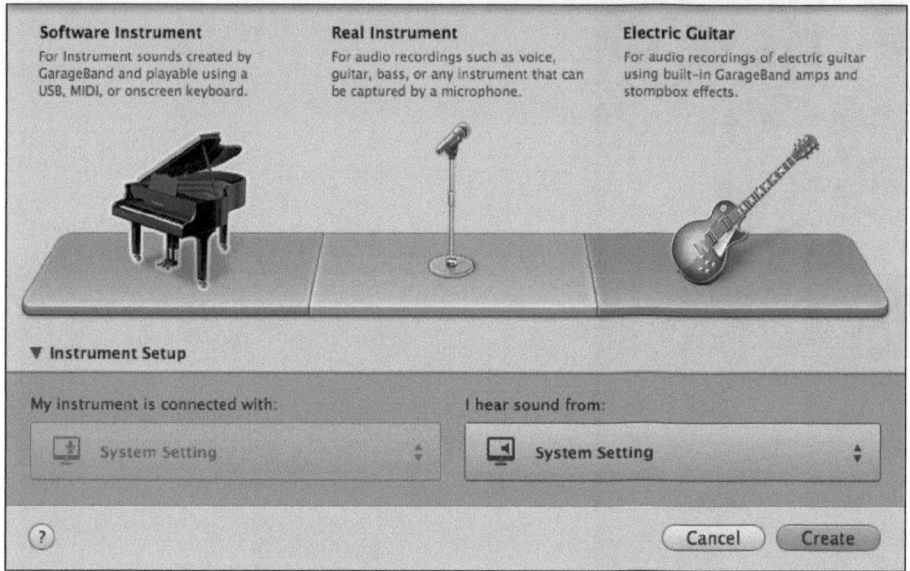

Figure 17–7. *The three types of instruments available for creating a new track*

View/Hide Track Editor

This button is located at the bottom of your project workspace next to the **Add Track** button. It allows you to access to the **Track Editor**, which allows you to move recorded notes individually. You can view the **Track Editor** in two different views. They are the **Piano Roll** and **Score** .

Piano Roll

Piano Roll views the notes in chart form with a piano at the left of the chart showing the layout of the notes available. This window is shown in Figure 17–8. Just highlight a note on this graph and move it to any other spot available on the scale or anywhere else in your song. If you select a note, you also have access to a few options that are listed on the far left of this window. They include: **View** (**Notes**, **Modulation**, **Pitchbend**, **Sustain**, **Expression**, or **Foot Control**), **Pitch** (a slider setting), **Velocity** (a slider setting), or **Quantize Note Timing**. This will move the selected note to the spot you select from a dropdown menu. The choices available in this menu are shown in Figure 17–9. This window makes editing notes and rearranging them as easy as clicking and holding down your mouse button. It's an instant musical arranger, thanks to GarageBand.

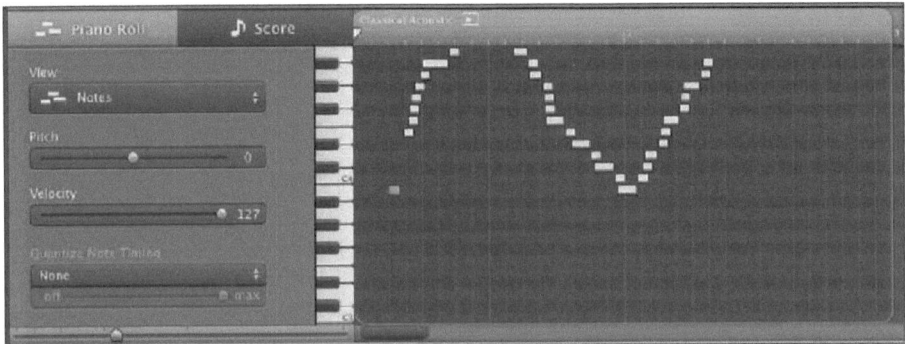

Figure 17–8. *Track Editor* window: *Piano Roll*

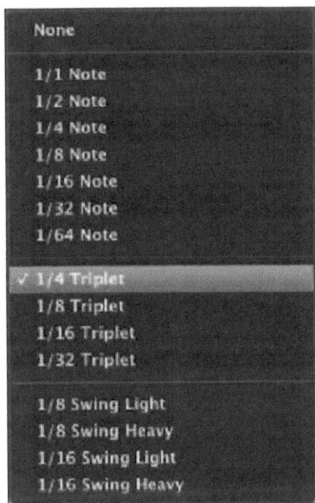

Figure 17–9. *Options available when accessing the* **Quantize Note Timing** *dropdown menu*

Score

The other option is the **Score** ♪ Score window. This displays all recorded notes as written notes. You must have some musical background to interpret these notes. This window is shown in Figure 17–10.

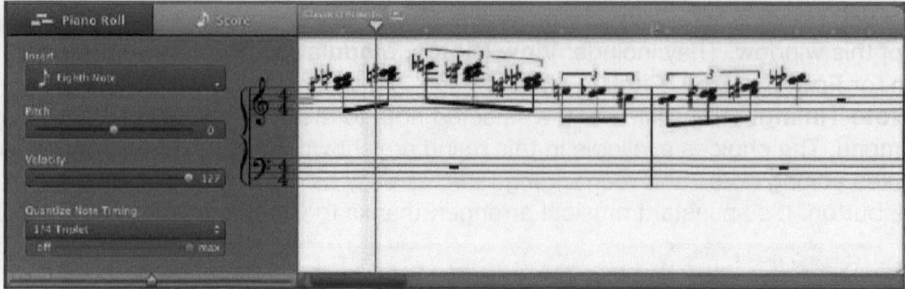

Figure 17–10. *Track Editor window:* ***Score***

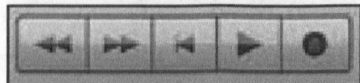

These five buttons are found at the bottom of your workspace, roughly in the middle of your screen. They govern your time indicator movement and whether you want to play your selection or record a new piece.

Moving Back One Measure

 This button will move your time indicator back one measure.

Moving Forward One Measure

 This will move your time indicator forward one measure.

Returning to the Beginning of the Song

 This simply returns your time indicator back to the beginning of your song.

Play/ Stop Button

This will either start playing your song or pause it. Pressing the spacebar can also stop playback.

Record Button

This button will start the recording process. Click on this button again to stop recording. You must stop the track manually by clicking on the **Stop** button or hitting the spacebar.

LCD Display

This screen is found directly at the bottom of your screen, in the middle. It displays various aspects of your song. Measures are shown in this example, which is the default. You can also show chords, time, or display in one window - the **Key**, **Tempo**, and **Signature** (project window). You can switch the info shown by

clicking on the small graphic (a musical note in this example) at the far left of the LCD display and choosing your selection from a drop down menu. You can also change the window by clicking on one of the arrows above and below this small graphic.

Turning Cycling On or Off

This button is located at the bottom of your workspace, to the right of the LCD display screen. When activated, this will display a yellow line at the top of your song. This region is called the cycle region. It determines where in your song you want to add a recording of a live instrument. You can drag this yellow area anywhere in your song or lengthen or shorten the region by holding your mouse button down on either end of the yellow line and dragging to the left or right. This area can also be turned on or off via hitting the C key. An example of the cycle region is shown in Figure 17–11.

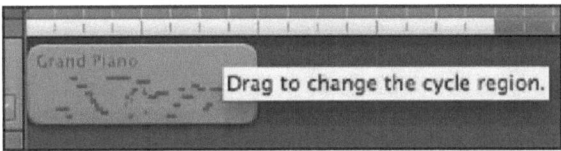

Figure 17–11. *Example of the cycle region turned on (yellow line)*

Metronome Button

This button is found at the bottom of your workspace, just to the right of the **Cycling On or Off** button. It will activate a metronome for your track. A metronome "beeps" out a beat in your song to help you keep the tempo as you record. It is not recorded in your recording. It is a tool that you might find handy to help create your song.

Volumes

This window is also located along the bottom of your workspace. It is to right of the **Metronome** button. It displays the left and right volumes of your song as it is playing (two green lines, in this example) and has a slider to adjust the volume of your playback.

Loop Browser Button

This button is located with a trio of buttons at bottom of your screen, at the far right. It brings up a **Loops** sidebar at the far right of your screen. Loops are small pre-recorded audio files that can be added to your project. Loops are mainly used to add drumbeats or other sounds to your song. As I stated, I am not a musician. With the addition of loops, I can add background music to my simple piano track in a flash. It's like having an instant back-up band. A loop can be chosen from one of the pre-recorded ones included in GarageBand, or you can create your own. A loop can either be made with a software instrument or a real instrument. The available loops are shown in Figure 17–12. You have three different views for loops. Figure 17–12 shows the **Column** view

Figure 17–12. *Column view of the Loops window*

If you click on the musical note icon , you chose the loops in a different way. This displays your options by genre, such as rock, jazz, electric, or dark. This view is shown in Figure 17–13.

Figure 17–13. *Loops organized by type/genre*

The last option is the **Podcast** view ![podcast icon]. This gives you many choices to enhance your podcast. A sample of this window is shown in Figure 17–14.

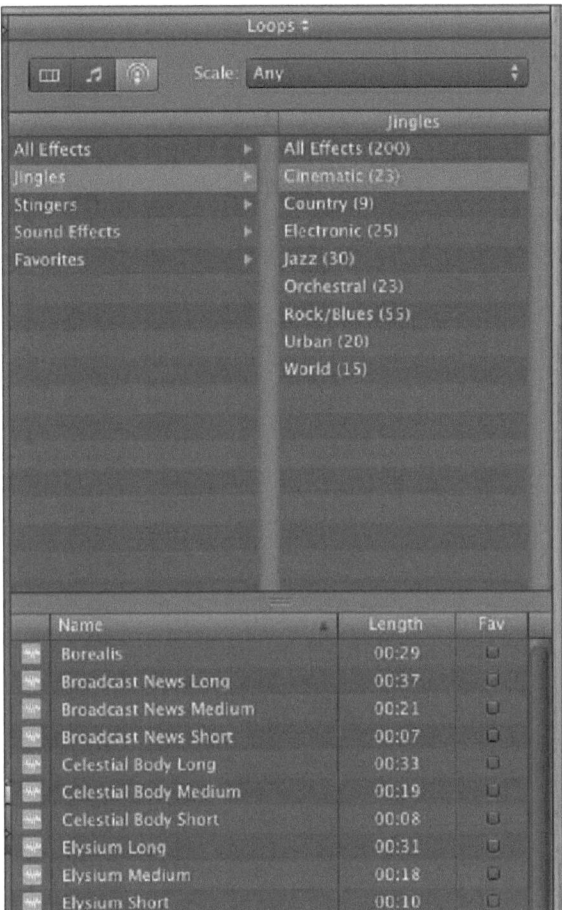

Figure 17–14. *Podcast view of the Loops window*

Track Info Button

This button is located at the bottom of your workspace, just to the right of the **Loops Browser** button. It was discussed in detail earlier in this chapter, when I discussed the elements of the main workspace.

Media Browser Button

This button is the last in the trio of buttons located at bottom of workspace. It gives you access to your audio and video files stored in various locations. For audio, it can be in a GarageBand folder or in iTunes. For photos, it has to be in iPhoto. For movies, it can be in an iMovie folder, Movies folder, or iPhoto.

Summary

GarageBand gives you access to a huge selection of software instruments. With it, you can also record live instruments and apply many effects to your music. The GarageBand workspace gives you an ideal environment to start to learn how to write a song or enhance your writing skills with more advanced options. With the power of GarageBand, the ability to record the next big hit is at your fingertips. Play, explore, learn, and have Fun. Let your creativity guide you like never before.

Chapter 18

Help Composing Your Song with Notes on GarageBand Menus

I hope you agree that, note for note, GarageBand is a truly amazing program. From beginners to professional artists, GarageBand has something to offer everyone. I will end this song about GarageBand by covering its menus. As with the other applications, I will start with the app-named menu (the **GarageBand** menu), which is located at the top left of your screen.

GarageBand Menu

The **GarageBand** menu, shown in Figure 18–1, contains a few important options and some minor ones. Let's start at the top of the list and work our way down.

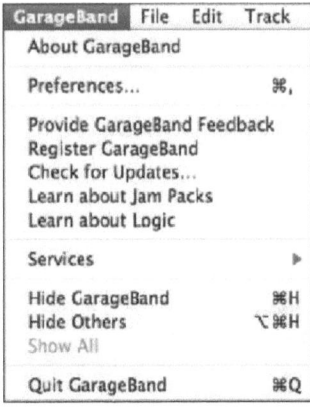

Figure 18–1. *GarageBand menu*

- **About GarageBand:** This tells you which version of the program you are running.

- **Preferences...:** This is an important menu item (see Figure 18–2). With it, you can choose from various settings to customize your work environment. As with the other apps I have discussed, these settings will be applied to the entire application.

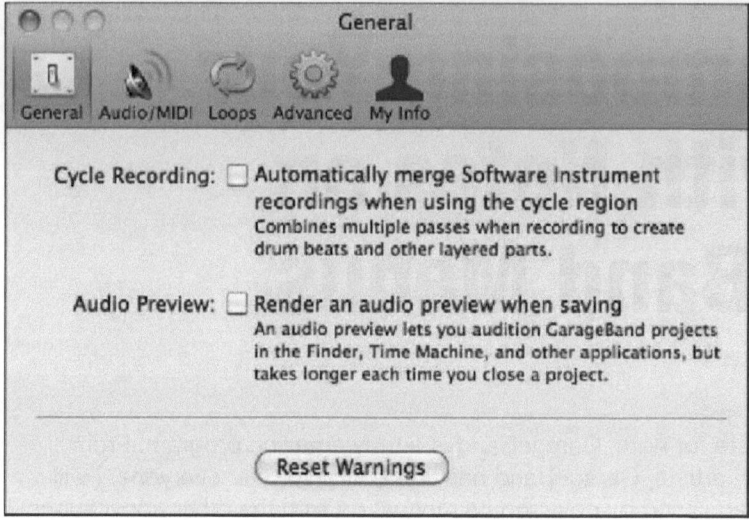

Figure 18–2. *General tab of the Preferences...window*

General Tab

This tab has the following three major elements:

- **Cycle Recording:** This is turned off by default. It will automatically merge Software Instrument recordings when you have chosen to add a cycling region in your project. This is useful, as it allows you to combine multiple passes when recording a live instrument. In the biz, this is called "mixing down."

- **Audio Preview:** The Mac has the built-in ability to preview many types of files, such as pictures or word processing documents. By default, it does not preview GarageBand files. If you want to add this functionality (which I think is a good idea), check the box next to **Audio Preview**.

- **Reset Warnings:** If GarageBand generates a error message at any time during your time using GarageBand, this will simply remove all of the warnings that appear.

Audio/MIDI Tab

This tab sets your default audio output. **System Setting** is the default, but you can also select **Built-in Output**. You can change the audio input here, as well. **Built-in Microphone** is the default, but you can also choose **System Setting** or **Built-in Input**. Below these two options, GarageBand provides a status line on your MIDI device. MIDI stands for musical instrument digital interface. MIDI is the common method by which instruments are attached to your Mac, but it requires additional hardware. The last option is **Keyboard Sensitivity**. This slide adjusts the velocity level of the notes you play. This window is shown in Figure 18–3.

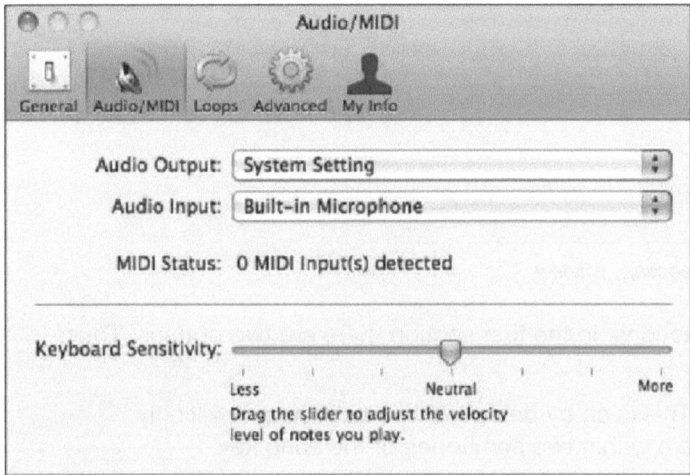

Figure 18–3. *Audio/MIDI* tab of the *Preferences...* window

Loops Tab

Loops are audio files that are prerecorded. They are primarily used to add beats and rhythm sections to your songs. The patterns in the loops can be repeated and extended for as long as you need. Figure 18–4 shows the **Loops** window.

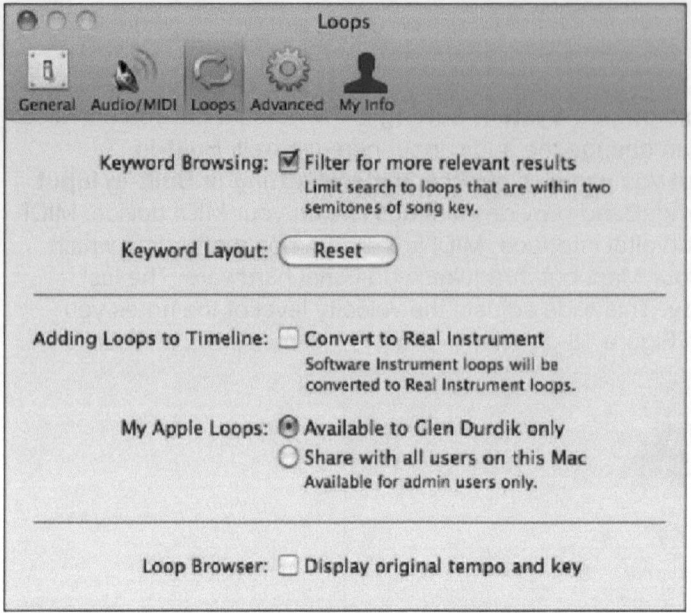

Figure 18–4. *Loops tab of the **Preferences...** window*

This window contains three sections. In the first section there are two options. These are:

- **Keyword Browsing:** This is on by default. When activated, it will only search for loops that are within two semitones of the song key.

- **Keyword Layout:** The names of the loops can be changed by clicking on them and selecting a new name that better describes them for your project. This button will reset the loops to their default names.

The second section contains the following:

- **Adding Loops to Timeline:** If you check the box next to **Convert to Real Instrument**, the loops you add to your project will be real instrument loops.

- **My Apple Loops:** Here, you have two options to choose from. Because loops can be purchased, you might want to be the only person with access to them. If you click on the circle next to **My Apple Loops**, your account name will show up and this will block other users from accessing your loops. The second option, **Admin Users**, will only allow admin users have access to your loops. This means that only certain users who have complete control over you Mac can see them.

The last option in this tab is this:

- **Loop Browser:** This will simply display the original tempo and key of the loop browser when selected.

Advanced Tab

This tab primarily deals with how sound is recorded. **Auto Normalize** will enhance your final project if needed, and **Audio Resolution** allows you to set the final quality setting of your project. This tab is shown in Figure 18–5.

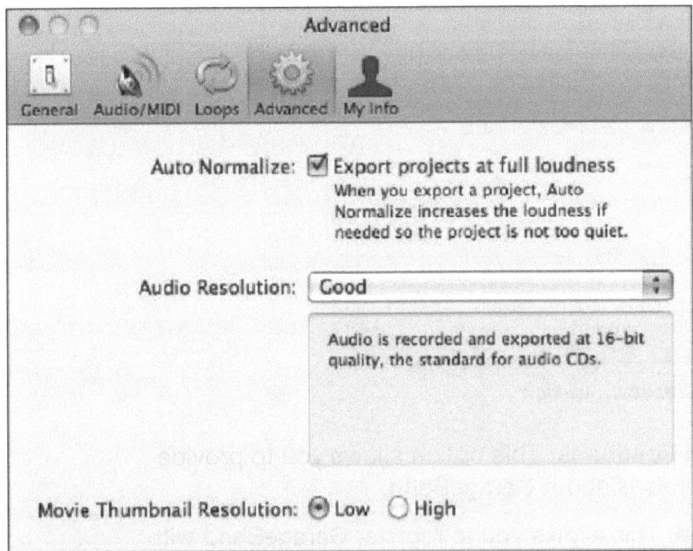

Figure 18–5. *Advanced tab of the Preferences... window*

This tab has three options in it. They are:

- **Audio Normalize:** This is turned on by default. When selected, GarageBand will determine if there are any spots in your song that are too low. It will then increase the volume of the "quiet" spots.

- **Audio Resolution:** You can select **Good**, which is the standard for audio CDs. This means it will be recorded in 16-bit. You can also choose **Better** (24-bit record and 16-bit export) or **Best** (recorded and exported as 24-bit). As you increase the bit size, the size of the file gets much larger.

- **Movie Thumbnail Resolution:** This determines the visual quality of the film clips you add to GarageBand. It is set to **Low** as default. This setting does not affect the audio portion of you film clips.

My Info Tab

The **My Info** tab (Figure 18–6) does not affect the quality of your songs. All of the items listed are items that help identify your project in iTunes.

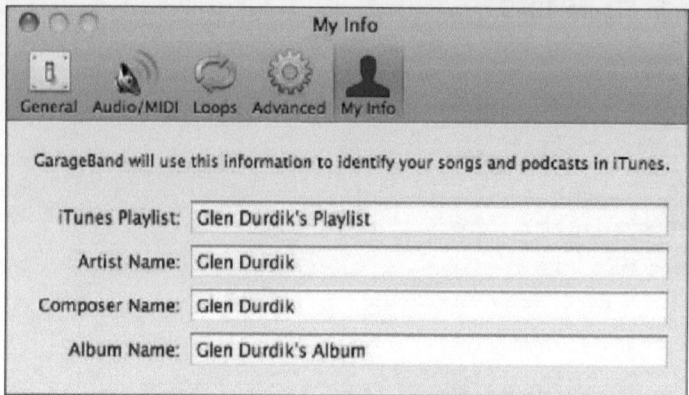

Figure 18–6. *My Info tab of the Preferences… window*

- **Provide GarageBand Feedback:** This option allows you to provide Apple with gripes or praises about GarageBand.

- **Register GarageBand:** This allows you to register GarageBand with Apple. This is not mandatory.

- **Check for Updates…:** This will seek out Apple servers and see if there are any updates available to GarageBand.

- **Learn about Jam Packs:** You can purchase so-called Jam Packs, which Apple states each include "thousands of Loops and dozens of playable software instruments." Choose from, for example, **Rhythm Section**, **World Music**, or **Remix**. You are taken to a website to get further details on what is available.

- **Learn About Logic:** Logic takes music creation to a whole new level. If you feel GarageBand is getting too limited for you, the **Logic** option offers everything a pro could need. Clicking this takes you to a website to learn more about this advanced program.

- **Services:** Some applications have built-in add-ons called services. By default, GarageBand does not have any.

- **Hide GarageBand:** This will make all of the windows associated with GarageBand disappear from your screen. To get them back, click on the **GarageBand** icon in your dock.

- **Hide Others:** This removes all other (non-GarageBand) application windows.

- **Show All:** This will show all open windows—GarageBand and other apps as well.

- **Quit GarageBand:** Want to end your musical journey with GarageBand? Click this. You will be asked to save any changes and if you want to include an iLife preview so that other iLife apps can see your song in the media browser found in that app.

File Menu

The **File** menu in GarageBand (see Figure 18–7) is similar to all other iLife apps and other Mac apps as well. Two of the common tasks are that we can create a new project (song) or save a song under a new name.

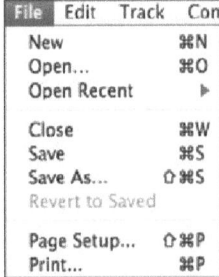

Figure 18–7. *File menu of GarageBand*

- **New:** This brings up the **GarageBand** sidebar. As I discussed in detail in Chapter 16: "Rockin' Around the GarageBand Sidebar", the **GarageBand** sidebar has a ton of options to get you started on the path of musical nirvana.

- **Open:** This will bring up a window to open a file anywhere on a storage device, including your hard drive or an external device.

- **Open Recent:** This will give you a list (up to ten) of the last songs you created.

- **Close:** This will close the project you are currently working on.

- **Save:** This will overwrite your saved song with the version you are working on presently.

- **Save As...:** This allows you to save your song with a different name. This is useful if you want keep each iteration of your song rather than delete all the earlier versions.

- **Revert to Saved:** If you select this option, you will be asked if you want to go back in time and remove all changes made after your last save. If you do, the last saved version of the song will then appear on your screen. Think of it as one big "undo."

■ **Page Setup:** If you want to print your project, this is where you choose your printer settings.

■ **Print:** This will allow you to only print the **Score View** of your project— not the **Piano Roll** view.

Edit Menu

The **Edit** menu of GarageBand is—you guessed it—similar to the **Edit** menu of pretty much any other iLife app. It does, however, contain several new features that only apply to GarageBand. The **Edit** menu is shown in Figure 18–8. A description of each option follows.

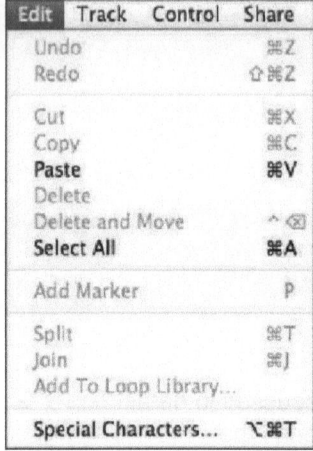

Figure 18–8. Edit menu of GarageBand

■ **Undo:** This "undoes" the last change you made in your song.

■ **Redo:** If you change mind after undoing a change, the **Redo** button will put it back for you.

■ **Cut:** This will remove the item you have selected in your song.

■ **Copy:** This will place the item you highlighted into your Mac's memory.

■ **Paste:** This will take the item you just copied and place it into your song at the location of your redtime indicator.

■ **Delete:** This will remove the item you have selected. (Remember, the **Undo** function is there if you decide not to delete the item.)

■ **Delete and Move:** This is used for podcasts. It deletes an audio region and moves the regions that follow it to take its place.

■ **Select All:** This will select all the notes in a selected region.

- **Add Marker:** If you are working on a movie project, you can add markers in the arrangement. With these markers, you can add URLs, URL titles, and chapter markers.

Let me provide a little background on regions before I discuss the next options. A *region* is defined as the section of audio you just recorded or added. Each region is color-coded. Real instruments are purple. Real instruments from Apple Loops are blue. Imported audio files are orange. Software instruments from loops, recordings, and imported MIDI files are green. The next two options deal with editing a region.

- **Split:** Splitting allows you to start playing a region from a point other than the beginning. It can also be used to take parts of a region and place them in different spots in the timeline. To split a region, move the timeline indicator to the location you want the split to occur. Then choose this command from the **Edit** menu.

- **Join:** You can join a Real Instrument recording (purple) into a single region, or join a Software Instrument recordings (green). Real Instrument loops (blue) and Real Instrument regions that have been transposed can't be joined together. To be joined, Real Instrument regions must be adjacent to each other on the same track. Software Instrument regions must be on the same track, or on adjacent tracks. Last, if you join compressed audio files, the files are converted to the AIFF format.

- **Add to Loop Library:** This allows you to add selected segments to the loops library. When you select this option, Figure 18–9 appears.

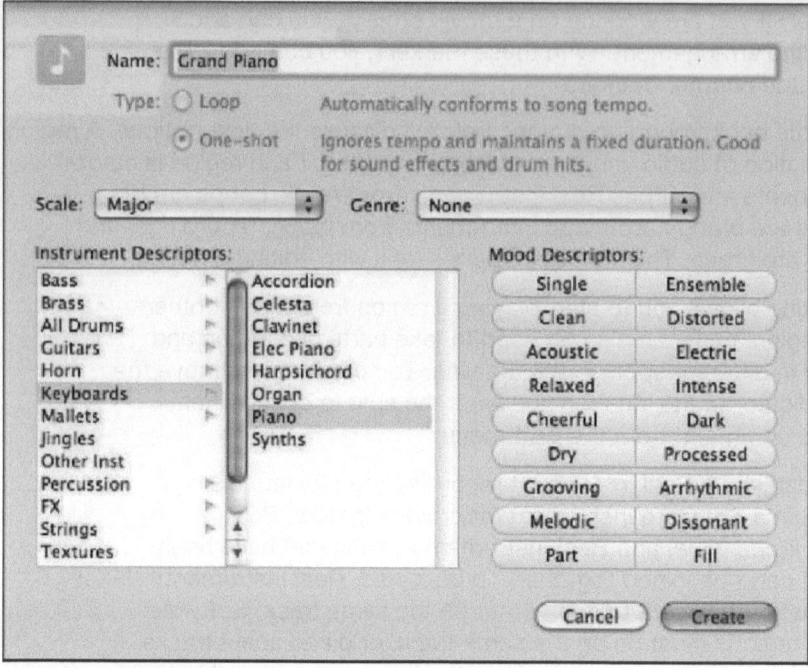

Figure 18–9. *Adding an audio segment to the **Loops** library*

You have a few options in this window. They are the following:

- **Scale:** Choose from Any, Major, Minor, Neither. or Good for Both.

- **Genre:** You are given eight choices, as well as **None** or **Other**.

- **Mood Descriptors:** You can add mood descriptions to your new loop. You just click on the one (or more than one) you want and the **mood** descriptor(s) is highlighted in blue.

Special Characters: If you want to place characters that are not on the keyboard, this option displays a window to help you find that unique character you want.

Track Menu

This menu rocks the house when it comes to viewing or editing a track in your song. This menu is shown in Figure 18–10.

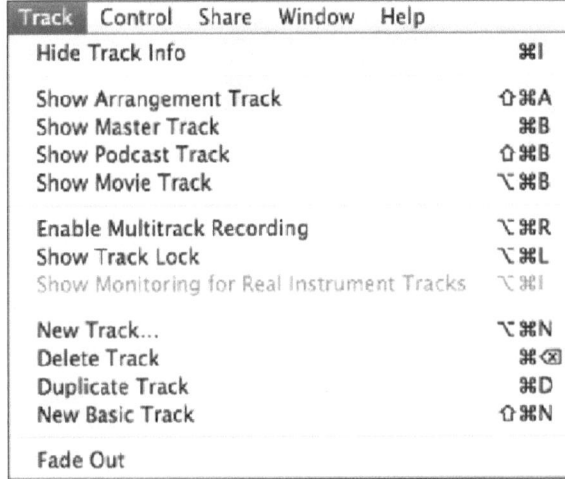

Figure 18–10. *Track menu of GarageBand*

- **Hide/Show Track Info:** This will either remove or place back into your workspace the **Track Info** sidebar.

- **Show/Hide Arrangement Track:** When you add arrangement regions, you can create sections in your song such as an intro, verse, or chorus. You can move arrangement sections easily in your project. The first arrangement appears at the start of your project. Each additional one starts at the end of the previous one. These regions are most beneficial if you add them to every section of your song, thereby allowing you to rearrange the entire song. When you first add an arrangement, it is eight measures long. You can customize it to match the section you want. In Figure 18–11, we see an example of a newly added arrangement track. Click on the small grey + (plus sign) to add a new arrangement region.

Figure 18–11. *Example of the **Arrangement Track***

■ **Show/Hide Master track:** You can view and edit the automation curves for the overall project in the **Master Track**. The master track is shown in Figure 18–12. There is a dropdown menu next to the speaker icon. Here you can choose to change the **Master Volume** (default), **Tempo**, and **Pitch**. You can also add curves for master effect parameters. These are **Echo**, **Reverb**, **Visual EQ**.

Figure 18–12. *Example of the **Master Track***

■ **Show/Hide Podcast Track:** This allows you to view and edit marker regions for a podcast episode. It also allows you to preview podcast artwork. This track is shown in Figure 18–13. When this track is chosen, the track editor workspace becomes a podcast editor workspace. This is shown in Figure 18–14.

Figure 18–13. *Example of the **Podcast Track***

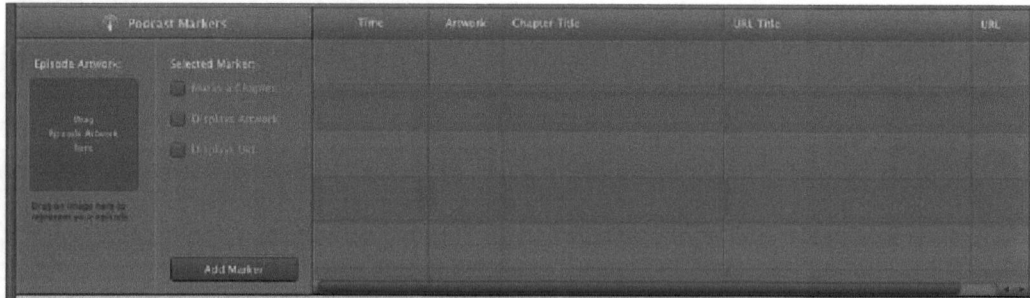

Figure 18–14. *Example of the podcast editor workspace*

■ **Show/Hide Movie Track:** You can create a soundtrack by importing an iMovie project or QuickTime-compatible movie file. You import a movie by choosing it from the media browser (the **Movies** section). Once imported, still frames from the video will appear in the movie track. This way you truly match the music with the action in the movie. This is shown in Figure 18–15.

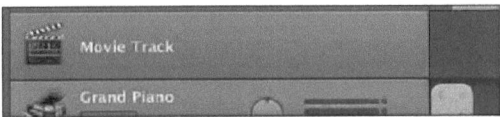

Figure 18–15. *Example of the **Movie Track***

- **Enable Multitrack Recording:** GarageBand allows you to record up to eight real instruments and one Software Instrument at the same time. To record on multiple tracks, you need an audio interface that supports the number of instruments you want to record.

- **Show Track Lock:** If you want to prevent accidental changes to a track, you can lock it. When you activate the lock feature via this menu option, a small lock icon appears in the instrument section of the workspace. This is shown in Figure 18–16. The lock icon on top is an example of an unlocked track. The green lock is shown in Figure 18–16.

Figure 18–16. *Example of an unlocked (top) and locked track (bottom)*

- **Show Monitoring for Real Instrument Tracks:** If you are going to record real instruments, GarageBand allows you to hear input from an instrument plugged in or a microphone. This means you can hear yourself play. This is useful, as it allows you to hear the part you want to record as accompanied by the instruments in your project. If this is turned on, there will be a small yellow icon added next to either the lock icon or headphone icon in your track.

- **New Track:** This allows you to add a new real or Software Instrument or vocal track to your song.

- **Delete Track:** This will deleted the selected track from your project.

- **Duplicate Track:** This will take your highlighted track and paste an exact copy of it back into your project. This might be useful if you want to have two very similar tracks in your project by just modifying the copy.

- **New Basic Track:** This will create a track that contains a real instrument recording, but without any effects added.

- **Fade Out:** If you choose this option, the sound at the end of your track will gradually get softer until it ends in silence. Nice touch to add, I think.

Control Menu

This menu mainly contains items that can be shown in your workspace. This menu is shown in Figure 18–17.

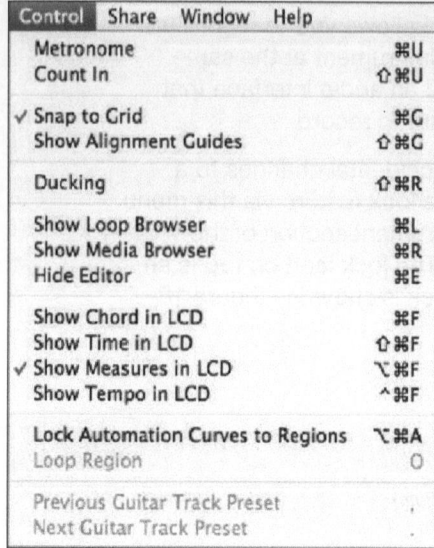

Figure 18–17. *Control* menu of GarageBand

- **Metronome:** When turned on, a ticking sound will be heard at specific intervals to help you keep the tempo of your song.

- **Count In:** If this option is chosen, GarageBand will start playing a measure ahead of the playhead location. This gives you a little time to get ready before you have to start playing. If you're starting from the beginning of the song, the metronome plays alone for a measure. If the metronome is off, GarageBand sits silently for a measure.

- **Snap to Grid:** This is turned on by default. When you cut and paste a section, GarageBand will snap it to a grid and won't let you adjust the section to the exact location you wish. This is because it automatically selects a new location at minimum of a 16th of a beat in length apart. If you turn this option off, you can manually move the section to any location.

- **Show Alignment Guides:** This is turned on by default. Alignment guides will appear when the edges of a region you are moving align with another region in the timeline. They also appear when automation control points you are moving align with other items in the timeline. The yellow alignment guides briefly appear as the edge of the region or control point aligns with other items in the timeline.

- **Ducking:** This is primarily used for podcasts. Ducking will lower the volume of the backing tracks to hear the spoken word much more easily.

- **Show/Hide Loop Browser:** This simply shows or hides the **Loop** browser.

- **Show/Hide Media Browser:** This will show or hide the **Media Browser** sidebar in your GarageBand workspace.

- **Hide/Show Editor:** This will show or hide the **Editor** window in your GarageBand workspace.

- **LCD Options:** In roughly the bottom middle of your workspace is a blue LCD display. It contains the following four choices, which are available in the Control menu:

    - **Show Chord in LCD**

    - **Show Time in LCD**

    - **Show Measures in LCD** (default setting)

    - **Show Tempo in LCD**

- **Lock Automation Curves to Regions:** This will lock your changes to the automation curves so that they cannot be changed.

- **Loop region:** This will take a selected loop and have it play over and over again until it fills the remaining musical time in your timeline.

- **Previous Guitar Track Preset:** You can save all of the effects you applied to your guitar. This will go back one saved setting.

- **Next Guitar Track Preset:** You can save all of the effects you applied to your guitar. This will go forward one saved setting.

Share Menu

Ready to share your musical masterpiece with the world? Behold: the **Share** menu. All will be revealed in Figure 18–18.

Figure 18–18. *Share menu of GarageBand*

■ **Send Song to iTunes…:** This option will take your song and whisk it over to iTunes, but you'll have to set a few options to make sure it is sent in a format that is good for you. These options are shown in Figure 18–19.

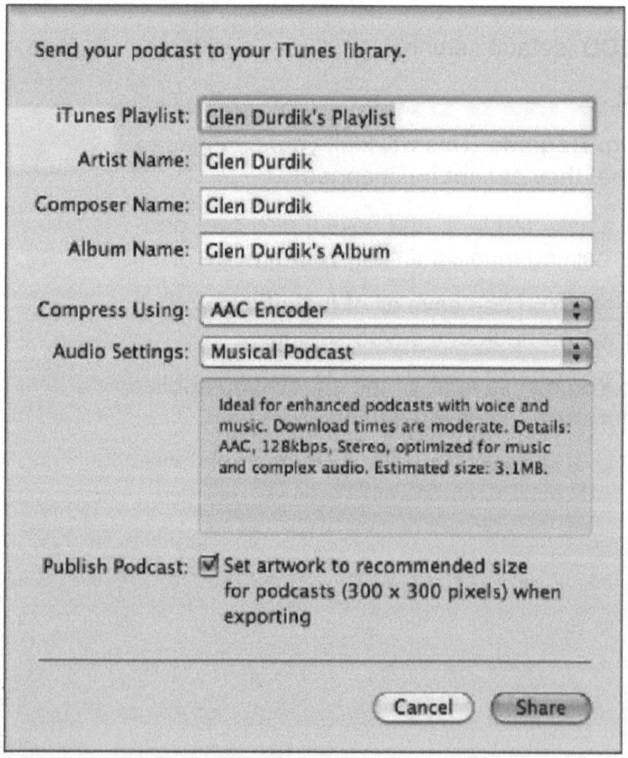

Send your podcast to your iTunes library.

iTunes Playlist: Glen Durdik's Playlist

Artist Name: Glen Durdik

Composer Name: Glen Durdik

Album Name: Glen Durdik's Album

Compress Using: AAC Encoder

Audio Settings: Musical Podcast

Ideal for enhanced podcasts with voice and music. Download times are moderate. Details: AAC, 128kbps, Stereo, optimized for music and complex audio. Estimated size: 3.1MB.

Publish Podcast: ☑ Set artwork to recommended size for podcasts (300 x 300 pixels) when exporting

Cancel   Share

Figure 18–19. *Send to iTunes* window

The first four sections of this window are automatically filled in with your name and the item it is describing.

The next two sections determine the final audio quality of the output.

- **Compress Using**: This can be either **AAC Encoder** or **MP3 Encorder**. For better compatibility with all other computer devices or portable players, I recommend that you change this setting to MP3, as it is more universal. You do not have to compress a file. However, if you don't, the file you end up with might be too large to share easily.

- **Audio Settings:** Choose from **Low Quality**, **Medium Quality** (default), **High Quality**, or **Higher Quality** for AAC files. For MP3 files, choose from **Good**, **High**, or **Higher Quality**. If you are recording a podcast, the options are **Mono Podcast**, **Spoken Podcast** (default), **Musical Podcast**, **Highest Quality**, or **iTunes Plus**. You also have the option at the bottom of the menu to create a custom podcast. Here, you can customize the audio settings yourself.

- **Publish Podcast:** This will adjust any artwork in your project to the recommended size when you export the final work.

When you are done, click on the **Share** button .

- **Send Ringtone to iTunes:** This allows you to send your song to iTunes to be used a ringtone. However, the length of the ringtone is limited to 40 seconds. GarageBand will display a message explaining this, as shown in Figure 18–20.

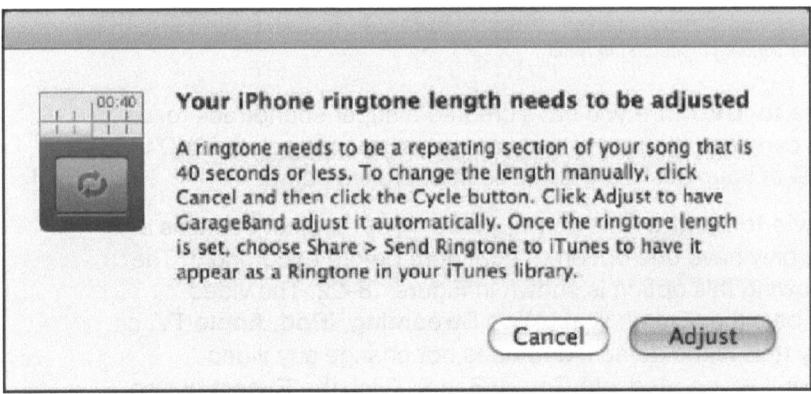

Figure 18–20. *Ringtone error message warning you if your song is over 40 seconds*

- **Send Podcast to iWeb...:** This will allow you to send your finished podcast to iWeb. This is shown in Figure 18–21. As we have seen, iWeb is a simple, yet powerful web page creation tool. As with sending a song to iTunes, you have a few settings to configure first.

- **Compress Using:** Can be **AAC Encoder** or **MP3 Encoder**.

- **Audio Settings:** Can be either **Mono Podcast**, **Spoken Podcast** (default), **Musical Podcast**, **Higher Quality**, or **iTunes Plus**. You also have the option at the bottom of the menu to create a custom podcast. Here, you can customize the audio settings yourself.

- **Publish Podcast:** This will adjust any artwork in your project to the recommended size when you export the final work.

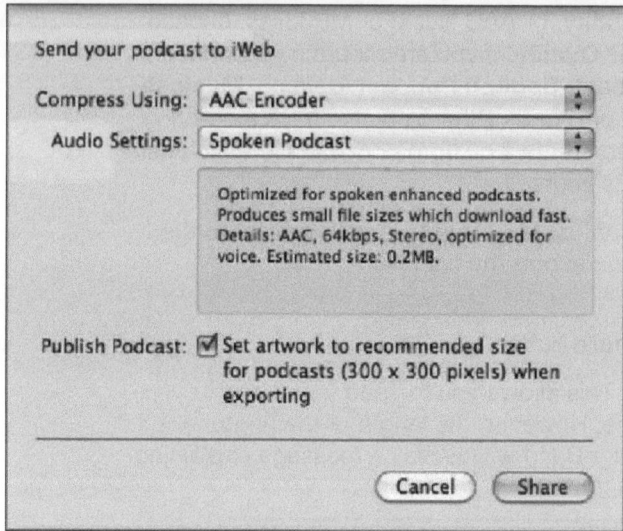

Figure 18–21. *Options for sending a podcast to iWeb*

- **Send Movie to iDVD...:** If you have created a super soundtrack for a movie, you can send the movie and completed soundtrack to iDVD to make a DVD of your finished work. Oscars, here we come!

- **Export Movie to Disk...:** This only appears if your project contains a movie. You only have one option to configure before exporting it. The window showing this option is shown in Figure 18–22. The video quality can be either **Email**, **Web**, **Web Streaming**, **iPod**, **Apple TV**, or **Full Quality** (this is the default, and does not change any video settings after it was added into GarageBand). Click the **Export** button [Export] to get the process going.

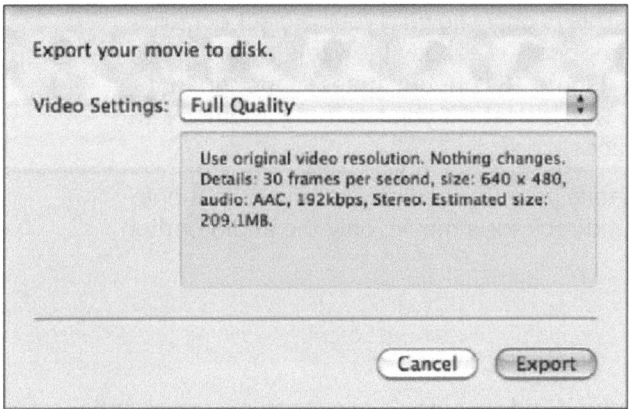

Figure 18–22. *The one setting that has to be selected before exporting a movie*

- **Export a Song to Disk...:** This is only shown if your project contains a song. Here, you can take your finished project and save it to your storage device. In some cases, this might make it easier to distribute than going through iTunes. The screen that appears is shown in Figure 18–23. Please notice that, if you do not compress the file and leave the song at its highest quality, your file will be saved as an .AIF file. If you do compress the file, you can adjust the audio quality. Click on **Export** Export to start the process.

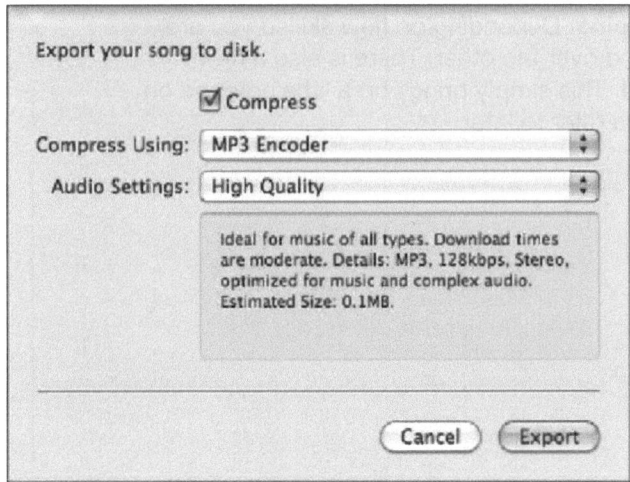

Figure 18–23. *Exporting song to disk* window

- **Export Podcast to Disk...:** This is only shown if your project contains a podcast. The window that appears is exactly the same as the **Exporting to iWeb** window (Figure 18–21), but states at the top that you are exporting to a disk. This is useful if you are using another web editor to create your web pages.

- **Burn Song to CD:** This will take your finished project and burn it onto a CD. If you are doing a soundtrack for a movie, only the audio portion will be burned.

Window Menu

Keyboard and **Musical Typing** are the **Window** menu's two most important options (refer Figure 18–24), as they determine how you input notes for Software Instruments.

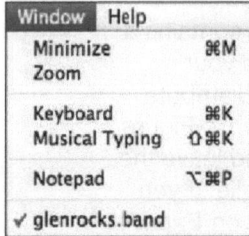

Figure 18–24. *Window menu of GarageBand*

- **Keyboard and Musical Typing:** Depending on how skilled you are, you might prefer one method over the other. There is also a new option here called **Notepad**. This simply brings up a little notepad on which you can write ideas to refer to later.

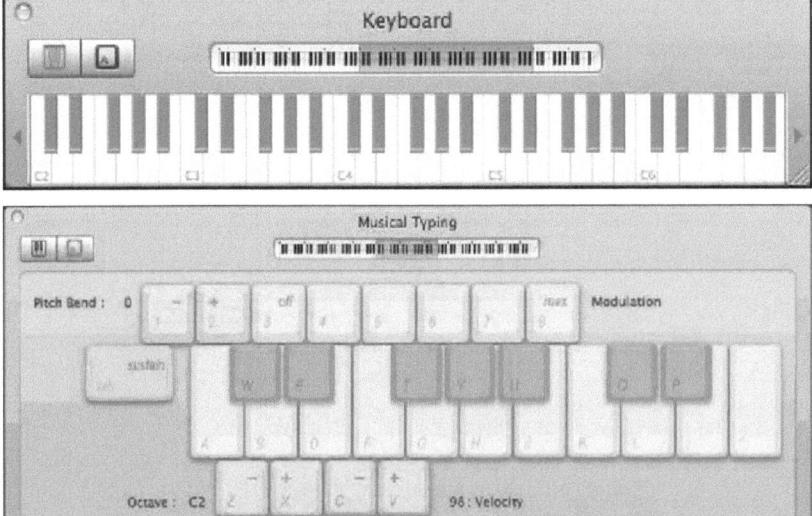

The other **Window** menu options are standard across most apps:

- **Minimize:** This will take your project and zoom it down into your dock. You must click on the small icon in your dock to return your project to the full screen.

- **Zoom:** This will take your workspace and make it as large as it can be. It does not take over the full screen.

- **Title of Project:** This simply shows you the current project you are working on (glenrocks.band, in this example).

Help Menu

The **Help** menu provides the answers to questions that you might have about various tasks or options in GarageBand. This menu is shown in Figure 18–25.

Figure 18–25. *Help menu of GarageBand*

- **GarageBand Help:** This is broken down into two sections. The first— **Get Started**—is shown in Figure 18–26.

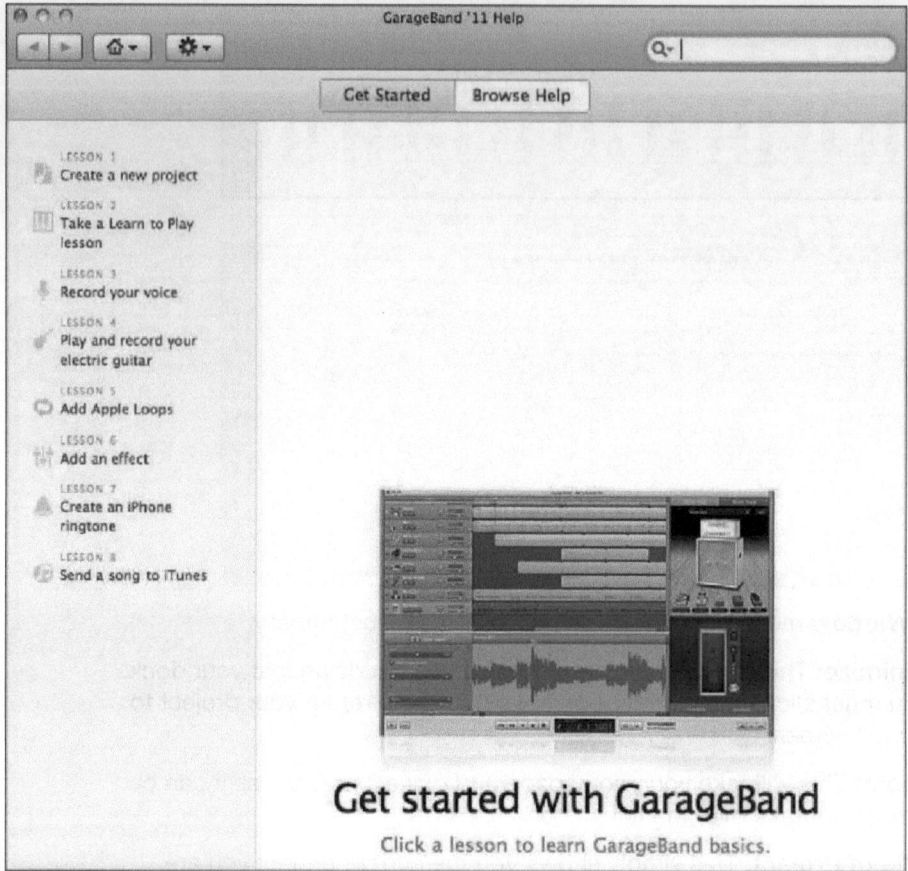

Figure 18–26. *The Get Started section of the GarageBand Help section*

The **Get Started** section guides you through some basic tasks that are needed to start you on the right track. The **Browse Help** section, shown in Figure 18–27, allows you to find info on other topics.

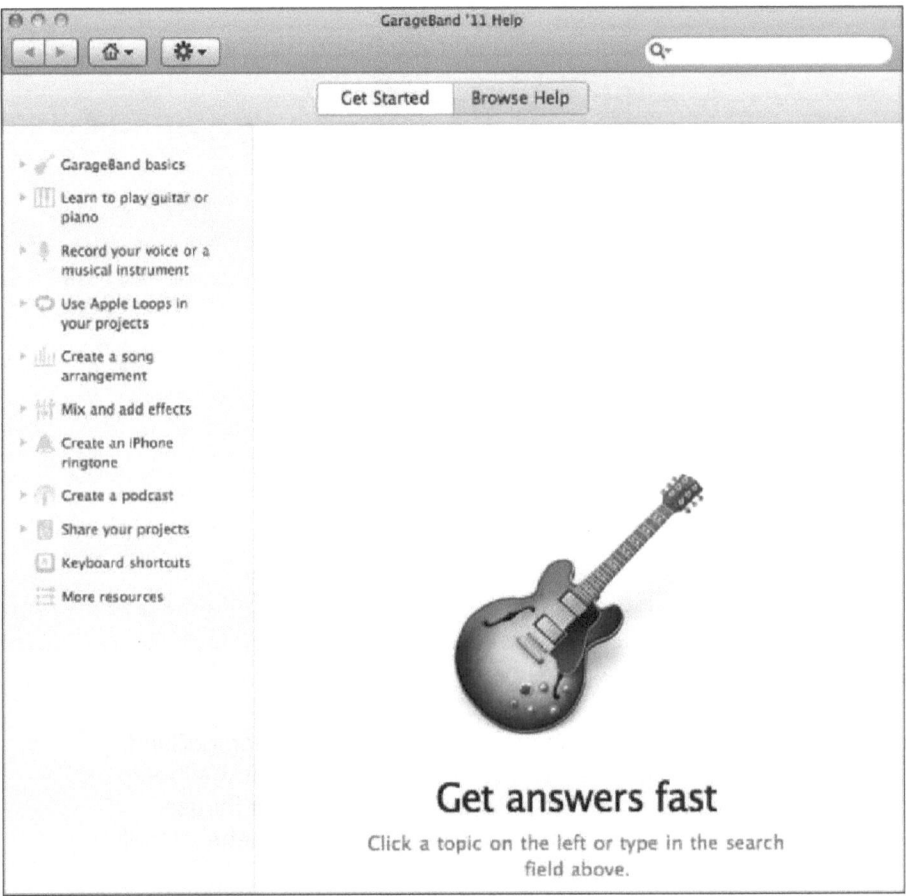

Figure 18–27. *The Browse Help section of GarageBand Help*

- Please remember that there is a search window located at the top of both windows.

Just enter a subject and, I hope, Apple has the information you need at hand.

- **Welcome to GarageBand:** This will show the opening screen of the program (see Figure 18–28).

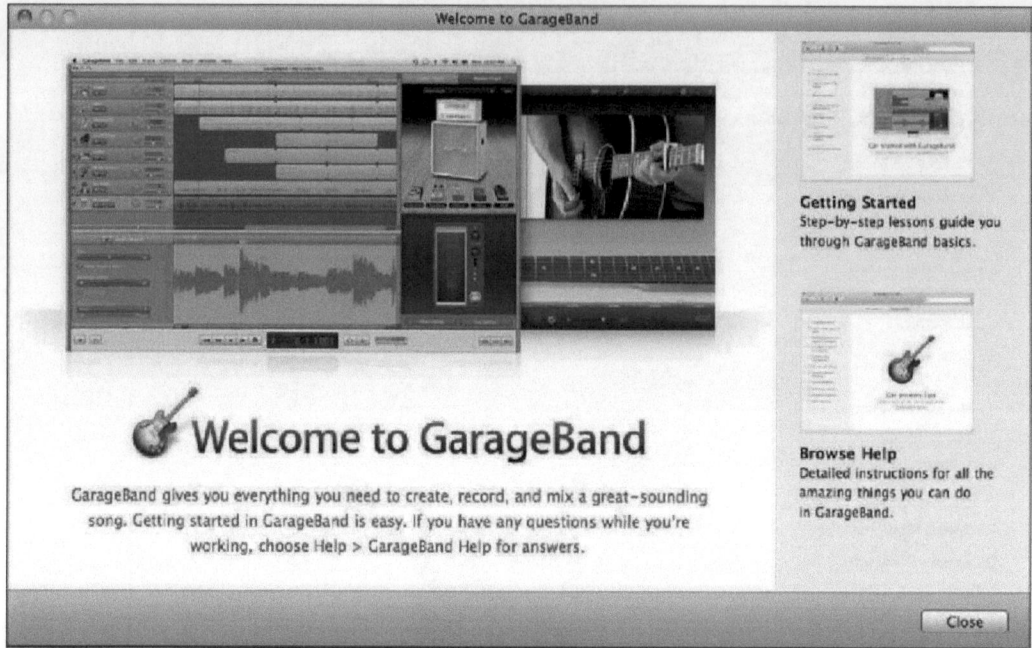

Figure 18–28. *Welcome to GarageBand* window

- **Keyboard Shortcuts:** As you become more familiar with GarageBand, you might want to make choosing various option a lot faster. Keyboard shortcuts allow you to use only your keyboard and not your mouse. For example, holding down the command key (⌘) and the letter "I" will hide or show the **Track Info** sidebar.

- **Service and Support:** This will bring up a website maintained by Apple to provide valuable and updated info on GarageBand.

Summary

And so ends my song about GarageBand. It is music creation made simple. It enables learning the guitar and piano in an exciting new way. You can learn from musicians and purchase numerous new loops and instruments. I hope that your future sessions with GarageBand will always end on a high note.

iTunes

iTunes is not part of the retail package of iLife '11. Rather, it is included with the bundled software that came with your Mac. As you go through this book, you will see that iTunes is accessed by many of the iLife apps. Therefore, I felt it critical to include this app to complete my coverage of the iLife experience. The following chapters cover the iTunes features accessed by iLife, as well as the program's many other uses. The program truly does so much more than just store music.

Navigating iTunes via Its Sidebar and Workspace Views

iTunes is automatically installed on all Macs, and can be installed on Windows machines as well. It began as a simple program to manage songs, and now it handles videos and apps for iOS devices. For the most part, the program is easy to use, but there is quite a lot to learn to become an efficient user. This section on iTunes will include a lot of walk-throughs, an in-depth discussion on the sidebar, a complete write-up on all its menu options and an explanation of how to manage media on an iPad. As I have stated before in this book, iTunes is not a part of iLife, but it does go hand and hand with iLife. It can be used for sharing items with friends or family that was created in other apps, and is used as a source location for media items to be used in iLife apps like iMovie or GarageBand.

So, let's begin the discussion with the sidebar. It is where you go to find your media, manage your iOS device, or even listen to Internet radio.

Getting to Know the Sidebar

Figure 19–1 shows you all the items in the sidebar. Please notice that the sidebar is broken down into several sections: **Library**, **Store**, **Devices** (if you have one), **Shared**, **Genius**, or **Playlists**. Each section serves a different purpose.

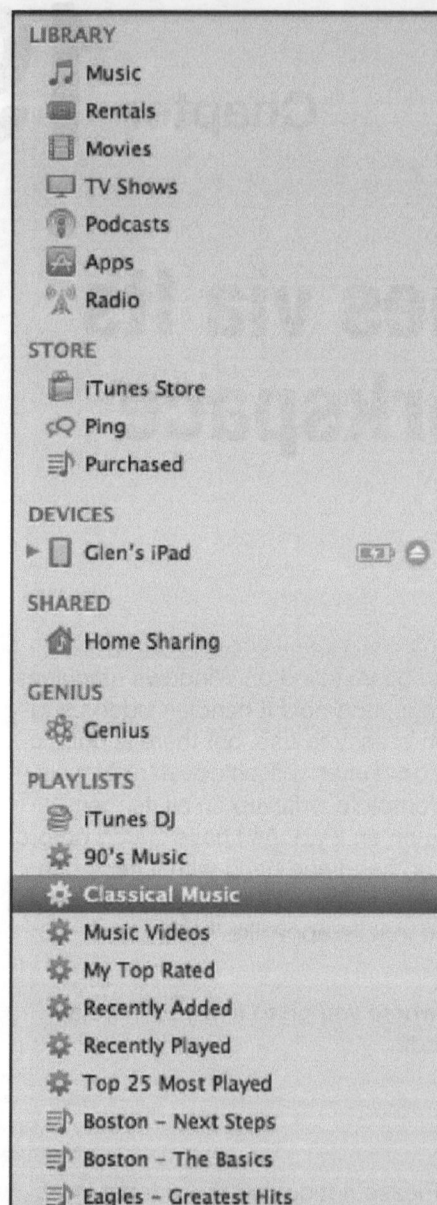

Figure 19–1. *iTunes sidebar*

Library Section

This section contains the master list of all the items stored in iTunes. It is broken down into **Music**, **Movies**, **TV shows**, **Podcasts**, **Apps**, and **Radio**. Okay, radio is not really stored media, but I guess this is the best place to put it.

Music

This contains all of the music in your iTunes library. In Chapter 20: "Getting Media into and out of iTunes," I will show you how to create unique playlists from songs in this library. But for this chapter, I just downloaded a few albums and all of the music is now in my library. You can view media in a few different ways. The default shown in Figure 19–2 is the List view. I will show you the other ways to view media after I cover all the items in the sidebar.

Figure 19–2. *Music section of the **Library** sidebar*

Please notice that, by default, the list view contains the following columns: **Name**, **Time**, **Artist**, **Album**, **Genre**, **Rating**, and the number of **Plays**. You can sort the list by any of these categories. This is useful if you want to sort your library by **Artist** (the default) or have the songs listed alphabetically. If you choose to rate your songs, you can sort by your ratings as well. Just click on the item you want to sort at the top of the screen.

Rentals

This will only appear if you download a video rental. A rental allows you to view downloaded material for only a specific time period. An example of a rented movie is shown in Figure 19–3. Please notice that you have only a set period to play the video— 30 days. This is shown in the top right corner of the rental window. To play the rented item, click on the picture of the video and then click on the small play button that appears, or just double-click on the picture instead.

Seven [R]
New Line
Run Time: 2:08:47
Expires in 29 days and 18 hours

Figure 19–3. *Rentals window*

When you click on play, Figure 19–4 will appear. This is telling you that once you start to play the video. you have 24 hours to watch it. Then the video is removed from your library. Click on **Play** to start viewing the video.

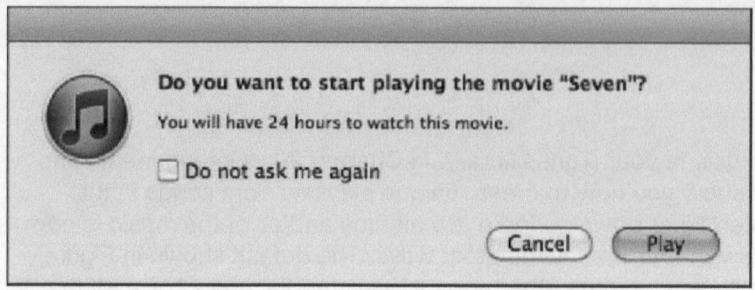

Figure 19–4. *You only have 24 hours to watch the video after clicking on **Play**.*

Movies

Here is where all your movies are stored. This screen is shown in Figure 19–5. Please notice that I have sent one of my movies created in iMovie to iTunes. It is called **My first Project 1**. To play the video, either double-click on the preview graphic or click on the preview graphic and click on the small **Play** button. If it is a purchased movie, a scene selector icon will also appear in the graphic .

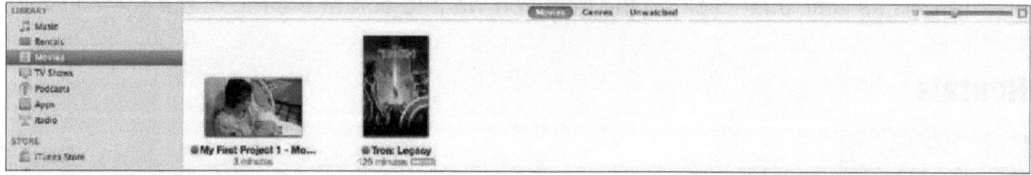

Figure 19–5. *Movie section—**Movies** view*

There are a few important items to take note of in this window. They are:

- The small dot next to the movies' title **My First Project 1** means that the video has not been viewed yet. It will disappear after you view the item. If the movie has not yet been completely viewed, a **1/2** button remains.

- You can sort the movies in three ways: **Movies**, **Genres**, and **Unwatched** **Movies** Genres Unwatched .

- You can shrink or enlarge the **Preview** graphics by using the slider at the top right of this window .

When you are playing the video, there is a set of controls that will appear when you move your mouse. This is shown in Figure 19–6.

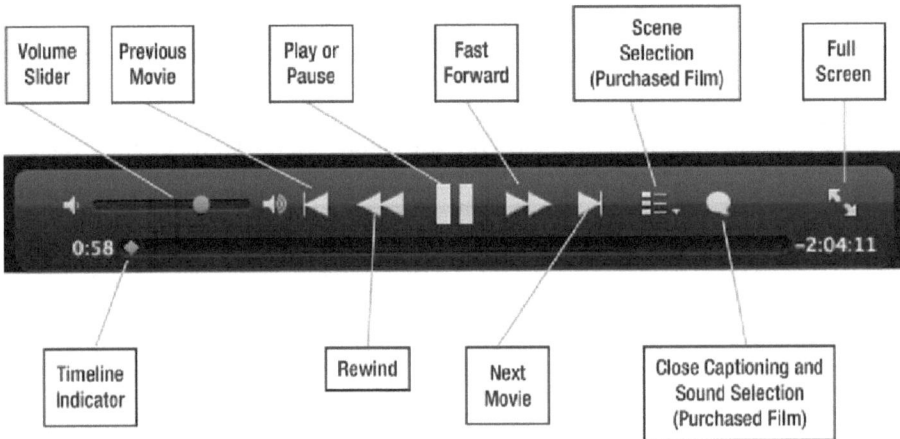

Figure 19–6. *Controls available when viewing a movie*

If you want to close the video viewer window, click on the small black **X** located at the top left corner of your viewer window.

TV Shows

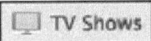

You can also purchase TV shows from the store. They usually are sold as a season set or one episode at a time. In Figure 19–7, we see one purchased episode's information screen. This screen is brought up if you double-click on the preview graphic of the show. Please notice that this screen tells you the series, the episode title, the parental guidance rating, length of the show, what season it is from, and a brief description of the episode. To play a TV show, you must go back or be in the **TV Show** home page. As with **Movies**, you can double-click the preview graphic to start playing the show or click on the graphic and then click on the **Play selected** icon inside the graphic.

Figure 19–7. *Example of a purchased TV show info window*

Podcasts

Podcasts are free audio or video programs that deal with a particular subject. The maker of the podcast usually creates new episodes on a regular basis. Podcasts are usually free to download. iTunes allows you to subscribe to these podcasts so that they download automatically and you therefore never miss a new one. An example of a Podcast is shown in Figure 19–8. Please notice that you again can sort and view the podcast list in three different ways: **Podcasts**, **Categories**, or **Unplayed**. As with **Movies**, there is a slider in the top right-hand corner to increase or decrease the preview graphic size on a Podcast episode.

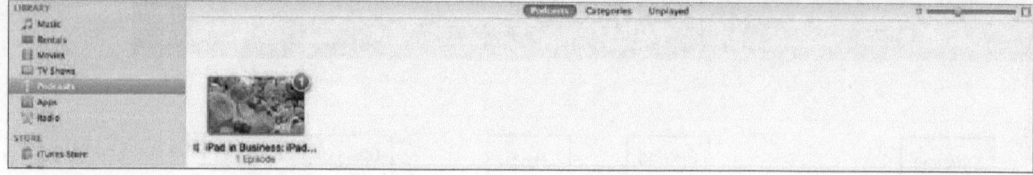

Figure 19–8. *Example of downloaded Podcast*

Apps

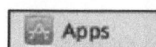

If you have an iOS device, such as an iPhone, iPod Touch, or iPad, you can download and use a wide variety of apps. There are a ton of games to choose from, but there is also a huge selection of apps that have more productive uses. In Figure 19–9, we see a list of apps that I downloaded for my iPad. You can choose between two different views: **Apps** and **Genres**. These two options are located in the top of the **Apps** window, directly in the middle. Figure 19–9 shows the **Apps** view. Notice that, in this view, it is broken down into applications that are designed for the iPhone, iPod Touch, and iPad or exclusively for the iPad. Below each application is the genre that it belongs in. You can see in Figure 19–9 that I have six applications installed and each is a different genre. These are **Games**, **Finance**, **Music**, **Entertainment**, **Social Networking**, and **Productivity**. The app store is the place you can find and download new applications and it is found inside the iTunes store. The iTunes store will be covered later in this chapter.

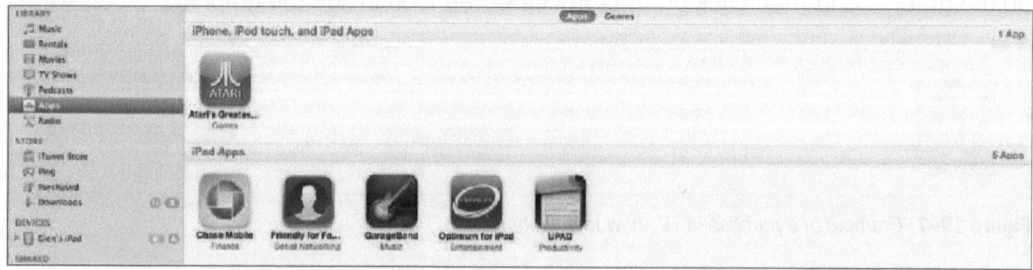

Figure 19–9. *Apps view of the Apps window*

In Figure 19–10, we see how your purchased apps will appear in the **Genres** view. Please notice that, in this view, the title of the app is not shown.

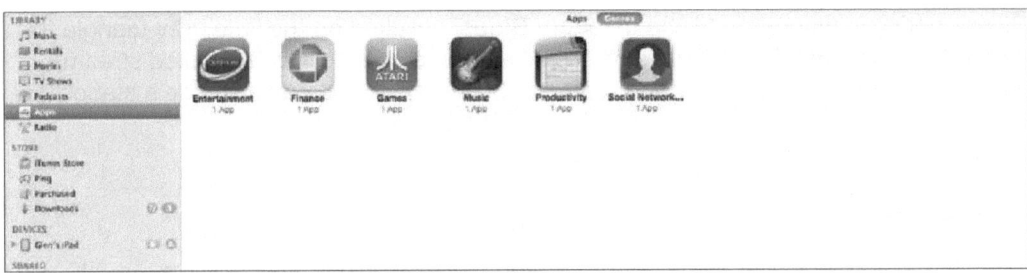

Figure 19-10. *Genres* view of the *Apps* window

Radio

This option gives you access to hundreds of Internet radio stations. As we can see in Figure 19–11, there is a wide variety of types of music available. It ranges from **Adult Contemporary** and **Alternative Rock** to **Jazz** and **Sports Radio**.

Figure 19-11. *Radio* option found in the *Library* section of the iTunes sidebar

Please notice in Figure 19–11 the category **Blues**. I clicked on the little grey triangle to expand the view of this category and see all available channels, or so-called streams. You can see that, for this category, there are 30 streams. You can also see a station name and a small description of what the station plays.

Store Section

This section contains two items related to purchases involving the iTunes store and Ping. Ping is Apple's social network that revolves around the music industry. It requires a bit more coverage, so I will discuss Ping in detail after going over the iTunes Store and Purchase function.

iTunes Store

The iTunes store is an online shop that allows you to purchase music, video, movies, and apps for your iOS device. It also contains a **Top Song**, **Albums**, **Music Video**, **TV Shows**, and **Video** list, a **New and Noteworthy** section, a **Discount** section, a **What's Hot** section, a **Recommended for You** section, and a few other sections. There is a lot to choose from. Finally, the program keeps track of your purchases to help make suggestions for future purchases.

The top portion of the main iTunes store is shown in Figure 19–12.

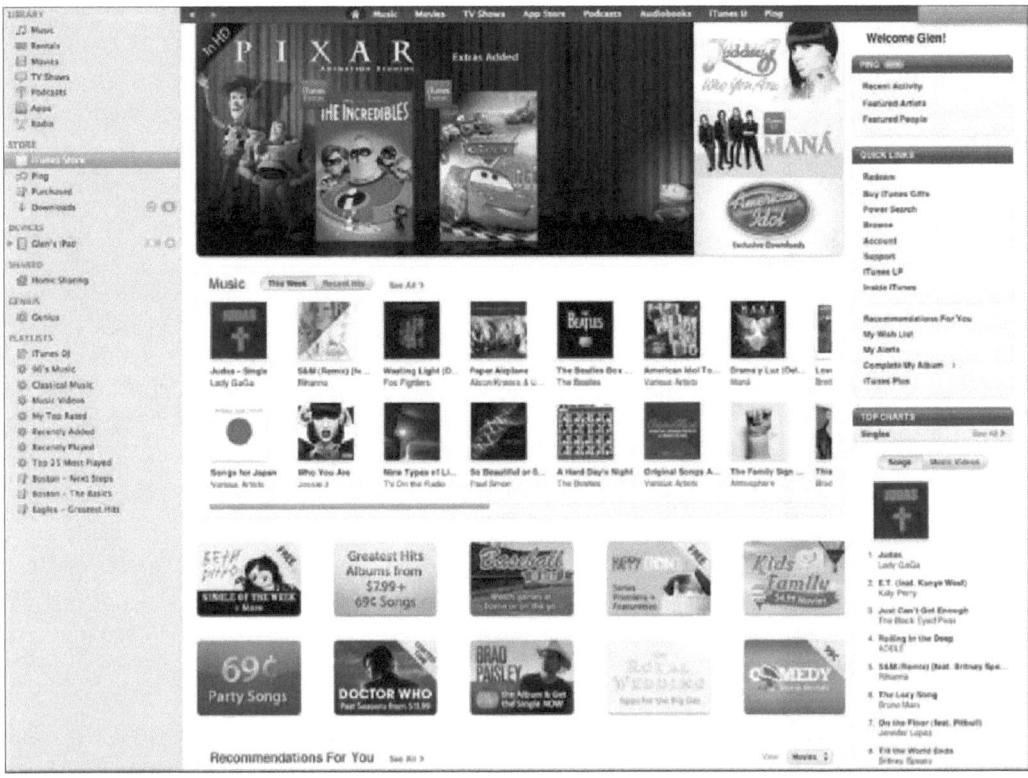

Figure 19–12. *Home* window of the iTunes store

Let's start the discussion of getting around the store by using the main toolbar located at the top of the screen.

This is the **Home** button. It will bring you back to the **Home** screen of the iTunes store.

This part of the toolbar gives you access to purchase **Music**, **Movies**, **TV Shows**, **Apps**, **Podcasts**, **Audiobooks**, **iTunes U** lectures (this section gives you access to educational material that is available for download), and **Ping**. Again, Ping is not really an item to purchase—it is a social networking service from Apple.

Each purchase category contains a dropdown list of more options. The **Music** dropdown menu is shown in Figure 19–13.

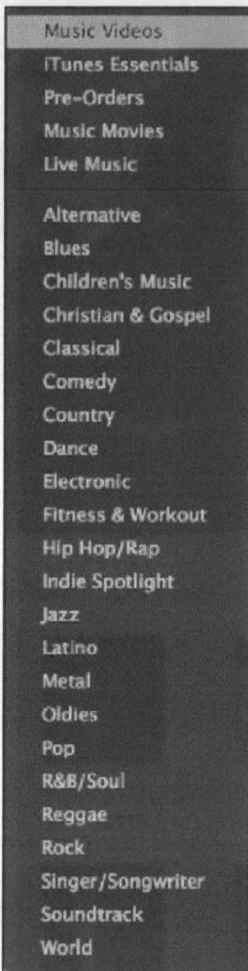

Figure 19–13. *Music drop-down menu accessed by clicking on the* **Music** *button found in the* **Store** *toolbar*

These arrows allow you to move either forward or backward through the store's windows.

Purchased

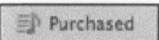

This option keeps track of all of the purchased media. Music is listed first by default and then movies and TV shows.

This section only appears in the **Store** section when you are actually downloading content. In the example I am using above, there are two spinning arrows representing a download that is taking place. The number 3 means that I am currently downloading three items. In Figure 19–14, we see that I am downloading three large items and that, on a wireless network, it is going to take about seven hours to download.

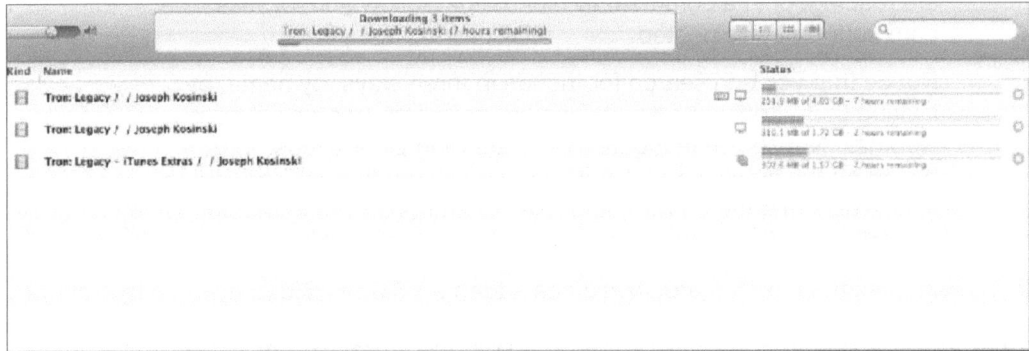

Figure 19–14. *Example of downloading content (a movie) from the iTunes Store*

Ping

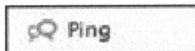

Ping is a social network set up by Apple to help artists communicate with their fans or to allow users of this service (which is free) to communicate with others. You must activate a Ping account to get started. A portion of the main **Ping** screen is shown in Figure 19–15.

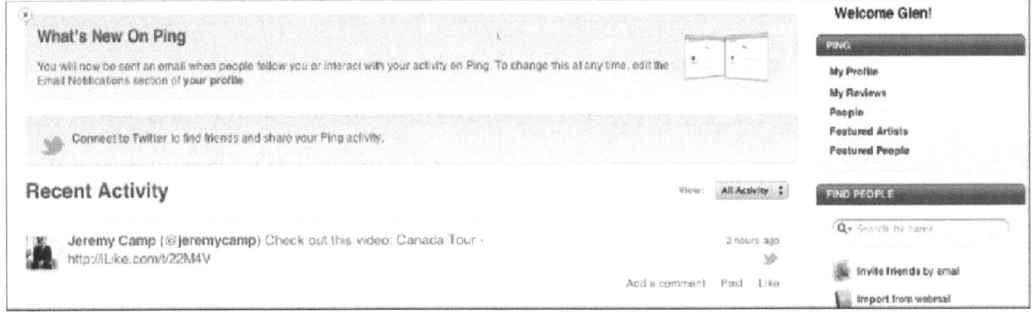

Figure 19–15. *Portion of the **Ping** window*

Please notice a few things in Figure 19–15:

- You can connect to Twitter to find friends and share Ping activity.
- **Recent Activity** is shown in this window.

■ You can access your profile, reviews, people you are connected with and your featured artists. In Figure 19–15, I got a message from an artist named Jeremy Camp. You can add a comment to the post you are reading, post a comment to friends that follow you, or "like" the comment that was posted.

■ Notice that you can search for friends in three ways: by name, by inviting them from your email account, or by importing a list from webmail. Not shown in Figure 19–15 are Ping Charts (customized based on the artists you follow), concert listings that may appeal to you, artists that are on tour, and a list of artists that Ping recommends you follow.

If you really like the Ping feature, Apple has added an **iTunes Sidebar** at the far right of your iTunes workspace. This is shown in Figure 19–16. You can turn this sidebar on or off by going to the **View** menu and selecting **Hide/Show iTunes Sidebar**.

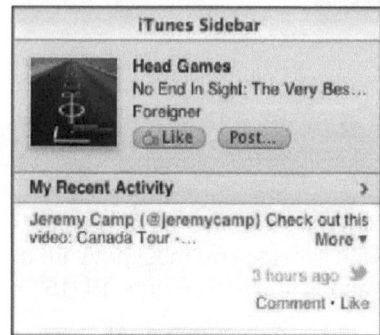

Figure 19–16. *The iTunes Sidebar*

When you click on a song in your **Library** or **Playlist** you will see a little **Ping** icon appear next to the song. If you click on it, you will get the dropdown menu shown in Figure 19–17.

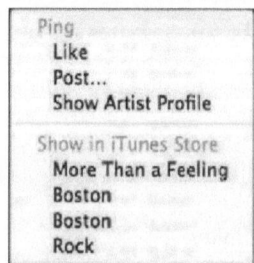

Figure 19–17. *Ping options for any song in your Library or Playlists*

Please notice that you can **Like** the song and post it on your Ping page, post a comment, or show the artist profile (if it exists). This menu also allows you to go find the song in iTunes, the band that recorded the song in iTunes, or you can go to the category of music in which the song belongs.

Ping is relatively new, so I would not be surprised if some of your favorite artists have not yet joined this online community.

Devices Section

This will only appear if you connect an iOS device to your Mac or Windows computer. In the graphic I used above, we see that the device **Glen's iPad** is attached. The **Plug** graphic [image] means that the device fully charged. The **Lightening** icon [image] means that it is charging. If you click on the **Eject** button [image], the device will be removed from the sidebar.

All of the options for using an iOS device will be discussed in a Chapter 20: "Getting Media into and out of iTunes,"

Shared Section

This will only appear before you activate this feature. If you click on **Home Sharing**, you are presented with Figure 19–18. It explains what Home Sharing is. Basically, it will copy new purchases to every Mac (in your home) that has this option turned on. You can also choose to copy any item from one library to another. Click on **Create Home Share** at the bottom right-hand corner of this window to start the process. You must use the same Apple ID on every Mac on which you want to be able to view and copy songs.

> **NOTE:** A few users have mentioned that sharing between PCs and Macs is not as straightforward as Mac-to-Mac sharing.

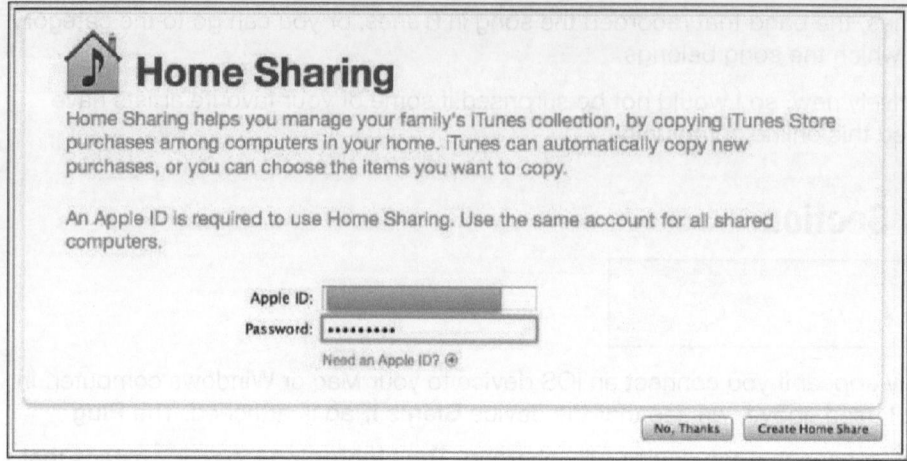

Figure 19–18. *Initial screen to set up* **Home Sharing**

Genius Section

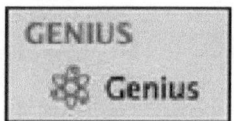

This feature is really cool if you want to find new music or movies that fit your personal tastes. You must activate this feature for it to work. If you click on the **Genius** icon, you are presented with the screen shown in Figure 19–19. This screen tells you all of the great things you can do when you turn on this feature.

Figure 19–19. *First screen to turn on the* **Genius** *feature*

The next screen asks you to enter a valid Apple ID account and password. After this is entered, the next screen will accept you to accept the terms and conditions of using the Genius feature. Click in the small box next to **I have read and agree...** below the legal message and then click on **Continue** to start the process.

The initial scan by this feature is shown in Figure 19–20.

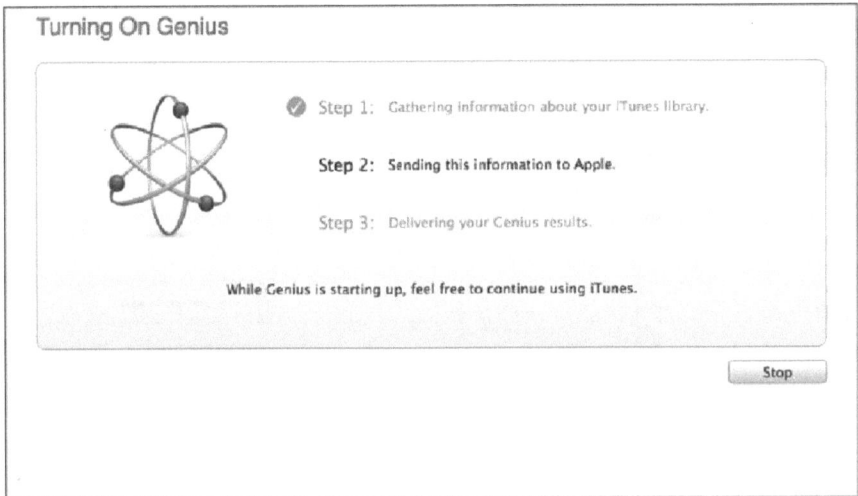

Figure 19–20. *Scanning your library to determine your favorite genres*

After this completed, the Genius feature is active.

If you click on a song or video in your Library, you will get a customized list of suggestions for future purchases called **Genius Recommendations**. This sidebar is located at the far right of your workspace and is below the **iTunes Sidebar** (if you decided to keep it visible). This sidebar is shown in Figure 19–21.

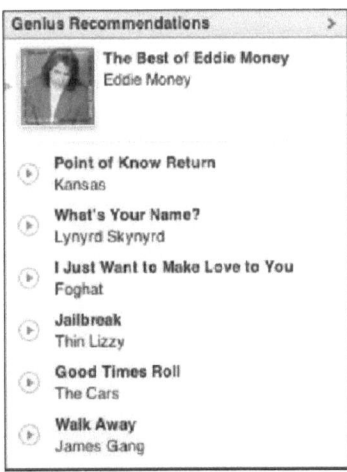

Figure 19–21. *Genius Recommendations sidebar*

Please notice the small arrow at the top of this sidebar directly across from the **Genius Recommendations**. If you click this arrow, you are brought to a much more comprehensive Genius selection page in the iTunes Store. This is shown in Figure 19–22. Please notice that this has tabs for **Music**, **Movies**, and **TV Shows**.

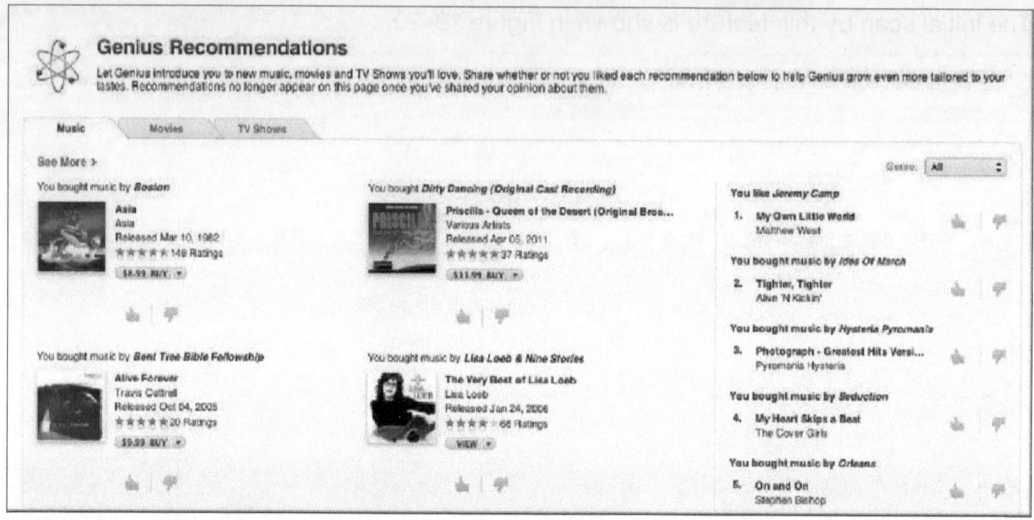

Figure 19–22. *Genius selections customized for you—iTunes Store*

Playlists Section

The image below shows all of the default Playlists for iTunes, plus a few that I added. There are three types of playlist.

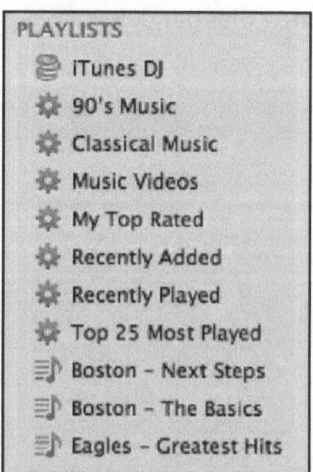

The first is a playlist that you create from purchased or imported media. This is designated by the **Musical Note** icon next to name of the Playlist.

The second type of playlist is a **Smart Playlist**. This is represented by a little gear icon

next to the name of the Playlist.

To create a Smart Playlist, you must go to **File** and chose **New Smart Playlist....** A window appears that allows you to specify what type of music you want to add. This is shown in Figure 19–23.

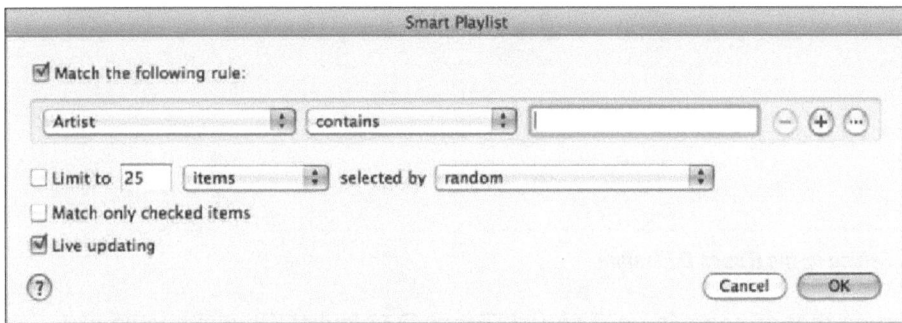

Figure 19–23. *Creating a new Smart Playlist*

Please notice that you primarily create the Smart Playlist by applying a rule. In Figure 19–23, it is by Artist. If you click on **Artist**, you see a dropdown menu of over 40 different elements. After you have decided on what material will be included in this playlist, make sure the check box next to **Live updating** is checked (it is on by default). With this checked, any new media that you add that matches the Smart Playlist settings will be automatically added to that custom playlist.

The third type of playlist is called the **iTunes DJ** playlist ⎡ 🐢 iTunes DJ ⎤. This playlist takes songs from your Library and creates a random playlist.

The first screen that appears when you click on the **iTunes DJ** icon is shown in Figure 19–24. One of the cool features of this option is that, if you have an iOS device and install the **Remote** app, anyone at a party can access to your iTunes Library and request songs from it.

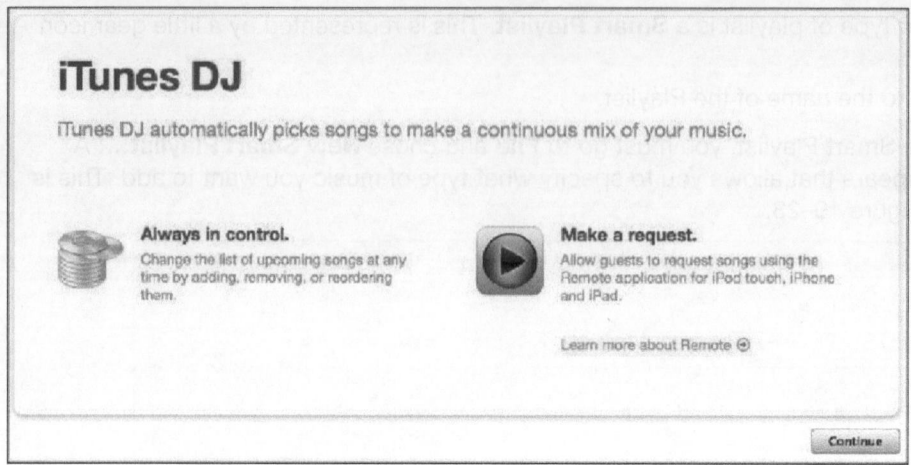

Figure 19–24. *Setting up the **iTunes DJ** feature*

The next screen that appears is your actual iTunes DJ playlist. This is shown in Figure 19–25. Please notice that is has two song lists. The top portion shows what songs have been played and below that are the songs that will play next.

	Name	Time	Artist	Album	Genre	Rating	Plays
	Desperado	3:35	Eagles	The Very Best of Ea...	Rock		1
	Love Will Keep Us Alive	4:02	Eagles	The Very Best of Ea...	Rock		1
	The Best of My Love (Ping ▾)	4:34	Eagles	The Very Best of Ea...	Rock		
1	Walk On	2:58	Boston	Walk On	Rock		
2	The Last Resort	7:29	Eagles	The Very Best of Ea...	Rock		
3	Tooth and Nail	3:57	Foreigner	No End In Sight: Th...	Rock		
4	Higher Power	5:08	Boston	The Full Discover P...	Rock		
5	Can't Wait	4:32	Foreigner	No End In Sight: Th...	Rock		

Figure 19–25. *iTunes DJ window*

At the bottom of this window, you have three options. This is shown in Figure 19–26.

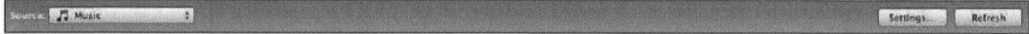

Figure 19–26. *Options available to customize iTunes DJ results*

The three options are:

- **Source:** This tells iTunes DJ where to find your music. You can select **Music**, which is all of your songs and is the default, or you can select a specific **Playlist**.

- **Settings** (Figure 19–27)**:** This is broken down into two sections. The top portion allows you to set what is shown in the Playlist. You can set the window to display a customizable number of recently played songs, a customizable set of upcoming songs, and, if you wish, play songs that are rated higher more often. The bottom section allows you to customize how users can interact with the playlist via the Remote app. The Remote app is a free download from the App store and works on all iOS devices. Check the box next to **Allow guests to request songs with Remote for iPhone or iPod touch** to activate this feature. Below this check box, you can set a custom welcome message. You have three other options to set.

  - **Restrict requests to source:** This can be turned on to only users to pick songs from a certain location. The **Music** section is the default.

  - **Enable Voting:** If you wish, users can vote on which songs they want to play. Very democratic.

  - **Require Password**: You can lock users from using the Remote app by giving it a password to restrict access.

Figure 19–27. *ITunes DJ Settings window*

- **Refresh:** This will update your playlist based on any changes you make to the settings governing what is to be played.

View Options of iTunes

The sidebar is a great start to learn about iTunes. Another important way to learn about iTunes is by understanding the different views available to show your media lists. To demonstrate these different views, I will use a playlist I created containing the greatest hits of one band. It contains a bunch of songs and a few albums.

To access the view choices, there is a set of four buttons located on the top of the iTunes workspace—towards the right side of the screen. The full top of the workspace is shown below in Figure 19–28.

Figure 19–28. *Full set of options above iTunes workspace*

The four view buttons are shown in Figure 19–29.

Figure 19–29. *The four view Options of iTunes*

List View

This view just lists the items in your library or playlists as one long list of items. This is shown in Figure 19–30. By default, it contains: the Name of the item, the Time of the item, the Album the song is found on, the Genre of the song, A rating if you choose to rate a item and the number of times it has been played. You can sort the list using any of these headings by clicking on the heading.

▲	✓	Name	Time	Artist	Album	Genre	Rating	Plays
1	✓	Can'tcha Say (You Believe In Me) […	5:13	Boston	Third Stage	Rock		1
2	✓	A Man I'll Never Be	6:36	Boston	Don't Look Back	Rock		1
3		More Than a Feeling	4:45	Boston	Boston	Rock		1
4	✓	Cool the Engines	4:23	Boston	Third Stage	Rock		1
5	✓	We're Ready	3:58	Boston	Third Stage	Rock		1
6	✓	Peace of Mind	5:04	Boston	Boston	Rock		1
7	✓	Don't Look Back	6:00	Boston	Don't Look Back	Rock		1
8	✓	Let Me Take You Home Tonight	4:47	Boston	Boston	Rock		1
9	✓	Smokin'	4:21	Boston	Boston	Rock		1
10	✓	Foreplay / Long Time	7:48	Boston	Boston	Rock		1

Figure 19–30. *Default List view*

If you go to the View Menu and select View Options, you can add a ton of other items to this list. I like to add the year the song came out so that I can sort the list by Year. The list of available options is shown in Figure 19–31. Click on the box next to the item or items you want to add.

View Options

♫ Music

Show Columns

☑ Album	☐ Episode ID	☐ Season
☐ Album Artist	☐ Episode Number	☐ Show
☐ Album Rating	☐ Equalizer	☐ Size
☑ Artist	☑ Genre	☐ Skips
☐ Beats Per Minute	☐ Grouping	☐ Sort Album
☐ Bit Rate	☐ Kind	☐ Sort Album Artist
☐ Category	☐ Last Played	☐ Sort Artist
☐ Comments	☐ Last Skipped	☐ Sort Composer
☐ Composer	☑ Plays	☐ Sort Name
☐ Date Added	☐ Purchase Date	☐ Sort Show
☐ Date Modified	☑ Rating	☑ Time
☐ Description	☐ Release Date	☐ Track Number
☐ Disc Number	☐ Sample Rate	☐ Year

(Cancel)   (OK)

Figure 19-31. *Complete list of items that can be shown in the list view*

Album View

This view highlights your lists by album and will show a graphic of each album's cover. This is shown in Figure 19–32.

Album by Artist		√	Name		Time	Artist	▲	Genre	Rating	Plays
	Boston	1		More Than a Feeling	Ping ▼	4:45	Boston		Rock		1
	Boston	2	√	Peace of Mind		5:04	Boston		Rock		1
	★★★★★	3	√	Foreplay / Long Time		7:48	Boston		Rock		1
		4	√	Rock and Roll Band		3:00	Boston		Rock		
		5	√	Smokin'		4:21	Boston		Rock		1
		6	√	Hitch a Ride		4:12	Boston		Rock		
		7	√	Something About You		3:48	Boston		Rock		
		8	√	Let Me Take You Home Tonight		4:47	Boston		Rock		1
	Don't Look Back	1	√	Don't Look Back		6:00	Boston		Rock		1
	Boston	2	√	The Journey		1:44	Boston		Rock		
	★★★★★	3	√	It's Easy		4:24	Boston		Rock		
		4	√	A Man I'll Never Be		6:36	Boston		Rock		1
		5	√	Feelin' Satisfied		4:12	Boston		Rock		
		6	√	Party		4:07	Boston		Rock		1
		7	√	Used to Bad News		2:57	Boston		Rock		
		8	√	Don't Be Afraid		3:48	Boston		Rock		
	The Full Discover Pa...	11	√	Higher Power		5:08	Boston		Rock		
	Third Stage	1	√	Amanda		4:16	Boston		Rock		
	Boston	2	√	We're Ready		3:58	Boston		Rock		1
	★★★★★	3	√	The Launch: I. Countdown, II. Igni...		2:58	Boston		Rock		
		4	√	Cool the Engines		4:23	Boston		Rock		1
		5	√	My Destination		2:20	Boston		Rock		
		8	√	I Think I Like It		4:07	Boston		Rock		

Figure 19–32. *Example of viewing a list using the Album View*

Grid View

This view is similar to the Album view. This view does give you a few options to customize how the grid is shown. If you look at my example shown in Figure 19–33, please notice at the top of the workspace—there are four ways to view the grid. The choices are: Albums (shown in example), Artist, genres or Composers. There is also a slider at the top-right of the screen to shrink or enlarge the preview graphics (album covers).

Figure 19–33. *Example of the Grid View*

Cover Flow View

This is the most visually stunning way to view your lists. It takes the preview graphics of your song or movie and puts it into a 3D environment. This is shown in Figure 19–34.

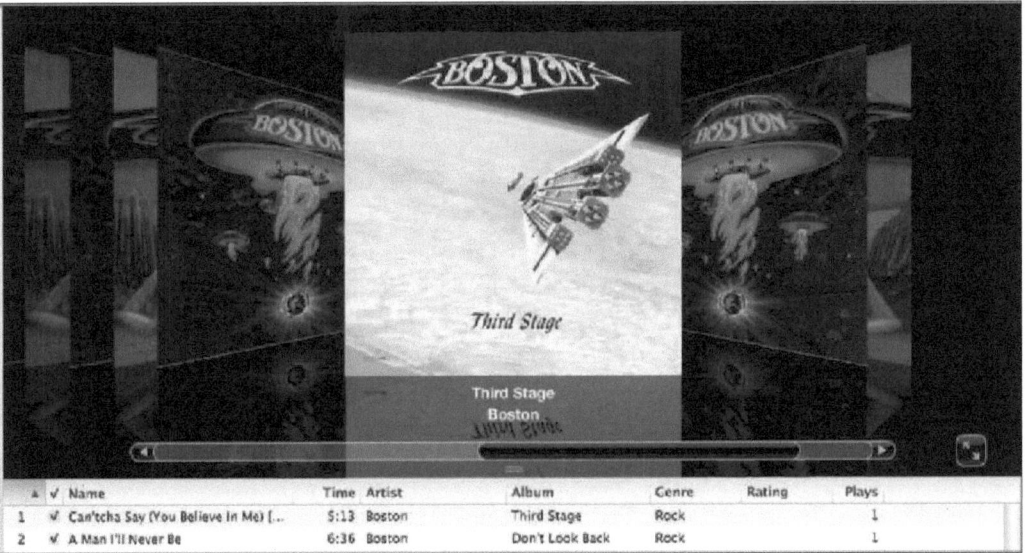

Figure 19–34. *Example of the Cover Flow view*

To navigate through this list, you could either use the slider located just below the preview items or click on an item just to the left or right of the item directly in front. Just below the slider is a small icon of three lines [image]. If you hold your mouse button on this icon, you can make this 3D view window larger or smaller.

[image] This button, located just at the far right of the **Cover Flow** window, will make the **Cover Flow** window appear infill Screen mode. You are then given a new toolbar to navigate. This toolbar is shown in Figure 19–35. The first three buttons at the left of the toolbar allow you to play the current album and navigate through the songs. The slider is the same as the regular view:- it is used to navigate through the **Preview** graphics. To the right of this slider is a slider to control the volume. Last, you can return to the regular view by clicking on the **Full Screen** button. You can also exit full-screen mode by pressing the **ESC** key on your keyboard.

Figure 19–35. *Full screen toolbar while viewing in the Cover Flow view*

Summary

This chapter introduced the very important topics of the iTunes sidebar and available view options. You should now be familiar with two key concepts for navigating through iTunes. In the next chapter, I will discuss getting media into iTunes as well as getting media out by burning it to a CD or putting it onto an iOS device.

Chapter 20

Getting Media into and out of iTunes

In the last chapter, I introduced you to two important navigations tools: the iTunes sidebar and the four different views available. In this chapter, I will explain how to get your media into iTunes and organize it, and then how to get media from iTunes onto a CD or iOS device.

Getting Media onto iTunes

Let's start with getting media into iTunes. There are several ways of doing this:

1. Purchase songs or videos from the iTunes store. I briefly covered this in the last chapter.

2. Import songs from a CD. Note that this could take some time if you have a lot of CDs.

3. Import media from other iLife apps, such as songs from GarageBand or movies from iMovie.

> **NOTE:** I covered exporting from the other iLife apps in detail when I discussed the **Share** menu for each app, but here's a quick recap:
>
> **iMovie:** Go to the **Share** menu and select **iTunes**.
>
> **GarageBand:** Go to the **Share** menu and select either **Send Song to iTunes** or **Send Ringtone to iTunes**.

In this chapter, I will focus on importing data from GarageBand.

Getting Songs or CDs into iTunes

Every audio CD is created in the same format so that it can be played in every CD player or computer. Think of this format as any other file on your computer. It contains information that only certain applications can understand. iTunes gives you the opportunity to play the songs or "files" found on any CD. It also gives you the chance to take these songs and translate them so they can be saved on your Mac. You can import your entire CD collection and then organize the songs however you want in iTunes. The following pages cover all the information you need to translate or import your songs into iTunes.

The first thing to know before you start to import CDs is what format they will be imported as. I will guide you through the menu items to achieve your import goals. I highly recommend that you import all of your song as MP3s. Most new cars will play MP3 CDs. An MP3 CD will contain a lot more songs than a traditional CD. A regular CD may contain 10 to 15 songs. A MP3 CD might contain around 100 or more.

Setting Your Import Settings

The settings that govern in which format iTunes will import your songs is found in the **Preferences...** window of the **iTunes** menu. I will cover all the iTunes menus in detail in Chapter 22: "How to Become an Efficient Media Mogul by Using the iTunes Menus," but it is important to cover this specific material before then.

In Figure 20–1, we see the bottom of the **General** tab of the **Preferences...** option of the **iTunes** menu. As you can see, there are a few settings that can be adjusted by the user.

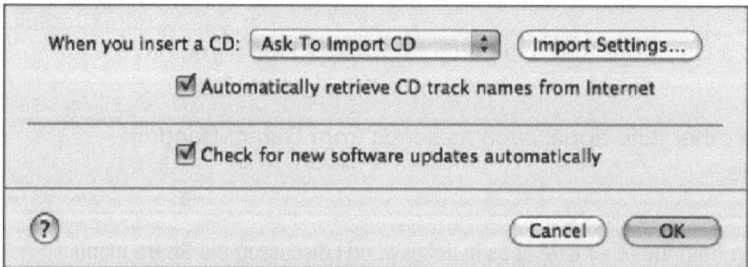

Figure 20–1. *Bottom section of the **General** tab of the **Preferences...**window found in the **iTunes** menu*

When you insert a CD, the CD will appear in the **Devices** Section of you iTunes sidebar. This is shown in Figure 20–2.

Figure 20–2. *Example of a CD inserted while iTunes is being accessed*

A drop-down menu presents you with a few choices of what to do with the inserted CD. **Ask To Import CD** is the default choice. The complete list of choices is shown in Figure 20–3, and explained below.

Show CD
Begin Playing
✓ Ask To Import CD
Import CD
Import CD and Eject

Figure 20–3. *Options available when you insert a CD*

- **Show CD:** This will display the track listing of the inserted CD.

- **Begin Playing:** This will display the track listing of the inserted CD, but it will also start playing the CD from track one.

- **Ask To Import CD:** You will be presented with the screen shown in Figure 20–4. Click **Yes** to begin the import process or **No** to not have it imported.

Would you like to Import the CD "Missing Links Volume 1 – 3 Finger Painting – The Sky Road – Time And Tide" into your iTunes library?

☐ Do not ask me again

No   Yes

Figure 20–4. *Ask to Import CD option*

- **Import CD**: This will automatically import your CD into iTunes.

- **Import CD and Eject:** This will automatically import your CD into iTunes and then eject it from your Mac.

Import Settings

This is a very important option to be aware of before you start importing music. The default settings for this option are shown in Figure 20–5 and explained below.

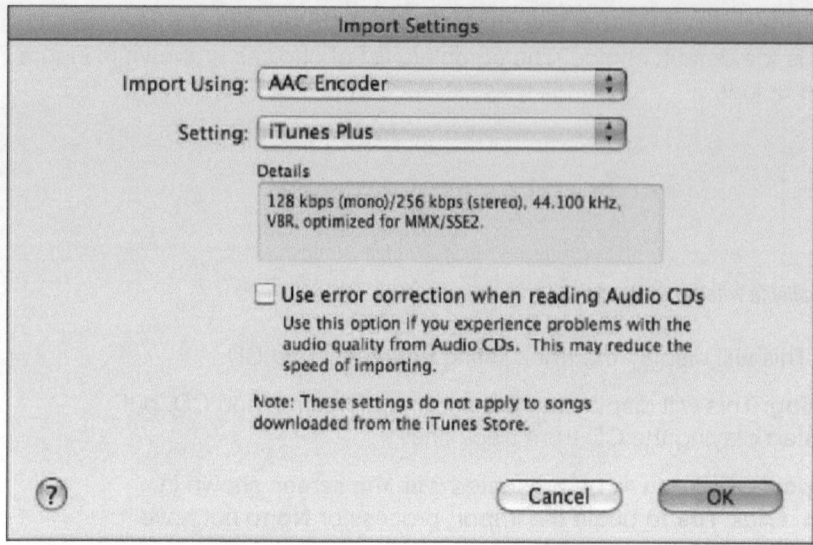

Figure 20–5. *Import Settings window*

- **Import Using:** This could be a wide variety of formats. Again, I recommend that you choose **MP3 Encoder**. However, if you do not plan to make MP3 CDs, some of the other formats might offer better sound quality. The list of available formats is shown in Figure 20–6.

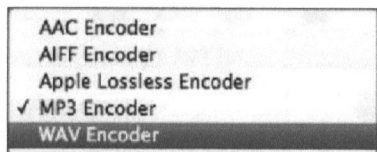

Figure 20–6. *Available sound formats for importing songs or CDs*

- **AAC Encoder** (default): You can play this format in iTunes, iPhone, iPad, or any iPod that came with a dock connector. If you plan to use another portable device, it is also recommended to use MP3. You can choose between three quality settings. They are: **High Quality**, **iTunes Plus**, or **Spoken Podcast**.

- **AIFF Encoder or Apple Lossless Encoder:** If you want to create high quality CDs, choose one of these options. Please note the size of these files will be much larger .

- **MP3 Encoder:** I recommend you use this if you plan to use MP3 CDs in a computer or in your car. You can choose between **Good Quality**, **High Quality**, or **Higher Quality**. The higher the quality, the larger the bits per second. **Good Quality** starts out at 128 and the **Higher Quality** settings tops out at 192.

■ **WAV Encoder:** If you plan to play your music on a device that doesn't support MP3 technology, use this format.

There is an option below the setting line that asks if you want to use error correction when reading Audio CDs. To select this option, check the box next to **Use error correction when reading Audio CDs**. It should only be used when you are having difficulty importing a CD. The time it takes to import a CD will be much greater if this option is used.

Importing the Material

When you import a CD, there are two status items to keep track of. The first is an information window located at the top of your window, directly in the middle. When you are importing music, this window will display the current status. This is shown in Figure 20–7. Please note that is gives a rough estimate of how long it will take to import each item. In the example shown, it is **0:09** for the song **Amazonas**.

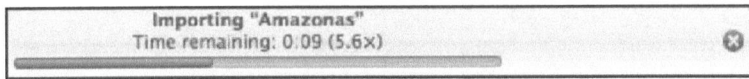

Figure 20–7. *The status of your import.*

The second way you can find out the status of the material being imported is to look at the CD contents. There will be a small green checkmark next to each song that is done being imported. An orange wavy line tells you that a song is currently in the process of being imported. This is shown in the third song in Figure 20–8.

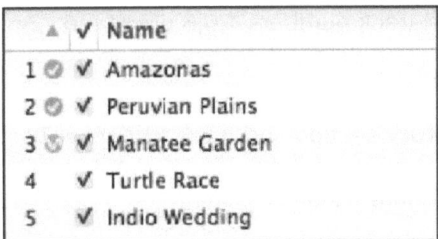

Figure 20–8. *Example of songs finished being imported (2 green checkmarks) and one song being imported (orange wavy line)*

If you did not select **Ask to Import CD**, **Import CD**, or **Import CD and Eject** (shown in Figure 20–3), then you can also import your music in two other ways: via the **Import CD** button or by dragging songs into the library.

Using the Import CD button

Click the **Import CD** button located at the bottom of your workspace at the far right. If you change your mind and decide not to import the material, or want to change

the import settings, the **Import CD** button becomes the **Stop Importing** button. Click it to stop the import.

As I have stated, it is preferable to set your import settings before you import any material. But, if you want to change the settings on the fly when you are importing using

the **Import CD** button, you can click on the **Import Settings** button just to the left of the **Import CD** button. This will bring up the **Import Settings** window shown in Figure 20–5.

Dragging Songs

Another way to import music is to select the tracks you want from the CD and drag the songs into the library.

To select all of the tracks of the CD, go to the **Edit** menu and use the **Select All** command.

To select random tracks, hold down the command key (⌘) while selecting the tracks you want to import. For example, you want to import track numbers 1,6,8 out of the 12-song CD.

Once you have selected the material you want to import, drag the material to the **Library** section of the screen. A border will highlight the **Library** section and track's name will move with your mouse into the section. Let go of the mouse button once the material is inside the **Library** section. This is demonstrated in Figure 20–9.

Figure 20–9. *Example of dragging new media into the Library section to import it*

Okay, so now it's time to organize my music into playlists.

Playlists

I briefly covered this topic in the last chapter. If you have a ton of music you want to add to iTunes or if you have decided to only buy digital versions of albums in the future, playlists are essential.

It is a very simple procedure to create playlists from material in your master **Library** section or to create an empty playlist.

To create an empty playlist follow these steps

1. Go to the **File** menu and select **New Playlist**. The top portion of the **File** menu showing this option is shown in Figure 20–10.

File	Edit	View	Controls	Store	Adva
New Playlist					⌘N
New Playlist from Selection					⇧⌘N
New Playlist Folder					
New Smart Playlist…					⌥⌘N
Edit Smart Playlist					

Figure 20–10. *Top portion of the **File** menu*

2. You will then see an **Untitled Playlist** appear in the **Playlist** section of the **iTunes** sidebar .

3. Type in the new name of the playlist.

4. Hit the **Return** button to finish the naming process.

TIP: You can organize your playlists in a myriad of ways. Organizing by the artist's or group's name is an easy and efficient way to sort your music. You can also organize your music by "mood." For example, you can create a playlist called **Romantic** that has all the romantic songs from various artists in your library.

To create a playlist from the songs in your library, follow these steps:

1. Highlight the items you want to add to a new playlist.

    Hold down the Shift (⇧) key to select a group of consecutive songs.

    Hold down the Command (⌘) Key to select more than one non-consecutive song.

2. Go to the **File** menu and select **New Playlist from Selection**. The top portion of the **File** menu showing this option is shown in Figure 20–10.

3. You will then see an **Untitled Playlist** appear in the **Playlists** section of the **iTunes** sidebar ![untitled playlist].

4. Name the new playlist.

5. Hit the **Return** button to finish the naming process.

Adding Songs from One Playlist to Another via a Contextual Menu

We can see in Figure 20–11 that, when I right-click on a song, a pop-up menu called a contextual menu appears. There are a lot of options to choose from here. Please notice the **Add to Playlist** option. If you choose this, you can add the highlighted song(s) to any of the playlists that you already created.

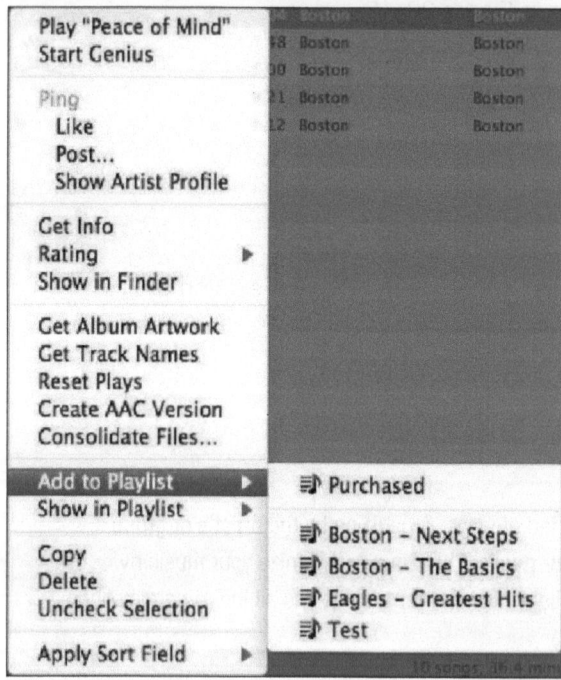

Figure 20–11. *Adding a song to a playlist that already exists*

Creating Playlist Folders

Folders are great if you want to create sub-playlists within a master playlist. An example is shown in Figure 20–12.

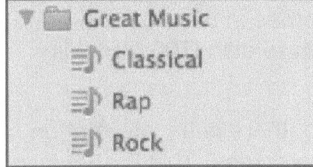

Figure 20–12. *A playlist with a few sub-playlists inside*

To create and modify a playlist folder, do the following:

1. Go to the **File** menu and select **New Playlist Folder**. The top portion of the File menu showing this option is shown in Figure 20–10.

2. You will then see a folder called **Untitled** in the **Playlist** section.

3. Name of the folder.

4. Hit the **Return** button to finish the naming process.

5. To add songs to this folder, click on the folder and follow the procedure for creating a new playlist mentioned earlier.

To delete a playlist or playlist folder, click on the item you want to delete and then right-click on the item. Choose **Delete** from the pop-up menu. You can also delete a playlist by going to the **Edit** menu and selecting Menu and selecting **Delete**.

Getting Media out of iTunes

We have just seen how we can get songs into iTunes. This is only half of what iTunes can do. iTunes allows you get whatever you import into it back out in a variety of ways. iTunes can take the songs in your library and re-translate them for other formats so you can copy them to a CD or other iOS device.

There are two ways to get media from your iTunes library available use on an iOS device:

- Copying or "burning" a playlist to a CD or DVD
- Copying all forms of media to an iOS Device

Burning a Music CD

If you want your CD to play on all devices (CD players and computers), you must use a CD-R disc. A CD-RW disc will not work. RW means the disc can be erased and have material added onto it after the initial burning process. A CD comes in two sizes. A 74-minute disc (650 MB in size) will hold about 20 songs. A 80-minute disc (700 MB) will contain more songs.

To determine the size of your playlist and see if will fit on a disc, there is an information bar at the bottom of the workspace, directly in the middle of the screen. This is shown in Figure 20–13. It tells you the number of songs in the playlist, how long the playlist is, and how big it is.

> 8 songs, 31.2 minutes, 66 MB

Figure 20–13. *Info bar of an iTunes playlist*

Pick which playlist you want to burn to a CD or DVD and follow these steps:

1. Click on the playlist's name in the sidebar.

2. Go to the **File** menu and select **Burn Playlist to Disc**. This is shown in Figure 20–14. You can also access the **Burn Playlist to Disc** option by right-clicking the playlist title. You will get a pop-up menu with the option to **Burn Playlist to Disc**.

Figure 20–14. *The **Burn Playlist to Disc** option*

3. You are presented with Figure 20–15, the **Burn Settings** window.

Figure 20–15. *Burn Settings* window

You have a few options to configure. They are:

- **Preferred Speed:** The default is **Maximum possible**. However, this setting should match the maximum speed of the CD that your purchase. It may be lower than the maximum available on your Mac.

- **Disc Format:** This can be any of the following:

  - **Audio CD:** Choose this if you want the CD to play in all CD players. You have three settings to configure:

  - **Gap Between Songs:** This will determine if there will be a gap between tracks. You can choose **None** or up to five seconds. The default is two seconds.

  - **Use Sound Check:** This will ensure that all your songs play back at the same sound level.

  - **Include CD Text:** If you play the CD on a computer or in car that supports CD text, this option will copy this info so that it can be displayed.

- **MP3 CD:** This will burn your CD as an MP3 CD. This allows you to store roughly 12 hours of music or 150 songs on a 650 MB disc. Again, if you want to use the disc on devices other than a computer, it has to be a CD-R disc, not a CD-RW disc. A lot of cars now have CD players that play MP3 CDs.

- **Data CD or DVD:** This gives you the option to potentially burn a disc that stores your songs in a long playlist. These discs primarily are only playable on computers.

4. After you configure the way you want to burn the CD or DVD, click on the **Burn** button 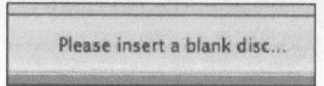 to start the burning process.

The window at the top your screen will instruct you to insert a blank disc. This is shown on Figure 20–16. If the disc inserted can't be used, this window will tell you to use another disc. If the disc is acceptable, the music will be written to the disc.

Please insert a blank disc...

Figure 20–16. *Insert a disc to start the burning process.*

Getting Media onto an iOS Device

You can also transfer music, videos, photos, and iOS apps from iTunes to an iOS device. This process is called syncing.

Follow these steps to transfer media to an iOS device:

1. The iOS device must be attached to your Mac or PC.

2. The device will appear in the Devices section of your **iTunes** sidebar. If you click on the small triangle next to the name, a more detailed list of media that can be stored on your device will appear. Please notice that it does not include everything like apps and photos. This is shown in Figure 20–17.

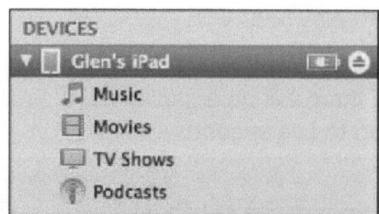

Figure 20–17. *Expanded view of media stored on an iOS device when attached to a computer.*

3. If you click on a category such as **Music** or **Movies** in this view, the list of media in each category will appear in the main iTunes workspace. However, you cannot edit the contents of the iOS device by clicking on the categories in the sidebar.

4. To edit the contents on your device, you must click on the device's name. In this example, it's **Glen's iPad**. This brings up a window that contains many tabs to configure. This is shown in Figure 20–18.

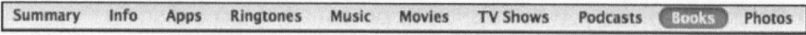

Figure 20–18. *Tabs available to configure or add media to an iOS device*

5. Click on the tab you want to modify: **Music**, **Movies**, **Photos**, and so on. I
    chose the **Music** tab, which opens the window shown in Figure 20–19.

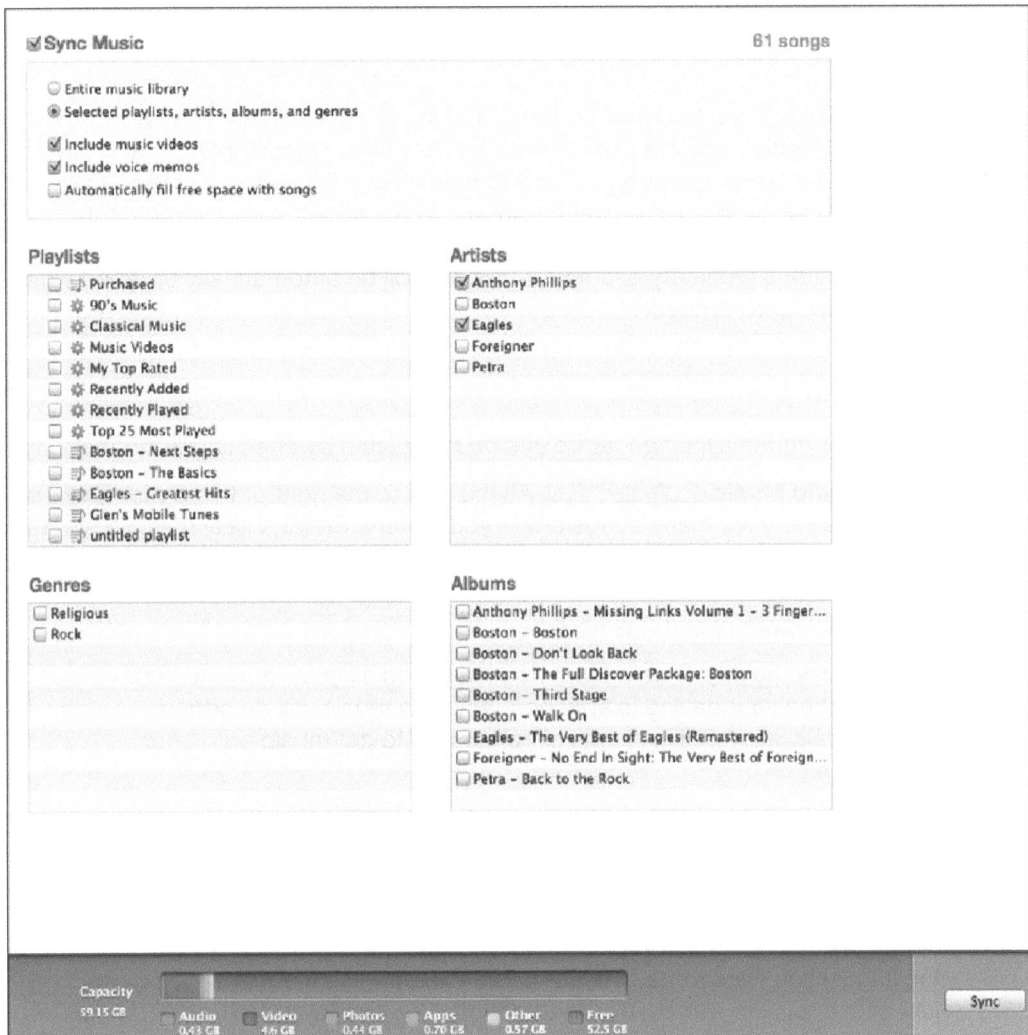

Figure 20–19. *The **Music** tab if you choose not to automatically sync your entire music library*

As you can see, the **Music** window is broken into several areas. In the following
sections, I'll review this and the other medium's syncing windows.

But before I go on any further, please notice the **Capacity Info** bar at the bottom of your
workspace (see Figure 20–20).

Figure 20–20. *Capacity Info* bar

This is a very useful tool, as it contains a bar graph (color coded) to let you know how much space each media item takes up on your device. Also, please notice that it tells you how many items are in category. In the example, I have 61 songs, 3 videos, 660 photos, 8 apps, and a small space used for **Other**. At the far left it tells you the total capacity of your device (59.15 GB in my example) and the amount of free space at the far right of the bar (52.5 GB in my example). This bar will be automatically updated when you add new media to be synced.

Syncing Music

You can turn on or off the syncing feature (it's on by default) by checking or unchecking the box next to **Sync Music** ☑ Sync Music . All the way to the right of this option there is a section that tells you how many songs are in your library. So far, I only have 61 songs 61 songs .

There are several important settings here:

- **Entire music library:** This will automatically add all your music to your device. When your device is attached, any new music will be added automatically as well. This is the simplest way to get music onto your iOS device.

- **Selected playlists, artists, albums, and genres:** This is what I used for my example in Figure 20–19. This window is pretty straightforward. You can choose different criteria for music to be synced. The **Playlist** section will contain all your playlists; **Artists** will contain all of the artists featured in your library, and so on. Just check the box next to the item(s) you want to be synced. In the example in Figure 20–19, I just chose to sync two artists—Anthony Phillips and Eagles. This means that on my device, only songs from these two artists will be added. All other songs will be removed if I previously chose to sync the entire music library or other options.

- **Include Music videos:** This will add any music videos found in iTunes to your device.

- **Include Voice Memos:** If you have an option to create voice memo, this will sync it as well.

- **Automatically fill free space with songs:** If you have a huge library of music, this will fill up any spare space with music until your device is full. This is off by default.

After you have decided which music, videos, or voice memos you want to sync, click on the **Sync** button Sync .

Syncing Movies/Rentals

This window is shown in Figure 20–21.

Figure 20–21. *Movies tab*

This screen is also broken down into several sections. The top two deal with rented movies. In this example, I have one rented movie. The **Rented Movies** section tells me the title and how many more days I have before the rental expires. If I click on the **Move** button Move , the rental will be moved to my iOS device. It can only be on one device at a time. Please remember that once you start viewing a rental, you have 24 hours to finish it. Also, please notice that it states you have to be connected to the Internet to transfer the rental back and forth.

The second section below the rental windows is the **Sync Movies** section. Please notice in my example in Figure 20–21 that I have one purchased movie and one movie I that I created in iMovie and exported to iTunes.

The **Automatically include _____ movies along with selected movie**s Option needs to be filled in. Your choices are shown in Figure 20–22.

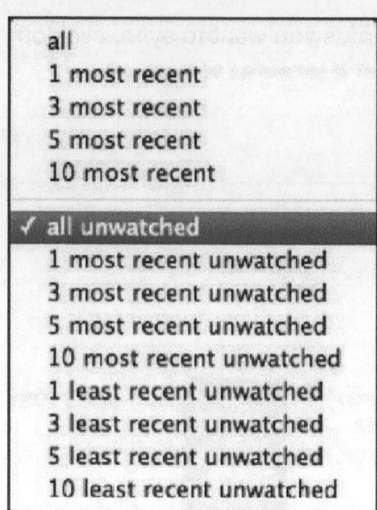

Figure 20–22. *Options for which movies you want sync*

If you want all movies to always be synced, choose **All**. If you want to sync only the movies you have not watched, you have a few options. You can choose **All**, **Most recent**, or **Least recent**. The last two give you the option of choosing 1, 3, 5, or 10 items.

When you have decided what you want to be synced, click on the **Apply** button
. To complete the process, click on the **Sync** button .

Syncing Photos

This window is shown in Figure 20–23. You have a few options to configure in it. The first is to decide where you want iTunes to search for your photos. This is determined by a drop-down menu next to **Sync Photos from___** . The easiest way and the default setting is to use **iPhoto**. It can also be the **Pictures** folder of your account, or you can specify a different folder on your hard drive.

☑ Sync Photos from [🖼 iPhoto   ⬦]   644 photos

   ○ All photos, albums, events, and faces
   ◉ Selected albums, events, and faces, and automatically include [no events   ⬦]

   ☐ Include videos

Albums   **Events**

☐ 🖼 Last Import   ☐ Baby Test
☐ 🖼 Last 12 Months   ☑ Baby Christian – Full   543
☐ 🖼 Baby Arrival   ☐ Jan 25, 2011
☐ 🖼 untitled album   ☐ Jan 25, 2011
☐ 🖼 Baby Arrival II   ☐ IMG_1052
                                                             ☐ Baby Test - 2
                                                             ☐ Feb 7, 2011
                                                             ☐ Feb 10, 2011
                                                             ☐ Feb 19, 2011
                                                             ☐ Feb 20, 2011
                                                             ☐ Mar 26, 2011
                                                             ☑ Baby Smiling   1

Faces

☐ 🖼 Baby Boy
☐ 🖼 Elisa Durdik

Figure 20–23. *Photos* tab

As with the **Music** tab, you can specify all items or specific items. For photos, you can select **All Photos, albums, events and faces** or **Selected albums, events, and faces and automatically include** ___ . The second option is shown in Figure 20–23. The blank line deals with events. The list of all event choices is shown in Figure 20–24.

Figure 20–24. *Sync choices for events found in your iTunes library*

If you imported videos into iPhoto, there is a check box to include these videos as well

☐ Include videos

Syncing TV Shows

This window is shown in Figure 20–25.

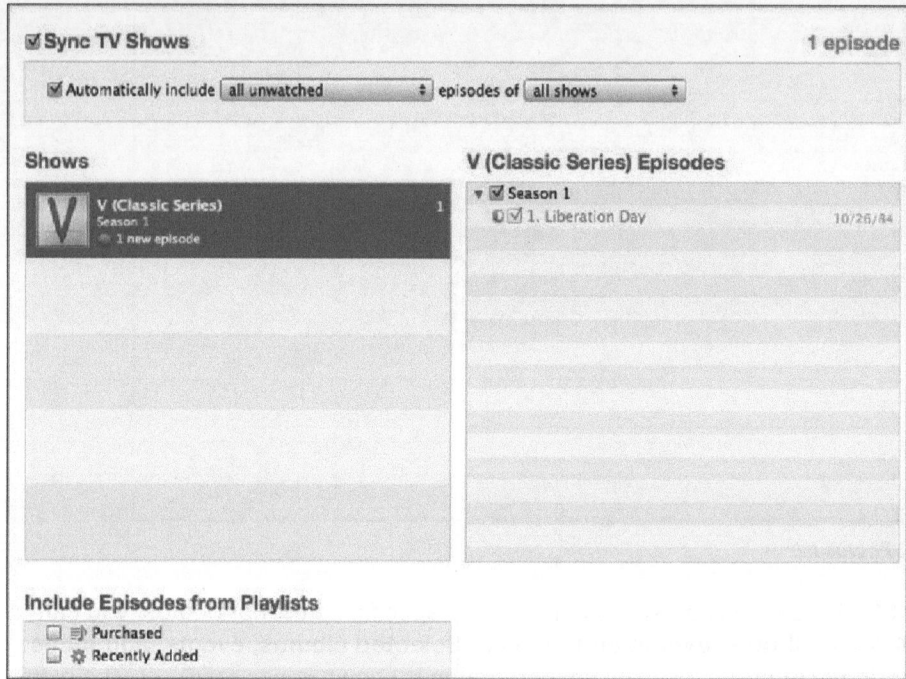

Figure 20–25. *TV shows tab*

There are two settings to configure in this window. The first is to select what you want to sync and whether you want to sync all shows or selected shows. The options available next to **Automatically include** is shown in Figure 20–26.

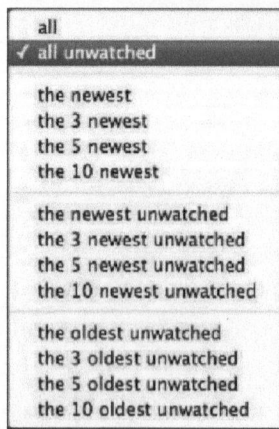

Figure 20–26. *Deciding what TV shows you want synced*

Syncing Podcasts

This window is shown in Figure 20–27. There is nothing really new to this tab. You have to decide what content you want to sync (see Figure 20–28) and if you want to sync all podcasts or only selected ones.

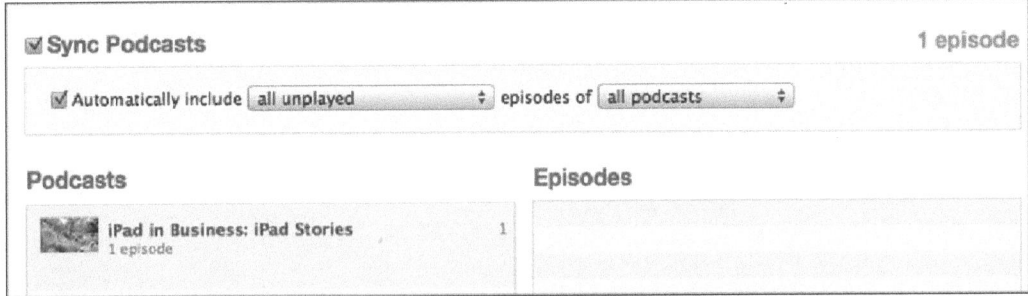

Figure 20–27. *Podcasts tab*

Figure 20–28. *Sync options for podcasts*

Syncing Books/Audiobooks

This tab is shown in Figure 20–29. I do not have any books or audiobooks at the moment, but as with the other tabs, you can select all items to be synced or just selected ones.

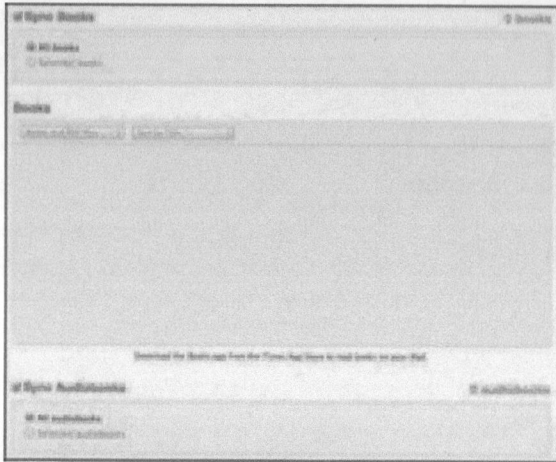

Figure 20–29. *Books/Audiobooks tab*

Syncing Ringtones

Remember that we can create custom ringtones in GarageBand and export them to iTunes for use on an iPhone. If you had ringtones, you could select all of your ringtones to be synced or just a selected set.

Syncing Apps

This will only be used if you own an iPod Touch, iPhone, or iPad, as these devices can run apps on them. The **App** screen is shown in Figure 20–30. On the left side of the window is sidebar listing all of the apps you have purchased. It does not include the apps already installed by Apple on your device. To the right of this sidebar is a visual representation of your device. It shows you where all of your apps are located on the screen and, if you have more than one screen of apps, it shows the different screens on your device. If you click on any of the apps' icons, you can move the app to any other location of your choice—you can even move it to another screen. In Figure 20–30, I can move Facetime to the top row of Apps or to the second screen. The screens available are shown to the right of the mock-up of your home screen.

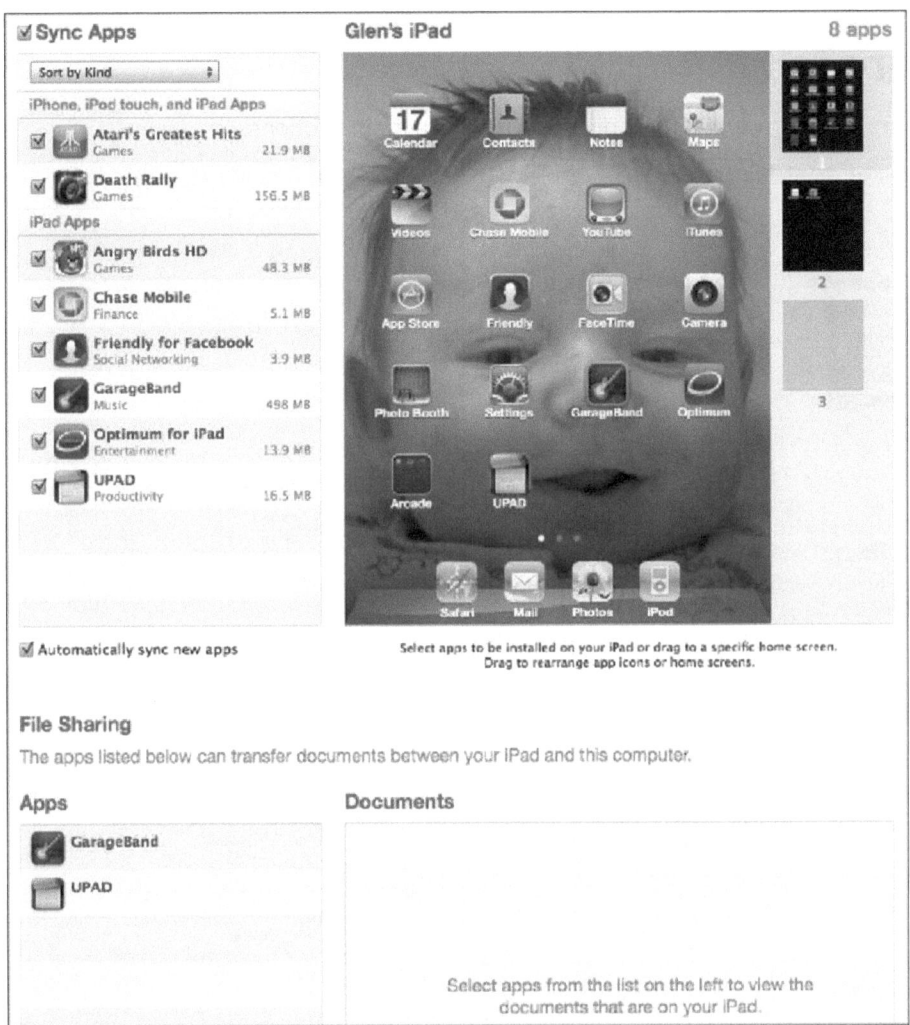

Figure 20–30. *Apps tab*

Below this section is the **File Sharing** section. The apps listed in this section can transfer documents to and from the iOS device to the your Mac or PC. So if you use a GarageBand on an iPad and create songs with its built-in software instruments, you can transfer them to iTunes. This will let you share your song(s) by burning them onto a CD.

That's it for the syncing media or apps. But before wrapping things up, let's review the two other tabs that configure your IOS device: device: **Summary** and **Info**.

Summary Tab

The **Summar**y tab (Figure 20–31) is divided into three main sections.

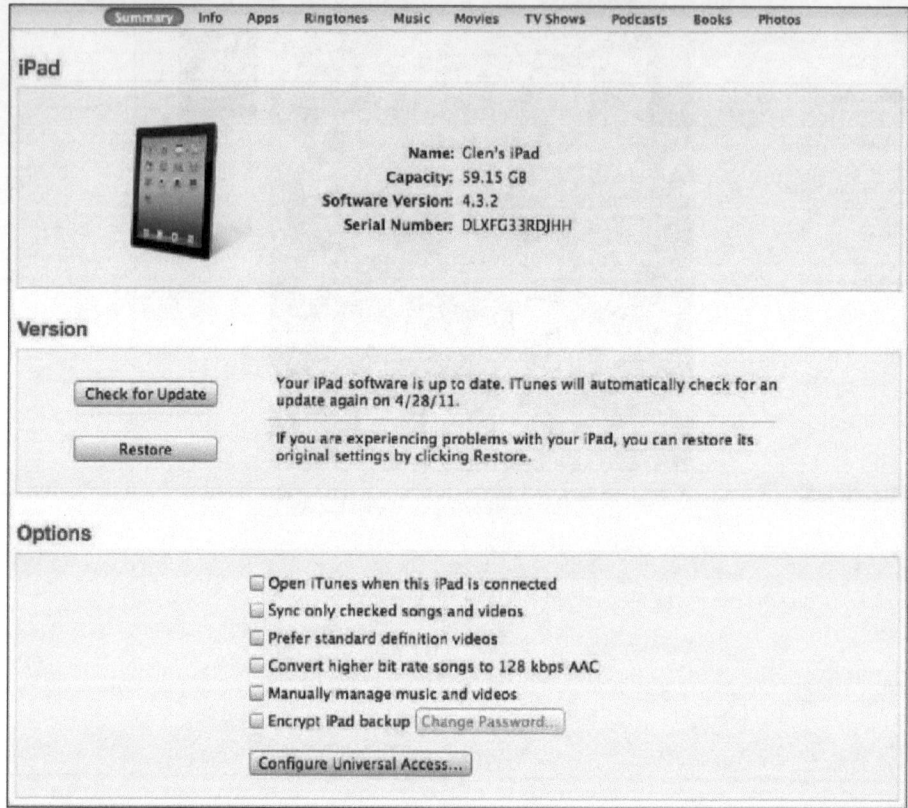

Figure 20–31. *Summary tab*

The first section of this tab tells you the name of the device attached, its capacity, what version of iOS it is running, and its serial number. The second section allows you to check for updates to the iOS or to restore the device. Restore is very useful. Sometimes this process will fix any unusual problems you might have. Restoring will set your device back to its factory defaults.

The third section is called **Options**. You have six choices:

- **Open iTunes when this (Device) is connected:** iTunes will automatically launch when this is selected.

- **Sync only checked songs and videos:** This will sync songs and videos only.

- **Prefer standard definition videos:** This will download only standard definition video to your device. The iPhone and iPod Touch require standard definition video.

- **Convert higher bit rate songs to 128 kbps AAC:** If you import your music with a very high quality convertor, the songs will take a lot disk space. With this option selected, the songs will be converted to a lower quality format so that you can fit more songs onto your device.

- **Manually manage music and videos:** If this is selected, you can just drag any song or video from the library onto the device. This will disable all automatic syncing. If you want to still automatically sync media for some media types, you just have to check the box next the **Sync** item.

- **Encrypt (device) backup:** This is very important to do. This will make the backup secure so it cannot be seen or accessed by others.

- **Configure Universal Access...:** This button allows you to turn on items that help people with visual, auditory, or other physical challenges. They are: **VoiceOver**, **Zoom**, **White on Black**, **Mono Audio**, or **Speak Auto-text**.

Info Tab

The **Info** tab consists of two main parts. The top of this tab is shown in Figure 20–32.

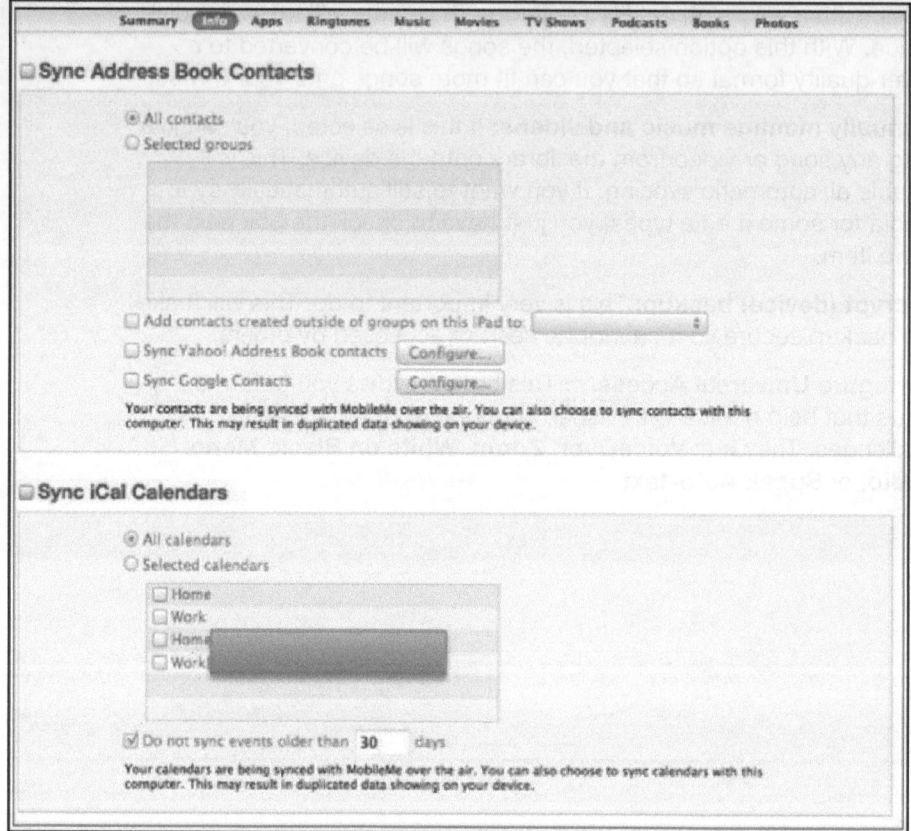

Figure 20–32. *Top portion of the* **Info** *tab*

Here you have two options: Sync Address Book Contacts and Sync iCal Calendars.

The bottom half of the **Info** tab is shown in Figure 20–33.

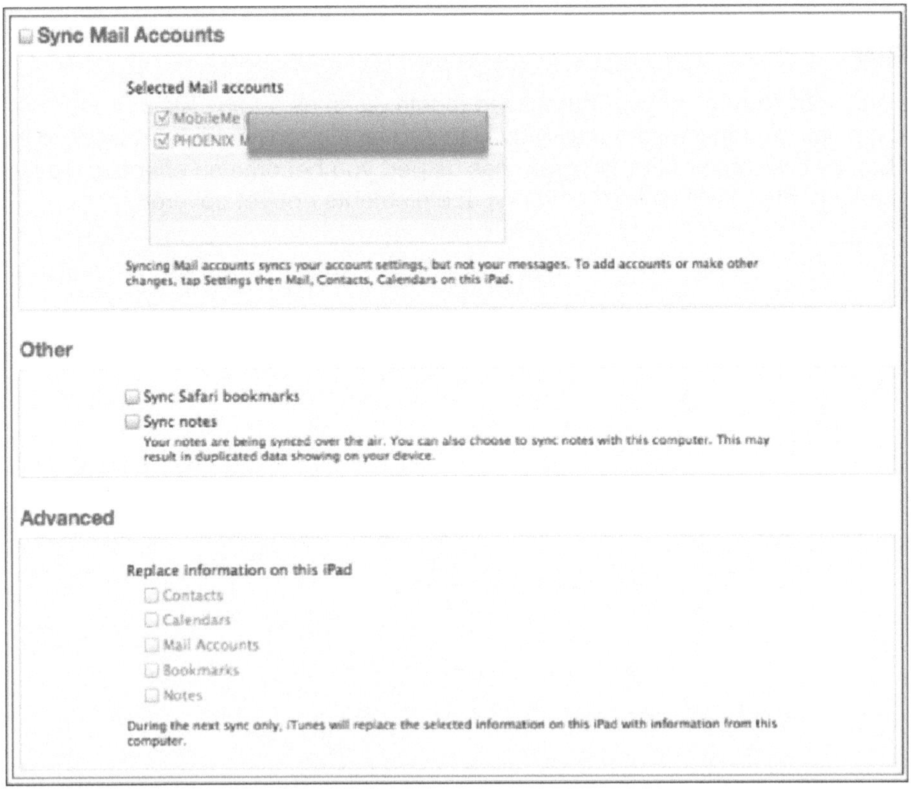

Sync Mail Accounts

Selected Mail accounts

☑ MobileMe
☑ PHOENIX M

Syncing Mail accounts syncs your account settings, but not your messages. To add accounts or make other changes, tap Settings then Mail, Contacts, Calendars on this iPad.

Other

☐ Sync Safari bookmarks
☐ Sync notes
Your notes are being synced over the air. You can also choose to sync notes with this computer. This may result in duplicated data showing on your device.

Advanced

Replace information on this iPad
☐ Contacts
☐ Calendars
☐ Mail Accounts
☐ Bookmarks
☐ Notes
During the next sync only, iTunes will replace the selected information on this iPad with information from this computer.

Figure 20–33. *Bottom half of the **Info** tab*

Here you can set to automatically sync mail accounts, Safari bookmarks, or notes. If you choose to sync notes here, you may see duplicated data, as notes are set to sync wirelessly.

You also have an **Advanced** section. This gives you the option to replace on your device your contents, calendars, mail accounts, bookmarks, or notes from your Mac. This will take place only once during the next sync.

Figure 20–34 will appear when your sync is done and it is safe to disconnect your device from your Mac or PC.

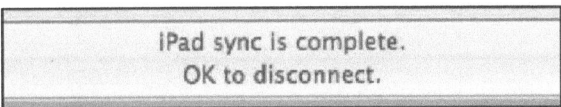

iPad sync is complete.
OK to disconnect.

Figure 20–34. *Sync is complete—it is now safe to disconnect device.*

Summary

With iTunes, you can store all of your purchased media, such as audio CDs or downloaded movies, and make them easily available to an iOS device or burn them to a CD. I hope that my coverage of this program has helped you become an effective iTunes user. In the next chapter, I will cover the workspace elements not yet covered.

iTunes—Everything about the Workspace Except the Kitchen "Sync"

This is a unique chapter in one respect. I felt I had to cover a few workspace elements and menu items in previous chapters to better introduce you to the simple, but feature-packed application called iTunes. In this chapter, I will go over all of the workspace elements that I have not yet covered. These elements are found at the top and bottom of the iTunes workspace. As you will see, this is also the shortest chapter.

Let's begin by discussing the top section first.

Reviewing the Top Workspace Toolbar

The top section of the iTunes workspace is shown in Figure 21–1.

Figure 21–1. *Top row of workspace elements*

I discussed the three buttons shown to the left in the Quick Start Guide to iLife. However, please notice that, for some reason, Apple has stacked these three buttons in iTunes. But, more importantly, the green button (the one on the bottom of the stack) gives you a **Mini-Player** window. This is useful if you want easy access to several iTunes functions while working in other apps. This **Mini-Player** window is shown in Figure 21–2. It features several buttons related to playing music:

Figure 21–2. *Mini-Player window*

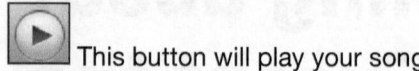 If you click this button once, it will start playing your song from the beginning again. If you click it more than once, it will play the previous song in your Playlist.

This button will play your song.

This button will pause your song.

This button will move you forward one song in your Playlist.

This is a slider control that sets the volume of the media you are playing in iTunes. Click and hold your mouse button on the circular object in the slider to increase or decrease the volume.

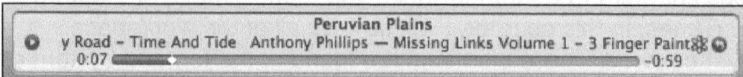

The screen capture immediately above shows the main display of iTunes. Notice that it states the song title ("Peruvian Plains"); and below that title, it shows a moving status line that states the artist and album. At the bottom of the window, it shows a visual timeline that indicates what point you are at in the song. And at the far left of this line, it shows the time that has elapsed (0:07 in this example). Finally, at the far right of this line, it shows the amount of time left to play (0:59 in this example).

At the far left of the main display of iTunes, you can see a small triangle . If you click this element, you will change the display window to an **Equalizer** window, which is shown immediately below.

At the far right of the two versions of this window, you will see the **Genius** button, which looks like the symbol for atomic energy. Clicking this button will activate the Genius feature previously discussed.

I covered the four different view options shown here in Chapter 19: "Navigating Through iTunes via Its Sidebar and Workspace Views." These four views are List, Album, Grid, and Cover Flow.

 This is a search tool to find a song in your Library.

Next, we will explore the bottom section of the iTunes workspace elements...

Reviewing the Bottom Workspace Toolbar

The bottom section of the iTunes workspace is shown in Figure 21–3.

Figure 21–3. *Bottom row of workspace elements*

This workspace also features several buttons related to playing music:

This button will create an "Untitled" empty Playlist.

This button turns the **Shuffle** feature on or off. The **Shuffle** feature will randomly play songs within your Playlist. This is nice if you have a huge Playlist and don't want hear the songs in the same order every time you listen to it.

If you click this button once, it will turn blue. This signifies that your entire Playlist will be played again and again.

If you click the button just mentioned, you will see a small "1" appear inside the button. This means that only the selected song will play over and over again. If you click this button yet again, the repeat functions I just mentioned will be turned off.

This button will either hide or show album artwork in the sidebar. You can see an album cover being displayed in Figure 21–4. The artwork will be displayed at the bottom of the sidebar. If you double-click the artwork, it will be displayed in a much larger separate window. One of the growing trends that many artists are now adopting is to include *Digital Booklets* and other special items when you download an album from the iTunes store. This usually includes unique photographs, artist information, and liner notes.

Figure 21–4. *Example of album artwork being displayed in the sidebar*

125 songs, 8.1 hours, 990.7 MB   This states some important info about your Playlist. It tells you how many songs are in it (125 in this example), how long in minutes the playlist runs (8.1 hours in this example) and how much disk space the Playlist takes (990.7 MB in this case).

This button will turn the Genius feature on or off. You might remember from an earlier chapter that the Genius feature makes suggestions for future music purchases based on what it finds in your Library.

This button will show or hide the iTunes sidebar. The iTunes sidebar is found at the right of your workspace. It primarily deals with the Ping service from Apple.

Summary

That's it for the workspace elements. Armed with your knowledge of the sidebar, importing and exporting media, and now all the workspace elements—you can get around and perform just about any task found in iTunes. The next chapter is the last chapter on iTunes, and it covers the only items I did not cover in detail thus far: the iTunes menus.

Chapter 22

How to Become an Efficient Media Mogul by Using the iTunes Menus

We've come to the last chapter on iTunes. I hope you have a good understanding of what iTunes does and how to navigate around it. As with the other iLife apps, some of the material discussed in the menu section is repeated, but some material is specific to each app. Let' start at the beginning: the **iTunes** menu.

iTunes Menu

This menu is shown in Figure 22–1. As with other apps, the key focus of this menu is the **Preferences...** option. In iTunes, this option has a lot settings that can be changed.

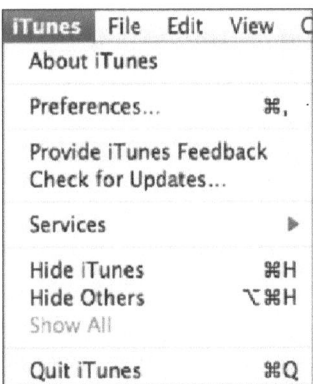

Figure 22–1. *iTunes menu*

About iTunes

This tells you what version of the program you are running.

Preferences...

This section is broken down into seven tabs. The first tab is called **General** and is shown in Figure 22–2.

General Tab

This tab primarily sets what items are to be shown in the sidebar. The other key element in this tab is the ability to configure the settings that determine at what quality you want to import a CD. Also, you can change the **Library Name** if you wish at the very top of this tab.

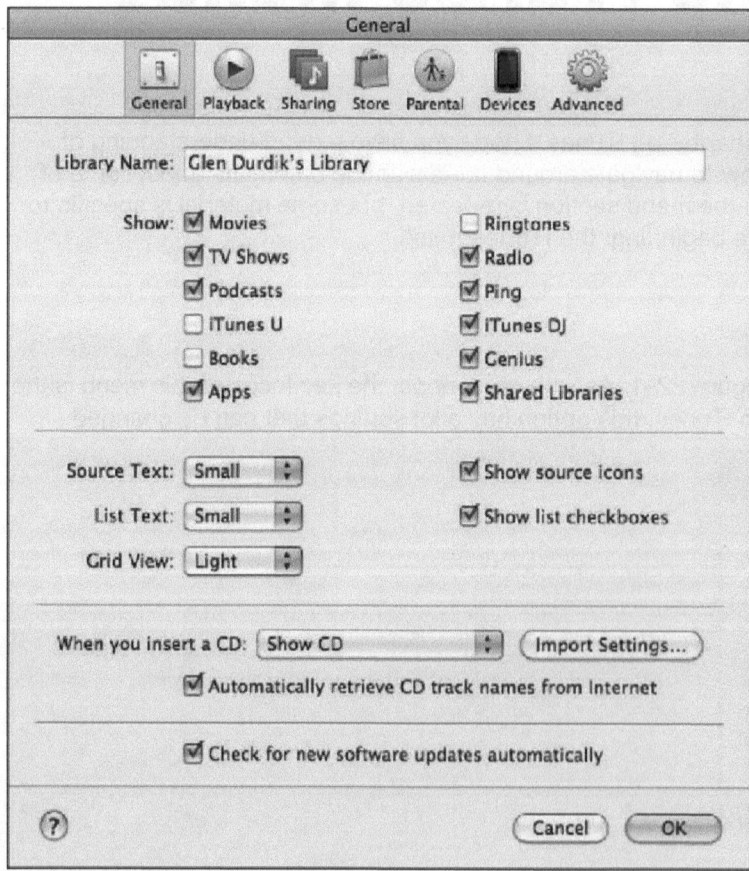

Figure 22–2. *General* tab of the *Preferences...* option in the *iTunes* menu

- **Library Name:** You can name your iTunes library here. This is important if you want to share your library with other Macs in your home.

- **Show:** The options you see selected here are the default items that iTunes will show in the sidebar. You can add **Books**, **Ringtones**, and **iTunes U**.

- **Source Text:** This can be either **Small** or **Large**. This is text that is used for your sidebar.

- **List text:** This can be either **Small** or **Large**. This is the text that is used for listing the items in your playlists.

- **Grid View:** This can be either light or dark. This determines the background color behind the grid of items in a playlist.

- **Show source icons:** Select this to see source icons (checked by default).

- **Show list checkboxes:** Next to each song is small checkbox. By default, each is checked. Check all the songs in a playlist that you want to play. Songs that you do not click will be skipped.

- **When you insert a CD:** This section was discussed in Chapter 20: "Getting Media into and out of iTunes."

- **Automatically retrieve CD track names from the Internet:** Your Mac does not know the titles of your CDs and tracks. Check this box and it will find the title and track info on the Internet.

- **Check for new software updates automatically:** When you first launch iTunes, this option will check to see if there are updates to it.

Playback Tab

This is shown in Figure 22–3. This tab deals with settings for audio and where media is played.

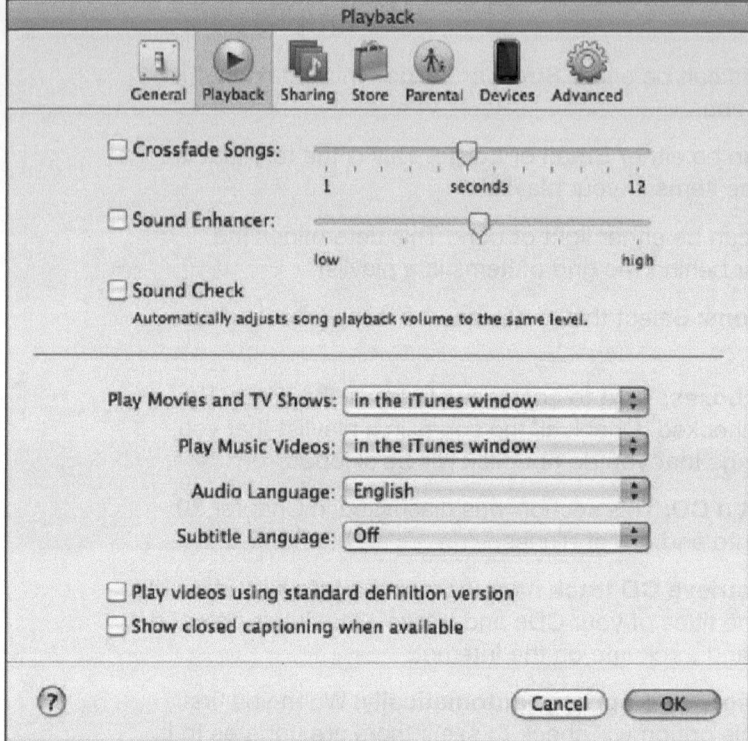

Figure 22–3. *Playback* tab of the *Preferences...* option in the *iTunes* menu

- **Crossfade Songs:** A crossfade will fade the volume of a song at the end, and then gradually increase the volume as the next song begins.

- **Sound Enhancer:** This can make the music played through your speakers sound better. It changes the treble and bass.

- **Sound Check:** This will play all of your music at the same volume level.

- **Play Movies and TV Shows** and **Play Music Videos:** These two options offer the same five choices shown in the following image:

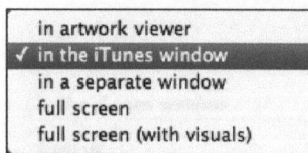

- **Audio Language:** This is set to **English** by default, but can be changed to any of 12 other languages.

- **Subtitle Language:** Choose from 13 languages to add subtitles.

- **Play videos using standard definition version:** Certain devices require standard definition video. This option means that iTunes will only play this media on your computer.

- **Show closed captioning when available:** This can be activated if you need to have the text of a program displayed on the screen as well.

Sharing Tab

This is shown in Figure 22–4. This tab determines what you want to be shared in your local network at home or at work. Check the box next to **Share my Library on my local network** to start sharing your media. Below this check box, you have to decide if you want to share your entire library or just selected items. Last, you can assign a password to your shared media so people outside of your home or workplace cannot access your library. At the bottom of this tab is a check box that, when checked, will update the play counts of your media when others listen or view it.

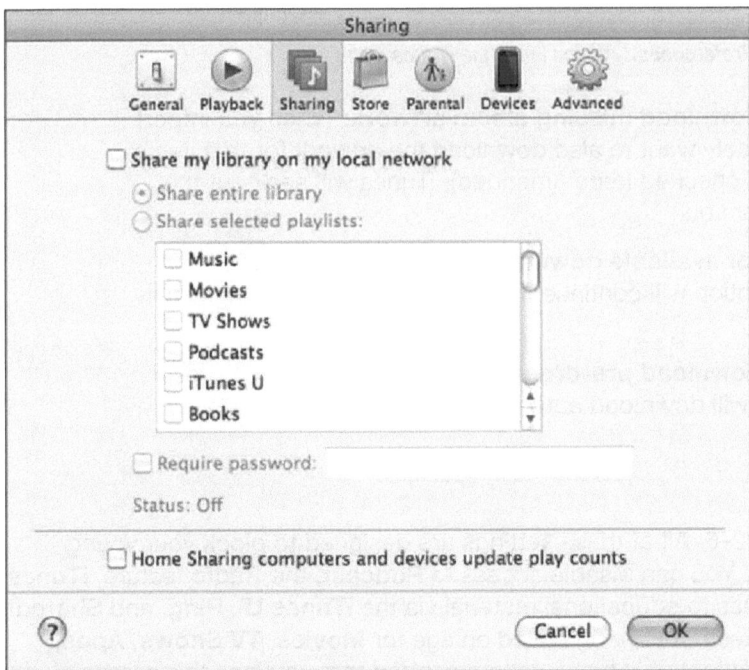

Figure 22–4. *Sharing* tab of the *Preferences...* option in the *iTunes* menu

Store Tab

This is shown in Figure 22–5. It contains three check boxes.

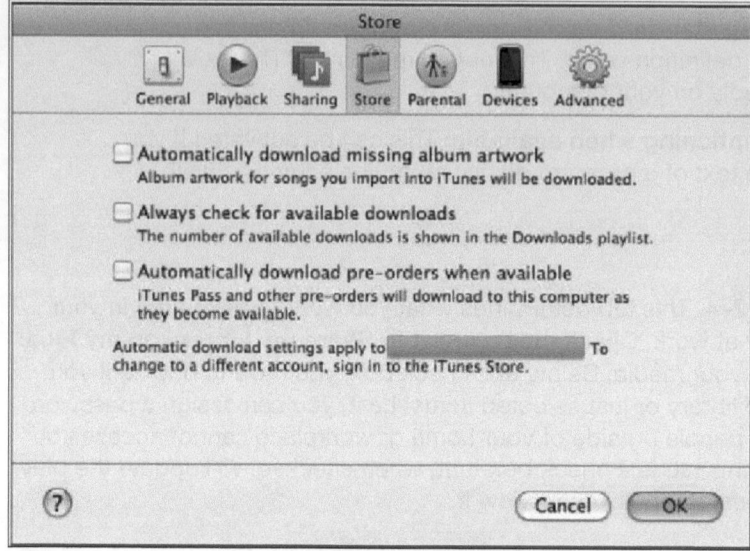

Figure 22–5. *Store tab of the Preferences... option under the iTunes menu*

- **Automatically download missing album artwork:** When you import music, you probably want to also download the artwork for that item. When this box is checked (recommended), iTunes will seek out the album artwork for you.

- **Always check for available downloads:** If a download failed to complete, this option will continue the process until everything is fully downloaded.

- **Automatically download pre-orders when available**: If you pre-order an item, it will download automatically on its release date.

Parental Tab

This is shown in Figure 22–6. All of these settings are designed to block your young ones from adult material. You can disable access to **Podcast**, the **Radio** feature, **iTunes Store** (but still have access to educational material via the **iTunes U**), **Ping**, and **Shared Libraries**. You can also restrict viewing based on age for **Movies**, **TV Shows**, **Apps**, and items with explicit content. It is highly recommended that you lock this screen by clicking on the small padlock icon located at the bottom left of this window.

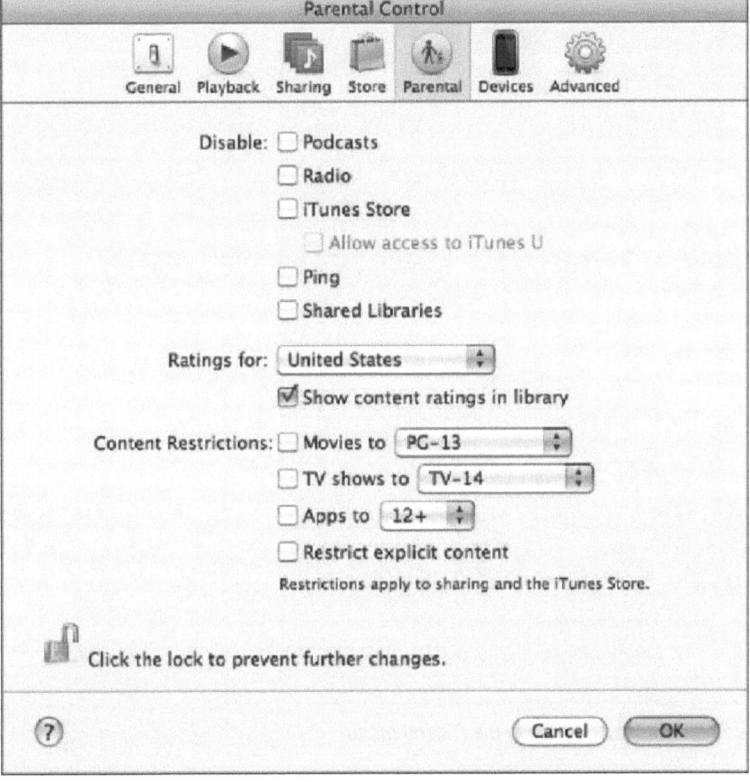

Figure 22–6. *Parental* tab of the *Preferences...* option in the *iTunes* menu

Devices Tab

This is shown in Figure 22–7. The top portion of this window shows you the latest backup of your iOS device.

- **Prevent iPods, iPhones, and iPad from syncing automatically:** If you do not want your iOS device to constantly auto-sync whenever it is plugged in, you can check the box next to this item to stop the auto-sync process.

- **Allow iTunes control from remote speakers:** If you have iTunes attached via an Airport Express, changing the volume of the remote speakers will change the volume of iTunes on your Mac.

- **iTunes is not paired with any Remotes:** You can download a free app called **Remote** from the **App Store**. This will make your iOS device a wireless remote for iTunes. In this example, I have no remotes synced with iTunes.

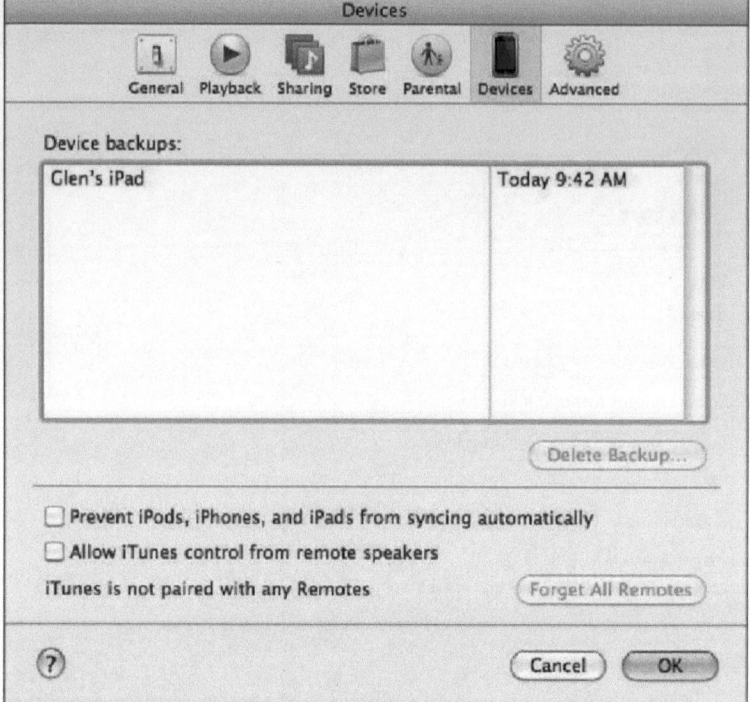

Figure 22–7. *Devices* tab of the *Preferences...* option in the *iTunes* menu

Advanced Tab

This is shown in Figure 22–8. This window is broken down into three sections. The first section deals with handling media. The first option allows you to change the location of your media library.

- **Keep iTunes Media folder organized** and **Copy files to iTunes Media folder when adding to library:** These two items should always be selected so that your library remains organized and consistent. The second section allows you to reset all dialog warnings and reset the **iTunes Store** cache. The third section deals with how certain items are displayed.

- **Keep Mini Player on top of all other windows:** This is nice, because it is always visible no matter what application or window you are working in.

- **Keep movie window on top of all other windows:** This is the same idea as the **Mini Player** option.

■ **Display visualizer full screen:** The visualizer is an animated graphic screen designed to change to the music that is playing. Think of it as a screen saver that syncs to music. If you check this box, the visualizer will always play full screen.

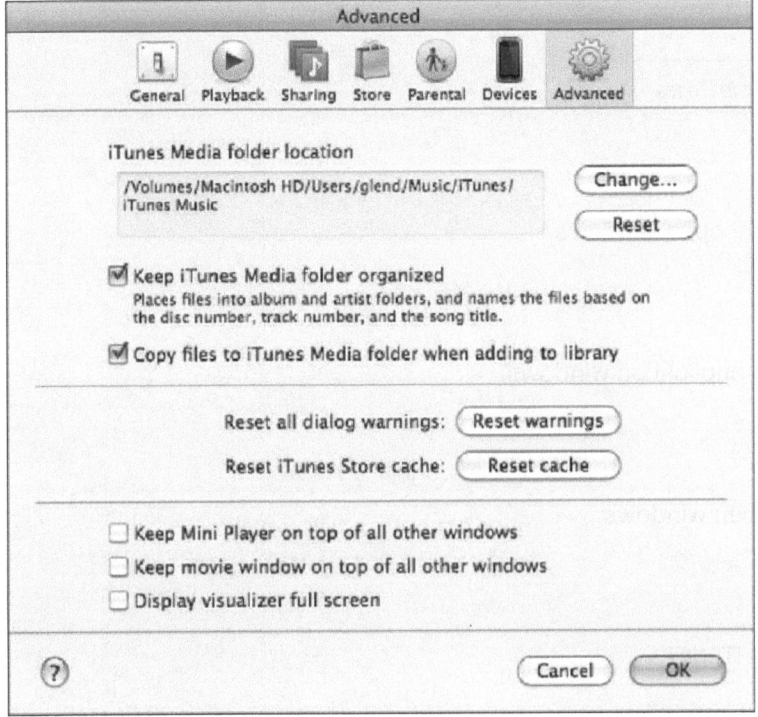

Figure 22–8. *Advanced tab of the* ***Preferences…*** *option in the* ***iTunes*** *menu*

Provide iTunes Feedback

This allows you to report issues or comments about iTunes to Apple.

Check for Updates…

This will access Apple's servers to see if there are any updates to iTunes.

Services

Finally, an app that has services activated. As we can see in Figure 22–9, we have a **Text**, **Searching**, and **Messaging** section.

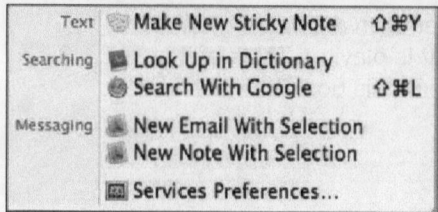

Figure 22–9. *Services available in iTunes*

Hide iTunes

This will hide all of iTunes' open windows.

Hide Others

This will hide other open application windows.

Show All

This will bring back all open windows.

Quit iTunes

This will end your time in iTunes.

File Menu

This is shown in Figure 22–10. The **File** menu allows you to create new playlists, modify your library, and even print CD inserts for your burned CDs.

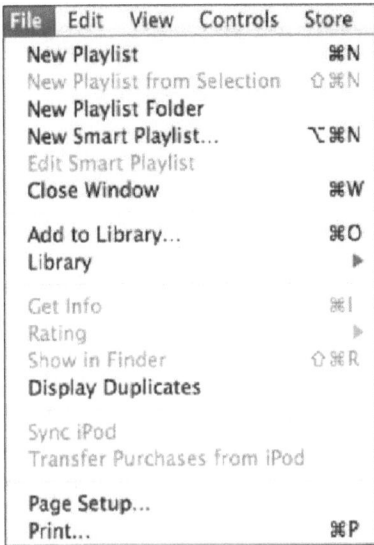

Figure 22–10. *File menu*

New Playlist

This will create a new, empty playlist.

New Playlist from Selection

If you select songs from your library and choose this option, a new playlist will be created of those selected songs.

New Playlist Folder

If you want to provide another layer of organization, this is a nice feature. You can have a folder called, say, **Favorite Rock Bands**. Inside it, you can put all the playlists that match this criteria.

New Smart Playlist...

This is useful as the contents are constantly updated to match the criteria you set. The **Smart Playlist** configuration window is shown in Figure 22–11. Besides **Artist**, you have over 30 different choices to choose from.

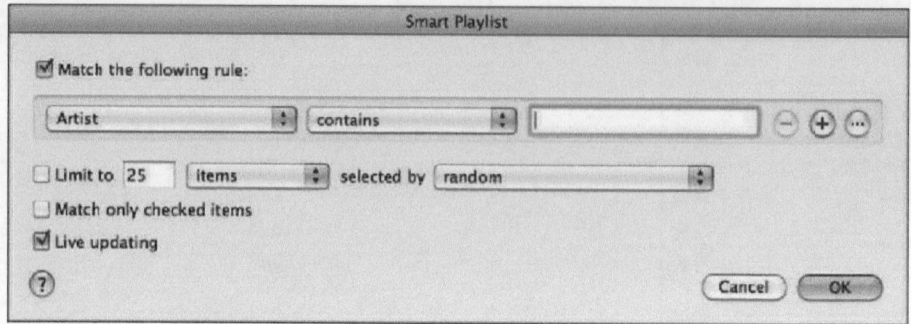

Figure 22–11. *Smart Playlist* configuration window

Edit Smart Playlist

This allows you to edit the settings for a **Smart Playlist** that has already been created.

Close Window

This will close the current window.

Add to Library

A finder window will appear to add new media to your Library.

Library

This window is shown in Figure 22–12. Its options are described below.

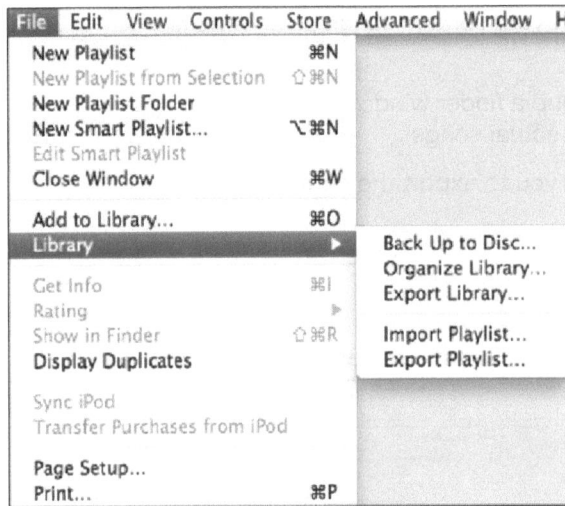

Figure 22–12. *Library option of the File menu*

- **Back Up to Disc…:** Backing up any of your documents is good practice. This option allows you to just back up your iTunes library. Your library may get very big; play it safe and back it up using this option or another backup utility to back up your whole hard drive. If you choose to use CDs or DVDs, the backup can take a long time to complete. But, if something happens to your hard drive, you will be thankful you did it.

- **Organize Library…:** This brings up the window shown in Figure 22–13. You can consolidate files. This takes all the media you imported and puts it all in the **iTunes Music** folder. You can also reorganize files in the folder called **iTunes Music**. This will create subfolders, such as **Music**, **Movies**, **Podcasts**, etc., within the **iTunes Media** folder specified in the **iTunes Advanced** tab found in **Preferences…** option in the **iTunes** window.

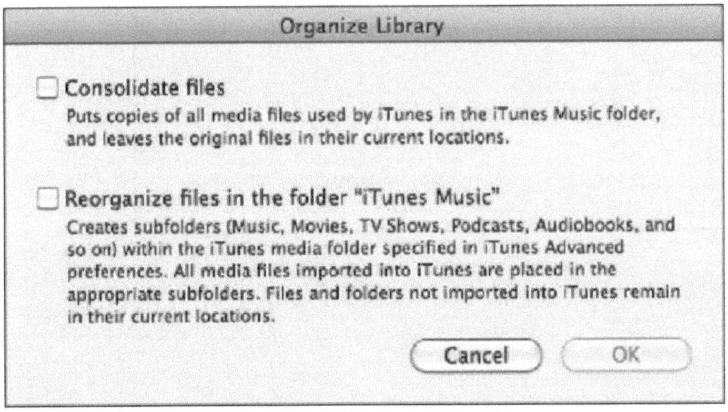

Organize Library

☐ Consolidate files
  Puts copies of all media files used by iTunes in the iTunes Music folder, and leaves the original files in their current locations.

☐ Reorganize files in the folder "iTunes Music"
  Creates subfolders (Music, Movies, TV Shows, Podcasts, Audiobooks, and so on) within the iTunes media folder specified in iTunes Advanced preferences. All media files imported into iTunes are placed in the appropriate subfolders. Files and folders not imported into iTunes remain in their current locations.

(Cancel)   (OK)

Figure 22–13. *Organize Library window*

- **Export Library…:** This will export your library listings as an XML file for use in a web creation tool.

- **Import Playlist…:** This will bring up a finder window to manually import your playlist—list (not the actual songs).

- **Export Playlist…:** This will allow you to export the contents of a playlist as a basic text file.

Get Info

This will bring up a comprehensive window of information about the item you selected. An example is shown in Figure 22–14.

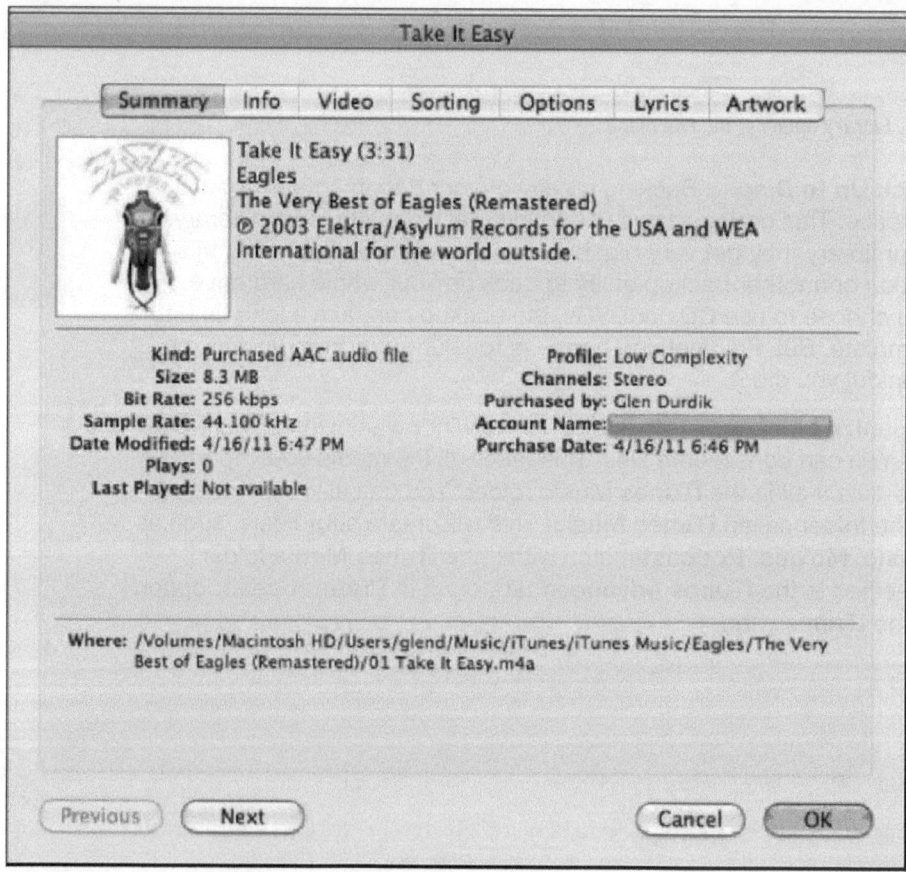

Figure 22–14. *Get Info window*

Rating

As with iPhoto, you can rate individual items in iTunes. The rating system starts at **None** and goes up to five stars.

Show in Finder

This is useful if you want to copy a song or songs from the hard drive and keep it as a computer file. You just might want to copy a few songs and not burn them to disc, for example. This option will bring you directly to the location where it is stored on your hard drive.

Display Duplicates

As your library grows, you might import the same song more than once. This feature will point out if you have any duplicates. Please read the results after performing this action very carefully. If there are duplicates, scrutinize which songs are the ones you want to keep and which ones you want to delete. The song title might be the same, but the quality or length of each song maybe different.

Sync iPod

If you made any updates to the items that go on your device, this feature will sync the media at that point in time.

Transfer Purchases from iPod

If you bought material on your iPod, this will transfer any purchases made back to the Mac that you use to sync your iOS device with.

Page Setup

This sets the settings for your printer. The same for every Mac app.

Print...

This will allow you to print CD jewel case inserts, a song List, or an album list. The main **Print** window is shown in Figure 22–15.

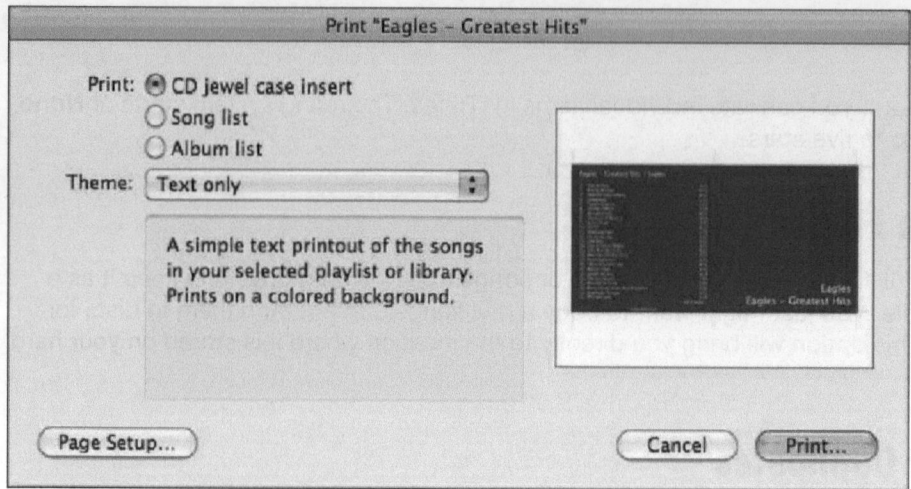

Figure 22–15. *Print options in iTunes*

You can also choose a theme for a CD jewel case. The choices available are shown in Figure 22–16.

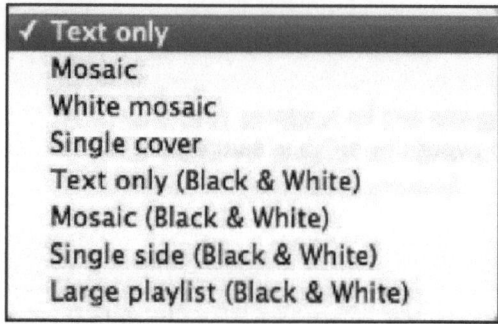

Figure 22–16. *Themes for CD jewel case*

For a song list you can choose: **Songs**, **User Ratings**, **Dates Played**, or **Custom**.

For an album list you can choose: **Songs by Album** or **List of Albums**.

Edit Menu

I think we have seen this before, right? The **Edit** menu (shown in Figure 22–17) contains the same options as in other iLife apps.

Figure 22–17. *Edit menu*

- **Undo:** This will undo the last action you have taken.

- **Redo:** If you change your mind, this will "redo" an action you just undid.

- **Cut:** This removes an item from a playlist.

- **Copy:** This will copy the selected item from a playlist.

- **Paste:** This will place what you just copied at the location of your choice.

- **Delete:** This will remove the item you have selected.

- **Select All:** This will select all the items in the window you currently have open. This is great if you want to copy all the items from one playlist and add them to another one.

- **Select None:** This will undo the **Select All** option.

- **Special Characters:** If you want to add a special symbol to your playlist title, this option will help you find it.

View Menu

This menu is shown in Figure 22–18. It deals with what is to be shown in the iTunes workspace. It allows you to activate the visualizer and set which visualizer you want to use, provides access to the Mini Player (remember the green dot does the same thing), and allows you to view items in full-screen mode.

Figure 22–18. *View menu*

View As: List, Album List, Grid, Cover Flow

These are the available views in iTunes, which I covered in Chapter 19: "Navigating iTunes via Its Sidebar and Workspace Views."

View Options...

By default, iTunes only displays a small set of info for every track. **View Options** gives you the opportunity to display a wide variety of info for the different views. The **View Options** window is shown in Figure 22–19.

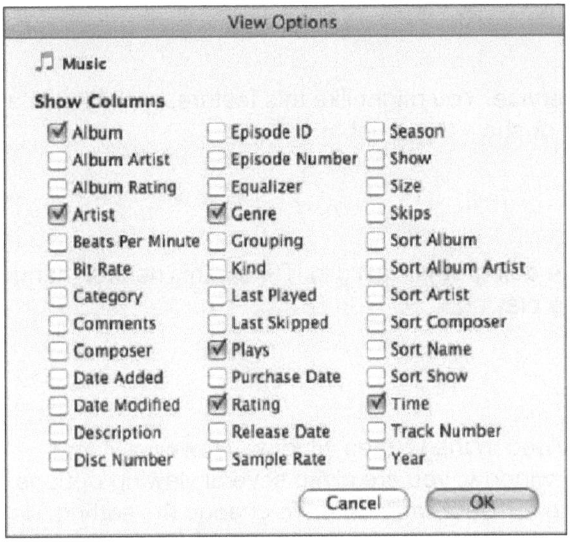

Figure 22–19. *View Options window*

Column Browser

This is not really a fifth view. It modifies the other views with a different layout. I activated it in the example shown in Figure 22–20. Notice that the layout starts with an **Artist** list at the far left.

Figure 22–20. *Column view*

Show/Hide iTunes Sidebar

The iTunes sidebar deals with the **Ping** service. You might like this feature, or think it is a waste of time. This menu option will hide or show this sidebar.

Go to Current Song

If you are currently playing a song, but are doing other tasks in iTunes, this helpful menu option simply brings you back to the song playing.

Video Size

This option is not available if you view a video in the **iTunes** window. However, if you choose to view your videos in a separate window, you are given several viewing options: **Actual Size**, **Fit to Screen**, **Increase Size**, or **Decrease Size**. To change the setting, do the following:

1. Go to the **iTunes** menu.

2. Select **Preferences…**.

3. Click on the **Playback** tab.

4. Select **In a separate window** from the drop-down menu next to **Play Movies and TV Shows**.

Visualizer

This will set the choice of visualizer that you want to use. You have five choices and you can download new ones (not from Apple though). The choices are shown in Figure 22–21.

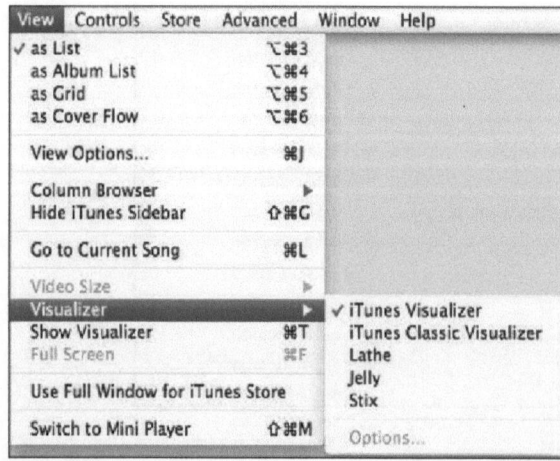

Figure 22–21. *Visualizer* choices

Show Visualizer

This will display an animated scene that syncs with your music. An example is shown in Figure 22–22.

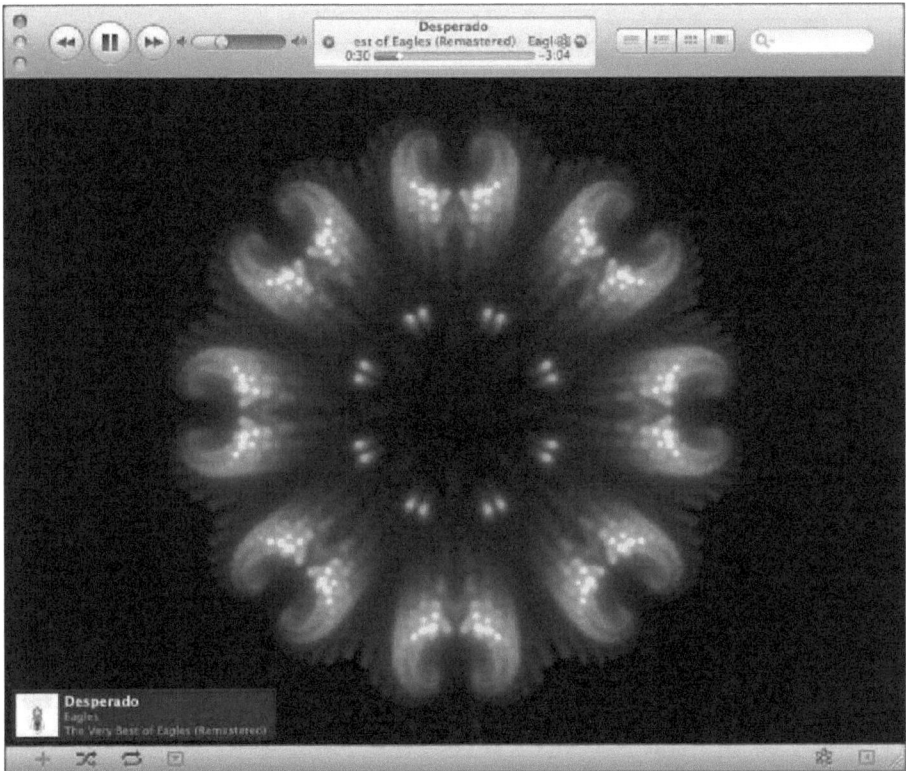

Figure 22–22. *A visualizer in action*

Full Screen

This will display the visualizer in full-screen mode. It's nice to play when you have a party and you are using iTunes as the source of music being played.

Use Full window for iTunes Store

The store has a lot of options in every window you access. You might find it easier to navigate if the store takes up your full screen.

Switch to Mini Player

This was discussed earlier. It is a nice little window to access commonly used iTunes commands. An example is shown in Figure 22–23.

Figure 22–23. *The Mini Player in action*

Controls menu

This menu is shown in Figure 22–24. The top section of this menu deals with navigating through your playlist. You can increase or decrease the volume here as well. The **Shuffle** and **Repeat** options are located here as well.

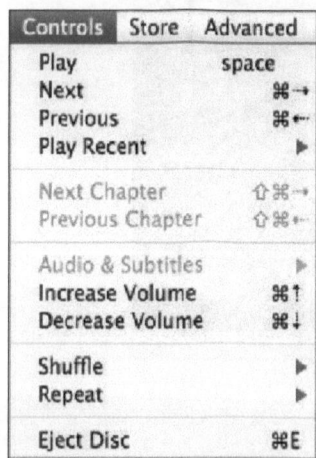

Figure 22–24. *Controls menu*

Play

Starts playing the track you have selected.

Next

Goes to the next track in your playlist.

Previous

Goes to the track before the one that is currently playing.

Play Recent

This is a nifty little feature. iTunes keeps track of what media you played recently so you can easily find it and play it again.

Next Chapter/Previous Chapter

If the media you are listening to has chapters in it (purchased movies, for example) these buttons with either go forward or go backward a chapter.

Audio & Subtitles

This applies to purchased media as well. You can set the audio settings here (stereo or surround) or turn subtitles on or off.

Increase Volume or Decrease Volume

These two items simply lower or raise the volume of the item you are listening to or watching.

Shuffle

This is a great little feature. If you have a huge playlist—you will probably be bored listening to the same songs in the same order over and over again. In Figure 22–25, we see that we can select the **Shuffle** feature, which plays the songs in random order. You can also set this feature to be based on **Songs** (default), **Albums**, or **Groupings**.

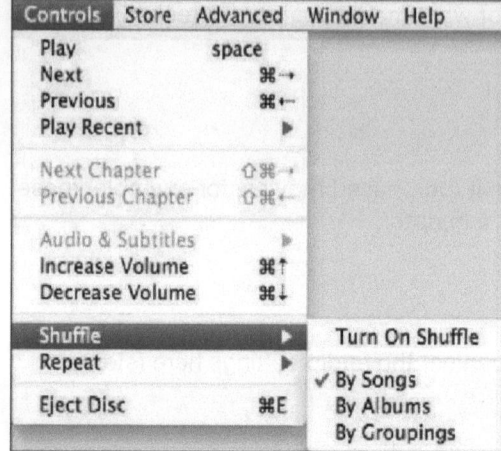

Figure 22–25. *Shuffle feature of iTunes*

Repeat

Want to play a song or playlist over and over again? You can choose to repeat **All**, which will be the entire playlist, or **One**, which will only play the selected song over and over again.

Eject Disc

If you have a CD inserted into your Mac, this will eject it for you.

Store Menu

This menu is shown in Figure 22–26. The important items in this menu are located toward the bottom of the window. If you purchased music from the iTunes store the songs have a set limit of how many computers they can be played on (5). You can also access your iTunes account here as well.

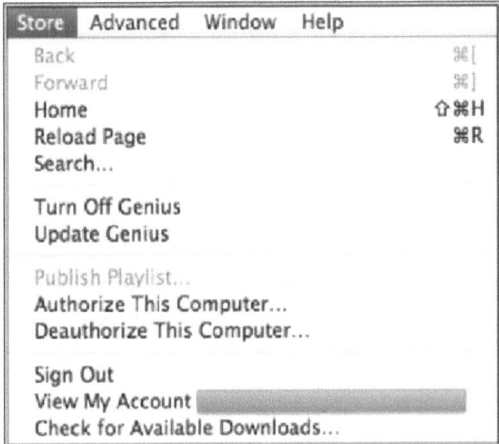

Figure 22-26. *Store Menu*

Back

Helps you navigate the store by going back to the previous screen you were viewing.

Forward

Helps you navigate the store by going to the screen just ahead of the one you are viewing.

Home

This brings you to the initial screen of the iTunes store.

Reload Page

This will reload the page you are currently viewing. This might be needed if something went wrong viewing the page.

Search...

This tool helps make it easier to find the song, artist, movie, and so on that you want.

Turn Off Genius

You might not like Apple constantly viewing what you have in your library. If you select this, the **Genius** option is turned off and Apple can't see what you own.

Update Genius

If you do the **Genius** feature, this will send new info about your library to Apple to update its recommendations for future purchases.

Publish Playlist…

You can publish any playlist you create to be seen by anyone accessing the iTunes store. You simply create a playlist, add a title and a description, and then click on **Publish**.

Authorize This Computer…

If you have material that has restrictions on how many devices it can be played on (the limit is 5), this feature will activate a computer so it can access this material.

Deauthorize This Computer…

If you disable a computer from viewing restricted material, this will de-activate your authorization on the computer.

Sign Out

This signs you out of your iTunes account.

View My Account (account name)…

This will bring up all the details related to your iTunes account.

Check For Available Downloads…

If your download gets interrupted, this option will resume it.

Advanced Menu

This is shown in Figure 22–27. This menu contains a varied list of options.

Figure 22–27. *Advanced menu*

- **Open Stream…:** In the sidebar, there are a lot of Internet radio stations available via the **Radio** option. If you have a specific address of one that is not included in this list, you can type it in via this option.

- **Subscribe to Podcast…:** Podcasts are usually updated daily or weekly. If you choose this option, you can have iTunes always download the latest episode.

- **Create iPod or iPhone Version and Create iPad or Apple TV Version:** iPods, iPhones, iPads, and Apple TVs have different screen resolutions. Choose one of these two options for playing your videos: **iPod/iPhone** or **iPad/Apple TV**.

- **Create AAC Version:** This will create an AAC version of a item that is in another format.

- **Turn On/Off Home Sharing (account name):** Home sharing allows you to share your music with other Macs in your local network.

- **Choose Photos to Share…:** You can select photos or videos to share via a second-generation Apple TV.

- **Get Album Artwork:** This will allow iTunes to search for an album's artwork online.

- **Get Track Names:** If you import CDs that import without track names, this feature will find the track names online.

NOTE: When you import a CD, iTunes should automatically go online to find the album artwork and track titles. The number one reason for these two items not showing up is that your Mac's connection to the Internet was down during import.

- **Submit CD track Names...:** If you have a very unique CD, it might not be in the online database used by Apple. This feature allows you to update this database with your own listings for the CD in question.

- **Join CD tracks:** If you have material that is meant to be played without gaps between songs, this feature will join the tracks and remove the built-in gaps from purchased music.

- **Deauthorize Audible Account...:** Audible is a service for downloading audiobooks. You can only use an account on one device. Use this feature to disable access on one computer so that you can activate it on another.

Window Menu

This is shown in Figure 22–28. The **Equalizer** is a cool new feature that I will explain below.

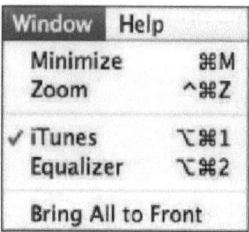

Figure 22–28. *Window menu*

Minimize

This will take the open **iTunes** window and place it in the dock.

Zoom

This causes the **iTunes** window to fill the largest amount of screen space as possible. It's not the same as full-screen mode.

iTunes

This is stating that iTunes is open. You can go to this menu option to restore your windows from the dock.

Equalizer

This is shown in Figure 22–29. If you click on the different vertical sliders, you can change various frequencies in the song.

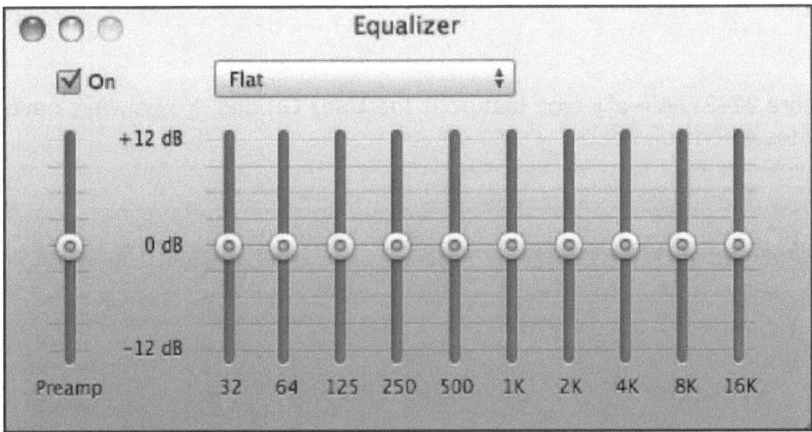

Figure 22-29. *Equalizer window of iTunes*

If you click on **Flat**, you will see Figure 22–30. Below is the complete list of pre-defined equalizers available in iTunes.

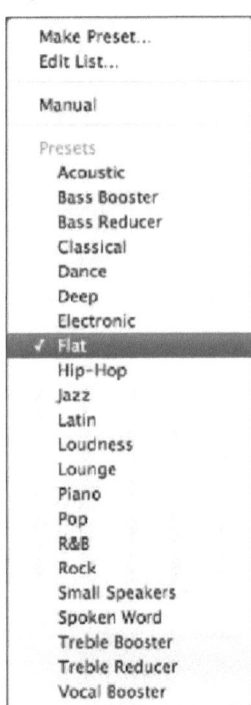

Figure 22-30. *Complete list of pre-set equalizer settings in iTunes*

Help Menu

This is shown in Figure 22–31. A really nice feature is the **User Guides**. You always have access to these guides when you need it.

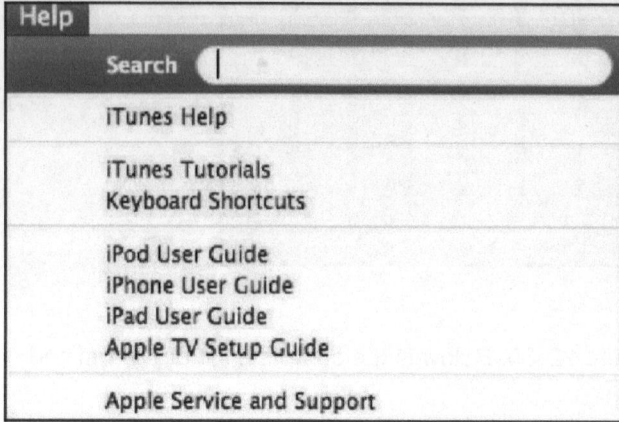

Figure 22–31. *Help menu*

- **Search:** This allows you to enter a topic that you have a question about.

- **iTunes Help:** This is shown in Figure 22–32. Notice that, unlike other iApps, it only has one section. There is a comprehensive list of hot topics to choose from.

Figure 22–32. *iTunes Help* window

■ **Keyboard Shortcuts:** As you get more familiar with your Mac, you truly can become a power user by learning these shortcuts. You can perform a lot of actions without using your mouse.

■ **iPad User Guide**

■ **iPhone User Guide**

■ **iPad User Guide**

■ **Apple TV Setup Guide:** Got an iOS device and need some help? Apple's got you covered with these guides in iTunes.

■ **Apple Service and Support:** This brings you to the Apple site to help you diagnose a problem that the default built-in Help system could not solve.

Summary

And so the music fades as we end our discussion on iTunes. I think iTunes is integral to iLife, but that is not as simple as it first appears. From storing apps and music to having the ability to share projects created in the core iLife apps, iTunes is designed to meet all your media organizing needs.

I have taught many people how to use a Macintosh and the applications available for it. In this book, I tried to explain how to avail of the power and ease of use of every app in a simple and concise way. All of the material I have covered in this guide is what any user should know to get started. My goal is to guide you and help you explore and have fun learning each app.

After reading this book, you should be ready to get out your digital camcorder, shoot your first video, and edit it **iMovie**; post your promo shots that you enhanced in **iPhoto** via **iWeb**; use **Ping** in **iTunes** to promote your film to all your online friends, and record your soundtrack in **GarageBand**. So put this book down and start exploring iLife to its fullest.

Bonus Pack

Innovation in the computer industry is a key to survival. What is possible now… was once considered fantasy. Apple was created by two individuals who had a vision of what computing should be at that time. The first invention of these pioneers was revolutionary, and Apple has never looked back.

These two appendixes deal with Apple's vision of what computing will be like in the future.

Apple believes that tablet devices will prove to be the mainstay of personal computing in the future. As a result, Apple has already created iPad versions of iMovie (iMovie also works on newer iPhones and iPod Touches) and GarageBand. While not as feature rich as the desktop versions, the initial releases of these programs for mobile devices can do quite a lot—anywhere. You will find an overview of these two apps in this section.

To further its goal of making iOS devices interact with desktops more easily, Apple has created its own "cloud computing" solution. This approach is different from cloud solutions by other companies because Apple hardware actually runs the programs on the device—not in the "cloud." Coming out this fall, the *iCloud* service will change the way you look at data or documents. All of your data will be automatically saved in this cloud and be accessible anywhere you log in with your Apple ID (this feature will initially work only with Apple's software). This section highlights what all the features of Apple's new iCloud paradigm will entail.

Will the approach taken with the iPad become the new standard? Will iCloud someday be called "indispensible?" Only time will tell. However, Apple has a track record of reinventing the computer experience.

Part X

Bonus Pack

iLife on the iPad

Apple and many other companies feel the tablet is the future of computing. While there are many games and special utilities for the iOS tablet, there are not many productivity apps at present. Apple is quickly moving forward in developing these essential apps. To that end, it has created iOS versions of word processing, spreadsheet, and presentation apps (Pages, Numbers, and Keynote, respectively). The latest to be released are two iLife apps: GarageBand and iMovie (iMovie also works on newer iPhones and iPod Touches). While similar in function and basic feel to their Mac desktop app counterparts, these apps have been optimized for the touch environment and truly make editing movies, learning to play a "pseudo" musical instrument, and writing songs a breeze. Let's start with the more feature-packed app: GarageBand.

GarageBand

Got the urge to write a song? Or want to learn how to play a new instrument without actually going out and buying one?

GarageBand for the iPad is a wondrous thing. Over the next few pages, I will touch upon the amazing things you can do with it. To start, go to the App Store and download the GarageBand for iPad app. In Figure A–1, we see the sample song included with GarageBand. As you can see, it is similar to the desktop version, but does not include all the features—yet.

Figure A–1. *Sample song included with GarageBand*

My Song Screen

There are four important buttons found on this screen (**Share**, **Copy from iTunes**, **New Song/Duplicate Song**, and **Delete**. Because the iPad is a touch device, you must touch a function or swipe your fingers to move an object. For example, if I wanted to open the sample song shown in Figure A–1, I would touch anywhere inside the song workspace. If I wanted to access another song, I would swipe my finger across the song workspace to get to another song.

Explore, as always. I am sure you will find new things to try every time you run GarageBand for the iPad.

The Share Button

This option allows you to either import your song into iTunes or e-mail your song. If you import it to iTunes, you can send it as an AAC music file or open it in GarageBand.

When you sync your iPad, click on the **Apps** tab in iTunes. Click on **GarageBand** and your songs will appear. This is shown in Figure A–2. Notice at the bottom of this screen that you can add music back to your iPad by clicking on the **Add...** button and saving your creation to any location you wish by clicking on **Save to...**.

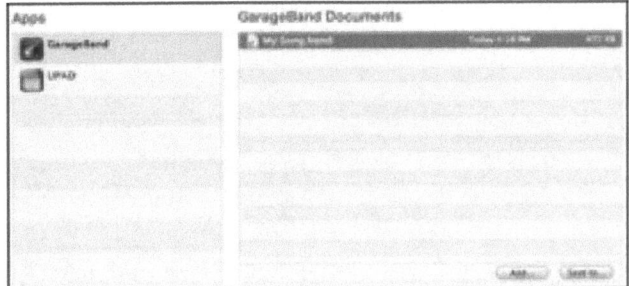

Figure A–2. *iTunes **Apps** window when iPad is attached to Mac or PC*

Copy from iTunes Button

 This button will import songs that you have in iTunes into GarageBand.

New Song or Duplicate Song Button

 This button will allow you to create a new song in GarageBand or duplicate a song.

Delete Button

This button will delete the song you currently have selected.

Instruments Available to Play in GarageBand

There are two main categories of instruments: **Plain Instruments** and **Smart Instruments**. Let's start with the former. To select any instrument, swipe your fingers to the left or right to select it. In Figure A–3, we see the the **Keyboard**.

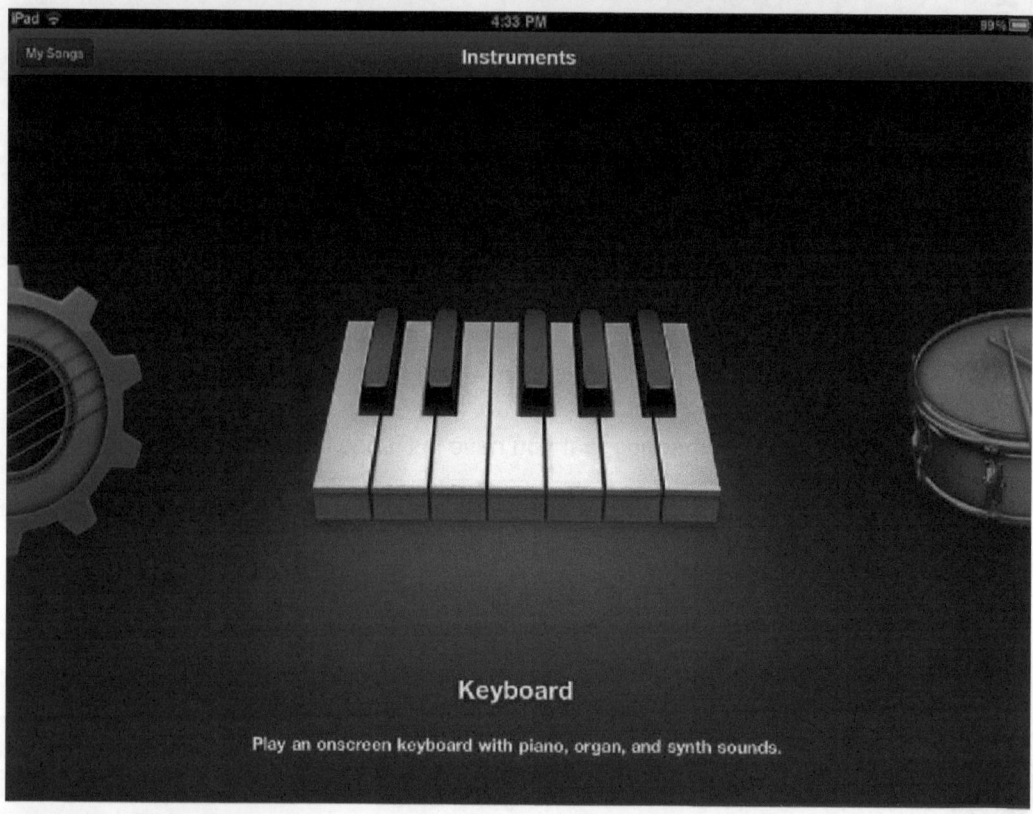

Figure A–3. *Keyboard* option

Keyboard

You are given the opportunity to play many types of keyboards. If you touch the one that is currently in use (the **Grand Piano** icon in Figure A–4), you can change the instrument type.

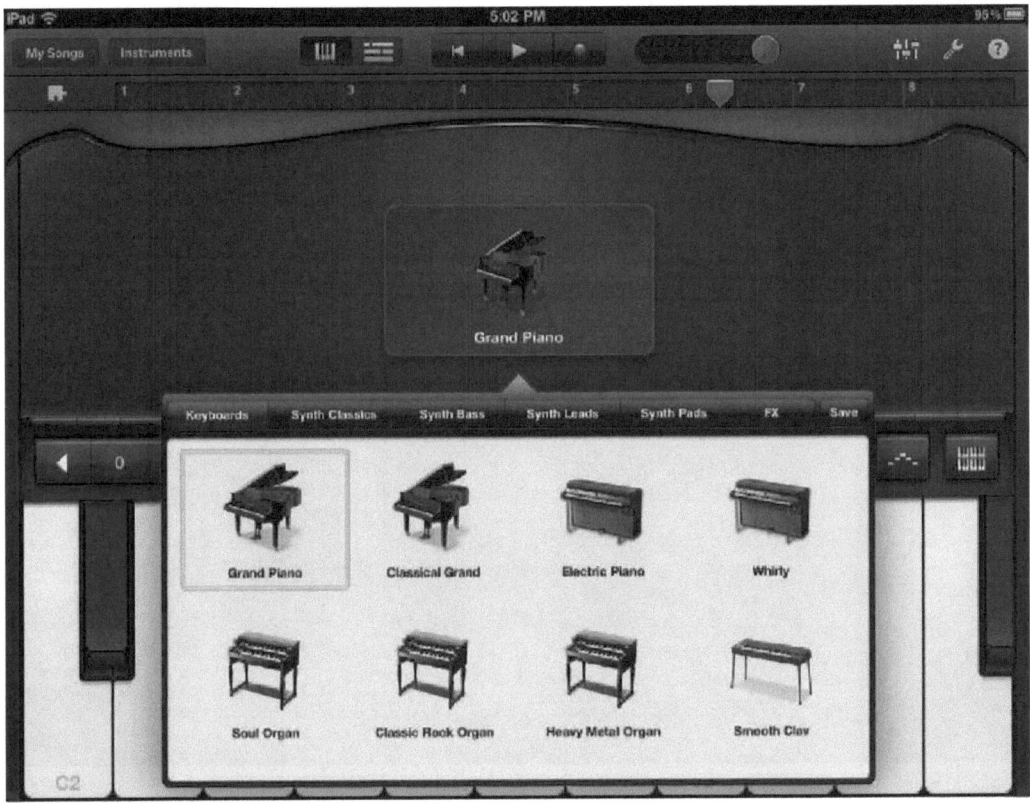

Figure A–4. *Different keyboards available*

Drums

You are given the opportunity to practice your banging skills on a complete drum kit. The graphic to access **Drums** is shown in Figure A–5.

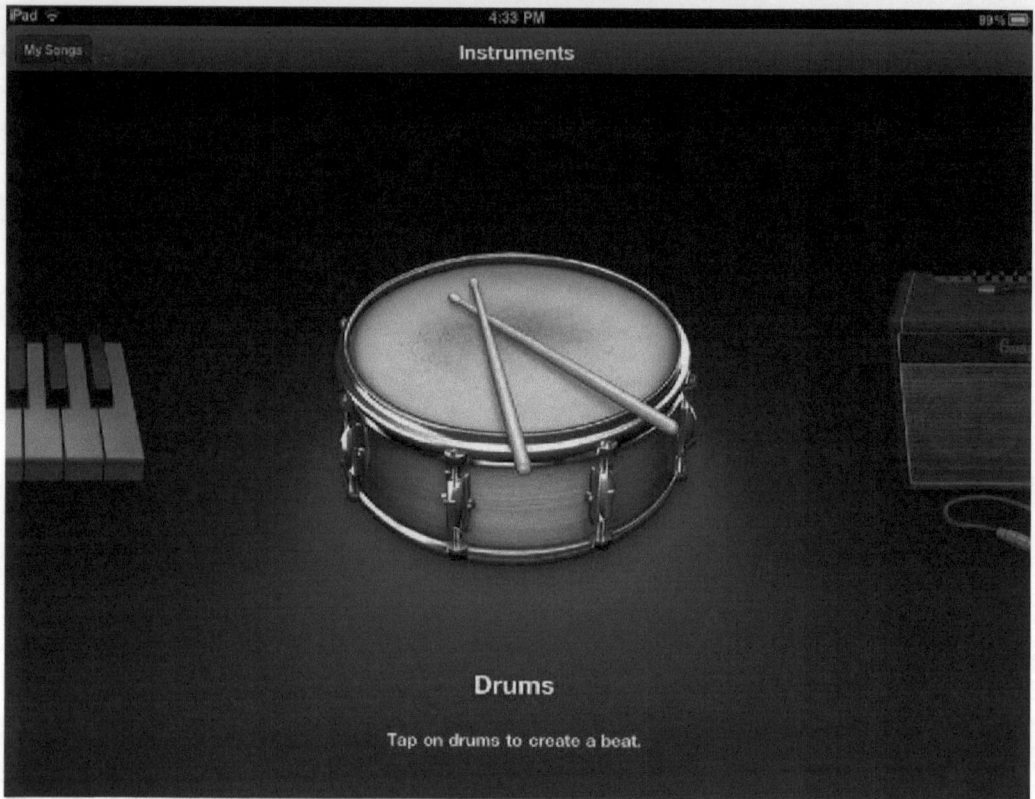

Figure A–5. *Drums option*

The **Classic Studio Kit** is shown in Figure A–6. You also have the choice of two other drum kits and three electronic drum machines.

Figure A–6. *A drum kit in GarageBand*

Guitar Amp

You can (with the proper cable) attach your guitar to the iPad. You can use a wide variety of guitar amps to customize your sound. The graphic to access this feature is shown on Figure A–7.

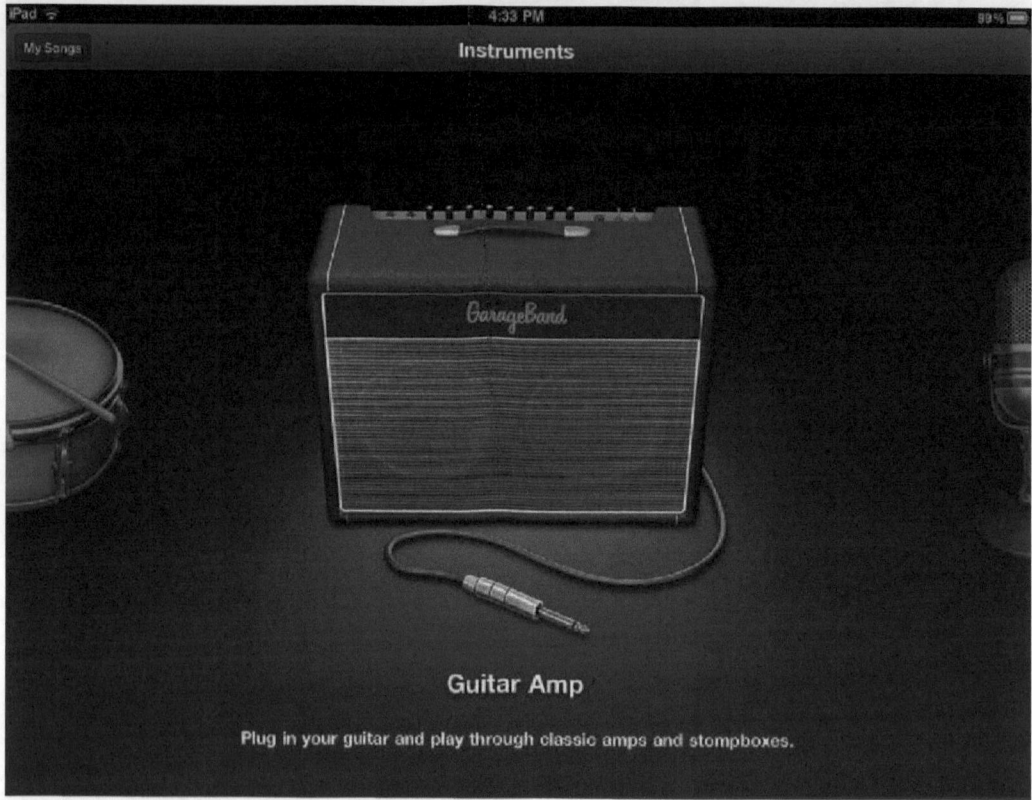

Figure A–7. *Guitar Amp option*

The selection window for choosing an amp is shown in Figure A–8.

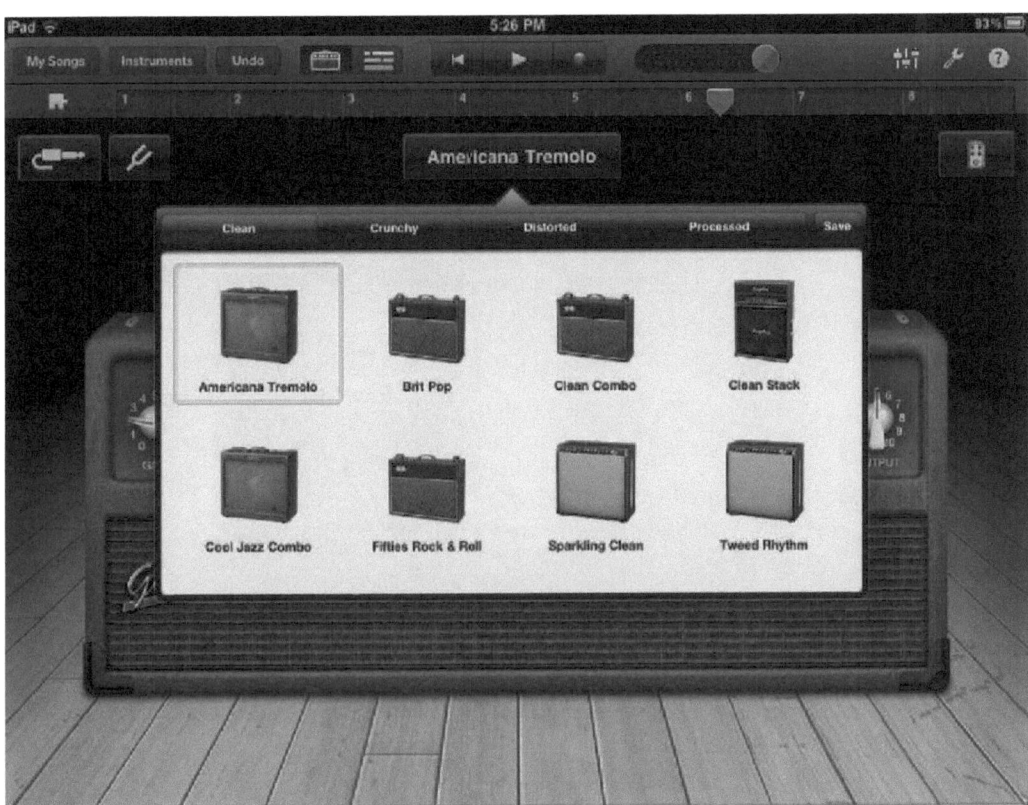

Figure A–8. *Amp choices available in GarageBand*

Audio Recorder

Want to record audio from your iPad's microphone? With this feature, you can record any audio you wish.

Figure A–9. *Audio Recorder option*

To access this feature, tap on the graphic shown in Figure A–9. The recording window is shown on Figure A–10.

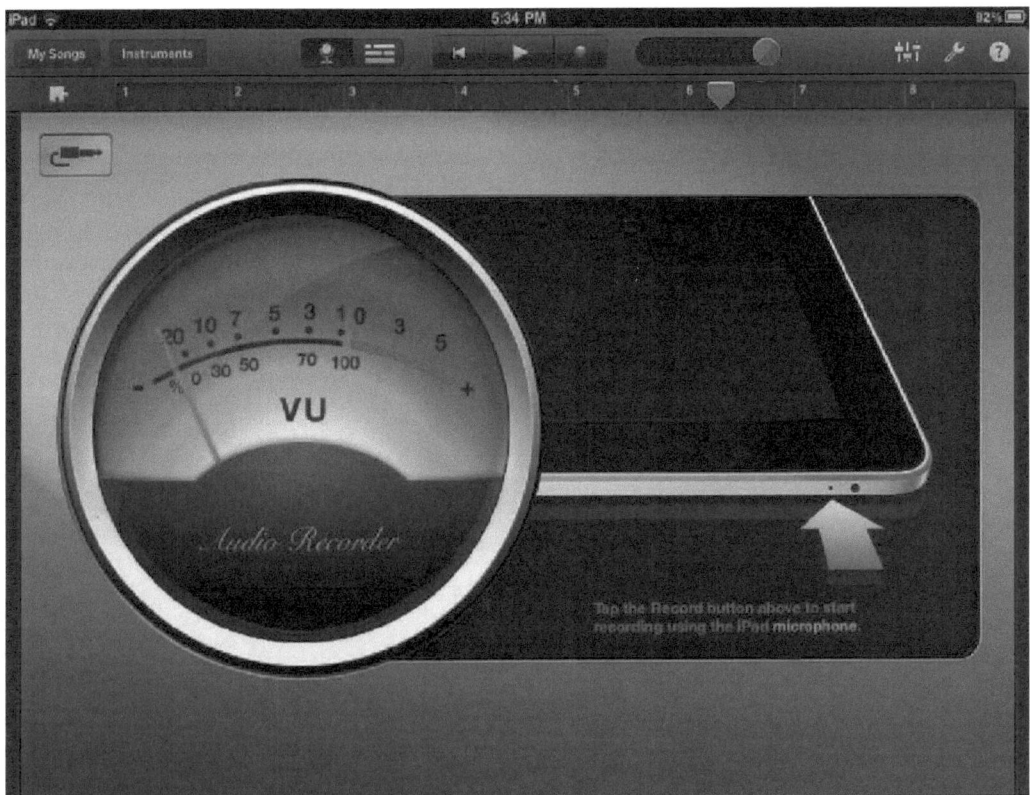

Figure A–10. *Recording window—built-in microphone*

At the top left of this screen is the **Noise Gate** button . If you click on this button, you will gain access to a slider that will help set the level for reducing input noise.

Smart Instruments

Let the learning begin! Smart Instruments are designed to help you learn how to play an instrument in a unique way.

Smart Drums

Easily create custom beats with this feature (see Figure A–11).

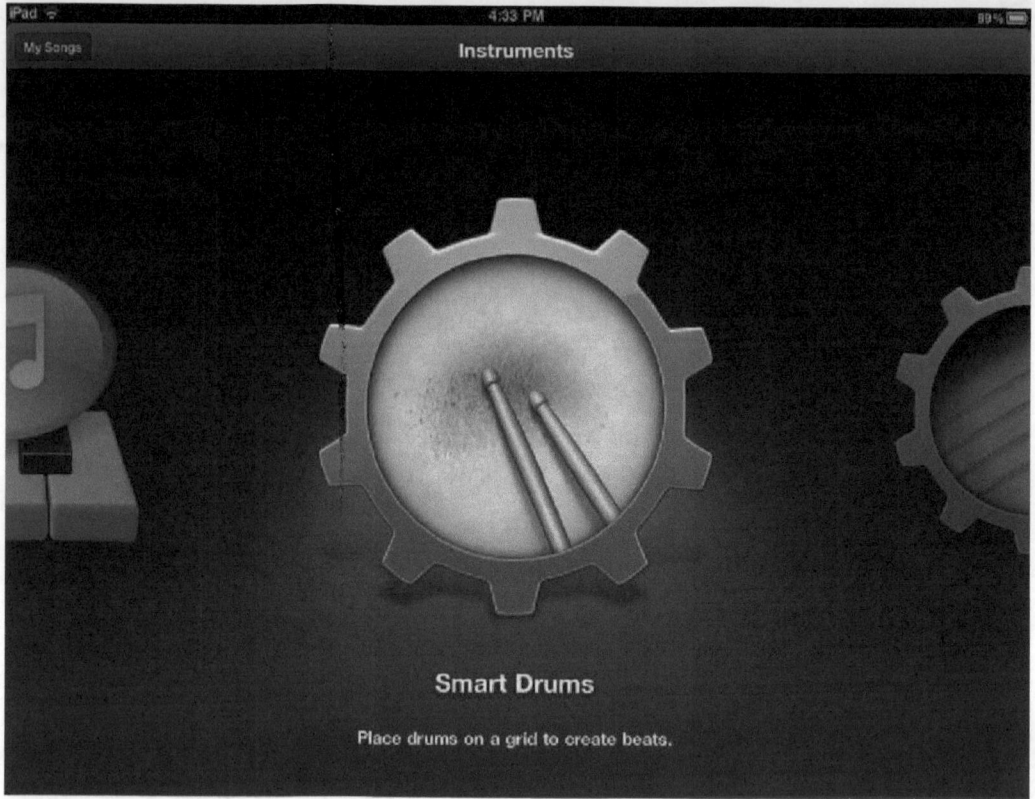

Figure A–11. *Smart Drums*

You are given a list of percussion instruments to choose from, and you can place each item into one of four sections. These sections are: **Loud** or **Quiet** (volume) and **Simple** and **Complex** (patterns). This window is shown in Figure A–12.

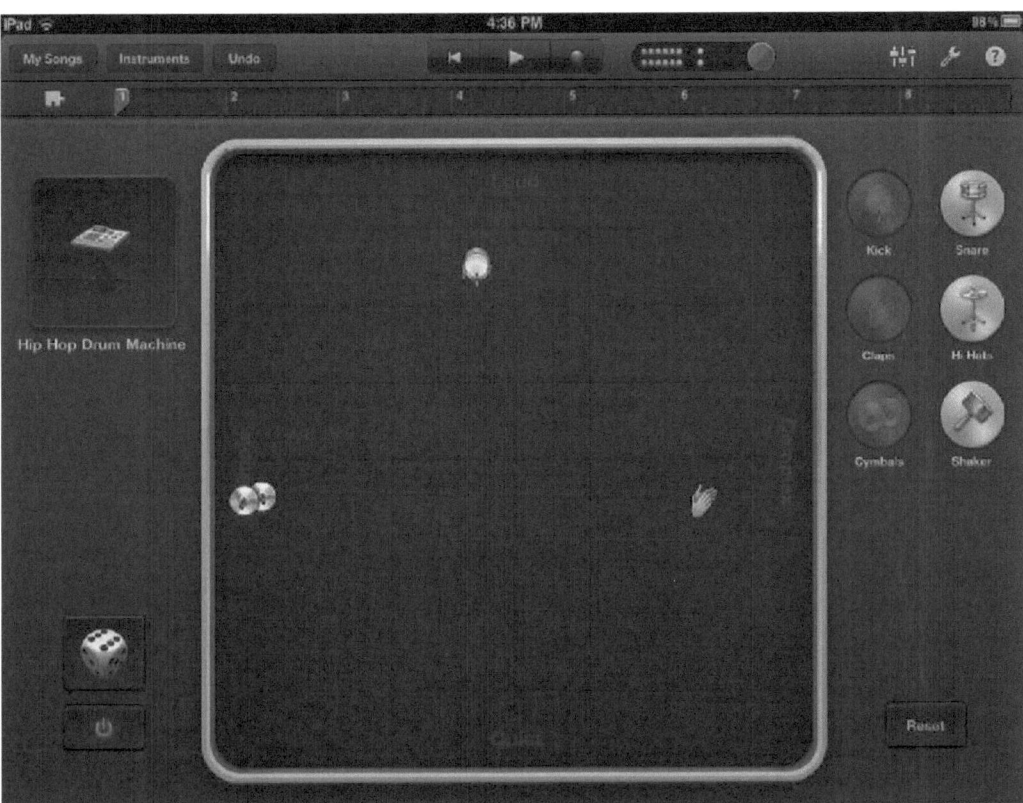

Figure A–12. *Smart Drum* workspace

Smart Bass

Learn to lay down some bass grooves (see Figure A–13).

Figure A–13. *Smart Bass option*

Click on the current instrument's icon to change the instrument. In Figure A–14, you see the **Liverpool** bass icon in the upper left-hand corner. Just tap on the strings to start playing. You have two main ways of playing: **Chords** or **Notes**. You can select either option at the top right of the bass workspace. The **Chords** environment is shown in Figure A–14. Please notice the **Autoplay** dial located at the top right, as well. If you move the dial to the right, the notes you play will automatically be repeated. As you go from one to four, the number of notes played back will increase.

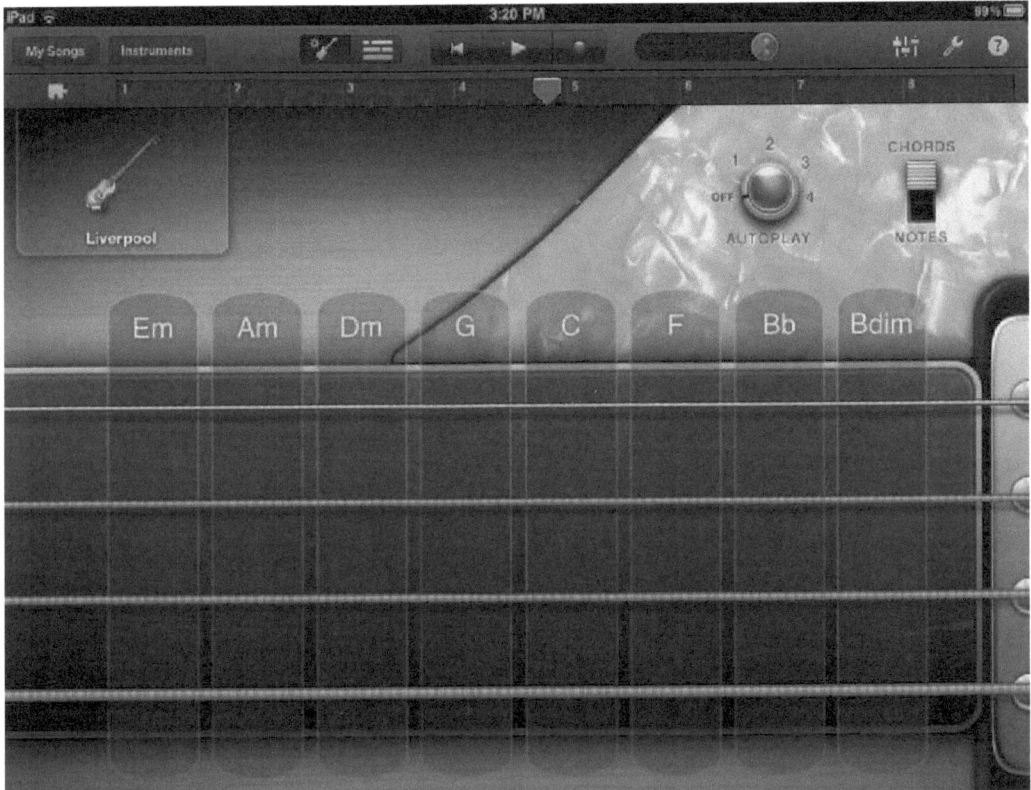

Figure A–14. *Chord workspace—**Smart Bass***

The other environment is **Notes**. This is shown in Figure A–15.

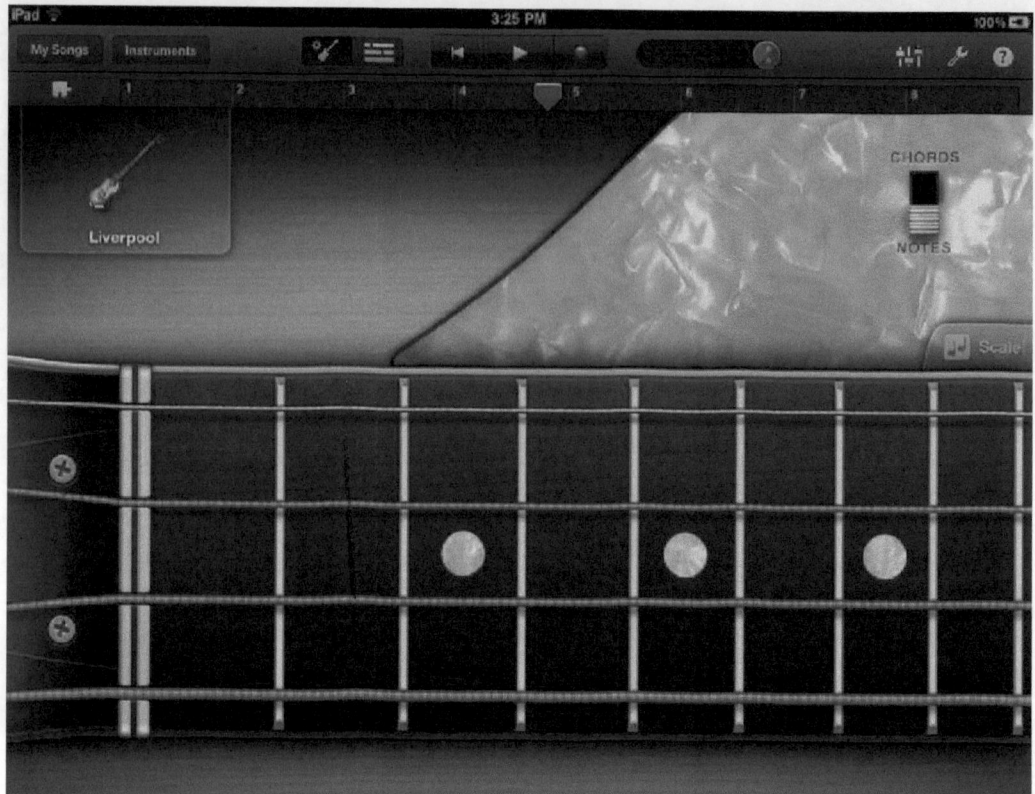

Figure A–15. *Notes* *workspace—Smart Bass*

Here you can compose note for note. Please notice the **Scale** button at the far right of the screen, just above the bass strings. If you click on this button, you get the screen shown in Figure A–16. It allows you to choose a selection of notes that best suits your tastes.

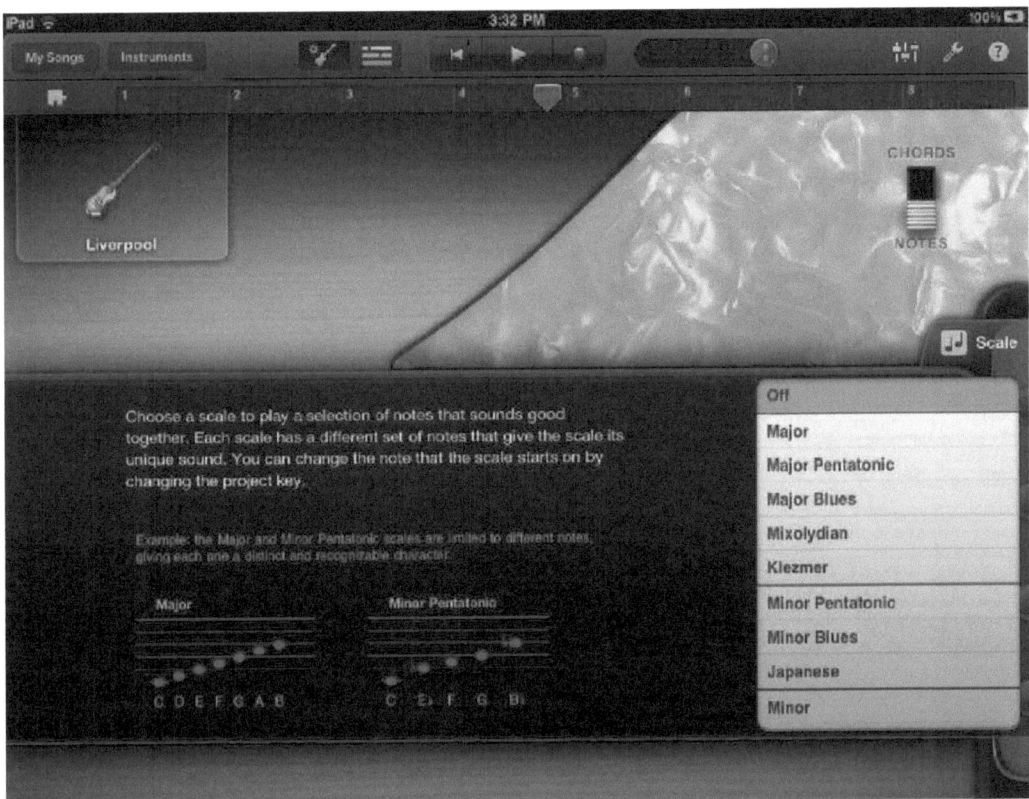

Figure A–16. *Scale* options found in the *Notes* workspace—*Smart Bass*

Smart Guitar

Prefer the guitar? Become a guitar rock hero with this feature. To begin your quest, tap on the graphic shown in Figure A–17.

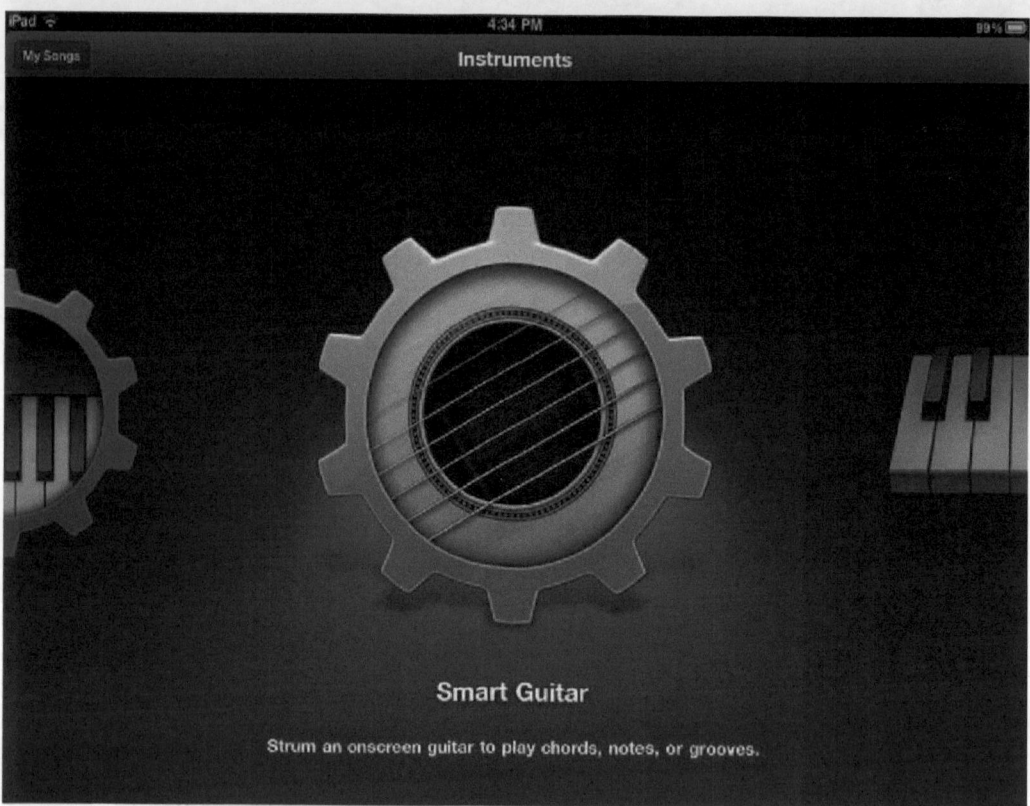

Figure A–17. *Smart Guitar option*

This instrument's options are the same as with the bass instrument. You can activate the **Autoplay** feature in the chord window and have the same scale choices in the notes window. The chords window is shown in Figure A–18.

Figure A–18. *Chord* workspace for the *Smart Guitar*

Smart Keyboard

Want to learn how to create keyboard grooves? Use the Smart Keyboard, shown in Figure A–19.

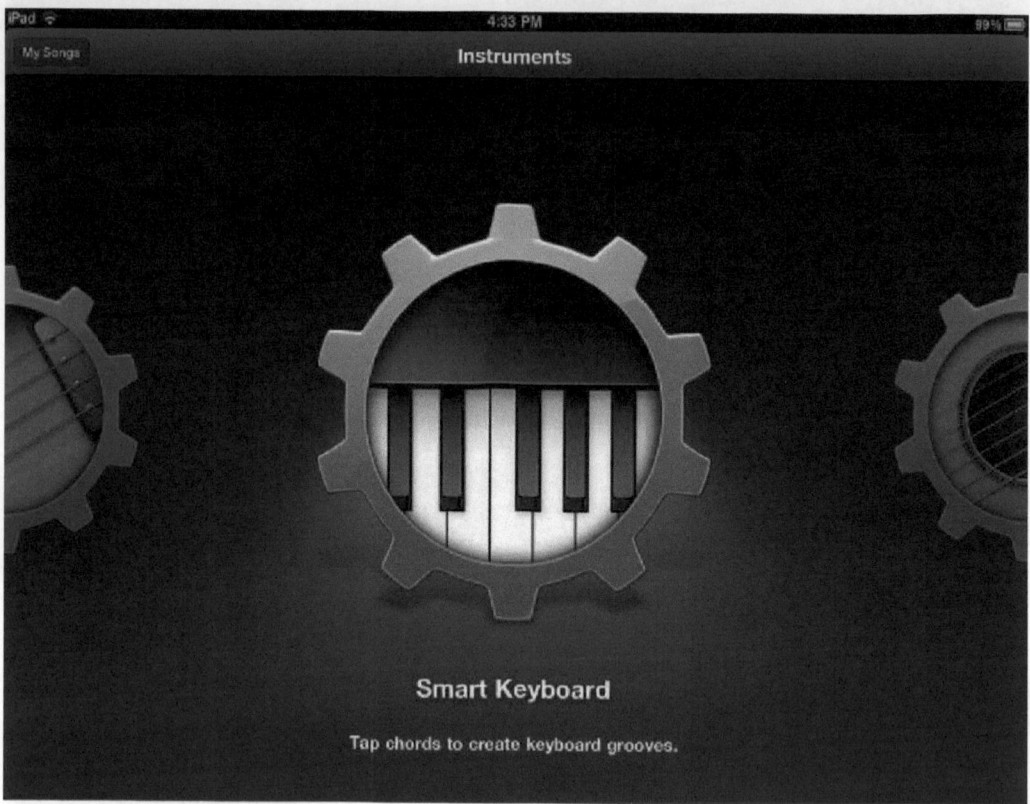

Figure A–19. *Smart Keyboard*

Start hitting the ivory keys by tapping on the graphic. The Smart Keyboard gives you the chance to easily create grooves by using the **Autoplay** dial found in this window. The **Smart Keyboard** workspace is shown in Figure A–20.

Figure A–20. *Smart Keyboard* workspace

Create Your Own Instrument—Sampler

Want to add a truly unique sound to your song? Is a bird's whistle the missing piece?
This cool tool allows you to record any sound and play it back on a keyboard. Pretty
nifty. Tap on the graphic shown in Figure A–21.

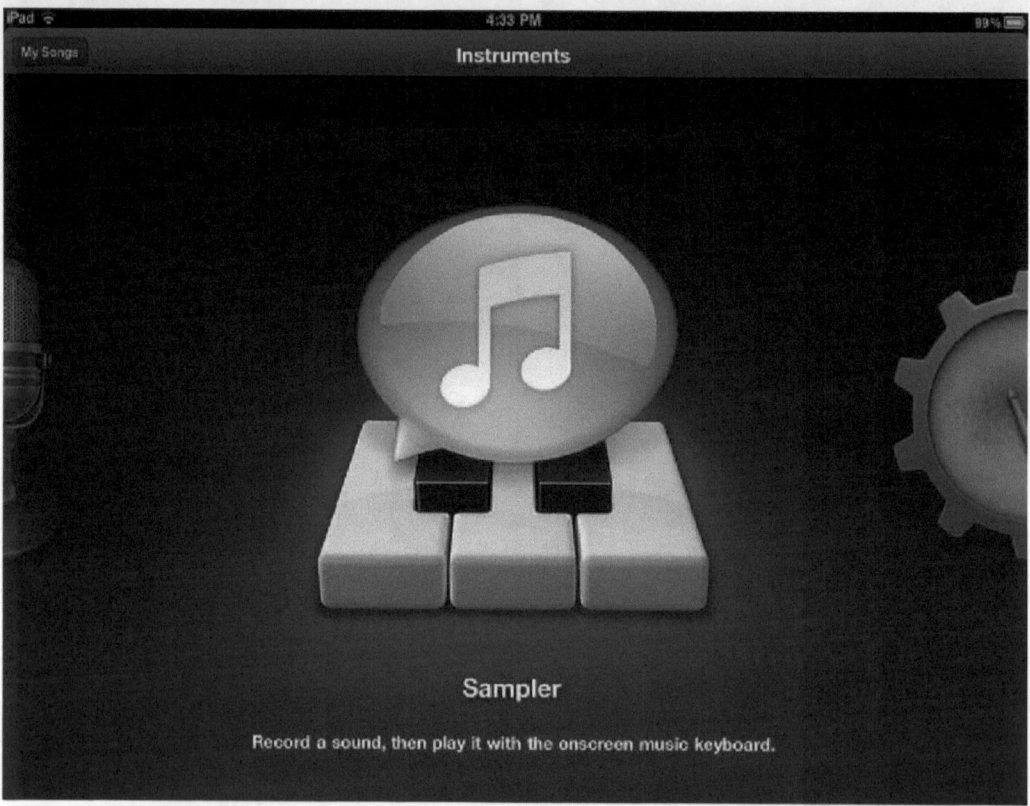

Figure A–21. *Sampler option*

To record a sample, just click on the big round **Start** button in this workspace. This is
shown in Figure A–22. To stop recording, click on the same button that now states
Stop. Please notice that you can access all of your recorded samples by clicking on the
My samples icon located in the middle of the workspace. GarageBand includes five
sample sounds, including a bark and a giggle.

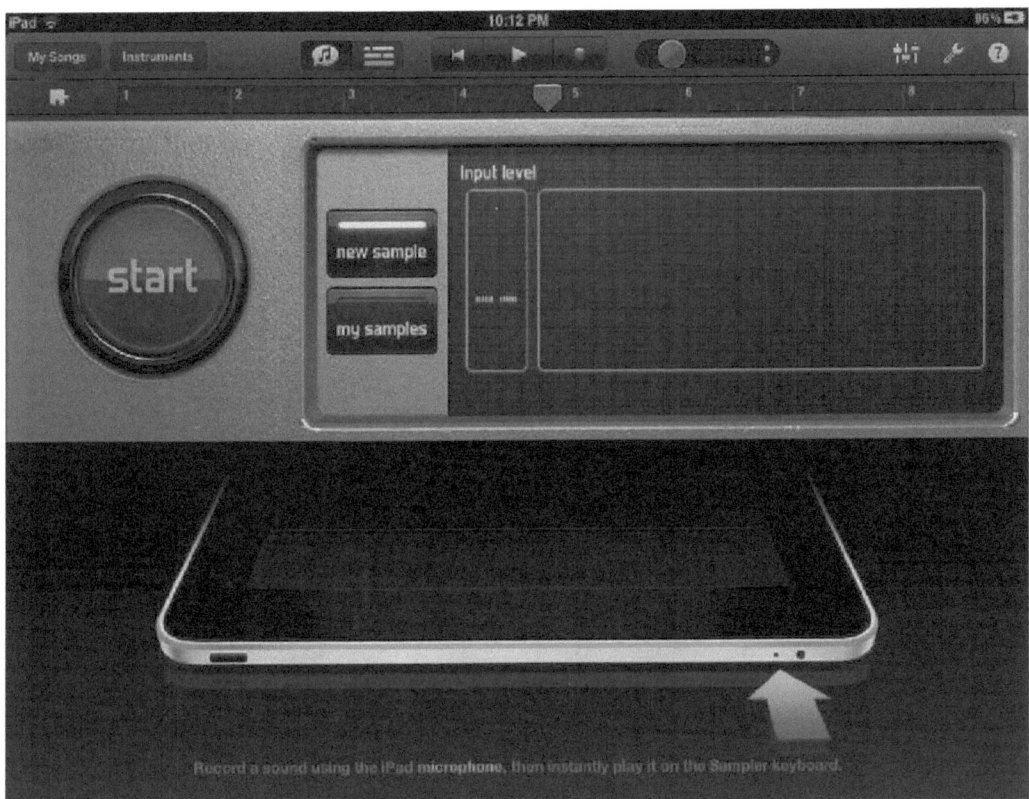

Figure A–22. *Recording window of the* **Sampler**

After you record the sample, the screen in Figure A–23 appears.

Figure A–23. *Keyboard playing of your recorded sample*

If you look at Figure A–23, you will notice that there are quite a few options for customizing your sound. In the top window located on the right side, you can change the actual sound of the sample or trim it. Just above the keyboard, you can lower or higher the pitch, add a sustain, change the scale, turn on the "Arpeggiator," which plays chord notes in a sequencer. At the far left, you have two dials that can either change the pitch or mood. I think this is the most fun instrument to play to experiment with.

Workspace Environment—Smart Drums

To demonstrate the working environment of GarageBand on the iPad, I have chosen the Smart Drums instrument to illustrate all of the options and settings available.

Instrument Control Bar

This is located at the top of the screen for every instrument. This toolbar is explained in Figure A–24.

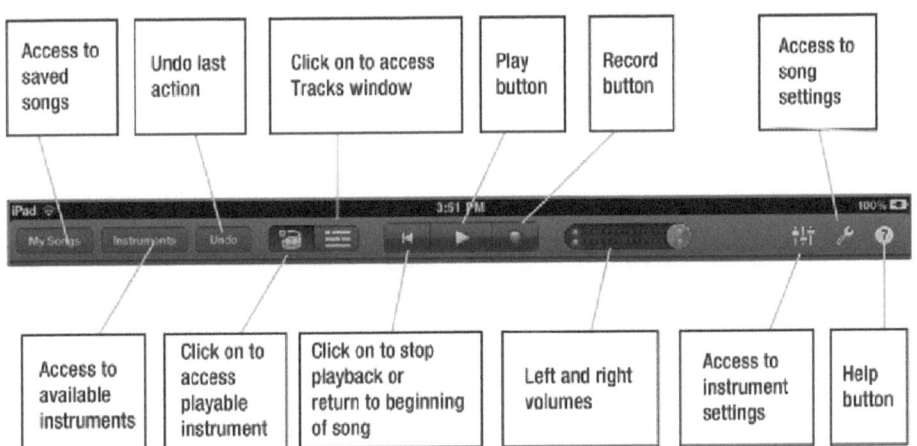

Figure A–24. *Control bar*

The last three options at the far right of Figure A–24 include more choices. These are **Instrument** settings, **Song** settings, and the **Help** button.

Instrument Setting Window—Smart Drums

Here you can adjust various settings for the instrument you are using (see Figure A–25).

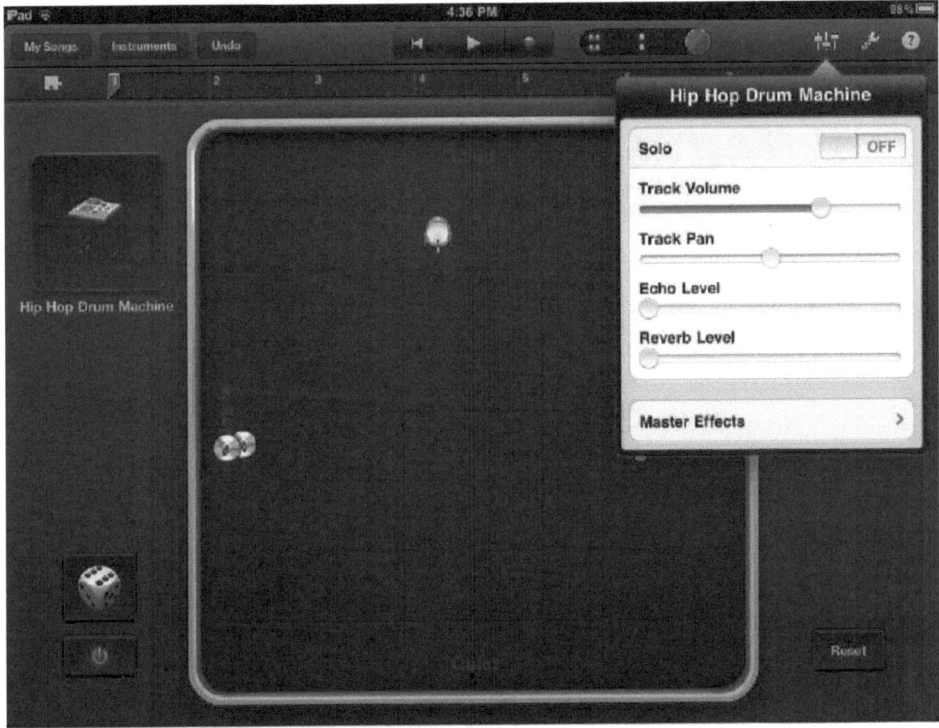

Figure A–25. *Instrument settings*

Song Settings Window—Smart Drums

Here you can activate the **Metronome** (Figure A–26), **Count-in**, **Tempo**, or **Key**. Please notice that this screen includes a **Help** button.

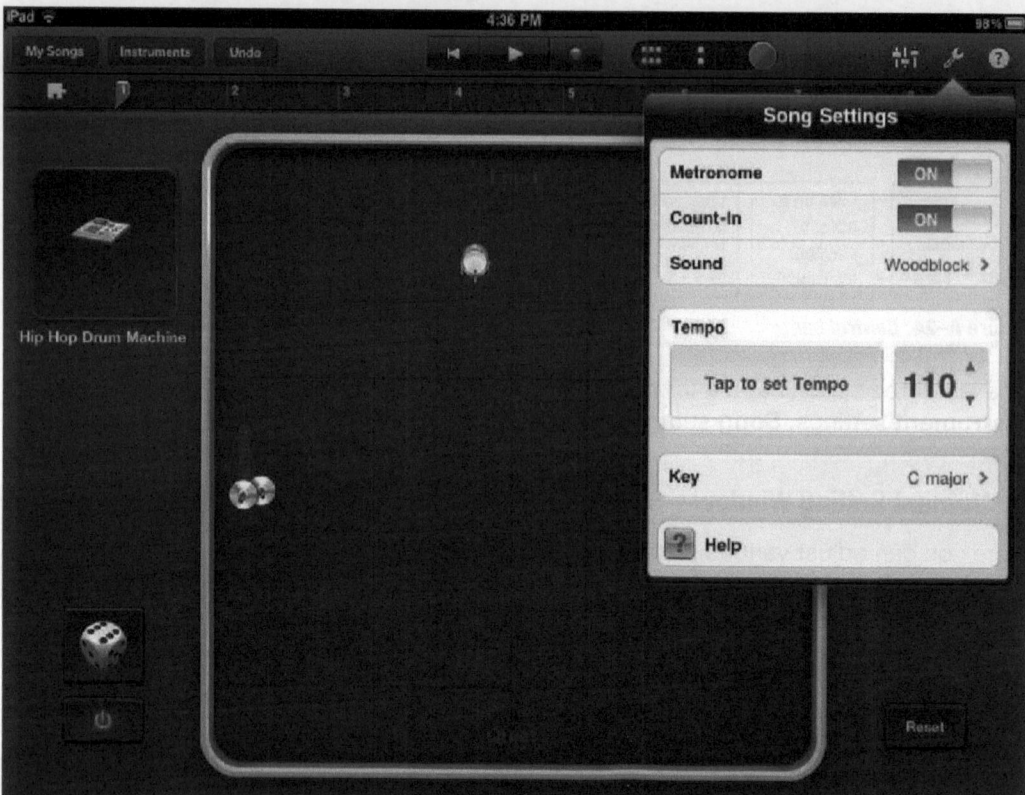

Figure A–26. *Song settings*

Help Button—Smart Drums

This is a great feature. When you click on the **Help** button on the top right of your screen, GarageBand provides explanations of items or ways to access more detailed help on certain features (see Figure A–27).

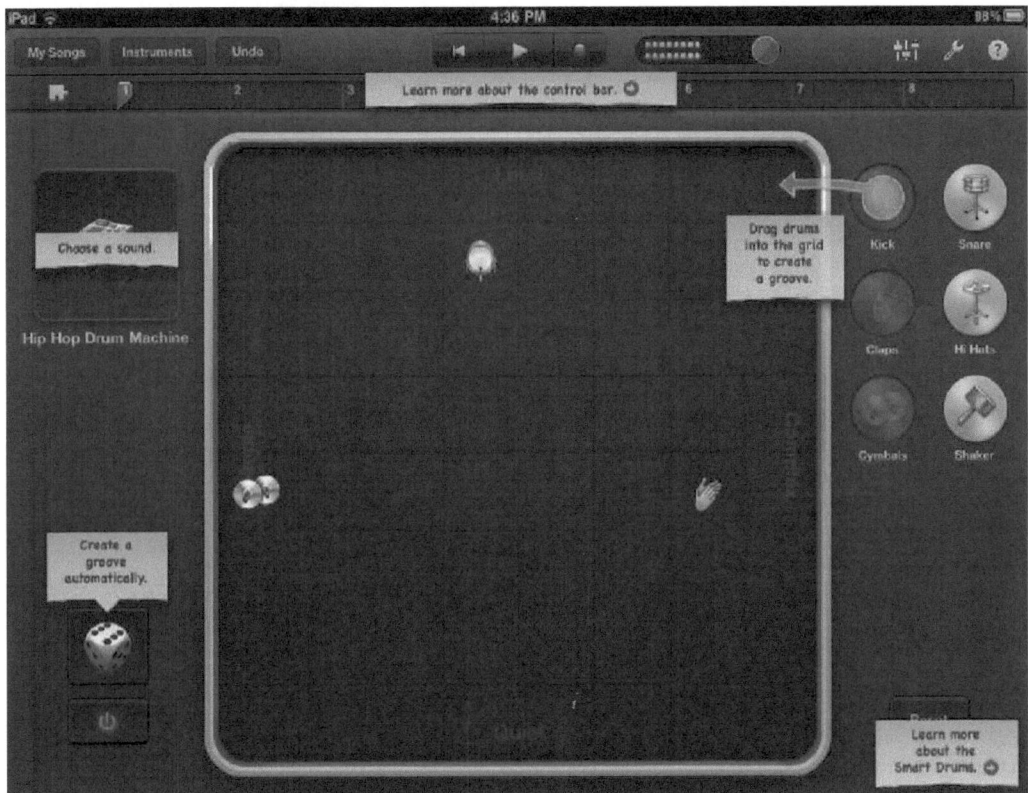

Figure A–27. *Help* button

Tracks Window

This is very similar to the **Tracks** window of GarageBand for the Mac. To make changes, you must click on the track you want to edit. This is shown in Figure A–28.

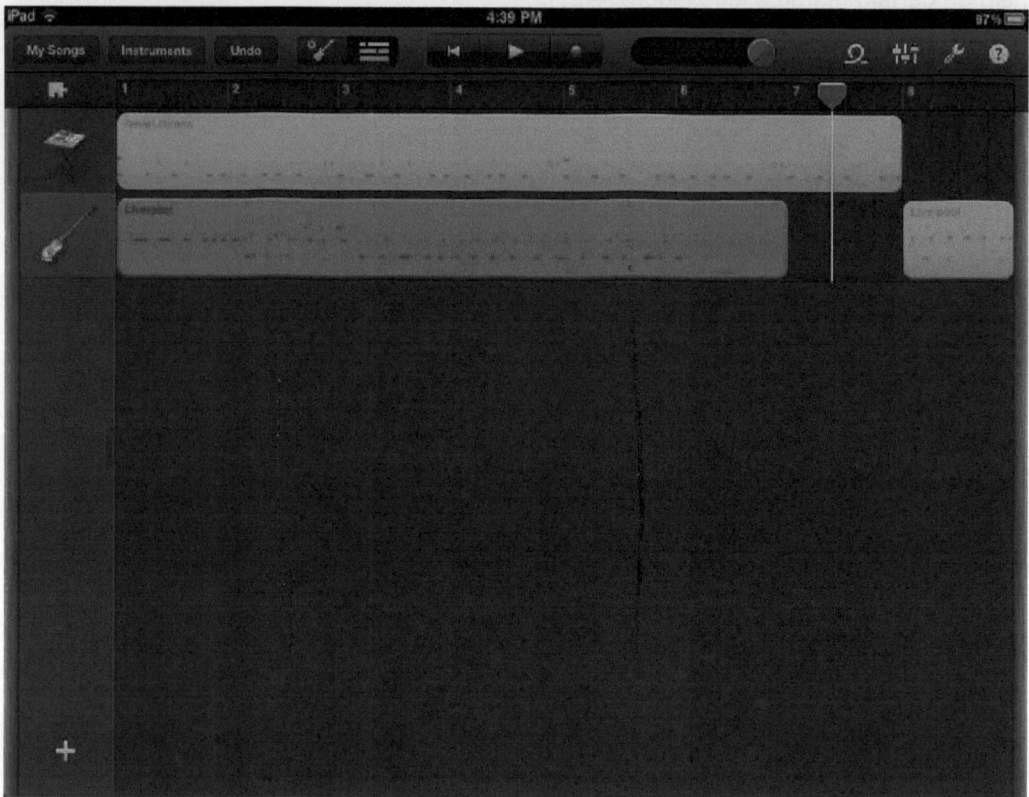

Figure A–28. *Tracks window*

If you want to lengthen or shorten the track, click on the track and drag your finger to left or right to achieve your goal. You can choose to **Cut**, **Copy**, **Delete**, **Loop**, or **Split** tracks. You can't edit the song note for note. You have to bring the song into the Mac version of GarageBand to achieve this. For serious writers, this is an obvious limitation when using the iPad.

The last item of interest found in the track workspace is the addition of the **Loops** button in the control bar found at the top of your screen. This is shown in Figure A–29. Loops allow you to easily add editable beats and rhythms to your song.

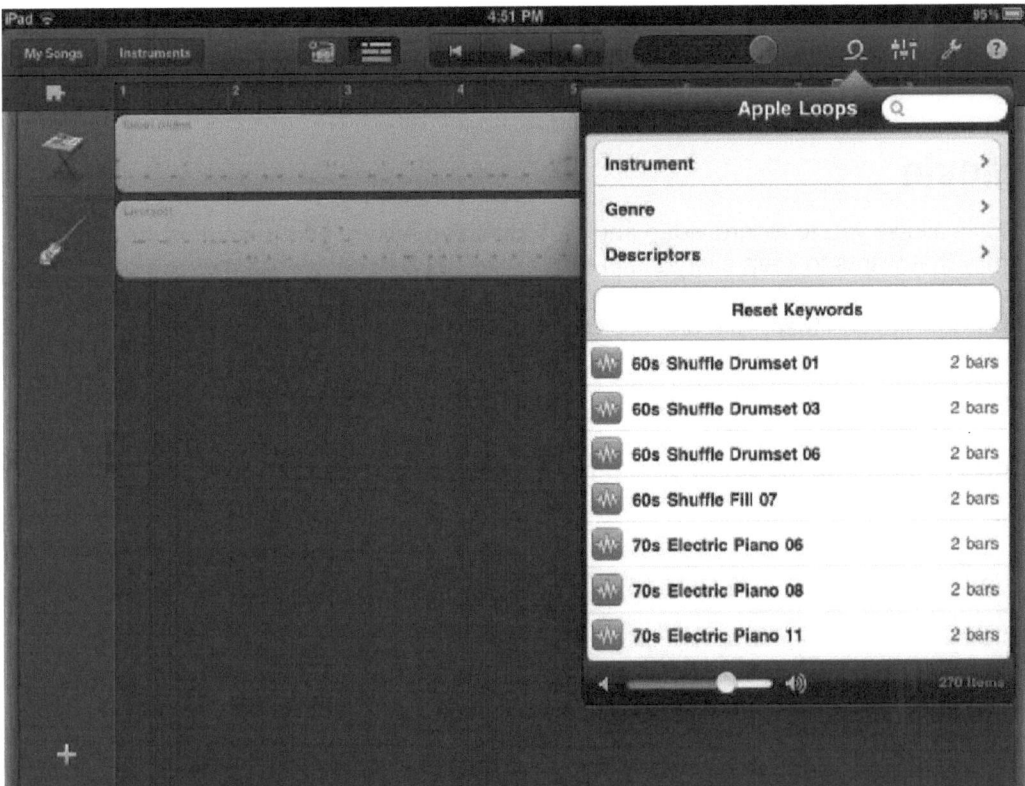

Figure A–29. *Loops* option in the tracks workspace

This Just In!

GarageBand has been updated with a few new features. You must manually update the app to take advantage of these new items. These are:

- The new version supports the importing of Apple Loops; AIFF, WAV, and CAF audio files; and uncompressed 16-bit, 44.1 kHz raw audio data (CD audio format). These new items make GarageBand more desirable to professionals who need to import these items to create commercial-quality tracks.

- Users can import audio data files into GarageBand on an iPad using the **File Sharing** pane of iTunes to sync the data to the device.

- Users can now also copy and paste audio into GarageBand projects from other iOS apps that support sending audio data to the clipboard.

- Support for audio playback via AirPlay, Bluetooth devices, and to HDMI devices when using the Digital AV adapter.

- Various bug fixes.

GarageBand for the iPad includes a lot of features to help you learn how to play a few instruments or write your own songs. It is not as full of features as GarageBand when it comes to editing your songs, so you may still want to edit in the Mac version.

iMovie

iMovie allows you to record video and perform basic editing on the go. It is great for the family that wants to keep everyone in their universe up to date while they are on vacation. What is cooler than making a short video of your family at a beautiful beach or a historic site and then, with one click, uploading it to YouTube or Facebook?

My Projects Window

Figure A–30 shows the opening window when you first access iMovie, or can be accessed at any time by clicking on the **My Projects** button located at the far left of the **iMovie** toolbar.

Figure A–30. *My Projects window—iMovie*

This toolbar is situated at the very top of the main workspace. Please notice the text **My Project** in the theatre marquee. Click on it to insert the title of your new movie. Clicking on the mock movie poster with a graphic from each project will open the project so you can edit it. Just swipe your fingers to the left or right to select the movie project you want to access.

The **My Projects** window contains several buttons at the very bottom of the screen. These buttons are described in the following sections.

Help Button

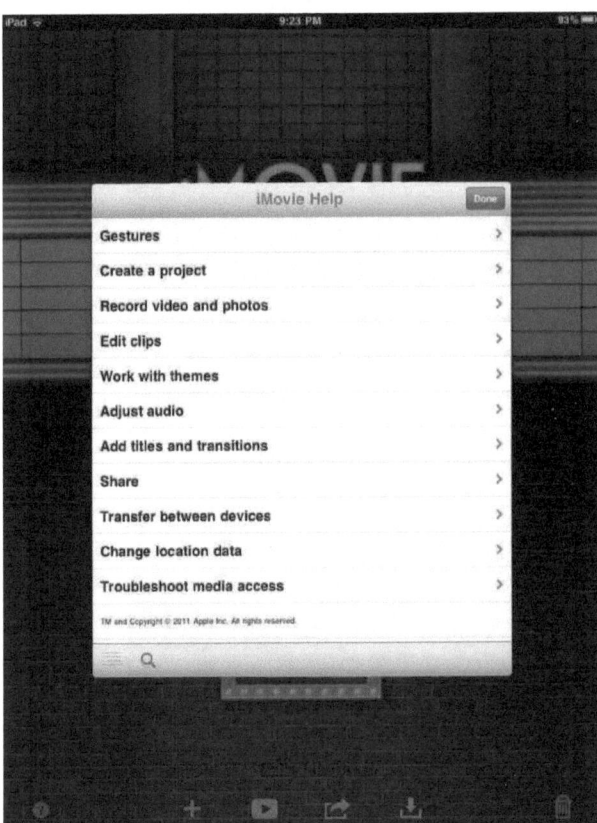 This button will bring up a great list of topics to help you get started with iMovie. The list of available topics is shown in Figure A–31.

Figure A–31. *Help topics for iMovie for the iPad*

Create a New Movie Button

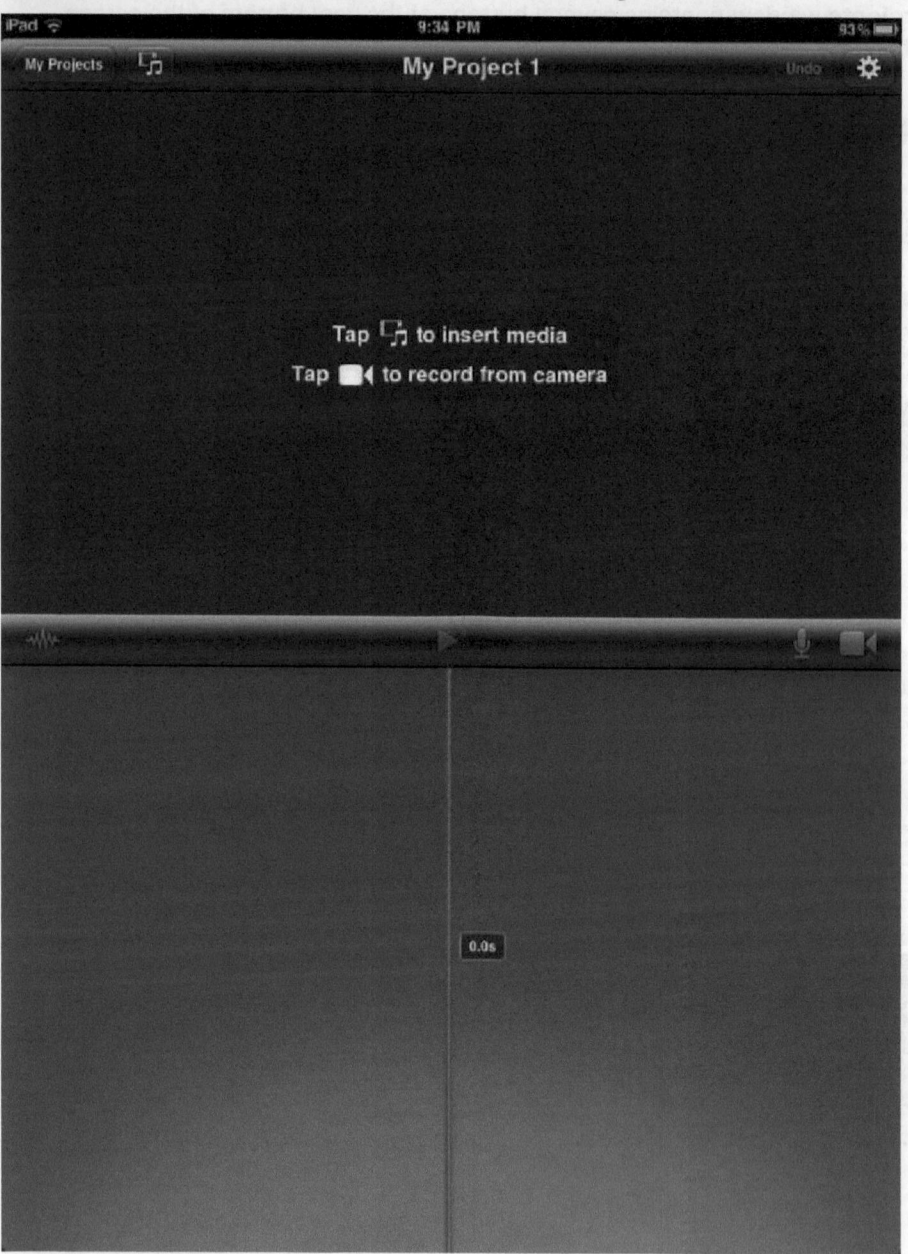

This button allows you to get started and create a new movie. The initial workspace environment that comes up is shown in Figure A–32.

Figure A–32. *Initial window when creating a new movie*

If you look at Figure A–32, there are two things to notice.

- At the top of the screen, it tells you the two ways to get video into your project. They are:

    - Accessing your stored files by clicking on the **Media** button

        ![Media button](media). This is located at the top of your workspace, just next to

        the **My Projects** button ![My Projects button](myprojects).

        Projects are stored as iMovieMobile files and can be accessed in iMovie on the Mac if sent to iTunes and then saved onto your hard drive.

    - The second method of getting video into your project is to record it via the built-in video camera. To do this, click on the **Video**

        Camera icon ![Video Camera icon](camera) located directly in the middle of your workspace at the far right of your screen. You can also you this button to take photographs.

- The workspace of iMovie for the iPad is very basic. Your options are far fewer then the iMovie app for the Mac.

Play Button

 This button allows you to play the highlighted movie in the **My Projects** window.

Share Button

![Share Button] This button allows you to send your project to a variety of Internet services, iTunes, or Camera Roll (the Photo app on your iPad). Each selection has a different screen to fill out. The Internet services all require a username and password to upload the selected video. The one universal setting each asks for is the video size. It can be **Medium** (360p), **Large** (540p), or **HD** 720p). The list of available options is shown in Figure A–33.

Figure A–33. *Share options for iMovie*

Copy from iTunes Button

 This button allows you copy iMovie files that are found in iTunes.

Trash Can Button

 This button allows you to delete projects you no longer want stored on your iPad.

iMovie Workspace

There are four major elements in this workspace: two windows and two toolbars. At the top of the workspace is the first toolbar. Below this is a large preview window. Below the preview window is the second toolbar. At the bottom of the workspace is the editing window. These elements are shown in Figure A–34.

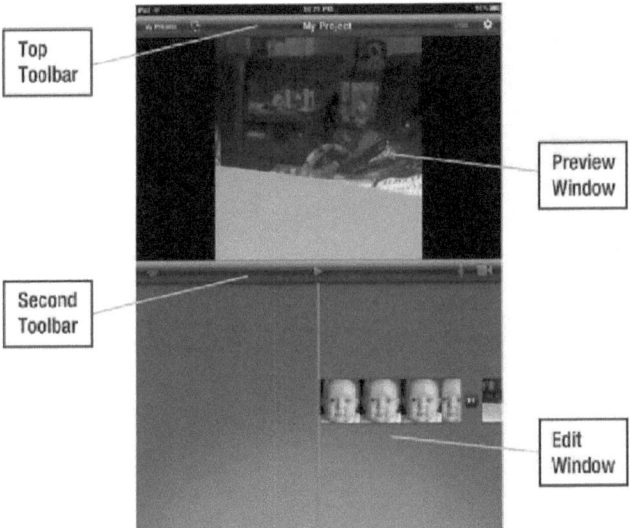

Figure A–34. *Four major elements of the **iMovie** workspace*

Top Toolbar

This toolbar contains four important items. You can access projects or stored media. You can also change project settings or use the ever-present **Undo** button.

My projects Button

 This button allows you go back to the **My Projects** screen. There you can share, play, rename, or trash all of your movie projects stored on the iPad.

Media Library Button

This button gives you access to all of your stored video, photos, or audio files created in iMovie. This screen is shown in Figure A–35. It shows the video section with only one movie stored.

Figure A–35. *Media Library window*

Undo Button

 This button simply undoes the last action you have taken.

Project Settings Button

This button brings up a variety of options. Just below the words **Project Settings** is a selection of eight different themes you can add to your project. Just swipe your fingers over the sample theme graphics to access your choices. Below the **Theme** window there are four other settings you can configure. They are:

- **Theme Music:** This allows you to turn **Theme Music** on or off. It is off by default.

- **Loop Background Music:** If you have added music to your project, this will play the audio track over and over. It is on by default.

- **Fade in from Black:** If you turn this option on, your movie will start with a black screen and then your video will gradually appear.

- **Fade out to black:** With this option, the end of your movie gradually fades out to a black screen.

Preview Window

This window displays your project as a movie at any time. To start the preview, click in the **Play** button found in the second toolbar in the middle of your workspace.

Second Toolbar

This toolbar accomplishes a wide variety of tasks. iMovie for the iPad does not yet have all the features of its desktop big brother, but the options found here are very useful and make recording or playing items a snap.

Sound Button

This button will display the audio section of your video just below the video section.

Play Button

 This will play your video so you can preview any changes you make.

Audio Recorder Button

This button allows you to record audio using the built-in microphone only. The recording screen is shown in Figure A–36.

Figure A–36. *Recording* screen—*Audio* button

Video Capture/ Photo Capture Button

With this button, making movies on the go is possible. You can record videos or take pictures. The camera in your iPad is fairly low resolution due to its size. Not horrible, but I was disappointed on-the-go the go projects. The camera window is shown in Figure A–37.

Figure A–37. *Camera function of iMovie*

At the top right of this window is an icon of a little camera.  If you click on this icon, you will switch which camera is to be used. The front camera or the one facing you. Directly in the middle of your screen at the very bottom is a button with a solid circle inside.  This is the **Record** button. Click it to start and stop recording. After the clip is recorded, it is not yet saved to your iPad. The toolbar at the bottom of your screen changes to what is shown in Figure A–38. Please notice that directly in the middle of the toolbar there is now a play button (a triangle graphic). This is key to use as you see exactly what you recorded and see if is exactly what you wanted. If you are not happy with item you just took, you can click on the **Retake** button at the far left of the toolbar to re-shoot the video or re-do the photo. Once you are completely satisfied with the new footage, click the **Use** button at the far right of the toolbar. This will then save the item and can be used in your project or other projects in the future.

Retake ▶ Use

Figure A–38. *Confirmation screen when recording video or photos*

> **NOTE:** iPads are very limited when it comes to storage capacity. It is highly recommended to delete items that you sure that you will never use again.

Edit Window

This is the bottom section of the iMovie workspace. As with GarageBand for iPad, your editing options are limited. To illustrate what is available, I have added a photo and video into a sample project.

Photos

If you click on the photo, you will see two circles at either end of the photo clip. If you then hold your finger on the circle, you can lengthen or shorten the time the photo appears on your screen during your video. If you double-click on the photo, you will bring up the **Photo Settings** window. This is shown in Figure A–39. There are only three options. They are:

- **Title Style:** Here you can add a title to your photo. You are given the choice to add the title to the opening, middle, or ending section of your photo.

- **Location:** You can add location data into your photo

- **Delete Clip:** This allows you to remove the photo from your movie.

Figure A–39. *Photo settings*

Movies

The options for editing movies are shown in Figure A–40. **Title Style**, **Location**, and **Delete Clip** are the same as for photos, but they are called **Clip Settings**. There is a new slider option to change the volume in the video clip or a button to turn the sound completely off.

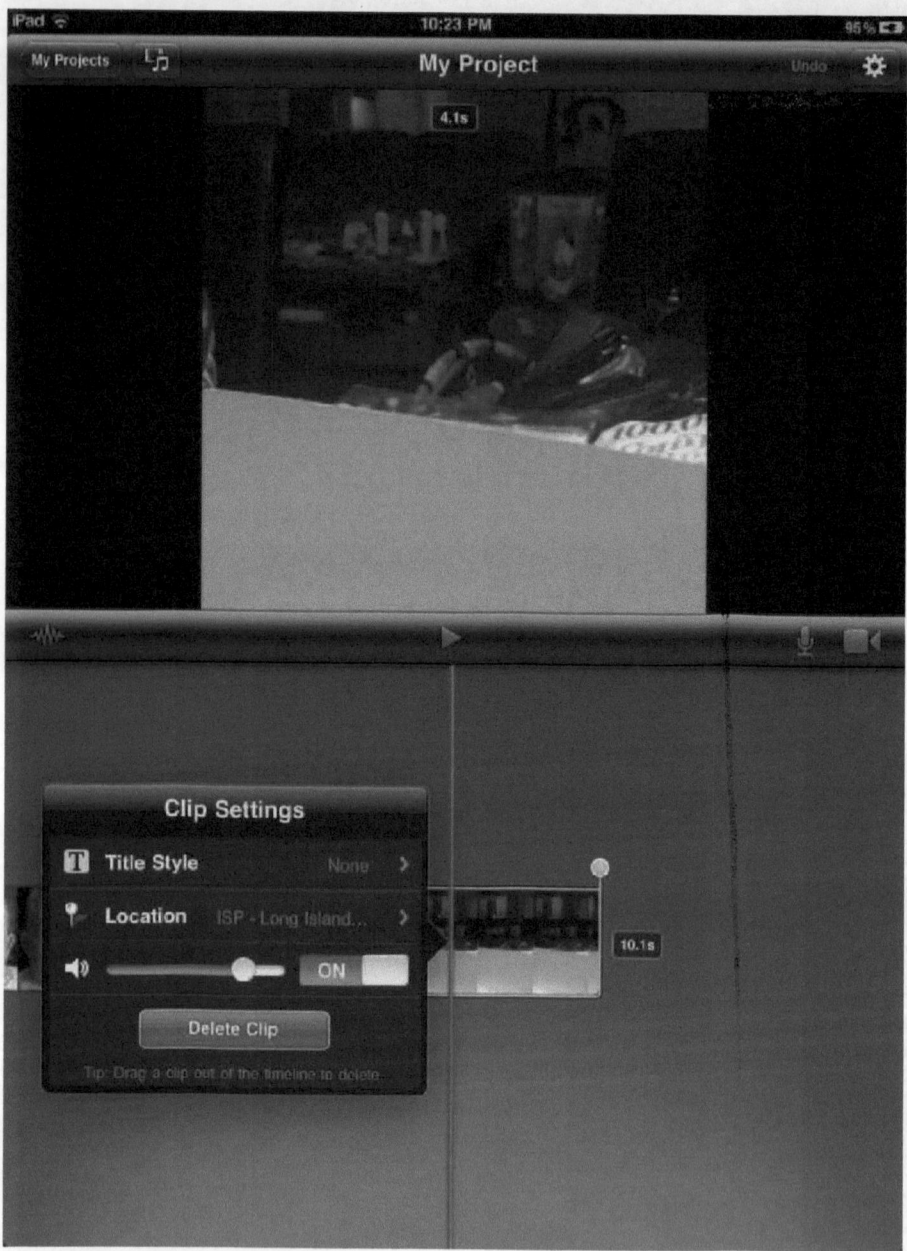

Figure A–40. *Clip settings*

This Just In!

The following features have been updated in iMovie. You must manually update the software to take advantage of these features.

- Delivers audio playback through the Apple Digital AV Adapter.

- Can play full screen videos to an HDTV from the Marquee page.

- Various bug fixes.

Summary

iMovie was designed to create movies on the go using an iPad or another iOS device. It gives you the opportunity to create basic home videos by using iOS devices cameras and provides basic editing capabilities to clean up and enhance your home footage. To me, iMovie shows a lot of potential. It is very new still, and I am sure that, as time goes by, Apple will add new features and make it more powerful. Tablet devices may someday be the computing choice for a lot of users. Apple is revolutionizing the market with each new hardware and software upgrade. What we can do now on an iPhone, iPod Touch, or iPad might just seem like child's play in the near future.

A Glimpse into iCloud

iCloud is a new (primarily) free service that Apple is rolling out in full in Fall 2011. There are a few different ways that companies define so-called "cloud computing." Apple's approach is to provide storage for your purchased music (and other music in your iTunes library, for a fee), as well as your photos, apps, and documents. It can also manage your e-mail, contacts, and calendars. It keeps track of all these items and makes them accessible on all your devices. Just log in with your Apple ID and all supported items are now available on every device. No more syncing required.

> **NOTE:** iCloud automatically gives you 5 GB of free storage. However, your purchased music, apps, and books, and your Photo Stream are not added to your quota. Therefore, only your mail, documents, Camera Roll, account information and settings and other app data will be go towards the storage limit.

Individual Services of iCloud

iCloud consists of several different services. Each service deals with a different type of media or data file, but all items are sent to iCloud for storage. Whether you want access to a new song you just downloaded from iTunes, important contacts, or constantly changing calendar events, iCloud will keep everything up-to-date on all your IOS devices and computers.

iTunes in the Cloud

Whenever you purchase new music from the iTunes store, it is stored in iCloud, which "pushes" or sends the new items to all of your devices. Also, new to iTunes is the opportunity to download all previously purchased music to all devices. These two features are now actually live after you download the latest iTunes beta software. It is beta software, so back up your hard drive before installing. Better be safe than sorry.

Downloading Previously Purchased Media onto Other Devices

The **Purchased** option in the iTunes Store is new, and is shown in Figure B–1. You use it to manage all of your past purchases and decide which items you want on each device.

Figure B–1. *The new* **Purchased** *option in the iTunes store*

After you select the **Purchased** option, you are presented with the screen shown in Figure B–2. Please notice that, at the far left, are the three items this option keeps track of: **Purchased Music**, **Apps**, and **Books**.

Figure B–2. *Purchased screen—Music*

Also at the top of this screen are two buttons: **All** and **Not in My Library**.

All | Not In My Library **All** will display all of your media and **Not in Library** will only display items not on the device you are currently using.

Getting Purchased Media onto Another Device

You have two ways of getting already purchased media onto a new device. You can use the **Download** button or the **Download All** button.

Download Button

This button will download only the track or item you have selected. It is found on the same line as the track you want to download, at the far right of the screen.

Download All Button

Download All This button will download all of the media that is not on the device you are currently using. Basically, it makes your iPad or other iOS device and Mac have the same media with just one click of the mouse.

Apple ID Name and Password Request for Download to Complete

After you have selected what you want to download and clicked on the appropriate button, you must enter your Apple ID and password to complete the download process. Then click on **Get**.

In Figure B–2, we saw the **Purchased** screen for Music. In the example I used, all items in the screen can be downloaded onto to the device I am currently using. If we look at Figure B–3, the **Purchase** screen for **Apps**, we see that some apps have **Downloaded**

Downloaded next to them. This means that the app is already on the device I am currently using and does not have to be downloaded again. This will appear next to any song, app, or book that is already on the device you are working on.

Figure B–3. *Purchased screen for Apps—Examples of already downloaded content*

Also, if you look at Figure B–3, you will notice that most elements are the same as in the **Music** example. You have the **All** and **Not in My Library** buttons at the top of the screen and the **Download All** button at the bottom.

iTunes Match

This feature allows you to store up to 20,000 songs in iCloud. The music can be taken from any source—not just purchased from iTunes. This feature has an annual fee attached to it. However, if you choose to use this option, iTunes will scan your library of music and give you access to a "256 kbps iTunes Plus" quality version of the song. This means that, if you imported a lower-quality version of a song or album a while ago, iTunes will automatically give you a much better quality version. If Apple cannot find your song among its 18 million songs, you will have to manually upload it.

Photo Stream

Take a picture on an iOS device or import a digital photo into iPhoto on a Mac or the Pictures library on a PC, and the photos are added to iCloud and ready to be accessed from anywhere. When photos are taken on an iOS device, they will appear in a Photo Stream album that can contain your most recent 1,000 pictures. iCloud then stores your new photos for 30 days. If you want to permanently keep these new photos, you must save them to your iOS device. However, the photos from this Photo Stream album are automatically saved to your Mac or PC, because storage space is not usually an issue on a traditional desktop computer. You just have to activate the Photo Stream feature on your computer to gain access to this new iCloud feature. Last, if you have an Apple TV, a special Photo Stream option is available so that you view your new photos on your TV via the Apple TV device.

Documents on the Cloud

iCloud will allow you to store your documents and have them available on every device. Currently, only Apple applications are supported, but other software companies can build iCloud support into their apps as well.

Apps, Books, and Backup

Apps can now be downloaded again for free to any of your IOS devices. When you purchase new apps, they can be set to automatically be pushed out to all your devices. Books will also be allowed to be downloaded to any device, and iCloud can even save your place when you are done reading by adding a bookmark. It can also save highlighted text or notes. Backup is a great application that stores all the daily changes made to the following items: purchased music, apps and books, photos and video in the camera roll, device settings, app data, Home screen and app organization, text and MMS messages, and ringtones. This feature is also helpful when setting up a new iOS device or restoring one that crashed. Just enter your Apple ID and the settings and media mentioned will be added to the device.

Contacts, Calendar, Mail

When iCloud goes live, you will have access to great productivity tools, from anywhere. If you store all your contacts in your Address Book app and use the Calendar app, iCloud automatically updates any changes to all of your devices. Apple is now also giving you the ability to create a new e-mail account that is automatically synced with all your devices.

Note to MobileMe Users

MobileMe was mentioned quite a bit in this book as it was used as a great way to share your media on the Internet. Shortly after the announcement of iCloud, it was stated that the MobileMe service will eventually be shutdown. However, free MobileMe access is being extended until June 2012. However, some features are not going to be included in iCloud. The biggest feature that might affect a lot of users is iWeb web site hosting. Users will have to transfer their web sites to other companies that host sites. iDisk is also no longer available, so you can no longer store any item in iCloud. iCloud can only store supported files. As more companies modify their software to accommodate iCloud. their app's files can also be stored in iCloud. Most other features are being reworked into iCloud. For example, Photo Stream is essentially a modified Gallery section.

Summary

The concept of what iCloud is meant to do is based on an old idea that Apple has reinvented for the ways people use their devices, today and in the future. Having the ability to access our data from everywhere without thinking about how to do it is a feature that I think we will all love, and wonder how we lived without. iOS devices are blurring the lines as to what people consider to be the best device for a task. Apple will be giving us the opportunity to have all our documents, apps, e-mails, contacts, and so on on all our devices updated automatically and accessible from everywhere we need without thinking of how to do it.

Index

S

X

Y

Z